D0856125

7e

1500

THE LAST FOOD
OF ENGLAND

THE LAST FOOD OF ENGLAND

ENGLISH FOOD: ITS PAST, PRESENT AND FUTURE

MARWOOD YEATMAN
PHOTOGRAPHS BY ANYA YEATMAN

EBURY
PRESS

1 3 5 7 9 10 8 6 4 2

Published in 2007 by Ebury Press, an imprint of Ebury Publishing

Ebury Publishing is a division of the Random House Group

Copyright © Marwood Yeatman and Anya Yeatman 2007

Marwood Yeatman has asserted his right to be identified as the author of this Work in accordance with the Copyright, Designs and Patents Act 1988

The publishers would like to thank the copyright holders for use of extracts from the following works: *The Book of Sausages* by A. and A. Hippisley Cox, published by Victor Collancz (a division of Orion), extract reproduced by permission of the Orion Publishing Group (www.orionbooks.co.uk); *Food in England* by Dorothy Hartley (copyright © Dorothy Hartley 1954), published by Little, Brown, extract reproduced by permission of Sheil Land Associates Ltd. on behalf of the estate of Dorothy Hartley; *As I Walked Out One Midsummer Morning* by Laurie Lee (copyright © as printed in original volume), published by Penguin, extract reproduced by permission of PFD (www.pfd.co.uk) on behalf of the estate of Laurie Lee ; *Love in a Cold Climate* by Nancy Mitford (copyright © the estate of Nancy Mitford 1949), published by Penguin, extract reproduced with the permission of PFD (www.pfd.co.uk) on behalf of the estate of Nancy Mitford; *Constance Spry Cookery Book* by Constance Spry and Rosemary Hume, published by Weidenfeld and Nicolson (a division of Orion), extract reproduced by permission of the Orion Publishing Group (www.orionbooks.co.uk)

All rights reserved. No part of this publication may be reproduced, stored in a retrieval system, or transmitted in any form or by any means, electronic, mechanical, photocopying, recording or otherwise, without the prior permission of the copyright owner

The Random House Group Limited Reg. No. 954009

Addresses for companies within the Random House Group can be found at www.randomhouse.co.uk

A CIP catalogue record for this book is available from the British Library

The Random House Group Limited makes every effort to ensure that the papers used in our books are made from trees that have been legally sourced from well-managed and credibly certified forests. Our paper procurement policy can be found on www.randomhouse.co.uk

Typeset by Palimpsest Book Production Ltd, Grangemouth, Stirlingshire

Designed by Two Associates

Printed and bound in Italy by Graphicom

ISBN 9780091913977

CONTENTS

CHAPTER ONE

THE MAP AND CALENDAR

THE FOOD OF ENGLAND is a product of trade and acquisition, of coal, peat, faggots and furze, of nets, traps, guns, hawks and hounds, of chases, parks, forests, dovecotes and warrens, of moorland, woodland and enclosure, of heaths, downs, marshes, meadows and commons, of ponds, lakes, rivers, fens, sea and sky, of inns, taverns and chop houses, of cottages, farms, manors and rectories, of long wet winters, short summers and twelve months in a year, and of a mixed race most absorbed and fulfilled when growing plants, grafting trees and breeding livestock.

On a superficial level, we find supermarkets, corn belts, woodland walks, heritage, leisure, and conservation. We go deeper to find reconstituted farmers' markets, the Soil Association, the WI, shops, dairies, allotments, specialist nurseries, and a seed library. We go deeper to find cattle markets, produce auctions, garden stalls, and people organic by birthright: commoning, wildfowling, trapping eels, picking laver, cockling, shrimping and casting nets on inshore waters. We go deeper to find frumenty eaten at Christmas, and salt cod on Good Friday, bacon up chimneys, and cheese made by renneting the pail. We go deeper still to find the quiet side of England's given history, where beestings pudding and pirate stills never disappeared.

Most of England, from the Surrey heath to the high fells, has supplied food, and may yet be required to do so again. Every county has or had its own breeding programme, its ways of trapping game or preparing fish, its herbs, fruit and vegetables, breads and biscuits, cakes and puddings, hop, damson, burdock and sweet-gale beers, blended cider, single perry and nettle drink, which local people made to live or lived to make, inheriting the knowledge and passing it on.

The map of England bears names that, before they acquired amenity status, meant something to the kitchen and even to the world: Hampshire, Hereford, Lincoln, Wensleydale and Yarmouth. There are cities and towns that are losing or have lost the vital connection: Bath, Dorking, Glastonbury and Southminster. There are hills that were known for their mutton, vales for their vegetables, and villages for their fruit or cheese: Cheviot, Pewsey, Barnack and Cottenham. There is a family of butchers engaged in their trade since graziers rode by in velvet and gold chains.

England has more breeds of livestock, fruit cultivars, and possibly vegetable seeds to its credit than any other country. The sheep may be lumped together as one like Cheddar cheeses, yet each in turn signifies an entire world to flockmasters, and traditionally cooks, which is separate from the next. A Romney Marsh longwool lamb grazed at sea level and a Swaledale ewe grazed on a hillside not only look different; they grow a fleece, respond to man, and eat differently too.

Sussex was known for its textbook repertoire of cockles, lobster, herring, mullet, trout, eels and wheatear, requested by locals and visitors alike. There was in addition middlehorn beef, Southdown mutton, speckled hen, apples, truffles, sea kale, cabbage and Tipper, Newhaven's seven-year-old beer, which was brewed with water from a single well.

'He who knows not Tipper knows not Sussex,' the saying went.

For every disease in every region, said historian Thomas Fuller, a cure was said to lie within that region's boundaries.* He did not know what the cures were, only that there existed in seventeenth-century England men and women who did. For nettle rash they prescribed dock leaves, as we still do; for eye complaints they sent the afflicted to Eyeworth Pond. Each bank had a purpose, each field a history, each bush or tree its own individual name, not a Latin or species name, but sufficient to describe an ash marked for cords or coppicing, an oak for a cruck frame, or a beech dropping mast for a bacon pig.

 Our knowledge is broad and universal; theirs was narrow, detailed and personal, intensely so. The same person who spoke of the next village as he did a foreign country, and saw no more than two hundred other persons in his lifetime, had the local knowledge of a modern zoologist, the learning of a botanist and the skills of a technologist. He read the forest floor like an Indian scout; he walked slowly enough to look for food, fuel or a sickening beast, silently enough to listen, and stealthily enough in order to surprise, gaining through the lessons learned a sense of place, and one place in particular.

A peasant did not just see a rib of beef (Hartley, 1954); he saw past it to the killing of the ox, the extraction of the tallow and the curing of the hide. His wife did not just see a loaf of bread, but past it to the corn crop. She felt the sun on her back as she gleaned the ears of wheat, the weight of the flour in the sack from the miller, and the softness of the dough in her bowl or pancheon. The boys took fish without rod or net, sparrows in traps, and rabbits with a bramble. The maids wove willow into baskets, kept herb corners and made broth with garlic from the hedge. They had to, or went without.

There were apples to eat, apples to store, apples for sauce, apples for pies, apples for mincemeat and apples for cider. There were pears for the plate, pears for the pot and pears for the press. The hooks in kitchens bore hams and bacon. The faggot ovens baked the daily bread. The supply of fish was limited only by the weather, the fowls were free range, the fruit and vegetables chemical-free. A hunk of home-made cheese or a bowl of wheat porridge, and a glass of beer brewed from a local strain of barley might be had for a small reward by any casual person riding by a farm.

---

* *Chinese acupuncture holds the same belief.*

Food had a provenance, and connections to a place and season which were automatically made. There was a time to keep butter and a time to eat it, a time to kill a pig, and a time for pork too. The understanding of where to go and what to do on the longest day, the shortest day, St George's Day and Lady Day, as well as the Glorious Twelfth and the First of September, implanted in the fertile grounds of childhood, lasted until death.

To those who know and love York ham, it is not like prosciutto, serrano or anything other than what it claims to be. To those who eat wild food, it has not 'caught on'; it is not 'enjoying a revival'; it never went away. To the farmers supplying markets, it is not a Californian or Canadian idea, but a right granted in medieval charters. To country people, we are not 'all suburban now': that is London mouthing off, partly out of ignorance, partly out of fright, and partly with an intention to make us all the same.

So, there may not be a food culture in England, but there was, and a subculture remains.

'What do they know of England who only England know?' More than any pen-pusher, I found out. The traveller and writer Celia Fiennes and The Reverend Woodforde said little or nothing of the barren, silent and mysterious world beyond the wicket gate, with its soaring kites, stooping falcons and weatherwise men trudging home through broom and furze bearing lichen for their pipes, bracken for bedding and fowls in traps for the landlord's table, the lady's cage or the cottage pot.

King and castle, squire and parson account for the greater part of history consumed; traditions old and new complete the package. For the artisan, who did the work and made the food, there was not the same protection or recognition. You can tell by the houses where the greater part of history took place; they may survive, but only as monuments of a humbler sort, only pretty shells: farms without farmers, mills without millers, and dairies without milk.

More has changed in the English countryside than it is given credit for; more has gone for good and more remains, obscured by persistent prejudice and myth. In my lifetime, some of the age-old functions have been suspended; food is one of the casualties. The sale of our past and the regulation of our present are delivering a new package. The risk to our future is from continued progress without improvement, ruptured connections, and lack of the will to fix them. The land, its people and its history are divided at their peril. The food is next of kin, a pleasure, a need, an opportunity and a lead; a link in a vital and fundamental chain. Without it, your death is hastened. Without enjoying it, a part of you is dead already. Without pride in its own food and resources, a country dies too.

CHAPTER TWO

English Food
and Cookery

1. Ceremonial, festive and Christmas dinner: roast ox or pig, saddle of mutton, dry salted hams, stuffed chine, 'the Alderman in Chains' (see page 228), whole salmon and turbot, half-Stilton, etc.
2. Domestic, local, seasonal and Sunday lunch: oven roasts, 'boiled' meat, stews, soups, fresh fish, vegetables and fruit, home-made pies and puddings, cakes and bread, unpasteurised milk, cream, butter and cheeses.
3. Proprietary: pork pies, brawn, haslet, potted shrimps, salt fish, Patum Peperium, etc.
4. Convenience: pasties, sandwiches, etc.

Categories two and three are the most important ones, where the everyday *pièces de résistance* are alive, if unwell and failing to pull in the necessary subscriptions. Seasonal foods continue to occupy an important niche. Local ones fall into three categories. Cheshire and Stilton cheeses, owing to the milk necessary to make them, are confined to one area in terms of production. Tripe, hog's pudding and saffron cake are amongst the items that used to be widely eaten, but retreated before change to a final stronghold. Pork pies did the reverse, emerging from their heartland to become widespread. Salt cod is an example of a dish that has become so rare in England it is not considered English at all, but French or Spanish, and known in its home country as *morue* or *bacalao*. Sourdough bread, which probably became extinct, is re-emerging as American or European.

The first principle of good cooking in general, and English cooking in particular, is that for good food to come out of the kitchen good food must go in. If it does, a cook can hardly fail; if not, he or she can hardly succeed. Faults at the source will certainly be found out, whatever the mask, as taints in the milk come through in the cheese. An elaborate creation cannot exceed the quality of the raw materials. To serve a chicken tasting of itself is at present harder to achieve than a fowl tasting of its marinade or sauce.

The fashion is to cook non-specific food in an increasing variety of ways. The English tradition, charitably expressed by the *Larousse Gastronomique*, was the opposite. It lay in choosing ingredients of the finest quality and 'serving them in such a manner as not to mask the natural flavour'. If that meant four years on the hoof, four months on summer grass and four weeks on the hook to bring a wing rib to perfection (see page 115), and treating the meat with restraint, it was done.

English cookery was and remains a vernacular pursuit, which relies more heavily on agriculture, horticulture and an awareness of the natural world than any other type. Not every pig makes first-class hams and pies, not every apple makes a fluffy sauce, not every milk makes clotted cream. Such products need time to produce and understanding to prepare. Spit and oven roasts, 'boiled' meat and steamed puddings must go to the table as soon as they are done, and did in the glory days. At the inns along the Great North Road, which fed hundreds of people every evening, spit-roast meat was served at eight and ten o'clock. Patrons waited for food; the food did not wait for them.

The classic dishes, 'though good to eat' and 'easily digested' (*Larousse* again), being ones in which 'deterioration takes place rapidly', are more suitable for serving in the home than to order in modern restaurants. With fewer people in England cooking, and a greater number eating out and at all hours, both dishes and their ingredients have been affected. Food, which appears easy to put on the plate, but is easily ruined at the same time, enjoys the worst of two worlds. In a three-year-old ewe, there is much potential misery and little glory for a high-profile chef.

The measured build-up to a clean and tasty result is a hard one both to follow and communicate. It could represent a life's work, a philosophy and an understanding of food committed to memory, which writers lacked the time or aptitude to investigate, and custodians lacked the inclination to reveal.

The food of England, even if it arrives at the top, comes from the toe, the earth, air and water. It is traditionally plain, but, rather than simple, of singular complexity, as anyone knows who has eaten herb-rich mutton the colour of shoe leather, hung for as long as it requires, cooked as slowly, and served in its own gravy enriched with a glass of wine. For this there is no convenient recipe or contemporary short cut. The best we can do is cherish, honour and build on the remains. They can suffer when updated and often cannot be born again.

Here is an English menu, which may be taken at face value, or more:

Potted Shrimps
Roast Chicken
Raspberry Fool
Cakes
Cheese
Bread and Rolls

The items listed, which seem ordinary enough, appeared on a menu for a luncheon held in the Town Hall, Lancaster, on 10 April 1951, complete with their provenance.

The potted shrimps were 'produce of Morecambe Bay caught by the Guides over Kent and Leven Sands being Fishermen . . . appointed to their office since 1538 by the Sovereigns in England in Duchy Right'.

The roast chicken was 'produce of Corless Mill and . . . Farms, tenants J. Fox and J. Cookson, on the Wyreside estate'.

The raspberry fool was 'produce of Kiln Trees Farm on the Winmarleigh estate and made by Mrs Freda Whittingham'.

The cakes, a butter biscuit from the village of Goosnargh, were 'produce of North Planks Farm on the Myerscough estate, granted to Edmund first Earl of Lancaster in 1267, and made by Mrs Elizabeth Crompton'.

The cheese was 'Lancashire Grass Cheese, produce of Cogie Hill Farm on the Winmarleigh estate and made by Mrs Betty Rossall'.

The bread and rolls were 'home-baked by Mrs Dorothy Marquis at Pepper Hill Farm on the Salwick estate'.

Behind this menu, there is pride, a connected mind, and at least one person whose second nature was to seek out 'fresh, local produce' fifty years before it became a battle cry, and go to any lengths to ensure it was traceable. Owing to the trouble evidently taken, we can assume that the shrimps were boiled in sea water and potted with farm rather than factory butter. The fowl was a 'spring' chicken, meaning a cockerel, from what would now constitute a rare breed, fed out of doors, home-killed and hung. The raspberries for the fool were bottled by the grower. The cream was unpasteurized and probably from Channel Islands cows. The Goosnargh cakes, which were served with the fool, were distinguished by caraway seeds. The cheese was made from milk, also unpasteurized, probably from shorthorn or Ayrshire cattle grazed between the months of May and September on permanent pasture. Even the bread and rolls were baked at home.

Every item and ingredient, with the exception of the salt, which is most likely to have been from Northwich in Cheshire, the pepper on the tables, the mace in the shrimps, the sugar in the fool, and a proportion of the flour in the bread and rolls, was produced for the moment and within a few miles of where the luncheon was held. The food was considered fit for:

His Majesty the King
in company with
Her Majesty the Queen
and Her Royal Highness Princess Margaret

The event, 'by command', was to celebrate the 600th anniversary of Lancashire's elevation to a County Palatine. I obtained the menu from my old Cornish mucker Philip Pendarves, whose grandfather held office in the Duchy and was present at the occasion, clad in black frock coat and matching knee breeches. The King, George VI, wearing only a grey suit himself, asked for whisky rather than the customary gin before luncheon, and Player's Navy Cut cigarettes. His only other request was not to be given salmon, which runs up the Lune past Lancaster, and was eaten so often by nineteenth- and twentieth-century landowners that they tired of it.

Like anything else, food reaches peaks. The Berkshire pig is a classic porker – you can tell by the way the skin crackles and the meat carves. A Cheddar can be a classic amongst cheese with a flavour many dimensions deep which, at eighteen months to two years old, eclipses all competitors. It is also a cheese of the lowest order, made all over the world and flagged up as 'traditional'. Below the pass mark there is a great raft of utilitarian products and copies of the genuine article, which compromise the whole of English food and its reputation. They may be part of folklore, get most of the exposure, and even be asked to represent the English kitchen, but only in error, or in order to confirm the prejudice against it.

Frenchman and Anglophile André Simon, former president of London's Wine and Food Society, said much the same about poor execution: 'To dub English cooking as bad is . . . nonsense. There is a great deal of food which is badly cooked in England, but it is not English . . . just bad cooking.' He added that there was good, bad and indifferent food in every other country, including his own. These points, made over sixty years ago, have yet to register with many critics.

CHAPTER THREE

THE ENGLISH CLEARANCES

ITH THE NEW MILLENNIUM, England entered another culinary phase. According to aficionados in the food world there was no 'vernacular cookery' or 'national cuisine'. Perceptions differ. Drabness and dullness went down as the everlasting blueprint of the postwar period. At the same time, André Simon, living in London, found the food 'as good as the best one may get anywhere else' and of 'the kind that is better here than anywhere else if and when given a fair chance by the cook'. The *Larousse Gastronomique* was equally charitable, citing ingredients fondly considered the best in the world: the 'beef, mutton, lamb, pork, salmon, sole, plaice . . . butter, cheese, etc. of a quality unsurpassed . . . and a greater variety of puddings than . . . any other country'.

For the food writer, P. Morton Shand, living in France, English cookery was 'dead' by the pre-war period. For R. Trow-Smith, his contemporary and author of a classic work on livestock husbandry, it would have been dead but for people 'fifty years behind the rest'. That meant the purists, perfectionists, conjurors and creatures of inherited habit and provincial backwaters: the English aboriginals who grew up and old with their food, drinking the same water and sharing the same land beneath the same sky.

The older the reference, provided it is made by a foreign national, the more positive it seems to be. For Louis Eustache Ude, another Frenchman living in London but a hundred and fifty years before Simon, English cookery 'when well done' was 'superior to that of any country in the world'. The agricultural revolution was under way, but the hunter-gatherer was still plying his trade. The breeding and finishing of livestock were reaching their peak. Meat was cooked to its greatest and simplest advantage by roasting, boiling or broiling; kitcheners had been invented (see page 98) though they were not in widespread use. Hams and Cheshire cheese were being prepared for export to France. Fish were taken from inshore waters and rushed to the capital, a development which Paris, having no railway, had yet to capitalise upon. There were wildfowl from decoy ponds, waders from the marshes, larks from the Downs, and plovers and their eggs from field and fen. People cooked both well and badly, but cook they did and without confusion.

None of the advertisements or slogans that sell foods today had been conceived; none of the phobias, taboos and superstitions that cap demand and supply. A fowl or fish was known and understood for what it was, and valued in more than terms of cash or alleged health benefits. Restraint and modesty had yet to be regarded as characteristic and hallmarks of civilised behaviour. The French writer François de La Rochefoucauld, who spent the year of 1784 in England, was 'astonished that people who have a good education and are capable of doing almost anything else, find pleasure, and a pleasure renewed daily, in joining each other to eat and drink'.

GOLDEN AGE

It existed! say romantics. It did not! say cynics. Both are right. The world is a different place to a man who goes from a supermarket to a leisure centre than to one who goes from a cattle market to a quiet campsite, swimming in a river on the way. T. E. Lawrence, in a letter to *The Times* at the outbreak of the Great War, said that everything he loved in England was finished. I have been down this route as well, but emerged cautiously and uncharacteristically optimistic. Some things are wrecked beyond redemption or gone for good; there will always be casualties. Others, missing presumed dead or imaginary, have a new and unexpected energy and lease of life. Every time I go to Bideford market, buy a saffron cake and eat it on the moors or by the sea, it seems the golden age is now.

LAND VERSUS LANDSCAPE

The land, which is physical and symbolic, came first. It provides work, resources and food if you are lucky. To try and live off the land without cash and comfort as a failsafe is to discover what 'pig earth' means. Since farming profits slumped in the late nineteenth century, land has been bought or maintained for prestige or sport and subsidised by its owners.

The landscape, emotional, came later. It is a term drafted into the English language from the Dutch, based on Arcadia, whose visual potential registered with romantic painters and poets from the late eighteenth century. The market was ripe for development. Subscribers did not want an accurate assessment of the brutal, dirty, tedious and threatening world beyond the drawing-room window and park gate. They required an untruthful, pastoral image, which provided a refuge from the towns, a model for garden cities, an ideal conveying peace, and an opiate. The 'countryside' acquired a dreamy, playful resonance, established itself in the psyche, and changed the nature of pursuits like shooting, fishing and keeping poultry. The cottage garden emerged as a design concept. Tourism blossomed, bringing money and people intent on recreation and seeking a glimpse of the flora and fauna.

Land and landscape rubbed shoulders for a generation or two. People went to Cumberland for the scenery, the walking, the ham, and the jugs of rich, creamy milk on the farmhouse tables. It was in the post-war period that food drifted out of the picture and leisure became dominant. Today, the two seem almost mutually exclusive – but they do not have to be.

A Hanoverian farmer saw only the land. A modern conservationist sees only the landscape; I see both every waking moment of the year. No connection, once made, is easier to make again.

1 Jersey cow + 1 species-rich field = milk, cream and butter of the highest quality, harebells, birds and butterflies too.

Town and Country

London, with a sixth of the UK's population, punches way above its weight. It passes laws, exercises controls, and beams out powerful messages from the media. Its view of the country, alternately sentimental and contemptuous, has not changed since 'landscape' was invented. The last working links were cut at the end of the hop- and fruit-picking era. However big the north–south divide is today, the one between town and country is bigger. The residual fear of rural England as a dark, threatening and inhospitable place, where people speak and act differently and there is no obvious entertainment laid on, is expressed in the swipes taken at it and the antipathy to country pursuits.

Londoners arriving in William Hazlitt's nineteenth-century Winterslow found themselves 'wondering and wondered at', meaning open-eyed and open-minded, rather than seeking the consolation and comfort of familiar objects. There are still plenty of questions to ask. No country in the world has so many cultural nuances and compartments as England, so many differences confined in such a small area. The more you look, the more you listen, the more slowly you travel and without a guide to prompt you, the more frequently they appear.

Try hitting market day or the boat coming in, and stopping at random for cider. Whether or not you are delighted by the result may be a question of building on inner resources and sharpening your skills. A junk shop, a foreshore and a gastronomic desert to one person can be a happy hunting ground to another.

Fashion and Fortune

The social structure in England has proved more fertile ground for fashion than for tradition. It is also far more mobile than in countries like India or France where caste and lineage matter. The boundaries are clear, and easily crossed with the right indoctrination and property qualification. Land, still symbolic, more or less equals rank. The fascination of owning it persists hundreds of years after feudalism failed. The first thing new money does is to get an estate. Continuity can be invented as easily as tradition. You only have to be there for three generations and it seems like for ever.

The advantage of the system is that anyone can jump the counter and, by observing certain rituals and wearing the right tribal insignia, land on his feet. The down side is the quick ebb and flow of people, its unsettling effect: the class casualties, and social aspirants eager to distance themselves from important but inglorious roots.

By the 1870s, the aristocracy amounted to 363 persons who owned ten thousand or more acres each (Newby, 1987), but who tended to live in London and who set the standards which others submitted to, copied, or perished in the attempt. The grandest of the grandees had a two-hundred-year-old tradition of employing foreign cooks, making them an enduringly fashionable presence and their food 'the thing'.

The gentry, owners of more than a thousand acres each, outnumbered the aristocracy by ten to one. They tended to live on and by their estates, but came and went with economic cycles, and were often too distracted by events in the drawing room to mind the stove. Employers either met their cooks once a day to discuss menus, or communicated through housekeepers and settled for the consequences. The atmosphere of detachment, a fashion in itself, was taken as grand. When the Reverend Collins praises Mrs Bennet's food in *Pride and Prejudice*, his hostess replies that she is 'well able to keep a cook', and that her daughter, Elizabeth, has nothing to do with the kitchen. Landowners did some excellent work in agriculture and horticulture towards the end of the nineteenth century, possibly provoked by a sense of imminent loss (Morgan, 1993). When friends, relations and labour departed for the war and never came back, their fears were realised.

The yeoman was an owner or tenant of less than a thousand acres: the backbone of rural England and its produce, self-sufficient in all things, from bread and butter to beef and beer, and rooted to the spot. His standard of living in the glory days compared 'to that of a baron overseas' (Harrison, 1968). The ethic changed with the creeping refinement that infuriated William Cobbett.* Prosperity slumped with the cheap food imported from the mid-nineteenth century to provide for the industrial working class. For every pound of New Zealand lamb or American fruit, there was one fewer from home. The ripple effects were terminal.

Then there was the peasant, the least fashion-prone in the social structure and the closest to the land, a prosperous and erudite fellow compared to his equivalent in France (La Rochefoucauld, 1988). He lived by open-field arable concessions and rights to a common, attached to houses like mine and granted by the owner of the land on which it stood. Dartmoor, Exmoor and the high fells are collections of past and present commons; Durham has commons, Dorset has commons, Middlesex and Surrey have commons: all remnants of the waste between England's towns and villages which provided grazing, wild food and fuel.

The enclosure of land for livestock, its improved cultivation or a mixture of the two began in medieval Kent and parts of the West Country. It persisted on a small scale until the reign of George III, then got going in earnest, swallowing up a fifth of England (Turner, 1980) in about a hundred years, mainly in Buckinghamshire, Oxfordshire, East Anglia and the north. The process increased production, but 'destroyed . . . the home-bred civilization of rural England' (Ernle, 1912). The peasant was undone by artful lawyers and act of parliament, which excluded

---

* *Cobbett's gripe was with women who had notions. He felt they should spend less time at the pianoforte and more attending to the responsibilities in the kitchen.*

him from ancestral haunts, ended his self-sufficiency and severed age-old connections never to be fastened again. He descended into poverty and made for the towns. His former occupation is a term of abuse.

By the turn of the twentieth century, only about 350 families were left in the whole of England (out of the 10,000 names in Walford's social directory) whose connection to their land pre-dated the Reformation. Sixteen hundred farms and smallholdings had sunk in some parishes to six. Thomas Hardy did not know of a single agricultural labourer who lived in the house of his birth. Colonists, displacing the thousands who moved on, planted their own ideas where others had grown before. The vernacular arts, crafts and customs were overcome: the dialects and stories, the words of songs, steps of dances, racial memories, the effects of the seasons on hunting and gathering grounds, and the little ways of using a plant or drying a plum.

So great and obvious have been the changes to the countryside, and to its personnel, that the gooey, 'timeless' image, plugged by poets, painters and TV, cannot have much longer to run. The sooner it is done with, the sooner the mist will clear. It helped me to discover that a sizeable chunk of England's much-loved patchwork, hedgerow and asylum for wildlife is less than two hundred years old. It was also designed by civil servants, developed by land-grabbers, and a scene of suffering for the dispossessed.

FRENCH CONNECTION: RESTAURANTS

The first time I went up to London, aged about ten and accompanied by my mother, I found that the food was described in a foreign language. That was in the fifties. The menus at Buckingham Palace, reputed to be the last bastion of haute cuisine, were in French until 2005. The culinary terms used in catering colleges still are. It is *boeuf* not beef, *veau* not veal, implying that English is not good enough, a legacy over three hundred years old.

Clergyman William Harrison complained about 'musical headed Frenchmen' playing an affected and comic part in English kitchens in the seventeenth century. Cookery writer Hannah Glasse made a similar remark a hundred years later. London had job opportunities for migrating cooks and servants. It was rich, licentious, libertarian, and politically stable compared to Paris, and also a source of inspiration to budding restaurateurs.

The London Tavern, located in Holborn, started the ball rolling. John Farley was the proprietor. In 1783, as well as feeding everyday patrons, he entertained City companies, Masonic lodges and charitable institutions, conducted sales, elections and feasts, and held twenty-eight regimental banquets in the month of May alone (Hutchins, 1967). The standard to which he aspired was uncompromisingly high. His *Art of Cookery* was published in twelve editions, having taken 'the greatest care to admit nothing inelegant or prejudicial to the [human] constitution'.

There were no equivalent places to eat in France, nowhere for passing or casual diners to feed except inns. A *restaurant* was originally a fortifying soup, served from a kitchen in Paris. The meaning of the word began to change with the opening in the 1780s of La Grande Taverne de Londres, which was based on Farley's establishment. The menu, one of which I bid for at auction, featured 'roastbeef' and 'Welsh rabbit'. The 'porter Anglais' fetched a higher price than Chablis.

La Grande Taverne closed during the Revolution and the Napoleonic Wars, but foretold a service industry with publicity laid on by the allies' occupation (Brillat-Savarin, 1973). The champagne trade, advertised by the looting of 600,000 bottles, recovered and prospered. Tourism flourished. Restaurants and auberges proliferated, gaining confidence and requiring personnel, who also had prospects in England. Careme worked in London during the Regency.*
Soyer arrived in 1830, paving the way for an 'invasion' of chefs in 1848.

The French food in England was neither good nor authentic, according to the *Encyclopaedia Britannica* of the early twentieth century more of a confidence trick, to which Belgium and Switzerland succumbed as well. 'By repeating that their cookery is the best in the world, which is not true for good cooking exists everywhere, they have given . . . gourmets from other countries complexes,' says Parisian Robert Courtine in his *Feasts of a Militant Gastronome*. The mistake we all made was to 'scorn our own . . . dishes' and replace them with 'imitations'; to copy French or global *cookery* rather than their ambitious, pure and protective, even nationalistic *approach*.

Terroire-iste

In Rouen and Beijing you eat the duck. In Gascony and Corsica, you eat the pork. In Pedrazza, Spain, you eat the lamb baked in 'ovens of wood' (*hornos de asar*). The whole operation is as slick as any city could make it for the streets full of people, enjoying a walk around the town before dinner. The same thing could happen in Lyndhurst, Lynton or Leyburn, just as it used to, making a trip to the Dales twice the 'experience' it is cooked up to be.

London is the self-styled food capital of the world, but on a wavelength where variety is paramount. In most other capitals and countries good food approximates to home cooking, relates to the host culture, and responds poorly to frequent or haphazard travel. The world's great gastronomies have all been enriched, but gradually and patiently. Hungarian paprika,

---

* *Antonin Carême (1784–1833), one of twenty-five children, was abandoned as a boy in Paris. He became the tireless 'king of cooks and the cook of kings' employed by most of the crowned heads and luminaries throughout Europe. He worked for the Prince Regent and Duke of Wellington while in London and designed the kitchens at Buckingham Palace, but left because of the climate and conversation, and would not be bribed to return. Carême combined architecture, which he considered one of the fine arts, with confectionery.*

Indian chillies, Belgian chocolate, French beans, Spanish oranges, and *sarlach salad Inglesi* took time to become established in what are now their spiritual homes.

The curries made in London by my friend and landlady Bengali Ela Sen were better than any Indian restaurant's, though not as good as her food in Delhi: she agreed. The curries in Japan, which arrived in Kobe via England, and feature on the 'bullet train', are a different thing again. It can be the same with drink. A Jack Daniels is somehow 'right' for a New York bar, a pint of Summer Lightning for a Hampshire pub. The reasons why cannot always be explained.

The drawback with travelling around England is the ever-present threat of a bad and overpriced dinner, unrelated to home cooking, time or place. Fashion dominates, repeating itself on menus in the unlikeliest of spots, meat is non-specific, and cheese absent from the world-famous epicentres of production – facts of provincial life that foreigners find impossible to understand. Pubs, no longer watering holes where people smoked a fag and had a chat, begin from a standing start as places to eat. Their change into gastro-destinations (an economic necessity I deeply regret) happened quickly. As in the case of the average restaurant, they have yet to make the giant leap that gets a Southdown chop or a cauliflower out of an adjacent field and on to a plate.

To re-establish itself as a place to eat, rural England needs relabelling as *terroire*, populated by *terroire-istes*, as in France and other European countries. It is already happening through the EU rather than because of any interest in food shown by the British government. The rest is up to customer participation and fidelity, a funny, old-fashioned idea thrashed into me by a pitiless parent. If you keep asking for the pork in Tamworth, you will get it.

ART AND SCIENCE

The French have a lofty and reassuring Minister of Culinary Arts, from whom it all seems to flow. He is up against rural depopulation, fast food, faster living and fashion, but is part of a structure pledged to support the national heritage, and farmers and fishermen large and small. Chefs are employed in schools, educating children about taste and flavour, and as advisers to the Department of Environmental Health. Instructors are seconded to smallholders, helping to maintain gastronomic traditions. EU grants, when it is necessary to discharge them, are matched by the government. The supermarkets work within the system rather than bestride it, out of control.

The UK has a Food Standards Agency with a scientist in charge, currently (in 2007) an informed and sensible one, but part of an Orwellian structure that is low on the list of government priorities, Treasury-led, and heavy-handed in crises. The Department of the Environment, Food and Rural Affairs (DEFRA) is regarded with fear or contempt by artisan producers and as an irrelevance by consumers.

For advice, particularly in moments of doubt, the government refers to science. The 'quality' of food is known to the microbiologist by its bacterial count; to the nutritionist by its contribution to a 'good' overall diet; to the technologist by its physical properties – elasticity, temperature, etc.; and to the legislator by its absence of banned substances and contaminants. The weak suit here is objective. A boffin with everything at his disposal except a love or belief in the food he produces, and its place in the landscape, lacks the vital piece of equipment. He may make a form of cheese, but he does not hold the office of cheese-maker, a difference recorded in 1912 (Ernle).

In the last few years, scientists seem to have risen to a priest-like status, interpreting the unknown, calling for prohibitions, and being asked to speak before they are ready. They scare the pants off me. A scientist can take a food that is indispensable to my quality of life and on the grounds which only initiates can question send its market into a tailspin. A lascivious press waits to pounce. The producers, especially the small ones, pay.

The act of dumping responsibility on scientists and the state has provided the UK with some of the most uninteresting and hazardous food in Europe, which seems cheaper than it is. You can eat as well in England as in France or Spain, but it is unconventional. It requires ingenuity, practice and education. We could start in schools by forgetting diet and nutrition, teaching appreciation, and calling cookery by its proper name rather than home economics, domestic science, food technology or even food therapy. Then we could invite applications for a Minister of Culinary Arts.

FARMING

Agriculture means more than food production. It has considerable side effects, helping to distinguish one county, village or community from the next. Farming has had a special resonance in England, the cradle of revolution, birthplace of Robert Bakewell[*] and company, and 'the stud farm of the world'. If the aim is quality, there is pride and a certain symbiosis.

In the first post-war phase, farmers were paid to produce as much food as possible, 'not wildlife' (Ministry of Agriculture, Fisheries and Food). In the second, having produced a

---

[*] *Bakewell (1725–95) was an ingenious and far-sighted agriculturalist, with an eye second to none for star quality in livestock. He let rams for colossal amounts, which affected most of the sheep in England, and favoured Longhorns, a breed still present in his native Leicestershire. His pupils included the Collings family, who went on to be great improvers themselves. Bakewell's farm outside Longborough, where he dug canals to transport feed and kept a menagerie, continues to attract visitors from all over the world. He neither made a fortune nor married, but lived with his sister at Dishley Grange. His memorial is in the ruined church adjacent to the house.*

surplus, they were paid to grow nothing and weedkill the land: a scheme entitled 'set-aside'. In the third, they are paid as occupants for more or less growing wildlife.

By the 1980s, farming and flora and fauna, united throughout their history, were mutually exclusive. The adoption of high-input, high-output monocultural systems, and precocious European livestock, had changed the face of England. An EU corn subsidy kicked in and that was more or less that for the birds overhead, the bugs underfoot, the ancient bloodlines, dreamy orchards and springy turf overlying the downs, embroidered with flowers, which grew the bite which fed the sheep that made the world-famous lamb and mutton. The Southdowns, the shorthorns and the Saddlebacks disappeared with the native vegetation, which underpinned the flavour of the meat and milk. The muted-green protectorate emerged as a nitrate-green desert, deprived of all but one living thing per field. The mood changed too. A corporate mantle spread across the countryside, and in the towns the consumer baby was born.

No nation on earth that had prospered so much from the tenets of good husbandry held them in such contempt. Farmers were blamed for the devastation wrought, pocketing the subsidies and causing the 'Silent Spring' (as 1960s environmentalist Carson called it), but were not induced to take any other course. For all the outpouring of emotion towards the 'environment', the British public took more from it with one hand than they gave with the other. By eating cheaply, they perpetuated the system that was abusing the landscape, wildlife and creatures they held so dear.

The bigger the farm, the bigger the financial gain from subsidies, and perhaps the bigger the spiritual loss. Nothing can be more soul-destroying than growing a crop destined for incineration, or poisoning land when the skylark breeds and cranesbill breaks through. Farmers stopped eating their own food, a strange situation for the bloke who grows it, especially in England. How odd it must be, to take an example from hundreds, for a New Zealand breeder of sheep to see what has been done with the South Downs and their mutton.

The larger landowners were easily persuaded out of agriculture and into agri-business. Few resisted the temptation even if they could afford to. That left the smaller, most vulnerable forest farms, hill farms and mixed family farms – out of habit, conviction or lack of an alternative – to carry the flag for the food of England. Half their number have gone in thirty years, say the statisticians, but it feels like more than that to me, with only one in fifty calling in the cattle as before, and one in fifty thousand making the butter. Rising costs, static prices, hostile governments, red tape and supermarket forces have helped them on their way.

The original objectives of government and EU policy were sound: to feed the hungry and keep agriculture in wraps in case it was needed. Conservation and recreation now have prior claims on the land. The assumptions are that finance, insurance and tourism will provide, and trade and surpluses continue without interruption. The concerns about energy do not apply

THE LAST FOOD OF ENGLAND

to food. I can hardly watch. Some shortages are already upon us, but hidden. Others are in the pipeline. Most are self-inflicted. 'The worst fate that can befall our countryside is that it should become a playground or waste,' said author and journalist H. Rider Haggard in 1902. For the third time in living memory it has happened.

INDUSTRIAL FOOD: THE LEGACY

Laura,* a Victorian country girl with a pig in the sty and a kitchen garden, could not understand what people in Oxford ate who had neither. When food changed hands in *Lark Rise* it was not for money, but given, a reward for a service, or loaned for repayment in kind. The industrialization of food meant that even people in the country could buy it. 'Johnny Fortnight' called at the cottage door with exciting packets, news and gossip, and grocers opened up in every market town. The effects were mixed. Village shops hit fairs and markets; the bottling of milk hit cream-, butter- and cheese-making; and tinning and refrigeration hit fish- and meat-curing. Imitations were permitted to bear the names of genuine articles, diminishing their reputation and confusing buyers.

Town-dwellers in general, for whom industrial goods were invented, bought their provisions. In gaining a price food lost a meaning. The cost was measured, the origin often obscure, a nd the condition a mystery. People seldom learned to choose food as expertly as they did other objects, I am not clear why. They turned their attention to eating cheaply instead, and the tradition stuck.

The rich in towns did not necessarily fare much better than the poor. In the increasing number of nineteenth-century houses that were able to afford servants, there were not enough good cooks to go round. Musty plovers, 'only' mutton,** and fowls packed in sawdust and tasting of turps were banged up in an industrial range by an untrained skivvy, whose alternative to service was the street. Meals were transformed from routs and feasts (*convivia* in Latin), gained from the fat of the land, into repressed and perfunctory occasions that were endured not enjoyed, and borne with indifference or fortitude. From the ashes of a culture, a majority emerged with a cauterized palate, stiff upper lip, and the inexplicable habit of eating bad food with good wines and wearing dinner jackets to do it.

For many in England, the only gastronomic heritage is a painful one: a hundred-year-old programme of broken connections and indifferent raw materials hastily put together. Industrial food is dominant, militant, advanced by the supermarkets and favoured by

---

* *Laura is the principal character in* Lark Rise, *in reality the author Flora Thompson, referring to herself in third person.*

** *i.e. 'It's only mutton for dinner, nothing special', though there was world-beating mutton too (see page 125).*

utilitarian grading standards. Words like 'quality', adapted to fit, were stolen from items with flavour and texture and pinioned to pretenders. The very fat in meat, complexity in cheeses and diversity in fruit and vegetables that traditionally put them above the rest, now put them below.

The imbalance between the vernacular art or craft representing the food of England and the industrial process is greater today than ever. It is clear and crucial, but seldom given the attention it deserves, even in a country that spends more on a tin of cat food than on a child's lunch. With so much going on in the cookery world, the secret should be out by now. If an item like Cheddar or custard is called for and an industrial product is chosen, rather than a mature farm cheese or a crème anglaise, it is not the English kitchen that is deficient.

SUPERMARKETS

Supermarkets are the major success story of the last thirty years, asset-stripping England, spoiling meadows and felling trees, a chalice that poisons rich and poor in equal measure. They have perfected every trick in the book, from locking producers into 'feudal' relationships (Blythman, 2004) to branding consumers, funding art galleries, and suborning TV chefs. They break bread with national and local politicians, speak the same language and share, it is whispered, 'a cosy relationship'. When the big players talk, even the government listens.

The supermarkets have the power to control what the farmer grows, and the price. They have the power to control what the buyer buys. They have the power to charge more for one leg of lamb than they pay for the whole beast. They have the power to make offers that cannot be refused, to welsh on them, to terminate relations, to create rare breeds of livestock, and to destroy competition with predatory pricing. They have the power to meet any law thrown at them and, in the case of Sunday trading, to ignore it. They have the power to increase the roads programme, conduct the flow of traffic, erect landmarks, and orchestrate the 'planning game': the means by which permission to build is bartered for civic facilities and the mirage of jobs. They have the power, when denied such permission, to brush a local authority aside and go to an appeal. The system is 'supermarket friendly', the mention of their names a free advertisement, the word 'shopping' almost obsolete. Their profit margins have been eight times higher in the UK than in America.

Kyoto, in Japan, has over 250 shops registered as heritage. Salisbury, in Wiltshire, has five supermarkets, no fishmonger and no greengrocer. Look closely at Winchester and other show places; they are more or less the same. Look at the cars at the out-of-town stores on Sunday mornings: the new religion.

The 'mind set' is currently in the supermarkets' favour. There appears to be no other way forward, nowhere else to go, no time to consider the implications, and no other way of life.

One of the easier predictions to make was that the quality, availability and traceability of milk and meat lost to the common tank and pile* would be wanted back. The common tank is the one into which most of the milk has gone with rationalization, as opposed to being bottled, qualified and sold by individual dairies. Perhaps the apples, the orchards, and the nutty, dewy, cylindrical clothbound Cheddars will meet the same fate. The danger is that the supermarkets, having shafted so many people, might lead a return to the promised land, but a token and illusory one. They could then emerge as the good guys, power undiminished. One prospect is worse: if the supermarkets start producing better food in response to public or celebrity pressure, even discriminating buyers may be driven to use them, and that means curtains for any residual charm English towns might have.

The threat from supermarkets is as persistent as ever, but now successfully challenged. One campaigner in Suffolk, Lady Cranbrook, calculated that in exchange for the hundred jobs magnanimously promised by a new store in her area, about three hundred traders and their families would stand to lose their livelihood. Thanks to her endeavours Saxmundham in Suffolk was spared. Freedom fighters in Louth in Lincolnshire continue their heroic ten-year struggle. Torrington in Devon is manning the barricades. A national movement is needed. The Federation of Small Businesses and Friends of the Earth are involved.

Supermarkets are big, bright, sexless sensory deprivation chambers, an impediment to human contact as much as they have been to the food of England. Anyone is free to take his or her own little stand against them and keep away. Anyone can retrieve the power lost, and enjoy the pleasure it can bring. Supermarkets promise and provide many things, but only on one level. They cannot make shopping the intimate, creative and saucy occupation it is for people who buy elsewhere.

REGS

The UK's admission to Europe could not have been better suited to the rationalization of the food industry or the conditions of entry more lethal from 1991. A great raft of hygiene 'directives', designed for the corporate sector and expensive or impossible for artisans to implement, took effect. The supermarkets, with friends in high places and representatives in Brussels, could not have done better if they had made the rules themselves.

The burden of rules mounted with the incidence of food poisoning emanating from the industrial sector. The government, obliged to act, responded by lashing out at soft targets, like

---

* *The common pile refers to the meat, good, bad and indifferent, which goes through the auctioneer and gets sold as beef, lamb or pork, rather than 30-month-old grass-fed beef from Meadow Farm, slaughtered by A. N. Other.*

green-top milk (see page 297), or some treasured possession, like buying eggs at a garden gate. A structure emerged that favoured corporate standards and unregulated food bought in from abroad. There was a horrid feeling in shops, slaughterhouses, dairies and markets that whatever traders did, it would not be enough to save their skins. It has not gone away. The laws continue to multiply, creating offences and putting blameless people out of business, without making food any better or safer.

The oppressed and disinherited are still blaming Brussels for making the rules rather than British executors for making the most of them. European law starts with guidelines or 'directives' from the Commission that pass through the administrative channels of member countries before they take effect, and may be adapted or challenged at any time. The tendency in some parts of Europe is to exercise tolerance towards the 'grey' areas. The practice in the UK, known as 'gold-plating', is to define them in black or white. The result can be a document up to ten times more onerous and riddled with anomalies than the original, drafted by unaccountable people whom the Minister of State cannot or will not control.

DEFRA and Environmental Health provide the law-enforcement officers, who are intermittently short in supply, borrowed from Europe and deficient in English. They can vary from worldly-wise, reasonable and encouraging to high-handed corporate pimps, intoxicated with the power to intimidate or close down a trader. In dealing with adverse regs and officious behaviour, more use could be made of the Federation of Small Businesses; a request to see a regulation on paper can also have an effect.

Germany has emerged in Europe with industry, France with agriculture, and Spain with fishing, legally and otherwise. The UK leads the way in Health and Safety regulations. May they keep us warm and fed.

THE FOOD WORLD

John Mortimer QC thinks that English cookery was 'ruined by egomaniac chefs and crippled food writers'. The temperate view (mine) is that they did little to promote it or help fight the power of the supermarkets and excessive regulation until journalists Joanna Blythman and Felicity Lawrence came along.

A movement began in the sixties with the likes of Fanny Cradock, escorted by her Johnny, whose mixture of cookery and farce, conducted in the casual dress of the period – satin for her, suit for him – makes increasingly riveting viewing. Cradock believed that all 'British cuisine' was copied from the French. Her career prospered until the infamous encounter with Gwen Troake, a cosy Devon farmer's wife, invited to serve a lunch in London, whom she treated with contempt. Cradock departed, but the vacuum was filled and the slots multiplied, creating celebrities and entertainment as they went. The French never fell for it, warned off perhaps by French food writer and critic Robert Courtine and the shortage of 'truly good chefs . . . anxious to leave their pots and pans in order to stand on their hind legs'.

In helping to make cookery a performance, the performers became part of the problem, adding to the confusion of those who could not cook, or churning out fashion victims. So few chefs practise the plain and simple message that they preach, or lead humble cooks down a path we can follow. Our worlds are too far apart, our priorities too different. Our motivation has also been becalmed. I never managed to hit white-hot 'hedge high' drives (described by golf correspondent Peter Ryde) by watching golfer Arnold Palmer, but I learned a lot from having a go. [*]

Food writing changed with Elizabeth David. Her approach was a new and beguiling one, based on her time abroad, and associated with being free, on holiday and without responsibilities in sunnier climes than England. The highest award she received was for her contribution to French gastronomy. She addressed Italian food with the same mixture of elegance and escapism and at the very moment it was wanted. The success of Mrs David's books was unparalleled and lasting. It drafted into her slipstream a generation of cooks and journalists with two ideas writ large: that an outward-looking approach was the one to follow; and that they could make a living from it too.

English cookery was not one of Mrs David's favourites. She found it 'extravagantly overpraised by . . . advocates and so bitterly and often so rightly reviled by those who have suffered from British hotel and restaurant catering'. There were no cherished memories of her childhood in Sussex, no references to the sheep-shearing suppers, the truffles, the Tipper or any other perk of living in the country. The nursery food was 'distasteful' and the vegetable matter 'soggy', personal recollections that are still common property, and doing the rounds.

Few writers on any subject have had such an effect as Mrs David. None opened a nation's eyes so wide to every sort of food except its own. Twenty years passed before she turned to the English kitchen. She wrote two scholarly books that were both well received, but, unlike her previous best-sellers, products of work at a desk rather than at the coal face. The pity is that she never made it to Ringwood, Bideford, Tenbury Wells or any other provincial market simultaneously packed with treats and dying of neglect, nor did any of her adoring fans. If she had, how loud the chorus in favour of English gastronomy might have been.

* * *

---

[*] *Palmer was not the best golfer of all time, but he was the most charismatic, virile and exciting, winning seven major titles before hysterical fans and losing in the same spectacular fashion. He picked up a sedentary game and made it look fast, changing it forever.*

David, when she started, is alleged to have told travel writer Norman Douglas that she was writing a book, 'not a real book – a book of recipes'. She did not do herself justice; she was a very good writer. It is a shame she stuck to food, a subject I have never liked reading about except when it is addressed in passing by non-food-writers, non-introspective, and related to other subjects. Recipes, as David seems to imply, have their limitations. Cookery needs nous, feel, imagination and an ability to adapt, which can all be developed. It is learned at home by understanding raw materials and how they perform when baked, boiled or stewed, not from a manual or by rote.

Recipes are necessary for baking, and for making things like marmalade and pastry that need precise measurements. Produced and reproduced every week, month and year, they are an easy and automatic way out for writers, largely ignored by readers and inhibiting to cooks. They can be a comforting list of commandments for fledglings to fall back on rather than taking flight, and responsibility for their own food. Recipes can also be unreliable, and may not even work. Betty Haywood, a friend of mine for forty years who nearly reached a hundred, told me that past generations of cooks might part with a recipe when asked – minus the vital ingredient. It still happens.

By the millennium, the UK had accumulated the largest number of programmes broadcast, books published and words written on cookery per head in the world, and the smallest number of people who could cook. The obligation to find new, sensational or global material is one that French and Italian gastronomy have not embraced and could not survive intact if they did. They look to proven assets and resources. There are no expanding pools of information, roving spotlights, or feeding frenzies. Their food is in better shape too.

Mentors

Dorothy Hartley is number one on many lists, the daughter of a Yorkshire farmer and a Welsh mother. She was not exclusively a food writer, but did write about food along with every other rural occupation, from cooking the 'market ordinary'* to building a garden privy. She travelled the highways and byways of England in a horse-drawn caravan, and so acquired the nickname 'scholar gypsy'. In her 'long and inquisitive life', Miss Hartley visited every part of the country,

---

*Market ordinary: a stronghold of English food, still in reasonable health before the war, now obscure. It was a meal served on market day at inns, mainly to farmers, automatically made from all the things we are trying to get back – 'fresh, local, produce' with no 'food miles' attached, well cooked and served in honest portions. Dorothy Hartley gave several examples from her travels around England, roast duckling with new potatoes and green peas, followed by a steamed pudding, was one.

every market town and almost every village, seeing where others saw not, finding good where they failed, and going to depths that few have ever plumbed. She gave recipes without peddling them, quoted from the archives, and drew with pen and ink. She painted literary pictures, addressing cookery as a component part of life and a complete life, not the isolated ritual and career opportunity she saw it become.

Hartley's honest and affectionate *Food in England* is an education – leading you out to seek and find. It was published within years of Elizabeth David's *French Provincial Cooking*, gaining a fraction of the recognition. It was not a book of its time, but a book for all time, and is now in its sixth edition thanks to an informed and loyal following in America. Hartley's *Land of England*, *Water in England* and *Made in England* are on my shelf too.

Dorothy Hartley has not left the rest of us with much to say about country cooking or the chance of saying it any better. Only Sheila Hutchins' *English Recipes and Others* comes close. The other writers on England who did it to me were George Borrow, John Fothergill, Geoffrey Grigson, Laurie Lee and Oliver Rackham.

Mrs Beeton's success must be partly due to having married a publisher. I am not clear why she has maintained a reputation as a cook. She died in her twenties with an impossibly large number of recipes to her credit, many of which were flawed, simplistic or cribbed. I never look at them now. The best bits of *Household Management* are the engravings and footnotes, which cover all sorts of subjects, from IOUs to the stabling of horses, and provide an insight into the threats to middle-class refinement in Victorian London.

HEALTH

A brand-new industry took off in the seventies. It preyed on superstitions, created fears and promised to take them away, provoking witch hunts and setting up icons. I was not in with scientists or qualified to argue with the salt police, but I was a statistic and living proof. I should have been fat, unhealthy and obsessed, but I wasn't. What was my secret? Nothing new, and it was no secret anyway. Eating regular and varied meals, not eating between them, not eating fast food or junk, not overeating, swimming in the summer, coppicing in the winter, gardening all year, walking whenever possible, and not sitting around in overheated houses then taking strenuous and pointless exercise. The dog wheel was banned for being cruel to animals (see page 318). A hundred years later humans are running on treadmills and paying for the privilege.

Cholesterol was the worst thing you could eat, but emerged in about 1990 as more of a mystery than previously thought. Inexplicably, a high consumption of animal fat affected men above women, though not all men, and not all men it affected were released from misery by a fat-free diet. Was it the consumption of cider made from the ripest apples, containing high levels of asprin that kept people healthy on West Country farms? (Patrick Adams). There is now a possibility that pasteurising and homogenising milk may be the problem, and meat varies according to whether it comes from a beast fed on grass or from one fed on concentrates. I do not know or care. I made my choice years ago, on the grounds of what both the creature and I would like to eat, where he would like to be, and the striking results obtained by obliging us both.

I eat a steak about six times a year and, whatever the future holds, cannot confess to feeling anything except better for it at present. But then the meat is the best ever, cooked over a fire in the dining room or garden and served with two veg. The memory lasts. The satisfaction is emotional, mental and physical. The effects of rounding off the day with a good dinner rather than a bad one are obvious if incalculable, and are waiting to get the nod from a boffin or 'lifestyle guru'.

In the meantime, omega-3 may be toppling from its pedestal. It is when you hear that wholewheat flour may *not* be easy to digest unless it is properly fermented (see page 75), reducing your most cherished opinions to nothing, that the bets are off. I would not mind laying money on one thing, though: that a commodity like butter with two ingredients is a lot better for you than a low-fat spread that comes with twelve.

The problem seems to be this: we are growing taller and living longer, but not becoming more acclimatised to what happens next. May I suggest an action plan, free of charge and confusion, unashamedly cribbed from the school of common sense?

Do eat one varied and regular meal a day – meat and two veg., fish or eggs and a salad; decent bread and butter; fruit and cream; nuts and cheese.
Do drink unpasteurized milk if you can get it.
Do swim in the summer (avoid swimming pools, unless there is no alternative) and walk all year.
Do not eat too much, then diet; buy commonplace white or brown bread; drink alcohol before 6 p.m.
Do not sit around in sealed and overheated houses.
Do not take the advice of any nutritionalist, or food therapist, whom you suspect of being unable to enjoy their grub or cook you a satisfying meal.

WHITEWASH, AND MOVING ON

The prevailing opinion is that food in England has improved since the post-war period. There is mostly jambon for ham, farmed salmon for wild, crème fraîche for cream, lots of butter substitutes and olive oil, unlimited volume, endless choice and every sort of cookery from Thai to Turkish. Not surprisingly, the people I know who know about food know their own least of all.

As a spectator I felt that a hatchet job was done on the living food of England. The pig bench, bacon loft and other lingering nerve centres were marginalized, left for dead, or declared nonexistent, paving the way for the process to continue. This was conveniently labelled an 'improvement' by interested parties. So was a two-hundred-year-old species-rich butter pasture, ploughed up and resown with a single crop of grass. It did not ring true, even for a person in denial. The increasing number of claims that products were 'like they used to be' and the campaign for 'slow foods' were not reconcilable with genuine improvement.

In my lifetime, we have sustained tens of thousands of casualties, from milk rounds to master grocers, like roly-poly Mr Smith of the County Stores, Taunton, who did an apprenticeship and written examination, tested hams, ironed cheeses, and chose the fruit for Christmas puddings. The losses, filtering out, include the 'exquisite beauty of the small . . . complex and unexpected . . . and also . . . of meaning . . . the record of our roots and growth of civilisation' (Rackham, 1986).

The countryside tells so much of the story. There are swine on the downs in the rightful place of sheep, crayfish on the loose brought in with disease, and pheasants killed for a 'pony a pop' that never make the cooker.* We have dairy bygones at one end of a showground and cows at the other masquerading as pets. The milk in the tent is anonymous, processed to within an inch of its life, and supplied by a supermarket van from a distant depot.

We can do better than this. Hobby farmers are having a go, rather than automatically crossing the Channel to satisfy desires. England, still with so much left, can offer many things the rest of Europe has got except the monotony of wall-to-wall sunshine. One in twenty incomers has only to put Sussex cattle in a Sussex field, keep hens or grow veg., rather than housing the customary loose boxes, etc., and there will be good food from the fringes of the system. Ancillary gains, actual and psychological, may follow. Even the experts are cottoning on. This is not a breakthrough or new-age nonsense, but a matter of getting a return from an emotional investment. Beatrix Potter did it, helping to save Herdwick sheep (see page 126) and perhaps herself as well.

As a consumer, it is encouraging to see quality (in the proper sense) prioritised French or Italian style. It is disappointing when people do all the right things, get a decent pig, feed it well, tickle its tummy, etc., then brine it, or load the sausages with rusk. Presentation in England is substandard as well. There is a lot of badly cut meat and cheese, manky labelling and asphyxiating packaging. Displays needs artistry. A peep through a butcher's or fishmonger's window abroad can show you how it should be done.

---

* 'Pony': slang for £25; 'pop': as in gun, i.e. the inflated cost of shooting a pheasant.

The only way forward is to change perceptions, to clarify the difference between the food of England, representing a gold standard, and its industrial big brother. From the top tier alone, it is possible to compete and favourably compare with other countries. For people intent on such artisan programmes, the challenges are considerable. The market is rigged against them. Until a radical change of direction occurs, anything which is not pasteurized, standardized and stabilized is liable to be victimized. It takes energy, guile and bloody-mindedness to make a ham or cheese that is an offence to the corporate hymnal, and survive. Those who do, however, enjoy the sweetness and added frisson which is a fact of country life: that their success was threatened by public servants and mean buyers every step of the way.

Buildings, badgers and beech trees have protection. Food and its champions have none. In the circumstances, it never ceases to surprise me that anything as battered, bruised and belittled as Victorian writer and libertine Frank Harris' 'high ideal' of English cookery manages to survive. The pickings may be thin compared to what they were, and hanging by a thread in the most unlikely and unprepossessing of places, and that makes them all the more baffling, thrilling and moving to find. It is not the choice that matters (Richardson, 2001), but the chase, and the knockout punch delivered by a tea cup full of brawn, an apple presumed extinct, or a whortleberry pie and a type of cream you can only get in England and that would take a Frenchman's breath away.

CHAPTER FOUR

JOURNEY

**I** WAS BAPTISED IN A ROBE OF HONITON LACE during the big freeze of 1948. The ceremony took place in a chapel attached to a house in Dorset, occupied by cousins who had married each other, producing two spinster daughters and a schizophrenic son. The incumbent, over ninety years old and another relation, had served communion to an antecedent of mine, who had been born before the French Revolution. The herd of fallow deer in the park outside was the oldest in England, people said; the rectory beyond the ancient oaks the most haunted of buildings. A troop of phantom horsemen galloped through the lanes, spreading fear amongst the children for miles around. There were tiger and leopard skins in my bedroom, toads in the cellar, swords in the hall, and bedtime stories of beautiful maidens, and fearless men who fought mighty battles and slew giant boar.

Petrol came in rations. The hounds met. Hoopoes pecked in summer on a blistered lawn. People stopped to call, leaving cards at the door. And a boy could play and hide in the stooks of standing corn. It was under the dark awning of a copper beech, with the sun baking the still and silent world outside, the house behind shutters and a blue-black obelisk rising from the hills, that I thought and therefore I was: a moment of precocious clarity followed by thirty years' confusion.

EDUCATION

My father and stepfather were both 'gentlemen farmers', i.e. 'hands-on' landowners of private means and enduring fascination, envied and copied the world over. Nicholas II of Russia, if he had not been tsar, would have chosen to be an English country gentleman. P. G. Wodehouse's fictitious Lord Emsworth was a good example, on the face of it an amateur playing at agriculture, yet proudly and successfully breeding the Empress of Blandings, his prize-winning sow, a Berkshire, of course!

Gentlemen farmers enjoyed a life and a style, as distinct from a self-conscious or borrowed 'lifestyle'. They loved their home patch, horizons and trees, shorthorns and Devons, pigs above sheep, and beautiful trappings, not just expensive ones: cars, clothes, shoes, guns, furniture, books and effects, thrown together in 'innocent confusion' (Lander, 1989). Gentlemen farmers hunted or fished, invariably shot, drank after six, and did themselves proud. They knew where to go, what to do and when, including how to eat, looking forward to meals for structure, and back with pleasure on chosen foods and favourite wines.

My father cooked and enjoyed it. My stepfather turned his hand to scrambled eggs and toasted cheese, never expertly, though bravely, wholeheartedly, and with pride in the results. They taught me to carve, to bone a kipper, and to 'leg' a woodcock in the field. They also kept orchards, walled gardens and working dairies for personal use and in defence of local traditions. The remnants of yeoman and peasant families who lived roundabout did likewise on a smaller budget. They had stronger racial memories than the landowning tribe and a more hardened attitude to the earth under their feet, but we gathered cider apples, shot rooks, and watched cricket side by side.

My mother's place in Somerset, run as a farm, stood with the Blackdown Hills before it and the Quantocks behind. Her cottage in Cornwall looked over a creek named Abraham's Bosom. Every summer we commuted between the two, sweeping through the lanes and on to the moors in a crimson Alvis, inwardly rejoicing at the rumble of the cattle grids under the car. A silver eagle mounted on the bonnet led the way. Buzzards resting up on telegraph poles marked the route. Grim summits, broken boulders and a solitary lake flanked by rushes passed by on either side. The wilderness meant freedom. The sea lay beyond.

There was conventional English history and one, like *Lavengro* by George Borrow, under the skin: a feared, fearful and magnetic place rich in customs, dress and language that could vary from one village to the next. A cob cottage, however poor it looked, was not impoverished to me. A lonely heath or brooding moor was pre-enclosure England. I did not live in a fantasy world, but a fantastic, magical and vestigial one, with giant, windblown, twisted trees, wild ponies and home-made pasties wrapped in napkins and eaten on the beach in a secret cove. The men milked cows with crumpled and elliptical horns, caught crabs and cricked the necks of rabbits in huge hands. The women pressed sheets on ironing boards, peeled apples and laid the tea. Together they made the difference and came to represent a way of living and a gold standard that increased in value the older I became.

I was up at dawn, rain or fine, and out until nightfall, except for meals, served punctually and dispatched without a fuss. We ate a cooked breakfast, a proper lunch and a copious tea, by the fire or on the beach, depending on the season. The vegetables came to the table fresh every day; new-laid eggs and clotted cream the following day. The butter was occasionally made at home, or bought with the cheese from the farm over the field. Sour milk was used in cakes. The skim from the scalding pan went to the pigs.

The apples from the orchard were hard, sharp and sweet. The grapes from the hothouse, hanging in bunches between the vine leaves, were black, pippy and luscious. The tomatoes were fragrant, and tasted of fruit. The asparagus and first broad beans were eagerly awaited. The beef was fat, the bacon was meaty, and mutton was preferred to lamb. At Christmas, a York ham stood on the sideboard with a ripe Stilton beside it. Puddings at lunch and savouries at dinner brought meals to a close. Strong flavours predominated, claiming my palate early on: two-year-old cheese, Patum Peperium, and the soy and chillies in Worcestershire sauce.

In winter we had wild duck and snipe from Sedgemoor, oven-roasted on tiny bits of bread. In spring we had sweetbreads. In summer we went shrimping or cockling at low water, and spun for mackerel, then fried them on board the boat. If my mother had grouse sent down from Scotland, Cornish lobster or Torbay sole – the best of the soles – my brother and I had them too. We were lucky, we were sometimes reminded, and for starving children everywhere we finished the helpings on our plates. Nothing was wasted or went unappreciated. Nothing was analysed or trivialized. Nothing arrived without an explanation of what it was and where it came from. Some foods were 'good', which meant good to eat, and others were 'good for you', which meant 'eat up'. Then you thanked God in a peremptory manner, getting away with it and hastily getting down.

Mrs Whaites did the cooking. She was ample, homely and dependable, with blue eyes and pinny, and large soft hands perfectly proportioned for making cakes, lifting cream, patting butter and holding wooden spoons. She rolled up her sleeves to cure the meat Somerset-fashion, rubbing it with the treacle in the tub until her arms were covered up to the elbow. Her husband, whom she called 'Whaites!', had an honest and trusting face, lined, worn and leathery from years outside. His strong, safe grasp was firm with horses, gentle with eggs, and certain to catch a boy who ran and jumped. The couple lived in a pink pebbledashed cottage overlooking the narrow lane that had once been the main coach road from London to Exeter and beyond. They had a chicken run, a potato patch, a few fruit trees and a whitewashed hive of bees, informed of Whaites' death when the old boy died. People round about said it stopped them swarming.

Mrs Ford took over when Mrs Whaites retired, going about her duties just the same. She piled the pots of jam on the shelf in the larder and cast an expert eye at the pans as they simmered on the stove. We met every morning for elevenses in the kitchen. Churchill, our cowman and gardener, clad in old cords, came in from the cold. Conks and Mary, his wife and daughter, who worked in the house, made hot drinks. Sometimes we were joined by Elkington, a hard old boy from along the lane who riddled the boiler, helped with the pigs and lived (by way of an explanation) with his sister and sister-in-law. The fish man called on Tuesdays and Fridays; then the butcher, Mr Baker, and the baker, Mr Hussey, in his red and black van and coarse-cloth coat with his huge creaking basket full of loaves. The bright eyes, weathered faces and rich, round West Country voices mingled with the sight of cream scalding and the smell of fowl boiling. The kitchen was the cosiest, safest and warmest room in the house.

Uncle Ned, a relation by marriage, residual grandee and patron of the living, belonged to the previous age but one. He was descended from a London banker who had 'downsized' in the eighteenth century and consolidated his rank in the age-old English way – by acquiring land from a family in decline. Now time was running out for Uncle Ned as well: his classical pile and its mighty columns, his fine possessions, overgrown garden and arcane and presidential way of life, which intoxicated me and everyone else. I liked the whiff of ritual, going to tea, and the endless dusty rooms. In the silent, crowded hall, a stuffed white fox and sixty sightless birds, imprisoned in glass cases, stood and stared at the world outside. The manor, church and banqueting hall nestled together in the distance. A pair of half-timbered cottages, custom-built to please a child bride in her native Cheshire style, clung to the hill.

The food was part of it all, neither a bit part nor an outsized one. It was part of an education, a picture and a design representing England that needed every card in the deck to make proper sense. It played an important everyday role, and came by routes that were of great fascination to an enquiring infant mind. By the age of eight I had driven the cattle to the cow house, seen the cream lifted, and eaten it with splits and whortleberry jam at mahogany tables, in cottage kitchens, and on woolly rugs spread in the heather or upon the sand. Even at school, the eggs were fresh, the milk was good, the ices were great, and cooking allowed a provocative three days a week.

The sum of all these parts was a kick-start. It proved an advantage to know in an urbanized society for what purpose a sheep or a tree occupies a field. I felt lucky to have registered the work and lives involved, even to eat: a fact and a privilege underlined in a Third World slum, when a shrunken, grey-haired woman with a plate of precious meat offered to share it with a man passing by.

PARADISE LOST

It was the late fifties, and the West Country seemed to lie untouched. Taunton had a gunsmith, a shoemaker, a master grocer, a shop that sold fudge – run by two jolly men in chef's whites who looked like French cook Paul Bocuse* – and the last hotel in any town with a working livery stable. The biggest excitement was the county cricket XI coming third in the championship and giving the mighty Surrey a nasty scare. The Churchills, having raised several children, acquired a bathroom; the Elkingtons refused one; and with the number of cars on the roads, the journey to Falmouth took as long as it can today.

My father had remarried, sold up and taken an Exmoor pub for a bit, but felt he had to move on, settling closer to London, where the changes to sweep across the rest of England had already taken place. Meanwhile, my stepfather and my mother stayed put. From the age of four to fourteen I travelled between parents six times a year, suffused with elation or desolation according to the direction of the train. The journey took me back and forth, like Alice through the looking glass, into and out of the long dark tunnel on the GWR, and the wonderland on one side. The old, magical and vestigial world where the cider 'dropped bright' and the weather was 'wicked' could not have been richer. The new and concentric one upcountry I was happy

---

* One of the greatest living French cooks, who was in the British Army during the war. He still has porridge
   for breakfast, and likes kippers with white wine.

to leave behind. I was making plans, aged thirteen, and preparing for the day. Then it all came tumbling down.

Progress descended on the west and quickened, creating and devastating with equal power, and working its way through the high-banked lanes to the farms, dairies, and kitchens like ours that lay beyond the long dark tunnel through the hill above the moors. The death of Uncle Ned and the sight of his house in its final moments, dark and empty one evening in late summer, seemed to betoken things to come that were borne on the wind. A year later, with even less warning, my stepfather sold up too. He may have sensed that gentlemen farmers were on death row with the yeomen, peasants, miners, fishermen, huntsmen, grocers and other master craftsmen. The mixture of egalitarianism and elitism, Thatcher style, that swept them away was just around the corner.

It is easy to see what happened. My parents relinquished a way of life, a package and dependants making up my world; I lost a paradise and, after a few false starts, spent the rest of my life trying to regain it.

NORMANDY STORES, LONDON

I drifted out of school to London and into various forms of employment, from tour guide to a runner of antiques, travelling in between. I took a Christmas job in Harrods, and got the sack, but emerged from the dairy counter with a slightly increased knowledge of how to make a living. A fellow spirit, Stuart Wood, brought up on a farm on the Surrey–Hampshire border, where the manager's wife made all the butter and cheese, had an idea. We should open a master grocer's, and a plan went into action, based on his obtaining the dosh and my obtaining the experience.

The Normandy Stores was one of the late, great ethnic food shops in the Portobello Road, cast in the same mould as the Epicerie Francaise and Gomez Ortega of Soho, and advertising for a position I was able to fill. The business had been started by a drunken and charismatic Pole and his glamorous Jewish wife, originally from Caen, hence the title of the business. The employees were a mixture that included two Lithuanians and a Czech. The customers were mainly expatriate Europeans and Russians, who jostled each other and pointed, barking orders in strange tongues. From each unintelligible sentence I learned to extract the single word, or two at the most, indicating what people wanted: '*Kartenrauch!*' '*Kruptczatka!*' '*Garbanzos!*' '*Tarhonya!*' or '*Edulsuss!*'

The Normandy sold over a hundred and fifty different types of sausages, salamis and chorizos, fifty cheeses, and up to five varieties of cheesecake, as well as salt herring, sauerkraut in barrels, ground paprikas, rye breads, Canadian flour, Turkish coffee, carp at Easter, and panettone at Christmas. A prize-winning Cheddar, stripped, washed and bearing its gong from the Bath and West, offered by the factor, took its place amongst them after the show.

There was little in the English repertoire to interest us at the Normandy, or so it seemed to one of the lads who worked by my side. But what did he understand, born and bred in London of Polish parents, and what did I? We were selling prosciutto, serrano and *jambon de Bayonne* while the last Cumberland sow had perished and with her the hams that went down on the *Titanic*. And I never knew. I was absorbed, far away, and amongst a ninth and tenth generation of town-dwellers. The loss meant nothing.

The enduring love affair with olive oil and European food had begun in London, but the Normandy did not last. It was too small, too specialized, too good in a sense, and went the same way as Powell's of Falmouth, Stokes of Salisbury and other master grocers smelling of bacon and coffee whose personal service, lacquered tea tins and marble counters were not required. If our plan to open a shop had passed the drawing board, we too would have gone bust. And the reasons? One of them was opposite the Normandy: a bog-standard self-service entitled Tesco.

Thanks to London weighting I dismissed the country and what it had to offer on all but the prescribed level of pretty pictures and given destinations, which often consisted of big houses. The bigger and grander, the better, it seemed, and opinion was with me. I, obsessively visual and now on the fringe of the art world, had gone down with a familiar symptom. I had got the classical bug and got it bad. Uncle Ned's Palladian mansion, its towering columns, high ceilings and eclectic mixture of contents, of all my childhood memories, had become the most blessed.

VERNACULAR AND CLASSICAL

Francesco Luzietti was an Italian journalist whom I met in Africa. We kept up, exchanged visits and used to argue about the relative vices and virtues of each other's countries. When I went to his, he showed me around. When he came to mine and asked to see an English house, I took him to a classical pile – one of the self-styled 'Magnificent Seven' – a couple of hours from London. I never recovered. It was a feeble and unimaginative choice, which Francesco tore to shreds. He found the building fraudulent, inappropriate, ridiculous and unlived in, neither English in conception, nor suited to its resting place a thousand miles from Rome.

We traded insults, retreated, regrouped, and started again on a summer's morning a day or two later with a different brief. The mission was to find anything indigenous and historic, but with life and breath still in it, to compare with the parts of Italy where Francesco had taken me. We made for the sea through a succession of villages with a superficially dreamy quality and pretty houses restored to within an inch of their lives, nothing more. The matter of food cropped up. What was Portland known for? Fish, said I, wheatears and mutton, but that was long ago.

It was late in the afternoon when we came to a gate with a box of plums labelled 'Help Yourself' and a sign saying 'Teas'. The garden beyond had a vegetable plot, fruit bushes, a rickety beehive, and a few fowls scratching around underneath the trees. The lawn was rough. The borders were random. An innocent cottage stood at the end of a curvy drive. It had faded blue paint, white Gothic windows and an open door. There were books at ten pence each piled on a trestle table, logs in a grate, swept floorboards, and promises of apple cake within. A woman appeared in a pinny, seated us and took our order. And could I have a boiled egg from one of the chickens? 'Course, said she.

Francesco was enchanted, but still on the offensive. It seemed to him, and seemed craven, that the English worshipped other cultures, customs and food to the exclusion of our own, and places like the cottage we had come to. Crane Kalman, founder of the Gallery of Naive Art in Bath, thought so too – blaming what he called the 'classical obsession' for thwarting 'interest in the heritage of ordinary people . . . seamen, farmers, innkeepers' – and cooks as well.

I had a personal stake in the debate, and divided loyalties until that moment. Uncle Ned himself had lived in an 'Italian' house with a Greek temple, Dutch paintings and French furniture. He favoured German music, Portuguese wine, Spanish dogs, Himalayan shrubs and Lebanese cedars. It was a queer and disconnected way to live, based on cribbed ideas, souvenirs and status symbols, which had helped to suffocate or weaken almost every vernacular art, artefact and achievement, and I had been programmed to look up to it.

I felt outraged by the suggestion, then chastened, and released from a process of conditioning which was twenty years old and all set to last a lifetime. I was treading an accepted route with blinds on either side which I could leave, or lift and peer behind. There was a universe and a parallel one between motorways and beyond city limits. The signal it sent out was growing fainter, but clinging on and waiting to be acknowledged. I had discovered through an Italian what to look for in England while the English looked abroad.

YEW TREE COTTAGE

Dark stories had filtered through to me in London. Great swathes of cow pasture, sheep walk, orchards and hedges had surrendered to efficient field systems and the plough. Yet on sporadic visits to Somerset and Cornwall, the view appeared the same as before from the train or car. Perhaps I wanted it to be. Was I being ignorant, or wilfully ignorant, of events taking place?

The time to move on and the place to go to chose themselves. It was one icy Christmas Eve in a part of England I hardly knew that I was taken by a friend to the back room of a pub, lit by candles, the power having failed in the storms and snow. The ceiling was treacle-bound from years of nicotine, the hip-high panelling black. The beer came from a row of barrels. A picture on the wall showed a large dog lying on its side and the owner regarding it sadly. 'Poor Trust Is Dead' said the words above the couple, and below them, 'Bad Pay Killed Him'.

Four men sat on benches, their boots dripping on the lino, pints on a table before them and pegs advancing round a cribbage board. The talk was of boundary fencing, pony drifts and cattle being rustled. A single oak log burned in the grate. When visitors came in and closed the door, depriving the fire of its draught, smoke filled the room and forced them out into the cold again. Above the huge bed of ash in the hearth, silhouettes of meat from an acorn pig, suspended from cross-sticks high above the grate, stood out in relief against the night sky. The pub had everything I desired. The beer was good, the welcome almost hostile, the paintwork struggling, the carpet absent and the food authentic, even if it was only for the landlord. This place would do. By and by, I fetched my own hams from the chimney too.

The cottage I rented, half-timbered, thatched, was similar and in similar condition to the pub. It had the beam for my bacon, a huge hearthstone and a stove for drying mushrooms that played up in the north wind. The previous occupants included the painter Gwen John, and a white witch and engraver who served a few teas. There had been no changes since the 1930s, and there were none with me. The doors, the walls and uneven brick floor, bathed every night in oil lamp light, cried out to be left alone. Behind the cottage lay the chalk and the downs, and before it the 'Queen of Rivers'. Beyond, there was a ninety thousand acre expanse of heath, scrub and cover, where a king was killed in a pagan sacrifice (Ross Williamson, 1974), and, deep in the greenwood I was told, the last incident of death by panic took place on English soil.

I never doubted how much I could learn from being in the cottage, or suffered a moment's illness, cold and primitive as it was. I remained through long frosts, snowdrifts, and floods bringing hundreds of duck to temporary lakes, and a bittern to the bed of waving reeds. The hurricane came through, uprooting eighty-foot trees and leaving them scattered and splintered across the main road. The garden suffered, but survived. There were apples until Christmas, blewits at the gate, and wild pears nearby. A rookery woke me in the morning, a sparrowhawk hunted at four. A wren, and a robin that attacked its own reflection in the mirror, came in and out of the house at will.

The meadow opposite the cottage was a hop over the road and stile. It was drained when the Avon was a moving swamp and drowned (i.e. irrigated) until the war. The old sluices, rotten but still in evidence, let in the river over the flood plain during storms. When it froze in winter, the ice creaked, groaned and splintered under foot. When it thawed, the swans cruised along the ditches, thicker than maggots apparently swimming on dry land. The cobs, drawing blood, fought to the death while I stood watching, thrilled and appalled by their struggle to force each other's head under water. I walked the ground almost every day for ten years and usually encountered something: owls and foxes hunting, redshank piping, snipe drumming, buck browsing, and a snake swimming the river. The meadow was the godliest place in Hampshire, inviolate from the traffic roaring by, but created by man to increase supplies of food – an early bite for sheep, a later one for cattle, plus venison, wildfowl, coarse and game fish, crayfish, eels, plovers' eggs, blackberries, wild mint and brooklime.

The most extraordinary thing about the meadow was this. The owner, paradise though he had, could not sell it. No one came up with an offer. So complete was the changeover to intensive farming in and around the Avon valley, as elsewhere, that soft or inaccessible non-arable land had no monetary value. The virtues that commended the land to a lover of birds, botany, beef or butter lopped thousands of pounds off the market price.

The New Forest, or simply 'the Forest' to its residents, a former royal hunting ground, lay across the Avon. It had a less forbidding presence than the West Country moors, but offered the same freedom of movement, and upheld the same independence. Jusserand, a Frenchman writing on England in the Middle Ages, felt he entered the Forest's precincts as he did another country. I did too, so different were its by-laws and customs from the surrounding countryside. Some people, used to polite and controlled fields and gardens, are threatened by the desolation and disorderliness of the landscape. Others cannot leave it without feeling confined, or even leave it at all.

The Forest owed its existence to those who honoured it, understood it, and fought a century of battles on its behalf to maintain a balance and continuity already rare in Victorian England. In an almost unprecedented defence of public interest in the early twentieth century, local grandees rose against their peers to protect the land from partition, clear-felling and agricultural development. Without their intervention, support and a well-run campaign, it would not have survived in anything but name, and would have merged with the surrounding countryside.

The Forest remained a collection of commons, utilised by commoners with a history of eking out a living on marginal land, or going to sea. Rights of pasture and mast (see page 143) helped to keep a working population and ways of life going which were imaginary elsewhere. Within a few miles of my door, there were cattle unconfined, swine amongst the acorn crop, sheep on the purlieu, geese on the marsh, three private cream- and butter-makers, three slaughtermen, three cider presses, two eel stages, two pirate stills, and a coterie of wildfowlers, in addition to several butchers and Women's Institutes, fish from the coast, and fruit and veg for sale at farm and cottage gates. There was only one way to discover and capitalize on such assets: by going cautiously native, staying awake, and taking people and places as I found them.

THE FRONT LINE

Ringwood cattle market was the place to go on Wednesdays: an animated remnant of pre-enclosure England, and the last trading place for the commoners, cottagers, smallholders, travellers and horse copers in and around the Forest and its outlying fragmentary heaths. People arrived by car, van, bike and trap, and visitors queued in the summer to take part in the same unscripted costume drama. A man came in with an owl on his shoulder, another with a dog that he wore like a shawl. The Bengalis from the curry houses in town bought fowls live and dead. There were ponies, pigs, and occasionally house cows too.

The produce auctions were held in the Egg Shed, a dingy, draughty crinkly tin shack painted green, reminiscent of a pre-war village hall or cricket pavilion. An overgrown garden rose behind, and a sprawling medlar tree with fruit for jelly. The bell rang at eleven. At Christmas, turkeys and geese from common and marsh were laid out in rows, feet erect and shoulder to shoulder. The rabbits, emptied but jackets on, one hind leg threaded through the other, were hung along the wall in pairs. You looked them over inside and out for wounds, and a nice covering of fat around the kidneys, then bought a couple with an option on the rest. There were hares in the winter, and every type of bird from pigeon to wigeon, all sorts of eggs, vegetables from cottage gardens, cress from the beds, Guernsey cream and local butter, lovingly churned and compassionately wrapped in plain waxed paper. Nothing was packaged. There were no guarantees, sell-by dates, false promises or lures. You bought every item as seen, knowing it was local, seasonal and the rest, and left the market feeling both rewarded and richer with dinner in the bag.

It was a muggy July day in 1988, promising thunder. While the county prepared for its best-kept village competitions, flower shows and fêtes, the hammer fell on the last pair of rabbits in the Egg Shed and the site was sold for development. As the man at my elbow said, the deed was accomplished at the stroke of an accountant's pen. None of us who gathered together and tried to prevent it met again. An inanimate wall and barn were saved by conservationists. The life that went on around them ceased. A supermarket rose upon the site. Where the cattle were auctioned there are now ranks of cars; where the ponies trotted out, bronze replicas. The medlar tree stood naked, exposed and abandoned, dropping its fruit on a pedestrian precinct, then withered and died. Across the dwindling heath, a £6 million Wessex World was proposed for Bournemouth.

By the 1990s, four out of five people in the UK lived in towns. A higher proportion lived as if they did. The cattle market was doomed because it failed to conform. Hampshire was not only blind to the auctions' charms, but unsettled by them. The Egg Shed was not for the urban-minded polite society or weekenders fearful of confronting taboos. It was too rough, too ready and too near a threatening 'front line'. With its mucky boots, crude banter and unedited mix of country life and death, no place on earth was less likely to survive.

I never got over the closure of the Egg Shed (which shut in the late 1980s), and was not allowed to, what with all the carry-on about life in Provence. It was not until the market had gone that Ringwood acquired a sign saying 'Ancient Market Town'. Then it opened up to European traders. Over a three-day festival many years later, wrote the *Forest Journal*, 'a host of stalls offering authentic French fare were set up', while can-can dancers provided entertainment. The organiser said: 'this time of year trade can be a little slow – but the market kept shoppers in the town for longer'.

Ringwood cattle market was nothing to the media, but famous far and wide. After it went I met a couple from the Midlands who made a point of dropping in twice a year on their way to the ports and the sea. When it emerged that I lived nearby, they became indignant – almost angry. How could an interested party like me have let the market go? By failing to convince the local MP, district council, county council, town council or historical society, said I, in a repetitive and gruelling correspondence which ended where it had begun, that there was anything of historical, social, educational or emotional, let alone culinary, importance worth hanging on to.

THE BOOK

After protracted trips around Europe, Africa and Asia it was time for America's east coast. I went to see New York, and, having been a tour guide in London giving out history, to get some of theirs back. The sight of North Devon oxen at Mount Vernon and York-type hams in Smithfield, Virginia, cherished more abroad than they were in their own country, led me to consider the position at home. If there was one image that had been distorted it was that of rural England, one contribution undervalued it was the rural artisan's, and one market struggling it was the beef, the butter or the fruit he produced. I had always wanted to write. I now knew what to write about and how, as a traveller and talent scout, to go about it.

The subject of English food proved even bigger and touched more subjects than I, a sympathetic voyeur, had thought. I was motivated by love, loss, and adverse publicity: critics who had eaten the worst food that England had to offer, relived it ever since and failed to find anything better or even to embark on the search. To such negative perceptions I never became resilient, but did become resigned. Plenty could be found below an acceptable level – everyone knew that – but I never let it divert or exasperate me, nor felt it represented the nation's sole capability, achievements or gold standards.

I responded to food like a Frenchman. I was also determined to find what I was looking for, and seldom disappointed. The advantage that restaurateurs, chefs and journalists had over me was that they were at the centre of things: in military terms, at headquarters. The advantage I had over them came from being in the field, amongst proven or wasted assets and remains. No new gastronomic phase or fancy could beat the personal discovery of a master butcher, or the annual rediscovery of the Guernsey cream, purple egg plums and half-wild pork that helped to make life in the countryside worth living. For the beau monde of cookery, work began when food entered the kitchen. Then, for me, it was more or less done.

I have never concerned myself with other people's eating habits, except when they threatened mine. Some folks do not like you to plough your own furrow; it must be like theirs. It is always worth protesting, but costly and distracting.

The 1990s were a bleak and horrid period. Often I finished a chapter only to cross it out, the star of the show having perished in battle. It looked as if English food was going the same way as the songs, dances and dialects. A culture was faltering, and with it my faith in its survival and my campaigning towards that end. The nosedive continued, the seasons came and went, and other work took over. Every two or three months, my stepmother, irked at not being rung herself, rang me.

'Still scribbling away in a damp little cottage for no reward?' she used to ask.

'We shall see,' I drawled. The rejection of my suit seemed more and more likely. I had no contract to fulfil, no deadline to meet, and no obligations except to my wife, whose faith in the project kept all three of us on the rails.

Most of my research was done at large. Many times my wife and I, returning home, were too full to speak of the brave, true, wise, wily, doomed or defiant souls who, for every two paces we took in their direction, took twice the number towards us. Many days thereafter, still in silence, we recalled the haunting and precious moments, mutual understandings and confidences exchanged in a draughty barn or quiet kitchen with night falling outside. No time spent could have been more affecting and absorbing, none more poignant than the trust given by men with values and women with vision, overcome by the interest a stranger took in their nobility, labours and lives. I could never have found out all they knew without reversing roles, but found out enough in brief encounters to fill the head, touch the heart and raise the occasional smile.

Writers do writing. The rest have a living to make, I was reminded by a sheep farmer from the coastal strip, with whom I got acquainted over his salt-marsh lamb. At close of play in Lancaster market, he asked me to hitch up his trailer while he reversed the car.

'Can you manage?' he asked.

'Of course,' I said, and added a little preciously, 'I am very strong.'

He looked me up and down.

'Must be all that bloody writing.'

Inevitably, I read – mindful of how 'unimaginably different' (as the poet Louis MacNeice wrote) the past must have been, and how open the present is to biased or inaccurate interpretations. It is not easy to understand what England was like when there was licensed rape, boys were 'tried out', and men knew everyone in their village but none in the next, nor what it meant to buy food, fuel or medicine. Secrets were transmitted by word of mouth and imitation, not written down, and prevented from reaching a wider audience by poor communication and social barriers: the lack of curiosity in some people, suspicion in others, and the mutual awkwardness town and country dwellers can feel in each other's company. We shall never know how much history was withheld from prying eyes or withered on the vine. The estimated twelve hundred folk songs lost to Hampshire and Dorset alone may be a clue.

I was in the fortunate position of not having to use culinary folk tales from the history of England to prove how good the food could be. We did indeed have less to be ashamed of than people imagined, but because of what endured in the present rather than what happened in the past. Dorothy Hartley seemed to be saying the same thing, but in a different era. Every time I dipped into her book, published in only 1954, one thing became clearer. Of her *Food in England*, the food *of* England was what remained. The question was whether there was room for English food in a country increasingly forced to defend itself from the safe, inclusive and culturally nondescript 'British' label, or would it be the last?

From childhood, I loved the continuity embodied in man and beast, the work they did, and the trail they left for us to interpret in forests and field systems, gardens, churchyards, churches, houses, and the public bars of ungentrified pubs. I suspected people and institutions to whom it all meant nothing. I despaired at the easy meat the public made for corporate interests, at economic and civic decisions, and at the zero consultation with people in the know. I despised political assurances, the calculation of votes, and the upturned noses sniffing the wind. I feared the shadow cast by London, its self-importance, lack of curiosity, and power to legislate for the state. I feared the influence of the media in its embrace. I feared even more received wisdom, the assumptions made and the insidious effect that a backward look could have on emotions, which a street full of traders never did. I feared most of all the people who, acting as imperialists and eager to colonize, brought their own set of values to defenceless places.

I am not a 'foodie' or a chef, but a feeder and a cook who neither eats to live nor lives to eat. There is a middle course: to live, and eat well too. To eat appropriately is even better: game in winter, plums in summer, crabs in Cromer, and sole in Dieppe. It is not much more trouble, no more expensive, and puts you in touch. There is so much more to life than food, so much connected to it, and so much to be missed by taking it for granted.

CHAPTER FIVE

ON THE ROAD

# ‘THE BUTTER,’ I said to the girl behind the chiller, ‘do you sell much?’

‘Quite a lot.’

‘Whey or full cream?’ It was a loaded question. You cannot tell at a glance.

‘I am not sure.’

‘Does the producer make cheese?’

‘No.’

Full cream, then. Hen's teeth. There were about six or so private butter-makers left in England, and here was another. I looked round. The shop was stocked with the usual packets, jars, biscuits and cheeses, but not bad, its mere existence a positive signal. The town, crammed with the shopkeepers who once made a nation, was still the 'lovely little place' that people remembered, and functioning as well, thanks to a supermarket's failure to buy and develop the site it wanted. For twelve years the council had fought off the constant pressure and financial incentives to give in. A heroic struggle due to be appreciated in the next phase.

I purchased a pound of the butter, expressing an interest in meeting the person who made it and brought it in. The girl sized me up. She said that would probably be OK and, after checking, wrote down the name 'Kitty' and an address. The farm I wanted was marked on the map, an oasis in broad sweeps of manicured land working to fill mighty barns. The telltale and contrasting sight of green grass and Jersey cattle emerged at the end of a sycamore drive: twenty or thirty well-kept girls lying down, chewing away, tame as puppies.

A path led through a courtyard to the back door of a red-brick house. I knocked. A woman in her fifties or sixties appeared, her face honest and her hair falling in grey ringlets. She was wearing a cheerful pinny over a blue top, checked skirt and walking shoes, and carrying a stick to help her get about. Kitty, having had a call from the shop, was expecting visitors. Come inside. The dairy was the first room on the left down a passage, next to a larder. It was equipped with a built-in safe with gauze over the doors, a brick shelf, and a cricket table, which stood on a concrete floor, painted over. There was a continuous-flow separator for removing the cream from the milk, with the familiar red body, cup and spouts; a wooden end-over-end churn, mounted on a stand; and an earthenware pancheon to salt the butter in: all museum pieces and in good working order. A pile of greaseproof paper was waiting. A north-facing window with muslin on one side and bars on the other let in a quiet light from the overgrown yard outside.

The house was pure throughout, never mind the butter. Apart from a post-war Rayburn, there was nothing amongst the fixtures, fittings and furniture, not a floorboard, not a lick of paint that postdated the Victorian era. The cast-iron range in the kitchen, the glass in the windows, the doors and handles, the pair of lace curtains hanging from the stair, the floral carpets and wallpaper, the mahogany tables and chairs, the clock, the black marble fireplace, the tiles, brass fender, plant pot and stand, the sideboard, the pictures and the china had all been put together a hundred years before.

Kitty's mother was reading the paper. She was confined to a wheelchair and in her nineties, but in full possession, and as strong in spirit as the room around her. Another house had stood upon the spot, which must have been of some importance. It was acquired by Sir James Lancaster, navigator, and left to charity in 1618. One of the Stuart kings stayed the night on his way north. A serving maid, fearful for her chastity, spent his visit in the well outside. The place had been known ever since as Maidenwell. An unlikely town council many miles away, who were subsequent owners, erected new buildings and let them with land to Kitty's family in 1903. Her father bought the freehold with sixty acres of trees and grass a few years before he died in 1981. Two stone tablets, recording some of the facts, were embedded in external walls of the house. A third covered the well, still in excellent order, but no longer used.

Kitty, born in the house, milked by hand from the age of sixteen. With all the men off to fight the war, she had to do their work. She had made butter twice a day for over fifty years, but, like a lot of country people, ate little of her own produce. She also made buttermilk cheese, which I had heard of in connection with sailing ships' provisions, but not encountered. On the Sunday before Christmas, the house opened its doors to a carol service. The fires in the hall and dining room, belching out the heat from solid, efficient Victorian grates, kept everyone warm.

My gaze drifted through the door and window to the field outside, returning to the room on each occasion. My voice when I spoke felt like an imposition, my presence a peculiar distance from the sacred surroundings. I stayed for about an hour, then rose to go.

'That butter has heart!' the mother said in farewell.

Elevenses: best meal of the day, especially on the road. It consists of home-made bread, marmalade or jam, and butter, Kitty's in this case, accompanied by a silky, syrupy half-cup of *veluto nero* brewed in a percolator in the car and topped up with hot milk. Tea is runner-up, provoked by the unfailing habit of even the swankiest venues to close at the moment you want them: between half past four and five. A kettle and a piece of WI cake, or splits and cream in Devon and Cornwall, come to the rescue.

The spots are carefully chosen, quiet, pastoral, by the seaside or a stream, perhaps on a moor, in an oak wood, or near an old building. England provides. The time arrives, the rug is comfy, the opportunity stolen, and the pleasure out of all proportion to the cost. Churches and churchyards are favourite, often wistful and worth half an hour of an unwatched clock. I read the writing on the gravestones, grouping families, matching names, and calculating ages younger than they might have been, younger than mine.

Where to stay? At selected boltholes and minimal campsites within reach of the sea or a river to swim in, a hill to climb, shops to shop in, and that all-important pub where knowing and 'secret'* people smoke, drink and talk or sing. Once, on a cold Christmas Eve, I left home in the dark and stopped to check out a place known as the Monkey House, which sold cider only: hatch for a bar, thatch for a roof, and no food – people brought their own if they wanted it. A woman was seated at a table, cutting bread, spreading it with dripping from a cup and sprinkling it with salt wrapped in a paper bundle. She asked me to join her: I must have been looking hungry, thirsty too. An old man with whiskers left me a pint. I never found out who they were. Angels probably.

On our way across England, my wife and I bought a Staffordshire bowl, a print, a rummer and various plants. Too early for evensong in Lincoln Cathedral, we looked at the arches and listened to the footsteps on the floor. There were black bullets in the sweet shop on the hill. The Jew's house looked ever older – will it last another 900 years? A travelling salesman had spoken of Spilsby market, which reminded me of Ringwood as was: strong faces, flat hats, coats, boots and similar banter, but a language of different lanes, and fields disappearing into the distance to match the mighty expanse of sky. Skeggy was bracing indeed: a place to see Ken Dodd, and see him you must, says writer Hugh Massingberd. They say there is a town out at, and under, the sea. A single fishing boat lay listing on the mud at Gibraltar Point, surrounded by dunlins and marine buckthorn growing from the sand. They get godwits out here, tall and red-breasted, which we do not in Hampshire. Norfolk looked like another country, and was, a dark grey belt of land imposed upon a light grey treacherous Wash.

Boston is an inland port still reasonably prosperous. Its grandiose church, called the Stump, is visible for miles. There is a smashing green caravan in the market, which people can lean their bikes against and pop into for tea. An Indian trader liked it as much as I did: 'Different, innit?' The fishmonger in the square must be crammed in season with some of the wildfowl which come in their millions to overwinter. A fish and chip shop with its original interior, front and sign above has closed. Perhaps the new owner will know what he has bought. Parts of the coastal strip, guarded by windmills, manned by immigrants and vacated by the sea, can bear three crops a year. Best soil in England, says farm manager Brian Martin.

To Gainsborough, a possible victim of civic decisions, and at the end of a downward cycle which had yet to resume an upward journey. In the middle of the high street, behind farmers' market stalls, stood a double-fronted butcher's shop. The name 'Surfleet', in sharp silver capitals, stood out from a black glass background above the door. From behind a counter on the left, two fresh-faced middle-aged women were serving brawn and haslet. On the right, a

---

* *G. K. Chesterton.*

lean, spare man in his sixties, wearing a white coat, shirt and tie, was cutting pork. A whole fillet of beef, and a wing rib on two bones, suitably black at the edges, lay in the chiller before him. There was bacon and the last quarter of a large dry-salted ham, with dark red meat and a hard, light brown skin.

The only signs in the shop indicated prices. The black and white floor was marble and the walls were clad in ceramic tiles. In the room out the back, under a steel unit, was a round hardwood chopping block on three short legs. It was probably made of sycamore – like my carving board at home – a former favourite with butchers and cooks for its close grain and failure to collect smells. The thick honey-coloured block, scarred and worn with age, looked nineteenth-century, possibly earlier. It barely reached the knee: people were short in those days, and boys did the work of men.

The shop was too busy to force a chat, the impulse too strong to resist. The proprietor was a testy man, who did not like me much – or anyone else, I guessed – but that did not matter. After a slow start, we got going. The business had been run by many generations of the Surfleet family. He, apprenticed to the last, took over after the war. He had learned to buy thriftily, to cook chitterlings, make brawn and salt meat in temperatures diminished by scalping winter winds. His beef had gone to Sandringham. Most of the customers knew what they wanted. A retired vet, taking delivery of pork bellies, liked to make his own sausages.

I wanted to make an offer for the chopping block, but held off. I did not like mentioning business either. Surfleet was not the sort of shop to court publicity, attract attention or entertain the beau monde. It was not only too serious: the proprietor did not feel he should have to. He still cured pigs for the older people, farmers and initiates, but not in the numbers he had. Demand and takings were down, the premises up for sale. People were paying to see the plastic hams mounted crazily on a spit in the Old Hall, an adjacent half-timbered building and museum, rather than to buy the real ones in a nearby butcher.

There were eggs for breakfast, and cheeses and tomatoes for lunch, all in the market. The season for samphire, sold in bunches from the coast, was over. Surfleet's brawn and radishes dipped in salt, plus a Beauty of Hampshire brought from home, would be dinner. The shopping done, we beat it cross-country for the warp lands further north which used to be flooded to enrich the soil. Belton, one of the only two houses in England left with an eighteenth-century painted floor,[*] I had been to. Brigg and its fair, immortalised in song, I still have not. We have a date with Bourne, its sheep sales, and a village shop too, painted in several shades of blue.

---

* *Crowcombe Court, Somerset, was the other.*

The Humber Bridge was empty, the view either side worth every ounce of steel. The river below was a life-supporting, penetrating and magnetic line, a smooth-flowing artery to England's heart. It brought birds and habitation, water to land, ships in the flesh, and spectral invaders watched by prying, fearful and hidden eyes. The town of Hessle, located nearby, gave its name to a seedling pear. The smell of fish and the sight of its imprint on the pavements greeted us in Hull. We were making for a campsite on Sunk Island, a spot I had liked the sound of, only to be detained. We joined a small and silent crowd glued to a shop window and a TV screen, but not to wickets falling or goals being scored. It was a day of discoveries, breezes and grey skies, memorable on several counts. The date: 11 September 2001.

How To Shop – Food Normality*

The best buyers are opportunists. If you want food, and pass a shop with a gleaming and fluffy bass just in or a brace of partridge on the hook, get them quickly. Then decide what for. To go out looking for such things can lead to disappointment, and makes no allowance for the possibility that the best fish on the slab might be a mackerel or a gurnard, there might be no fresh fish at all, or there might be something better in the butcher's on the way.

Your aim is to be able to shop regardless of labels, recipes, advertising, fashion, food scares, gossip, health claims or other propaganda; to discriminate; and to buy on your own initiative – and on sight. Load the meter, ask questions, scout about, have a chat. No one buys a car without knowing what it is. They make it a priority and take the time to find out. Shopping for food can be a hunt for treasure, rewarding and creative – a pleasure that continues when you get home.

Most people think they have the best butcher, but however good he may be, there is less to be gained from letting him choose for you than from learning to do it for yourself – initially with his help. A good man will assist. Genuine experts, with nothing to hide, rarely hide much. They are only too pleased to share their knowledge, explain why and when their food is good, what conditions to look for, and how to test a ham or try a cheese.

The place helps. There are oatcakes in Staffordshire, kippers in Craster, cheeses in Yorkshire, and shrimps freshly boiled next to the sea. Many items do not travel. Anyway, it is fun to collect. The seasons positively limit the choice. A dinner in June, to take one month, need not feature anything imported or frozen. It can be built around spring lamb, sweetbreads, asparagus, new potatoes, rhubarb, and the raw deep-coloured Guernsey cream and farm butter that comes from cows in young grass.

---

* *Adapted from* Memories of Food at Gipsy House *by Felicity and Roald Dahl.*

In 2006, I met a girl of Czech extraction living in Devon and very pleased with her local plum. She was recording the 'lost flavours' that members of the public felt they missed. The funny thing was, she said, that most of the items people mentioned were still available.

From listed or endangered buildings, temporary stalls and rough auctions and farm gates, I have pounced on roasting hens, Muscovy and tufted duck, teal, snipe and woodcock; red, fallow, roe, sika and muntjac deer; salmon from the Taw, Tamar, Severn, Tyne, Lune, Wye and Hampshire Avon, sea trout, eels and every other type of fish; black puddings, hog's puddings, tripe, elder, cow heel, sheep's trotters, bag, and chitterlings; apple cake, barm cake, cider cake, dough cake, fat cake, heavy cake, white cake, yellow cake, cut rounds, muffins, pikelets and parkin; honey, marmalade, lemon curd, and high dumpsie dearie jam; bullace, damsons, medlars, quinces, mulberries and whortleberries, filberts, chestnuts, mushrooms, laver, salsify, samphire, scorzonera, sea kale, and baskets of other vegetables pulled or picked that day and good enough to enter the local show.

It would be unfair to take the credit for finding these things. They were not hidden: they presented themselves. All I had to do was stay away from the food giants, make an appropriate purchase, and be careful not to ruin it when I got home. This approach cannot be seen as going back to basics until people know what the basics are. If there must be a slogan it amounts to cooking and eating normally: food normality.

Two Cheers for Organic

The use of chemicals in English farming is not new. They have been put on the land since the nineteenth century. According to David Howard, the Prince of Wales's head gardener at Highgrove (quoted by Nigel Blundell in the *Daily Telegraph* in 2003), 'the rot set in after the First World War when stocks of sulphate of ammonia, previously used in munitions, were converted to inorganic nitrogenous fertiliser . . . this produced taller crops with better yields, but at the same time it left the plants weaker and more susceptible to attack by pests and diseases. So you suddenly needed two applications of chemicals . . . a fertiliser then a pesticide.'

Evelyn Balfour was one of the first people to appreciate the danger. In 1946 she responded by cofounding an organic movement entitled the Soil Association. Today it is a vocal minority with a niche market, a good record, exacting standards and a symbol that commands a premium on registered items.

Without the organic movement, even fewer traditions, lores, seeds and unspoiled patches of our green and pleasant land would have survived. Apart from rumours of squabbling within its ranks and the expense of obtaining separate licences for lamb, chicken, vegetables, wheat and the rest, there is only one thing for which the Soil Association can be criticized – and it is not its fault. Followers tend only to look for the symbol, and buy goods because they are labelled 'organic', with no further considerations.

However, to be a producer of organic vegetables involves much more than being chemical free. It means composting, saving or acquiring seeds, likewise organic, and meeting a long list of requirements that amateurs need not bother with and that may not make any difference to the quality of their produce.

The best cauliflower I have eaten happened to be organic. The best runner beans happened not to be. In my experience, the types of beans, peas or spinach matter more than anything else, but they need the right conditions and treatment in order to perform well and gain the desired amount of flavour. My neighbour's organic potatoes were delicious, whilst mine were not, yet we had grown the same type. The land, the weather, the fertilizer and the way the crop was kept and cooked, both individually and collectively, influenced the results.

Meat is another complex subject. Some beasts have the inbred potential to taste good as meat, whether they are organic or conventionally reared and slaughtered (see page 154). Others do not, regardless of how they are fed, hung and cooked. Game is organic in everything but title in its wild state. So are fish and shellfish caught at sea. So are England's ancient meadows, chalk downs and high fells. And so are the dwindling number of families who have farmed them in more or less the same way, and without recognition, since the pre-organic era.

Yet everything that lives or breathes in developed countries is subject to acid rain and various forms of pollution. The paradoxes deepen with man taking chemical doses for his ailments, insisting that his beef and lamb should not, and ignoring the food miles on goods flown in from the ends of the earth. And what of organic standards in countries which may be unreliable?

At present, only a tiny percentage of the goods eaten in England is organic and only a third of those home-grown, so the benefits to the nation's health and well-being are negligible, and largely ignored. Simultaneously the movement represents a better life, a way forward and also a way back to the time when food tasted of itself and rural England was more like the place it is imagined to have been. The label is honest, minimal and serious. Whilst it may not mean everything, it means more than lists of ingredients, sell-by dates, emotive words and cuddly or pastoral images cooked up by psychologists.

'Organic' is a battle cry worth supporting. It is an invitation to make connections and dig deeply into issues that affect the well-being of both man and beast.

CHAPTER SIX

RIGHT ON

WAS WALKING THROUGH A MARKET with a brace of wigeon, acquired in a market, slung over my shoulder when a woman accosted me. Her expression was one of outrage, and her message that 'it' – pointing to the birds – was 'cruel'.

We spoke, sensibly and logically, waiting for each other to finish before starting ourselves, emerging from the meeting as more conscious and enlightened human beings . . . I don't think. She was in no mood to stop, let alone listen, and nor was I: a pity for both of us.

From my point of view, the birds were obviously dead: they were not hanging live from the string around their necks and suffering. They had also enjoyed a free and fulfilled life, unlike the chicken in her shopping bag. She was a hypocrite. I knew better.

In May I hired a garden contractor. After work, he invited me to try the digger and have some fun. So I cleared some scrub. Ten minutes later I turned off the engine to hear shrieking. It came from a golden-crested wren – not the rarest bird in England, but a pleasing one, a harmless one, a tame, tiny and defenceless one with a green coat and cheerful hat, high on the list of charmers. Her nest still lay where she had built it in the brambles. The eggs were smashed, and by the digger with my hand on the controls.

I was no better than the woman at market, the average petrolhead, or a man with a hygiene fetish transferred from house to garden who mows his lawn rather than leaves it to grow up and burst into flower, providing food and cover for all manner of wildlife. I was a hypocrite too.

Many of us claim to be animal-lovers, green or greenish, but even the most sentimental are inclined to distance themselves when it comes to facing the consequences or changing direction. The addictions to mobility, comfort, tidy gardens and other forms of death-denial ensure that wildlife will suffer. As an afterthought it is protected by laws that may be neither enforceable nor effective, and might even have a negative result.

The collection of plovers' eggs took place every spring for hundreds of years, proving that the harvest was sustainable. Men and boys walked out in a line to breeding sites, looking hard and treading carefully. Their method was to take north and south eggs from each well-camouflaged clutch of four, followed by east and west the following day, leaving the mother to complete her maximum of eight and safeguarding supplies for the following year.

It was not until man did a long list of things an awful lot worse than harvesting the eggs that numbers plummeted; whereupon, as a token gesture, collecting was banned. There was no post-mortem to see whether the prohibition had worked, and no decriminalisation of the scapegoat. Today, nothing could be more morally reprehensible than taking a wild bird's egg (except lighting up a fag). Meanwhile, the number of plovers continues to decline without the causes being addressed, and poultry is kept in misery in order to feed the public.

Humanitarian issues can become political, with different social groups standing in opposition, firm in their prejudices, and experts – rather than men on the spot – giving advice. The future of deer, foxes and commons can thus be decided. Yet to someone who grows roses or beetroot and someone who does not, a roebuck is not the same beast.

Here are a few facts of country life and death (as they appear to me) that make the simplistic 'right on' routes so difficult to follow.

Man is a hunter born with his eyes to the front, whether or not the instinct is recognised, condoned or suppressed. The motivation to hunt has proved intolerable to Parliament, but not to the animal population. No English bird or beast has been hunted to extinction in the last three hundred years except the bustard and wild boar, and they were already on the way out.

Hunt abolitionists, including the RSPCA, got their way – but without contingency plans for the animals. They are now pledged to uphold the ban, monitor operations and produce evidence to prosecute anyone breaking the law and causing perceived cruelty to animals – but only from the fraternity that rides to hounds or follows them on foot.

I have not heard of any plans to monitor:

1. The urban poachers on Exmoor armed with infra-red rifles who kill deer for trophies in and out of season and leave the bodies decapitated in the field.
2. The owners of game cocks trained for fighting.
3. The owners of dogs ditto.
4. The owners of dogs that have coursed hares persistently and to the death at illegal meetings over the last hundred years.
5. The owners of dogs that kill without detection, in and out of season:
    (a) leverets, partly accounting for their fall in numbers;
    (b) ground-nesting birds, including nightjar, plover, redshank, etc., ditto.
6. The cyclists who disturb the above, putting mothers off their eggs.
7. Motorists, who are by far the biggest primary killers of mammals in England. The tally of animals hit, unreported, and left to die includes:
    (a) 100 ponies in the Forest every year;
    (b) 50,000 badgers throughout the UK;
    (c) an unspecified number of deer, foxes, hedgehogs, field mice, etc.
8. The closure of small abattoirs (see page 93).

Shooting and fishing are next in line for prohibition. Meanwhile, the cruellest things you can do to an animal are:

1. Occupy its breeding ground.
2. Change its climate.
3. Pollute or steal its water.
4. Kill its food.

Livestock are happiest in conditions they would choose for themselves: an open space for sheep, and access to cover for pigs and chickens. Farmers may be praised or blamed for the way their animals are kept, but they are doing as commanded by market forces. The buck stops with payer, not payee. Welfare-friendly meat is usually home-grown and expensive. To shirk the cost is to bolster production abroad – and in countries where the UK's regulations and priorities do not apply.

Wildlife is happiest where there is little or no intensive farming or public access. As a result, the Army is the nation's greatest gift to conservation. Ramblers are one of the greatest threats. The reasons why are hardly secret, but usually shoved to one side. I do the same every time I get into an aeroplane or a car. The best thing would be to get out and stay out, living for the environment and in the most challenging way possible since the eighteenth century. We may have to. The alternative, much more convenient and less effective, is to prop up worthy causes.

CHAPTER SEVEN

INDUSTRIAL FOOD:
THE FLIP SIDE

AKED BEANS

My guess is that baked broad beans, dried on the vine and cooked after the bread in the declining heat of a brick oven, constituted the original dish. Haricot beans were introduced to England in the sixteenth century (see page 349), and commonly eaten with pork (i.e. bacon). Home-grown haricots continued to be cultivated throughout the Victorian period, and featured in fish and chip shops between the wars (John Walton, 1992), but lacked the popularity of peas and came to be replaced in the nation's diet by US Navy beans. *Callos* in Spain and *cassoulet* in France, also baked beans, have maintained their rank.

Baked haricot beans come into their own at the end of the winter, when game is over, stews are called for, and home-grown potatoes are declining in quality (see page 365). Young, home-grown beans may need only a couple of hours' soaking in cold water. Otherwise leave overnight.

1lb (450g) haricot beans, 2lb (900g) bacon belly in a piece or a hock, 1 onion and at least 1 clove of garlic, peeled and sliced, 1 tsp tomato purée or sweet paprika, watch the salt and season to taste with pepper.

Cover the lot with water, bring up to simmering point and commit to a slow oven (150–170°C/300–325°F/gas mark 2-3) for up to 6 hours or until the beans and meat are tender. Serve the following day. Improves with age.

To vary: instead of the bacon use an oxtail browned on all sides, pieces of ox kidney or tripe, pig's or lamb's hearts, pig's chitterlings or bag, or salted duck or goose. For a kick, replace the tomato puree or sweet paprika with ½ tsp harissa or ½ tsp chilli powder.

Another recipe, looking authentic and cribbed from a tea towel, was brought home by a friend of mine from Jersey.

4oz (110g) broad beans, 4oz (110g) small haricots, 4oz (110g) large haricots, 4oz (110g) butter beans (runners).

Soak in water overnight, drain and add one pig's trotter or 2lb (900g) belly pork, sliced onions and carrot, salt and pepper. Place in earthenware crock pot. Cover with water, put on lid and cook in a slow oven (150–170°C/300–325°F/gas mark 2–3) for 7–8 hours.

TOMATO SAUCE

To eat, chill or store. I make about a dozen pots a year for spaghetti (see page 264), salt cod, aubergines, marrow, etc. Choose the biggest tomatoes you can grow or buy – it saves time and trouble. Some whopping fruits are available weighing over a pound each, and tasting grand in spite of their size.

6lb (2.6kg) tomatoes, 6 cloves of fresh garlic, 3 medium-sized onions, 3 tbsp olive oil, a glass of red wine, salt and black pepper.

Drown the tomatoes in boiling water. Remove and discard the skins. Squeeze the pips into a sieve, using a wooden spoon to extract the juice and a bowl underneath to catch it in. Slice the flesh and set aside. Heat the oil in a pan. Add the onions and garlic, peeled and chopped, and brown lightly. Mix in the tomatoes, the juice and the wine and season to taste. Bring up to simmering point and cook gently for half an hour. The sauce should end up the consistency of porridge. If too thick, reduce it. Otherwise, thin with a little boiling water.

To vary: for a hot, rich sauce, add 1 freshly chopped chilli or ½ level tsp chilli powder to the lightly browned onion and garlic, and cook gently for a minute before adding the tomato and 1 tsp soy.

For a herb-rich sauce, add a bunch of freshly chopped parsley, chervil, basil or chives before serving. If you are going to store the sauce, you need clean jam jars preheated for ten minutes in a cool oven, with lids to fit. Fill them while the sauce is still boiling and screw down the lids immediately.

GRAVY

Making gravy is a rare gift, an art and a challenge equal to almost anything in cookery, a chance to experiment, show off, and conjure up a result from what is in your cupboard and comes to hand. You need ingenuity, a gravy separator – skimming the fat does not work – and to get into the habit of hoarding any leftovers and by-products of your cooking which may be recycled and useful. My fridge often has a little pot in it containing a past gravy, no more than two or three tablespoons in quantity, which will make all the difference to a future one.

In addition to salt, pepper and sugar, look to the following items to build up the flavour.

For volume: stock is customary, but may not be on tap, which means improvisation; vegetable water – saved from boiled cabbage or sprouts, carrots, beans, peas or leeks – is better than water alone; tea from a pot, malty but not strong or aromatic, is underrated.

For colour, body and piquancy: soy sauce (contains salt, so watch the seasoning); wine, preferably red (port may be used but tastes stronger and sweeter).

For colour only (in dark sauces): the skin of a brown onion, left in for at least 20 minutes and discarded.

For acidity: cider or perry; wine vinegar.

For piquancy: angostura bitters (suggested by wine writer Oz Clarke); cayenne pepper; chilli sauce of the sambal or harissa type; home-made mushroom ketchup (see page 406).

For sweetness: jelly – redcurrant, whitecurrant, medlar, crab apple, etc. – it does not matter which one.

Be sparing with strong flavours like bitters, vinegar, and bought sauces, using only drops at a time. Gravy browning is not necessary. Honey comes through. You want the different constituents to blend in, not stand out.

If the meat is going into the oven, put a tomato, a peeled and quartered onion and a clove of garlic in to caramelise with it. When the meat comes out and goes on to a dish, pour off the contents of the pan into a separator. Add a glass of red wine to the pan and boil up, mashing the tomato etc. with a fork, scraping up any bits of caramel and stirring until they dissolve. Strain through a sieve into a saucepan, pressing through as much of the juice as possible. Add a further two glasses of liquid for every four people – stock, vegetable water or weak tea. Bring up to the boil again. I stretch for the pepper and soy sauce first, then taste the gravy, usually melting a small knob of medlar jelly in it and adding the salt last. Aim to reduce the quantity by about half before serving.

A quarter of a pint (150ml) of gravy should do four people. Keep it thin, keep it hot and put through a separator. Finish off with any juices leaching out of the meat when it is carved.

With practice, and without even wine or stock, you can acquire the confidence to make a perfectly good gravy.

Sauces may be made by reduction, the same as gravy, but also thickened. The best way to do this is with a *beurre manié*. This is an equal measure of plain flour and butter worked together on a side plate with a kitchen knife until thoroughly amalgamated. It is easier if the butter is softish (i.e. not straight from the fridge) and the knife is rounded at the end. An ounce (25g) of *beurre manié* whisked into a pint (600ml) of simmering liquid gives it a pleasantly thick and silky consistency.

PASTRY

A school friend of mine returned from a trip to the old Huntley and Palmers factory in Reading greatly impressed by the sight of two men folding pastry like sheets on a king-sized bed. Industrial pastry can be very good owing to the way it is mechanically handled; air is incorporated into the mixture, making the texture light and open. Bread is the opposite, though the two have one important thing in common: you can do better at home.

There are several types of pastry. Here is an all-purpose shortcrust which does not require any mysterious lightness of touch or arduous manhandling, but needs a little work after the water is added to bring it together. A broad-bladed flexible palette knife is an essential piece of equipment. Butter, which may be grated when frozen, has the best flavour. This is the fat to use. Some people add lemon juice to the water: we did not find it made any difference.

Get to work in a cool and airy place if you have one, preferably with a china mixing bowl and rolling pin, a broad-bladed kitchen knife and marble slab. This amount will cover an 8in (20cm) pie dish or tart tin without leaving too much over.

Shortcrust pastry
6oz (175g) plain flour, 3oz (75g) butter (frozen, rock hard), 1 pinch fine salt, and 2 ½ tbsp ice cold water.

Sift the flour into the bowl and spread it out, having added the salt. Place a grater in the middle, making sure it is stable. Coarsely grate the butter on to the flour, stopping occasionally to mix it in with the knife, making sure that the flakes are coated. Do not rub it in. When the butter has been used up, add the water all at once. Pull the mixture together with the knife and form into a ball with your hands. Dust a slab or board with flour, knead the pastry lightly for a few seconds. Flatten out a little and put in a plastic bag and leave to rest in the cool for 30 minutes. Roll out away from you, i.e. in one direction, applying more flour to the underside of the pastry if it starts to stick. Turn as often as you want to arrive at the desired shape.

To vary: for a sweet pastry sift 1 dsp of icing sugar with the flour. For a suet crust which is nice and crisp, use self-raising flour and stir in the suet. Lard, which we use with suet in pasties, and vegetable fats, make the shortest crust.

Cooking pastry: pies are no problem – you need a hot oven 220°C/425°F/gas mark 7. Wet the rim of the dish with water to provide grip. Roll out the pastry after it has rested in the larder and drape over the dish, press down the edges, then trim neatly with a knife. Use a double crust of pastry on the rim to seal more tightly.

For tarts, we tried everything in the hope of avoiding the dread soggy bottom: nothing worked except self-raising flour which produces a cake-like texture. The only solution was to use a fluted tart tin with a removable bottom placed outside and underneath the rim. Put the two bits of the tin on a table, roll out the pastry and line them carefully. Prick the surface and refrigerate for 30 minutes. Line with tin foil (beans are not necessary) and place on a wire rack keeping the loose bottom underneath. Cook in a pre-heated oven 220°C /425°F/ gas mark 7 for 15 minutes. Turn down to 180°C /350°F/gas mark 4. Remove foil and ease away the bottom of the tin, keeping the rim and pastry together on the rack. Return to the oven for a further 10 minutes before filling.

PASTIES

The Paget family made our pasties. I was taught by a lifelong friend, Anthony Rogers of Carwinion, near Falmouth, who took second prize in a hotly contested local competition. We ate our pasties at home, at point-to-points, and on the beach by a mump called 'the giant's grave'. A path leads to the church where my mother lies buried, a spectral bird man has been sighted, and a prehistoric wood of evergreen oaks leads down to the sea. Arthur Christophers, who gardened at Carwinion for years, ate a pasty for croust, a snack between his nine o'clock lunch and midday dinner. A robin that came into the potting shed and stood on his knee shared the crumbs.

A pasty was originally a meal cooked throughout England in a flour and water paste which acquired local forms and followings, a convenience tag, and an edible crust guaranteeing safe passage from farm and cottage kitchen to field, factory, meet and famously tin mine. The pork pie is a type of pasty that has increased in popularity. The checky pig of Warwickshire and collier's foot of Lancashire – plural 'foots' – seem to have disappeared. Is this true? I wonder.

With change creeping out into the provinces from London, the pasty was relegated to the West Country together with saffron cake, though it is now re-surfacing in commercial forms. The word is that the pasties in Cornwall, owing to the persistence of the open hearth, were cooked under cover on a bakestone or brandis (see page 116) and crimped along the top. The pasties in Devonshire, at least from the nineteenth century, were cooked in a 'down' oven underneath the firebox on the local ranges, turned once, and crimped along the side.

My mother-in-law, a Cornishwoman, will have none of this. She says that the crust of a pasty was originally the handle to hold it with, often grubby from a labourer's paw, accounting for its position and the habit of throwing it away. The Rogers and the Pagets crimped their pasties along the top – there is no explanation why. I am neutral on the matter of the crust, but concerned about the items made in factories and sold as pasties, and the number of important counts on which they go wrong, particularly with the pastry, and by chopping rather than thinly slicing the vegetables.

The crust for a pasty must be firm, not flaky, which means using lard, though some cooks add a little suet. The meat in the filling is invariably skirt of beef, for which cream was substituted during rationing. The vegetables include 'turnip', the Cornish term for swede, which has led to confusion, and has implications. The swede did not arrive in England until the nineteenth century and is not available fresh except in winter, yet pasties were never seasonal. The rest of the year people improvise, as they always have done. I have never met a pasty with apple at one end for 'afters', but the mother-in-law does make tiddlers from leftover pastry (very thrifty, the Cornish) filled with jam.

You can't judge a cookery book by its cover, but you can by its pasty. For diehards, incidentally, the 'a' is long – as in Penzance . . .

Makes 4 pasties: 1lb (450g) plain flour, 4oz (110g) lard, 4oz (110g) suet, pinch of salt, 1lb (450g) skirt of beef, 1 large potato, 8oz (200g) swede (turnip), 1 onion, dripping, scant 5fl oz (150ml) ice cold water.

Make the customary pastry by rubbing the lard into the flour and salt, adding the suet and mixing to a dough with the water. Rest in the larder. Peel potato, swede and keep in water. Chop up the meat and onion finely. Divide pastry into four and roll into circles 9 inches (23cm) across. Pare equal amounts of potato into the middle of each pastry circle then swede. Put the onion and meat on top. Dot with dripping and season well.

Now comes the tricky bit. Brush the rim with water and gather it up into a sausage. Holding the pasty in shape with one hand, press the edges together with the forefinger and thumb on the other. This, with practice, will get you an upper crust. By shifting the ingredients, you can acheive one on the side. Bake in a hot oven for 40 minutes at 200°C/425°F/gas mark 6. Eat wrapped in a napkin the customary way – standing up.

CUSTARD

An old English preparation recorded in 1450 that appeared in a pastry crust or coffin, often of considerable size, and allegedly a target for the running jumps of jesters. By and by, custards were eaten from elegant glasses and china cups and subtly flavoured with orange- or rosewater, nutmeg and almonds, emerging as the luscious crème anglaise. 'Boiled' custard it may be called – boil at your peril!

Vanilla, the commonest of added values to modern custard, is a fleshy Mexican bean or pod and a type of orchid that appeared in Europe in the sixteenth century. The real thing accounts for only 5 per cent of the market. The rest, 'essence' and 'flavouring', is produced from material like wood pulp (Vaughan and Geissler).

There are two ways of extracting the flavour from a vanilla pod: (a) Steep it in milk and bring up to scalding point, then leave to infuse for 15 minutes. Remove pod and reheat liquid, before adding it to the custard. You can dry and use the pod again, or split it for a more intense flavour. (b) Make a vanilla sugar – leave the pod or bean in a sealed jar with caster sugar for at least three days before using. This is more convenient than infusing the custard and more subtle in effect.

Cinnamon, a native of Sri Lanka known to the ancients, is another ingredient used in custard. Either leave a stick to infuse in warm milk for a couple of hours, or make cinnamon sugar by the same method as vanilla. I have a Sri Lankan box made from cinnamon bark that the sugar lives in and more conveniently achieves the same effect. Cinnamon is better in custard, vanilla in ices.

Custard is useful, particularly if a supermarket is your only option. The cream they sell, filthy as it is, will make a form of custard. It is not the best, but not the worst either, considering the liberties taken: about middle of the range.

For custard: take 3 egg yolks, 5fl oz (150ml) double cream, 5fl oz (150ml) milk, 1oz (25g) cinnamon sugar.

Beat the egg yolks with the sugar in a bowl. Heat the cream and milk in a pan to scalding point. Add this slowly, whisking all the time, to the egg mixture. Put the bowl over a saucepan of boiling water and cook, whisking continuously until you can feel it thickening. You don't need to pass it through a sieve if you have made it carefully. Serve hot or cold. To prevent a skin forming, cover with a disc of greaseproof paper in direct contact with the custard.

CHAPTER EIGHT

Bread

THE JOHNSONS' COTTAGE lay up a track on a silent reach of the River Fal. He, Sylvanus, was a quarryman who played the organ in church. She, Annie, was a creature of habit known for three things. She refused the offer of the water and electricity which passed along her lane, made legendary bread, and baked it in a domestic faggot oven – the last of its type to be used in Cornwall, possibly in England.

People spoke of the Johnsons in the present, as living at home and still baking bread. I was looking forward to meeting them, but missed the opportunity by twenty-five years. Their son had moved on to a farm nearby, which had once been a hospital for lepers. Their garden gate was rotten and hanging on one hinge. The path was overgrown with elder and brambles, the pump collecting ivy, and the cottage standing open to the wind and rain. The windows gaped and the door gave.

The kitchen was dark, empty and musty, the floor strewn with flaking paint and fallen plaster. A jackdaw's nest, spilling twigs, occupied a shelf in the only cupboard. The oven was in the hearth, crammed with wood cut a quarter of a century before. Sylvanus brought the fuel and lit the fire. Annie mixed the dough, leaving it to prove as the heat got up, and made a few pasties perhaps, and put them all in. Then she walked round the garden, peeping through the trees for a sight of the sea, and back up the path. By the time she returned to the kitchen, the bread was done.

Ovens

England has a history of baking as varied as any other country. Manorial ovens gave way to domestic ones, though I have not seen any pre-dating the eighteenth century, and a communal oven (cited by John McCann) was built in the nineteenth at Papworth St Agnes, Cambridgeshire. The cloam or clay chambers like Annie Johnson's were made until 1957. They are of ancient Mediterranean origin and, as far as manufacturing in England is concerned, peculiar to one region. The potteries of Bridgwater in Somerset, Barnstaple and Fremington in north Devon, and Calstock and Truro in Cornwall were the only producers. Their ovens were fashioned in horseshoe moulds about a yard long and two feet wide, with high crowns, low foreheads, thick walls and flat, heavy soles. They look like huge, unoccupied classical helmets in rough earthenware, and weigh a ton, but were also free-standing, considered portable, and travelled widely throughout the West Country, to Wales, and even on board ship to colonial America.

Most clay ovens were built into the fireplaces of farms and cottages. They are often located underneath a staircase, a convenient cavity. If enclosed in an external buttress attached to the side of the house, a cracked or damaged oven could be removed and replaced without disturbing the kitchen. In both cases, the chamber was loaded from indoors. The majority of West Country houses more than a century old have or had a bread oven. Some have two, even three, entombed for generations in the masonry.

To find and expose the huge clay carapace of an oven is amongst the joys of reopening a chimney. Forgotten, empty and often walled in, each dark chamber holds in quiet keeping the history of countless loaves and fireside secrets. Once, I found an oven unlike all the rest – abandoned on an outhouse floor. It had the gaping mouth and characteristic presence, but no past, never having brought forth bread. It was good as new, unused, and still waiting after more than a hundred years for its host cottage and kitchen to be completed.

The ovens in Cornwall, notably Cotehele, can be made of granite and stopped with slate. Upcountry, they are narrow tunnels or igloos built in brick on a timber frame that burned away with the first fire. The clay or masonry is bedded on rubble and fuller's earth or sand (one of the best natural insulators). There is no chimney in a faggot oven, but its customary location in or near an inglenook provides an escape for the smoke and a place to put the ash. The door can be on hinges and made of cast iron, or loose and made of hardwood, usually scorched. The oven works like an inverted bonfire, which sounds baffling, yet with a good blaze cannot fail. The heat of the fire, having permeated the walls of the chamber, is retained in the fabric for a number of hours.

The mass or solid heat of a cloam or brick oven, a favourite with bakers, is different from the scalding flash heat of an electric fire or even a coal range. It is a breath-like, enveloping, radiant, almost tangible heat, which is contained in the masonry and imprisoned in the chamber when the door is closed. The crust it delivers to the bread is thin and strong, even the crumb chewier than usual. When the temperature is at or over 230°C/450°F and high enough to bake, it tickles the hairs on your arm. The custom was for cobs and tin loaves to go at the back where the oven was hottest. Steep top-and-bottom or cottage loaves went in the middle, or else they could lean towards the walls and scorch. Pasties fitted at the front in a dish. When the door was closed, if old and worn, its holes were stopped up with dough, or clay from the garden.

The enlarged peel ovens used by village and municipal bakers, also brick-built, were named after the long wooden spade with which the trays of dough, festive dishes and Sunday lunches were loaded. The earliest burned faggots in the usual way. They have the same-sized mouth as a domestic oven, but an interior that can be five feet wide and fifteen deep. The chamber takes days to heat from cold, and days to cool down. The crowns, fractured by age and grinning like broken teeth, disappear into the darkness. The sole underneath can be worn and weathered as a garden path or kitchen floor: it is the first part to go. Repairs were costly to the owner, and uncomfortable for the men paid to do them in considerable temperatures rather than wait for the glass – and business – to drop.

Side-flue ovens, also brick, have a grate to the right or left that is filled externally, and a chimney opposite: the fire rages through the chamber. They date from the beginning of the nineteenth century when coal was forthcoming and wood getting short, but occasionally took offcuts from sawmills.

Steam-tube ovens are the industrial descendant of faggot ovens. They have cylinders running front to back heated by coal, coke or oil, cast-iron interiors and often proving chambers underneath. The brick housing may be glazed in white enamel. Side-by-sides are not uncommon. Draw-plate ovens, a variation, have a retractable metal sole on rollers. One baker used a donkey to draw the plate loaded with bread in and out of the oven, and to pull his cart on the daily round.

The grandeur of a peel oven can come as a surprise – especially in unlikely surroundings – emphasizing the former importance of our daily bread. They lurk behind modest shop fronts in remote villages, polite suburbs and every sort of thought-provoking and historic site from Essex to Exmoor, the Wirral peninsula, the Forest of Dean, and central London, a short walk from Westminster Abbey. Southern England, which was less progressive than the north in terms of industrial development, has most of the remaining ovens.

By the 1990s a fringe market had emerged in brick ovens imported from France, while the number in England continued to dwindle. For every one in use, thousands must have been demolished. Six peel ovens have gone near me in the last ten years, three in farms and cottages, and two as I arrived to admire them. Owners think nothing of it. Builders fill them (and unused chimneys) with concrete. There must be hundreds more ovens lying idle, up to two centuries old, saved only by the inconvenience of demolition and carting off tons of rubble. None is listed.

The last English peel oven, fired with wood, ceased to be used when the baker retired. It is still in existence, but condemned to a life after death in a National Trust tea room. Coal-fired units were hit by the miners' strike in the 1970s, which held up supplies of the quick-burning type of fuel they needed. Since then nearly all the working ovens have been converted to oil and gas, though new equipment is favourite, particularly with Environmental Health. Apparently a brick chamber gunned up to 1000°F, in which baking takes place at nearly 600°F, can still constitute a health risk.

Plymouth has one brick oven on top of another, located amongst the gift shops in the Barbican: a double-decker. The bottom part is said to have baked provisions for the *Mayflower*. It fell into disuse when a new quay was built by the Hanoverians, causing Southside Street – and its oven – to flood on the spring tide. A replacement was called for and built in the only place possible, on top of the original oven. The business was run by the Warren family for two centuries, then the late Hugh Jacka, who continued to make ships' biscuits until the war.

In a country as eager to modernize the interiors of buildings as England, it is unusual to find an artefact two hundred years old that continues to be used for its intended purpose and looks its age. A brick oven that a baker has loaded all his life is a known quantity and reassuring presence in the bakehouse – the two of them a pair: he all hands and shoulders from years of working and stooping to the dough; 'she' monumental without, and behind her foundry door, cavernous within.

It is a curious, twilit, lonesome world, the baker's. He rises at night in the dark and cold, while others are warm or going home to bed. The light shining from his window is the only one on in the street. He works at high speed and without distractions – many bakers like it that way – weighing, measuring, pouring, kneading, scaling off and tinning, almost all at once. The oven is like a theatre, its door the curtain, which closes on dough and spectacularly opens on all manner of bread. A two-man team with a mixer and bun divider will produce three hundred loaves of different descriptions, splits or rolls, tarts, fancy cakes and more, in sickness and power cuts every day of the week but one. Obliging bakers lend their ovens too.

Fordingbridge in Hampshire had a pair of brick ovens built in the Edwardian era. Steve Evans, the proprietor of Mellors bakery, for the cost of his favourite tipple, allowed me to cook a pig in one of them for a local wedding.

The late George Allen, baker, of Scalford in Leicestershire, whose oven had cooked many pigs, Christmas hams and turkeys in its time, told me how to proceed:

Lay on a suitable pig from one of the leading pork breeds: I chose a Middle White. Get the nearest capable metalworker or smith to build a tray and rack large enough for the pig, small enough to fit through the modest mouth of the peel oven, and deep enough to retain the fat. Make the gravy and prepare vegetables in advance. Enlist at least one person to help you carve. If you do not know how, approach the local butcher.

Score the skin of the pig with a Stanley knife, and stuff it if you wish (I filled mine with three legs of venison and a few partridges, confident that owing to their location inside the pig and the particular heat of the oven, they would not dry out). Sew up the belly with string. Wrap the beast from head to foot in tin foil, and allow up to twelve hours for it to cook: i.e. for a dinner at 8 or 9 p.m. commit the pig to the oven at around 8 a.m. when the heat is still around 230°C/450°F, and the baker has finished work. Remove the tin foil at half time, then when the pig is cooked put it back over with some towels on top to keep the meat hot until it gets to its destination.

In 1990, Steve moved on and sold his bakery to Belinda's. Within days his ovens were demolished. There was no opposition. Simultaneously, the street outside acquired an 'Edwardian' look identical to many others in Hampshire and funded by the New Forest District Council: a 'Conservation Enhancement Programme' whose cost ran into six figures.

PHASE ONE: BREADMAKING

The Campaign for Real Bread, hoping to follow in the steps of beer, had not got off the ground. The average loaf was a shocker: fluffy, tasteless and of negligible value, an iconic food torn from its pedestal and subjected to abuse. 'Without wishing to disparage the skills of bread makers by trade,' said Eliza Acton in 1845, they were in effect making you ill. It was the same a century later. In 1999, according to aficionados in America, the English (and Australians) made the worst corporate loaf in the world.

The Chorleywood process dates from 1961. It started out with the soundest of intentions: to reduce the UK dependency on imports. It is now perceived by the baking fraternity to have the following 'advantages', all economic and none of them connected to the obvious reasons for eating good bread: additional yield, processing time and space-saving (calculated in percentages), lower staling rate and greater control.

After milling, the flour receives a cocktail of interdependent chemicals that is the largest in Europe. Ascorbic acid, which is only vitamin C, but vital to the Chorleywood process, speeds up fermentation and ensures a specious bulk. The mixing is brutal and hectic, incorporating air. The dough is injected with gas in order to make the additives perform with maximum efficiency. The supermarkets sell it. The public, conspiring in their own malnutrition, eat it. Animals consume the healthier by-products. As for the future, one thing is certain: the way forward in corporate baking circles will be science fiction turned fact, profit-led all the way.

Rather than making bread as slowly as possible, giving it the fermentation it deserves (see page 75), and selling it daily, the plan is to make it ever more quickly and prolong shelf life. According to *Kent's Technology of Cereals*: 'baking using microwave or radio frequency energy alone produces a crustless bread'. However,

> 'a crust can be developed by applying thermal radiation, in the form of hot air, simultaneously during a total baking time of less than 10 mins for a standard loaf . . . Mould development can be delayed by the addition of propionic acid or its sodium, calcium or potassium salts . . . other means of preservation include the use of sorbic acid-impregnated wrappers, y-irradiation . . . or infra-red irradiation. The use of impermeable packaging to prevent the entry of oxygen is very expensive; a less expensive alternative is to include an oxygen absorbent, such as active iron oxide, in the packaging: by this means the shelf life of crusty rolls has been increased to 60 days. A so-called '90 day loaf' is packaged in nylon polypropylene laminate and the interior air partly replaced by carbon dioxide. The packaged loaf is then sterilised by infra-red radiation. None of these methods prevents the onset of true staling.'

It continues.

According to the Technology Assessment Consumer Report addressed to the whole of Europe, the wise 'will not break bread with the British' (David, 1977). In the meantime, the Belgians, faced with similar post-war sociopolitical problems, went for a wholewheat sourdough – healthy, palatable and lacking only the voluptuous bottom line.

Back in the seventies, there were few bakers of any sort making an honest loaf. Floris Gruhn of Soho was one, a Polish expatriate who supplied the Normandy Stores and ultimately retired. The South London Bakers Co-operative (SLBC) was another, a producer of a wholemeal loaf as good for the tummy and teeth as it was for toast, which performed in every department. The crust was firm, the weight substantial, and the crumb naturally sweet and close, neither rock-solid, nor falsely elastic, and inflated by vitamin C.

The SLBC was founded in 1978. It was a genuine trade union with a constant turnover of staff who enjoyed equal status in the company and passed on, leaving the heat, smell of the dough and quality of their bread undiminished in the slightly alternative atmosphere of Eversleigh Road, Wandsworth. By mid-morning on the day of my visit, baking had finished. The premises were manned by a lad in a woolly hat who said he had worked there and returned to help out. Every few minutes a customer came to the door and, for less than the price of a pint, he handed over a loaf.

The calm, emptiness and quiet were a contrast to the furious activity for which bakeries are renowned in the small hours of the morning. The electric ovens, blackened tins and racks of trays were nothing special: it was the middle-aged Artofex mixer standing upright in the corner, and its deportment, which caught the eye. We stopped in front of the cream-coloured torso and domed head, and bent over the bowl. The lad pressed a button. Two sturdy dough hooks moved into action. They plunged and scooped, up and down, relentless and thorough, a mighty metal housewife forbearing in its movements as machines can be. The next best thing, it seemed, to a pair of hands or human feet. I wanted to know about their bread. Sure. The loaf had only four ingredients. Why did it taste so good? Because of the wheat, the lad supposed, and the part of England it came from. The SLBC did nothing to the flour except add the essentials for bread, then clear and tin the dough, and bake it off. Who devised the loaf? Some guy way back, last seen heading for Glastonbury.

The SLBC bread had gone through several stages. It evolved from a 'suffocated' loaf, which was baked in an inverted tin with holes in the bottom – a method designed, by restricting the size, to concentrate the texture. The baker who made it was called David Fuller. His employer, Barry Wookey of Rushall, Wiltshire, an organic farmer, writer and long-suffering contributor to the Ministry of Agriculture, Fisheries and Food's legendary slush pile, supplied the flour. The yeast was manufactured by British Fermentation Products (BFP), and activated by the addition of warm water and sugars present in the flour. There was nothing special about the salt. Oils and fats were surplus to requirements.

The SLBC was taken over after my visit and moved. They expanded in the process and implemented changes. Their loaf came out of it spongier than before, but remained better than most of its competitors. Here is the recipe for the original, which I left the bakery with, written down on a scrap of paper.

The original South London loaf
   50lb (25kg) bag of wholemeal Rushall flour
   6oz (175g) BFP yeast in summer; 8oz (225g) in winter
   2 buckets (20 l) warm water
   12oz (350g) fine salt

Cream the yeast and a little water in a mixer, pouring in the rest of the water gradually. Add the flour and mix it gently for 5 minutes. Scatter the salt and mix for a further 10 to 15 minutes. Grease loaf tins. Scale off the dough into the required amounts, sufficient to half fill each tin. Knead into tidy shapes and pack in. Prove in a warm place for about 1½ hours, or until the dough reaches the top of the tins. Bake for 30–40 minutes in a preheated oven at no less than 220°C /425°F/gas mark 7. Turn out on to perforated trays.

I liked good bread and disliked making it in equal measure. The two would not have been reconciled unless I had moved out of the SLBC's catchment area. The three bakers whom I approached, intending they should copy the loaf, never got close. Their every instinct was like that of a builder in a cottage, intent on results I was anxious to avoid. Whatever my instructions, they would not change direction. The only solution was for me to try and make the loaf myself. I would keep the number of ingredients to four, experiment with measures and method, and dig a little deeper into the subject of bread.

Grains

Many cereals have been used for bread. Wheat, which predominates in the richer countries, makes the most palatable. It is a type of grass domesticated thousands of years ago, possibly prior to livestock, on the Syrian–Turkish border, where a similar wheat grows today (Kent). Its arrival in the West with crops like barley was accomplished by neolithic farmers. Oats crossed the Channel, possibly as a weed in wheat, a role they persist in playing today. Rye, an inhabitant of northern Europe, was cultivated and spread by German tribes from the fourth century BC: it has a long and proven relationship with sourdoughs (see page 80). Spelt, a relation of wheat, lower in yield and more difficult to process, but liked for its flavour, was introduced by the Romans.

From a very few early forms of wheat, tens of thousands evolved. The durum wheats (from the Latin for 'hard') are used for pasta and couscous. The less hard wheats are for breadmaking, the soft ones for cakes and biscuits. The spring wheats tend to be harder than the overwintered wheats, but lack the flavour, yield and mineral content, and require a long hot summer. Growing conditions can matter more than variety.

'There it sits – a single kernel of wheat,' says *Robertson's Kitchen Bread Book,* moved by the sight alone, 'maybe three sixteenths of an inch long, creased along one side and rounder on the other. At the bottom nestles a tiny oval compartment, the minute beginning of the plant's rebirth, called the germ' – this is the mystical 2 per cent of the grain with most of the goodness and flavour. 'Above is the endosperm, a protein and calorie rich food . . . that will fuel the plant as it germinates' – 85 per cent and a miller's bread and butter. 'Enveloping both is a hard seed coat, impermeable for decades to anything but the warmth and moisture that will bring the seed to life' – 13 per cent, consisting of four fibrous layers including an inner one containing more goodness. A nutritional package second to none.

The grain of the hard or strong wheats is steely or flinty when ground, fine and easy to sift. The grain of the soft ones, not so easy, is mealy or starchy. Their consistency, hard or soft, is dependent on the amount of protein in the grain. This turns to gluten when combined with water, producing the elasticity and extensibility required in an English loaf. Tests determines whether wheat is millable or not. There is no other grading system in the UK.

England has had its fair share of varieties, but struggled with its climate to produce milling wheats that bakers liked to work with. Good weather brings forth 'cheesy' crops and a dough that stays firm on the bench. A wet summer, which causes the berry to germinate, brings forth animal feed and hectic trading in the grain market come September – or it did. Great advances have been made in the breeding of wheats in recent years and strides towards making East Anglia the UK's bread basket. The dependence on grain from the Urals, Australia and North America, a source of supply since the Corn Laws were repealed, appears to be over.

None of the English wheats used for breadmaking today and credited with flavour are very old. Maris Wigeon, the niche market leader, was bred in 1965. It came from the same stable as Maris Huntsman, Maris Otter malting barley and the Maris trio of potatoes (see page 365): the Plant Breeding Research Centre located in Maris Lane, Trumpington, near Cambridge, which succumbed to government cuts and now, ironically, houses GM wizards Monsanto. To complete the denouement, some of the land has been sold to Waitrose.

Wigeon is distinguished by its height, which can reach six feet on fertile ground. If you see a man out working on a binder or making stooks in our corner of Hampshire, it will be Pete

Barnaby preparing the straw for thatching or a cidermaker's 'cheese' (see page 440). Wigeon is scarce, but triple-purpose, and has caught the fancy of conservationists, 'foodies' and Prince Charles. I cannot bake with it, but plenty do. Maris Dove, a wheat considered to be the finest of the lot, has not been as lucky as its fashionable cousin, Appel[*]. Unless there are a few pounds left somewhere in a jar, it is extinct.

MILLS

The hand-operated quern was the earliest type of mill, smashed in England by medieval landlords who objected to their tenantry grinding (and baking) their own wheat. Asian querns, comprising two horizontal stones about a foot in diameter and three inches thick, still exist. There is one at Burcot Mill in Somerset which you may play with (if you have the strength).

Watermills arrived under the Romans, suffered after their departure and re-emerged. Six thousand were recorded in the Domesday Book, serving three thousand communities in the south of England (David), an enduring link between town and country in growing cities, and a focal point of village life after the manor and church. The number fell with industrialization to about a thousand by 1900, and twenty-eight by 2000, including one or two reconnecting to the national grid. Eling, near Southampton, has the last of the tide mills, still in operation but kept in existence by opening to the public. Judiciously placed astride great rivers, amongst willow and alder, watermills can also be tucked away on the meanest-looking streams and still succeed in doing what they were built for. 'Calm as a millpond', the saying goes, and so it is, the current barely moving under the ducks, then crashing urgently through a sluice and on to the scoops of a giant wheel. The inside is like a ship's galley or primitive engine room, with beams, props and a subterranean atmosphere, creaking, groaning and reverberating to the sound of wood and metal turning in their grooves.

Windmills have occupied the English landscape since the twelfth century, foreign as they seem, and were a mixed blessing, with landlords owning the earth they stood on and claiming the air space – or wind – above. Many suffered from the erection of tall buildings that interfered with their power supply. Now, again, about twenty-eight remain. How proud and prominent a windmill is, a show-off with a distant presence, of colossal size up close, a landlocked lighthouse or queen of the castle moving in on defenceless pawns. Windmills crop up in scattered locations from low-lying fens to high-flying hills: one airy attic after another, and a provocative one if you are a climber, each with a view more elevating, thrilling and scary than

---

[*] *Robin Appel of Warminster Maltings.*

the last. How strange the summit, a brainbox from within, but irregular without – a skullcap, hexagon or even an inverted dinghy, ready to turn and meet the breeze. The smock mills are brick, the post mills rotate. The sails, rotating too, go faster and faster as the wind gets up. People get obsessed. 'Ride the storm and get to work,' says Nigel Moon, nicknamed 'Old Windmill' at the age of six. Now he has the one he wants, in Whissendine, Northamptonshire, which came complete with the only porcelain roller in England. His mother, aged eighty-seven, helps out. A woman in the village objects to the mill: 'We don't want that sort of thing here.'

Mill stones weigh a ton, considerably more, in fact – the harder the better for grinding wheat. French burr stones are the most frequently used in England, and will have to last now that the supply has come to an end. They arrive in sections set in concrete, which are bound with metal straps. German lava, Baltic flint and emery from Greece, the second hardest material in the world, may also be used – but I have not seen them. Derbyshire gritstone is employed for oats and barley. Softer stones can be used for bread corn if the grain is heated first.

The language of the mill flows as smoothly as the wheat. A hopper feeds the grain into a shoe, agitated by a damsel, and into the eye of a horizontal runner, turned by a quant, located on top of a stationary bedstone. The meal is ground between the lands and emitted by grooves to the rim or skirt. The millers, still dusty after all these years, either dress their own stones as the grooves wear out or consign the job to an itinerant millwright, equipped with hammers and chisels, a small and select body of about sixteen people. I have liked most millers I have met, whether they are born, made, or converts from office jobs.

The lie of the stones may be altered to produce a fine, medium or coarse meal, the coarsest making the heaviest bread. The process is a cool one, which shears the grain and produces wholewheat flour in full possession of its constituents. If white flour is required of a wind- or watermill, sifting or 'bolting' follows.

Roller mills, a nineteenth-century development, are the quicker and more efficient industrial end of the market. Their *modus operandi* is to put the wheat though break, scratch and reduction rollers. The endosperm is separated from the 'offal' and pulverised at up to 300 rpm. The process is a hot one that produces a white flour. Roller-milled 'wholemeal' is rebuilt and unlikely to be more than 98 per cent of the grain. The bread it makes, which is sold in the supermarkets, may contain some of the chemicals permitted in white flour.

The refinement or 'bolting' of flour through cloth, a service provided by millers for which they charged accordingly, has gone on throughout English history. It entered a new phase in the eighteenth century, a great step forward for cake- and pastry-making, thanks to the manufacture of silk by Flemish immigrant weavers. The subsequent invention of roller mills enabled the fine and costly white breads to fall into line with the coarse and cheapest brown ones, emerging – at a cost to public health – as a treat that anyone could afford.

The majority of bread flours in England are milled from a mixture of wheats. All may contain dried or synthesized gluten, a by-product of glucose manufacture, which need not be declared on any flour – organic, wholemeal or white – could be causing the allergies attributed to ordinary wheat. One hundred per cent stoneground wholemeal is the only flour with nothing taken away. Organic flour may contain non-organic foreign wheat. Sell-by dates, which are pointless on most things and preposterous on rice (the older it gets, the better), should be noted on flours. You are unlikely to get a bag that is past its best, but it may linger in a kitchen cupboard or larder and fail in baking. The more of the whole grain a flour contains, the less time it keeps, owing to the fat in the germ going rancid. Prepare for the quality to vary and for different varieties to absorb different amounts of water.

I use only wholemeal or white flour or a mixture of the two. Some brands perform consistently well for me, regardless of the weather and their origin; others badly. It is worth paring them down to the one you like and sticking to it, with the odd excursion into the unknown. And that, to anyone embarking on a study of breadmaking, is around the next corner. Plant-breeders, growers, millers and bakers are all involved in producing a loaf, but seldom to the extent of being able to tell you about each other's jobs.

Bread falls into two classes (*Blackie's Modern Encyclopedia*, 1896). Unleavened bread was the original sort, a flour-and-water paste cooked forthwith that persisted in the agricultural community of Lincolnshire possibly into the twentieth century (Hartley, 1954). Leavened (from the French *levain*) bread was discovered probably by accident between four thousand and eight thousand years ago when a dough fermented producing gas and a risen loaf, which was more digestible. It is not clear how much time elapsed before people learned to initiate the process and keep it going, using a leaven from one batch of dough to 'plum' the next.

Yeast, or barm, as in 'barmy', is all around us and is whacky stuff that used to be associated with corruption as well as growth. It is on things and in things, giving great performances, yet invisible to the naked eye in its natural state. Yeasts are self-replicating in the right conditions, only failing when starved or poisoned. Bread may be leavened with either native yeasts, as in sourdoughs, or manufactured ones. I brew beer with crushed Maris Otter barley, and, like countless generations before me in England, have used the lees in the bottom of the fermenting bin to make excellent bread.

Some of the nineteenth-century handwritten cookery books and kitchen diaries I have seen contain recipes for home-made yeasts, usually featuring mashed potato cut with hops, which were believed to help them keep. Patent or manufactured yeast emerged in the same period. Compressed yeast, known to the Victorians as 'German' or 'dried', and which we call 'fresh', is descended from brewer's yeast. It is grown in controlled conditions, fed on molasses and looks like milk chocolate.

Fresh yeast is available from bakers. It stores for a couple of weeks in the fridge before going sour, and freezes well. The larger the batch of bread, the smaller the proportion needed, but it is not worth worrying about or modifying the amount used from summer to winter in a domestic kitchen. Dried yeast is twice as strong as fresh and has a detectable taste. It will do in emergencies.

Salt is necessary for flavour in bread. Coarse salt should be dissolved in water. Household salt contains a chemical to stop it caking. However, the different types do not have a significant effect on the taste of bread.

The water used in yeast bread (unlike in a sourdough) does not matter. The temperature should be normal in medical terms or thereabouts. Let your finger be the guide. In a conventional dough, one measure of water (in fluid ounces) is used to two of flour (in ounces).

WHOLEMEAL BREAD

Doris Grant's eponymous loaf (so easy 'husbands can make it') went three-quarters of the way to becoming mine. It also yielded a vital piece of information. The laborious process of kneading and knocking back is not appropriate for everyday wholemeal bread. A dough made from unrefined flour, containing the entire wheat grain, is more unstable and full of natural flavour and gases than a dough made from sifted flour. It does not require or benefit from the same fermentation when working with compressed yeast. It should be mixed, left to rise and baked forthwith, a fact that the SLBC seemed to have absorbed. The whole process need not take more than a couple of hours. Again, two things were reconciled: the notion that one could cut corners, like an industrial baker, and to good effect.

The Grant loaf has been around since 1944, and has stood the test of time. I was happy with almost every aspect of it, but cut out the sugar and decreased the water. The dough is still a wet one, but the flavour and texture of the bread are as desired and compare to the SLBC's. The ingredients have been scaled down to a formula that both works and is easy to remember (provided you keep to imperial measures).

4-3-2-1 Loaf: 4lb (1.8kg) stoneground wholemeal flour, 3 pints (1.8l) warm water, 2 heaped dessertspoons salt, 1oz (25g) fresh yeast.

Cream the yeast in a bowl with a little warm water. Add the rest of the water and, using a wooden spoon, enough of the flour to make a porridge. Mix well and leave for half an hour. Grease loaf tins. Scatter salt over the mixture in the bowl and add the rest of the flour: as the quantity increases, it is easier to mix by hand. Either put dollops of the dough in tins, or pour it in, cutting off the lava-like flow with a knife when each tin is three quarters full. Leave in a warm place until the dough starts to show signs of life and rise a little (about 15–30 minutes), do not wait for it to double in volume. Bake in a preheated oven 220°C/425°F/gas mark 7 for 30–40 minutes. If you want a softer crust, wrap it in a towel. Eat the following day. New bread is delicious, but hard to digest. It freezes well.

WHITE BREAD

The promises of a 'No-Time Dough With Real Bread Flavour', which industrial compounds claim to deliver in one hour flat, are mutually exclusive. For George Ort, author of *The Modern Manna* and a fourth generation of master bakers, who entertained experts from all over Europe at his plant in Bedfordshire, the secret of white bread was 'all in the fermentation'. This is a process that cannot be compromised.

White flour is luxuriant to handle as dough, more delicate to eat as bread and essential for cakes and pastry (strong white flour is used for puff and choux). It is also deficient in constituents compared to wholemeal and without the husk.

Stone mills leave some of the germ behind in white flour, giving it flavour and a speckled, slightly golden colour. Roller mills are more ruthless, leaving around 70 per cent of the grain and producing a whiter flour. In order to compensate for the loss, it must by law contain chalk, iron, nicotinic acid and vitamin B1. These additives do not have to be stated on the packet. More may be on the way, notably folate, a further blow to opponents of mass inoculation. Ascorbic acid may be present in white flour but since it is not compulsory must be declared. Bleach is no longer permitted.

Some roller millers pass flour through token stones and sell it as desirable 'stoneground', a deceit which is permitted by the law.

Francillon and Dent's[*] recipe (adapted) for slightly less than a quartern (4lb) of white household bread is as good as any:

3lb (1.3kg) strong plain flour, 1½ pint (900ml) lukewarm water, 3 tsp salt, 1 tsp sugar, 1oz (25g) fresh yeast.

Sift the flour and salt together in a bowl and leave in a warm place. Cream the yeast with the sugar, gradually adding half the tepid water. Make a well in the centre of the flour and pour the

---

* *Francillon and Dent,* Good Cookery.

liquid slowly into it, stirring with a knife or the fingers of one hand. Work in enough flour to produce a batter, keeping it to a pool in the middle. Cover with a cloth and leave, again in a warm place, for about 15 minutes or until bubbles appear in the mixture. This is called 'the sponge' and the process 'setting the sponge'. Then work in by degrees the remaining flour and water. Knead lightly for up to 10 minutes. The dough will become firmer and more stretchy. Cover and leave for at least another hour. This is called proving, i.e. that the dough is alive. When the volume has doubled, turn out on to a floured board and knead again for a further 10–15 minutes in order to integrate the texture and eliminate holes. The dough will squeak and pop in response to being handled as the gases depart.

Divide up the dough; fold it from underneath, except in the case of plaits, to make any shape you want. Grease and dust the trays or tins with flour, allowing sufficient room for the dough to double in volume. Cuts in the surface are a change from a plain top and throw up a secondary crust. Perform the operation with a sharp knife or razor, preferably in one slick movement. Bake in a preheated oven 220°C/425°F/gas mark 7 for 30 minutes.

Split tins are cut from end to end, oblongs diagonally. Mark cobs with a cross or a trellis and you have a 'Fancy Rumpy'. Cottage loaves, which are liable to keel over and should be bottom heavy, take the most practice. Try playing with a warm white dough the size of a puffball, the colour of china, the texture of suede, solid, and compliant with your every wish.

A 'stotty' or oven-bottom cake was originally a piece taken from a batch of dough while the rest was left to rise, and cooked forthwith to provide a quick bite. It was sometimes placed on an iron trivet a bit like an artist's easel (Howey, 1971), and left on a shelf or windowsill in order to dry it out, which hardened the crust and made it more digestible. Stotties originated in the north-east of England, but travelled with Geordies working elsewhere, who used to collect them in stacks from the bakers. The first I encountered was in Durham, going back a bit now, on the way up to see the greatest of cathedrals.

A good stotty has a dense and chewy texture that makes the best sandwich of the lot. A bad one is produced from the same pre-mix as ordinary bread, fluffy, pointless, and identical except in shape. To make a stotty, take an 8oz (225g) piece of white dough that has risen once. Knead it well and roll out into a round, flat cake. Allow it to prove for no more than quarter of an hour. Invert onto a baking sheet. Poke a hole in the middle and bake in a hot oven for ten minutes on either side.

Swimmers are Norfolk dumplings remembered by the parents and grandparents of today's young farmers. Pat Graham of turkey fame (see page 228) says they were made until recently by some families, but declined with home baking, and she last saw them in the 1960s prepared by her mother. Swimmers are pieces of proven bread dough, weighing about 4 oz (110g) each, rolled in a little flour. Mrs Arthur Webb, breezing through Norfolk after the war ('fascinating!'), admired the dexterity with which the swimmers were transported on saucers from kitchen table to cooking pot (Webb, 1947).

Dinner in Norfolk took place at noon (in Suffolk at half past twelve and in Essex, being closer to London, at 1 p.m.). In Pat's household, the swimmers went on at a quarter to twelve. They took exactly 15 minutes to cook in simmering water, stock or boiled beef broth. It is vital to keep the pan covered, not to peep, and serve them straight away. I have made swimmers twice, not with great success, but perhaps it takes someone from Norfolk to do it. Eat before the meat, pulled apart with two forks, preferably soused in gravy from a stew.

Toast, from *The Book of Food*, 1927, by P. Morton Shand (a posthumous relation by marriage to the future king of England): 'Only public school fags can make perfectly golden . . . crisp . . . and spongey toast for the simple reason they are beaten should any one of the decrusted triangles . . . evince the faintest signs of scraping, uneven cutting, excessive thickness or . . . imperfect saturation with butter . . . Club toast is a pale imitation of fag-labour toast, for one cannot cane a club waiter.'

In other words, a man so excessively kind, reasonable and politically correct has no one to blame for 'imperfect' toast except himself.

PHASE TWO

Kenilworth, a visit! Perhaps the slogan has been used already. What were we going there for? You never knew, apart from the castle, of course, and to cast an eye on the area. I spent a few weeks on the canals one year, in a barge belonging to a friend. We coasted into Leamington Spa on a summer's evening, peeped at the royal tennis court, partook of a film and a curry, and coasted back into the countryside, waking to mist and quiet only broken by the puffing and blowing of cattle. Warwick, elegantly recovering from a fire in the sixteenth century, had another castle and a little pork butcher in the middle of town. It still has. A wingco, indifferent to closing time, ran a pub on the 'cut' with a life-sized model of a Spitfire in the garden – or was it a real one? Our boat was known as the *Hesperus* by the other barge owners.

Kenilworth had a market on, and a promising-looking artisan baker. A young man was selling the only good bread I had seen anywhere in England apart from in London, Canterbury, Harrogate and Penzance. His son, aged about eight and already prospering by the language, described my purchase – a sourdough – as 'piquant'. I was so impressed by its crust, colour, weight and flavour (which turned out to improve with time), I tried selling a loaf to a bloke rendered speechless and inert by the modest premium he was being asked to pay for it. Not my business and a waste of time. I should know better by now.

The Rawlings brothers, makers of my Kenilworth loaf, were a pair of strapping farmer's boys who lived on the borders of Oxfordshire and Northamptonshire. Matthew was the elder, a man whose career seemed to have been inspired by childhood visits to the local bakehouse, its closure, and partial collapse downhill when the last fire died and the oven went cold. Richard, the younger, joined him and Bread and Co. was formed. After two hours in their company, reminiscing about mutual watering holes and discussing sourdough, the wife and I left realising we had to make this bread ourselves. It was not a joint decision or even a decision at all, merely a case of an order unfolding as it was supposed to. I had produced an excellent wholemeal loaf in a gas oven for ten years, and would have continued but for the feeling that there was a destination in baking and I was only halfway there.

Sourdough

A true sourdough is leavened only by natural yeasts. Flour and water mixed together provide the medium in which friendly bacteria can thrive and attract and feed the necessary wild and local yeasts.* Fermentation is balanced and prolonged by punctual replenishments of flour and water, and temperature control. The acid build-up from the bacteria protects the yeasts from contamination, and gives the sourdough its characteristic tang and irregular open-textured crumb. The custom of baking it on a tray or bread oven bottom provides a loaf with a 360° crust that belongs on the high table. Manufactured yeast has been useful, but it is designed for speed rather than flavour, and its effect on bread, particularly white, may be costive. Great nutritional and digestive claims, attributed to slow fermentation, are made on behalf of sourdoughs.

Sourdough bread, the original form of leavened bread, is thought to have emerged in the near east and reached Germany between the first and sixth centuries AD, spreading through the Church and guilds (Kent). The word 'sourdough' was recorded in medieval England, but could have been pejorative, and meant the opposite of sweetness in bread as well as a product of fermentation. The term 'leaven' was also part of the language in the Middle Ages.

The circumstantial evidence is that being great drinkers of beer, the English used ale yeast in the best breads. We also grew large quantities of rye, which has an affinity with sourdough, particularly on the Gloucestershire–Worcestershire border, the home of the 'ryeland' sheep. If the grain came with German invaders, then so will the manner of baking it. North Country

---

* *Using grape skins or similar material to propagate your leaven is quicker, but unnecessary, and presents a different environment for the yeast and bacteria from the one they will inhabit.*

oat breads are known to have been a product of natural fermentation (see page 75), it is unclear for how many hundreds of years. In the seventeenth century, Gervase Markham gave a recipe for baking a sourdough with wheat flour, but the only one as far as I know. There are no clues as to whether such bread was too vernacular, subcultural, rare or common for other writers to bother with.

The next reference to sourdough (at least that I have found) was the most significant one. Blackie, author of *Blackie's Modern Encyclopedia*, said it had been 'superseded' by manufactured yeast. That was in 1896, after a period of great change, with large amounts of imported wheat, roller milling and industrial units coming in. Meanwhile, American sourdoughs, thanks to the shortage of yeast, and to immigrant bakers, had become world-famous – also a nickname for the prospectors with whom they were associated. Around sixty years on, sourdoughs re-appeared in England, but modernized, more controlled and bearing an attractive San Franciscan or Polish identity: a bit like Bob Curtis's* salt cod, reborn in polite circles as *bacalao*.

England's new breed of artisan bakers is making some excellent sourdough and other loaves. The outlook is rosier for them than it was twenty years ago, though problems remain the same. Incomes are static, overheads rising and a spectre hovers above us all: the threat of consumers being swamped with specious bread at knockdown prices 'skilfully compromised to fit the established supermarket system' (Wing and Scott, 1999).

Matthew gave us some of his leaven to start us off, which we named after him, and fed, cosseted and rocked to sleep in the warmth and comfort of our spare room. Even so, the first sourdoughs we baked – intending to christen them collectively Richard – were a disgrace to his name. It took eight efforts to arrive at the intended destination, and along the way we had to weather the interim storms (common to us both) of joy, sorrow, delight and despair.

The craft of making sourdough at home is heavily dependent on knowing your leaven: recognising when it is ripe and maintaining it carefully. 'Matthew' was a great success when we learned how to treat him. The next step was to start our own leaven. The ultimate aim was to produce a crusty country loaf, moist, chewy, tasty and indulgent, and to give it time. We did not intend to make the slowest loaf on record or subscribe to the slow food movement, but that is what happened. Sourdough takes longer to master and make than yeast bread. My advice to shrinking violets is not to bother. Get on with those grand designs you have for the time saved.

---

* *Bob Curtis: Fishmonger in Fordingbridge for 34 years, a man I would consult about fish, poultry, and game before anyone else.*

General notes on sourdough

The flour: wholemeal, 100 per cent stoneground, has a high mineral content, so it ferments quickly. So we used it to kick-start our new leaven and for flavour and goodness in the finished loaf. About 20 per cent goes into the bread recipe.

Rye flour supplies colour, flavour, a strong crust and a persistently moist crumb to sourdoughs. It also tolerates the acid build-up that occurs in natural fermentation. We used rye to start the leaven with wholemeal, and in the finished loaf. About 10 per cent goes into the bread recipe.

White flour is more stable than wholemeal or rye. It has to be strong and unadulterated for sourdough. We used exclusively white flour to maintain the leaven after it got going. About 70 per cent goes into the bread recipe, providing a nice light crumb in the finished loaf.

Hand milling: the advantage of this is that a supply of grain, which keeps longer than flour, can be bought in and processed at any time. Purists, in pursuit of the live bacteria on the berry and the flavour from the freshly ground kernel, mill their own wheat. We tried it but found that large amounts make the performance of a dough unpredictable. So if you want to use hand-milled flour, start by putting no more than 20 per cent in your bread recipe.

Water: non-chlorinated.

Salt: Maldon.

Quantities and equipment: (a) start with 1 bag of wholemeal flour, 1 of rye and 2 of white, 3 pints (1.8l) of water, and 1 packet of salt; (b) good scales are useful; (c) utensils: no metal – plastic bowls and spatulas; (d) flat baking trays; (e) temperature gauge; (f) houses that are cold or without an airing cupboard might need a plant propagator or heated mat; (g) timer; (h) razor blade (with which to slash the dough after proving).

Measurement: everything by weight, including the water. Sorry, but this one is easier in metric only.

Starting a new leaven

Day 1: mix 60g wholemeal flour, 60g rye and 120g water to a paste in a bowl. Put it in a plastic bag and leave at 15–18°C/60–65°F for 48 hours.

Day 3: the leaven weighs 240g. Discard (compost) half and make it up with 30g wholemeal, 30g rye and 60g water to regain the original weight. Return to the bag and a temperature of 15–18°C/60–65°F for 24 hours. There will not be any visible signs of life yet.

Day 4: repeat day 3.

Day 5: repeat day 4. The leaven should be alive and starting to bubble. It might be advisable to withdraw the wholemeal and rye flour and convert to white, slowing fermentation for the purpose of storage.

Day 6: repeat day 5. The leaven should be light, airy, slimy, fragrant, elastic, tenacious and ripe within 6–10 hours. If not, feed every 12 hours for the next week at 15–18°C/60–65°F until it is. The leaven must be stored in a jam jar with a fitting lid, and put in the fridge so that it ripens slowly and does not become too acid. The alternative is to use it straight away.

Maintenance of new leaven
Feed it or bake with it at least once a week.

To feed: discard half the leaven and replace with equal weights of flour and water. Leave it out for an hour at kitchen temperature to get going before returning to the fridge, if you are not going to bake with it.

Feeding the leaven too often leads to incomplete fermentation. Feeding it insufficiently starves it. Leaving it out of the fridge and in the warm for too long causes the leaven to become too acid: you can smell it. In each case, the result is weakness and loss of potency. Reviving a stored leaven: throw away and replace 80 per cent, and wait until it ferments out at 21–24°C/70–75°F. Then triple the volume each time it gets bubbly until this point is reached within 8 hours. It is now healthy enough to be stored or used again.

Sample baking routine
Producing three loaves, and replenishing your leaven

A new leaven does not perform well, but stabilises over a couple of months. The more frequently you use it to start with, the better. A mature leaven, made acid and sleepy by storage in the fridge, needs three big feeds to bring it to ripeness and provide the quantity needed.

Temperature has a big effect on timing.

Amount of flour etc. needed to refresh the storage leaven (150g) and make the bread:

1,675g flour (1,175g stoneground strong white, 300g wholemeal and 200g rye), 1l unchlorinated water, 30g Maldon salt.

Amounts needed to make the bread:

1,600g flour (includes 250g from leaven), 1l unchlorinated water (includes 250g from leaven), 30g Maldon salt.

Thursday 9 p.m.
10g stored leaven
20g strong white flour
200ml water

Take 10g of stored leaven from the jar and mix with the flour and water in a bowl (leaving the remainder in the fridge for now). This is your first leaven, weighing 50g. Leave for 12 hours at about 21°C/70°F covered loosely with a plastic bag.

Friday 9 a.m.
50g first leaven
100g strong white flour
100ml water

Take the the first leaven and mix with the flour and water. This is your second leaven, weighing 250g. Remove 150g as storage leaven waiting for an hour before returning it to the fridge. Leave your remaining 100g of second leaven for 12 hours at 21°C/70°F covered loosely with a plastic bag. This is the leaven that makes the bread.

Friday 9 p.m.
100g second leaven
100g strong white flour
100g rye flour
200ml water

Take the second leaven and mix with the flour and water. This is your third leaven, weighing 500g. Leave for 12 hours at 21°C/70°F covered loosely with a plastic bag.

Saturday 9 a.m. (ready for baking at 3–5 p.m.)
500g third leaven
950g strong white flour
300g wholemeal flour
100g rye flour
750ml water
30g salt

It is time to make the dough. Take a large bowl, put in the flour, dissolve the salt in the water and mix in. Add the third leaven and work first with a spatula and then by hand.

Kneading: turn the dough out on to a table lightly dusted with flour. Begin and continue by pressing down with the heel of the hand, using the weight of your body rather than the strength of your arms, to condition the gluten. Fold it and fold again until smooth, silky, swollen, springy and elastic for 20 minutes. The firm and rhythmic way in which you treat the dough will become instinctive. Then leave in a bowl as before, covered with a plastic bag in the kitchen for about 3–5 hours depending on temperature. It will spread, rather than rise like yeast-leavened dough.

Dividing: deflate the dough in the bowl with your hand and ease it out on to the kitchen table, dusted with flour as before. Divide it into three by weight (about 800g each).

Rounding: this stage is much more delicate than kneading, and a crucial one. Flatten each piece gently into a thick pancake with the heel of the hand. Fold the edges of the dough into the centre, forming a ball, and apply minimal pressure to seal the joints. Tease it, do not tear it. You are building tension and aiming to create a smooth, unbroken surface underneath, which will ultimately form the crust on the bread. My wife completes this operation by holding the dough in one hand and working it with the other.

Resting: leave the dough for 20 minutes to gas up and relax.

Shaping or moulding: the same action as rounding but still more gentle. Make the dough as plump as possible and turn it over, so that the creases are underneath. Lift each ball on to a floured baking sheet, allowing for expansion. Cover with a bowl to prevent the dough drying out (the more humidity, the better the crust will be).

Proving: leave for 3–5 hours at kitchen temperature. The dough will spread but should not be allowed to 'double in volume' if oven spring is going to be achieved. Better to underprove rather than overdo it, causing the dough to collapse. Keep an eye on it.

NB If the timing is awkward, you can leave the dough out for 1 hour at this stage, then retard it in the fridge for up to 24 hours. Leave out for 3–5 hours before baking. This makes *even* slower and better bread. Already close to the limit of our endurance, we have yet to experiment.

Baking: uncover the dough, dust the top with flour and slash half an inch deep, preferably with a razor blade, to release the tension and control the burst. Let artistry take over. Commit to an oven preheated to 230°C /450°F/ gas mark 8 for 35–45 minutes, putting the dough as close to the top as possible to help the crust, allowing for a 5cm spring. Do not bake below this temperature.

Comments: home bakers can produce better yeast bread than professionals with a commercial end in mind. The same cannot be said of sourdoughs, which are easier to make every day because the leaven is continually used, fed and kept ripe. You can create different textures by varying not only the combinations of flours, but the amount of leaven in the dough. The more leaven there is in the recipe, the more moist and chewy the crumb, the flatter the shape of the loaf, and the less time the dough takes to prove. Experiment, keeping to the same proportion of flour, water and salt. Leavens can have an infinite number of inoculations and live on. You may buy them dried, with all sorts of interesting tales to tell. You might benefit from a chat with the other sourdough nuts on the internet. There are plenty out there brandishing photos of bouncing baby home baked loaves.

The crust on perfect sourdough hearth bread is created by moisture, and the heat supplied by a clay or brick oven. To try and mimic the effect, we baked the loaves underneath terracotta flower pots with matching bases, ten inches wide and seven high.

This involved proving the dough upside down in eight-inch round wicker baskets lined with napkins dusted with rice flour (to prevent it sticking). Meanwhile the pots were heated in the oven. When ready for baking, the loaves were gently inverted on to the floured base of each pot. The lids went on top, holes covered, to be removed after 20 minutes' baking. The bread remained in the oven for a further half-hour.

It worked, and quite well, but we had still not taken enough punishment. That meant repairing the faggot oven that had come with our house, exposed by restoring the fireplace.

My wife pugged the holes in the masonry, rebuilt the hearth and repointed the mortar with one part of lime putty to three of builder's sand, a horrible, uncomfy and claustrophobic job carried out upside down, and which took her three days.* Adam Batty, our local chippy, made a hardwood door with two stout handles and a metal face, which weighed a ton. I collected the kindling and cut spokes, dry and up to an inch thick, for fuel: gorse and ash for heat, willow and hazel from our own coppices and dead hedge**. Blackthorn and hawthorn are good too, but vicious.

Nearly forty years earlier, Peter Whiteside, an Anglo-Canadian father figure, had picked me up from the airport in Montreal. We went for a drink at Ruby Foo, a Chinese restaurant and dimly lit bar haunted by glamorous businesswomen. A few days later we drove through the snow to St Sauveur, I think, a village in the Laurentians, where an old Québécois was unloading bread from an even older wood-fired oven. I did not understand what he was doing or know the questions to ask, but could not help absorbing the cold and dark outside, the warmth in the bakehouse, and the smell of the loaf in its white paper wrap.

I had used a faggot oven myself since then, but only twice. I needed a dress rehearsal to sharpen my skills, test the heat and assess the risk of fire to the staircase above. The results were both positive and negative. The house did not burn down, but the temperature failed to reach more than 200°F. Next time I would have to gun up the fire and allow two hours from lighting it to loading the bread.

My wife's sourdoughs, proving and pregnant in their linen-lined baskets, were corkers. I put paper at the front of the oven to utilise any draught, covered it with twigs and filled the chamber to the walls and the crown. The wood caught and the flames leapt up and out of the open doorway, licking the bricks without and working their way deeper into the cavity within. A red-hot furnace was burning in an hour. I continued to pile wood into the middle and back of the oven for a further hour, using the smaller bits to rekindle the blaze and the gorse for a grand finale. The flames died down, and I spread the embers over the sole. I closed the door for about thirty minutes to stop the flow of lava-like heat from spilling through the threshold, bottling it up in the darkness beyond. The leading edge of the door started to smoulder, but stabilized.

I used the iron rake for the coals, which had come with the house, to empty the oven. It was a mucky business, better done wearing a hat. Then I put in a thermometer. What would it say,

---

* *'Pugged' is Hampshire parlance for plugged with clay or lime mortar. The disused clay breaker in our wood is a puggy mill. The complaint which local men contracted in the clay pits was known as pug fever.*

** *I.e. made of dead wood. A live hedge is usually planted alongside. The principle is that the first, woven in situ like a hurdle, acts as a fence or boundary until such time as the second and live one gets going. The second then makes kindling and faggots for the oven.*

300–400°F? Get away. The temperature read an incredible 580°F, causing some excitement. We wiped the oven out with a damp household mop (or scuffle) to help even out the hot and cold spots, and put a crust on the bread. A final rest of about half an hour and everything was ready. The loaves were turned out of their baskets on to a garden spade, used as a peel, and dusted with coarsely milled flour. They were slashed on top, then with a deft little flick offloaded into the oven. The door, kept shut for as much of the time as possible since the fire had died down, closed like the lid of an Egyptian tomb. We charged our glasses and mentally prepared for the wait of forty minutes and we knew not what.

It is the absence of control that, in the twenty-first century, makes the process difficult to absorb. You could not speed it up or slow it down, and should not peep either. The temperature, which is everything apart from the bread, is not at your command. You are helpless; the dough is hidden and fighting for its life against hazards unknown. I wondered whether it would come out half baked, or had even disappeared. I almost expected to open the door and find an empty chamber, rather than three loaves perfect enough to paint, and ready for the journey from darkness to soft light. Each bore a 360° crust from the all-round heat, and a seemly birthmark inflicted by my wife on the crown of its oven-sprung tricoloured head.

The heat of the oven was falling slowly. Next time we shall put in a leg of lamb, a stew, a gratin of potatoes, or fruit to bake, leaving in pinhead oatmeal or rice pudding until the morning. Country people did not waste things, particularly food and fuel. So the chances are that there was a whole raft of cookery accomplished in the declining heat of a faggot oven, from 'two penn'orth of bits' (see page 118) to 'creed wheat' for frumenty. Again, little is recorded. A further development is that the embers of the fire which did not burn right down, having been deprived of oxygen in the time-honoured way, emerged as charcoal.

So there is a bread oven in the corner of the room rather than a TV. To fill it, except with dough for bread, or food, would be to dishonour it. When out of use, the door is in position. It closes with a conclusive and hollow sound, providing the house with a new acoustic and a genie that consummates and alters the spirit of the room. The oven, put to bed and out of sight, is not out of mind.

A neighbour who is interested in such matters was present at the initial firing. Another, approaching the house with her daughter, saw the blaze through the front window. It was the first time such a sight had been seen probably since the train came to Fordingbridge in the 1870s, bringing coal and the new technology to which the natives had converted. The local mill, working then, is working now, and even grinding English wheat.

If the ghost of Annie Johnson had approached the house instead, she would have been amused. To bake bread as we had was no more for her than a second fire to light on wash day.

Watching us do it, she would wonder what all the fuss was about. It was not clever of us to fire the oven, nor was it convenient. Yet so much was involved: the house, the crafts of building, carpentry, woodmanship and baking, and everything connected to them; the breast ploughs, the horses and oxen, the tractors, the seed, the shoots, the golden corn on flat fields and sweeping slopes framed in blowsy green; Pete on his binder, stacking stooks and loading his pink wooden threshing machine; the mighty combine, the Euro bales, the giant prize-winning ricks, the cob walls, the thatch and thatchers, the huge trade in straw, the Hertfordshire whites, the Bedfordshire bonnets made of plait, the Devon and Somerset cidermakers' 'cheese', the archers' targets, the bee skeps, the finials on houses, and the table mats; the carts, the barges on canals, the ships, the lorries, the mountains of subsidized grain; Jack and Jill, the mills on the Floss, and floating on the Thames in Elizabethan London; the miller and his thumb, the baker, his dozen and percentage; the flour, water and pancheon, and the cats and dogs drawn to the heat building in the oven.

My wife, torn from her devotions, was told there is more to life than bread. But not much compared to other things. In importance it is between water and salt, which, with flour, make up the baker's holy trinity (Sams). Bread is a sacramental and symbolic food, present at the dawn of civilisation and at Christ's last supper, a food which every government knows it must provide or it will fall. If you cannot connect with that, you cannot connect with anything. And to think I might never have known.

CHAPTER NINE

BUTCHERS

ABOVE AND TO THE WEST OF CUTCOMBE sales lay the open moor and the Devon border. The heather was dead around Dunkworthy Beacon and the wind beginning to strip the beech hedges of their curled and crinkled copper-coloured leaves. The cattle, breathing steam, were wearing winter coats. A cow cleared its pen, landing on the concrete to shouts from waving stockmen clad in overalls and boots. Farmers came and went opening and closing the metal gates behind them, or stood in twos and threes stroking weather-worn cheeks and scratching hairy heads. Hot drinks were going down, along with the odd nip. The bids rang out from the barn across the yard. Trade was brisk and prices were steady.

A butcher stood amongst the dealers, his arms resting on the rail of the ring. He was waiting for some beasts he had seen outside, sent in from a nearby farm on the moor. The lots passed by in which he had no interest, then six red Devon steers, colour-matched, frisky and fit, spilled over the gantry beneath giant scales and through a gate to take centre stage. A man scrawled their weight on a rotating board. A girl wrote it down. An auctioneer beside them on the rostrum, watching the faces intent on the cattle, or on him, called a sum of money in the musical and repetitive language of the trade.

A lad in a cloth coat moved the cattle on and around the ring. The butcher's eyes never left the six beasts as he signalled with one finger to the auctioneer. The price rose slowly at first, then more quickly as bids came in from high in the stand, low by the door and off the wall. It faltered and recovered, regaining momentum; it peaked and hung in the air. Two final challenging calls rang out from the rostrum, bringing no reaction. The hammer, poised for an instant in the hand of the auctioneer, descended with a sharp and conclusive tap. Another lot, completed in seconds. The butcher's name entered the book for the third and last time that day. He had seen what he wanted, bought it and now made for the office in order to settle up, exchanging the odd remark with people on the way.

The sale ended within half an hour. The ring fell quiet for another week. The barn emptied, the mist collected and people disappeared in mud-spattered cars, pick-ups and lorries. The butcher's partner loaded the steers and drove them to his farm to be housed in a barn for the wet weeks to come. He would be trimming their coats the following day and checking their condition. Then two months of feeding began.

The beasts were intended for Christmas. Their final journey was another few miles to the butcher's abattoir. Their final week was spent in lairage. Their final act was to die well, anticipating nothing. There was no stress, no panic and no hurry to get the next animals done. They were stunned one at a time, hoisted and bled, gutted and flayed, all by expert hands.

The butcher, Gerald David, who started in milk, was master of a model operation. His wife, Jenny, was the mistress. Their three sons are all in the business, their grandsons coming on. In addition to the abattoir, the family has several retail outlets and now a cutting plant. The welfare of cattle is automatic. The beef is hung for a month with its history pinned to the side. The breed, traceability and quality are assured. All the things that successive governments, their hatchet men and supermarkets combined to rationalise or destroy, which people now regret, have been taken as read since the couple started work with the sum of £7, and I stopped at their shop nearly thirty years ago.

A master butcher is a cattle breeder, feeder or fancier, humanitarian, craftsman, shopkeeper and often a show judge, who knows as much about livestock and lairage as any farmer and more about meat than any chef. If he is licensed to slaughter, so much the better: he is at the mercy of no one except his customers, and regulations both flawed and flawless he is obliged to follow.

The Balson family are the oldest butchers in England, having traded in Bridport in Dorset since Cardinal Wolsey's father dealt in cattle. The business moved from the shambles in the centre of town to its present position on the Axminster road in the nineteenth century, just after the high farming period, which proved such an auspicious time for breeding livestock and selling meat. There was plenty of money about, a growing population and, for perfectionists, every incentive to rise above the chain retailers and purveyors of foreign and colonial beef who were setting themselves up with saw, block and brine tub.

Butchers in England and Wales, known as 'fleshers' in Scotland, proliferated. In the West Country they tended to specialise in beef, in the Midlands in pork and manufacturing, and in the north in mutton and lamb, as they do today. Traders exhibited their wares inside and outside their shops with particular pride and artistry on the Christian feasts, market days and at weekends. The 'quality', farmers, merchants and cooks walked the streets admiring each display and returned to buy at the one they found the most alluring.

There were dry salted hams, sides of bacon, rounds of veal run with snow-white dripping, loins of mutton kidneys rampant, and prize-winning beef from the local shows. The meat was good enough to paint, the stuff of still life and the cameraman. Many shops were built for the part, with carved bullocks' or rams' heads, blue and white tiles and a wooden cash booth. Some of the survivors are listed. The majority have fallen to property developers and regulations.

Everyone has a favourite butcher tucked away, or had, but only a fraction are left from the UK's thriving infrastructure. Whilst the demand for beef has increased, it is for indifferent beef produced to industrial standards. When the book is thrown, regardless of their record and intentions, it is the craftsmen who suffer.

The UK abattoirs 'especially those in private hands, even though small in size, are the impeccable, mechanized and efficient units for which the British trade is noted' (Rouse, 1970). In the 1950s, the UK had 3,500 slaughterhouses serving 45,000 butchers. Animals did not travel more than a few miles to slaughter. The supermarkets helped to change all that. Still, there were over 1,000 plants left in 1992. In the run-up to entering Europe, it emerged that the knives were out for the smaller plants, regardless of the implications for animal welfare, rare breeds, rural economies and the roast beef of old England. An estimated eight pages of directives were increased to eighty in one of the first and most brazen examples of Whitehall 'gold-plating' rules they could legally have amended or torn up.

About 300 plants closed without contingency plans owing to mainly structural deficiencies as perceived by persons unknown. From a back seat in the Palace of Westminster (where I had gone to add to the objections) it was clear that neither the Lords nor the Commons would or could do anything about it. Radio 4's *Food Programme*, the Country Landowners Association and animal-lovers did not get involved either.

The situation was summed up in the title of Richard North's *Death by Regulation – The Butchery of the British Meat Trade*, which, as it happened, was only halfway through when his book came out in 1994. He blamed the 'veterinary caucus' within MAFF, now DEFRA (Department of the Environment, Food and Rural Affairs), intent on giving themselves jobs, which helped to double the costs of operating plants. The number of abattoirs fell with every draft of new regulations to 450 in 1997, butchers to fewer than about 15,000. Enter Compassion in World Farming, which, having taken a long hard look at the industry, came to the same conclusion as every licensed slaughterman. Lists of regulations, mandatory new equipment and posses of meat inspectors and vets are no substitute for skill and good management, experts and expertise.

The campaign to stop the closures, a disparate one, was doomed from the beginning. Indifference, rationalisation and a lack of positive publicity weighed against it. A slaughterhouse is not a sexy topic except in a negative sense, being the easiest thing to make a horror story out of. The tales of ruffians and condemned carcasses, handled by the dead moon, tarred all abattoirs with the same brush. They also caused the public further to avert its gaze from the realities of eating meat. The country was divided, but unequally. On the one hand there were people like me who wanted to know all about their beef and lamb; on the other were those who bought it in a packet and preferred not to know.

It was no use trying to plug the humanitarian angle. The RSPCA, I was told on the telephone by head office, were interested in animal welfare, not carcass quality.

'But can't you see,' I said after fifteen enervating minutes, 'they are the same thing?'

Most of us claim to love animals, though not enough to give them a decent life and save them from a long and debilitating journey to a distant slaughterhouse and a hectic production line. A beast seldom anticipates death: he fears it instinctively and reacts to a fuss. He also comes at a price, and serves a practical purpose. Only the rich are able to keep land or livestock for sentimental reasons. Farmers have a living to make. Their cattle convert food we cannot eat into food we can – like milk and cheese, which people must buy for those cattle to survive. If the demand dries up, so does the supply. However well-intentioned vegetarians may be, it is omnivores who keep livestock in the fields where they belong, animating the countryside.

As long as meat is eaten in England, the best that animal-lovers can do – even if they are vegetarian – is to prevent further rationalisation of the trade. The fewer and bigger plants there are, the greater the pressure on the smaller ones that are left. The Humane Slaughter Association keeps its eye on developments in the trade. I do not believe that everyone should eat meat, but recommend a visit to an abattoir to those who do.

By 2005 the number of slaughterhouses had fallen to about 180 with a full through-put, and 110 artisans. Retailers are down to 7,000. Meat consumption continues to rise through the food-giant retailers, while the industry sheds the skills, assets and people it needs most. The supermarkets were well on the way to commanding the whole structure and flow of business when BSE and foot-and-mouth played into their hands, killing off exports for their competitors in the medium term.

DEFRA thinks there are too many slaughterhouses. For the animals, there are too few – a detail that should have registered during the last crisis. Large areas are deprived of any facilities at all. Cries go up to save the smaller plants (*The Times*), a matter of nearly fifteen years after the majority closed. The remainder cannot be saved without controlling the number of regulations and training new apprentices. The National Federation of Meat Traders has much to consider.

The positive news is that Environmental Health seems to have taken kindly to home killing. You only have to do it their way, though this does involve planning, co-ordinating personnel and keeping to your own stock. Future Farms (see page 468) are looking into it. In some parts of the country, mobile units are operating too.

Many people do not go to butchers because they fear their ignorance might be exposed. It will, but it is no great humiliation, and is soon forgotten on the way to finding out what good meat looks like and how it is obtained. The history of England as the 'stud farm of the world' unfolds on the way. The language and terms that butchers use are riches in themselves. You may find backslang in London, a bread-and-butter cut in Hampshire and Dorset, a box-heater cut in Cornwall, and the Pope's eye in Scotland, as well as chaps, chines, chits and cowheel.

If a town has a butcher today, it is a positive signal, and there are likely to be other independent retailers too: perhaps a baker, fishmonger, grocer, ironmonger and draper rather than a corporate high street with supermarkets ruling the public's lives and gobbling up their cash. If a village has a butcher it is blessed: he is a link between city and country people with a finger on the rural pulse and an inside knowledge of what is going on. If a farm shop has a butcher it is an extra dimension worth a day out, and a place to stop and chat while the old man is otherwise engaged. More sauce goes down over a butcher's counter, missus, than in any restaurant, chippy or gastro-pub.

CHAPTER
TEN

SPIT, FIRE AND FUEL

S PIT ROASTS

The town was celebrating. Nine hundred years had passed since its name appeared in the Domesday Book. There was a carpet of flowers the length of the nave in the flint and stone church, a St George's flag flying, and a crowd milling about over the road. Months in advance of the event, the organisers had decided to roast an ox. They had also found out it was one of the most complicated matters in cookery. With no flash ingredients, recipes or manual controls to fall back on, there had to be plans for every contingency. Nothing could be left to chance.

Meat, building and engineering trades were all involved, as well as visits to medieval kitchens. A watertight brief emerged. The ox, a suitably finished one, was pinioned to a custom-made spit. A former motor mower, attached by a belt to a flywheel, provided the necessary power. A tray caught the tallow dripping from the beef. The fire was contained in an elongated basket, heaped up at either end with fuel, in order to cook the fore and hind quarter more than the sirloin. A temporary breeze-block shelter protected the whole operation from any wind and rain.

Two men, fortified by food and drink, took it in turns to pile on the coal and baste the meat over the course of a day and a night. The master of ceremonies, a builder, undertaker and on his own modest admission the handsomest man in the county, gave a short speech. The feast began as the clock struck one. The butcher and carver stepped forward with his knife. The first slice of beef went not to a celebrity, dignitary or the lord of the manor, but to a woman attired in a long skirt and white headdress whose family had lived in the parish since the kings of England spoke Norman French. The outside of the meat was slightly charred, the inside pink and juicy, and if the rump was underdone for some, it was just right for me.

Primitive spits are worked by hand. The horizontal ones in Hanoverian England, made of caste iron, were operated by a boy or dog on a treadmill, and mechanically by the end of the eighteenth century. The 'smoke jacks' in places like Brighton Pavilion and Saltram House were linked to a chimney fan, rotated by the hot air coming from below. The vertical danglespit progressed from a simple manually operated cord, nailed to a beam above the fire, to a clockwork 'bottle jack' which was either enamelled or made of brass.

Open ranges developed from coal-burning baskets in the nineteenth century. A portable 'dutch' oven or 'hastener' a light metal apparatus on legs, holding a piece of meat suspended from a bottle jack, stood in front of the fire. It had a domed head, a tray to catch the dripping, a rack underneath to warm the plates on, and a door in the back for ventilation and temperature control. However, ingenious as it was, the hastener did not save the art of roasting.

It was no match for the convenience of heated cupboards with the up-to-date benefits of griddles for oatcakes, drawers for pasties, and broilers for kippers, let alone gas or electricity. So the door closed on English meat, and the Australian 'baked dinner', an expression still used, was allowed to hijack the title of 'roast'.

I have seen two ranges in everyday operation, in Northamptonshire and the Lake District, and several employed as ornaments or, too heavy to move, gathering dust in kitchens. Hasteners, which were easier to dispose of and trashed wholesale, are more uncommon. It took me years to find one, plus a bottle jack to fit. There was a mystery to solve. 'When kitcheners came in,' a Miss Heath of Tonbridge had written to Florence White in the early twentieth century, 'good cookery went out.' What did she mean?

It is ten times easier to bang up meat in an oven and pull it out acceptably done in a calculable amount of time, but without the pleasure of seeing it turning and browning, tantalising and thrilling, drawing a little crowd and creating the chance of getting extraordinary results. An open fire heats the meat directly and from the outside, sealing in the juices. The steam can escape and the fat runs clear. There is no better and more artful way to cook beef or mutton, bred, fed and hung to perfection, than on a spit. Do not dismiss an authentic English roast until you have had one.

You may be a born *rôtisseur*; the French do not think they can be made. You may have a hastener sitting around as an ornament, a bottlejack or a piece of string and a beam over the fire to nail it to. An unhocked leg of lamb or mutton, suspended from the shank, is the easiest cut of meat to roast. A rib of beef, a duckling or a chicken, a little more fiddly, needs support underneath.

The weather, a major consideration outside, is not a problem indoors. With an efficient and well-built fireplace, you are halfway there. The fire itself needs at least forty minutes to get going, a ready supply of dry and suitable fuel (see page 100) and constant attention. Hang the meat a couple of feet away from the blaze or basket. You will have to turn it if you have no jack, so that it twists back and forth cooking evenly rather than burning on one side and cooling on the other. Put a pan underneath to catch the fat, basting when it starts to run. Four to six pounds of meat on the bone, emitting steam and firm to the touch, will cook in two to three hours. Fry some boiled potatoes in the dripping. Have vegetables, hot plates and a carving dish ready. Serve the joint or fowl as soon as it leaves the spit, with its own juices and Maldon salt.

CARVING

The Savoy, Claridges and the Connaught hotels all had a meat trolley. Simpson's in the Strand, another famous name and a much-loved place, has one still. It is a restaurant not just for tourists and reactionaries, but for social historians, expatriates and fugitives from the beau monde. You order a pint of Harley Street, a mixture of Newcastle Brown and Guinness, and the beef or mutton, warming to the courtly atmosphere, clean white tablecloths and muted colours, the pitch of the voices rising to the lofty ceilings and the absent pace of change. A trolley glides over the carpet and stops at your table. A man, or even a boy, also in white, rolling back the lid, asks how you want your meat. He plies the knife to the relevant part of the joint, committing each slice to one of the plates stacked on the trolley, which is heated by a flame underneath. He ladles the gravy over the top, and picks up a piece of Yorkshire pudding on the end of his fork. He advances your plate and graciously pockets your tip. Then he and the trolley move silently and seamlessly away between the seated suits and mahogany chairs to make their next appointment. It may not go on for ever; it does not even matter if the food is any good. But when it stops, we shall want it back.

Carving is one of the oldest arts. Carving vegetables, which I have seen the Chinese doing between shifts, is part of their culinary repertoire. Carving meat is no less of an accomplishment, a tradition in England conducted by men of rank or appointed to the task, and practised with respect for the beast before them. When hunt servants 'unmade' the deer in the Forest, as one of the local girls put it, 'you could see that something was going on', by which she meant a ritual.

The last lesson in a well-heeled Frenchman's education, delivered by a tutor, was how to carve. The executor at banquets was an *esquire tranchant*, occasionally the king himself. One of the greatest maîtres d'hôtel and past masters of the art was the restaurateur Joseph Dugnol, who carved a Rouen duckling while holding it impaled on the prongs of a fork – so that it fell in thin fillets and perfect order on the dish underneath – and in less time than it took to tell the story (*Larousse Gastronomique*).

The fifteenth-century English *Boke of Carving*, attributed to a Dame Juliana Berners*, may not be any more reliable or serious than her comments on hawking, but has it uses and survived more than four centuries of repetition. The later manuals, like J. H. Walsh's *Manual of Domestic Economy*, published with diagrams in 1879, are more informative. The head of the family carved at the head of the dining table in the Victorian and Edwardian periods, as he might today, and sat in a chair entitled a 'carver', a degree larger than his wife's. Otherwise the butler, the next most important man in the household, carved from a sideboard. The upper class started to eat as soon as they got their meat, while it was hot. The middle class waited, they thought politely, until everyone was served and the food was cold.

---

* *Dame Juliana Berners or Barnes is credited with works on hunting, hawking and heraldry, etc., printed by a pupil of Caxton at the end of the fifteenth century. She has been quoted ever since by people (including me) who have never seen so much as a reproduction of her text, and cannot be sure of anything about her.*

The huge knife and fork in Harrogate's museum are more than decorative. They were used by a local grandee to carve an ox during Queen Victoria's Jubilee. The Japanese ability to temper steel, which overtook Sheffield, is partly due to their failure to discover gunpowder. They fillet tuna with knives like samurai swords. One man holds the handle and another the end of the blade bound in cloth, enabling him to grip, just as they did in woodcuts that are now two centuries old. I watched at 4 a.m. in a freezing market until the last of the meat was parted from the bone. Silently and softly, implying applause, I put my hands together. Then we returned each other's bows.

I have a collection of knives and forks chosen as carefully for looks, weight and balance as any glass, jug or teacup. The majority, acquired in antique and junk shops, have specific uses and pre-date stainless steel. The grandest, ceremonial as well as functional, occupies a leather scabbard. The meat knives have long, thin blades almost as flexible as a foil. The game knives are shorter, with sturdy handles, often made of horn. I lost one of my favourites in a moment of forgetfulness, and covet another the owner will not part with.

I learned to carve not from my father, but from my friend Anthony Rogers. He taught me that the knife is more important than a knowledge of anatomy. If there is one kitchen gadget you need above all others, it is a set of knives, including carvers, which no one else may use. Keep them away from bread, which needs a serrated blade. Sharpening knives is an art in itself, says our local butcher, who has promised to do a couple of mine. A few grinders are still about, of Italian decent and operating from vans. The experts have whetstones, moistened with water, which preserves the temper of the metal. A steel is fine for everyday use. Employ it to sharpen each side of the knife equally, all the way from tip to handle. You cannot carve with blunt knives, yet people do, spoiling in minutes meat that took years to arrive at the table. Carve across the grain and towards the bone, using the point of your knife to its full advantage. A butcher will always show you how.

FUEL

Coal can be used to roast meat, but needs confinement to burn efficiently and a barrier to stop it going through pots and pans. The seams that broke at ground level and the coast provided the earliest and most accessible supplies. The first pit of any significance was dug in the thirteenth century, the first fire basket was recorded in the sixteenth, and the first range in the eighteenth. The quantity of coal available from English mines in the nineteenth century was estimated as sufficient to meet the country's needs for a thousand years . . . The quality and type varied, but it enabled furnaces to reach the temperatures at which world-beating iron and steel could be produced – a natural advantage that took manufacturing into the fast lane.

The down side was that the cost of the coal, a cheaper resource than wood, led to the neglect of woodmanship and woodland, and the filling in of draughty inglenooks in farms and cottages in order to accommodate a stove or grate. My hearth and 'bacon loft', modernized twice in the course of a hundred years, contained an enclosed and fitted coal burner with controls, vintage about 1950. In the course of restoring the inglenook I excavated a ton and a half of bricks: an indication of how keen my antecedents must have been to get rid of it.

Peat is immature coal cut over the centuries from the high fells to the low-lying parts of Norfolk that filled with water and became the Broads. A peat spade had a long blade with a sharp edge that parted the turf like butter and enabled them to be piled up in mumps and left to dry out over the summer for household use or taking to market. My mother and stepfather in Somerset used to burn peat when I was a child. It was light, brittle, the colour of dark chocolate, and left an earthy smell on your hands. The turfs were about a foot long, a few inches wide and thick as a telephone directory. They caught slowly, giving out lots of pleasant smoke and a good heat in time, breaking down into contemplative red-hot layers. Peat briquettes came later.

A New Forest commoner's right to peat, no longer exercised, was called turbary. The policy, self-regulated, was to 'take five and leave four' (squares), allowing the bells of heather to reseed the ground: a process that took about thirty years. The extraction of peat for compost persists on a small scale in England. It is more heavily monitored than in Ireland, and possibly okay, but still unpopular with conservationists and unlikely to clear its name.

A commoner's right to wood, now seldom exercised, is called estovers. The allowance was one cord of fallen timber per dwelling per year, a cord being 8ft x 4ft x 4ft, a half cord 4ft x 4ft x 4ft, measurements that are still observed regardless of metric martyrdom. The wood was taken in pieces no bigger than a man could carry, which usually meant no thicker than his wrist. Licences were also given for standing deadwood and the stumps left after the controlled burning of the gorse that is necessary to bring on new growth. 'Assignments' were located in new and inconvenient spots during the twentieth century, with the effect (desired by conservationists) of wood rotting down for beetles, etc. rather than going for fuel.

The different types of woods have different characteristics and uses. You get to know how they behave, store and burn, a detail that a *rôtisseur* should be aware of. Logs dry out more quickly in the wind than the sun, and more quickly than cords. Green wood is easier than seasoned wood to saw and split and, once a fire gets going, belts out more heat: use the two together for maximum effect. The rhymes about wood are more or less true; for example:

Beech wood burns bright and clear
If the logs are kept a year . . .
Oak and maple dry and old
Help keep out the winter cold.
Ash wood wet and ash wood dry
A king shall warm his slippers by.

Gorse is the best of the remainder, a former favourite in faggot ovens. Hawthorn is close, but spiteful to render. Juniper is aromatic, fruitwood also scented, a pleasant addition to an after-dinner fire. Elm burns extra hot in a furnace, slowly in the hearth, and smoulders. The mid-range fuel woods include alder and willow, hazel and holly. Birch soon rots: leave it a year and use quickly. Poplar and the pine family spit. Elder is the worst wood of the lot: hard, heavy and not very combustible.

I have commissioned a yew mantelpiece, and a sycamore carving board. I have found a turner for some wild cherry and seen teams of horses moving trees that machines cannot get to. It is a pity to waste such a sustainable resource. The act of cutting an ash in winter, and permitting regrowth in summer, can extend its life almost indefinitely (Rackham, 1986). This is called woodmanship, and is a light industrial craft I encountered on the job in the Forest. My mentor, Robin Roper, said that all he wanted was his own patch to work upon. I wondered why, finding out by accident when I acquired one with a house (see page 378).

An acre of deciduous woodland, used and used again, was reckoned to be enough to keep a man warm and sheltered for his lifetime (Hartley, 1979). An oak beam might start as a sixteenth-century ship's timber, progress to a Jacobean house and end on a fire centuries later. People knew their trees, what the various ones were for, and how much could be made from standing woodland. I have less than half the requirement for my lifetime, but with coppicing, pollarding, shrouding and clearing fallen branches it is remarkable how far the material goes. There have been cords for over ten years, guards for deer, poles for beans, fans for peas, stakes, binders and brash for hedges too.

England has a huge amount of woodland that is unmanaged. It also has a forthcoming energy crisis and large numbers of stressed, overweight and mentally unstable people who only need a hook, a saw and a pair of loppers to help sort things – and themselves – out. It works for me. An afternoon in a quiet wood has all the benefits of a keep-fit programme, with emotional and visible results. You can see things, hear things and get into a trance-like state and consistent pace, while the cords and the kindling pile up for the fire. The birds and beasts get used to your presence. The work keeps you warm. The trees drip on to the forest floor. The dusk arrives too soon. For woodmen, the English winter is not long enough.

Charcoal is a derivative of hardwood, burned off in enclosed heaps, pits or kilns, and used in manufacturing for thousands of years. Being lighter and easier to transport than wood, it has a history of being made in England's forests. The artisan charcoal-burners, rendered sooty by their occupation, solitary by their location, and romantic by posterity, overwintered with wives and children in huts near their work. The first mass producer and still the main distributor, the Shirley Aldred organization, started in 1796. Domestic output today, having fallen, appears to be creeping up again with rural diversification. From woodland that would otherwise be unmanaged, I can now get local charcoal to grill my local meat on. It retains the heat compared to other fuels and does not smell, smoke or scorch. The chop houses in London and Dublin cooked over charcoal until the war.

CHAPTER ELEVEN

THE ROAST BEEF OF OLD ENGLAND

I T WAS A BRIGHT AND WINDSWEPT EVENING in the border country where the English fought the Scots, the Scots fought each other, and feuds between families were endemic. The castle, heavily fortified and wonderfully decorated, bore amongst its ornaments pictures and trophies of the wild white cattle in the hills above. A print of about 1840 depicted a couple of swells dressed in top hats and frock coats creeping up on a bull, unwisely I thought, armed with only muskets. History does not relate whether man killed beast or whether it, wounded and crazy, killed him.

The trickle of people, up to see the cattle from the castle, had ceased. The park was situated in a high and lonely spot, steep in places, a mixture of oak woods, coarse grazing and sufficient water, with higher hills and a dark belt of trees beyond the stone wall. It was enclosed in the year 1260, to keep marauders out and the beasts in, the latter for the joint purpose of providing for feasts and the most thrilling and vainglorious form of sport: the hunting of wild bulls. To an original three hundred and sixty acres, five hundred were added. Of the twenty locations in England, Wales and Scotland where cattle are thought to have been emparked, it is only here in Chillingham that conditions have remained unchanged.

My wife and I were the last of the visitors that day. The warden, Austin Widows, offered in the soft burr of his native Gloucestershire to take us through the park and out of the top gate, then back down to the lodge. We would be safe from the cattle in his Land Rover, and undetectable, but not on foot. The bulls attacked when man came close. The cows killed their calves if they bore his scent. The herd formed a group as the hunt went past, taking the cries of hounds for wolves. When aroused, they trampled, hooted and trumpeted, a foghorn of a call that occasionally broke the silence.

We moved among the beasts, who stood watching but uninterested, their necks and faces freckled, foreheads woolly, noses black, ears fox-red and coats a shining white in the evening sun. The latest gossip, yet to be confirmed, was that the herd was of pre-Roman origin: a possible mixture of the mighty aurochs and domesticated cattle that came together in the neolithic era and reverted to or persisted in a wild state until now. The cattle were small by domestic standards, light in the rump and strong in the shoulder, and would have provided tough, dark and lean beef with little or no fat but considerable flavour. Bullfights were conducted on horseback, barren cows also engaged. With the invention of firearms and supplies of butchers' meat increasing in the eighteenth century, the hunting parties petered out. Honoured guests of the castle were invited to shoot a beast instead.

The horns of the females, comely and sedate as they chewed their cud, were lyre-shaped. Those of the males were set wider and pointed forwards, as if anticipating combat. The king bull, half-heartedly challenged while grazing with his family, turned to see off a young pretender. His reign was due to last up to three years and end in exile with the other adult males on the fringe of society. The calves lay curled up in the bracken and grass, fed in secret by their mothers for the first few days of their lives. They were then brought forth like debutantes and, cautiously and ceremoniously, introduced to the rest of the herd.

The Chillingham cattle have been of increasing interest to scientists, including Charles Darwin, who examined one of their skulls. More than unique, they are clones of each other and have been inbred since enclosure, confounding all the principles of husbandry. Nature has arranged it so that a bull's reign is too short and a cow's fecundity too delayed for father and daughter to reproduce; the weaklings are rejected, and only the strongest breed. The herd may get hay in a bad winter, but no other form of help. Compound feeds are neither given nor accepted.

From the thirteen head to which they fell in the blizzards of 1947, the number of beasts recovered to fifty and continues to thrive. All they have to fear is man, foot-and-mouth, and a government hell-bent on the slaughter policy pursued in the last couple of outbreaks. In 2002 the disease reached the farm on the ridge above and within sight of the Chillingham herd. Austin Widows, a cattle man all his life, employed by the park for nearly fifteen years, did not sleep while it threatened. In case reason has not prevailed by the next time disaster strikes, some of the beasts have been moved to other locations.

The cattle lay or stood in perfect repetition of the sight I had seen fifteen years earlier, enjoying the last of the day's warmth on their hereditary hillside. I thanked the warden and, on his recommendation, made for the church and a glimpse of the quietly coloured soft marble effigies that have lain on its tomb since the park was enclosed. The following day my wife and I crossed the causeway to Holy Island. Another castle, an older church, a garden by Jekyll, and upturned 'cobles', past it as boats and serving as huts, looked out over men pulling pots from the sea. So little impact did the crowds make, you could almost see the Vikings landing on the beach. Durham Cathedral, heather-fed mutton, and a B and B with original Fenwick's bathroom, and even cotton sheets, were yet to come.

The history of England is the history of cattle as much as sheep, of Chillingham Park, the Durham ox, blood lines, breed societies, barons of beef, chop houses, and the network of ancient roads that left their stamp on the names of lanes, the signs of pubs, and in the words of songs and stories. Some of the former droves, now empty and grown over, were in the glory days a furlong in width. They took a hundred thousand cattle or more a year, to say nothing of the geese and turkeys, sheep and pigs, to the finishing pastures of Sedgemoor, East Anglia, the Midlands, the Home Counties, and finally London. The trails might be marked with a lonesome pine or yew. The pubs acquired names like The Drovers. The ground gained a fertility where the cattle stopped that it retains today.

The beef, rising far above the means of the majority whom it passed, went on to Smithfield. The drovers brought news and gossip, ate and distributed wild fruits, and kicked up a cow when short of a bed, sleeping in the warm hollow she left behind. They took months to move cattle south or east, and days to drink their wages in London. The drovers' dogs, having been dismissed, returned home unaccompanied to Scotland or Wales. The innkeepers fed them on the way.

The domestication of cattle is thousands of years old. Invaders brought them on arrival and left them on departing. Plunderers killed the men, took the women and hamstrung their beasts, the next things in importance to life and limb. Wales had the cattle, Scotland had more, and England had the pastures to put flesh on their bones, plus bloodlines of its own. A herd of harmoniously marked or coloured cows confers a meaning on the landscape that can be older than the hedges and deeper than the topsoil. The colossal presence of a bull brings gravitas to shows. As he lumbers from the ring like an overgrown puppy, with a rosette on his halter and a ribbon round his girth, led by an owner flushed with pride, the crowds part and silence falls except for the odd gasp, low murmur and respectful sucking of teeth. Over the centuries, more than wealth has been counted in cattle.

Beasts have long been earmarked for meat or milk, which they cannot give in equal measure. The 'fatted calf' was killed in the Bible, but only for special occasions and the few, a situation that did not change until the agricultural revolution. For the majority, the roast beef of old England was rare, seasonal, and came from beasts no longer fit for breeding or work in the yoke that had been turned out to fatten for the summer and knocked down for the harvest home or village feast. The rest of the carcass was salted and boiled when required. While there is no evidence in seigneurial records of 'the great autumn cull so frequently described by social historians' (Trow-Smith, 1959), the owners of cattle were faced with a thin time of it in winter and an annual decision about which beasts to keep and which to dispatch.

With a growing population and demand for food in the Tudor period, steers were bred with an increasing eye on meat. Retired plough oxen continued to tempt graziers, but vanished as the horse took over in the yoke, reducing the average age of slaughter. The cattle from upland pastures driven to the lowlands and London, that rose in numbers after the Act of Union in 1707 and kept rising, were butchered at four or five years old. The 'buss' beef, housed in custom-built stalls at Barrington Court in Somerset, with no expense spared (Ayrton, 1980), were finished at the age of most cattle today – one to three years.

The size of the average beast, the business done at Smithfield, and the season for beef all doubled in the eighteenth century with better winter feeding. An accomplished dealer could tell by the feel of an ox how many stone of beef and tallow it would bear (a stone of meat weighed 8lb rather than the customary 14). His wife could too. The women involved with cattle are famously capable. In Cheshire I ran into a grazier and butcher who, when his boss died, completed his apprenticeship under the man's widow.

'And was she equal to her husband?' I asked pleasantly.

'Indeed she was,' he said – also pleasantly – 'and the very last person in the north-west of England to pole-axe a bullock.'

Cattle have been known by their colour throughout history, and in the eighteenth century mainly by their horns or lack of them. In all but a few cases programmes were undertaken to 'improve' beasts in commercial terms, for which Robert Bakewell – pioneer, visionary and lateral thinker – gets much credit. The purpose was not only 'to breed animals which weighed heaviest in the best joints and most quickly repaid the cost of the food they consumed' (Ernle, 1912) but 'to develop and perpetuate . . . beauty combined with utility of form, quality of flesh and propensity to fatness'. To add to these virtues, bull and cow were marked for their placidity, longevity, hardiness and thriftiness. The former plough oxen amongst them are noted for strong legs and feet. The 'beeves', an expression Dorothy Hartley ran into, that comprise the leading suckler herds are as follows (with milkers on page 310).

Longhorns were Bakewell's favourite from the Midland counties. With their magnificent heads, 'finch' backs and broken or brindle coats, standing amongst ancient oaks or by a colossal barn, these are beasts from Merrie England made real. The unpredictable sweep of their characteristic horns belies an ease of movement and a pleasure taken in man's company that make them an increasingly popular choice for parks. The triple-purpose Longhorns make interesting crosses, good sucklers and great converters of grass. Their skins are making increasingly popular rugs, hangings and throws. Their meat has a false reputation for laying on fat that is not distributed throughout the tissue. It is up there with the best, only needing time to grow.

Herefords are the much-loved and represented cows of Staffordshire pottery, with woolly white faces and stockings, matching eyelashes and golden-brown coats. If you are not sure whether dream England exists, proceed to the top of a church tower on a warm autumn day with plants for sale in the churchyard below, gardens open, teas in the hall, and Hereford cattle spreading unhurriedly out to graze in their native enclosures. The oldest bloodlines have horns and short legs, but all have the docile disposition of retired plough oxen and cows with a little milk that could grow to great weights. Time was in the Welsh Marches when every farmer large and small seemed to keep Herefords, more graziers bought them, and more people asked for the meat. From having the world at their feet in the nineteenth century, numbers crashed in

England in the twentieth. Promotion is needed. The beef will not sell itself, great as it is. To 'Ricky the butcher' of Cheshire it is the greatest every time.

North Devons, Devonshires or red rubies are stout-hearted, uncomplaining beasts that have stood for centuries in the thickening mists rolling in from the Bristol Channel. The familiar sound of ploughmen urging them on was compared to the plainsong in Exeter Cathedral; the colour of their pelt was like the earth under the plough; the sparse upland grazing that fed a hundred thousand beasts was 'a handful of thin air'. Devons are well travelled and connected beasts, put on the map by the farm in Molland that still has them today. The Massachusetts oxen present at Mount Vernon come from the same stock. Thomas Coke had a herd, and so did Prince Albert. The Isle of Lundy's was evacuated to Somerset in a drought and is now on the Dorset coast. Devon beef, a former favourite at the Lord Mayor's gluttonous banquets in the Mansion House, is equal to Hereford.

Sussex cattle bear a superficial resemblance to Devonshires, and also to the Wealden clay. Stalwarts in harness they were too. The crude painting of eighty-six beasts pulling a giant windmill up the Downs out of Brighton, watched by a tiny crowd in the year 1797, is my desert-island work of art. The practice of using oxen for draft continued until the 1960s. The last pair in the yoke belonged to a former landlord of the Three Cups pub, near Heathfield. The herd in the Forest, which cropped the heather and stayed out all year – complete with horns and an immunity to the local tick – were like the primitive ox on its native heath. The Sussex breed society, also strong in Kent, is full of proud men who seem to get on. Some of their butchers, and some of the best, do not sell any other type of beef.

Welsh Blacks, like their Devon and Sussex peer group, have curly coats and white tips to their tails. They are a distillation of breeds and embody a trade in livestock conducted since outlaws and wolves threatened the drovers. The scattered presence of these cattle in parts of England today is a reminder of the routes they took to hill positions and pastures near London. Welsh blacks are easy calvers with a good supply of milk, which not only look grand on their native mountainsides, but are able to cope with the conditions both early and late in the season. The meat is increasingly popular and deserves to be. The beef continues after centuries to reach the capital.

Shorthorns vary from white to brown. The classic ones are marked by a pale broken coat on a rust-coloured background that grows more pronounced towards the head. The breed is divided into milk and meat suppliers of equal merit and historic significance to England, Scotland and

Ireland. They are part of an ancient, widely distributed and varied family that emerged in the eighteenth century from its Teesdale heartland to heroes' receptions and to thrill the crowds. The Durham or Wonderful ox was a shorthorn standing five foot six and weighing a ton and a half. A bull entitled Comet, the most famous of all time, was the first to reach a thousand guineas. No other type of cattle has been so closely watched, so appealing to artists like Sidney Cooper, and of such wide benefit. The breed society is not as proud and rigorous as some, but the milk is economically produced and creeping back, and the beef legendary.

Lincoln Reds are a colour-matched type of shorthorn minus horns, but a handsome one out at grass on their native Wolds. The darker beasts were noted for meat, the lighter ones for supplying the milk – no longer called for – that went into Stilton cheese. Lincolns were calculated to stand the exposure of their heartlands to the biting winds of winter and occasional drought in summer. They have also developed a resistance to the tsetse fly. Lincolns have prospered in Canada, Hungary and Jamaica, populating a ranch owned by McDonald's that claims to be the largest in the world. The owners of the cattle, representing England's most agricultural of counties, have coupled pride with vision to keep their flag flying. The Lincoln Red breed society is another proud one, starting a promotional beef week in 1995 as part of their centenary celebrations and repeating it each October. The meat is sold in the restaurants and pubs recommended by members for that period, and by accredited butchers throughout the year. It has beaten all comers in competition.

Aberdeen Angus, which are naturally polled, have a smooth black coat which comes through in crosses. The occasional red one (which I have not seen) turns up too. The breed needs no introduction as meat producers, in spite of a dual-purpose past and having risen to eminence in a shorter time than most of their peers – a triumph of good marketing as well as selection. Since the end of the nineteenth century Angus cattle have won a wagonload of prizes and gained a conformation that has made them an almost automatic choice for large numbers of producers and consumers throughout the world. The bulls yield smallish calves and the cows have milk to give them. The steers respond to feeding and supply a prime carcass at an economic age. The beef is all it is cracked up to be.

Galloways are another polled breed, black as the Angus, but wilder, woollier, tougher and more skittish, with a distinctive teddy-bear head and ears. They make excellent crosses with a shorthorn bull, yielding a calf entitled a 'blue grey'. Belted Galloways, which have a white sheet around their tummies, are rare but creeping back. Their antecedents were of great value to hill farmers and drovers, being tough and independent, but able to finish well in the right conditions. From their native Scotland, Galloways and their crosses have been a welcome introduction to Exmoor, Dartmoor, the Forest and other poor soils in England. They supply small and succulent beef. One of my favourites.

Highland cattle are the hairy ones, erect of horn and an eye-catcher, that come in a variety of colours from black to ginger. They used to be called Kyloes, a Northumbrian word that in Old English meant 'cow pasture'. Highlanders are the former foundation stone of the droving trade, and are excellent foragers, proven swimmers and much less ferocious and uncomfy in warm weather than they look. The breed was overtaken by beasts that proved quicker to mature, but came south in modest numbers with the Scots on the move during the Depression, and are on the way back thanks to positive marketing. Try the beef.

Wild or feral cattle and their blood brothers, which might have become extinct but for the fantasies encouraged by Landseer and Sir Walter Scott featuring brave hunters, trembling maidens and savage beasts. On a sliding scale of ferocity and purity, the Chillingham cattle are at the top. The others have been changed by seven centuries in different environments, and are distinguished by black noses and ears and tamer dispositions.

Chartley Park! The castle I had heard of in connection with the cattle, and there they stood. The castle was crumbling, the cattle approaching in response to our pit stop on the busy road past. A winning, conscious and curious, even glamorous, creature came forward, calf-proud, horns erect, unafraid and knowing; I, as a man, called her a beast – though the look she returned was not a beast's at all.

According to the records in Leek, a number of white cattle were grazed in the Peaks a few miles away at Mixon, which was claimed by Dieulacres Abbey but occupied by Hulton Abbey in Stoke on Trent. Between the years 1260 and 1270 they were stolen by the local sheriff and his deputy, no less, and driven to Chartley. The castle fell down, and the cattle remained. The hall was built, burned and built again, twice, and the cattle, fortified with longhorn blood, still remained. It was only in 1904 that they left with the Earl Ferrers to begin a new life at Ditchingham in Suffolk. A fire on the train killed half their number en route. The rest survived, continuing as the Chartley herd.

In 1990, David Johnson, a Staffordshire man, and the second member of his family to do so, bought the estate, the buildings and the ruined castle. That Christmas he acquired two descendants of the park's departed cattle and with his wife began the Chartley Hall herd. The park, originally two or three thousand acres, is down to two or three hundred, but the number of beasts – no, beauties – has risen to nearly twenty in fifteen years. The beef has gone to the Savoy. Mary Queen of Scots, imprisoned in the house, may have eaten it too.

British White cattle are another park breed but hornless. It is not certain for how many hundreds of years they resided at Whalley Abbey in Lancashire, near a looming Pendle, before dispersal to Cheshire in the late seventeenth century. Their presence in Norfolk since the reign of George II, and in Sussex since 1907, has not been interrupted. British Whites were considered of such importance during the Second World War, a number were sent to the US on government orders if you please. From former status symbols they made the jump to milk production, then into beef. The meat in available in selected shops. I cannot wait.

Park cattle are dotted around England like Norman churches: there to be wondered at, though not by anyone racing by. If you want to see them you will – amongst medieval ruins, feeding in Nidderdale, and moving through the grassland towards Stonehenge – as though they were making a long journey home.

The Second World War might have been expected to test English and British cattle. Yet the *Champion Herd Book* of 1948 is crammed with stirring black-and-white photographs of prize-winning Devons and Lincoln Reds, as well as Oxford Down rams and Middle White pigs. It is also an historical document.

In 1970, Professor Rouse of Oklahoma University confirmed that 'Foremost in England's agricultural progress has been the development of her cattle industry.' In those parts of the world where there were no indigenous cattle, 'the British breeds account for most of the beef and many of the dairy herds seen today'. How shocked Rouse will have been to hear what happened to their bloodlines. How surprised a visiting American, Australian or Hungarian historian or farmer would be to find so little evidence of England's famous livestock out in the Herefordshire fields, the Hampshire woods and in recommended restaurants, let alone in heritage literature.

For the sake of quantity over quality, English 'rosbif' had sold out to French overgrown veal by the mid-1970s. The move was orchestrated by the supermarkets and government, carried out by farmers, ratified by a utilitarian grading system made to fit, and paid for by the British public. The coincidental input of the health-food industry in targeting fat, which supplies meat with texture and flavour – but need not be consumed in lethal quantities – helped the downward spiral.

Many beef producers who had not converted to French bloodlines used them to procreate a weight gain in the native cattle. They also imported descendants of livestock that had been shipped to the New World, and acquired the fashionable advantage of becoming taller and leaner to achieve the same thing. This was called 'breeding up', a programme that took time to register with societies, divided members, and now has them back-pedalling.

In the case of Herefords, Lincoln Reds and Aberdeen Angus, 'breeding up' has created rare and original breeds within breeds, entitled 'traditional' by the RBST and entered as 'pedigree' or '100 per cent' in herd books. Shorthorns, Sussex and North Devons have also been affected. The loss of meat and other qualities to a gain in weight may not be significant, but is already perceived. The purest cattle are fetching a premium at sales, as is their beef at the butchers'.

Retailers have over thirty years to make up for, a period in which 'the mainstream meat market has lost all semblance of caring for eating quality' (*The Ark*, Autumn 2000). The breed and feed are irrelevant provided the carcass is lean and uniform, the weight quickly gained, and the turnover speedy. The meat cannot be hung because it lacks fat and therefore dries out, and profits need to be realised, though the damage to the texture and flavour is done long before the beef, cherry-red, slack and wet, is imprisoned in a carbon-based wrapper on the shelf. However good a steak or joint may look to unpractised eyes, and however cheap it appears, the supermarket price is not worth paying.

Yet with a little effort, it is possible to buy the beef which takes its name from an English cathedral city and went to the bishop's palace, trod the moors with big Jan Ridd, and may even have fallen to the Druids' knife. The meat from pedigree suckler herds may be for the few, but it goes to a club that anyone can join. Supplies have been stabilizing, even on the increase. All native cattle are conservation grazers. They are economic to keep, stirring to look at, and have low stress levels. A new generation of hopeful breeders is taking them on. There has been restocking after the dreadful toll taken by foot-and-mouth. The thirty-month rule is due to come off too, releasing three- and four-year-old beef across the board. All the market requires is for the public to pay a fair price for inflated quality.

COOK'S ORACLE

Here is 'a perfect beef recipe' acquired from the Beef Shorthorn and Galloway Cattle societies at the Bellingham Show, Northumberland.

Ingredients:
One beef Shorthorn bull
One herd of Galloway cows
One rough hill (a field will do)

1. Mix bull with cows, using hill.
2. Slow-cook for approximately 9 months.
3. Watch as perfect creation emerges unaided (no utensils required).

4. Add milk, then forage and leave to mature for 18–24 months.
5. ENJOY.

Yes! Yes! YES!

Beef needs three things in order to eat well, the sayings go, whether it is organic or not: breed, feed and hanging.

So the meat should have 'at least half native blood in it' (Gerald David, butcher). The mixture of a Hereford or Devon bull and a dairy cow is an old commercial and propitious one. Heifers, which possess a higher percentage of beef to bone than steers, are preferred by some butchers. A beast that has calved once and been allowed to fatten is better still (the word from the inside track is that a 'freemartin' or 'willjill', i.e. neither a Will nor a Jill – a non-breeder – is the best beef of the lot).

One advantage of native beasts is that they can thrive on grass, their natural diet, whereas the continentals need barley and concentrates. Two or three summers in a field or on a hillside, ending with a month indoors, gets the optimum result. So, 'a lot of breeding goes in at the mouth'.

The fat on a side of beef, coyly redefined as 'finish' by the Meat and Livestock Commission (MLC), and a fallen idol, is usually a sign of good breeding and feeding. The Longhorns, Middlehorns, Shorthorns, Red Polls, Angus and Galloway cattle carry both surface and intermuscular fat, or 'marbling', a network of veins which indicates sweetness and succulence in the meat to come. Park and Highland types lack the marbling but have the compensation of primitive blood, making their beef more like venison in texture, but tastier.

Fat protects and lubricates the meat, enabling it to be hung, which concentrates the flavour through drip loss. Some butchers keep forequarters for two weeks and hindquarters for a month in order to bring out the best in the most expensive cuts. The fat does not visibly change in the mean time: it should remain firm and dry, and lie at least half an inch deep across the loin. The lean will acquire a dark or light brown crust and cut almost purple, turning a deep red on exposure to the air. The tallowy patchlessness of one and the scent of the other, a combination of 'cream and almonds', is what to go for.

In 2004, the English Beef and Lamb Executive (Ebtex) published a nice little pamphlet entitled *Cooking with Beef*, which tells us that 'English cuts have evolved through the centuries to match changing cooking methods and tastes in English homes.' The choices available from butchers and the uses they can be put to are as follows:

Sirloin: taken from the middle back; knighted or not? Sounds about as likely as Alfred burning the cakes; comes in a piece on or off the bone, or as steaks, known as 'porterhouse' (*entrecôte* in French); roast or grill.

Fillet: taken from inside the ribs next to the sirloin; the most tender and expensive cut, not the tastiest – one I seldom buy; boneless; comes in a piece or as steaks; roast or grill.

T-bone: the sirloin and fillet on the bone; an American import requiring a large appetite that tends to be too much and wasted, or cut too thin for choice; comes in steaks; grill.

Rib, wing: taken from above the sirloin – one of my favourites; comes in a piece on or off the bone; roast.

Rib, fore: adjoins the wing rib; may be a little cheaper, but presented and cooked the same way.

Rib, eye: the lean core or 'eye' of the rib – another American import; boneless; comes in steaks; grill.

Rump: taken from the lower back or chump in a lamb; called the Pope's Eye ('popseye') in Scotland; preferred by many to the sirloin for flavour and texture; boneless; Michel Roux's last supper? English rump steak and chips (surely with *sauce Béarnaise*).

Skirt: taken from inside the flank; boneless; the thick piece, known as the 'rump', is creeping up in price; slice thinly and stir fry or cut into cubes and stew; the smaller piece is the 'goose', used in Cornwall for pasties.

Topside: taken from the outside of the buttock; boneless; an awkward cut and one I seldom buy, but popular, carrying little fat or marbling, which needs prolonged hanging and dries out when overcooked; comes in a piece; oven roast – best eaten cold.

Silverside: adjoins the topside, but is even leaner; boneless; usually salted in a piece; 'boil'.

Brisket: the chest; comes in a piece on and off the bone, pot-roast fresh, 'boil' when salted.

Leg: taken from the hindquarter; boneless; comes in a piece or pieces; stew.

Chuck, blade, neck, clod, shin: taken from the forequarter; stew.

GRILLING

'Sometimes, on a day off, I'd walk into the City along the Embankment and up the Strand, pausing at the Victorian chop-houses to sniff the red sides of beef hanging on hooks in the steaming windows. To me such food was like a mountain of Sundays, or the hot gravied kiss of Mammon, strictly reserved for plump brokers and bankers – it never occurred to me that I might eat it' (Laurie Lee).

I worked not in a chop house, but in a place that grilled meat as it should be done: a wine bar (now demolished) in the former stables of the Kensington Barracks in London. The proprietor, a genial giant who claimed to have been the longest-serving captain in the British Army, rented a flat in the Russian Embassy. The chef, a part-time Shakespearean actor with a beard and an uncontrollable temper, used to get drunk, bawl his head off and trash the kitchen – then sober up and ask who had done it. The staff were a succession of odds, illegal immigrants and sods, including a highly strung but not unpleasant cove who was late one night, we learned from 'the force', on account of committing a murder. The customers were a social mix who boozed all afternoon regardless of the law, talking drivel at full volume, having eaten better than they realised. The day concluded with song, the occasional scuffle, and the departure of a dog that came in with its master and returned home alone on the bus. All human life seemed to be there.

We lit the fire at 10 a.m. with a bag of coke, cooking around fifty steaks and chops on a tray over the embers to go with a joint of roast mutton or boiled bacon and a date pudding. Another bag of fuel went on in the afternoon for the evening shift. One busy day in August I looked up at the thermometer on the wall next to the fire and it read 120°F. By the time the 'long hot summer' had drawn to a close, I was down two stone in weight, but committed to the rigour and ritual of grilling meat over a fire.

At home, I have a three-legged Cornish trivet or 'brandis' which goes in the hearth and a sustainable supply of hardwood. I also have an open-topped South-East Asian stove made of cast iron for charcoal (see page 103), which is used outside.

Give a fire up to an hour to reduce to embers. Make sure that the plates are hot, the vegetables or salad ready and a pair of tongs handy for turning the beef.

Before grilling a sirloin steak, snip through the fat and adjoining layer of gristle with a pair of scissors or else the meat will buckle from the heat.

As an alternative to a fire, use an old-fashioned grilling pan – a heavy cast-iron implement with ridges on the bottom. Brush with oil and heat until smoking before use.

Obviously, try and cook a steak evenly on both sides. You can time it, but not accurately. Get acquainted with the 'rule of thumb': once the principle is learned, it will not let you down. Meat is rare when tender to the touch, becoming increasingly firm as it cooks through. The side that is grilled first should be served facing up. It cooks more evenly than the other half.

OVEN ROASTING

Nature, nurture and butcher have done most of the work for you. The only things left are to identify and purchase a prime piece of sirloin or wing rib to eat hot, preferably on the bone, chined and tied up, or topside to eat cold, and have the decency to cook and carve it with consideration. Weigh the beef: 15–20 minutes per lb. (450g) in an oven preheated to 200°C/400°F/gas mark 6, turned down a couple of notches after a quarter of an hour, will produce beef for most tastes – pink towards the outside and rare in the middle. Allow a little longer for meat off the bone. There is no evidence to suppose, says the British Pig Executive (BPEX), that resting meat after cooking has a beneficial effect on the tissue. But it does not have a bad one either, and gives you time to make the gravy.

Lord Welby's sauce for roast beef: a substitute for horseradish, better than the stuff in the bottle, and named after a patron and admirer of the sauce. It is easily made and keeps for a couple of days. 'Mix 1 heaped teaspoon of mustard powder, 1 tablespoon of wine vinegar with 2 tablespoons of cream, 1 tablespoon of grated parsnip and a little salt . . . no sugar is required' owing to the sweetness of the parsnip (Hutchins, 1967).

Mustard sauce for steak: 1 shallot, knob of butter, half a glass of white wine, 5fl oz (150ml) cream, ½ tsp of made-up English mustard, heaped dessertspoon chopped parsley, or chives. Melt the butter and sweat the shallot until soft. Pour in the wine and boil up for a minute. Add the cream and reduce by half. Then stir in the mustard and herbs. You may not need seasoning. Do not reheat, otherwise the flavour will suffer. Serve immediately.

Carpet bag steak: *recherché*. For 2, take 1lb (450g) fillet steak from the thicker end. Make a slit in the side with the point of a sharp knife, but not all the way through or top to bottom, so as to form a pocket. Open half a dozen oysters and empty them in with their liquor. Bind or sew up with string. Brown quickly in butter all over and commit to a hot oven for no more than 15 minutes. Remove the string, carve and serve with its own juices (Hutchins, 1967).

POT ROASTING

A way of cooking the tougher cuts of beef, which you may wish to serve whole. Brisket is a lovely one to use, but any piece from the forequarter, which the butcher may sell as braising steak, will do. A gravy separator helps to get the perfect result.

Brown the meat in a piece on all sides. Place in a pot with a peeled onion, shallots or garlic, and season to taste. Add half a pint (300ml) of stock or red wine and commit to a cool oven,

150°C /300°F/gas mark 2, for the afternoon. Remove and keep warm while you pour off the gravy and reduce it by up to a half before serving.

STEWING

My father's stews, put sharply into focus by the ones at school, were the best I have known. The meat, which he cooked to rags, they hardly cooked at all. The sauce he enriched with whatever was handy. Their condition improved over the course of two or three days, if they lasted that long. Everyone, everywhere had their own stews. Lobscouse had a name.* My mother-in-law's had none. It was made with 'two penn'worth of bits' from Roy Toms, the butcher in Polperro, whose late lamented shop was decorated throughout with blue and white china.

Stews in England, with exceptions, are thickened with flour. The easiest ways to do it are as follows.

Basic stew: Take 3lb (1.3kg) from the forequarter, hindquarter or skirt of beef, and some ox kidney if you wish, or dripping, 1 onion and 1 clove of garlic, peeled and chopped, stock, wine or vegetable water, salt and pepper to taste, plain flour.

Trim the meat of excess fat, and cut into 1 inch (2.5cm) cubes. Put some flour on a plate and roll the cubes until coated. Heat the fat until smoking in a frying pan and brown the meat on all sides in batches covering no more than the bottom of the vessel. Remove the meat with a perforated spoon to a pot with a lid as you go. Add the raw onion and garlic. Moisten with almost enough liquid to cover. Bring up to simmering point and season well. Bake in a pre-heated oven at 150°C/300°F/gas mark 2 and cook for 3–4 hours or until tender. Taste the sauce when finished, adjusting the flavour if necessary. This method is the easiest to translate into mutton, venison and hare stew.

Sussex stewed steak: Elizabeth David takes a single piece of beef, dusted in flour and browned as above. She then adds equal measures of port and ale or stout and a slightly smaller quantity of mushroom ketchup to cover, making 'a rich-looking and interesting gravy'. The sweetness of the port and the bitterness of the beer cancel each other out, leaving the residual flavours to come into their own.

* *Lobscouse: 'A sailor's dish of meat stewed with vegetables and ship's biscuits or the like,' says the* OED. *There have been other ingredients not so choice. The dish seldom travels beyond Knotty Ash (Poulson), though it may originate in Holland or Denmark. Loblolly was a gruel, or slang for a boor.*

Exeter stew, a latter-day version of *Everyday Cookery**, uses a slightly different method. Brown the meat in the fat first, remove, and fry the onions. Then stir in a dessertspoon of flour, stir and cook gently until a light brown. Reintroduce the meat and add the liquid, etc. Similar result, different route.

To vary: you may begin a stew with fried bits of bacon, adding mushrooms, dried ceps or bay leaves, and vegetables too. Carrots are best, gaining as much from the flavours around them as they give in exchange. A single Jerusalem artichoke, peeled and grated, does wonders for the gravy.

It is fun tweaking stews and reassuring to have one on the go. Serve with mashed potato and cabbage, Hungry Gap (see page 362) or greens. Make it one cold, wet night with booze on the table and a fire halfway up the chimney. Kill the electric light. The best food of its type and a simple pleasure, outrageously easy and inexpensive to lay on. Someone should ban them.

Steak pie: a stew with a lid on it. I tend to eat half a stew first, then make a pie from the rest. Commit a warm cooked stew to a close-fitting dish and cover in shortcrust pastry (see page 60). Bake in a hot oven for 20 minutes at 200°C/400°F/gas mark 6, turning it down to 170°C/325°F/gas mark 3 for another 20 minutes. If the pastry is getting too brown, cover with greaseproof paper.

Steak and kidney pie used to be served cold at Huntercombe Golf Club. Delicious.

Steak pudding: more from Laurie Lee:

The café downstairs was a shadowy tunnel lined with high-backed wooden pews, carbolic-scrubbed and exclusively male, with all the comforts of a medieval refectory . . . my favourite was . . . a little basin of meat wrapped in a caul of suety dough which was kept boiling all day in a copper cauldron in a cupboard under the stairs. Turned out on the plate, it steamed like a sodden napkin, emitting a mournful odour of laundries; but once pricked with a fork it exploded magnificently with a rich lava of beefy juices. There must have been over a pound of meat in each separate pie – a complete working man's meal . . . Arnold, the proprietor . . . a man in his early thirties, was a rounded dandy with heavy cream-white jowls and delicate parboiled hands. He did all the work alone, both cooking and serving, and moved with the rolling dignity of a eunuch, dressed in tight cotton gowns, buttoned up to the throat, which also gave

---

* A curious book with plenty of acknowledgements but no ascribed author, published in 1972.

him the appearance of one of his cloth-wrapped puddings. He was bald, large-headed, red-lipped and corseted, and was given to abstractions, silences and revelries and he seemed clearly to be a cut above his clients, though if he thought so he never showed it. Each day, before breakfast, he padded around the tables laying out the morning newspapers like hymn-sheets . . . I have never known a man who gave to this particular job such a sense of modest almost priest-like dedication, advising and serving the labourers at his table and taking their coppers like a church collection.

This purveyor of Toads and Squeaks was something of a mystery. One might have imagined him to have chosen the job as a purge, an act of self-abasement, but certainly not for the money . . . I knew he had another life . . . about the two pretty children who visited him briefly each Saturday night. And that he kept in careful seclusion a young and beautiful wife. Sometimes as I climbed to my room I saw her standing in her half-open doorway, a tantalising strip of voluptuous boredom, her hair piled high and elaborately set, her eyes burning like landing lights. She wore a white silk wrap . . . and her toenails were painted green. She was about my own age, but she never spoke. Nor did Arnold ever mention her.

Goulash: a word which had become anglicised by 1900, borrowed from the Magyar *gulyasch*, meaning a herdsman, and a glorified soup. A few expats used to patronise the Normandy Stores: proud and vigorous people who breed the sweetest-tempered horses, speak the most difficult language and make the most piquant of salamis, called *csabai*. I visited their country. You can ride all morning in the *puszta*, the beginning of the steppe, seeing nothing but the elevated nests of storks – until a whitewashed farmhouse, long, low and thatched, rises from the grass two hundred yards away. The apricot colour of palatial buildings, the apricot scent and taste of Barac, an eau-de-vie, and a shave with a cut-throat razor goes a long way at 8 a.m.

The stews, which co-exist with the soup, were brought to the attention of the rest of Europe by the Viennese. There are many types. Potato, veal and pork are common, but beef, specifically shin of beef, takes the laurels. The paprika used in a goulash is of the sweet rather than hot variety, introduced to the region in the nineteenth century, a reminder that the world's gastronomies all exchange cards. The colour is high, but the taste a lot less spicy than it looks. *Edulsuss*, I was told by a friend, Inge Sprawson, who is half Hungarian, half Austrian, is the one to use (see page 364).

Goulash is good with boiled rice or mashed potato. In Magyar circles it is eaten with *tarhonya*, a soft and short-lived form of pasta described as 'egg drops', which used to be imported into England by a bookseller near the Normandy. He would turn up unannounced, with a consignment of *tarhonya*, then stopped coming and I never saw either of them again.

2lb (900g) shin of beef, half the quantity of peeled and sliced onions, 1 peeled and sliced clove of garlic, 1oz (25g) lard or dripping, 1 dsp powdered sweet paprika, ½ tsp caraway seeds, half a lemon rind, grated; salt.

Melt the fat in a pan. Add the onions and garlic and lightly brown, then the meat, sealing all over. Collect the solids on one side of the pan. Tip it so that the fat collects on the other side, sprinkle the paprika over it and stir well. Cook gently until it foams and turns a dark red, then mix with the rest of the ingredients including the caraway and lemon. Add sufficient water to almost cover the meat and salt to taste. Simmer for 3 hours or until tender, loosely covered. Moisten with water when necessary.

Oxtail and kidney stew: bake with beans (see page 57).

Heart

An ox heart weighing around 2lb (900g) will feed up to eight people. The meat is close-textured, lean and in shorter supply than fillet of beef, but a fraction of the price. It is highly underrated. Some, swearing they do not like heart, will not even try it. For others, it is an old favourite, even ceremonial. A stuffed heart used to be called 'love in disguise'.

To prepare a heart, cut out the cartilage and the larger pipes. Soak for 12 – 24 hours covered with cold water, adding 1 level tsp of salt and 1 of vinegar for every pint (600ml) of liquid, then drain. This gets rid of the blood.

To cook, take the usual suspects – 1lb (450g) carrots, ½lb (225g) onions and 2 cloves of garlic, peeled and sliced; 2 glasses of red wine and up to a further 2 of stock, vegetable water or even plain water, 1 bay leaf and salt and pepper to taste.

Put the heart in a close-fitting pan. Drown half the meat in the liquid and season. Cover and cook at 150°C/300°F/gas mark 2 for 3–4 hours or until the heart can be pierced with a fork. Add the vegetables at half-time. Put the gravy through a separator and dish up with the heart carved in thin slices like a rib of beef.

Cowheel: 'stew and hard' – the middle classes particularly, south of the Trent, can hardly restrain themselves at the thought. What could be funnier (*Private Eye*) or more tasteless. Fear and group solidarity may be amongst the reasons; ignorance certainly, based on an acquaintance never made. It can be the same with anything from tripe to *rosbif* and 'rabbit food', anyone from 'cheese-eating surrender monkeys' to 'froggies' whose habits and programming are not the same as yours. So, the foot of the pig is used in fashionable restaurants but the foot of the ox or calf, the principal ingredient of the 'sumptuous' jelly made in *Lark Rise*, is not.

The cowheel used in England today, mainly in Yorkshire and Lancashire, has come from Ireland since BSE. It is stripped and bleached like tripe (see page 158), unappetising to look at, and does not make a worthy dish on its own, nor is it asked to. Cowheel is used to enrich beef. The pie is as follows: 'Cut half a pound of stewing steak and cook slowly with carrots, barley and half a cow heel, chopped up. 30 minutes before the end of cooking time (up to 4 hours), put a thick suet crust on top . . . sticks to your ribs in winter' (Houlihan,1988).

A dish known as 'stew', which has a flavour off the Richter Scale, is made by selected Lancastrian butchers. It is presented in a bowl in jelly, cut or spooned into wedges, and preferably eaten with a North Country oatcake known as 'hard' (see page 463): an old favourite increasingly difficult to find. By the time I got wind of the partnership some years back, it was easier to find the stew than the hard. The recipes are secret, but this is how I would attempt to make the stew.

Take a cowheel and about 3lb (1.3kg) of lean beef, like silverside. Judging by the pinkish colour of the stew in the butcher's, the meat is given a preliminary salting for two days and a soaking in water for one (like brawn). Commit to a pan with the cowheel, cover with fresh water and simmer for up to four hours until the beef is soft. Skim constantly, remove the bone from the cowheel and stir until the meat breaks up. Reduce the liquor or add more water if necessary, aiming for the consistency of a soup. Leave in the cool for at least a day to set. I look forward to hearing from any butcher who may be keen to put me right.

SALT BEEF

One of the first culinary folk tales I ever heard was about two rich New Yorkers who felt they had one thing left to do in life. So they caught the boat-train to London via Liverpool, ate boiled beef and carrots for lunch, and re-embarked for home that afternoon, a round trip of nearly two weeks. Now, the journey takes hours, business is the incentive, and salt beef is more or less confined to sandwich bars advertising 'pastrami on rye', a label cribbed from America itself.

The salt beef in England, in spite of any transatlantic or Jewish connotation, fed generations of people on ship and shore and lingered after refrigeration. Huge 'rounds' from the buttock, weighing up to 30lb, partnered hams at festive occasions and hunt breakfasts. Of the smaller cuts, silverside was frequent, topside occasional, and a boned brisket, which has more fat, the aficionados' choice.

It was only in the 1980s that Phyllis Hitchcock, my stepfather's housekeeper in Somerset, looked up at the frost on the Quantocks one November morning and remarked it was about the time of year she used to salt the meat – beef as well as pork. The advantage of home curing is that you can choose the cut: approach the task as you would bacon (see page 179). Otherwise refer to the butcher: he may do the honours or have what you want already prepared.

To cook a 2–3 lb (900g–1.3kg) piece of salt beef, soak overnight. Then bring up to the boil in cold water and poach (i.e. barely simmer) for one hour per pound, or until it can be pierced with a fork, with a few peppercorns, bay leaves, etc. until tender. Remove to the oven and keep warm. Boil carrots or cabbage and potatoes in the broth, serving a little with the meat and saving the rest for soup.

Cold salt beef is usually pressed under a weight for 24 hours. It is still sold by butchers up north.

Tongues are salted, otherwise they lack flavour. There is not much to be gained by doing it yourself: a butcher with a brine going will be able to supply you. A pickled tongue does not need soaking unless it has been smoked, which is rare today. Cook it for at least as long as you would salt beef, until the meat is beginning to fall apart. Allow it to cool a little, then remove the skin and gristle. This is important. I ordered tongue at a highly recommended, expensive, and fashionable restaurant in London in 2004 to find it had not been skinned. A job half done.

Tongue is one of the foods you can eat hot, but is better cold as the meat can set. A tongue with gristle attached will make its own jelly, otherwise – if jelly you want – cook a pig's trotter with it. When done, put the tongue into a pudding basin. Cover with some of its own liquor. Place a saucer and a weight on top. Leave in a cool place for at least two days. To serve, turn out with a palette knife on to a plate.

So what have you got – an ordinary ox tongue? No – a delicacy hiding in a smooth, cool and crystalline jelly, and 100 per cent improvement on the tasteless, wafer-thin slices available from cooked-meat counters. Crown with a sprig of parsley, and carve horizontally. Serve for lunch on a hot summer's day, or beside a Christmas ham. A home-cooked tongue is a rarer sight than it deserves to be. When did you last have one?

VEAL

The received wisdom is that the horrid Normans were great eaters of veal and the good old Anglo-Saxons were not, preferring the stronger flavours of beef, mutton and game. A sentimental projection perhaps, though there does seem to have been a town and country divide in the eighteenth and nineteenth centuries, with farmers in the environs of London producing the lion's share of veal for habitués of the City. Cromwell liked his veal, Defoe said the best veal in the world came from Copthall, Maldon and Waltham Marshes in Essex. Farley cooked it in his famous tavern, and so did Fothergill at the Spreadeagle. Supplies from the West Country increased with the railways.

Calf's head was very much the thing. It was also the symbolic centrepiece at the annual banquet to commemorate the execution of Charles I attended by republicans carrying axes, wearing masks and sporting hankies dipped in wine (i.e. blood) that continued for a hundred and fifty years after his death (Beeton, 1968). Eliza Acton gives ten recipes for calf's head, including one called Burlington Whimsy.

The mode of growing and slaughtering veal, in order to arrive at a delicate white meat, is not surprisingly what got to people. England was not amongst the worst offenders, but was equated with the trade in general and regulated out of the market. This delivered the business into the hands of farmers abroad who were still operating crate systems. As a result, the demand for veal was met with imports. The potential supply – obtained from bull or 'runty' calves from dairy herds at home – was knocked on the head at birth and wasted.

Now that the industry is being asked to conform throughout the EU, English producers are regaining confidence and returning to a playing field that is closer to level. Paul and Ruth Kimber, who have a dairy farm and shop on the Dorset–Somerset border, and do most of the local markets, specialise in veal. Animal welfare is higher on their priority list than anywhere else in Europe, and the regs are more likely to be met. The calves live in social groups in and out of doors and go locally to slaughter at seven months old, almost the age of beef. The purchase of their meat has brought an end to its waste.

English veal, white no longer, is referred to as 'rosé'. It is hung for between seven and ten days, tender and lean. Some of the cuts have different names from beef, providing escalopes from the top of the leg, and knuckles (the Italian *osso bucco*) from the bottom, fore and aft. The French and Dutch way of dividing the meat across the grain, which prevents escalopes from buckling, is more elegant than the English method, but easily learned. Calf's head is off the menu for now and may be passé, but the kidneys are available. Let us hope that the sweetbreads return.

The prime joints of veal are usually oven-roasted like lamb, until pink. The secondary cuts are stewed like beef or mutton – my favourites are breast and brisket. Coat escalopes in flour, egg and breadcrumbs and fry in butter until golden on both sides. Alternatively, fry uncoated, cover in cheese and grill until it is melted.

CHAPTER
TWELVE

THE ROYAL MUTTON,
AND MACON

THE HIGH STREET lay under a brilliant sun and more than a foot of gusting snow. A raven held up in the wind.* There was nothing and no one else about, no ghosts of Roman soldiers marching, capes flowing and breastplates glinting, to swell the number people have seen. The domed heads of the opposite fells were smooth, clean and whiter than skulls, their faces pockmarked with rock. The lakes were iced over, the silent becks as well. The valley floor, warm, green and way below them, was basking in a different season. Off to the east lay an eagle's nest, due to be vacated for the next few months. Winter was closing in on Herdwick country, home of the famous sheep, the shepherds who counted in Celtic, and the faithful dogs of whom tales are told, all unlikely and all true. I started my descent. It was late afternoon and the cold was beginning to bite. I had an hour to get down the mountain before the light failed and the temperature dropped to well below freezing for yet another night.

The history of sheep is the history of England, of North Country abbeys and fells, south-country fairs and downs, East Anglian churches, Shropshire farms, Cotswold villages and the chalk fringe of Thomas Hardy's Egdon Heath. The ewe and ram, sheet anchors of agriculture and industry, filled both the Chancellor's woolsack and the coffers of dynasties wealthy as the King. Driven or driving, they were a blessing on one house, a curse on another, a cause of enclosure and rebellion too. Men ate sheep. They also said that sheep ate men.

'Herdwick' is thought to have been a Norse term for a farm or pasture. It was attached by the nineteenth century to a breed of sheep, obscure in origin and tough as they come, that is peculiar to the Lake District. The lambs, born black with white spectacles and flecks, acquire silver faces and feet, and a thick dark staple that grows back lighter when clipped. The rams have the legs of a carthorse, and a fine fighting head that can deal fatal blows. The ewes can live on coarse or dead grasses, and bear young to a great age. You come upon them in the highest and most unlikely spots, look up and see them even higher, gazing down at you almost forlornly, but certain to survive the cold and the night. A hefted sheep, emotionally attached to its heaf (heath) or birthplace, has the strongest of homing instincts. It will climb any mountain or swim any lake in order to return. A Herdy knows where it belongs, crag-fast or buried under snow in England's empty winter quarter.

The life and movements of a Herdwick flock are governed by the seasons. The ewes, primed and painted with the red and blue smit marks of their owners, spend most of the year roaming

---

* *The High Street: the highest Roman road in England, which winds across the fells above Hartsop in the Lake District.*

on the commons. They are gathered in for tupping, lambing, dipping and shearing, when the lucky ones get an extra bite from the ash pollards. The rams are kept on their own until required in November. The lambs spend their first winter, rather than on the fells, in the comparative comfort of lower altitudes, returning around Hog(get) Day – 5 April, and Lady Day elsewhere in England. The gimmers, the females, are reserved for breeding. The wethers, or castrated rams, ringed at birth, gain weight for the autumn sales. At the end of the season, the shepherds meet and the shows take place between glowering, steep and bracken-bound fells, with running, wrestling, and the singing of songs over pints round a fire which men long dead used to sing as well.

The fells, more than they might appear to walkers, are divided up into large commons covering thousands of acres, and smaller allotments. The owners of land are called 'statesmen' (estates-men). The parcels are 'stints' or limited to a maximum number of sheep, lambs and other livestock permitted to graze them. The dry-stone walls mark the boundaries between them, defying gravity and clinging to the mountainsides like giant scaly slowworms making for the heights on the High Street.

Life in the Lake District had no heyday. The fells have no practical purpose other than that of providing food for sheep, which is one of the slowest into profit. Herdwicks provide not lamb, but 'mature' lamb, from hoggets, or mutton, until their second year. The wool, hardly worth shearing, came to be overtaken by softer, cheaper and man-made fibres. If it had not been for the Reverend Rawnsley, a founder of the breed society, and Beatrix Potter, a subsequent chairwoman and hobby flockmistress, Herdwicks might have become extinct. Today, they pass with Lakeland tenancies from one generation of farmers to the next.

Potter's estate at Troutbeck, consigned to the National Trust, was controversially carved up in 2005. Meanwhile, Herdwicks are recovering from the horrors of foot-and-mouth, and not doing badly. The meat is better known thanks to improved marketing and acquiring a European AC tag.* The wool, warm and waterproof, is making a modest comeback too. Once, I stopped a man in the street and asked him about the interesting-looking jersey he was wearing: Herdwick, says he. I now have a tie. The cloth was mentioned by Shakespeare and Burns, and made 'the coat so grey' worn by huntsman John Peel – it produced carpets as well.

Arthur Weir filled me in on Herdwicks. I sat by the range in his cottage near the beck, where he had survived infantile paralysis to farm for fifty years. He talked of sheep, and the breed he knew, and of the dark, sweet, half-wild meat, raised on the bilberries and aromatic grasses

---

* Appellation contrôlée *status is granted to wines, cheese and other agricultural products. It binds them in law to where they originate and rules relating to manufacture. Some English foods have this protection. For others it is too late.*

bursting through the snow on the High Street. The mutton he referred to as 'royal'. I asked why. The answer, Arthur said, was that Herdwicks had been ordered and supplied for the Queen's coronation.

I wrote to the Palace about it, receiving a prompt and courteous reply. Two banquets were held, on 3 and 4 June 1953, and *carré d'agneau à la Windsor* had indeed been served, but from what source they could no longer be sure. I wonder if the family or descendants of the chef, Ronald Aubrey, can confirm that it was Herdwick, or whether a tattered copy of an invoice, addressed to the Royal Household and marked in £.s.d., still exists.

I was not brought up with sheep, and thought little of them until converted. A Dartmoor Greyface ram belonging to Terry Hoyland did it. Monty had stature, presence, attitude and nothing but disdain for the human race. To the indignity of being dipped he responded with outrage. To the pittance he had fetched at the Hatherleigh show and sale, he was indifferent. Monty bore himself like a champion who had run a syndicate up to forty thousand guineas.

Not long after meeting Monty and being given the brush-off, I rented a cottage in Yorkshire and occasionally saw the farmer up the lane drive his sheep through the beck. The flock, which he knew as individuals, moved as one down the bank, nimbly over the stones, and up the other side in the morning sun. Slowly, a crude picture emerged of a world in which sheep are paramount and, for a few days every year, Kelso, Bourne, Lazonby, Masham and Priddy, where farmers gather to buy and sell are the most important places on earth.

The UK has over fifty breeds of sheep. They may be lumped together, but the contrast even between flocks – even adjacent ones – can be startling. It is hard to believe that the great Romney Marsh ewe and the compact little Southdown tup, its neighbour, are jointly able to produce offspring let alone claim descent from the same wild ancestor that came out of Asia thousands of years ago. Sheep have adapted more quickly and evidently to their new situations and the vagaries of soil, climate and diet than any other livestock. Yet they still respond to a dog as they would to a wolf and to man as a predator.

Until two or three hundred years ago, the sheep in England were a mixture of lean, active and rangy heath-croppers with black or tan faces, longish legs, horns in both sexes, dark wool and gamy flesh. Flocks were kept for their fleece, milk and golden hoof – the capacity to fertilise the ground they trod. Meat did not become a prime consideration until needed by a rising population in the eighteenth century. The blood of the quicker-growing, heavier prototype, with which Bakewell responded, infused most of the native English breeds, many of the Welsh ones, and projected commercial flocks into parts of Scotland where there had only been cattle before.

A system of sheep farming evolved, designed for the UK's different altitudes and microclimates. It breaks down into mountain, hill, moorland, downland, and lowland breeds. For the longwools, a lowlander with upland characteristics, there are scattered locations too. The primitive types, once universal, though their characteristics live on in many sheep, are relegated to parks, islands, and the locations from which they take their names today.

Every commercial breed of sheep has a reason for being where it originated and adapted to its surroundings. A tough and independent slow-growing mountaineer is not well suited to a valley floor: he will run to fat on grass richer than he is used to, and resent confinement. A precocious lowlander is the reverse, lacking the hairy fleece, the woolly forehead and the taste for coarse vegetation to keep him alive on a demanding hillside.

You can travel around certain counties, passing from one culture to the next in the space of a few miles and the drop of a hundred feet, and, from the surrounding sheep, tell you are no longer in Muker but Masham. You notice the colour of the Herdwick, meaning Cumbria, the horns on the Hexham Blackface, the knees on the Gritstone, the legs on the Wiltshire, the mask on the Hampshire, and the wig on the Clun. You hear of the Cheviot's kindness to the shepherd, of his white Roman nose, of the size and fleece of the Cotswold 'Lion', and of flocks in the west of England closed for a hundred years. You see the paths to invisible destinations etched in the turf by the single files of many thousand feet.

The stratified system of sheep farming is a thrifty and ingenious one, simply and efficiently executed for a hundred and fifty years. It is held together by good management and the judicious introduction of ageing but serviceable lady sheep to gentlemen on lower and more comfortable pastures. Meat, wool and hybrid vigour are thus obtained from every available genetic resource and altitude. There is no structure like it, nor as many breeds, half-breeds, cross-breeds and mules to the square mile anywhere else in the world.

With too many subsidised sheep on the fells, the number of birds (notably grouse) has suffered. With too few, farming and food production cannot be sustained. The loss of lambs to crow and fox, house dogs and traffic is an occupational hazard; the loss of ewes, price fluctuations and rustling, regular disasters. Yet, the young come through and a way of life continues. Sheep farmers can now look forward to being subsidised as land occupiers, marketing a balanced number of sheep, and exploiting the different breeds and the virginity of their pasture. It is all organic up there on the mountainside and moors, there is no chemical drift and the water comes from the earth and sky before man can get his hands on it.

As in the case of other livestock, promotion is needed. It should not be so difficult to get some of the best lamb and mutton in the world.

THE UK BREEDS OF SHEEP

The mountain breeds include: Herdwick, Swaledale, Blackface (Scotch and Northumbrian), Black Welsh and Badger Faced.

The hill breeds include: Blue Faced Leicester, Border Leicester, Cheviot, Dalesbred (Yorkshire), Whitefaced Woodland (Penistone), Lonk (Lancashire), Gritstone (Derbyshire), Rough Fell and Beulah Speckle-Face, Kerry, Lleyn and Radnor.

The moorland breeds include: Dartmoor Whiteface and Exmoor Horn.

The upland breeds include: Clun Forest, Shropshire, Devon Closewool, Dorset Horn, Wiltshire Horn, Llanwenog

The downland breeds include: Southdown, Dorset Down, Hampshire Down, Oxford Down and Ryeland.

The lowland sheep are dominated by the Suffolk and European commercials.

The longwools, a lowland sheep with upland characteristics, include: Teeswater, Lincoln, Cotswold, Devon and Cornwall, Dartmoor Greyface, Romney Marsh (Kent pure-bred) and Wensleydale.

The heath-croppers, wild cards and primitives include: Portland, Norfolk Horn, Jacob, Manx Loghtan, Castlemilk Moorit, Hebridean, Orkney, Shetland, Soay and St Kilda.

Considering the number of sheep in the UK, their history, differences and the food they have provided, few are mentioned in dispatches.

Portland sheep retain the tan face that is said to indicate primitive blood. The rams are agile, bright and look you in the eye. The ewes drop fox-red lambs, though seldom in pairs. Their antecedents fed on the cliffside grasses and herbage adorning the rocky plateau that rises from the sea. The Isle of Portland is divided into Tophill, where the stone comes from, and Underhill. It is an inviting place in summer, but barren in winter, with a fear of rabbits (see page 192), and battered by storms of hurricane force. It is separated from the 'country' by a channel entitled the Gut, where the dipping of sheep used to take place.

A number of Portland families, employed by the quarries, persisted for hundreds of years. So did the sheep, until they fell on hard times. Too small and slow to mature for the Victorian market, they were relegated to photographs in the museum. Grazing was lost to the naval base, building and disinterest. Portlands were down and almost out, but were kept going by a handful of enthusiasts in the country and reintroduced to the island by the prison service. They provide some of the best small mutton in existence, which was a feature of Hanoverian Weymouth, and a favourite with George III. One of the local restaurants used to serve this meat, only for it to vanish again. An opportunity indeed.

Welsh mutton was mentioned by George Borrow, praised by John Fothergill, and brought to Windsor Castle by rail from Llanidloes. There are more than half a dozen breeds of sheep in the principality, black and white, from the temperate Lleyn peninsula to Plynlimon and high altitudes. Some of the victims contiguously culled during the foot-and-mouth outbreak came from blood lines impossibly old. Unlike Herdwicks, the mountaineers are generally recalled in winter, or brought to their age-old fattening pastures in England. The Beulah Speckle-Face, which thrives on coarse grasses, is a favourite with conservationists. There are several Welsh flocks near me in Hampshire and Wiltshire, including amenity ones used as lawn-mowers. The meat, which a London chef would give his eye teeth for, is a matter of indifference to locals. It drives me bonkers. Another opportunity . . . surely?

Southdown mutton was the market leader for more than a century. It came from the voluptuous chalk hills that run from Beachy Head across Sussex to the Hampshire border. By Roman times the land was stripped of trees in places, for building and to feed the furnaces in the Weald. Livestock invaded, preventing regrowth. Sheep, then rabbits, with their close and constant nibbling, created the unique and exquisite stretches of turf that are the texture of baize from a distance, and a star-studded cast of miniature perennials from inches away.

The Southdown was created to graze the hills by day, and to fold on the arable crops at night. It had to be round in the leg for meat, but also to walk well, and withstand the moderate degrees of heat and cold, strong winds and driving rain that come in from the Channel. John Ellman, the breed's improver, who entertained the rich and dined with his labourers, started newly-weds with a cottage and stock. The tups served the ewes in Romney Marsh. Their blood lines helped to form the other downland sheep – the Hampshires, Dorsets, Oxfords and Ryelands – and ancillary ways of life.

Southdowns were a triumph of selective breeding, feeding and marketing. By the beginning of the nineteenth century, Arundel, Petworth and Goodwood carried flocks of a thousand each. Average-sized farms kept three or four hundred. Their focal point, the lambing pens, stood next to the house. The spirit and economy of Sussex rested on the sheep and the singular race of shepherds whom they followed to the hills and back to the fold. The shearing suppers were famous too. There was Black Ram Night to start with and White Ram Night to finish, the captain of the gang with his gold hatband, the winder, the colt, the lieutenant and the tarboy* feeding and fighting together in pubs. The Tipper flowed, the men danced and the 'swanky' sang the songs.

The South Downs were one of the first parts of the English countryside to register as pleasant as well as productive. The shepherds who trod the turf between clumps of furze and scattered dew ponds, seemed to come under a magic spell. They were more confined in location than the average occupant of Sussex – a county on the move by the end of the nineteenth century – but covered more ground, saw further into the distance, and lived closer to the earth under foot every day. From this they emerged as unusually plant- and weather-wise, and practised at bearing solitude, charming hares, calling birds and commanding sheep as well as dogs. The tidy rattle of canister bells and clucketts was music to the shepherd. His Jew's harp and reed pipe were music to a flock he counted in pairs in a language of his own: 'One-erum, two-erum, cock-erum, sha-erum, shitherum, shatherum, wine-berry, wag-tail, tarry-diddle, den.'

The Southdown shepherd wore a painted felt hat, a boat-type cloak, leather boots, leggings, and a round smock frock in grey or butcher blue, white for best, waterproofed with linseed oil. He carried a stick, in order to defend himself from roughs, and a huge umbrella, opening it over the mouths of dugouts to keep himself dry in the worst of the storms. The earthly possessions of a shepherd were divided between cottage and hut, and amounted to little, but his badge of office was older than the sword or the farmer's plough. In life, he was worth a stone of beef at Christmas. In death, he lay with a single lock of wool placed gently on his chest. Michael Blann, with his great prophetic beard, was amongst the last of the legendary Sussex shepherds and folk heroes. Few names, in the right company, can be dropped to greater effect.

The highest-ranking butchers in Victorian London sold no other type of mutton but Southdown, and only sold the hindquarter – bark removed and kidneys rampant – with rosettes sculpted in the fat. The feet were displayed on each carcass, so customers could identify the one and only breed they accepted. The conformation was and remains world famous. The carcass cuts up more neatly than any other type of mutton. The meat, delicacy itself, justifies its former premium.

---

* It was the 'ship' in Sussex parlance you did not spoil for a ha'porth of tar, i.e. the sheep, not the ship as in sea. But, the failure of incomers to understand the dialect created confusion.

Between the wars, however, Sussex became the focus of more topographical books than any other part of England. It was a convenient escape and distance from London and one of the first rural areas to feel the urban influence. The agriculture suffered, the culture with it. Recordings of the dialect were made, but only for American academics, and rest with Brown University, USA.

Southdowns fell in number during the wars and did not recover. They maintained a diminished presence in Sussex and their other heartland, Cambridgeshire, until about 1970 providing the premium Sunday joint for small families. Demand fell further when the supermarkets went for larger, cheaper beasts, cut into convenient pieces. Breeders sold some of their finest rams to countries only too delighted to have them, leaving blood lines depleted and one of the world's most celebrated sheep and sheepwalk divided for the first time in two hundred years.

The permanent pasture that the downland breeds helped to create and that sustained them for centuries now occupies a minute fraction of the area it covered in Ellman's day. The surviving patches have not so much been spared as forgotten. There is one near me appropriately known as 'Pleasure Grounds'. The only other downland in the area is either protected by grants or owned by the Army – the country's least likely, and leading, conservationist. The turf elsewhere has yielded mainly to corn subsidies and welfare-friendly pig units, to gallops, golf courses and concrete or tarmac. Twyford Down was sheepwalk.

A chalk down, ploughed, is called 'bake'– a descriptive term indeed. It can be reclaimed at considerable expense, but becomes more fertile in the process, and is then classified as calcareous grassland. Even so, it is a backward step worth contemplating. The turf returns to a springy, natural grey-green, summoning perennials from the seed bank and its former population of birds and bugs. It is obvious ground to make for and gawp at in the summer and – once again – for farmers to grow their meat upon. An opportunity going begging, which breeders of downland sheep are once more taking advantage of.

Mrs Beeton praised the mutton of Banstead Heath, near where she was brought up, a former weekend destination for sportsmen and bon viveurs, covered in wild thyme, which is now overgrown or built on and bisected by the A217. Surprisingly, she did not mention the 'celebrated mutton of Bagshot Common' (Poulter, 1969) served by the inns judiciously placed in a westerly direction a day's journey from London and another from the coast.

In 1937, when George Poulter's *History of Camberley* was published, there were still a few oldies in Chobham and Windlesham who could remember what the meat was like. The dwarf black sheep it came from, roaming wild on the common and feeding on the heather and sedges, were either prehistoric or descended from medieval flocks driven from Wales and the Thames

Valley to Blackwater Fair and Crondall. They might, with management, conceivably have survived on land that is only enclosed at the edges and has no use to this day. Spare a thought for the panelled dining rooms, oak floors, pine settles, boisterous company, shining faces, pewter plates, foaming tankards, rush tapers, roaring fires and rotating spits as you whizz by with a sandwich on a hellish M3.

COOK'S ORACLE

It would take a lifetime to register the virtues of the UK's different sheep as meat. I am not familiar with all the breeds, but cherish memories of Blackface, Whitefaced Dartmoor, Whitefaced Woodland, Exmoor Horn, Oxford Down, Romney Marsh, Jacob and Shetland – in addition to those mentioned.

As in the case of other livestock, it is the combination of breed and feed that makes mutton and lamb. An upland sheep, unsuitably nourished, can taste disappointing: diet is important. A precocious lowland weight-carrier, intensively fed, can taste of nothing: a strange and discomforting experience for the consumer. Primitive blood helps, but so do the heather-clad moors of the north and west, the white bent grass of the Pennines, and the promise of salt borne on the wind to the south side of the Downs, and on the rising tide to marshes around the coast.

Mutton is one of England's best-loved dishes. Until about 1950, it was the most common sort of meat next to pork, the most expensive next to beef, and fluctuated more in price than any other food. The trade in mutton was a minefield of broad and fine distinctions, snobbery and calumnies, underwritten by a number of sheep that rivalled the human population of the United Kingdom. The rarefied mutton of the London clubs and chop houses was legendary for its flavour. The 'only' mutton of the bourgeoisie was legendary for its dullness. The braxy mutton of the slum kitchen, spent rams and cull ewes, now considered unfit to eat, was legendary too.

Mutton embodies all that is best and worst about English food. The meat takes time to supply, which ties up farmers' money. It also takes time to understand, which finds out inexperienced cooks. With an increasing emphasis on cheap home-produced or New Zealand lamb, proper mutton – and the knowledge of how to treat the different varieties – was forgotten. Good mutton was spoiled, converting it to bad, and condemning them both to the same low status.

Mutton disappeared from fashionable menus for forty or fifty years, but remained a favourite with a small number of farmers, who kept it back for home consumption, specialist butchers and ethnic communities. The price rises with the quantity on offer to meet the demand at Muslim festivals. The quality still varies, but some well-finished meat is coming through, restaurants are getting interested, and the future is rosier than it was.

The best time for mutton is the autumn. 'Baked' meat in terms of weather – obtained after a dry spell – is superior to 'boiled'. Wethers are preferred. Ewes are more of a risk, but a calculated one. An empty sheep in middle age with a summer behind her on the hills and flesh on her bones can be fit 'for the Gods' (Hutchins, 1967). This sort of mutton can be dressed as lamb. Ram mutton is bigger, tougher, stronger and unlikely to be encountered in quality butchers.

Lamb, though it does not have the flavour of good mutton, is more quickly produced and much easier to come by. The season starts with Dorset horns, which can give birth in the autumn and provide meat for Christmas, or used to, but now tend to continue to greater weights. Spring lamb is a mixture: a small amount is new-born, milk-fed and goes to a niche market; the rest is overwintered and reared indoors until the grass comes through. Pasture lamb, a safer bet, gets going in the lowlands during the early summer and continues until the autumn. The year closes with the slower-growing light lambs from the higher altitudes, which enjoy little recognition in England but a great deal in Greece and Spain.

The older, darker and richer the mutton, the more time it should hang. The younger, lighter and more delicate the lamb, the less hanging it requires. The cuts are as follows.

Loin: taken from the back, or sirloin in beef, used to be 'barked' or skinned by master butchers; it is usually split and divided into conventional chops, or boned and rolled; it can also be unsplit, providing two-in-one Barnsley chops, or a saddle, also known as the 'Alderman's Walk' – a former favourite in City chop houses; grill or roast.

Chump: taken from the bottom of the sirloin, top of the leg, corresponds to the rump in beef; meaty; grill.

Leg: cut short when eaten fresh without the chump, and long when salted like a ham (see page 175) look for joints in Cheshire and butchers up north, wrapped by them in a pig's caul for spit; the shank, having performed on TV, is currently overpriced; spit or oven-roast, or stew.

Shoulder: comes as is, with or without the fillet; fatter than a leg – eats sweeter as a result; a nifty butcher will pare the meat away from the bladebone, leaving you to pull it when the shoulder is cooked – a trick that facilitates carving; oven-roast; stew the fillets.

Neck: the best end comes from next to the sirloin and is sometimes 'French'-trimmed, i.e. of surplus fat; grill as cutlets; alternatively oven-roast in a piece or 'rack' on the bone, chined by the butcher; the scrag end is cut up – stew.

Breast: fatty, but cheap and full of flavour; usually comes boned and rolled. Oven roast.

Partnerships: mutton and lamb used to be served with the same partners that a sheep meets or eats in its habitat: thyme, rowan and mint, though the variety of mint used in sauce is cultivated spearmint (*Mentha spicata*) and pork may have got there first (see page 156). Redcurrants, rosemary and onions are stretching a point, but are excellent with mutton too. Pickled capers and samphire have the bite to lift commonplace mutton. Laver is good with almost any sort of meat. The point of mutton is the gravy it brings forth.

GRILLING

Do cutlets and chops like steaks, preferably over a fire, outside until you get the hang of it. Most people like lamb and mutton better cooked than beef, and charred on the outside.

OVEN ROASTING

A lean joint needs fat and basting; a fat one needs it taken away. Place a leg, shoulder or rack on a tray, on a bed of fresh rosemary if you wish. I cook lamb and mutton like beef. Commit to a preheated oven for 15–20 minutes per pound at 220°C /425°F/gas mark 7, then turn down to 180°C/350°F/gas mark 4 for a pink result. For something different:

(a) 'Bark', bone and roll 2lb (900g) loin, trimming it to a width of around 5 inches (12cm), then tie it up, roll in flour, egg and breadcrumbs and fry before cooking.
(b) Incise a leg or shoulder with freshly boiled cockles rather than the usual slivers of garlic.
(c) Cook a breast (boned and rolled) on a rack in a preheated oven 150°C /300°F/gas mark 2 for 2 hours.

Mature mutton can be left in a cool oven or Aga for eight hours over a day or night until it falls apart.

SPIT ROASTING

Take a prime leg, well hung. Do not allow the butcher to hock it (i.e. break the shank). Nerve and preparation required. Instructions on page 99.

STEWING

Trim a boned leg or shoulder, and cut into cubes. Proceed as for beef (see page 118). For the best results, add at least one glass of red wine to the liquor.

Irish stew or Lancashire hotpot? My mother, when in London, used to lunch at the old Berkeley Hotel in Piccadilly. The head waiter was a Mr Viccelli, who, in spite of a petition signed by hundreds of his patrons, was interned during the war. Undaunted, he re-emerged in peacetime and resumed his lofty position, his shirt as starched and tailcoat as unruffled as ever. Mr Viccelli was the grandest man alive, with elegance, poise and a sense of occasion second to none. My brother, aged ten and going through a 'tiresome' stage, was sent to bed for calling him 'Viccelli!' when everybody knew that the head waiter at the Berkeley was nothing less than 'Mister Viccelli'.

One day at luncheon, my mother, thinking perhaps of a chicken bone, asked for some food for her dog – a malcontented Pekinese called Chinky who had lost an eye in battle and who lay on the velvet couch beside her. Mr Viccelli, inclining his magnificent head, noted the request and swooped away like a ballroom dancer. Minutes later, the swing doors of the kitchen burst open and he reappeared flanked by two waiters dressed in livery and no less stately and composed than himself. Each of the waiters bore an oval tureen with a cover and ladle on a large silver salver.

Silence descended on the Berkeley. The London traffic hummed outside. The entourage, negotiating tables, chairs and meat trolleys to perfection, crossed the lofty and sumptuous dining room, watched in silence by over a hundred motionless people with food halfway to their mouths. The three men came to a halt before us, bowing deeply to my mother and her one-eyed Peke. At a discreet signal from Mr Viccelli, the waiters, supporting the trays with their left hands, whisked the lids from the tureens with their right. Steam rose through the chandeliers to the ornate ceiling. Mr Viccelli paused. Then, with one of his courtly gestures and another inclination of his magnificent head, he asked in respectful tones:

'I wonder, madam, would the little dog prefer Irish stew or Lancashire hotpot?'

A Lancashire lad told a mutual friend of ours, Julia Skinner, how the hotpot has changed. It used to be the remains of the Sunday mutton joint, thrown into a pan of salt water with root vegetables, and kept simmering on the range until the end of the week. Food and broth were taken out every evening as required; they were replaced the following afternoon, and the vessel returned to the hob. Finally, on Saturdays, when family and friends were together, the hotpot was improved with any meat available, scrag end of neck, sheep's feet, kidneys or black pudding. The dish was finished off with slices of potato, then covered and cooked in the oven. The lid of the vessel was removed for the last half-hour, enabling the top to brown and look its best on the table.

Contemporary hotpots have been kicked upstairs. Pieces of scrag end are usually rolled in flour and fried before committal to a pot with sliced onion and carrot, crushed garlic, and stock all but to cover. A cook may add anything else he or she wants – people did anyway – before the potato hat. Red cabbage, as served with hotpots at Russells in Bolton, is de rigueur.

Tatey pot is the Cumberland version of a hotpot, similar in principle. It is associated with the great days of hunting with the foot packs, when two or three hundred people turned out, climbing so high to the tops of the fells it gave you a crick in the neck merely to watch. A university graduate I met, employed as a part-time milkman, went home to the sound of singing in pubs and came back to it in the morning. To provide for the big occasions, a couple of lambs might be killed, one of the hill breeds because of the locality, which means Herdwick or Swaledale. This advice comes from farmer's wife Laura Brough:

1½lb (700g) stewing lamb or mutton (better than neck, say best end), 8oz (225g) black pudding, 2 large onions, 2 carrots, and potatoes to cover. Beef may be used, though it is not the custom.

Cut the meat into pieces and place in a shallow ovenproof dish. Add the sliced black pudding, carrots and onions. Season to taste with salt and pepper. Cover with water, then sliced potatoes. Brush the top with melted butter to help it brown. Cook in a heated oven at 180°C/350°F /gas mark 4 for 2–3 hours. Add more water if necessary. The gravy is never thickened.

Curry: a probable corruption of *kari*, a Tamil word, anglicised by 1598. Over the next four hundred years, the British introduced curry to Japan – and probably other countries – and funded a multitude of restaurants. The Ganges in London's Gerrard Street (now exclusively Chinese) opened in about 1906. Considering the length and intensity of the affair, the curries in England have been a disappointment for most of their history. I did not 'get' them, could not even eat them, and booked a passage to India wary of the food.

Conversion took place on the South Circular Road, Calcutta, months later. I arrived at a house anticipating dinner, along with a school friend from England, his wife and her mother, Ela Sen, who was putting us up. It was 8 p.m. and Martinis were served – several times. Two hours later, we were half cut, faint with hunger and desperate on a dozen counts. I had given up hope of any munchies when our host, having heard I did not like Indian food, offered me – for Christ's sake – an omelette instead. I panicked and, fearing a further delay, turned the offer down. We went through double doors to eat.

The dining room had a high ceiling, ebonised furniture, plants in pots and four bearers in attendance wearing blood-coloured livery, white jodhpurs, gold turbans and matching sashes. The table bore two mountains of rice, plain and pulao, columns of chapattis, and dishes containing dhal, cauliflower, bhindi and pottles, fish curries of becti, hilse and king prawns, meat curries of chicken and mutton, yoghurt and chilli pickle. Alphonso mangoes, constituting 'afters', lay in beds of crushed ice on the side. Talking and drinking were over. The party had moved on. The eyes of the guests shone with single-mindedness. We helped ourselves and ate in the customary fashion, with our hands, standing up and in silence apart from the odd grunt of approval. Halfway through the meal our host came over to the English contingent with some advice. It was better, he said, to try the dishes separately (like a Bengali) rather than to put them together (like a Punjabi), then return to your favourite and make a pig of yourself.

Ela Sen wrote a cookery book but did not live to see it published. She cooked for me every day in India for months and once a week in London for years. Her medium-hot 'basic meat curry', made in a wok, is as follows:

2lb (900g) of mutton off the bone trimmed of excess fat and cut into cubes, 1lb (450g) onions and at least 1 large clove of garlic, peeled and very finely chopped, 1 heaped tsp chilli, 1 heaped tsp haldi (turmeric) and 1 heaped tsp tomato paste (not essential, but improves the colour), salt to taste, and 1 oz (25g) fat, oil or ghee.

Fry the onions and garlic in the fat until soft. Add the spices and cook gently for a few minutes, stirring well, followed by the tomato purée and the meat. Continue to cook and stir for a further few minutes until the ingredients are well mixed together and the meat begins to stiffen. Do not let them catch or burn. Barely cover with water, and salt to taste. Simmer very gently for at least 2 hours or until tender, topping up with water when necessary. Keep for at least a day before eating.

To vary: add a bay leaf, a few cardamoms, cloves, or strips of peeled fresh ginger. This method may be used for venison or chicken curry.

BOILING

'Boiled' mutton is another misnomer. It should be poached, otherwise the meat will dry out. Take a prime leg, well hung. Again, do not allow the butcher to hock it. Bring the water up to simmering point in a suitable pan, immerse the meat and cook very gently for 20 minutes per pound. The mutton is done when firm to the touch. On no account puncture it to see, or the juices will leach out. Boiled mutton is not appetising to look at and seldom encountered today, but smothered in onion or caper sauce is one of the 'traditional glories' of the English kitchen (Hutchins, 1967). Make sure you have enough people to finish the meat while hot. 'Cold boiled mutton', Oscar Wilde's description of a French prostitute acquired for him by Frank Harris, is not worth the investment.

BITS AND PIECES

Sweetbreads: the pick of the bunch, a gland in two parts, thicker towards the heart and thinner towards the throat. They are found in young lambs (calves and kids) not in adult sheep, making them in season in the spring and early summer. The punctual appearance, delicate flavour and subtle texture of sweetbreads call for asparagus, broad beans and fresh peas.

2lb (900g) of lamb's sweetbreads, 1 small onion or 2 or 3 shallots, 1 glass of white wine, ¼ pint (150ml) of cream, salt and white pepper to taste, and *beurre manié* made with ½oz (10g) flour worked into ½oz (10g) butter.

Blanch the breads, i.e. pour over boiling water, return to the boil and simmer for a couple of minutes. Drain and remove any fat (though not the membranes or else they fall to bits). Add the onion or shallots, the wine and season. Commit to a preheated medium to cool oven, say 170°C/325°F/gas mark 3, for an hour (or until the meat can be pierced with a fork). Drain off the liquor, keeping it hot. Whisk in enough *beurre manié* to make it thick as a soup. Finish with the cream and reintroduce the 'breads, shaking the pan to coat them with the sauce. White rice is best, new potatoes next.

Any wild mushrooms, possibly St George's, sliced and fried in butter until soft, may be added to the sauce with the cream.

For a pie – put a lid on it (see page 119).

Kidneys are another favourite, which tend to be grabbed by restaurants, making them hard to come by at times. Allow 4 per person.

(a) The conventional route is to peel off the suet and membrane, cut the kidneys in half and remove the gristle. Fry them in butter on the round side first or else they will buckle; turn and continue cooking until firm. You may eat as is or take out the kidneys when done and deglaze the pan with red wine and/or leftover gravy in the pan when the kidneys are cooked.

If you want a feast, serve the kidneys with sweetbreads, prepared as above.

(b) Alternatively, grill kidneys in their suet over a fire, letting the fat burn away. The outside emerges black and crisp and the inside pink. Eat with mustard or chilli sauce.

Liver: prepare to pay more for lamb's liver than for pig's, enjoy it less and cook it the same way – gently in butter, in thin slices, until pink. Remove while still slightly tender to the touch.

Haggis: started out as an English word. It is made of liver, lites and other trimmings – a faggot in sheep's clothing; bound with toasted oatmeal and highly seasoned, it is sometimes baked in a pan rather than boiled in a paunch.

Heads were made into brawn or broth in certain areas, and on hill farms that did not keep pigs. Otherwise they were committed to a string bag, lowered into a chalk stream and removed the following day with crayfish attached.

Feet: very popular in Victorian England, and almost too expensive in London to be had (J. H. Walsh). Feet appear on the crest of Bolton Wanderers FC, whose nickname is the 'Trotters', though in local parlance a 'trotter' is a wag or a joker, rather than attached to a leg. A well-known Lancashire dish of the past, last seen in Yorkshire (by me), sold in the customary gangs of four – 'Stew until ragged, luv.'

Tails: gelatinous and fiddly to prepare, but a favourite with lowland shepherds (upland sheep keep their tails) and not unknown in polite circles (White). My parents ate lambs' tails during rationing in Somerset. Many did, skinned, blanched and added to hotpots and stews.

MACON

Mutton bacon, invariably the ham or leg, more widely eaten in the past than it is given credit for. Shoulders were salted too, and loins were up for it (Cobbett), though not recorded. In Northumberland macons were buried (a practice I have encountered in Spain and which improves their keeping qualities). In the Lake District they were eaten for 'breakshear' (as opposed to 'breakfast'). The rashers, fried up, constituted the tangy 'summer dry'. The shank, cooked with vegetables, made the nourishing 'winter wet'.

If mutton hams died out after the war, Harry Fellows of Corney Fell in Cumbria, helped to bring them back before retiring in the 1990s. He tried curing heavier breeds of sheep, but only Herdwicks passed the scrutiny of locals. Macons are hard, flat little customers which, when properly cut and dried, weigh six to eight pounds. The practice of smoking them, provided the meat is dry salted, is acceptable on the grounds of improving its appearance. The flavour, more like ham than mutton, is loved by those who know it when cooked, and gaining fashionable status when raw. Demand is creeping back.

Curing a leg of mutton or lamb is less trouble than doing a leg of pork, being smaller and unlikely to go off. Proceed in winter following the same rules as for a York-type ham (see page 173), leaving the limb entire and using only half a pound of salt and a pinch of saltpetre. The meat can be removed from the tub in two or three weeks, wiped down with a scalding cloth as usual, and hung up to dry. It will be ready to eat within three or four months and keep for longer, deepening in colour.

CHAPTER
THIRTEEN

ACORN AND OTHER PIGS

HE WALLS OF THE COURT were coloured cochineal, and bore a coat of arms, an iron stirrup, and trophies taken from fallen deer. Rows of wooden benches were arranged like pews on a cream and terracotta tiled floor. Two large windows shed a moody light. A door led to the Queen's House, another to the street outside, the queue of cars and the twenty-first century. A complement of ten men, entitled verderers, sat abreast behind a table on a platform. A further four, called agisters, wearing green livery with crested gold buttons and black gaiters, were stationed by the dock. The court is a remnant of Forest law with ancient and modern statutory powers, complete with its own language. It meets about every two months to hear 'presentments' and to address matters of local importance, including the acorn crop, its volume and its readiness to fall for the local pigs.

The original purpose of the court was to preserve deer for the Norman kings (see page 186) – and emphasise their power – in a calculated area called Ytene (pronounced 'Ittany'), which became the New Forest. The rule and system, unfair as it was, acknowledged rights of usage relating mainly to the gathering of fuel and feeding of livestock exercised by locals since time out of mind. The Forest included a number of commons. The beneficiaries of the rights granted throughout were called commoners, though the land they used was not in common ownership, nor were they subject to common law. The freedom to turn out swine for the beech and oak mast was entitled common of mast.

The pigs, an important part of the system, fulfilled the two roles of growing fat on the acorns and clearing them up for animals susceptible to poisoning. The crop was called pannage. The season originally ran from 26 September until the winter heyning, the period in which, under forest law, livestock was removed in order to preserve food for the deer. With the passing of the centuries and the failure of the oak seed to ripen at the desired moment, the feast became a movable one.

When the fall of acorns is heavy or precocious, pigs may be turned out early into the woods and left until late. The dates, decided by the verderers, are announced in the cochineal court with the Tudor stirrup and the tiled floor. The dues are collected by the agisters. Sows and shoots (their young) must be paid for and ringed. Boars are forbidden. The rights are contained in atlases bound in green leather. The households entitled to depasture livestock were confirmed in the New Forest Act of 1964. The by-laws relating to such matters can vary from one common to the next. They are complex, irregular, illogical to casual observers, and to legal minds delicious.

On manorial commons within the Forest, 'pig rights' as opposed to Forest rights are claimed. This means that sows and shoots may roam all year – in addition to the pannage season – if they come in at night. On adjacent commons formerly outside the Forest, vicinage is claimed – a sort of freedom to trespass amounting to pig rights. Got it? Matters are confused by failures of registration that can be centuries old, and failures of the Act to mention common of mast and pigs along with common of pasture and other livestock. There is also the question of to whom the owners, not having been mentioned, pay their dues.

Some want animals removed from the Forest on the grounds of 'progress', but there are legal, ecological and emotional obstacles. A sow has a right to a common, to feed and wander, to enter unprotected gardens, and to respond to provocation. There is no point in claiming damages. The magistrates' hands are tied by laws upheld for a thousand years. The pig will win if it comes to court; you will lose, and face a bill for the costs as well. It is great stuff, England at its best, merry at times, and an untapped supply of legendary pork that producers have no current interest in selling and consumers none in buying.

England has a history of pigs, counted as domestic, that are half wild in their habits. They were housed and fed by the Norman Conquest (Rackham, 1986) but continued to roam in the streets, the wastes beyond, and woodland already diminished by clearing. Some wore a collar to prevent them breaking into enclosures, or a harness attached to a stake. The swineherd employed to manage the pigs, the rent of their feeding grounds, and the tithes due to the Church, were paid in kind by the owner. Breeding stock and young hogs (castrati) were wintered over. The remainder were slain and salted. The value of a carcass was proportionate to its back fat, rather than the lean of today.

The pig's connection to its woodland resort was kept alive in medieval art and, owing to the favourable conditions, in Hampshire more than any other county. Both seventeenth- and eighteenth-century sources remark on the quantity of swine kept in the Forest. Writers recorded herds of five or six hundred collectively owned 'brutes' summoned to showers of acorns brought down 'by hook or by crook', and suborned by the comfort of a sty around the trees where they fed. Come the winter a few ran free, reverted, and possibly cross-bred with wild boar. The offspring William Gilpin knew as 'forest-pigs'. His eerie pencil drawing of these creatures, black and bristly silhouettes on faded cream-coloured paper, depicts a fearsome and tricky beast, ready to turn on man or dog, with 'broad shoulders, a high crest and thick . . . mane which he erects on any alarm'. The last survived until a hundred years ago.

The Forest accumulated cottages with custom-built sties until the 1930s and emerged as one of the only two former royal hunting grounds to remain in working order. Having survived clear-felling, partition, plantation and the Forestry Commission to date, it is now up against eighteen million visitors a year hell-bent on recreation, and the political will to 'fix what ain't broke' by transforming it into a National Park. The number of pigs has already fallen from a maximum of over six thousand to an average of two hundred a year. Further obstacles to their continuity are property prices that tempt commoners from the Forest, and exclude their dependants from returning; the disinterest of new home-owners in their rights of mast; and the failure to grasp an opportunity.

Hampshire's chosen logo is its hog. It stands outside the council offices in Winchester, fashioned in bronze, while Eric Gill's naughty little pug of a pottery pig waits in the hall. The porkers they represent are wild of diet and live in conditions in the Forest much more to their liking than a closed unit or an ark in a treeless field. The meat they produce is rich and dark from their diet in the woods. It has ticks in all the right boxes, provenance and fashionable potential, but has yet to be exploited – a point made by Thomas Fuller three hundred years ago.

The combination of pigs and acorns in Spain equals fresh and salt pork, repeatedly cited by London-based journalists. Each ham imported into England is worth more than two sides of bacon. Meanwhile, the presence of the same resources in Hampshire, the pigs and the pannage, amounts to nothing. None of the pork available, even through new incentives like Forest Friendly Farming, comes off the Forest. There can be few other cases of such a wilful and exasperating indifference to a proven, historic and sustainable asset, which a Frenchman would die for.

By 2005 I knew what I wanted in a pig. I had tried to get it from the Forest on several occasions, involving commoners, their wives and even an agister, and gave up. The connections, promises and undertakings made had come to naught. I could have persisted, but did not feel inclined, acknowledging the rarest of defeats, and on my own doorstep. It was time to find someone who wanted to do business, and for me to go about it the easy way – by contacting one of the better-known schemes involving pigs in woodland. There were two near me on the Hampshire–Dorset border, and at least two more upcountry.

Ray Harris, a forester, kept pigs as a sideline and lectured on the subject at Holme Lacy in Herefordshire. He was well known in the press, but was referred to me by the field centre at Burnham Beeches, which used two gilts for conservation purposes. Strange as it seemed, Ray confirmed that pigs can be good for woodland. They prepare the ground for uneaten oak and beech mast to take root, clear the vegetation from around saplings and, unlike sheep, do not bark or nibble fully grown trees.

By the time I caught up with him, Ray had been watching his pigs at work, in repose and avoiding poisonous plants for fifteen years, rotating the herd, and getting them ready for slaughter. The old supposition that forest pigs 'go out lean and come home fat without care or cost to the farmer' was not true. They need four to six weeks indoors in order to relax and finish well, a detail to be borne in mind by any producer.

There are thousands of acres of unmanaged woodland in England. The owners or tenants could do worse than build a fence and put in a few suitable pigs. An ancient speciality and a modern niche market are waiting. The danger is that meat given a couple of weeks out at mast will be thrown into a brine bath, committed to a smoker and sold as 'acorn-fed', discrediting the whole venture. If the product is to compete with Spain, it must be on level terms.

The wild boar is the ancestor of all domesticated pigs. It is a tough customer with a short fuse which fled before hunter and hounds for as long as it felt inclined, then turned and attacked, eyes red, tusks bared, and ears flat to the head. A young man's rite of passage was to get in the way, inviting a boar to charge and impale itself on his lance, either killing it or dying in the process. Wild pigs, having been reduced to nothing by man's invasion of their territory, were reintroduced to England on more than one occasion in the last four hundred years and are now thriving out of captivity. I have seen evidence of their rooting in the Sussex woods and their carcasses on the hook, black, bristling and scary, lifeless as they are.

The first tame pigs were porklings, either snatched from their mother while she slept or deliberately orphaned, and brought up in civilisation. Their descendants adapted to man's company over the centuries, and enjoy it, but retain their independence and revert when threatened. They are strong, quick and independent, also intelligent, affectionate, contemplative and engrossing creatures with a knowing look in the eye, that have been taught to count, spell, jump, pull carriages, and point game. If cattle are prized and sheep are valued, pigs are loved, particularly by women. They will clear a bramble patch, and convert food more quickly than any other beast into meat, and richer meat, which goes further and cures better. You can watch a pig all day snoozing, rooting and at the trough: a beast of enduring fascination, great amusement and good value, at home on the loose and in heaven being scratched.

By the end of the eighteenth century, the old English types of pig were proving too light in the areas that mattered. They needed more meat, acquired more quickly, and got it through the animals stowed away on ships along with homeward-bound porcelain, fabrics and other cargo. The intermingling of breeds was not universally condoned; it was poorly recorded and often confused, but panned out to produce families of national importance, world renown and thrilling sizes. The legendary boar of Rudgwick in Sussex was as tall as a half-hunter and heavier than an ox. Its hams were twice the size of a modern porker. Its weight amounted to 127 score, 182 stone, or nearly one and a quarter staggering tons. Sadly, no painting exists.

The various pigs were bred for different uses and conditions: to flesh early, as sucklings; less early for pork; and later for salting. A dark skin protected the beast from sunburn, a long snout helped him to root, and lop ears, which obscured his vision, enabled his owner to exercise control. Dished faces are supposed to indicate Chinese origins. The walkers, making a painful five or six miles a day, muzzled and shod, wound their way up over the Forest to the Southampton train. The sluggards stayed at home and fattened in the sty. Each type of pig aroused strong loyalties amongst fanciers and strong disagreements amongst farmers, judges, butchers and cooks as to which was the best in their estimation or for their purpose. The rivalry and arguments persist.

The Berkshire is descended from the rough, tough variegated pig of William Shiels' oil on canvas, improved for the Victorian market. It has retained prick ears, but acquired a black skin, white points, and long eyelashes. This pig is a hardy and alert creature with an elegant stance, which is said to bestow a better-proportioned early-maturing carcass in her young than any other sow in the world. The Berkshire came to represent the great triumvirate of English farming, along with the shorthorn cow and Southdown ewe: an obvious choice for Burnham Beeches' wood pasture, but an inspired one too. P. G. Wodehouse's Empress of Blandings was a Berkshire, the late Emperor Hirohito an admirer of the breed. My wife's favourite. The pork is unsurpassed.

The Middle White is another connoisseur's prick-eared beast, this time of Yorkshire origins. It is the most distinguished member of a trio that included the precocious Small White, a suckling pig now extinct, and the commercial Large White, a renowned baconer (see page 172) and father to millions worldwide. Behind the acutely dished and almost comic faces of Middles, especially ringed with mud, there is a history of champions second to none and a rooter, forager and grazer better than he looks. The breed is a favourite with the Emperor Akihito and leading chefs, and me too. I have baked a whole Middle White in a peel oven (see page 67). No crackling was ever more crisp, no lard more clear, and no meat surrendered more easily to a knife. The original London porker, equal first with the Berkshire.

The Large Black is a composed and stately butterball of a pig, lop-eared, tame and co-operative, which waddles rather than walks and beats all comers on looks alone. Oiled, combed and beribboned, it can hardly be kept from the show ring – but is equally at home in an orchard or paddock. The dark hair and pigmentation of its skin enable the breed to withstand hot weather and open sites exposed to the sun. It is found in the Forest, domiciled in Suffolk, and known in America as the Cornwall, and has also made the journey to Hungary and Italy for Parma ham production. The Large Black is considered by aficionados 'good for pork, good for bacon, good for everything'.

The British Lop is said to be like the Large Black pig, but white, and with a more local distribution. It comes from the Tavistock area in Devon, and is rated for its friendly temperament, excellent conformation, long back and well-developed hams. The Lop is not a conspicuous or well-known breed, but has a loyal following in the West Country and admirers in London. The bacon is renowned, the pork has gone to the Dorchester Hotel.

The Gloucester Old Spot (GOS) is another with a regional presence, but a wide distribution and fashionable status partly thanks to royal patronage. If there is one rare breed people have heard of, it is the GOS, though uncertainty surrounds the number of black spots on its white rump the creature should have. Dorothy Hartley describes this pig as producing 'two litters a year . . . scuttling under the blossom in the . . . shadow dance of the . . . apple orchards', the delectable pork in time for the young spring beans and the thick belly bacon ready for winter breakfasts.

The Tamworth is an active, prick-eared ginger pig, long in the leg and snout, and capable of walking and ploughing for hours on end. The breed was established by an ancestor of Anne Petch, a noted pig-breeder herself, and was brought to public attention by the escape of two crosses from a Wiltshire slaughterhouse. There used to be a Tamworth trio in the Forest, an environment the breed is built for. A wholly wild boar has only a fashionable advantage over a half-wild Tamworth: their spirit, stance, profile and meat are much the same. The pork is increasingly popular, the bacon and brawn are top drawer, and the head is the one for feasts. I have cured the hams (see page 175).

The Oxford or Axford Sandy and Black is a bit of a mystery, prick-eared in the past, lop-eared at present, and similar in looks to a GOS–Tamworth cross. The word is that the original boar line died out, but the sows did not, and the breed has been welcomed into the British Pig Association (BPA). Their progenitors seem to have varied from region to region and have thrown up a number of names, including the Oxford Forest – a clue to the pig's capabilities – and the Plum Pudding. There is now renewed interest in this good-tempered and striking pig, its mottled coat and winsome piglets. The carcass is leaner than its peers'. The long, well-covered back provides plenty of pork chops and bacon rashers of excellent quality.

The Saddleback, entitled British since the 1960s, is a black lop-eared pig with a white belt across its shoulders, good out of doors and great as a parent. The Wessex type of Saddleback is more numerous. The Essex type, brought back from the brink, was kept in being by a handful of enthusiasts in the heart of England and north of Ireland, emerging on TV in the ownership of Jimmy Doherty, hero of the BBC television series *Jimmy's Farm*, himself a product of Essex. Saddlebacks travelled to America, becoming the (New) Hampshire hog in the nineteenth century, and more recently to the kingdom of Bhutan. They make fine pork, and finer still when crossed with a Middle White. I was brought up on the bacon.

English pigs came under early attack from the Danes, who do not eat bacon themselves, but who sent huge quantities to the UK from the early twentieth century onwards. After the war, the supermarkets, utilitarian standards and fat probes added to the distress of the native breeds. The European Landrace and Piétrain pigs, long, lean and emaciated creatures with a fifteenth rib, swept the board, and the order of merit for pork was reversed (as it was for beef). The black breeds lost added ground in a world of fair complexions and through being more difficult to process in slaughterhouses.

The casualties, worse than those of cattle and sheep, were feeding through by 1960. The lonely fate of the last Cumberland sow, Sally – living out her life like the last Tasmanian – is one of agriculture's tragedies. In 1972, the Curly Coat pig, a testy one-off fed to great weights in Lincolnshire, also became extinct. It was such a close call with some of the other rare breeds that reinforcements were summoned from America and Australia to swell the numbers of parent stock.

The Japanese will cross the world for English pigs that we, the English, do not cross the road for. The Berkshire and Middle White remain top of the class abroad and simultaneously bottom at home, enjoying a critical status shared by the Large Black. The Lop and Tamworth are endangered, the GOS at risk. The Saddleback has an economic value as a hybrid, though it suffers in a commercial market, which is notoriously volatile and under pressure from animal rights groups. We all want pigs grown in 'welfare-friendly' conditions, but not the expense handed on. Intensive pork, reared abroad, is the supermarket leader.

Still, the prospect for English pigs is rosier at the start of the new millennium than it was at the end of the previous one. Breeders have found out that the only way to sell their pork and bacon is to do it themselves rather than through a predatory retailer or an auction. The meat quality of native pigs is beginning to re-register at last, along with the pleasure of having such engaging and amusing creatures around.

CHAPTER FOURTEEN

PIG KILLING AND PORK

**T**HEY CAME AT FIRST LIGHT, as agreed, the man and his brother, whom I knew. We shook hands, climbed into our cars and set off for the hamlet where my partner in pigs kept our three gilts in an outdoor pen. The land occupied a south-facing slope with a winterbourne at the bottom, a village upstream and a hump in the distance called Soldier's Ring. The day broke as the five of us gathered, the first time for my wife at such an event, the last for the pig.

The slaughterer, a large and graceful man, walked to the pen with his brother and greeted the pig, surveying the ground and choosing a spot. He confirmed what we needed: water, a groundsheet, a hoist and some straw, soon made ready. Then he stripped to his vest in the biting north wind, put on a waterproof top and trousers, and strapped to his belt a black-handled steel and metal holster containing knives.

The pig, anticipating food, followed our movements as we approached the pen. The slaughterman led her to a patch drier than the others, located in one corner, and dusted it with meal. Then he leant over the wire as the creature moved forward and, without changing pace, held the gun to her temple. Would he turn and check with me that the beast was to die, wait for a signal, or delay a moment longer? The answer in my heart I already knew. A man had been engaged to kill and dress a pig, and kill it he did.

A shot rang out, which troubled the pig. Something had happened – she did not know what – and something to me as I watched. There was no going back, suspending time or escaping from the events predestined to unfold, and nothing to be said. The blood started to flow on the forehead of the pig, slowly but relentlessly welling up as she stumbled and fell, running hard, running nowhere, and running in vain.

A second, precautionary shot rang out. The pig, on the ground and senseless now, eyes closed, kicked and twitched with decreasing vigour, then lay still. It was done in seconds. Then the brothers took the body fore and aft, bearing it out of the pen and over to the hoist, where a rope and pulley raised it aloft, legs outstretched and nose to the ground. Again without changing pace, the slaughterman took a knife from the holster at his belt. Considerately, even gently, he inserted the blade into the pig's throat and drew it up through the middle of the chest. The blood flowed out more quickly now and into a bucket that he had placed underneath. There was not much of it.

With the light increasing, we lowered the pig and wrapped her in straw, then lit a fire. The flames, gunned up by the wind and travelling from nose to tail, left a crust of black and glowing embers against the skin. We singed both sides, scraped off the hair and swabbed her down, then hoisted her again. The slaughterman sharpened his knives on the steel at his belt and opened the carcass from top to tail, removing the entrails, the maw (tummy), the pluck (heart, lites etc.)

and the fine, lacy caul. The liver, he said, unmarked by white spots, was good and clean. A healthy pig we had kept and fed, a pig in the prime of life, and a life I had taken.

For the rest of us the day continued. It was bright, fine and gusty – perfect for drying the meat as it hung. I asked the slaughterman to remove the head, split the carcass, and unravel the guts, taking the chitterlings off for a wash and allowing myself a moment of reflection. The water in the winterbourne was clear, swift and warmer than the wind. It rattled in the sun and rippled over the pebbles and brilliant grass, going one moment and gone the next, passing as quickly as the life of the pig.

We tidied up, putting the entrails in a bucket and leaving the meat on the hoist for collection later. I paid the slaughterman, thanking him and his brother for the clean, professional and ceremonial job they had done. My partner in pigs felt as neutral about the event as a child, unencumbered by its parents' prejudice. My wife was disturbed, but brave. And I? To kill or be an accessory to a killing, which happened every time I ate a pork chop or non-organic matter, mowed the lawn, and drove a car, confirmed me as a member of the human race. I had loved the pig and in time-honoured fashion betrayed and killed her. I had acknowledged my role in her death and not denied it. I had learned what a sacrifice meant. I had found out why in some religions it is the role of a priest to take a life, why prayers are said beforehand and thanks given when meat is on the table.

A Victorian farmer reckoned to keep his family in meat on two litters of pigs a year. One they ate and salted, the other they sold to pay for the sows' winter meal. The cottar bought at market in the spring with summer ahead, a free and easy time for livestock. Feed was a mixture of kitchen refuse and washing-up water (detergent-free), acorns, hogweed (of course) and whatever else could be gathered by children in the lanes. The average sty consisted of logs, which dried out in hot weather, the bedding of leaves or bracken. The pig within was almost a member of the family (Flora Thompson, 1939), who entertained visitors and featured in letters to and from home. His time, when it came, saving countless peasant families from starvation, was eagerly awaited. A pig killing was anything but sentimental. It meant plenty to eat for once, and a well-stocked larder.

The pig was dispatched in the full moon, when he fed at night and consequently gained weight. The victim was starved for a day beforehand, just like ours, but given water, ending his short and contented life without a journey or prior warning and on his own patch. Pigs tended to be singed in the West Country, particularly for bacon, and scalded in the north, then either hoisted or laid out on one of the hardwood benches now reborn as decorators' items.

The field men who went round the farms and villages with gun and bag might receive the fifth 'quarter' for their services: the feet, head and pluck. Meat was a gift and also used as a currency to repay debts. The liver and kidneys were eaten fresh with perhaps a few chops or a spare rib. The rest of the carcass was rendered or salted and stored beyond the reach of rats and dogs. Even the 'clees' (or claws) went to children as chews. The eyes and the gall bladder, which tastes bitter, were the only parts of the animal thrown away.

The pork or manufacturing butchers who emerged in the nineteenth century took the cottage culture to the towns: some were German immigrants who had fled to England rather than face military service. They sold 'meat', meaning pork, the only meat the poor ever saw, and in the same or a similar variety of forms encountered in villages. The beef and mutton stocked by 'high-class family butchers' were often known as 'butcher's meat' – a distinction that hardly exists any more.

A number of towns that had up to six pork butchers a hundred years ago have none today. In addition to the usual pressures, a pig takes a long time to process. The work is attracting few trainees, being manual, but provides a long list of *pièces de résistance* that the English kitchen is famous for and people no longer make at home. Pork butchers have many skills, often handed down and practised in historic shops, still bearing German as well as English names. They tend to favour knives rather than saws or choppers (Maynard Davies, 2003), keep chaps and chitterlings going, and get better results with hams and pies than you can yourself.

The cottage pig industry, despite its social and economic importance to the rural economy, was undermined by blanket legislation (intended for the towns) that prohibited sties within sixty feet of a dwelling house. The singeing or 'swaling' of pigs is still practised in abattoirs equipped with furnaces. It is not permitted over bonfires if the pork is for public distribution, but continues on private property. A farmer or smallholder may kill one of his own pigs a year, though the job is usually done by a licensed slaughterman. If a vet is present and the necessary regulations are met, there are no restrictions on the sale of the meat.

COOK'S ORACLE

Pork, smeared by the prophets and favoured by the poor, has a different cachet to beef and lamb. 'And the swine, though he be cloven-footed, cheweth not the cud; he is unclean to you,' says Leviticus. Yet there is a mule-footed pig, and the Jews ate pork, or they would not have kept the Gadarene and other swine mentioned in the Bible (Beeton, 1968). Whether or not the meat constitutes a health hazard is down to diet and climate, the pig being an omnivore and its flesh quick to deteriorate in hot weather. Even in the temperate English climate there used to be a season for pork. It ran from St Bartholomewtide to Lady Day, or 24 August–25 March. Country people, in spite of refrigeration, still observe the dates.

At the start of the twentieth century, large numbers of pigs were fattened in London and a residual population was foraging in the streets. The rich, wary of their condition, bought country-cured hams, but no fresh pork except sucklers, which were guaranteed to be milk-fed and were eaten at two to six weeks old on the day of dispatch. The meat was either sent round to the nearest peel oven for baking, or roasted in front of the fire protected by a pig iron, a shield over the animal's midriff that stopped the loin cooking before the legs and shoulders.

Over 50,000 sucking pigs were eaten a year in Victorian London: 'one of our most esteemed national dishes,' wrote Florence White in 1932. I have cooked them twice – to cries of dismay that turned to delight at the first mouthful. The meat is white and delicate, the crackling like brown paper, and the cost considerable. Sucklers are still a speciality in Spain, particularly Segovia, where they are displayed in the windows of restaurants.

A porker weighs up to 130lbs, after which it is classed as a cutter or baconer but can obviously make mature pork. The feeding of skim milk, buttermilk or whey, a practice that linked pigs to cream, butter and cheese production, is not as common as it was – owing to the demise of mixed family farms and the inconvenience of transporting liquids – but continues on certain enterprises. The whey, rather than going to waste, is intelligently used to supplement barley meal or compounds. The pigs like it, and their condition benefits. Mine were fed, amongst other things, on grain from the mash tub, Jerusalem artichokes (a menace in the garden) and a Chinese cucumber/marrow that went berserk. Swill, a favourite with the army, prisons and in wartime, which made the best pork of the lot, is no longer permitted except under licence.

Commercial pork, the supermarket choice, comes with little or none of the fat it needs to eat well. Over 50 per cent of what the UK eats is not only imported from Europe, 'it comes from farms that operate welfare practices which would be illegal in Britain although they do comply with EU standards' (MLC). Animal-lovers please note.

Home-fed pork is so superior to commercial it is almost another meat: better as chops, better in sausages, better in pies. Organic pork bears a premium owing to the price of feed, and may benefit the environment, but it does not on its own guarantee meat quality. Free-range pork has been developed in response to public demand, and implies 'happy' or 'contented' pigs. However, they can get sunburnt in an open field, and there is no evidence to suppose they like former sheepwalk any more than a Southdown ewe enjoys an oak wood. Freedom pork, the cleverest and most meaningless of labels, dreamed up for the food giants, is applied to pigs both extensively and intensively reared.

Taint in pork, which is present in a boar's fat and makes it smell 'pissy' in the oven and on the plate, is one of the biggest problems today. The Meat and Livestock Commission has said it does not exist in pre-pubescent pigs. So did the Danes – with drastic effects on their export market to Japan and a hectic reappraisal after four years. Taint is avoided by castrating males, which can be humanely done at an early age but is no longer common – and is forbidden by the Soil Association – making pork from non-'organic' sources or gilts the inevitable choice for me. Check on the sex of the beast with your supplier.

The best butchers hang their pork for a week to ten days in the cold until the skin has dried and the meat begun to set. The supermarkets, we are proudly told, move it in and out of their stores within forty-eight hours. The cuts of fresh pork are as follows.

Loin: taken from the back as in lamb or a sirloin of beef; it is chined (ask the butcher to do this and watch him) for roasting on the bone, or cut into chops and grilled.

Tenderloin: the inside of the loin excavated from bacon pigs and sold separately; it is equivalent to the fillet in beef; stir fry.

Leg: often cut into two for oven roasting.

Shoulder and foreleg or 'hand': difficult to carve – either boned and rolled for roasting or made into sausages.

Spare rib: left when the shoulder and foreleg have been removed; divide and grill or oven roast whole.

Belly: fatty, but full of flavour; oven roast.

GRILLING

Cook individual ribs, well seasoned, over a fire. Barbecue sauces are made from something sweet (like honey), spicy (black or chilli pepper, ground ginger) and salt or soy.
Cook chops, trimmed of skin and excess fat, under the grill on both sides until firm.
Pork (or veal) chops with cheese: when the meat is done, spread a heaped dessertspoon of Welsh rarebit (page 338) over each piece and grill until melted and brown.

OVEN ROASTING

(a) Use the loin, leg, rolled shoulder or hand, or spare rib. Try incising it like lamb with slivers of garlic. Cook in a preheated oven for 25–30 minutes per pound (450g) at 180°C/350°F/gas mark 4.
Like other rich foods (duckling, crab, lobster, salmon, etc.) first quality roast pork is excellent cold.
(b) Use the belly. Cook, like a breast of lamb, on a rack in a pre-heated oven for 2 hours at 150°C/300°F/gas mark 2.

Crackling is an English speciality almost unknown abroad, which owes nothing to cook, chef or recipe. The skin of a pig will crackle when it is young, paper thin and dry, and has a layer of fat underneath that the native breeds are able to provide. The scoring or 'spining' of the tissue, which can be done by the butcher or at home with a Stanley knife, enables the fat to run out over the surface causing it to crackle. A dressing of oil or butter is not needed on a suitable porker, it is not much help to an unsuitable one, and none at all to a pig whose skin is too old and hard to crackle. So, you can have crackling or mature meat, which is more tasty, but not both. A piece of pork, whether it is the leg or loin, needs at least an hour in the oven to make proper crackling.

STIR FRYING

Use the tenderloin. Cut into slices about half an inch thick and cook until just firm in a little fat with chopped onion and garlic. Remove with a perforated spoon to warm plates. Deglaze the pan with red wine, stock and any left over gravy, and pour over the meat. Season well.

Mint sauce (Hartley) was the original partner for pork, its refreshing sweet-sour taste the perfect foil for meat so rich. An apple sauce made from fruit like a Bramley or Golden Noble, which is high in acidity and breaks down to a froth, falls into the same category: try it without sugar. Chilli sauce of the Chinese or Arab type is for those who like something stronger. The Victorians made a currant sauce.

A sage and onion 'stuffing' for pork, baked in trays, is sold by some of the butchers in the north of England. A pudding that goes in with the meat takes its place in some parts of the country. The Derbyshire version contains equal amounts of self-raising flour and oatmeal, lard, a grated onion, an egg, salt, milk and water; sage is optional. The more of the pudding you ate first, families were told by poor but crafty mothers, the more pork you could have. Children fell for it every time.

Husbandry and cooking turn to ingenuity when it comes to dealing with the rest of the pig, though interest in the proceeds is not what it was. An estimated fifth of England's population will eat offal, and a fifth of them will kill for it: the remainder, swooning at the mention, do not want to be converted. It might help them to follow the American example and think of the body parts which they find offensive as 'variety meats'.

The blood: an ancient food source, a necessity to some and a treat to others, spilt and wasted in huge amounts every week. Blood is unfiltered milk. In consistency and usefulness to man, it varies from one beast to the next, The Scots bled living cattle until the war:* the Masai still do, a sight I have witnessed near Nairobi. The English took blood from slaughtered pigs and farmyard geese for puddings, and from hares (see page 191), carp and eels for sauces. Lambs' blood, which is high in fat and extra quick to set, is the least popular.

Blood (or black) pudding: has been eaten, universally and by all classes, for as long as England has existed. It had a seasonal resonance in cottage economy, connected with pig killing, and remains a festive dish on Guy Fawkes Night in parts of the West Midlands. From rural roots, such cheap and easy preparations spread to the towns and emerged as victims of a well-known divide. To the south 'black' pudding is industrial and unfashionable, almost contemptible. Up north, it is a gold-medal-winner in Europe, which has vanquished *boudin noir*, and a family friend.

Home-made black puddings are usually baked in trays: Dorothy Hartley counted nine in Bideford market in 1954, all made by different people. The industrial version is committed to ox runners (pigs' casings will rot), which were lacquered with blood after cooking in order to toughen, preserve and embellish the skin, turning it black. The name stuck, though the colour is obtained today by adding household soda to the puddings' boiling water, and a pale imitation of what it was.

It is *not* illegal to use fresh blood in black puddings, but, if transported, it requires a licence. The burly and accommodating Richard Chesters of Derby, who works all hours in the subterranean confines of George Stafford and Co., a well-known name in the business, has made sure to get one. Most of his competitors are content with a dried and imported mix, deprived of white corpuscles in processing, which is reconstituted with a meringue type of mixture. The choice of manufactured black puddings is lean or fatty – a welcome sight emerging from a gleaming, steaming cauldron on a cold winter's day. A bad pudding is mealy, a good one is moist, and can have meat in it, making it a blood sausage.

Pig's blood does not coagulate as readily as it is supposed to, but needs straining. A variety of spices may be used to beef up the flavour, from ground pimento to pennyroyal or 'pudding grass', a species of mint (*Mentha pulegium*) and one of the oldest English medicinal and culinary herbs. I have not made black pudding yet (the bucket of blood fell over) but intend to. Laura Brough, a farmer's wife from Cumberland, told me how to proceed.

---

* *A keeper near Caithness told me how they opened and closed the jugular vein. One bowl of blood was taken from each cow, no more, usually in the hungry gap before the harvest home. He also remembered transhumance as a boy: the movement of cattle to summer pastures, and through the remains of bonfires – to ward off evil spirits, they used to say.*

4 pints (2.4 l) of blood, strained, an equal amount of milk, ½ lb (225g) barley, boiled until it bursts, ¾ small white loaf, 2 handfuls of rolled oats, 1 handful of dried mint, 1 handful of salt, 1½ tsp pepper, a close-fitting dish and enough caul fat, cut in squares, to cover the bottom.

Mix the ingredients together. The seasoning should be all right, but you can put a teaspoon or two of the pudding on a dish, bake it for a few minutes and check to make sure. Then pile the lot into the dish and cook for about an hour in a medium oven or until set in the middle. If the edges are getting too hard, turn down the heat.

The usual way of serving such a pudding is fried, in slices. The French eat black pudding with apple sauce rather than mustard.

The tripes are eaten every time a sausage goes down, but, separated from the sausage, regarded with horror – and a great deal more horror than the worst industrial banger or low-fat spread with fifteen E numbers. The small intestine is about sixty feet long and entitled 'the casing'. It is unravelled, squeezed and flushed out – by tap or in a stream – then turned inside out on a stick or the handle of a wooden spoon. Soak for several days in fresh water, changing it twice daily. Cover in a strong brine and keep in the fridge. English intestines are used for chipolatas, Danish ones preferred for sausages. Both can be obtained from the Natural Casing Company, or a local butcher.

The large intestine or chitterling, the French *andouillette*, is many times shorter and wider than the casing. It is washed and salted, the internal fat having been removed, then simmered for three or four hours. The ready-cooked chitterlings available in shops may be bleached, plaited, pressed or vacuum-packed. They are more popular in the north of England than the south, and tiresome to process, but can still be found in the occasional West Country butcher.

The maw, often prepared by tripe dressers (see page 460), is called the 'bag' and sold on their stalls in the north of England. It is prepared and eaten like chitterlings, the fat having been removed, but tastes meatier. Another delicacy in Yorkshire and Lancashire, and a victim of divides.

Eat chitterlings and bag hot from the frying pan with mash and mustard, cold with pickles, or add them to 'baked beans' (see page 57).

Lard comes from the flair, flead or flick fat, surrounding the kidneys of a pig. It can be beaten into flour to make a form of pastry – something I have not tried – but is usually rendered. A modern porker has little fat and therefore little lard, so most of it is imported, while the native breeds can provide several pounds per beast. Country people used to store their lard in a cleaned and inflated pig's bladder, called upon when butter ran out.

Some pork and family butchers render their own lard. The best way of doing it at home is to hang up the lard in front of the fire, catching the drips in a bowl underneath: a sprig of rosemary, placed in the bowl, keeps it nice and fresh. Lard will keep for months in a cool dark place. The scratchings left by the rendering process, dusted with salt, make a thirst-provoking snack.

Lard can be eaten on bread, and used in hot-water-crust pastry and shortcrust for pasties (see page 63). 'We don't want to go back to cooking with lard!' said Radio 4 in 2005. Back? Some of us who still are should, according to received wisdom, be dead by now. Anyway, everyone who eats bacon or sausages consumes a form of lard.

Living in north Wiltshire for a bit, I used to wait in the village shop on Friday mornings. At around ten a.m. a local woman would deliver home-made lardy cakes of the simplest sort and the best ever. The 'recipe' consisted of a white bread dough (see page 77) rolled out and folded up in layers with lard, raisins and a little caster sugar in between, brushed with a syrup and baked for 30–40 minutes in a medium oven. Perhaps it was the walk to the shop and back that kept me in trim.

The caul is a fatty membrane resembling a lace hanky, also known as the veil, surrounding the stomach, in which babies are sometimes born. Human cauls, which were thought by country people to protect the owner from drowning, fetched high prices from seamen. My late uncle was born in one. On modern porkers, cauls are less well developed than on native pigs, and so are becoming harder to obtain than they were, though they are still used as wrappings for faggots and haslet (see page 160), and by butchers in the north and north-west to cover legs of lamb.

The fry, a corruption of 'frill' or mesentery, is an organ that fastens the intestines of a pig to its tummy. It is shaped like a ruff. This insignificant detail of English gastronomy is easily scorned but eagerly claimed by those who know it. The frill is seldom available in butchers today, though still requested, and should be cooked until crisp in a dry frying pan.

In the wider sense, the fry or pluck refers to what is left of the internal organs when the tripes, stomach, caul and flair fat have been removed.

The liver is the age-old 'best bit'. It is a little cheaper than from a lamb and a lot cheaper than a calf but next to it in taste and texture. For the conventional fry-up, lightly cook thin slices. Then deglaze the pan with a little red wine and soy sauce, and you have some gravy, or squeeze half a lemon over the top. For something different, which I have seen in the south of France, dust a thick piece of liver with salt for a week, drain and wipe with a scalding cloth. Hang up in a cold, airy larder to dry or keep in a jar, immersed in oil. Slice as thinly as you would fresh liver, and eat raw with a drink – extra tasty.

For the pâté I was brought up on:

1lb (450g) of pig and chicken livers, 2 shallots and 1 clove of garlic, peeled and chopped, a good 4oz (110g) butter, 1 glass of brandy or Calvados, a pinch of allspice, nutmeg or mace, and salt and pepper to taste.

Fry the livers in a little of the butter until firm with the shallot and garlic. Remove with a perforated spoon, add the brandy or Calvados and reduce by half. Melt the rest of the butter in the pan with it. Liquidise the lot until smooth with the seasoning. Pot and seal with more melted butter. Leave a day or two before eating.

The kidneys can be fried when cut in half, but tend to be a little tough. It is better to roast them on the loin, detach for a stew, or, if they have a good covering of fat, leave them in the lowest possible oven for a couple of hours.

The rest of the 'fry', the heart, lites or lungs, and melt or spleen, misleadingly, is not suitable for frying – or even eating on its own – but is used in familiar dishes.

Haslet, harslet or acelet, mentioned by Pepys, is one. It is rare in the south of England today, but remains common in manufacturing butchers in the Midlands and the north. Get it warm from the oven if you can. The following recipe for haslet, very-old fashioned, was contributed to *Farmhouse Fare*, the country recipes from *Farmers' Weekly*, by a Mrs Rogers of Wrexham.

> Wash and dry some [chopped] liver, heart, lites, melt and sweetbread if any, fat and lean bits of pork, beating the latter with a rolling pin to make it tender. Season with salt, pepper, sage and a small finely shredded onion. When mixed, put all in a caul and fasten up tightly with a needle and thread. Roast it on a hanging jack or by a string.
>
> This is a very old recipe of my mother's which she used when they killed pigs. She dished the haslet with a sauce of port wine, water and mustard (already made) just brought to the boil. Served in slices with parsley sauce, it is also very good.
>
> N.B. If the weight of the meat threatens to tear the caul, which is flimsy on a young pig, bake the haslet.

Faggots, meaning a bundle, in this case of meat, they are also known as 'savoury ducks' or plain 'ducks' (see page 456). Butchers sell hundreds a week, often their own. The sight of the statuesque Stan Holdaway in white coat and grey beard standing in his shop in Hampshire making faggots, lit by a single bulb on a winter's evening, was one of the great pictures never painted. Faggots vary from one maker to the next and have gone through several changes of identity, but emerged as miniature haslets. For every pound of pork take a quarter pound of liver and a quarter pound of lites or breadcrumbs and a small onion, mince, mix together and season well. Roll each quarter pound of the mixture into a ball, wrap in caul fat if available, and place cheek to cheek in a dish. Bake in a preheated oven at 170°C/325°F/gas mark 3 for an hour and serve with gravy and two veg. The pairing of faggots and pease pudding may be 'traditional', but is too much for most people.

The fifth quarter: the feet are not alike. The front pair are lean and good for little but stock. The rear ones are more versatile and meaty, if gelatinous. Miss Janet Morris, who missed her green-top milk in Leeds (and wrote to the Association of Unpasteurised Milk Producers about it in 1988), also missed her pig's feet: 'A dish I like, which I now have trouble in getting as my butcher throws them out . . . they do, however, need lots of cooking – about three hours covered in water with a pinch of salt – until the bones drop out. They are eaten with vinegar and bread and butter. When I was a child we had them for Sunday morning breakfast.'

In Leeds today, as well as Bolton, Bury and other towns up north, pig's feet are available in the covered markets. In addition to boiling, they may be committed to brawn or baked beans (see page 58). Alternatively, boil until tender, then egg-wash, coat in breadcrumbs, deep-fry and serve with mustard or *sauce Béarnaise*. A former favourite with taxi drivers, insomniacs and women of the night, eaten at Au Pied de Cochon and Chez Vatier in Paris.

The ears are a former component of mock turtle soup, valued for its gelatine, that degenerated into a dog chew, and now appears to be making a modest comeback. Prick ears contain more gristle than lop ears. The MLC recommends that they be boiled or steamed, then sliced thinly, dried and deep-fried until crisp. Alternatively, try a 'Ragoo' from *The Complete Housewife* (1737): 'Take a quantity of pigs-ears and boil them in one half wine and the other water [for 2–3 hours]; cut them in small pieces, then brown [in] a little butter . . . and [add] a pretty deal of gravy, two anchovies, an eschalot . . . a little mustard . . . some salt and nutmeg: stew all these together and shake it up thick.' I would leave out the 'slices of lemon' and 'garnish of barberries'.

Parson Woodforde's pigs got drunk on the 'cheese' from a local cider press. So he had their ears slit – the obvious thing to do, it seems. Any ideas why?

Tails are straight and 'swishy' on wild pigs, curly on domestic ones in general. They do not contain much meat, but are useful when hoarded and still have a role to play in country kitchens. Half a dozen tails, boiled until tender, are an age-old snack. Otherwise commit to brawn.

The stones are another titbit beyond city limits that is eagerly snapped up. In his *Description of England* Harrison warns that the testes provoked in women a fond curiosity and 'desire for fleshly lust' (really). The recommended mode of preparation was to take a quantity of 'stones', wrap each one in a bulrush and stew them in a pot until tender enough to be penetrated by a straw (ouch!): pickling sometimes followed. Frying is easier, but remove from their protective sack and split first. The smell and taste are similar to kidneys, the colour paler, hence the cosy title of 'white kidneys'.

The pig's head was a festive and ceremonial dish for hundreds of years, and one of the few to have had songs composed in its honour. Wild boar, until they ran out, provided for royal banquets – regardless of any taint – but a Tamworth did as handsomely, and the common and cottage pig made hearty peasant fare. The head was cleft in two, apart from the skin that connects the top, salted and soaked, boiled and boned, reconstituted and glazed, the tongue having been skinned, the brain and ears cooked separately, and the eyes discarded. The whole operation would seem a palaver today, but used to be considered worth it. I look forward to having a go.

Most heads today are split. They cost little or nothing, but to initiates, are the sum of the following delicate parts.

The top quarter is the eye piece. It includes the snout, which is like tongue in texture, and another old favourite. The brain, also in two parts, used to appear in little bundles in butchers' windows. Soak in cold water for two days in order to remove the blood, refreshing at intervals. Then, fry in batter or flour, egg and breadcrumbs until firm to the touch.

The lower part of a split pig's head is known as the 'face', 'jowl', 'chawl', 'cheek', 'chep', or 'chap', a corruption of 'chop' as in 'licking your chops'. A cut with mixed fortunes. I have heard of two butchers commanded to submit chaps for inspection until Environmental Health 'found something wrong with them' – a threat that had the desired effect, i.e. concentration on meat perceived as 'safe'. Fortunately, there are traders who are not so easily bullied and the way remains open to obtain one of the acknowledged best bits.

Rare as they may be to Londoners and the BBC, chaps 'walk out of' butchers' north of the Trent and west of the Severn. They have an extra-sweet and special quality of fat, which does wonders in a sausage, and a history of accompanying beef at Sunday lunch, and being sold in the occasional fish and chip shop. Chaps may be boned, scored and freshly baked, or salted, sliced and fried.

The environs of Bath were well known for pig keeping but no more so than other parts of rural England. I submit that 'bath' chaps, which are universal, were cured in a butchers' brine bath and salted as opposed to fresh. A muddle arose through speakers of Received Pronunciation failing to understand local dialects and terminology.*

Brawn is amongst the oldest of English dishes, and one that the French had not encountered until they occupied Calais (Harrison, 1968). It was originally made from the more muscular parts of wild or domestic pigs – as its name suggests – cooked, stored and presented in a 'shield' of skin. Ceremoniously treated as a plate of brawn could be, my guess is that it only achieved culinary greatness when the head – the best part of the pig, remember – came to be used.

'English brawn,' wrote P. Morton Shand in 1927, 'can be sublime.' First prize goes to Mary Hedden, who sold it from teacups in Bideford market – wintertime only, when the jelly is disposed to set. She retired in 2005 without having parted (despite ardent wooing from me) with any of her secrets. The second-best brawn was made by Taff Jones, who worked for one of the butchers in Fordingbridge. He retired too. Mine is not as good as theirs, but not bad either. To the head, which can be fat, some people add lean beef: not me – stick to pork (or include a rabbit). To the stock, they add vegetable matter: don't bother.

To make brawn: Take half a pig's head and a pound of the hock or hand, plus the heart, tail, tongue and any other trimmings if you wish. Dust either side with 1oz (25g) of sea or bay salt (i.e. 2oz (50g) salt in total) and leave for a day. Rub occasionally. Turn and repeat for another day. Wash and leave to soak in cold water for 2–3 hours. Cover with fresh water and boil gently for a further 3 hours or until the tissue is falling apart. Remove the meat. When cool enough to handle, pull the meat from the bone with the fingers and break up into smaller pieces (do not mince). Skin the tongue. Discard the bone, and some of the fat for rendering if there is too much, aiming for about 10–15 per cent in the brawn. Meanwhile, reduce the liquor to about two pints. Reintroduce the meat and commit to bowls, teacups, etc.

SAUSAGES

Typical of English food – something to be proud of when well made, but a product which has gone through several phases, most of them diminishing. By 1880, the quality was suspect, Mary Jewry, nineteenth-century food writer, urged readers to make their own sausagemeat at home 'in order to be sure of the ingredients'. The proprietary brands already contained a

---

* *I live in a former pub called 'The Ship', originally 'The Sheep' in Sussex and Hampshire parlance, although it happens to contain re-cycled ships' timbers, adding to the scent of a classic red herring.*

large amount of cooked rice or 'toke' in the Midlands, rusk or breadcrumbs moistened with water, and such material as the 'paddywhack' (the neck tendons of an ox), alternatively used as dog chews.

Two world wars and intervals of rationing ensured that the standard would be maintained by most manufacturers. The Great British Banger, made ever more cheaply, rose above censure to become a sure sign of the nation's indomitability and a patriotic logo. It was also one of the two foods, along with chocolate (lowest cocoa content in the world), defended by Westminster from the EC's attempts to raise their quality to the level of other European countries (well done, chaps!). So, the mass-produced English sausage remains the worst on earth, with a meat content as low as 60 per cent and a detectable binder, failing on the counts of taste, texture and the number of ingredients used to try and disguise them.

Meanwhile, the archives hold the secret of what an English sausage is, was or should be: an article of food with the highest possible proportion of meat, or mixture of meat, which, in spite of the invention of mincers in the nineteenth century, was often chopped by hand. It could be skinned or skinless according to custom.

Oxford sausages: there was one producer in the city's splendid covered market in the 1930s, and there is one today producing a modern version.

Free equal quantities of pork and veal from all sinews and skin. Take half as much beef suet. Chop finely and season with salt, pepper and minced sage and thyme. 'Work it up with one or more eggs and as much water as you see is good.' Roll into sausages, dust with flour and fry (White, 1932).

Cambridge sausages: 'Chop half a pound of pork, of bacon, and of suet, and a quarter of a pound of beef and of veal, the fat as finely as possible. Season highly with pepper and salt, a few minced sage leaves and sweet herbs. Take a delicately clean skin, fill it . . . and tie the ends securely [with string]. Poach it for twenty minutes in water not quite boiling' (Jewry, 1880).

Epping sausages: mentioned by Borrow in *Lavengro* (1850), were originally (I guess) from commoners' pigs. An updated version is available from butchers in the area.

From Ambrose Heath's *Pig Curing and Cooking*:

Put six pounds of young pork through the mincing machine and paste it in a mortar. Spread the meat out on a board. Scatter over it a handful of finely shredded sage leaves and the grated rind of a lemon, with thyme, herb savory and marjoram finely chopped.

Then sprinkle with a spoonful of pepper, a large spoonful of salt, and two finely grated nutmegs. Now mince six pounds of beef suet and scatter it on top, mix all well together, and press it into a basin til wanted. Bind with egg, make into sausages and fry or grill.

One of England's most successful sausage manufacturers, after ten years in the business, is still unable to reach the standard he wants. On a domestic level it is less difficult. Home-fed meat makes a colossal difference, so does chopping it by hand, though most of us mince it, shamefully trading off quality for convenience. A coarse cut manhandles the meat less and produces a better, chewier, juicier and more sophisticated sausage in my experience, but a fine one is more popular. Here are some guidelines and tips.

Any joint of pork can be used in sausages. The shoulder and spring or hand, which are difficult to carve, have become the most popular cuts. The head, boned and skinned and added to the mixture, makes the finest sausage. Surprisingly little salt is needed to season the meat, particularly when it is confined to casings kept in brine. Purists, keeping the fat separate, apply salt only to the lean (Maynard Davies, 2003), then mix the two. A binder is recommended, but should not make its presence felt: egg is the least obtrusive. The herbs and spices to have played a part in sausage-making, other than rubbed sage, include black, chilli and cayenne pepper, sage, coriander, ginger, garlic. Experiment within reason, keeping to subtle amounts unless you prefer a gimmick to a sausage.

Home-made sausages: 2lbs (900g) of pork, 80 per cent lean and 20 per cent fat, minced coarsely, 1 egg, ½oz (10g) salt, and ¼ tsp ground black pepper, ¼ tsp mace.

Mix well together in a bowl. If using skins soak for 2 hours in tepid water before piping in the pork. Alternatively roll up into sausages. Cook until firm, no longer or the meat can dry out. Pour the fat from the sausage into mashed potato or over veg.

For a sausage roll to die for (Hippisley Cox, 1987): insert sausages one by one into rolls made from a white bread dough that is ready for the oven. Bake off, eat warm for lunch with English mustard and resort to an armchair.

Hog's or groat pudding is another old and comforting dish, delightful to find and long since relegated to the south-west of England: I have not seen any hog's pudding in butchers east of Bridport. The proprietary versions are usually a mixture of cooked pork, barley meal and seasoning, wrapped in ox runners. Home-made puddings tend to use hulled oats or groats, which have yielded to bulgar wheat and couscous upcountry but are still available in Devon and Cornwall. Here is a recipe from the WI, using half a pig's head or knuckle of pork, recorded in the 1960s and lent by Brenda Mills:

Half cover [the pork] with water and simmer for 2½–3 hours til tender. Remove meat from bone and mince. Weigh, then put less than an equal quantity of groats in a pan with the strained liquor. Cook gently for 20–30 minutes, stirring occasionally. Mix with the meat, season, and commit to a dish.' Remember to keep the pan loosely covered and top up the liquor when necessary. Some shred the meat with a couple of forks, and boil the groats in a muslin bag in water. The proportion of cereal to pork can be as little as 1 to 5.

The hog's puddings in Bideford market, home made by the Smale family came in slices. Being pre-cooked and cold, they only needed heating through in the oven: good with mustard, laver, tomatoes, mashed potatoes or swedes – a Saturday lunch much missed, gunning you up for a walk on the cliff.

Pork pies are a culture and subculture, vilified and beatified, with connections to the ancient pastry case or 'coffin' and to modern cheese production and whey-fed pigs. The trade, using leftovers from the ham and bacon industry to provide a ready-made meal or snack, took off in the Midlands and the north during the nineteenth century. The south does not have the same track record of pies, with exceptions, since the skill of the maker anywhere can count. A member of the Berkshire WI called Mrs Tomkins was said to have baked the best pork pies on earth. I was informed of this fact by some friends of mine who lived next door to her for several years, but only after her death, a tragedy in more ways than one.

The average pork pie, obtained in a supermarket, is bland, inoffensive and not worth the attention it receives in sporadic competitions. The good ones are effectively home-made in large, medium and even cocktail sizes either by butchers or by small shops and industries who supply local retailers. The Melton Mowbray pie has AC status. It has sloping sides and a light grey interior, thanks to being hand-raised and containing fresh meat, plus a small proportion of anchovy essence.

A pie with straight sides has been cooked in a metal ring. If the pork within is pink, it is lightly cured. Jelly between the meat and pastry, injected through a hole in the lid, and superficial glazes, are not universal. The demand for pies rises in winter, peaking in cold weather. Wardle's in Buxton was the place to go on a chill Christmas Eve.

I have the lot: a wooden dolly to raise the pies, metal rings, and the best of pork. I have minced the meat, chopped it, and seasoned it morning, noon and night, and done everything I can think of to the pastry – without getting satisfactory results or finding out why. The secrets of pie men come with the business if at all, and writers repeat methods that are flawed from the start.

The only information I have been able to glean is as follows. The texture of hot-water-crust pastry is improved by adding 1oz (25g) beef dripping to 2oz (50g) lard, melting it in ¼ pint (150ml) of warm water and/or milk, and introducing it all at once to 1lb (450g) strong white flour or self-raising flour. Some butchers make the pie immediately, others wrap the pastry in a plastic bag and leave it to cool. The permutations are not inexhaustible. May you do better than me (and tell us all why).

A pork pie is one of the only safe bets for a traveller in England. It is typical of our cookery that such a simple combination as pastry and meat can be so complex, rise to such heights, attract such scorn and get so many people going. If you are ever cornered by a Yorkshireman with nothing to discuss (unlikely), you can always fall back on cricket, the relative merits of Wednesday and United, and who makes the best pork pie. What is the most memorable thing I have ever eaten other than at home? The sturgeon in Moscow or the beef in Kobe? No. The *foie gras* in Reims, the lamb in Pedrazza or that first Alphonso mango, at teatime in Bombay? Not quite. The crisp and unexpected pie from the London Road in Sheffield, made of succulent pork, golden without, pink within, and warm to the touch as the day was cold? Indeed it is. The Japanese would not have let that little shop go.

CHAPTER
FIFTEEN

Hams, Bacon and Chines

**I** WAS ON THE EAST COAST OF AMERICA, seeing the fall, the houses and the furniture: the new wing at the Metropolitan Museum of Art had just opened. Up in New England there was Salem and Newport, down the eastern seaboard colonial Williamsburg. A sale was on at Monticello, Thomas Jefferson's former house and garden in the hills. I left a couple of bids, both productive, and moved on to Smithfield, Virginia, Edgar Allan Poe's home town. The attractions included a manor house transported from England and reassembled, and an elegant quarter entitled 'The Fan'. There was also Gwaltneys, a leading producer of the famous hams.

I went to the factory shop and asked to see one. An engaging girl recommended the left leg (or was it the right?) because a pig scratches with the right (or was it the left?), making the meat tough. No kidding. Some light-hearted banter passed between us on the subject of pigs and their habits. The girl fetched a ham and put it on a table.

The specimen before me, hard of skin, dark and flat, neat at one end and round at the other, was a familiar sight. It looked like an English ham, of the sort my parents bought and old-fashioned grocers hung in their windows particularly at Christmas. And it would, said the girl. There was no change at Gwaltneys. The hams they sold today were cured the same way as they had been by the settlers three centuries before. We were serious now.

What about the pigs that Gwaltneys used? Some were a Saddleback type, name of Hampshire. Was that a place in England? You bet. So was Devon, the original name of the cattle at Mount Vernon, the Massachusetts oxen, and the beasts in the ring with Walt Whitman's 'Tamer'. The word was that an old woman up in the Appalachians used to make a form of Cheddar cheese too. Well, well.

I bought two right legs (or were they the left?) and arranged for them to be sent home. The girl asked where English hams came from. York and Suffolk, says I, grasping at names I had heard of, distinguished names, passing from household use into obscurity. I made a mental note to find out why on returning home.

There were not only hams up north but classes for them, beside the cakes and other produce, at the shows in the Dales that transformed their host village. The tents were like a Field of the Cloth of Gold, but white, laid out on the crimson moors. The sheepdog trials started at noon, then the cricket, and a steam train left. There was country dancing too, 'Count Your Blessings' and 'A Real Princess'.

In the huge, hot produce tent between monster gooseberries and beetroot as big as your head, six honey-coloured hams lay face up on a trestle table. There were two categories: under 25lb and over, with 40-, 60- and even 70-pounders drawing a trickle of people wondering in silence at their magnificence and size. The entries were home-fed, traditionally cut and dry-salted since the previous show, and had to be in order to compete. In the early afternoon the marquee closed for judging and opened with coloured rosettes pinned to the winning entries.

A man came and collected his ham, which bore second prize. Robbed, he was, according to us both, but happy with a first for eggs. His farm was located in a hamlet partly infiltrated by 'one-summer people' who came and tended to move on – after the following winter. Even in August I could see why. The house was made of the customary stone, the tea and cake were warming, and the meat was more or less everywhere. Bacon and hams were enjoying the comfort of his sitting room, the company of his pictures and the stability of the hooks outside his kitchen, jostling for position in dimly lit surroundings with coats, gumboots, trays, mirrors, and ornaments dating back to the previous age but one. Two other houses, similarly furnished, emerged over the course of the next few days.

I was kindly offered bacon to take home, but had seen the promised land in hams, lifted from a Victorian textbook, that gave words like 'farmhouse' and 'traditional' their proper meaning. Obtaining one that had not been earmarked for a special occasion was a different matter – the prospect of failure becoming increasingly real after several false starts. It was years since I had re-registered English hams in Virginia, months since I had planned an expedition to their heartland, and weeks since I had left on the round trip it included. I was days behind schedule and late setting out to see one Henry Ford, no less, a butcher all his life, and known as the best in the business, whose father had salted pork for a living.

The shop was in a remote village, neat, small and well staffed. I arrived just before it closed, breathing hard. The proprietor, a lean, dark man in a cloth coat and white hat, came out from the cutting room to serve. In response to my enquiries, he said that he had some hams – but cured and maturing to order and awaiting collection. They were all bespoke.

So, I was several hundred miles from home, deep in the heartland of York hams, and unable to buy one. The butcher said he was sorry and spread his hands. Was there anything else I would like?

People came in; I let them go before me, standing back to collect my wits. When they had gone, I made a suggestion. Would it be all right for me just to see a ham or two? I would be so interested. The butcher hesitated, wondering why and to what end, then signalled for me to follow him out of the shop.

The hams were hanging in a cellar at the back, done up in feed bags. We unhooked a couple, returned through the cutting room with one each and put them down. The butcher undid the string and took each ham out of its bag and muslin caul, revealing the elegant shape and crusty skin. He ran a skewer in and out of a spot below the aitchbone on the bigger ham, sniffed it and handed it to me, his expression unchanged. I took the skewer and sniffed it too, out of politeness; I had yet to learn what for. Then he took the skewer back, wiped it clean and tried the other ham. This time, he smiled. The smell was quite different, more mellow and sweet. He hung the first ham on the scales, looked at the weight, and took it down. He hung the second, watched by me. I told him I had to have that ham.

The butcher looked startled, but collected himself and almost sadly shook his head. I did not understand. The ham was already sold. We stared at each other in silence.

There were noises outside the shop, a bit of a commotion further down the road. Some lads from the local stable were riding horses up to the gallops. Amongst them, tossing his head and swishing his tail, was a grey-white gelding of no particular parentage who had captured the nation's heart. It was Desert Orchid, the butcher said, looking at him through the window, training on the moors in a secret location.

'My neighbour in Hampshire,' I told him.

'You've come a long way,' the butcher said.

The ham, suspended from the hock, hung motionless on the scales between us. I touched the skin with the point of the skewer, gave a little push and the meat began to turn on its piece of string, watched by us both.

'I'd love to let you have it,' the butcher said, 'but I can't. Why not take some of our bacon, or pies? We are renowned for pies. We make 'em every day.'

I hardly heard him.

'You must let me buy that ham.'

'Look,' the butcher said, pushing back his hat, 'it's promised to a company director for the big day at his shoot. He entertains some very important people, invited from all over. There'll be no expense spared.'

I was nearly in tears.

'Please.'

The sound of Desert Orchid died away. I waited. The butcher was torn. Eventually he took the ham down from the scales and muzzled it. Then, sighing deeply and shaking his head, he wrote out a bill.

'They'll kill me for this,' he said.

On the way home, I stopped at the grocer in Sandbach in Cheshire, and fell into discussion with the proprietor, Godfrey Williams. It emerged that I had a York ham on board. Which leg? he asked. Here we go, I thought, preparing for another tall story, but no! A 'yorker', I learned, was a pig in the habit of standing with one of its back legs toe to the ground. It could also be the leg itself, for which people paid a premium, believing it to be more tender. Time was when master grocers in England were required to complete a seven-year apprenticeship, and sit a written examination with such knowledge at their disposal.

To cure food is an art, possibly learned by the Romans from the Gauls. It involves removing the moisture and drying the tissue, usually by the application of salt: wind and smoke hasten the process (see page 182) but are not essential. The reason for curing is to prolong the life of fish and meat, making it easier to store for the months of want and also to carry. The effect is to transform the taste and texture and, according to many, improve the palatability of herring (see page 259) and pork.

Curing, a habitual and seasonal occupation in England by the Middle Ages, developed into a farm and cottage industry. On the church misericords in St Lawrence's, Ludlow, polished by generations of 'holy dusters'*, you may see the meat being salted hundreds of years ago, then walk round the corner to a butcher and buy the same thing.

A vast number of local and personal cures were used, different in detail, but of two basic sorts. Dry-curing was best suited to dry and cold environments, in which pork can lose moisture and age like hard cheese. It was only attempted in wet or humid conditions when the salt was rubbed into the skin of the meat for a sufficient length of time to make it sweat, an occupation undertaken by families in the Forest and possibly shopkeepers. Brines were easy by comparison: non-weather-dependent, non-labour-intensive, and more economic in terms of weight reduction, but unable to deliver the same result. And so the ways divided between one region and another, quality and quantity, artisan and factory.

The cuts of pork change their identities on being salted. The leg, the grandest and biggest cut, festive and ceremonial, becomes the ham when individually cured and matured. It is a gammon (correctly, 'jambon'), cheaper and often sold in pieces – middle, corner, slipper and hock – when attached to a side of bacon. Purists think of a ham as dry-salted, a gammon as brined. One is a thoroughbred, taut and sleek, the other a carthorse, fleshy and round, a distinction already blurred when Sheila Hutchins pointed out the difference in *English Recipes and Others* in 1967. Shoulder 'hams', which are rare but not extinct, muddle the issue.

Yorkshire had or acquired all the advantages necessary for curing meat: cold, crisp winters, quality salt, and a large white pig with the desired conformation, fed extravagantly on boiled potatoes or thriftily on the whey from cheese-making. The legs were cut long and rounded off in order to include the 'sweet' bone ('oyster' bone or aitchbone), please the eye and present a smooth face impenetrable to flies. They were salted in the wintertime only, one season for the

---

* *An office held by cleaners in some of the cathedrals.*

next, and left to cure, a natural process which took place in any dry location, windy or still. They were not smoked. The finished hams were sold at the gate or to qualified grocers, covering the cost of the bacon and brawn obtained from the rest of the pig.

York hams are mentioned by the eighteenth century: they went to London, for export to France, and fed royalty, partnering boiled eggs at breakfast, game pie at lunch, and pickled beetroot later in the day. Tea, to J. B. Priestley, meant a home-cured ham tea. It was one of the things you found in Harrogate and went to the Dales for, which added to the joys of sightseeing, walking, the shows and the cheese. 'It is difficult to say which ham is the best, but . . . for delicacy of taste the first place goes to . . . Prague ham, if served hot,' says the *Larousse Gastronomique*, 'and to York ham, if served cold.'

Lincolnshire and Shropshire produce hams of a similar type, which may lack the sweet bone but enjoy the same rigorous dry-salting and maturing. Cumberland hams, another former favourite with walkers, a fixture at the Ritz, and a casualty of the *Titanic*, claimed their own identity through a different breed of pig, which was taken to great weights and is now extinct. Suffolk hams, in common with those of their neighbours and the south-central counties, were often cured with molasses. Somerset hams, also black, were the best that P. Morton Shand (a French resident) had ever seen. There are Welsh, Belfast and Limerick hams too.

With the collapse of farming, changing food fashions and the failure to protect their name, English hams degenerated from niche market material to an almost invisible role. 'There's a lot of dry-cured bacon about,' said *New English Cookery* in 2005, 'but virtually no culture of dry-cured ham.' Prosciutto, serrano and iberico had concealed its very existence. Parma hams, produced in England, were praised for filling the perceived vacuum.

To find English hams alive, well and hanging in a shop, especially unannounced, is all the more thrilling as a result. It is like picking ceps, a pleasure that never seems to pall. They will not bear labels like 'air-dried' (a statement of the obvious), but they are difficult to mistake. Look north of the Wash and west of the Severn, in agricultural areas, not in supermarkets or fashionable delis. Coats vary from a pale gold to a deep honey colour or matt black, depending on the age and cure, perhaps glistening with salt or exhibiting a bloom, and hiding an inch of fat or 'cover' beneath the skin. Buy, regardless of price, minding the cost of petrol if you need persuading. Clock the butcher: you are lucky to have found him. Unwrap any ham imprisoned in a material, courtesy of real or imaginary regulations, that prevents it from breathing.

Tens of thousands of English farms have or had curing rooms, equipped with slate shelves, stone silts or salt-imbued wooden containers to lay the pork in. The granite and earthenware vessels used in the West Country were for brines. I have a Doulton ham bath the shape of a pig's leg, but a short one, more likely to have been used for chaps. The hooks that protrude from my ceiling are to hang meat on. The bigger the house and former household, the more hooks it will have.

Refrigeration and the mild winters make a nonsense of the rules, but in normal circumstances salting takes place when a man can see his breath – beginning in November and ending in February. The temperature should not fall below freezing, which inhibits curing, or rise above about fifty degrees Fahrenheit. Warm weather is an invitation to unfriendly bacteria: there are also flies to worry about.

A hog has always been regarded as the best pig for 'indoors', or salting. A gilt is broader in the beam, which means the hams. A sow is sometimes used if she has failed to breed well from her first litter, and has fattened well, but will reject the salt if she is in season. Pigs' fat is said to change in consistency as they grow older, making them better for curing. Boars are avoided.

COOK'S ORACLE

To cut a ham is an art, and a challenge to a novice. Bacon curers Jeff Sheppard and George Seed, with blows of a cleaver and sweeps of a knife timed to perfection and precise to a degree, showed me how. I cut two hams a year, both badly; and with nothing to practise on until the next season, took several years to do it properly. There are two invisible joints to find and to part, below the knuckle and through the sweetbone. You then have one shot at rounding off the ham. This is best done by laying it over the corner of a table – and taking heart.

The alternative is to funk it and go for a short-cut ham. Again, tens of thousands did. Take a fresh, well-covered leg of pork weighing not less than 15lb. Saw off the trotter, Remove any lard or loose fat. Turn the ham over and run the heel of the hand up over the skin from the shank, pressing down hard, to squeeze out surplus blood from the main artery.

Fine salt is normally used for curing. It must be dry. Sea salt is considered to have a better flavour, but ordinary household salt is just as good, and cheaper: a mixture of the two has the advantage of not caking. The old blocks of salt from the Lion works at Nantwich in Cheshire, which was ideal for rubbing into the skin of hams, are greatly missed.* Avoid kitchen salt, which contains chemicals to make it pour freely, and may offend the meat.

---

* Salt was obtained from the brine springs in Cheshire over 2,000 years ago. It was mined from about a hundred and fifty feet below ground in the seventeenth century. The Thompson family of Marston, who had been trading in salt for over 100 years, started an open-pan works next to the Red Lion Hotel in 1894. They remained in business, employing 'lumpmen' and 'walkers', until 1986. Closure was due to the civil war in Nigeria and loss of the West African market. The factory is now a museum up for a grant, provided it can be matched. How I miss the blocks of salt that were sold at the chemist's in red and white bags. There was nothing better for rubbing into hams.

Saltpetre, potassium nitrate, an impurity in natural salt, neutralizes any traces of blood in hams and gives them an appetising pink colour. Very little is applied, no more than will fit on a fifty-pence piece, but as a constituent of gunpowder it has become difficult to obtain. Try the chemist and prepare to sign a form. The 'sal prunella' of the old cookery books is an unrefined version of saltpetre, and much stronger. Do not bother to ask for it.

Molasses, sugar and honey are said to tenderise hams, but cannot improve upon good pork and salt. Herbs and spices are unnecessary too. The vinegar mentioned in old cookery books kills bacteria. Beer and cider, with their high water content, constitute brines.

As in the case of cheese, to credit entire counties with first-quality hams is to imply a consistent image where none existed. Every family salted meat with considerable freedom of expression, and kept its own counsel and secrets.

E.J. Perrin of Birmingham worked for a firm that had traded for one hundred years and salted a thousand legs of pork a week. He was watching Albert Rees curing hams for his shop and stalls in South Wales when he noticed something was amiss. He promised to explain what it was before he died. Then the two men lost touch.

Years later, the Reeses' telephone rang in the middle of the night. It was Mr Perrin calling to keep his word. He spoke briefly and hung up. Within forty-eight hours he was dead, the information lodged where he had intended. It was something to do with getting a consistent colour in the meat. I pried, but got no further.

To cure a ham: lay the meat in a container – I use a plastic one – skin side up for a day. Turn over and dust the cut surface with salt. Leave for a further 24 hours and drain. Rub a little 'petre around the shank and the rest around the sweetbone. For every stone of pork, take a good pound of salt and scatter a handful over the ham. Rub that in too, leave, drain again and repeat. Turn occasionally, gathering up salt and rubbing it into the skin. When the salt is used up, continue to rub the ham every 48 hours or so.

'Taff' Jones dusted hams with an ounce of salt, brushed it off the following day and repeated the process. My grandmother (Anglo-Irish), in common with many others who live in damp houses, chose to heat the salt.

A 15–25lb ham needs three to four weeks in salt. Then rinse with a little cold water, and wipe all over with a scalding cloth as hot as you can bear to handle. Select a spot for your ham that is safe from cats and dogs, indoors or out, and hang up by a cord attached to the knuckle. Any dry location will do.

A ham then embarks on a voyage of its own. How long it takes to mature is not in human hands. Some legs, salted in the autumn, can be ready by Christmas. Others need the 8–12 months they are given by artisans. The taste improves and intensifies up to a reasonable age.

I have eaten a ham of three years old that was sensational, and seen one of nearly eight, crusty but still edible.

A well-cured ham shrinks as the moisture departs. Knock the skin on the outside towards the middle as you would a door: it should sound solid. A hollow report indicates fly-strike. If the ham can be heard to 'tick', it is heavily infested.

To test a ham: lay it on a table skin side down. Take a skewer and run it into the thickest part of the meat. Leave for a couple of seconds, withdraw, and sniff. If the skewer smells salty or of bacon, the ham is not ready to eat. If it smells pleasant, of apples or hazelnuts, it is ready. If it smells high and the ham is puffy and sticky around the aitchbone, it has rejected the salt within the first few days of curing and 'blown' from the inside out. The meat is not bad, merely strong. The condition overwhelms most palates, but is greatly liked – every pork butcher will tell you – by travellers. A fruity ham will always find its way to a gypsy's table.

I cure two hams a year. One is eaten raw and thinly sliced, as they do in southern Europe. The other is cooked English fashion, which makes it more presentable, but perishable too. In the north, people sometimes bought a ham, left it with the butcher, and took it home in quarters, saving the last piece for when the peas and beans came in.

To cook a ham: hams destined for cooking are normally soaked beforehand to make them less salty. Remove any bloom, dust or mites with a scrubbing brush. Then submerge in a bath or container of cold water for two or three days, refreshing it twice to prevent stagnation. If you need a ham quickly and you have not been able to soak it, bring it up to boiling point in water, and drain before cooking.

Hams should be poached, never 'boiled', however they are described, or else the outside is done before the middle, and the meat contracts (a chilling spectacle), leaving it dry and tasteless. Commit a small or medium-sized ham to a Burco, a large one to a metal dustbin mounted on a gas ring. Cover in cold water; it does not matter if the shank sticks out. Bring the ham up to boiling point, no more, which will take up to an hour. Then *poach* at a temperature just hot enough to be able to stir the water, giving the ham 15 minutes per pound. Allow a morning or an afternoon to complete the operation.

If the ham is properly cooked and retains all its flavours, the water will taste of nothing. In my experience, putting cider, hay or vegetables in with the meat is a waste of time and material. The only good ham stock is made from the bone.

Boiling a ham in a plastic bag, or steaming it, averts the chance of overdoing it, but takes a further 10 minutes per pound to cook the meat. Hams may also be baked, and were by obliging village bakers in the run-up to Christmas. Soak as usual first, find a big enough tray and commit to a preheated oven 150°C/300°F/gas mark 2. Wrapping the ham in tin foil (or a flour-and-water paste) does not make much difference provided it is fat enough. Give a 20lb ham most of the day.

To find out whether a ham is done, insert a metal skewer by the knuckle – not haphazardly into any part of the leg, or valuable juices will leak out – and run it up to where the pork is thickest. Leave it for a few seconds, and remove. Feel the instrument. If the heat has conducted itself to the blade, it has also reached the middle of the ham, and the meat is cooked through.

Cold ham is preferred to hot and always seems to taste less salty. Leave it in the liquor overnight, and drain. Remove the meat to the larder for a couple of days to set, protected from flies. Then either 'vandyke' the skin with the point of a knife, which looks attractive on a treacle-cured ham, or remove it carefully – and bake the Christmas turkey underneath it.

When skinned, trim surplus fat. Avoid studding the ham with cloves, which get stuck in your teeth, or orange breadcrumbs, on the grounds of appearance. Smear the ham with honey and dust with demerara sugar. Bake in a hot oven for 20 minutes and allow to cool. Carve towards the knuckle in paper-thin slices with a long, supple and razor-sharp knife. The blade should be visible through the meat, the fat as clear and translucent as lard. The lean, pink and opaque, varies from one muscle to the next, improving towards the sweetbone. The flavour of a mature dry-salted ham, given the right treatment, will put you off substitutes for good.

You cut the ham, cured it and matured it, or found it and chose it, then cooked it. In between times, you came down every morning and back every night to the stand-by and comfort of a ham hanging quietly from the hock, its craggy face awaiting inspection and its contours inviting the customary slap. If I could paint and fancied still life, I would know where to start. No colour on a plate is more beguiling. No trophy on a table is more distinguished. No English kitchen is complete without its hams.

Cumberland-type sauce: easy to make and worth it, against the salty taste of a ham. Melt a pot of redcurrant, medlar or crab apple jelly in a pan. Moisten with the juice of a small orange, and half a lemon. Add a dessertspoon of the orange and lemon skin cut into strips (minus pith), and a chopped shallot, both blanched. Boil up with a glass of port, a good pinch of salt and pepper or ginger, and allow to cool.

Pea or pease soup: the 'London Particular', thick as the smog: split peas were the thing. To make a ham stock, cover the bone in water and simmer for six to eight hours on the lowest of heats, topping up when necessary. Drain off the liquor, but do not skim: the grease, absorbed by the peas, helps the flavour. For every 3 pints add half a pound of lentils, an onion and a clove of garlic, peeled and sliced, and a stick of celery if you wish. Cook gently for half an hour until the vegetables are soft. Season with pepper. Do not add salt. The Victorians put pieces of red herring in this soup (wow!).

To vary: you may substitute the liquor from salt beef or tongue for ham stock. Pease pudding is thicker than soup, that is all.

BACON

I have a little book called *The Strange Story of the Dunmow Flitch* by D. Carter. The custom of giving a side or flitch of bacon to a couple that had neither 'repented of their marriage' nor exchanged cross words for a year and a day dates in England back to the Middle Ages in Great and Little Dunmow, Essex. The obligation to deliver the award, which could also be a gammon, is thought to have been imposed on the local priory by one or more contributors to its coffers or even by the Crown. After the dissolution of the monasteries, it fell to the lord of the manor. A jury of spinsters and later bachelors, a judge, counsel for the claimants and counsel for the bacon, collectively known as 'homage', asking penetrating questions, hearing the answers and suitably attired in robes, convened for the event. The happy couple were borne aloft with the flitch or gammon through cheering crowds of up to five thousand people before their benefactor, who sat enthroned in a monastic chair, and knelt on special stones to receive their due. Drinking, feasting and liberal helpings of slap and tickle followed. The occasions were commemorated in paintings, a print, a novel, an operetta and verses from Chaucer to *Punch*, and reported in the *Spectator* and the *Gentleman's Magazine*. There is or was an overmantel featuring a side of bacon in Wychnor Hall, Staffordshire, carved in oak and commemorating a similar custom.

The first ceremony in Dunmow was held in 1445, the second in 1510, according to documents in the British Museum. The last in legitimate terms was in 1751 with a triumphant Thomas Shakeshaft, weaver, and his thrifty wife selling slices of their award for considerable sums. The lord of the manor shut himself away in 1763 and forbore to hand the bacon over. It happened again in 1851, but the party continued, with 'rich and poor, gentle and simple' folk attending the customary knees-up. Two couples came forward in 1869, one of whom did not like being cross-examined, the cut of the judge's jib or his red smoking hat, and left in disgust to write letters of outrage. Queen Victoria was offered the bacon (no cross words with Albert?) and did not want it. From 1870 to 1906, the event, regarded as a mixture of a fun day out for Londoners and locals and an 'attempt to clothe with flesh the skeleton of an obsolete habit' cum 'anachronistic farce' loosely connected to Robin Hood, took place every year. It limped on until 1949, with claimants appearing or applying from as far afield as Kent, Norfolk, Northamptonshire, Devon, Wales, Dublin and New York. One of the couples registered (much giggling – can't think why) as a Mr and Mrs William Willie.

The Dunmow Flitch Bacon Company, a farmers' co-operative capitalising on their location and selling Priory Brand rashers and gammons, came and went in the twentieth century. The trademark included the monastic chair.

The term 'bacon', used by Falstaff to describe a rustic, pre-dated *le rosbif*. It was the food of the poor, but also a tithe and a bequest in wills, and it rose in the Victorian world to be regarded as a country-fed, country-cured product that was safer than London pork. When the English breakfast of bacon was established as the perfect partner for eggs or kidneys, its humble origins were soon forgotten.

The frustrating thing for Mrs Beeton and her contributors was that the best home-cured bacon remained where it was needed: in farms and cottages. There was no effort to increase or market the supply, even from the Buckinghamshire beech woods into London – a distance of twenty-five miles linked by rail and covered by millions of duckling. The factories stepped in with not a bad product, smoked or 'green' (originally from traces of saltpetre), clamped by portly grocers on to giant Bizerba slicers whose hypnotically smooth comings and goings preceded the contemporary packet. Up to eighteen cuts of bacon fell slice by slice in their millions over the years, into outstretched hands as clean and scrubbed as the district nurse's. A flitch with the gammon removed was – and still is – quaintly called the spencer, in memory of a close-fitting jacket worn by an earl of the same name that became a fashion item in the eighteenth century.

The Wiltshire Bacon Company, in spite of its need to be commercial, adhered to the local customs of singeing rather than scalding their pigs and curing the meat in hot salt. Then came Danish bacon, and brine injection. By the post-war period, 'one of the greatest discoveries in the science of gastronomy' (Escoffier, 1907) was spitting rather than sizzling in the pan, and emitting the water which consumers had paid for.

I first went to Suffolk in the 1970s. There were the voices to ponder, the churches and the half-timbered buildings in the occasional strong colour with gables as high as a witch's hat and roofs to match. Planks of come-hither bacon hung in the butchers' windows, black outside with snowy white fat, a sight that is now conspicuously scarce. The Bacon Shop in Chippenham went too (along with the only forked bridge on earth), but there has been loss adjustment elsewhere. As in the case of hams, dry-salted bacon is what to go for. If you are economising, look out for 'bits'.

To cure bacon (simple as winking, simpler than ham): take a piece of belly, or loin with the backbone removed, weighing a couple of pounds. Dust with a handful of fine salt, rub each side and turn every day or two (when using the loin, mix a pinch of 'petre with the salt). You may add a small quantity of demerara sugar or black treacle after 48 hours. Leave for one week in the cure for every inch thick. Then rinse and wipe with a scalding cloth as you would a ham and hang in a safe place.

Bacon is ready to eat when dry, keeping well for a couple of months. Eat before the fat turns yellow and reasty. The condition does not improve with age like a ham, though people used to say their bacon survived when buried in bran. I have yet to experiment.

The best way of cooking bacon is to toast rashers in front of the fire. There used to be vessels to hang it up in and catch the drips. Otherwise, bake a piece with beans (see page 57).

CHINES

The Webster family, butchers by trade, left their native Devon and moved upcountry during the Depression. They took a shop in Baston, Lincolnshire, a county with fowling, fishing, and its own breeds of cattle, sheep and pigs, as well as York-type hams and a cut of bacon called a chine. A good place for curing meat, the fens, owing to the uninterrupted and burnishing east wind that comes in from the North Sea, up the village streets and through every crack in every defenceless window and door. The Websters hung their chines up to dry from the rafters in their garage.

A chine is the backbone of a beast and, in culinary terms, the adjoining meat on either side. On a pig it is a cut from the neck down as far as and including the fifth rib, minus the shoulders. It weighs at least twelve pounds, but can come in two halves, split down the middle, and needs a good covering of fat. The custom with a chine of pork is to salt it and incise it with finely chopped parsley or any other suitable herb or veg. Thyme and marjoram, along with raspberry and currant leaves, leeks, spring onions and lettuces, have all been used. The chine is then cooked for up to seven hours in a close-fitting bag, so as not to disturb the stuffing, and served cold. The slices fall from the knife in resplendent pink and green stripes, fresh-tasting and finger-width.

Stuffed chines were more or less confined to Lincolnshire by the nineteenth century. They are a yeoman's food that never made it to London or, I feel – and could be wrong – on to the tables of the 'quality' either. They might have disappeared with the Curly Coat pig, but never did, enduring in memory of mop fairs, sheep-shearings, village feasts, christenings and family occasions, and taking pride of place in the centre of groaning tables. Chines today play a part as important as pies, sausages, acelet and chawl in the pork butcher's repertoire. They feature at shows, but pubs are missing out. Buy them in Lincolnshire, and have them sent for parties.

'*Jambon persillé?*'

'In spades, my lady.'

SALAMI AND SO ON

Salami: an omission from the English repertoire that the beau monde (unimpressed by the French failure to make bacon or hang beef) finds of great frustration. A word nevertheless that entered the language in 1852. The following variations are recorded.

Saveloy, a corruption of 'cervelat', meaning originally brains, arrived in 1837 and persists (admittedly in a bastardised form) in fish and chip shops. For the home-made version (Hippisley Cox, 1987):

> Take 3lb of tender pork free from skin and sinew; rub it well with ½ oz saltpetre and 8oz salt. Leave for 3 or 4 days, rubbing and turning it every day. It is then minced finely, mixed with ½ lb fine breadcrumbs and seasoned with 1 heaped teaspoon of white pepper and 6 young sage leaves chopped very small' – an English variation, the French do not use sage in sausages – this fills the casings. They should be boiled and smoked and are sometimes baked before serving.

I would leave out the breadcrumbs.

> An excellent sausage to eat cold,' said food writer Mrs Rundell in 1806. 'Season fat and lean pork with some salt, saltpetre, black pepper and allspice, all in fine powder, and rub into the meat: the sixth day cut it small; and mix with it some shred shallot or garlick, as fine as possible. Have ready an ox-gut that has been scoured, salted, and soaked well, and fill it with the above stuffing: tie up the ends and hang it to smoke as you would hams, but first wrap in a fold or two of old muslin. It must be high dried. Some eat it without boiling, but others like it boiled first. The skin should be tied in different places, so as to make each link about eight or nine inches long.

Polony: a corruption of Bologna, is not made well in my experience, but made it still is by pork butchers in the north of England. Its first official appearance was in 1764: this from *Delights for Ladies* by Sir Hugh Plat, 1602:

> Take fillets of an hog, chop them very small with a handful of red [purple] sage, season it hot [well] with ginger and pepper, then put it into a great sheepes gut, then let it lie three nights in brine, then boile it and hang it up in a chimney where fire is usually kept, and these sawsedges will last one whole year. They are good for sallades or to garnish boyled meats, or to make one relish a cup of wine.

Smoking: a pat question frequently asked, 'Do you smoke your own meat?' Not necessarily; nor does anyone else. Smoking is far less common than imagined. The hams in my house, like most of the others in England and the rest of Europe, are not smoked: their dark and crusty skins are due to age. The bacon is smoked from time to time. It makes a change: opinions are divided as to whether it equals an improvement. If pork is to cure and keep, it must be salted first. To many, that is more than sufficient. None of the dried meats we sold at the Normandy Stores were smoked except Westphalian ham, and a lacquer-black Austrian salami called *kartenrauch*.

Smoking is an ancient craft that helps meat and fish to lose moisture, gives them a protective coat, and can make them palatable without being cooked. It is also a device to bump up the flavour of tasteless foods that usually follows brining. The label 'smoked' applies to items that have been processed over wood, but also painted with a solution of pyroligneous acid, a practice permitted for more than a hundred and fifty years.

The decision to smoke meat in England seems to have been a regional one, dependent on tastes, with the fuel available having mixed effects. The black hams in Norfolk, masquerading as smoked, were merely treacle-cured (Webb, 1947), while the ones in Suffolk were smoked both at home – occasionally over bog oak – and over wood shavings in chambers adjoining the workshops of coopers and turners. In Yorkshire and Lincolnshire, the consumption of coal may have helped to invalidate smoking, but in Bowerchalke, Wiltshire, it provoked the building of a village smokehouse (demolished in the 1990s).

The former landlords of a pub near me smoked meat in the simplest way – up their chimney. The pork they obtained from their own pigs, which ran in and out of the door. The wood they gathered in the Forest, according to commoners' rights. The fire, smouldering all night against a backstick and kindled with bellows in the morning, stayed in all winter. It protected the meat from flies, rats and dogs. The rain, dripping from above, hardly seemed to matter.

My inglenook was built with the front part of the house on to the original in about 1800. The owners filled it in when the railway came, bearing coal, obscuring behind tongue-and-groove panelling a mud floor, bread oven, the cosy retreat where old folk sat – protected by a curtain – and in Hampshire parlance, 'the bacon loft'.

I arrived a century later to excavate the space brick by brick, peered up the chimney and saw the hooks. My bacon now hangs, home-cured and A4 in size, nine or ten feet above the hearth. It remains overnight and comes down in the morning, leaving me free to gun up the fire during the day without melting the fat and cooking the meat. Hardwoods or fruitwoods, not too combustible, provide the smoke. Softwoods and pine cones are occasionally burned for the last couple of shifts, their resin giving the meat a lacquered finish. The operation takes two to three weeks. The alternative would be to hang the bacon twice as high and leave it for half the time. Try it either way.

CHAPTER SIXTEEN

GAME: FUR

I T WAS A FINE SPRING AFTERNOON when Dave called. He was a man of medium height and advancing years, tough but not hard, with an incomplete circle of white hair on a brown head, clear blue eyes, and a country voice. I liked him on sight. Brenda, his wife, still had family in the Forest. Her father went aboard the *Titanic* as a boy to deliver a message, then, luckily for him, returned to his job in the telegraph office.

I had been promised a day's stalking and dressed accordingly. Dave said the boots, cords and flat 'at would do, but not the tweed coat, and lent me a combat jacket from the back of the car. A rifle lay next to it in a leather case, and a box of ammunition, calibre .125. The quarry was roe deer. Does had finished, and bucks had begun.

We set off in a westerly direction and crossed the county boundary. Dave, habitually observant, commented on everything we passed: an isolated cottage, a buzzard prospecting or a hedge mangled by a council contractor. Later in the day, he would be pointing out the slots of deer on patches of mud. He shot from a high seat in the Forest and on two farms, taking meat for his services and sharing it out with the owners of the land.

After about an hour we turned off the main road, up a lane and through an open gateway. We disembarked from the car, scouring the horizon for deer, but only saw rabbits nibbling near cover on the slopes of the hills. After coffee, Dave unlocked the boot and took the rifle from its case and the bullets from their box. He slipped a pair of binoculars into his pocket and handed me a stick about five feet long. The journey and pleasantries were over. The hunt was on.

We crossed the lane into a large field, occupied by horses, and made for a gap in the overgrown hedge beyond. There was still no sign of deer, but they were known to lie up in cover the other side. Dave sank to his knees and I followed suit. We crawled through the gap and saw what appeared to be three pairs of dock leaves rising from the grass, eighty yards away and thirty yards apart. They were the does, I was told. No bucks yet.

We needed to make ground and rose to our feet, scattering the deer – it was not important. We crept to the top of the hill, still in the shelter of the hedge, and stopped with an open view of the slope down towards the next valley. Three hundred yards away, with its head poking up through the grass and eyes half closed, enjoying a snooze in the sun, a roebuck was resting against a bank. Dave, quick as a hawk, saw it first.

'I know him,' he said, peering at the buck through binoculars. 'The one with the ear. Must have had it chewed in a scrap with a dog.'

We were down wind of the buck with the sun behind us, and protected by the silhouette of the hedge – perfect conditions for moving forward. Dave needed a full-frontal: a shot from close range, he told me, straight at the heart. He would crawl off through the grass and take up a position at fifty yards, ready for the buck to rise to its feet and present the necessary target. I was to keep down and wait to move forward when the summons came.

I took stock of my surroundings. Away to the south was the well-trodden path to Thomas Hardy's door; to the north, the comforting profile of a church he might have known, nestling in the trees near the customary manor, rectory and village street. New names in the graveyard, though, new farm buildings, an empty sky, an absence of people, corn for sheepwalk and a vanished carpet of wild flowers. What was left now from a century ago that Tess would have recognised, and what would be left in a century hence? Two hours passed. The shadows lengthened and it started to get cold.

Dave lay still in the longish grass, intent on the buck, while the creature looked through slit eyes into the sun, and in his direction, but seeing nothing. At last he turned and signalled for me to approach. I advanced on all fours, taking my stick and pausing once to rest, and lay down beside him. Thanks to the wind and coming season the grass was dry and lush. The gun was mounted and pointing at the target. Dave whispered that it was getting late. He had waited long enough. If, by the time he had counted to fifty, the buck had not moved, we would get up and go home.

Deer lie up all day in locations they consider safe, unless disturbed, and make off to feed in the evening. This one had done nothing all afternoon except flick his ears and chew his cud. Then, without looking round or giving any other signal, he tilted forward. The hind legs unfolded, raising his beam end, followed by his forelegs and his head. With eyes open and chest bared, poised and almost posing, the buck stood before us. Dave, who had counted to within two or three seconds of his deadline, clasped the rifle. He put his chin to the butt and eye to the sight. Then, after the briefest pause, he pulled the trigger.

The shot was like a thunderclap, almost knocking me sideways with its report. The deer, hit dead centre, was thrust off its feet by the power of the charge and into a backward somersault, collapsing out of sight. I stood up instinctively, eager to move forward, but felt a restraining hand on my arm.

'Leave him be,' Dave said. 'Let him die.'

Even a mortally wounded deer can flee at the sight of man. The combination of fright at what has happened to it, and fear, gripping the beast in a terminal adrenalin rush, provides the physical resources.

We stood in silence for a few moments, then walked down the hill. I expected the deer to jump up and clear the hedge, or somehow to have vanished, rather than to find him lying on his side, still and breathless in the young spring grass. Dave touched an open eye with the point of his gun. The lid did not respond. There was no wound either, no blood flowing from the creature's chest, only a tiny partition in the grey-brown pelt where the bullet had entered. Man shall have dominion.

We slit two of the legs front and back and pushed the other two feet between bone and tendon, raising the buck on my stick to our shoulders. It was quite a long way back to the car, the body was heavy and Dave had to rest a couple of times. So did I. The cold was increasing, the evening wild, the grass bent and shining in a strong, chill wind. In the next sunlit valley, oblivious to the events in ours, two or three does continued to graze.

Back at the car, Dave 'unmade' the deer like a Norman king. I, hunt servant for the day, claimed the liver and kidneys – but dug a hole with the spade provided and buried the umbels*. It was hard going in the flint compared to the heavy clay at home. We washed the blood from our hands in a puddle, crossed the road with the deer, and loaded it up when the coast was clear.

'It's funny,' said Dave, 'the girls at the farm all eat meat – but get upset at the sight of a dead animal.'

He, on the other hand, ate everything he killed or made sure it went to a good home. He did buy meat, but preferred to shoot it. Looking down at the deer beside us in the field, I felt neither triumph nor remorse, neither in the right nor the wrong. I did not feel neutral either. I was involved in an act as old as man, and a conditional one. The buck had stopped with us. It would not be wasted.

Deer: England has five species, native or naturalised. The red, the fallow, and the roe deer we had killed enjoy an order of merit originally based on grandeur and a job description sprinkled with Norman French. The sika and muntjac are comparatively recent arrivals, imported from Asia, that have escaped from captivity and bred.

Red deer, driven into enclosures for slaughter, became royal property in the Anglo-Saxon period. With the greater glorification of hunting, protection of the hunted increased under the Normans. The areas with the highest concentration of stags and other desirable quarry were effectively taken over for the king's pleasure and entitled forests, or used by favoured subjects and called chases. Fallow deer were farmed in parks, and less important but manageable beasts and birds, notably hare, rabbit, pheasant and partridge, were organised in warrens.

Some of the royal forests covered entire counties. There were twenty to thirty chases, hundreds of parks (though a number fell to looters during the Civil War), and thousands of warrens. All concessions of land came through its sovereign overlord, the king.

Deer were a valuable commodity. They provided an excuse to create forests and extend royal power, sport and military exercise for horsemen and bowmen, along with trophies, hides, hartshorn, and the most exclusive food in English history. The meat of deer, entitled venison (from the Latin *venatio*), was a gift from the sovereign that 'money could not buy' (Rackham,

---

* The innards of a deer, given to hounds today, but originally to hunt followers and the poor for humle pie.

1986). When unfit for the royal circle or military, it went to the poor, the sick and lepers. None is on record from the medieval period as having been bought or sold.

The forests had their own courts and officers charged with protecting not only the venison, but the vegetation or 'vert' on which the deer depended, and threats to their existence from man, his dog, or livestock competing for food in the winter period known obscurely as the 'heyning'. It is unlikely that any king of England visited all his forests, took advantage of them or caused anyone to be blinded, maimed or executed for poaching. Transgressors were usually fined (Tubbs, 1986). Forest law was not especially punitive. It was loosely administered, open to abuse, and yet, cited as so iniquitous that the coincidental deaths of William Rufus and his brother out hunting were regarded as divine retribution for their tyranny. England's forests acquired a reputation. They were independent places where outlaws collected and, in folk story and song, 'Jacky was hanged for stealing the king's deer.'

A vestigial resentment, coupled with land-grabbing in the nineteenth century, caused most of the royal hunting grounds to be sold off – whereupon their assets, integrity and history were destroyed. The New Forest lived on thanks to a democratic mixture of residents, who combined to protect an identity fast becoming unique. It also survived, through lack of money, poor execution and the impossibility of the task, a Deer Removal Act of 1851 aimed at making life easier for the farmers and commoners competing for space with wild animals. Today, they rub along together.

The walls of the verderers' court are lined with the trophies of deer, single and double, their antlers locked in the fatal embrace that can do for both contestants in the rut. A Tudor stirrup recalls the alleged crippling of dogs (by clawing or hambling) that were unable to pass through it. Outside there are cattle and pigs at large, great grey shrikes, one of the last developing peat bogs in lowland Europe and freedom of access to it all because of the deer and the hunting that a king grabbed for himself almost a thousand years ago.

The buckhounds, under pressure, were disbanded in 2001. The deer population is now maintained at a level the land can support: a Deer (preservation) Society acknowledges the need for control. A far greater number are killed by motorists. I have taken home several carcasses from the side of the road. I once saw one on the hard shoulder of the M3, came off at the next exit and scrambled up the motorway bank to where it lay. I was carrying the beast back to my car Robin Hood style when the law turned up. The two policemen inspected my vehicle for any damage, muttered to each other, then waved me on. They had to. Under the laws of the land, the creature, dead already, was mine from the moment I picked it up.

I hoisted the deer at home, disembowelled it and removed the jacket. The hind quarter was damaged, which it often is after a road accident, but the rest was fine and as free-range as you feel when you cross the cattle grids into one of England's former forests.

Deer can browse and graze. The males exfoliate every year and regrow their antlers, increasing in majesty and, as they multiply, in nuisance value to farmers and gardeners. Each new set of antlers is subject to irritation and covered in fur or 'velvet' which the deer rub off on trees, causing damage to the trunks. This habit, coupled to a healthy appetite for certain shoots, leaves, plants, flowers and vegetables, makes them difficult to live with.

'I love deer,' said a neighbour of mine 'on a plate with a bit of gravy.'

Look for the following deer at large and their meat in shops and at markets, noting the type and where you are: they can be linked. I have given them a 1–3 star rating, based on flavour.

Red deer are indigenous, at home in the wilderness and 'At Bay' before hounds, the 'hart royal' of legendary chases. They retreated from the sixteenth century to Scotland, Westmorland and parts of the West Country. Numbers plunged on the Quantocks with the decline of hunting around the time of the First World War. But in 1917 Somerset County Council (no less) restored the balance with imports from elsewhere, twelve couple of hounds and two huntsmen. As well as a wild population, there are colonies in parks and several escapees, plus a single case of a red deer having coupled with a horse and produced a hybrid. A mature stag is a magnificent trophy, though not the innocent he appears. He is wily and cynical – a 'rascal' in adolescence and a seasonal danger to both man and his own kind. The hinds quit the herd and conceal their calves to protect them. The meat of the red deer provides the largest cuts of venison 2 star.

Fallow deer, a casualty of the last Ice Age, are thought to have been reintroduced to England at around the time of the Roman occupation (Whitehead, 1964). They colonized the southern counties and were farmed by landowners, particularly after the conquest. An estimated two or three hundred remain in existence. Fallow deer respond to management better than red and have long since replaced them in the Forest, rising to numbers in the nineteenth century that the land could not support. Despite their title ('fallow' means pale), there are many strains and colour variations from black to white. Menil (spotted) is the optimum camouflage in dappled sunlight. The buck has a wide set of antlers or bracket head, he rolls in muck to impress the does and can be heard groaning at competing males, a fearful sound if you have not heard it before out at dusk in the autumn woods. He can be dangerous too. For the rest of the year the herd sticks together, creating the browse line visible on ridges. For their wedding feasts, country brides sometimes got a fawn from a benevolent squire. The haunch was served with the slot or foot intact so the age of the animal could be identified. The meat is 1 star.

Roe deer are compact and elegant natives. They were relegated to the north by the nineteenth century, but possibly reintroduced and have not looked back, multiplying where fallow herds are scarce. The buoyant numbers, coupled with an infuriating appetite, take gardeners to the limit. Do not coppice hazel, plant whips, or grow roses, geraniums, beetroot and runner beans with roe in the vicinity and expect to retain your sanity and humour – unless you take precautions, and consider a neatly nibbled holly hedge a fair swap. The buck is the size of a large dog and has two points on each antler set in a pearly ring, more appreciated by European than English marksmen. The does are independent except when the sexes couple, which, unlike other deer, happens in the spring. They are also monogamous. The meat is light and close-grained with a mild flavour – 1 star.

Sika are the more common of the water deer in England, imported from Asia in the nineteenth century. The number of escapees is increasing in the New Forest and Poole basin, having swum to Purbeck from Brownsea Island on their first night in captivity and commuted ever since. Sika are often mistaken for fallow, but are closer in size and disposition to red deer, with whom they hybridize, endangering the purity of both species, even in Scotland. The stag is an increasingly desirable trophy, with a fine head, now limited to a season. The meat is darker than other types of venison and superior in flavour – 2 star.

Muntjac deer have spread a considerable distance from Woburn Park since they first arrived in the early twentieth century. They are even smaller, shyer and more secretive than roe deer, and almost as tiresome, particularly in ancient woodland, being delicate feeders with a liking for berries and bluebells. The buck has little tusks. I have never seen a live muntjac, nor the fly it attracts, but I did find one dead in my woodshed from causes unknown. My wife and I buried the carcass and, in time-honoured fashion, planted an asparagus bed on top. Muntjac can mate every few months and at any time of year. The meat is increasingly common and is of excellent quality – 2 star.

COOK'S ORACLE

The season for wild stags and bucks is from the start of August until May. Roe bucks, an exception, are shot from April through October. The season for hinds and does is from the start of November until March. Park deer are less restricted. Muntjac are not protected at all. So, the meat of at least two types of deer is permanently available. It has the added fascination of varying between species. Soyer put venison second to turtle in English gastronomy's order of merit, which seems rather mad, but it is free-range, naturally grown, and comes in sufficient quantities to keep home and export markets supplied.

Venison in England was salted down for much of its history, and still is prior to smoking, but is more frequently eaten fresh. It is easier to skin the beast as soon as possible after dispatch, making it lighter to handle in the field, and better for the meat – which can cool more quickly without its jacket on. The guts should also be removed. The liver and kidneys of deer, regarded as the best bits, often go to keepers and hunt servants. If you are lucky enough to get them, fry them in butter.

Farmed deer come to market at about eighteen months. A younger beast need only hang for three or four days, especially in hot or humid weather. An older beast, killed in winter, can be kept for three or more weeks. Suspending a carcass by both legs from hooks or a trivet enables the haunch to acquire its desired and customary shape. Select a dry and airy place for the meat to hang in, preferably a safe that excludes any flies. If the surface begins to sweat, wipe with a vinegar-and-water solution and cook immediately.

Venison is not marbled. In the autumn it can carry surface fat that helps to prevent the meat from drying out, but does not improve the flavour, and congeals at a low temperature. Make sure that gravy goes through a separator, that plates are extra hot, and that people are ready to eat.

The prime cuts of venison, a secret that does not seem to have got out, should be cooked like lamb, i.e. rare or pink, *not overdone*. Grill the chops and serve while still tender to the touch. Oven-roast the saddle and leg or haunch for 15–20 minutes per pound at 180°C /350°F/gas mark 4, basting frequently with dripping. Serve with a jelly.

The secondary cuts, the neck and shoulder, should be cut up into pieces and cooked like stewing beef (see page 118) for 4–6 hours or curried (see page 139).

It is not necessary to marinate venison in wine or buttermilk, an almost automatic habit that England has copied from other European countries. It does not make the meat any more tender and juicy than it is when properly hung and cooked, and may even draw out more juice than it puts in. The original purpose of a marinade was to preserve the flesh in hot weather.

GROUND GAME

Hare: nothing is more unsettling on an afternoon stroll on a path in open country than for a wild animal accused of madness and witchcraft to race towards you at full tilt. The hare drew ever closer. At the last moment it seemed to sense that something was wrong. It stopped – I had already – inclined its head to the right and looked sideways in my direction, then it sped off at right angles into the distance.

Hare have all-round vision, which is part of their defence as a quarry species (unlike man), but suffer from a blind spot straight ahead. They are also built with legs that enable them to run faster up hill than down dale. There is no end of stories about what a hare will do: hold parliaments, box clever and cry like a baby when wounded or threatened.

The mountain hare is native, bluish in summer and white in winter, with an Achilles heel of black tips to the ears that an eagle can pick out in the snow. A modest number are found in the north of England, sharing the Derbyshire Peaks with the moor game, the dippers and the Gritstone sheep. A larger population breeds in the highlands of Scotland, feeding on heather and allied plants, and occasionally resorting to outlying turnip fields. The odd mountain hare is picked off by parties on the way home after they have finished with grouse.

The brown hare is naturalised, a possible Roman introduction from southern Europe and escapee, which provided sport and material for puns used in art[*] and hunting sermons.[**] The number of hares in Victorian England rose with efficient gamekeeping and an increased food supply, only to recede after the Second World War. The leverets, born naked and above ground, fall to biocides, modern machinery, traffic, foxes and undisciplined dogs. The hare population in the Forest, which followed the same routes for at least a hundred years, dwindled with increased public access and the first car parks. With the ban on hunting, it is due to fall in the areas covered by regulated coursing clubs.

As food, hare has a mixed record. It was banned by Leviticus, and classed as a rodent, but reserved for the 'quality' on tenanted land until the Ground Game Act of 1888. Women of sense and sensibility applied powder to their faces with a hare's foot, and liked the rest of the animal cooked whole and set before them, ears erect, teeth bared and sitting on its haunches.

The only blue hare I have seen on the hook, and purchased, was in Salisbury cattle market many years ago. The brown one is larger, more common and similar to eat. An adult buck weighs several pounds and feeds many. He has a rough coat, large yellow teeth and the characteristic hare lip. A leveret is no bigger than a rabbit.

Hare may be shot all year, but not sold in the breeding season. An adult should be hung as long as pheasant, up to three weeks in cold weather, and by the hind legs. A leveret needs only a few days, the meat is as dark as venison and more succulent. The blood is appreciated, as it is with duck. It collects in the breast and may be gathered in a bowl for use in the gravy when skinning and gutting take place, but goes to waste on an animal that is dressed and vacuum-packed. The liver is also worth keeping. Fry.

To stew hare, proceed as for chicken (see page 220), using either the whole beast cut into joints or fore and hind quarters, vegetable water and red wine. The meat should be cooked in about 2 hours. When done whisk in any blood to the sauce. Keep warm, but do not boil or it will curdle.

Recipe from *The Sportsman's Cookery Book:*
For 2: take only the saddle and remove the membrane. Put it in a saucepan, and 'cover it half-way with fresh cream. Add two dessertspoonfuls of red wine vinegar and two tablespoonfuls of finely minced shallots. Cook it on a slow fire for an hour and a quarter, stirring frequently and without dismay if the sauce appears curdled, as this does not make any difference. Do not

---

[*] *The depiction of hare commanding and man obeying, their roles reversed in a medieval setting, commissioned by the Eyre dynasty, is another of my desert island paintings.*

[**] *i.e. 'This is the heir, come let us kill him.'*

add pepper, but salt lightly before serving' (Pollard, 1926). Alternatively, commit to a medium oven for the same period. The meat should be pink. Carve lengthways and serve with mashed potato or noodles.

RABBIT

Rabbit is an everyday event in England, given a cuddly status by Beatrix Potter from which it may never recover. The control of the numbers was 'needless and heartless', said a subscriber to the Avon Advertiser. The flip side is that the creature eats better than Third World babies and contributes enough in crop damage to fund a cottage hospital. On Tophill, Portland, rabbits have a record of burrowing in the quarries, and causing cave-ins and loss of life: they are bringers of bad luck. If a member of the Stone or Mason families met one in the morning, he would turn round and go home.

Rabbits in England have changed from weak to strong, cosseted to carefree, and valuable to valueless. The population had risen to an estimated one hundred million when myxomatosis struck. The disease, a seasonal one carried by fleas and possibly manmade, hit Cornwall in the innocent and unsuspecting summer of 1954. I, aged seven, saw the blind and wretched victims make for the beach and stop, waiting for the tide to end it all. At low water a fortnight on, the foreshore was littered with skeletons stripped and blanched by the sun and sea.

Rabbits were introduced to England via the Scillies by the Normans. The adults, or coneys, a term still used in the fur trade, were farmed by the church in conigries or warrens. The rabbits, brought to a colder climate than they had been used to, were given food to sustain them and hospitable slopes or manmade 'pillow mounds' to burrow into. They were taken with dogs, ferrets and nets, or in pitfalls with revolving doors baited with hay and known as 'tipes'. The harvest of meat was modest by contemporary standards, amounting to only ten rabbits per acre per year, but it more than covered the cost of keeping a warrener. The pelts were valuable too, especially the black ones. The grand fortified lodge, a two-storey keep which rises from the sandy soil of Thetford Forest, housed an important man.

Over the centuries the escapees developed a resistance to the cold and an appetite for the vegetation, and 'bred like rabbits'. With their close and constant nibbling they infuriated farmers, gardeners and heath-dwellers, but helped to create the sward of the South Downs, to control scrub and to provide both town and country with meat. An experienced trapper in the dunes, reading the runs with ease and competing only with short-eared owls, could take two hundred rabbits a day. He stretched them and 'thumbed' them towards the tail (emptying the bladder), then left the gut for foxes and hung the dead around his caravan or piled them in bales ready for the train. The market and way of life held up until after the war.

The blind eye turned by landowners and keepers to poaching rabbits distracted the culprits from precious game. On the same territory today, the creature is more likely to be shot and slung over the hedge than hung from the handlebars of a bike and sold around the villages or cooked in a pub. People should eat wild rabbits, they are too abundant, a healthy feed and, if ever there was one, a free-ranging animal from 'environmentally friendly' conditions. Do not worry about disease. Myxy may repeat, but no infected rabbit is going to interest a game-handler or dealer.

A buck and three does will keep a family in almost as much meat as they need per year. A wild rabbit will feed three to four people – and for the price of half a pint in total. A net kills more cleanly than a gun unless the rabbit is struck well forward. The animal is paunched straight away and hung for no more than a couple of days. Look for a healthy covering of fat around the kidneys. Chop into six: two fore quarters, two legs and the saddle cut in half. Some like to leave the meat in water overnight in order to make it whiter.

Rabbits are available throughout the year. Stew like chicken, expecting drier meat, especially on the saddle, but a better sauce. Go heavily on onions. It is customary to cook the head of the rabbit with the rest (for the extra flavour) and remove it before serving, often with mustard. Alternatively, make into brawn with pork (see page 163). Farmed rabbits, usually imported, are bigger and more expensive than wild ones. They are more tender to eat but can smell stronger.

Squirrel

The life and times of the red one are reasonably well recorded in English history, its fur making warm, useful and colourful hats. A mystery surrounds the depletion of its numbers in the eighteenth century in Scotland and Ireland, to which it was reintroduced, and its preference for coniferous woods in England – which did not exist prior to that date. The population, now protected, is confined to Brownsea Island in Poole Harbour and the environs of Formby (one of the most pleasant seaside golf links).

The grey squirrel, charged with giving the red one a virus, was imported into England in 1876 and, the lesson unlearned, in 1929 (Game, 1999). It is a nasty little chap, a rat needing no protection, cheeky, greedy and vicious when cornered, which plays merry hell on a bird table, ring-barks trees and takes all the nuts in your garden. Brillat-Savarin, the French 'Philosopher in the Kitchen', ate and enjoyed grey squirrel on his visits to America. The USAF wartime personnel in the Forest, stationed at Stoney Cross, ate them too. A restaurant in Brighton used to take a proportion of the many thousands of squirrels evacuated from their dreys and shot in Hampshire.

Do not handle the creature when wounded, and, obviously, skin and gut before cooking. The meat is white, pleasant, 'free range', low in cholesterol, etc., but tastes of surprisingly little for a consumer of nuts. Only the lower back and leg are worth cooking. Allow at least one squirrel per person. Prepare like chicken or rabbit.

CHAPTER SEVENTEEN

GAME: FEATHER

**T**HE END OF A SEASON that seems too short every year. We pulled into the estate cottage for the last time. Paul, a builder and fowler known as 'Hardy', had plucked and waxed, to the minutest feather and wisp of down, the geese and ducks he had shot with us. Each bird was neat and clean as a newly bathed baby, and packed proudly in its own little tray. A message read, 'I have also left the Pintail's final meal in the bags. It has fed on the small snails, but mainly seeds, so should eat well. I hope you have enjoyed yourselves.'

Hardy and I had discussed, amongst every other aspect of wildfowling, the feeding habits of geese and duck in relation to how they tasted. Pintail was one of the birds where varied diet was apparent in its meat.

I also left a message, saying that our lives had changed in two and a half days. From now on, my wife and I would forever look up at the sky on winter mornings and think of the fowl coming over the east of England marshes. We would miss Winnie too, her crinkle-crankle coat, her indifference to the cold, and the four webbed feet that Nature has given to Chesapeake retrievers.

We would remember the seventeen roundabouts on the A12, the gates on the level crossing, the yellow strap of distant street lighting and the lizard of a night train sliding by. The decoys, made at home of roofing felt, were mounted on sticks under cover of the dark, and left shuddering in a bitter wind. A camouflaged net was erected on rods in a muddy ditch filled with water and waving reeds, which became our hope and refuge. The darkness lifted, drip-fed by the dawn, the mystery with it. An icy light brought a rebirth of the land, falling on the fens, farms, churches and wind pumps in between. There was the promise of geese, the threat they might not come, the scouts they sent ahead, and the skeins right and left that descended on the crops beyond the main road. A lull followed, and passing disappointment, arrested by the vast and disturbing cloud, two thousand strong, that rose like giant bees from the waters by the castle, circled and swarmed. Then it made straight for us, cruising overhead in big black squadrons, rippling ribbons, loose threads and sharp silhouettes against the pink and blue board of a January sky. The birds, deceived by Hardy's call, looked and lingered. He raised his gun and fired, shooting one that folded on the wing and spiralled to the earth in the weak morning sun.

Winnie watched the birds in flight, followed their descent, then crashed through the reeds, up the banks and through the thistles, cheered by us, to pick up the fallen from distant clumps of grass. An old man stopped by in a pointed woolly hat, gun under arm and out for a stroll. A labourer followed the long and sweeping drive that led to a lonesome house. We broke and regrouped further down the marsh as the afternoon advanced, searching the splashes for signs left by duck, their down and grazing, finding also the tracks of snipe. We took up positions for the evening flight. The wind mounted and the plover wheeled by in the renewed and bitter cold, failing sun and half-light known as the crack between the worlds. We finished with a torchlit walk through frozen puddles, a full bag from the morning, limit of six, and an empty one from the afternoon. For Hardy, there were two hours' plucking still to do. For us, a bath was waiting, drink in earnest, then dinner and collapse, before another meeting at 4 a.m.

Day two: a giant had lived in the pub by the creek. He appeared in a photo standing on the ground shaking hands with a woman leaning from a first-floor window. A path led over a scaffolders' bridge, through an unlikely patio gate and along raised duckboards into a marsh, lit by the newest of moons and parted by channels where the tide came in. A boat was waiting. Pushed from behind, it slithered down over the mud into an apparent chasm, but only a slick of sea water leaking away. We rowed to a point and round to a desolate island, beaching where you may run in waders, not stop, otherwise you sink. You can also be driven offshore by increasing wind and degenerating weather, and meet an ice-cold death on shifting sands. It had nearly happened to Hardy the week before.

We set up the hide in the boat this time. We prepared for the wait as the mournful cries of curlews, sensing a new day, started up in the dark and cold. I could have done with a nip of sloe gin. My feet were freezing, fingers stinging, and ears only saved by a Deputy Dawg hat left by Father Christmas.

'Bags o' time,' Hardy would say as he settled himself and the glass fell further. 'We got bags o' time. Warm enough, mate?'

Occasionally there would be a little squeak from me.

The temperature dropped before dawn to its lowest, then rose with the sun to bring in a winter's day more like the spring. Hardy opened the bidding with three booming shots that echoed round the marshes and brought birds in tens of thousands up from the ooze and on to the wing. The wigeon and teal raced hither and thither with hundreds of Brent geese, golden plover and flocks of dunlins, or circled and strayed towards the hide. The chances were few compared to the numbers of fowl, the shots on target fewer. The stricken hit the water for Winnie to fetch; the survivors wheeled off. There were shelduck, oystercatchers, whimbrels, and avocets too, both feeding on the pipeweed and flying by, their backs arched and legs clumsily arranged behind them. A seal joined in, rising from the water with its coat as smooth and shiny as a manmade fibre, its whiskers like brushes and face all doe-eyed and beguiling, but ready to fight in defence of its young and drown a dog for the hell of it. By the time the tide had covered the mud and stolen up the gulch, the samphire and sea grass lay basking in the warmth. The marsh was a different place to the one we had arrived in.

The day ended by a wide stretch of river up the coast. John, a courteous and observant red-haired chef employed in a local club, came too. The verges were covered in alexanders, already in leaf, early in the year as it was. A luminous white owl, his black and baleful eyes turned occasionally towards us, was hunting the saltings. A line of pheasant-poppers stood waiting in a field as we took up position below them, two contrasting groups of people, close together, that came under the same banner. Hardy made off in the failing light and falling tide, and vanished. He returned in the dark an hour later, held up his bag and produced from inside, like a rabbit from a hat, the pintail. He had fired one shot and hit the one duck, the only duck I had never tried.

The following morning we met at the usual time. For the third time in three days I did not know where I was and could not see. The pub and houses at the water's edge were dark as the hour. John, the chef, and Dave, another builder, came too. The five of us piled into dinghies unloaded off the cars, and started rowing with the tide but against the wind into an increasingly choppy river. We made for a single twinkling light set amongst trees – it was impossible to tell how far away – and a sea wall with a field beyond in which the geese liked to roost. The banks were low and dark, the water was inky and the silence broken only by the lapping of oars, the rolling of rowlocks and the odd call of an early bird.

Dave tired. John took over. He did not look like an athlete – but how that man could row! He dipped the oars with no apparent effort or bodily movement, talking as he did so, and never even paused to catch his breath. With the three of us and a dog in the boat, and a dinghy trailing, he rowed and rowed past tiny promontories, little coves and the bend in the river until we came to the other side. We beached and took up positions. The party split up, the others moving on and out of sight.

John remained with us. His father, a local police chief, used to shoot the foreshore before him, then go to the pub, lean his gun against the bar and sink a pint, while his dog warmed itself by the fire. His brief as a chef, John said, was to obtain the best ingredients and do his utmost not to bugger them up. He ate game all the winter, spun for bass in the summer and spoke of a vicar who did the same, giving away fish to fortunate parishioners.

The geese, disturbed by gunners, farmers or walkers the previous evening, never came. They had gone elsewhere: that was wildfowling for you. Only two birds flew over, and from behind us, one of which John, swivelling right, brought down with his second barrel. The bird crashed into the river too far from the shore for the dog to fetch, drifted into deeper water and started moving down on the current towards the sea. John ran down the foreshore and went after it in the boat. It took him several minutes to reach where the goose had been, by which time it was a quarter of a mile downstream, hidden by the waves and almost impossible to see. He rowed and rowed – he would never catch it, but on and on he rowed, plying the oars in even and economic strokes, his large frame and small dinghy getting ever smaller.

It was against the backdrop of a lonely farm, outlying fields and church tower that had come into view with the light that John found the goose on the far bank of the river. He brought it on board aided by the dog, and started to row back against the current, silently encouraged by me. He beached the dinghy as Paul and Dave returned half an hour later, held up the bird, then disembarked and brought it up the foreshore.

John had risen in the dark and cold, like us, then rowed for three miles to shoot a goose and a couple more to fetch it. Next week he would cook the bird, then sit down to eat it with a glass or two of his favourite red wine and perhaps another two of whisky.

'There's nothing wrong in that,' he said, 'is there?'

We returned to the slipway in the light, finding beach huts, a yacht club and signs of life where there were none before. We hauled out the dinghies, loaded them up and prepared to re-enter the mainstream of the new millennium. Later, I met Hardy in the plucking shed and chose the pick of the wildfowl he had done. How to shop, taken to the limit. My conscience was as clear as it could be for a paid-up petrolhead, cat-owner, and member of a race that is wilfully destructive and would rather not know. The birds I bought were scarcely a pinprick in the population. They had enjoyed a longer, better and freer life than the factory-farmed animals killed out of sight, had fed more naturally, and tasted like it.

Wildfowling: For all the aggression and abuse they can get, fowlers are an observant, grounded and reflective bunch, good naturalists and great ornithologists. They are conscious of the age-old hunter-gatherer lying dormant in the rest of us, but unafraid to move on. I asked one fowler where he shot. He replied with the number of a motorway exit, where the Germans had dropped bombs, leaving craters that filled with water and became duck ponds.

Wildfowlers must be up early and out late, hardy, stealthy, patient, aware of wind and tides and quick to tell one duck from another, to open fire or – as a protected species – let it go. The law is clear and the responsibility clearer. I have known people commit fraud, drive dangerously and threaten murder, but never known a gunner wilfully kill a bird that is not a legal target and in season. They have a compassionate side too. In continuous frosts, when shooting is suspended and everyone else is warm at home, fowlers will go out and feed the duck. In spring they monitor nesting sites. In summer they watch the young. It may be hard for many to understand, but it is also an approach to farming more sympathetic than the one most of us subscribe to.

Fowling is as old an occupation as fishing, and an habitual quest for food carried out in every accessible wood, waste and marsh for centuries before the gun arrived. It provided meat for all classes in medieval England's pecking order, but, like many rural and commonplace activities, hardly got a mention from men of letters. If it were not for a handful of writers like

Markham and Willughby, who is buried in Southwell's magnificent cathedral (do not miss evensong), we would know nothing about fowling, the birds caught for table or cage, and by what ingenious methods.

Fowlers were providers and pot hunters: shepherds, labourers, longshoremen, fen tigers and amphibians, whose lives and occupations brought them within sight, sound and striking distance of pocket money or dinner. They knew from experience, watchfulness and the bush telegraph where birds fed, roosted and collected for migration and how they behaved when trapped or under pressure: the ones that played dead or threw their voices (corncrake), pretended to be crippled (partridge, plover), or struck at the eyes of an unwary man or boy (heron, bittern).

My first trap consisted of the usual bait, box and pull rope. I caught a blue tit, which clawed me nastily, and thought twice before trying it again. In addition to such elementary devices, fowlers used an assortment of 'gins' (engines), nets and snares, stalking horses, blinds and bird lime (a glue made from mistletoe) to an end almost certain of success. Victims could panic and fly off, but, with exceptions, did not wise up or learn to avoid a commotion, acted as predicted, and were 'caught by their own curiosity' (Collins, 1876) day and night. A fowler needed only to know where partridge lay up after dark and, by holding up a lantern and ringing a bell, he could drive them into captivity. He took fledglings tethered to their nests and fed to table weight by dutiful parents. He took plover, duck and geese with whistles, calls and decoys, live and artificial. He took an owl with a counterfeit mouse, and the birds that came to mob it. He took the fish that an osprey caught for its young.

Hawking: For the rich, there were grander pursuits than fowling. Hunting was one (see page 186). Hawking was another, a two-tiered occupation possibly as costly in time and money.

The dark-eyed longwings, the hawks 'noble', made high flights in open country. They were trained by a falconer to provide sport first, in this case a thrilling spectacle and good gallop, and food second. The aloof and aristocratic peregrine was the most desired of native birds. Hobbies, merlins and kestrels were elegant trifles.

The golden-eyed shortwings, the hawks 'ignoble', made quick, impulsive flights in or near woodland. They were trained by an austringer (from the French *autoursier*) to provide food first and sport if at all. The powerful goshawk was the best of the pot hunters and 'cook's birds', a sparrowhawk useful to have in reserve.

The small number of birds that showed spirit, and responded to investment or intervention, were entitled game and conceded by the king to favourites and the Church. The list maintained a long association with pheasant and partridge, but gained and lost members over the centuries, including swans, and possibly kite and heron, the highest of flyers and mightiest of targets valued for hawking. The remainder were fair game and free for all – a complement of over five hundred species freely available to anyone for cooking or selling.

The record gets stuck with *The Book of St Albans*, which coupled hawks to rank. It is not a favourite with the experts. Nor (I guess) are its 'terms of art for carving', though they do shed light on what went down in Tudor England. There does not seem to have been any such thing as a fowl unfit for the table, any fear, prejudice or sentiment to compromise their edibility or create a taboo.

The rich ate a wide range of both game and fair game, favouring ruff, dotterel, knot, wheatear, lark, the thrush family and greenfinches (a plump and greedy little chap, I have noticed), in addition to birds cooked today. The poor ate what they could, large or small, thin, greasy, or fishy in coastal communities, and sent the pick of the bunch to market or up to the manor. 'A curlew lean or a curlew fat carried twelvepence on its back', as the East Anglian saying went, and not long ago. Half curlews were the waders that fetched sixpence. Captives, finished on scraps and dairy wash, were sold as 'fed'. First-feather birds, cooked with their feet on to advertise their age, realised twice the price of adults.

In Lincolnshire, Cambridgeshire and Sussex, fortunes were made from the proceeds of a self-regulating trade in fowls that did not prove unsustainable, however brisk, until man invaded their nesting sites, cleared their woods or drained their bogs for his own use. The fens were ague-ridden reed beds and marshes crossed on stilts that sheltered the spotted crake and crepuscular bittern. The flood plains of rivers were swamps where the harrier could hunt. The Downs had an inn and at least two farms named after bustards. There were butcher birds in thickets, land rail in the corn and cranes overhead. The days and nights were undisturbed, and the summer evenings silent but for the incessant shrieks, whistles, hoots, trills, churrs, croaks, booms, and the eerie whaup of the stone curlew, which, in spite of all the heartfelt concern for animal welfare, I have only heard once in fifty-eight years.

Shooting: The goalposts moved in the seventeenth and eighteenth centuries. The 'haves' embraced shooting and dogging, armed with muzzle-loading guns on stands, which, clumsy as they were, marginalised hawking. They also acquired property through enclosure and drainage, and planted with quickthorn and buckthorn as much to keep the public out as livestock in. The Forest laws decayed and game laws replaced them, creating little princelings where there was one prince before (Camden). The 'have nots', deprived of the right to take birds on former common and marsh, took them anyway. The offences multiplied with every new estate and poaching entered a golden era.

An undercover market took off, supplied by conniving inns and coach-drivers, particularly from the Great North Road catchment area, which provided game in abundance and a quick getaway for handlers. The authorities and clergy were complicit, and consumers in London addicted to the frisson of food from a country estate that was not legal tender. United sullenly against their landlords, the poor worked with great effrontery and none of the merriment implied in 'The Lincolnshire Poacher'. Game was less likely to be noticed than a stolen sheep, more abundant, and increasing with the growth of corn and improvements in agriculture: an invitation in a violent age. Skirmishes were common and mantraps used. The 'Black Acts' made crimes committed by night a capital offence. So was the sentence for raising arms to a keeper. You may as well, as the ballad went, kill him.

The mood changed again in the nineteenth century. The law started to relax. The sale of game was legalised. Poachers turned keepers with legitimate money to be made, swelling their numbers to over twenty thousand. Guns were licensed, ending hedge-popping, and making a stroll a less hazardous occupation. The integrated cartridge with standardised shot and a percussion cap, made for breech loaders, enabled men to fire more quickly, more successfully and also more safely. There was no need to look down the barrel to see (surprisingly common, by all accounts) what had happened to your charge.

The old school ranted against the feeble demand on man's abilities of a shotgun compared to a flintlock, and the meat on the table peppered from close range. A structure was called for and put in place. A new and exclusive sport emerged with driven birds, which was tailor-made for the increasing number of prestigious estates. It provided something to do at house parties, required skill, and presented men at arms in warrior posture and uniforms, clasping the most beautiful mixture of walnut and steel ever engraved by English craftsmen, for women to admire.

The shared use of guns brought game shots and pot hunters briefly together in enthusiasts like Colonel Peter Hawker.* Fowling then reverted to a fringe activity for gentlemen, practised by Cambridge undergraduates (Trevelyan, 1944), rough diamonds and latent hunter-gatherers, or continued with professionals in punts and on mud pattens (Gilpin, 1798). The occupation might have died out, since most of the fowlers were landless, but continued on friendly farms, tidal reaches and reserves acquired by the clubs. The bag went to waterside cottages or the London train.

The ancestral nets, traps and tricks were superseded by the gun, then gradually prohibited, reducing targets to birds that were compatible with shot. The ones that were easily blown to pieces, and troublesome to prepare, vanished from English kitchens. For over 95 per cent of

---

* Colonel Peter Hawker: a landowner, overgrown adolescent and a Peninsular War victim – active, curious and easily drawn into feuds. Hawker went down as the last and greatest of the flintlock gunners and the father of modern game shooting. He was not a bad musician either.

species complete protection followed in the twentieth century, or at least the partial protection of a close season.

The term 'game' is today used loosely to describe any quarry species, but confined in law to the pheasant family and covered by the latest Game Act. The remnants of fair game come under the Wildlife and Countryside Act of 1981. They comprise duck and geese, or wildfowl, selected waders, curiosities and vermin. Over twenty birds may legally be shot. Of these about six are star performers and a further six worth cooking.

Tastes have changed with the law, availability of food, and conditioning. In some cases it has happened slowly, in others not at all. The distinction between sport and pot hunting in game shooting and wildfowling continues to exist. They also determine who eats what. It is remarkable, because of their different status, how many people, including farmers, have never tasted pheasant, and how many 'sahibs' have never tasted a pink-footed goose. Meanwhile, with the mutual consent of landlord and tenant, sporting rights continue to be exercised. In at least two cases I know of, one a solicitor, their abolition over a century ago has yet to register.

Shooting, a matter on which the RSPB is 'neutral', has proved as good for conservation as it has for the English kitchen, the Exchequer and the economy. A ban may be on the horizon, but is not yet on the agenda. Between gunners and twitchers there is a truce, albeit a bad-tempered one at times. All the quarry species are on the increase, except where they have fallen foul of biocides, pollution, disturbance and development.

GAME BIRDS

The *Gallinae*; related to the Asian jungle fowl and farmyard hen. I have given the birds a 1–3 star rating based on flavour.

Pheasant: *Phasianus colchicus*: a native of Colchis, home of the Golden Fleece and modern Georgia, a probable Roman escapee and subsequent reintroduction to England. Originally a marsh-dweller, it has long since adapted to the woods. There are many strains of birds, from gaudy to dark green, which fly fast but not too fast, high but not too high, and make a large, inviting target. They are easily reared. If keeping pheasants magnified class divisions in the countryside and caused the destruction of their alleged predators (Rackham, 1986), it also provided a rival crop that 'limited the excesses of prairie farming' and helped the rural economy. Pheasants are compliant in their own fate, conspicuous and unwise. They do not have any road sense either: keep a penknife in the car to dispatch the wounded. A boy at my school claimed to have shot birds on corps days by loading his army-issue .303 with a blank and a pencil. The meat is subsidized by the cost of joining a syndicate, is often wasted, and varies owing to the wide distribution of pheasants and the difference in their diet: cheap and versatile – 1 to 2 star.

Grey partridge: a plump little cracker, brave, bonny, spirited, loyal and a native in soft colours. The hen will fight off crow, fox or cat at breeding time, and share her pretty nest; the cock will incubate the eggs in her absence. The young form into coveys, then pair off. After falls of snow on bright nights in open fields you may see them clustered together for warmth and security or 'jugging'. The rarefied 14-bore was the premier gun for partridge, the opening day of the season one of the most important in the calendar. Birds lived off the 'emmett heaps' opened up by badgers on permanent pasture until the corn subsidy levelled the landscape. The adults need insects, and the fledglings need more, so biocides have taken a heavy toll. Bags of a thousand dwindled to less than a hundred and kept falling. The 'common' partridge is no longer common; it is modestly shot at present and does not respond to management, but is getting some of the help it needs, and to good effect in places. The meat, very delicate, is outstanding – 3 star.

French or red-legged partridge: of Mediterranean origin, it has been introduced to England on more than one occasion since the seventeenth century. It is half the grey partridge in terms of charm and bottle, but larger, more promiscuous, unwilling to travel and easier to rear. A covey occupied the roundabout on the A9 outside Perth in Scotland until a few years ago. The number of birds now reaching the market is considerable, accounting for their modest price. The meat is not bad – 2 star.

Red grouse: with his furry trousers, crimson eyebrows and indignant babble, this is a type of willow grouse peculiar to England, Wales and Scotland. He is also cult. The promise of 'heather, feather and weather' (Payne Galwey) and the prospect of hitting a target that can reach 90 m.p.h. downwind have combined to make the Twelfth 'Glorious' and the most cachet-ridden day in the sporting calendar. The number of grouse is well known to fluctuate. It rose with scrub clearance and controlled burning of moorland in the nineteenth and twentieth centuries, but has fallen since the pre-war bag at Broomhead in Yorkshire (owned by the Wilsons of Sheffield, a tribe of great amateur cricketers) gained its place in the *Guinness Book of Records*. The causes are said to include worms; an increase in predators, notably peregrine falcons and hen harriers; and the flocks of sheep introduced to moorland that compete for food and bear a transmissible tick. The situation may improve when farm subsidies are lifted. Their diet of purple shoots and berries makes grouse one of the finest birds to eat, regardless of where it comes from – 3 star.

Black grouse and grey hen occupy the margins where moorland, woodland and farmland meet, coming down off the tops and over the trees in a cold winter and in the autumn to snaffle the corn. He, almost glossy, has a fan tail and displays at a springtime 'lek', while she, modest and retiring, feigns indifference. Up north, black game were sometimes known as moorcock, down south as heath poults. At one time they inhabited every county in England, including Middlesex, and have given their name to pubs in Durham, Derbyshire, Lancashire and Somerset, but they have dwindled to nothing in age-old strongholds, retaining a close season in Hampshire by default. The blackcock, which my stepfather remembered on the Quantocks, vanished during the war when the area was used as a tank training ground. Their attempted reintroduction to the New Forest did not work and never will, thanks to the pressure of the human population and the number of dog-walkers. The survivors are confined to the dales of the Goyt and Tees and to Wales and Scotland, and are of more interest to bird-watchers than gunners.

White grouse or ptarmigan, which turn brown or grey in summer, occur on the shale above two thousand feet. Confident in its own camouflage and unused to man, it is very tame. I saw one on the hook in Leadenhall Market many years ago. Ptarmigan used to be trapped in pitfalls dug in the snow and baited, which the victim once in could not escape from. The bird still enjoys a game season in Scotland, but an academic one, being on the edge of its range and threatened by global warming.

Of the former game birds, the wood grouse (capercaillie), corncrake and quail are protected, though Chinese quail are farmed – I have served them impaled on a swordstick. The bustard has been extinct in England since the end of the nineteenth century. A second attempt to reintroduce it has been made on Salisbury Plain. You may go and have a peep at certain times of year.

Wildfowl

Duck come from a large and amusing family with a mixture of habits and coats of many colours in the drakes. The females lack the dress. They range in size from a goose to a thrush. The best walkers are not the best swimmers, and vice versa. The majority feed by night and roost by day on salt or fresh water, flighting to and fro at dawn and dusk. The imposition of a ban on netting wildfowl when they are flightless and in the moult, which took effect in the seventeenth century, was one of the first parliamentary acts of nature conservation. Decoy ponds or 'pipes', a Dutch idea based on a canine lure, which are now illegal too, were dug in the same period to supply duck in feather for the country markets and London train. The modus operandi is explained in detail in the opening pages of Wilkie Collins' romantic novel *The Two Destinies*.

Duck provide the most varied range of birds for wildfowlers and cooks in England, but being mostly omnivorous and driven by the weather, they vary more than other birds. The pick of the bunch are dabblers, grazers and gleaners, predominantly vegetarian, which have fed in the stubble or on barley provided by gunners. The divers are stronger medicine, especially if they have been in salt water. The crop of a duck will tell you how he has been feeding and what to expect. Fat is a good sign. There are nine quarry species, which happen to be the fastest on the wing. Of these, seven may be sold and five are recommended.

Wild duck, or mallard: the best known of the tribe. The drake has a bottle-green head, and insignia. One is a credit to the other. The female appears in the paper every year, crossing a road with her young while a policeman holds up the traffic, and covers her nest sadly with down when she deserts. They are a talkative and sociable pair, easily led, fed and tamed, and thus became domesticated. The wild duck's diet varies from grain and berries to shellfish in the creek-dwellers: for meat 2–3 star.

Teal drakes have striking chestnut heads and green eyebands, and emit a short whistle. They are the smallest and most nimble of the duck, plump little ground-huggers and speed merchants who jilt, flinch, land with precision and 'spring' from the water, giving them their collective title. Teal are amongst the most abundant of duck, but not an easy target and so are in short supply. Their preferred diet is seeds, including those of marsh samphire, and their breast is disproportionately deep for their size. The meat, a luxury, is 2–3 star.

Pintail drakes have a long pheasant's tail, which the females lack, and an attenuated white neck visible in flight. They are slender and elegant with an acute profile – *Anas acuta*. Numbers are healthy, though not as visibly as some of the other duck. As food, pintail are regarded as the poorest of wildfowl, and also the finest, according to whether they have been amongst the sea snails or gleaning barley and linseed. The fat, when present, can be translucent and buttery: 1–3 star.

Wigeon drakes have a rust-coloured head, silver-grey plumage and a white front. Their call, a longer whistle than teal, is mimicked by fowlers. The females purr. They collect in rafts of thousands, ride rough seas, walk well and run fast. Wigeon used to be known as half duck, being half the price of mallard, and equally variable. They like to graze or glean, which makes them fat and white of skin, but resort in cold spells to mud-sifting, making them lean and brown: 1–3 star.

Gadwall[*]: are sober-looking duck, dressed like a female mallard but smaller. Originally migrants, they were pinioned and encouraged to breed. These birds do not cause much of a stir, but eat well: 1–2 star.

---

* There is a prohibition on the sale of these birds.

Of the remainder, pochard, with their red heads and bluish skin, are the best of the divers. Tufted duck, the black and white ones, are more to ask of modern palates. Shoveller have an undulating flight, a spatulate bill and delicate meat, but a strong smell which some people find offensive. Goldeneye* is fishy and usually avoided.

WILD GEESE*

Geese have a muscular build, a swan's neck, and a flight of consistent power. They migrate long distances at great heights, and commute from salt or fresh water at dawn and dusk like duck, but feeding by day rather than by night. An airborne flock is a commanding skein, a grounded one a restless and wary gaggle that takes off at the slightest provocation. For centuries there were more manageable birds to trap and easier ones to go after. If a goshawk was indeed a goose-hawk, it did not do much for the reputation of a wild-goose chase.

The extent to which geese were and are eaten by country people is not part of mainstream history. The quantity rose with the shotgun in the nineteenth century, stabilising with the restricted number of quarry species in 1954, and modest bag limits. The huge flocks of birds now coming to East Anglia for the intensive crops, and their pestilential habits, have not yet caused the law to change. Until they do, in order to get in on the secret of 'flying beef' and first cousin to swan, you must either befriend or become a fowler.

Wild geese are vegetarians and greedy ones, whose diet includes grass, grain and sugar beet. They dress neatly for a bird that looks so large and formidable in feather, and have the same advantage over farmyard geese as the mallard over domestic duck: a deeper breast on a smaller frame, and superior meat. Wild geese are preferred by fowlers to mallard or wigeon and are less variable to eat. A total of four may be shot, one black and feral, the rest grey. In descending order of merit, they are:

Canada geese*: imported as ornaments three hundred years ago, these are the largest of the targets and the one you are mostly likely to encounter at present. They migrate around England, honking in flight, and have established patterns that any wild goose would be proud of. The Canada geese in Regent's Park will commute over the rooftops and out of London every day in order to feed. Their meat, to which I was introduced in Baltimore, is highly rated by fowlers in America. Wounded birds have been known to attack, a fearsome sight in the half-light with a mist coming down. A youngish one weighs about five pounds when dressed: 2–3 star.

---

* There is a prohibition on the sale of these birds.

Pink-footed geese[*] are as described, with a brown head and neck and another honk of a call which carries for miles. They arrive in East Anglia every year up to 50,000 strong, clean up favoured spots including old potatoes, then leave to breed in the Arctic Circle. A youngish bird weighs about three pounds when dressed for the table: 2 star.

White-fronted geese[*] have a small white facial patch around the bill, orange legs and black pectoral bars acquired with age. Their call has occasioned the ornithologist's nickname of 'laughing goose'. They will consort with pinks, but are more of a marsh-feeder, with gamier meat, yellower fat and a smaller carcass. A youngish bird weighs a couple of pounds when dressed for the table: 2 star.

Greylag geese[*] have pink legs and an orange bill. The 'lag' is a possible corruption of 'lake' or 'lea', or what it implies: a dawdler, slowcoach and reluctant migrant. This bird is larger and more approachable than the other geese, and so became the farmyard goose and watchdog. The greylag bred in England until comparatively recently (see page 225). It is not considered the best goose to eat, but worth a shot. A youngish bird weighs about four pounds when dressed for the table: 1– 2 star.

WADERS

Woodcock have boot-button eyes, bracken-coloured plumage and such confidence in their own camouflage that they will freeze in the silliest and most obvious of places. Cock are credited with many eccentricities, from rotating on their nest to carrying young. In summer they embark on a punctual, eerie, owlish and mysterious flight to distant haunts and back, croaking all the way, their long bill pointing earthwards: the occupation is called roding. Migrants collect in France every year for a favourable gale (or allegedly boat) to help them to England. Birds gain weight as the season progresses, rise silently and keep low, seldom permitting an early shot. A prize for killing two woodcock with a right and a left was awarded by Bols, the manufacturer of liqueurs until 1983. Sir Francis Chantry, sculptor, did it with one charge. A monument to this unique achievement was erected in 1829. The pen feathers, proudly worn, used to go to limners. Leg (i.e. remove each leg plus tendons) in the field. The meat is a taste that is unlikely to be acquired, but a sexy and evocative one to those who know it: 3 star.

Common snipe are flashes of white and brown, up and away quickly, tilting and screeching as you invade their bog or marsh. They are like diminutive woodcock, equipped with the longest

---

_* *There is a prohibition on the sale of these birds.*

bill of any English bird. The sensitive tip enables them to seek out food, leaving tiny holes in the mud next to the delicate imprint of their feet. Numbers have suffered from drainage and the deterioration of water quality in certain areas, but have held up in millions near the Wash. In summer snipe take to the afternoon sky and 'drum' overhead, a sound created by the passage of wind through their tail feathers. In winter they glide not quite silently in on the wind to feed. The flocks are called wisps. A trio, held between the fingers of one hand, is a 'finger'. A snipe was the first bird I ever had to myself as a child and the one I would choose for my last supper, preferably in triplicate: 3 star.

Golden plover have the characteristic bill and legs of other waders, but a golden speckled mantle and a black horseshoe breastplate. They feed on the estuaries in winter and often come up to the downs and moors in summer, consorting with other waders, notably the dunlin or 'plover's page'. Goldies are fast and unanimous in flight, swishing to and fro like radar on a screen, but diving towards danger in suicidal response to being shot at. To minimise the chance of hitting each other, gunners used to stand in pairs, back to back, for plover. Bags are negligible, but the meat is 3 star.

Curiosities and Vermin

The woodpigeon or ring dove, which acquires its ring after one year, is the commonest of a loved and loathed partly protected family. It is heavily armoured, strong on the wing, wary, rapacious, and seems to benefit from all man's endeavours to grow food, good and bad. Pigeons are capable of laying two eggs in any month up to four times a year. Guns can kill a hundred a day per head without making any apparent difference to the locust-like clouds that descend on corn, crops, clover and beech mast. Most of the birds shot in England go to France.

Woodpigeon accounts for nearly all the dove eaten today in England, small as the quantity is, owing perhaps to the variable condition of birds and the damage done by overcooking them. Country people tend not to eat adult pigeons unless they are pampered and 'plump on stolen corn' (Hartley, 1954) gleaned in the summer and autumn. Even so, squabs of up to four months old, identified by their pink rather than red feet, are superior. Birds acquire their characteristic ring after one year. The feathers are easily removed. The skin is dispensable. The breasts should be detached and cooked. The meat, when pink, is worth a star.

The rock dove is an habitué of cliffs and ledges that nests with the gulls at sites like Flamborough Head. It is also the progenitor of the carriers, fantails, tumblers, jacobins and the rest, so easily handled and housed, that have been of much use as messengers and a delight to fanciers. The rock's homing instinct and turn of speed are its greatest assets. The Lincoln Blue, the swiftest, was used as a target at London gun-club meetings in the Victorian and Edwardian periods –

a catholic mixture of high and low life with much heavy betting. Escapees flew off to populate the railway stations and Trafalgar Square; the casualties were eaten. Feral pigeons are still legitimate food, but dropped off the menu when banned as live targets after the Great War.

The rock inhabited the approximately twenty-five thousand humble, grand and architectural pigeon houses dotted around England. A large number were located in Northamptonshire (Fuller). Until the agricultural revolution, dove provided landlords with some of the only fresh meat besides venison on tap throughout the year, and their eggs were protected, but at the cost of the surrounding crops. The grumbling of farmers and gardeners, and increased supplies of butcher's meat, caused nearly all dovecotes to be abandoned in the nineteenth century. I have known only one from which birds were taken, which was circular in shape and equipped with its original ladder. The light inside was restful as a church, the cooing muted, and the stench enough to lift the lantern from the roof. The dung, which has been used to make saltpetre, is higher in potash than any other fertiliser.

The collared dove is the second tamest member of its family, and the latest arrival, having swept across Europe in the 1950s and 60s. You may shoot and eat it, but few bother on account of its defencelessness, modest size and low rating as a pest.

Here is a recipe for pigeon, as cooked by Germaine Greer while a student at Cambridge (*Daily Telegraph*, 12 February 2005):

> Buy three or four pounds [of fresh peas] and shell them . . . pack . . . thickly basted birds breast down in a baking dish and then bury them in peas, pour over an inch or two of rock salt and shove them in a medium oven for as long as . . . necessary. Take the dish out [half an hour before serving] and let it sit. The fun was to break the crystalline salt crust and smell the rich aroma, as each little bird was lifted, placed on a sippet and surrounded with the essence of melted pea.

Rooks are merciless and sinister-looking creatures, which occasionally call a parliament and impeach a member, and banish the wounded from their nests. They are also soothing to wake up to, hear overhead and see blowing around the sky. To 'go and watch the rooks of Trelawne' was Quiller Couch's answer to a troubled mind. The population is stable, but suffers in spring gales, and had to relocate in many parts of England after Dutch elm disease. Rook-shooting takes place in the first two weeks of May. The adults are scattered with 12-bores, leaving the branchers (the young) for the table. A powerful air gun is the weapon of choice. One of the former rook rifles was a .3 with a hexagonal barrel used in the Boer war. The appropriate rimfire cartridge is no longer made.

It is customary to remove the breasts of birds in the field, and leave the carcasses for foxes and badgers to clear up. The meat may be steeped in milk or buttermilk overnight. Rook pies are re-emerging, but in a few cases never went away. One West Country butcher, who sells all he can produce, has made them throughout his life and in the most traditional of guises – with the feet sticking out. Pies come in two forms. They can be a steak and kidney type, covered with shortcrust pastry, or hand raised in a hot-water crust for eating cold. Recipes tend to contain equal amounts of rook and stewing beef, rabbit or bacon, pre-cooked until tender.

Coot and moorhen* are still occasionally shot and given to ferrets. They have long since made an exit from even local diets as far as I know, but did come in handy when food was short and rose in price during rationing. Moorhen, a corruption of 'mere-hen', an amphibious corncrake. Used to be highly rated as food, they are better to eat than coot.

My neighbour in Dorset, the late Sid Newman, in common with the rest of his village, used to trap sparrows in a cage activated by a bramble, which he called a 'nicky van'. He also netted them under the eaves of cottages at night. House sparrows, regarded as a nuisance, fetched 1d each from the Ministry during the war: the scheme was colloquially known as the Sparrow Club. You sent up the feet and kept the breasts for the pot. There was not much on a 'spadger', but, as Sid confirmed, 'you might have bugger all else to eat'.

COOK'S ORACLE

Game birds and wildfowl are shot over the autumn and winter though the dates of their seasons can vary. Grouse are first in during August. Goose and duck from below the high water mark are last out in February. Birds can be cooked the day they are shot, but are usually hung as killed, one at a time, in a cool, dark, airy meat safe or larder, at least until rigor passes off. The rule is to suspend a fowl from the neck, though there are exceptions. In the fat years a cock pheasant was hung by a single tail feather, and when he dropped to the ground you ate the hen (a high bird indeed). The female of any species is smaller than the male and regarded as superior.

Hanging game and wildfowl is an art that is better understood in England than in any other country I have been to, including France, where the mode of preparation is perhaps more important. There is an optimum but variable time for most birds to hang, decided generations ago. A badly shot fowl does not keep, especially in the Indian summers and muggy winters we are now getting, except in a cold room. When the feathers are easily removed from the legs it is ready to eat. Beyond such vague if established facts, there are no ways of telling whether a

---

* Another bird which may not be resold.

bird would be better hung for a few more days or not, no scientific aids and consequently no regulations to enlighten or burden you. Environmental Health is short of information on game and steers clear of it, leaving us all free to decide how fresh or high we want our meat.

All birds should be plump and well rounded over the breast. The first frosts can produce a natural fat, but a prolonged cold spell is debilitating. The pheasant family excels when it has come from the wild, fed itself and is not too fat. Duck and pigeon are the reverse – better from feeding.

Dressing a bird yourself is a chore, but worth a free dinner. Pluck from the neck down. Either do it in the garden or on a walk, scattering the feathers, or into a bin bag. Remove the head, neck, windpipe and, without breaking it, the crop. From the other end, cut round the vent, put your hand inside the cavity and pull out the entrails. Reserve the neck, liver and gizzard, sliced open and washed, for stock. Singe the bird with a lighted candle and wipe all over with a scalding cloth.

Woodcock, snipe and plover, which do not carry food in the manner of other birds, and shit on take-off, need not be drawn as they are eaten guts and all.

A good game-dealer takes the pick of the birds, plucks them mechanically without tearing the skin, and waxes the wildfowl to remove the down. The premium is well worth paying.

Young birds are more delicate to eat than old ones, softer in the beak and more sober in colour, but difficult to tell from adults when dressed for the table – and most of them are, today.

GAME AT A GLANCE

	Hang (days)	Oven roast (minutes at 180°C/350°F/gas mark 4)	Grill	Fry (minutes – breasts)
Pheasant	Up to 14	30	–	10 (skinned)
Partridge, Eng.	3	15	10	–
Partridge, Fr.	3	20	10	–
Grouse	6	20	–	–
Mallard	3	25	–	–
Wigeon	3	25	–	–
Pintail	3	25	–	–
Teal	3	15	10	–
Wild goose	14	40 +	–	–
Woodcock	7	15	–	–
Plover	7	15	–	–
Snipe	7	10	–	–
Pigeon, dove	2	–	–	5–10 (skinned)

The age of game matters, though not as much as the treatment you give it: the important thing is not to cook birds too quickly or for too long, otherwise the meat will dry out.

Game is one of those foods that can do it for you. There are recipes galore, but nothing so good as a bird in prime condition treated with restraint. All game birds and wildfowl are excellent cold, in particular partridge, grouse, the duck family and wild geese.

Spit roasting

A horizontal spit is the easiest to use and was the commonest. The smaller birds, stacked nose to tail, were 'shown the fire'. The fatter ones, like geese and duck, were self basting.

'Canard au sang', English version, a wigeon caught in decoys and roasted on a spit, preceded by oysters, were two of the local treats served at the Essex Coursing Club's annual meeting in the King's Arms, Southminster, during the 1880s (the building is still there: you can imagine the menu). One fowl per person was *de rigueur*. The 'recipe', reproduced by Harding Cox, correspondent for *The Field*, was as follows:

> You wring the bird's neck, then cut an incision in the skin and lay a piece back all round. With one quick stroke you . . . chop off the head and sew the skin over, without allowing a drop of blood to escape. The bird must be drawn very quickly and the place instantly sewn up. Ten minutes before a hot fire and the trick is done. When dissected the flesh is quite blue, but no one who has eaten wigeon as . . . described will ever care for them done in any other way.

Alternatively, take any type of wildfowl. Hang it by the legs, so that the blood collects in the chest, tipping it into a bowl when dressing the bird. Oven-roast and make a gravy, as usual, and remove from the heat. Whisk in the blood along with any that has collected inside the carcass. Heat the sauce through, but do not boil otherwise it will curdle. Rich as Croesus.

Oven roasting

Rashers of bacon, draped over pheasant and French partridge, kept in place with toothpicks, help the breasts to keep pace with the legs and also to remain reasonably moist. The precaution should not be necessary with other birds. Feel the meat occasionally and remove from the oven when just firm to the touch.

Grilling

Use English or French partridge, brushed with butter, or teal. Either 'spatchcock' birds, i.e. cut down the back (I use garden secateurs) and open out, or cut in half. Cook until just firm.

FRYING

When using pheasant and pigeon, melt some butter in a pan. Cook the breasts over a gentle heat, turning two or three times: the little fillet will detach itself and cook more quickly – put to one side. The meat is done after a few minutes while still a little tender to the touch. Alternatively, cover in flour, egg and breadcrumbs and deep fry.

When using the duck family, commit the breasts to a hot, dry frying pan, skin side down. Brown until the fat runs, turn down the temperature and cook on the other side until just firm.

Partners: Game chips, home-made crisps, swede, parsnips, sprouts, laver with all game birds. Celery and celeriac with pheasant. Cabbage with partridge.

Bread sauce: for pheasant, partridge and grouse. Always make sufficient. Sweat a small chopped onion or shallot in a little butter in a pan. Tear up or liquidise a quarter to half the crumb of a small white loaf, cover with milk and add to the onion. Simmer very gently for an hour until the bread has broken down, stirring occasionally and adding more milk if necessary. Season to taste with salt, white pepper and mace.

Fried bread is an alternative, if you do not have time for the sauce. Put triangular sippets on a plate with duck that have been cooked in its fat, and rectangular rafts under woodcock, plover and snipe to catch the juices while the birds are cooking.

Blood and other oranges go with duck and goose. The tartish hybrids, like ortaniques and mineolas, are worth looking out for. To prepare a fruit, take a sharp knife and cut away the peel and pith outside, then cut out the 'pigs' from the membrane inside. Put the juice in the gravy. If you are short of time, serve the duck or goose with home-made marmalade.

Wild rice is customary with goose (in America) and also good with duck. Brown rice, at a fraction of the price and easier to get, is a surprisingly good substitute.

Gravy: grouse and grey partridge, woodcock and company hardly need gravy (provided they have bread sauce). Thin is the norm for roast pheasant and French partridge, achieved by reducing vegetable water and seasoning it to taste. The duck family and pigeon can take something stronger.

Cook the bird or breasts as above, draining off any excess fat. Throw a sherry glass of brandy, Calvados or whisky over them. Boil up the liquor, stand back and set it alight. When the flames have died down, remove the meat and deglaze the pan with a glass of red wine and add a little redcurrant or whatever jelly, a spoonful of soy, some tea or any stock or vegetable water. Season to taste. Tip over the game to mingle with any juices before serving.

To vary: damson or sloe gin, or port, may be used instead of the red wine, but taste sweeter, so go easy on the jelly. The juice of an orange may be added too.

STOCK

Game carcasses make the best. They are also available when you want a good soup – in winter. Hoard in the freezer if necessary, until you have enough. Woodock, snipe and plover make an unforgettable stock (and a legendary consommé if you can be bothered – consult Escoffier). Grouse, partridge and pheasant come next. Duck, provided they do not taste or smell too strongly, are close behind with geese. Pigeon can be musty.

Cover the bones with water and bring up to simmering point. Skim until the froth is white. Add salt, peppercorns, a bay leaf and any leek or celery tops that might otherwise go for compost. Cook very gently for four hours, adding more water when necessary. Strain through a colander, then a fine sieve. Make a chicken, duck or turkey stock the same way.

SOUP

To the stock, add chopped garlic, onions or leek, plus carrot, or dried mushrooms. Simmer for 20–30 minutes, adding 1oz (25g) porridge oats, pinhead oatmeal or couscous to every pint (600ml) liquid to thicken the soup. Shredded cabbage and sprout tops can go in at the end. Adjust the seasoning. To beef up the flavour, try a little soy or wine vinegar. To heighten the colour, use sweet paprika (see page 364). The flavour improves over a number of days.

SALMI OF GAME

An abbreviation of salmagund, anglicised in the seventeenth century. The process takes a little time, but is not much trouble and is convenient to dish up. A salmi is the only way of cooking a whole pheasant guaranteed not to be dry.

For 6: start the dish a day or two in advance. Oven-roast a brace of pheasants for half as long as usual. Remove the breasts and thighs and reserve. Make a stock, as above, from the carcass and legs. Strain and skim off the grease, or remove by means of a gravy separator. Add a glass of red wine to the liquor, a chopped shallot, or a few dried mushrooms. Reduce to a good half pint. Thicken with a little *beurre manié*, and adjust the seasoning. Alternatively, add a glass of white wine to the stock and finish with 2 tbsp cream. Introduce the meat and heat through without boiling for five minutes. This is an equally good way of cooking French partridge and guinea fowl, but eat the legs and wings along with the breasts.

CHAPTER
EIGHTEEN

POULTRY AND EGGS

I T WAS IN A FRENCH-CANADIAN log cabin operating as a restaurant, surrounded by snow and burning a huge fire, that I first encountered 'Rock Cornish hen'. How peculiar to have travelled so far and to be sitting with West Country friends who did not recognise it either. We joked, drank, ordered, ate, and having failed to discover the origin of the bird, forgot about it. The next time I heard it mentioned, thirty years later, was by John and Sylvia Cook, breeders of bantams near Luton.

Jungle fowl, the progenitor of the chicken and relation of the pheasant, are a native of South-East Asia still found in the wild. They live in small flocks, four or five females to every male, foraging for food by day, and roosting by night. They were tamed by man thousands of years ago. It is not clear whether the domesticated bird was brought to the province of Britain by the Romans or found on their arrival. The cocks acquire spurs at about six months, which, coupled with an aggressive instinct, made them useful for fighting. The sport was banned in England under public order offences in the mid-nineteenth century, but continued near county boundaries. It still goes on.

Poultry-keeping in England, a commonplace and poorly recorded affair, has a more accomplished and successful history than it is given credit for. The medieval hen-wife expected from each fowl a hundred eggs per year and half a dozen layers. The surplus cocks were castrated, becoming capons, and kept separately in monastic and other houses. 'Sister Pernell was a priest's wench,' says Piers Plowman. 'She had a child in the capon-cote and all the chapter knew it.'

In the seventeenth century, Sir Hugh Plat, a Hertfordshire farmer and author of *Delights for Ladies*, came through with up-to-date advice on how best to fatten birds for the table. Daniel Defoe, a little later, cites the quantity of chickens raised in the environs of Dorking. The local breed, easily identified by its five toes and mentioned by the Romans, is one of the most enduring in existence. The imponderables are whether it was not a Dorking but a 'darking', and what a pub called 'The Dorking Cock' was doing in Droitwich, Worcestershire.

The Old English game fowl, possibly as old as the Dorking, maintained popularity through its capacity to fight. This divided poultry-keeping into two factions, sporting and culinary, which temporarily merged in the 1830s. The story is that Cornish miners, intent on a prize fighter, crossed the native champion with two of the most likely-looking birds from the east. One was a Malay, the other an Asil, originally from India and used in the pit for a couple of thousand years (Hawksworth, 1994).

The result was a bird entitled Cornish Game in North America and Indian Game in England. It was too heavy for fighting, but had an unequalled amount of richly flavoured muscle across the breast, which got more guineas from bidders upcountry than a breeding ram or north Devon bull.

Since its rise to eminence, the fortunes of the 'Indian' game cock have been mixed. In America, it combined with a breed called a Plymouth Rock to produce the 'Cornish hen', a fowl the size of a poussin, for an appreciative niche market. Not so in England. The renowned 'Surrey' chicken (Haggard, 1902), a product of the game cock and the 'barndoor' fowl of Sussex and Kent, which developed into the Sussex breed, was commercially abandoned. There is nothing in London's Leadenhall market, apart from listed and empty hooks, to show for seven hundred years of selling poultry.

CHICKEN

With the 1849 ban on cockfighting, energy was diverted into showing poultry. Again, the ways parted into practical and diversionary camps. The first pair of Cochins had just arrived from China. They took up royal patronage and caused a temporary sensation. They also swelled the number of acquisitions from Europe and Asia whose names did not always tally with their origins, whose colours could be startling, and whose points varied according to fashion. What miniatures and bantams* lacked in size and magnificence, they made up for in beauty. I am no judge, but who could be indifferent to the combs, quiffs, trousers and tails, or a ride in a brougham to Turnham Green to see the gold or silver pencil pattern feathers, so perfectly arranged on Sir John's Sebright's fowls?**

Utilitarian poultry is divided into meat and egg producers. Capons of up to a couple of years old, and younger caponets, were available at more or less any time. Cockerels were in season five to six months after hatching, which meant the back end of the year. Immature hens or pullets, mostly needed for laying, were rarely eaten. Autumn or 'bramble' chicks, which matured into 'spring chicken' and were calculated to come in when game went out, began to emerge with incubators from 1854. Throughout the nineteenth and early twentieth centuries, production was confined to the smaller farms, cottagers and higglers (traders), who looked to the hunt for compensation after losses to foxes. The quality of birds varied considerably. A good one was a festive and accredited treat. A bad one, breast broken to make it look larger, tasted of turps from the sawdust it was packed in for the London train. The force-feeding or 'cramming' of poultry persisted until 1939.

The whole thing changed with the Ross Cobb, an eating machine developed in America and predominant in the UK since the Second World War. Provided it is housed in a battery, deprived of the freedom to exercise and kept in a living hell, it can be ready for the table in a

---

* *Bantams are a small and spirited group of fowls with no large counterpart, originally named after a town in Java. A standard-sized fowl, bred small, is not strictly speaking a bantam, but a miniature.*

** *Sir John Sebright was a breeder of bantams which are still in existence today.*

quarter of the time taken by traditional breeds. The result is a fowl so incapacitated it may not be able to stand, identifiable by hock burns (sores) on the back of the legs and other disabilities inflicted on it as a matter of course. It was over twenty years ago that Ivy, wife of Ted, a beekeeper who supplied me with honey, noticed that something was up with the chicken in the supermarkets. Not even the colour of the bones was normal, said she: it was black.

This abominably reared offence to humanity, ornithology and gastronomy is the worst food of its type. The grieving at the loss of giblets (courtesy of EC directives implemented by MAFF) was way off target: the chicken almost universally eaten, gutted or otherwise, was lousy in the first place. The only thing in its favour is a price, dependent on serial abuse. Despite the TV programmes, the articles, the coverage and information, the message has not got through. If a chicken is cheap, it has paid for it in suffering more than any fox hunted, any hare coursed, any mouse injected, any mink farmed, or any cabbage or carrot fly submitted to a spray by public demand. It happens all the time. So, if your top priorities are animal welfare and subscribing to good causes, pay more for chicken and enjoy it more too. Even if you are not interested in eating well, it is the only way to end the misery.

A supermarket chicken lives for about thirty days, or one eighth as long as a veal calf. It is wet-plucked, eviscerated and wrapped, encouraging bacterial growth. The carcass cannot be hung to improve any flavour it might have. It does not matter whether you boil, curry or stew this bird, or make it into the ubiquitous tikka.

Poultry shows began as shop windows displaying carcasses, and this continued until well into the twentieth century. They have now gone to the other extreme, with birds grown for exhibition only. This has maintained interest, as in the case of other livestock, but created breeds within breeds whose looks do not necessarily translate into meat or eggs. Given the opposition to their survival, like many English foods, it is remarkable the star performers have come this far. The next ten years will reveal whether or not, after two millennia, they have further to go.

All the fowls on the current list of rarities have culinary as well as ornamental uses. Old English, Modern and 'Indian' Game, and Dorkings are amongst them. The others include (most endangered breeds first): Pheasant Fowl (Yorkshire, nineteenth/twentieth century), Marsh Daisy (c.1910), Ixworth (Suffolk, 1920s), Derbyshire Redcap, and Buff Orpington. The Scots Grey and Scots Dumpy are having a tough time too. The biggest perceived threat to these and other naturalised breeds comes from DEFRA embarking on a Mass Animal Destruction policy, appropriately known as MAD, rather than vaccinating against avian influenza. The mere possibility is already forcing people into early retirement.

The positive news is that a modest number of part-timers and professionals who are keeping poultry and waterfowl need only turn their attention to the rarer sorts to ensure their survival. All you require is a fox-proof run, preferably electrified, and housing. Do not, like so many enthusiasts, wait for an accident to happen. Unless prevented, it will.

England's highest-quality roasting chickens were obtained by crossing a gamecock with a long-in-the-back breed like a Dorking or Sussex, or vice versa. It is still done. Anne Terrell of east Cornwall goes further, observing the old season for chicken, hatching birds in the spring and keeping them through the summer until the flies have gone and the carcass can be hung. These are principles that may be out of date, but they put meat on the table that Queen Victoria, a chicken-fancier herself, would have recognized.

COOK'S ORACLE

I have never bought chicken in a supermarket, except a *poulet du fermier* as an experiment in France. At home in England I go to private suppliers, encountered by chance and by keeping an eye open, or bid at sales. I also get a fowl killed at Christmas and Easter. This involves two pleasant trips to one of my favourite neighbours, the first to order, the second to collect. For those who are not so disposed or lucky, a good roasting chicken has been the most difficult thing to find for the last forty years. This is now changing, with excellent birds turning up at farmers' markets.

A free-range bird tastes best, given exercise and the opportunity to grub about, though a barn-dweller can be fine if it is old enough. Ask the age. A decent chicken will be about fourteen weeks old, cost the same as four pints of beer and weigh around five pounds. The traditional breeds are slower, more expensive, superior in flavour and may have darker meat on the legs. Like a pheasant, the longer a chicken is hung, within reason – up to two weeks in cold weather – dry-plucked and with the guts in, the better the result will be. A good fowl emits fat when cooked, not juice.

Roast chicken: Spit-roast chicken, given the raw material, and basted and served with its own juices, is best. Some cookers have horizontal spits to which the fowl may be pinioned. On dangle spits like mine it must be supported underneath and suspended on a cord through the cavity. Proceed as on page 98, allowing time to lay in the fuel and up to two hours to cook the bird. Worth the palaver when you have great expectations of a chicken.

Oven-roast chicken: if you are gutting the bird yourself, take some of the internal fat and slip it from the tail end between the skin and the flesh. The skin, tougher than it appears, will not break. Alternatively, use slices of fresh truffle *au français* or rashers of streaky bacon, or spread butter over the top. You may put herbs or a lemon in the cavity. Season with pepper. Give an average-sized bird an hour in a pre-heated oven at 180°C/350°F/gas mark 4, basting it two or three times. A fowl can sit around without spoiling while you make the gravy.

Cold chicken: if you want one for a summer picnic or party to go with an ox tongue, cook it like a salmon, but for longer. Put the chicken in a close-fitting pan, and add a heaped teaspoonful of salt. Cover with cold water and bring up to the boil. Simmer for fifteen minutes, remove from the heat and leave over the day or night in the same water to get cold. Drain and dry. Boil up the carcass in the liquor for an extra tasty stock.

Stewed chicken: The procedure is similar to a beef stew. But, you need stock from a previous bird or at least vegetable water to make a decent gravy, and do not have to cook the meat for so long. There are two ways of making this dish.

For a dark stew, 1 chicken, cut into eight or 10 pieces (ask the butcher to do this, and show you how, if you do not have the confidence yourself), plain flour, oil, butter, 1 onion and 1 clove of garlic, peeled and chopped, liquid almost to cover, 1 glass of red wine, 1 dsp soy, seasoning.

Roll the chicken in flour and fry until crisp on all sides in a little oil and butter. Remove to a pan. Pour in enough liquid almost to cover, bringing it up to simmering point and agitating the pan so that the meat and sauce get acquainted. Add the onion and garlic. Season well. Cook gently on top of the stove or commit to a pre-heated oven at 180°C/350°F/gas mark 4 for about 1 hour or until the meat is tender.

For a light stew, use white wine instead of red, omit the soy, and add some cream when the bird is done.

To vary: fungi go well with chicken – dried ceps are best. Add to the stew after the chicken. If using fresh mushrooms, use the firmest, youngest specimens and slice and fry in butter first. Try horns of plenty in a dark stew and chanterelles in a light one. Field and horse mushrooms can go in either.

Curried chicken: proceed as for mutton (see page 139).

Boiled fowl: a former favourite, which dropped off the register in the 1960s. Laying hens, at the end of their short reproductive cycle, are now disposed of, an extraordinary waste of resources that has become routine. The carcass of a boiler is usually lean and scrawny, and the meat dry, but the flavour is better than a roasting bird. If you ever see one at market, it will probably be yours for the price of half a pint. Cover in water, bring up to the boil and make a stock (see page 214), adding peeled carrots, garlic and leeks or onions at about half time. After a couple of hours, or when the chicken is tender, take the meat off the bone. Reduce the liquor by half. Add half a cup of unwashed white rice or some potato peeled and cut into cubes. Re-introduce the chicken:

cook gently for 10 minutes and you have a soup. Reduce the liquor a little more for a stew. Mix in freshly chopped parsley or chives if you wish. Adjust the seasoning when necessary. There was no recipe for this sort of food, nor should there be. Real farmhouse cookery.

Guinea Fowl

A native of west and northern Africa related to the turkey. They were spread by the Romans with peacocks and pheasants, and probably reintroduced to England in the sixteenth century. I have seen them whizzing around in the semi-desert sands of the southern Sahara; collectively conscious earthbound bundles of fluff and feathers with scrawny necks, mechanical voices and hysterical alarm calls, spindle shanks invisibly whirring at 40 m.p.h.

The guinea fowl and the turkey traded names at least until the 1650s (*OED*). Confusion arose through their similarity, and the use of the latest jargon to describe anything foreign. 'Guinea' happened to be appropriate, 'turkey' was not. The bird is also known as a pintado, after the spots on its grey plumage (from the Latin *pingere*, to paint), or a 'gleeny' in the West Country (from the Latin *gallina*, hen). There are two or three types, including an occasional white one.

The guinea fowl in England are regarded by their owners as neither truly wild nor domesticated and are usually ornamental. They are not disposed to lay indoors, are vulnerable to foxes and magpies, and occasionally struck at shoots. Birds are encouraged to wander less in the company of hens though they can antagonise each other. They are underrated as food. The black legs that Victorian gourmets looked for in a chicken are present on the guinea. The flavour is partly due to the life it leads. The meat is a welcome sight when game is not in season. The carcass is smaller than it appears before plucking, but heavier in certain strains, and ready in a respectable fourteen weeks. The weight is around three pounds: a nice feed for four people. A guinea is best prepared like pheasant: hung in feather for as long as the weather permits and made into a salmi (see page 214). Alternatively, oven-roast as you would a chicken, allowing less time. Forty-five minutes should do it. The breasts are small, it is better to lift off each one in a single piece rather than trying to carve them.

Duckling

To Aylesbury, Vale of. I lived up there for a bit, on the south-western fringe of the Chilterns. Beech is the thing, planted to keep the capital and its bread ovens in fuel generations ago. Kites are back, a little too close to Heathrow Airport for their comfort and safety. A Victorian monument marks a strange and lonely spot where a man on a horse was struck by a bolt of lightning, which killed them both. A gentleman farmer's boy took off with the gypsies, never to return. One of the pubs' tenancies has been in the same family since the 1780s. Richard

Waller's antecedents, on the distaff side, were already keeping ducks by then. He still is, not far from what is now the London Underground.

The domestic duck is descended from the mallard, tamed in Mesopotamia thousands of years ago (Chris and Mike Ashton, 2001). By the eighteenth century, it is not clear how long before, an 'English white' was bred selectively from the common duck of the village green and pond. It was appreciated for its feathers, down and meat by the London market, and farmed at a convenient distance in the valley of the Thame. The undercarriage was not like other species, but parallel with the ground. The neck was long and the head large. The legs and feet were a bright orange and the bill, from the consumption of local grit, as 'pink as a lady's fingernail' (Alison Ambrose, 1991).

Without the ducks, the tastiest in the country, Aylesbury 'would be another little-known town in the south of England'.* As it is, the name is to table birds what Bramley is to cooking apples. The duckers were divided into two lots. The breeders tended to be farmers in outlying villages as far away as Oxfordshire and Bedfordshire, who kept the stock birds and supplied the eggs. The growers were the labourers and poor of the town, who relied on the trade and mostly lived in 'Duck End' (now Friarage Road). In conditions that called for a scented hanky, they shared cottages with 400 to 1,000 duckling a year. Broody hens hatched the eggs. Women did the rearing, feeding with a compound called greaves ('graves'), and plucking the customary ten minutes after killing and hanging. During the eighteenth century, carcasses went by cart or packhorse to London, and from 1839 by railway via the Cheddington branch line. Agents or salesmen completed the transactions.

Duckling was expensive, too expensive for most Buckinghamshire folk, but popular with the rising metropolitan middle class. The Aylesbury started laying early, in November, ate voraciously, and went to the table at less than eight weeks, mostly in March and April. It originally filled the gap between game and spring chicken, with prices falling away after Ascot and reviving at Christmas. Between 1850 and 1890, up to one ton of birds could be dispatched for Smithfield in baskets or 'flats' three times a week in season.

The Peking duck, arriving from China in 1873, interrupted the party. It provided the Aylesbury with a good cross and its progeny with hybrid vigour, but pure-bred fowl with strong competition. Complacency, neglect, and the disruption of two world wars hit the heartland of duck as Lancashire, Lincolnshire and Norfolk started to take over production (Alison Ambrose, 1991). The passing pub fancy for 'half a duck', for which the Aylesbury was too big, made another dent in its fortunes. One of the best-known names in the business,

---

* Says Alison Ambrose in her charming publication The Aylesbury Duck, sponsored by Ron Miller, dairyman (2nd edition, 1991), and sold by the Buckinghamshire County Museum in the town.

the Weston family, a combined breeder and grower near the station, went out of business in the 1950s.

Richard Waller is left amongst the characteristic beeches, a golf course behind him, a valley below, and the pleasantest of views of the Buckinghamshire countryside unfolding in the distance. His grandfather, a keeper, planted the trees adorning the slopes of Chesham Bois. His father, fondly remembered for his dialect, and indifferent to showing the local duck, possibly kept it going for the table. His mother brought to their marriage a dowry of one drake and six ducks. Richard plans to breed from the birds with a few coloured feathers, and in ten years arrive back at the Aylesburys his family might have recognised centuries ago. The last of the duckers.

There are other heavy ducks bred for the table in England. The Rouen has been around in the southern counties probably since the early nineteenth century. It had the dress of a mallard and the size of an Aylesbury, but hatched later, took six months to mature, and appeared at market from the autumn until Christmas. Respected poultry-breeder Reginald Appleyard, who lived near the river at Ixworth in Suffolk, developed his eponymous 'silver' duck from the Rouen in the 1930s. Like his chicken, it has been used commercially.

Muscovy duck arrived in England from Nicaragua around the mid-eighteenth century (*OED*), probably via Europe. It is said to be named after a tribe of Indians entitled the Muysca, or possibly the Mosquito coast, but called a Barbary or Cairo duck in France (*Larousse Gastronomique*). There are several colours from chocolate to lavender. Unlike the other domesticated species, this one likes to perch. It is also a bully in the farmyard and around village ponds and is better kept apart from smaller duck. A young gander, ugly as he looks with his red mask, is a favourite for the table with country people.

COOK'S ORACLE

A duckling is a 'first-feather' bird sold before its initial moult at about eight weeks old, whereupon its strength goes into making plumage and its body loses condition. A duck obtained a year later when stock birds are rationalised is a more enticing prospect – but hard to come by. The fat on both is plentiful and prized. Get it to set by freezing a fresh bird for 24 hours, thawing it out for another 24 and hanging it up to dry. The Chinese, a dab hand with ducks, immerse them in boiling water for a minute before drying and submit them to a fan. Then prick the skin all over with a sharp fork, particularly around the legs and the parson's nose.

Duckling is a favourite all over the world: in Beijing, Guangzhou, Rouen, and at various restaurants in Paris, notably La Tour d'Argent, Lapérouse and Chez Allard. You enter the French Horn at Sonning in Berkshire. I did as a schoolboy, fumbling with a fag, perspiring over a wine list, and paired with an equally stupefied girl. The duckling were turning and browning on a spit. They still are, uniquely in my experience, but causing no more of a stir than they did forty years ago. They are carved at the table. The dish is a combination of 'classic French . . . and traditional English cookery' – it can be done – significantly called *canard à l'Anglaise*.

The fat, running from the duckling and the heat of the fire into a tray, is saved from burning. This can also be achieved by placing the bird on a rack over a pan in a *bain-marie*, and draining the fat off every 15 minutes. Not many do: you have to be committed to take such courses, and fully appreciate the fat obtained.

There are two approaches to the timing of duck. The advantage of cooking it pink is to the meat, and of cooking it through is to the skin. Give it 220°C/425°F/gas mark 7 for 40 minutes, turning the oven down to 180°C/350°F/gas mark 4 if you wish to leave it for another 20–30 minutes. Make a gravy with red wine (see page 59). Boiled new potatoes and green peas are customary, old potatoes and turnips not so good. Apple sauce may be a cliché, but it goes very well. If you do not have time to prepare it, or lack the fruit, use a home-made marmalade.

The flavour of a duckling, like other rich foods – crab, lobster and salmon – is almost better when cold.

Stuffing a duck: imagine my surprise and admiration when, having taken some duck for boning to 'Taff' Jones,* he held them up like pullovers without a mark on them. He never so much as broke the skin. It is not difficult to do, but fiddly. You work away with the point of a very sharp knife, loosening the carcass from the meat, removing the wings and thighs but leaving the drumsticks and gradually turning the bird inside out. Be careful not to puncture the skin where it is thinnest – along the breastbone. The cavity will take 2–3lb of sausage mixture (see page 165), including an egg, half a glass of red wine and some extra seasoning, i.e. the ingredients of a French terrine. Sew up the top end with string, comfortably fill the duck, and sew up the tail. Bake on a tray in a preheated oven at 180°C/350°F/gas mark 4 for about two and a half hours. Allow to cool, then chill for a couple of days before using. If the skin bursts, which it can occasionally along the top, enlarge the wound, and fill it with soft fruit. Then cover with a little melted redcurrant jelly or similar, and you have a decoration. Remove the string and carve crosswise; cut in half if you wish. Handsome, and surprising to those expecting a conventional duck. Feeds at least a dozen.

COMMON GEESE

They appeared in the summer on a marsh near me and probably had done since the church was built and the abbey owned the land. They went at Christmas, and came again when the

---

* *Taff worked for the butcher David Price in Fordingbridge for years.*

sun had crossed the line, competing for attention with the village cricket, thatched pavilion and cattle grazing. Eddie Trim, the estate carpenter, discharged his right to keep geese until he died in the 1990s. There is a chance that a local lad, who has rented a cottage nearby, will continue the tradition.

Geese are noisy birds that react to movement and strangers, easily drawn but easily driven by a pint-sized girl to market or fair. Their plumage has been used for arrow flights and quills, the down for quilts, and wings for brushes, a present made to me, and whose tips get nicely into crevices and corners. The indigenous farm goose of Europe and North Africa is descended from the greylag, a more amenable and wide-ranging bird than the other species. It was tamed even before the duck – in the same way as pigs – by stealing the young from their mothers and bringing them up in civilization. The natives were already doing this when the Romans arrived in Britain with the first of the selectively bred white geese on record. The English continued to plunder goslings for the table until the last nesting sites were drained in the nineteenth century and birds migrated to breed elsewhere.

The advantage of white geese is in the perceived quality of the feathers and down. The English bird went one better. The goose was the desired and pristine white, and the gander had a grey 'saddle' back, enabling owners to identify candidates for breeding or meat almost at birth. This useful characteristic is called 'sex linking'. It has been known in England for at least two hundred years, probably four hundred, and possibly since the Roman occupation. The facts are not clear. There are still keepers with an encyclopaedic knowledge of waterfowl who are too busy to write them down.

By the Middle Ages, the goose was an important part of the rural economy. It was payment in kind with the quarterly rent to the landlord at Michaelmas (29 September) and declared a festive dish by Elizabeth I. Geese were cheap to keep on the wastes around the village commons and easy to house, residing like Aylesbury ducks in the cottages of their owners (Chris Ashton, 1999) and in colliers' pits. They could make the journey from Norfolk to London, shod in tar and feeding as they went, and attain a great age. In 1771 a gander in Grimley, Worcestershire, was still alive aged seventy-five.

The imports of the nineteenth century included ornamental and other waterfowl from Asia and Europe that caused great excitement. The Embden (German) and Toulouse (French) geese stole the limelight in culinary terms, and, hatched in Norfolk, remain far and away the most important commercial cross. The natives hung on mainly in Devon, the Shetlands, and abroad, emerging as the Pilgrim in America and the Settler in Australia. The West of England breed, as it is now called at home, admitted to British Standards in only 1999, is amongst the rarest of rarities. Geoff and Sue Chase, not quite neighbours of mine, have kept them for years. He is a schoolmaster and judge of waterfowl, she has always liked geese. They live not on a common or farm but in a house next to others, with a long, thin garden occupied by birds of little value and no obvious distinction whose bloodline may be older than England itself. We are all looking out for other sex-linked geese, which may be hiding somewhere and waiting to swell numbers that are critically low.

A 'green' goose is between six and nine weeks old – a foolish bird, according to the Somerset proverb, 'too much for one, too little for two'. Dr William Kitchener said the best goose appeared from the second week in June until the first week in September.* Gleaners, let loose in the stubble, came next. The season closed with Christmas geese, upstaged by turkey but returning to popularity.

Goose fat is even better than a duck's. It was declared full of cholesterol in the 1990s, but lo! It does not kill those who eat the most. The English waste quantities of goose fat every Christmas; the French tin it, and some rub it on their chests for colds. There is a lot inside cuddling up to the liver (the best bit of a goose) that may be slowly rendered in a frying pan. To extract the subcutaneous fat, treat the bird as you would a duck.

Some years ago, Bob the Fish was asked to dispatch a vicious gander aged about eight, which he put in the slowest of ovens from six in the morning till six at night: delicious, he said. A younger bird does not take so long. Prick it all over as you would a duck. Oven-roast on a tray for 15–20 minutes per pound at 180°C/350°F/gas mark 4. The breast is shallow for so large a fowl, but the meat is rich and needs something tart to go with it. The gooseberry is available for sauce in summer, the cooking apple in autumn and winter. The leftovers make plenty of excellent stock.

Salted geese are an example of a food that was seldom recorded but was probably common amongst country people and was prepared like hams. Here are some instructions taken down from a Mrs Machen (Stevens Cox ed., 1961): 'take the fairest and fattest goose you can gett, dry . . . within . . . beat . . . and salt him well and let him lye a fortnight . . . tye him up . . . and hang him . . . in a chimney [for as long as 3 weeks]'. The goose will be ready to 'boyle', i.e. poach in water, immediately, or keep. Eat cold.

TURKEY

I met Dennis and Margaret on a campsite in the Yorkshire Dales. He was easy-going, undemanding and little trouble. She, tough and vicious when roused, had to get her own way.

---

* The son of a London coal porter and merchant, who made a fortune, sent Kitchener to Eton and left him a rich and cultured man. He gained a medical degree in Glasgow, which excluded him from practising in London, and devoted his life to study, music, entertaining and experimenting with food. Kitchener wrote The Cook's Oracle, which was first published in 1817.

The 'Iron Lady' bore not two children, but fifteen eggs, which mostly hatched out. Sarah Pearson, the owner, who was known to like turkeys, received one as a present from the home where she worked. She called him Dennis after a man she had nursed. Margaret was a later acquisition; her name chose itself. Armed with a camera, I watched my wife playing grandmother's footsteps with the happy couple and family. When she took a pace, they took one. When she took two or more, so did they, travelling in a circle and finishing where they had begun. It went on for about an hour.

Turkeys are another noisy bird, but one that reacts to sound: doors closing, keys dropping, or the clatter of pans. They are queer, suspicious-looking creatures, not half as stupid as they are supposed to be, but can have suicidal tendencies. Turkeys are also comic, stately, posturing, entertaining, and signal changes of mood with changes of complexion. They have an aversion to red, the colour of their combs, good eyesight, and tend to be more wary in the wild. A Virginian told me that an older bird can tell whether or not you are carrying a gun, and behaves accordingly.

There are five sub-species of North American wild turkey, *Meleagris gallapavo*, ranging from the East Coast to the Midwest and from Canada to Mexico. They have had more than one misleading name, including 'guinea hen', applied to females, and *coq d'Inde*. The story is that one Pedro Niño introduced the first birds in Europe to Spain in 1498, and their descendants spread through France with priests, accounting for their nickname 'Jesuit'. There is another form of turkey in Yucatan with a culinary past, *Meleagris ocellata*, which misled me for a bit, but it prefers to remain at home.

The rhyme about carps, turkeys, hops, heresies, piccarell, beer, etc. 'coming to England all in a year' is more than half untrue, but believable in terms of the date: around 1520. It appears that Yorkshireman Walter or William Strickland went to North America with Sebastian Cabot, returned with domesticated turkeys, which he had acquired from Indian traders in exchange for glass beads, and sold them in Bristol. I have two things to check: whether the lectern in Strickland's local church is a turkey; and whether there might have been a feral population. Whilst looking around Holkham Hall in Norfolk, I found a curious entry in the gun room's game book. It read, amongst the usual pheasant, partridge, etc.: '1 wild turkey'.

The size of the turkey made it the ideal festive bird and replacement for swans, peacocks, cranes and bustards, except, ironically, in Strickland's home county, where a capon was preferred (Hartley, 1954). Having established itself in England, it left with the settlers, ingratiating itself at Christmas on one side of the Atlantic and at Thanksgiving on the other. The bronze turkey, showing the original colour, is associated with Cambridgeshire. The black turkey, a sport, established a heartland in Norfolk. The two can hybridise. Large numbers massed at the autumn sales in places like Aylsham and Attleborough, then made the annual, terminal pilgrimage to Smithfield Common, goaded by red flags and gleaning at the margins on the way. Pat Graham, née Peele, of Thuxton, one of the greatest and most enduring names in the world of turkeys, knew a woman whose grandfather remembered the flocks leaving on their journey south. The A11 was then one mile wide, mucky and muddy, the pace painful, the babble incessant, the hungry watching, the city waiting. The end came on 15 December.

Turkeys are now divided into commercial and standard birds. The industry was revolutionised by the 'double-breasted' heavyweights developed in the US after the war and introduced to England via Ireland. The birds are farmed indoors and, tipping the scales at more than a Cheddar cheese, can barely stand, let alone breed without assistance. The skin is fashionably white, the plumage uneventful, and the meat unsurprising, but eaten by the ton. The standard Cambridgeshire bronze turkeys are 'single-breasted' and far closer to the wild bird: darker, firmer, tastier, a different proposition altogether, weighing around fifteen pounds. The word is that the Norfolk black, slightly smaller, pips it by a short head. Try both.

To cook a standard bird, put it in a preheated oven at 170°C/325°F/gas mark 3 after breakfast, baste well, and remove half an hour before lunch to a warm place. A turkey presented on a dish with a garland of sausages at nineteenth-century City banquets was called an 'Alderman in Chains'.

Eggs

We met at seven 'down quay'. Chris, a fit man in his fifties, born and bred in the village, was the son of a wildfowler. He had already been out. He swung the boat in, helped us aboard and moved off into the morning mist, hailing a fisherman on the way. The dark line of marshes, passing right and left, linked and divided the sea from the sky, and the dry land hidden beyond the horizon. Fifteen minutes later we beached on an empty spit peppered with clear saline ponds and strewn with coarse maritime grasses and clumps of purslane waiting for rebirth. I knew not to linger on the smooth muddy patches left by the tide. If you do, you sink.

Black-headed gulls are noisy, fractious and sociable birds with red bills, matching legs, and face masks dipped in ink. They inhabit tidal flats, venturing forth to feed inland and along the coast particularly in the morning and evening. They are the smallest, least evil-minded and most abundant of the gulls, more like a tern in size and deportment, but they feed mainly on insects and do not dive for fish. Their nests are a subtle collection of grass, reeds and twigs built on the ground uncomfortably close to high water. The eggs are pointed, mottled and greenish. Clutches are repeated if washed away by spring tides, eaten by foxes or jackdaws, or removed under licence by human hand. The season is short. It opens in early April, gets under way in the middle of the month, and closes in early May.

It takes time and concentration to see the eggs, they are so well camouflaged in their tidy and invisible palette of a nest. You start by blundering forward, almost treading on a clutch, freeze at the thought, and proceed in slow motion, looking hard and seeing nothing until the mind behind the eye learns to separate an egg from the surrounding vegetation. Meanwhile, Chris worked the ground as quickly as a spaniel, occasionally stooping to the right or left and rising with an egg to put in his bucket. For every one I found, he found eight or ten, moving in straight lines back and forth across his imaginary grid towards the edge of the marsh. The birds squawked a bit – gulls and terns do – but did not seem to resent the intrusion: like chickens, they were free to lay again.

He tested the eggs in a pool. You put one in and if it remains horizontal it is fresh, fit for the London market. It will be boiled for five or six minutes, until the rich deep orange yolk is firm and the white translucent. Eggs that tilt remain at home. Chris likes them fried, with a bit of brown sauce. Curtain-twitchers resent what he does and occasionally confront him, but he is even-tempered, philosophical, and has even made people see reason.

A swan's egg is a meal. Once, I surprised a fox carrying in his mouth one that he had stolen from a nest. On seeing me the fox dropped the egg and ran off. The shell was blue and covered in an opaque film scarred with toothmarks. I was not sure of the legal position. It would have been misguided to try and return the egg to an angry bird the size of a swan, and pointless to leave it among the kingcups and wild iris. So I took it home and, since it was too addled to cook or blow, mounted it in a glass on a shelf. The egg and I remained together for about eight years, and survived several changes of address. Then, without warning, it exploded.

Wild birds' eggs have been used for food throughout English history. Only a few, like peregrines', were protected – though it did not prevent them from being eaten. Size, beauty, flavour, richness of yolk and accessibility made certain varieties more popular than others, and likely to be met in specific localities. A springtime traveller would find the eggs of one group of waders at markets and on tables in the Peaks, of another in Norfolk, and of finches at cottages in Northamptonshire, beaten into cups of tea (Flora Thompson, 1939).

Shirley Lavis, a Yorkshire lass who lives near us, had an uncle in Bempton near Flamborough Head. Every May to July, the climmers worked the sheer four hundred-foot cliffs that descend to the North Sea, and house on their ledges thousands of eggs. They operated in gangs, each keeping to its own ground, with baskets, ropes, winches and harnesses or bosun's chairs. The landowners charged the climmers in kind for access, and visitors 2d a head for watching part-time fishermen and labourers walk backwards over precipices in their hard hats. There were hairy moments and falling rocks, but no fatalities. The eggs, raised in baskets, could be found in the local shops and markets as far afield as Hull.

Guillemots' eggs were the pick of the bunch (Martin, 1994): no two are alike, though the pear shape is consistent. The bird lays one, and if required another: large, tough, long-lived in storage, and designed by Nature to roll around in a circle rather than fall over a ledge. Razorbills' eggs were the next in size. Kittiwakes', the richest, went to local bakers and into custard tarts. Puffins bit in defence of their nests. Fulmars vomited oil. Patches were rested to ensure the return of the birds to nest. A wage could be made, weather permitting, year after year.

The green plover incubates four eggs at a time, but will lay up to eight crosswise in a hollow in the ground, allowing half to be removed without effect. The custom was to take two, say north and south, followed by another two, then leave the birds to breed. The number of people returning home with eggs, and how they found the nests, was of great fascination to correspondents in past issues of *The Field*, and also to André Simon. The occupation was subject to licence in 1954, and banned after 15 April, which effectively killed it off. But, signalling changing attitudes and where priorities lie, it is permitted to destroy both plovers and black-headed gulls, and their nests, on the property of the Civil Aviation Authority at any time. Hawks are used to help implement the law.

In the years since these precautions were taken, the plover population, in common with that of many other birds, has collapsed. There is protection, but not from the things that hurt most, and when it comes to sacrifice, the soft targets go first.

I was listening in to a conversation between two fishermen on the Kent river bank in Lancashire who ate moorhens' eggs as boys, and felt in retrospect that they had transgressed. In modern England, a mental barrier exists between the acceptable practice of pricking the eggs of pests like Canada geese and herring gulls and the shocking one of taking or selling them for food.*
At the same time there is nothing politically incorrect about building a landfill site on a plover colony in Hampshire, which, by attracting traffic, rats and foxes, did more damage in two years than hunter-gatherers had accomplished in the previous two hundred.

To clear up any moral confusion (I hope), collectors of eggs are criminals. They are engaged in a vicious circle of their own deliberate creation, intent on rarities, and motivated by greed. I know. I was one as a boy, and though it was not illegal, it had a bad record and did not feel right. At the risk of being mauled, I robbed a tawny owl's nest located in the crook of a Somerset cedar tree. I often think about it.

Chris, a harvester of eggs, is in a different category. He takes a sustainable amount. His occupation is older and a million times kinder than chicken farming. Black-headed gulls are

---

* *Probably very strong and fishy. I would not bother unless starving.*

free-range, feed organically, live for as long as Nature intended, and die naturally. If I had to choose between laying eggs for Chris and for a supermarket, I would know which one to go for.

The authorities are doing a three-year survey on black-headed gulls and, by implication, the egg harvest – not a good sign. My predictions are these. The study will come up with information that licensees, if asked for it, could have provided in the first place. It may also be inconclusive. Egglers may have to fight for their rights regardless. The big picture is unlikely to be mentioned. The black-headed gull and its young have lots more to fear from container ports, oil refineries and rising sea levels inflicted on them by man and his appetite for holidays, comfort and mobility, than from a handful of people encouraging them to lay more eggs.

The ancients thought that an egg represented the elements. The shell was the earth, the yolk was fire, the white water, and the air contained in the compartment in the shell. And it's true – you can squeeze an egg as hard as you like lengthways, and throw it as far as you can on to grass, and it will not break.

All eggs are or were seasonal, including hens'. They arrive in the winter or in the spring to be eaten fresh or stored, and were usually rubbed with lard or butter and buried point downward in barrels of sawdust. The invention of electric light enabled man to deceive a chicken into thinking it was time to reproduce, and lay for longer periods. By the 1870s, aided by Australian and other imports, eggs entitled 'fresh' were sold for most of the year and eaten in much larger quantities than they had been previously.

Throughout the nineteenth century the supply of eggs in England was way behind demand, but it was a low-cost investment with great opportunities that were realised after the First World War. Egg-laying competitions, dating from the 1920s, sorted out the most efficient hybrids. Production rose from 900 million eggs a year in 1913 to 2,956 million in 1934 (Ernle, 1912). An industry developed that is still with us today, riding boom, slump, disease and sporadic salmonella scares that are unlikely to go away or teach anyone in power a lesson.

Chickens are sociable and adaptable birds, at home wherever they stop, in an Irish or West Country kitchen dresser, or go in compartments underneath gypsies' bow tops. My stepfather kept two lots of hens, one in deep litter indoors, the other outside in an orchard, providing about eighty eggs a day. You might open the lid of the nesting boxes, count five empty ones, then, holding your breath, find a clutch of seven, eight or even ten eggs, brown, warm and inviting in the sixth. It was not a job collecting them, but a daily pleasure and thrill, experienced in the half-light of winter afternoons, which delivered the occasional double-yolker. Only pulling carrots or lifting new potatoes comes close.

One of the things I missed living in London was decent eggs. The yolks were pale, the texture slack when raw and strangely emulsified when scrambled, regardless of any claims or premium. Now you can get such eggs at country supermarkets too, shored up by the usual consumer-friendly jargon and sell-by dates as long as your arm. So, beware labels. They have been negotiated. They occupy the twilight world between fact and fantasy or fiction. The main thing to remember is that supermarket hens do not have much going for them, and nor does the egg.

When Ms Currie made that remark about mass-produced eggs in the 1990s, plunging the industry into crisis, it left the way open for dicey foreign producers to fill the void. The effect on the subcultural life of England was to hit the small fry, depriving me of the right and pleasure to buy eggs at a garden gate, another perk of living in the countryside. Fortunately, reason has prevailed – it can happen – and we are back to where we were. Here is the message left with the eggs at a house in Suffolk:

Return of boxes appreciated
Save trees & help keep prices down
Produced at Naughton, Near Ipswich

The hens are free-ranging on grass and clover
They are kept in small numbers with plenty of space
They are fed on a mixture of grains milled locally, with no meat or bone meal added
The good yolk colour comes from eating grass, not chemicals in the food.
No antibiotics are added to the meal or water.

It was sad to see the makings of a security system next to the honesty box.

COOK'S ORACLE

Hens' eggs, described as 'mild' by the Victorians, are the best suited to popular taste. The size increases as a fowl gets older. Pullets' eggs are smaller, bantams' smaller still. The colour of the shell varies: white from Dorkings, brown from Welsummers (Dutch), blue or olive from the Araucana (South American) and speckled from Marans (French) and Rhode Island Reds (New England). Chickens' eggs are the most widely used, but mainly because of the quantity on the market. There are better and more imaginative choices.

Duck eggs are one and a half times the size of most hens' eggs and abundantly supplied by the light breeds. They are white, greenish or bluish and famously porous, but have never troubled me or anyone I have heard of. The effect on a horse of a bad duck egg is to put fire in its belly, a practical joke at country house parties (nothing more hilarious than a guest with a broken leg). The good ones are excellent boiled, low in water content, high in protein and do wonders for cakes, puddings and custards.

Goose eggs are equal to three hens' eggs, and are the largest on the market. The shells are white, torpedo-shaped and ideal for anyone with Fabergé in mind. They start arriving on or around St Valentine's Day and can continue until June. A Cambridge undergraduate's favourite, according to Jane Grigson, was a fried goose egg and chips. Mine is scrambled or an omelette. The yolks are very rich: another star performer in cakes, puddings and custards.

Turkeys' eggs are one and a half times the size of most hens' eggs. They were a favourite with the Victorians (*Blackie's Modern Encyclopedia*): light in colour, speckled and mostly to be found in the east of England. They are available from March to August and promoted by breeders. I bought some from a house on the outskirts of Southwold, in Suffolk. Free-ranging turkeys, as in the case of hens, provide the best eggs. Good for general use, great in meringues.

Guinea fowls' eggs are the size of a bantam's, broad and elegantly pointed. The colour is a greyish brown. The shell is tougher than any domestic bird's. They are not usually available in England until about June. Another former favourite, they were sometimes used as a substitute for plovers' eggs 'and sent to the table [hard-boiled] embedded in . . . moss in the same manner' (Hutchins, 1967).

Pheasants' eggs are similar to guinea fowls', but not as tough. Partridge eggs are smaller. The 'French' ones are speckled. They come from birds reared by the shoots, not from the wild (illegal). Very occasional at market. We ate them at home, hard-boiled in salads.

Quails' eggs are from the Chinese birds raised on farms in England. They are the size of a thrush's egg, heavily mottled with black, and seem to have a certain cachet. Hard-boil.

And peacocks' eggs: they and the chicks must be about, but you only ever see the adults and hear them calling at dawn and dusk. A neighbour of ours has peacocks. One day I shall ask him for an egg.

Eggs laid in season, indoors or out, says Hartley, are best. A new-laid egg should be given a day to 'set' before use. Fresh eggs feel warmer at the rounded end where the air is trapped than at the point: place them against your lips to test. When broken on to a plate, as at the shows, the yolk sits proudly on the surface. The deep colour of duck and goose eggs, compared to the average hen's, is due to their preference for grazing.

Coagulation of eggs takes place at 158°F (70°C) – one of the few scientific facts I know.

Boiled eggs: surprisingly, not mentioned until the sixteenth century, long after baked and fried. Fresh eggs should be barely covered in water or else the shell will break (owing to the air retained). The fresher the egg when hard-boiled, the more difficult it is to peel.

Fried eggs: cook them one at a time in a wok – the shape, containing the white, does the work for you.

Scrambled eggs: probably early nineteenth century, and a luxury in their day. Some people cannot help overcooking them. To return the texture to normal, break in another egg.

For an Indian 'rumble tumble', fry a chopped chilli and a shallot in butter before adding the eggs.

A true encounter in a pre-war New York diner (Nick St Germans, storyteller and friend):

Proprietor: 'Whaddya want?'
Englishman: 'Poached eggs on toast, please.'
Proprietor, shouting to the cook: 'Adam and Eve on a raft!'
Englishman, after deliberation: 'Can I change that to scrambled?'
Proprietor to cook: 'Wreck 'em!'

Omelette: 'first, steal six eggs . . .' (Hungarian recipe).

A primitive way of cooking eggs without the aid of fire (Mrs Beeton): 'the shepherds of Egypt . . . placed them in a sling which they turned so rapidly that the friction of the air heated the eggs to the exact point required for use'. Could be useful in a power cut or energy crisis.

CHAPTER
NINETEEN

Pages 236–55

S E A   F I S H

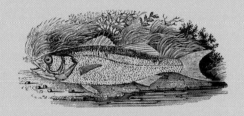

CHAPTER
TWENTY

Pages 257–65

S A L T   F I S H

A FIVE-FOOT WHITE PRAM, low in the water and almost too small, emerged from the cluster of boats next to a crowded quay. There were two middle-aged men aboard, dressed in yellow fishermen's waders, one plying the oars, the other with the net in the stern. They headed out into the deep and furious channel fifty yards wide that bore the water from the queen of English rivers, its lagoon of a mouth and feeder streams to the sea. The current, used to the boat's advantage, washed it over to the nearside shore.

The men beached the dinghy and disembarked. My wife and I, watching from the shadow of the tarred coastguard cottage, awaited their arrival. It was the final moment of a short season, starting on the first day or June and ending on the last of July – August upcountry – in which the seine fishing of certain estuaries is still permitted. Sea trout were the intended catch. The migrants congregate on the run-off tides that ebb along this part of the English coast and, thanks to the Isle of Wight, occur four times a day rather than the customary two.

Sea trout are brown trout that migrate to sea, where the food and exercise increase their size, and return to spawn in the rivers of their birth. They are caught at night with a fly, by day with a net, cast in Wales from coracles. They are also taken by hand – a feat witnessed by Bob the Fish as a boy in the Forest. The grilse are released to breed. The population is monitored and the fishing controlled by the Environment Agency. Only a handful of licences are left. They can be renewed every season, though not passed on under current legislation, and have mostly been bought out by the game fishermen who operate up river. Reviews take place every few years. It is hoped that in the next, the fishing grounds off the port of Rye, closed for years and now recovering, will be reopened.

The banksman, John, made his way up the shore – hat on head, rope over shoulder, and hauling the dinghy like a bargee's horse. The taller of the two, Tony, followed him. They stopped at a stretch before the jetty known as 'back shoot'. The one lower down, taken by other fishermen, is 'front shoot'. The beach huts and café on the dunes close by were heaving. The ferry came and went from the quay on the other side. The breeze ruffled the feathers of the swans across the water. Children skated on an exposed mudflat, and in the distance white modern houses and a grey medieval abbey rose from behind the willows on a marsh.

John released the dinghy and took one end of the net and bobbins, folded as neatly as a blanket in the stern. Tony climbed back aboard and rowed out into the deep channel. Using the current as before, he made an unhurried semicircular course with the boat, tripping off the net as he returned to the shore, then disembarked. With the tide working for them, and a man holding each end of the distended net, the bobbins closed on one another, forming a tunnel.

While John stood anchoring the net, Tony, hands continually crossing over without changing pace, pulled it in. A gleaming silver fish leapt out of the water and to freedom over the side. The bobbins on their rope, lapped by the waves and bringing nothing with them, piled up on the beach in the afternoon sun. The net was empty. The two men, showing no reaction, folded it up as neatly and considerately as before and tried again.

The second attempt yielded flounders and a bass, too small to eat and returned to the water. On the third, a fat, youngish man in long shorts, driving a speedboat, appeared from downstream. He was keeping to the limit of four knots and saw the bobbins, but slowly, certainly and with no explanation, he cruised up and into the middle of the line. The snarling of his engine stopped, throttled by the net. His boat stood still in midstream, impotent and helpless, before drifting on the current towards the shore. John and Tony stood watching and waiting, then walked into the shallows and without so much as a rueful smile or shake of the head freed the propeller. They had seen it all before.

The tide and afternoon were ebbing away. The net was damaged, but cast twice more. The boat went out and round on the same gentle course, followed by the bobbins, and returned to the shore for the last time, on the last tide, on the last day of the season. A huge silver salmon, muscular and gleaming, came in with the net. Tony held it gently and briefly, then, bending down, returned it to the sea. The fish, released under an agreement with the rods on the Avon, made its way upriver. I was consoled with a large grey mullet, not my favourite fish, but fresh and free. I gutted and scaled it in the water, ready for the pan that evening back home.

A well-built man in shirtsleeve order watched over the proceedings. He looked official, but I gave him a chance, quickly to learn that he had drunk from springs where I had taken only sips. There was nothing that the man, who turned out to be the bailiff, did not seem to know. He stalked, farmed, and made black pudding from the blood of his own pigs. He cockled, fished, and out in his boat had met sika stags crossing Poole Harbour for the land the other side. He could also tell, ten paces from the net, that Tony's bass was not worth keeping. The Environment Agency were lucky to have landed him.

The haul of fish never materialized. The gauge, used by the bailiff to measure fish, lay uncalled for on the beach as the empty nets came in. None of us watching seemed to mind. The little crowd of old folk, young mothers, waifs and strays with enquiring minds, torn from the all-day breakfasts in the café and the comfort of huts, were not disappointed. We had been silently absorbed by the timeless choreography of two men born to fish, fishing in retirement and going through the motions of St Peter and St Paul.

Man's dominion over fish conferred on Adam by God is as old as hunting or whoring. The net, gaff hook and spear, and pools for storage, are mentioned in the scriptures. An interpretation of how the fish became an emblem of the Christian Church can be found in Cassell's *Bible Dictionary*. You take the first letters of the words 'Jesus Christ Son of God Saviour', translate them into Greek, and they spell 'fish'.

Excavations have revealed that the Anglo-Saxons cooked all the fish consumed in modern England. The medieval kings claimed the right to porpoise, whale and most of the sturgeon, but, rarely able to take delivery, farmed it out to favourites or the Church (Fort, 2002). The Luttrells in their castle matched hounds against the conger marooned under boulders at East Quantoxhead (Ayrton, 1980). The poor men at their gate were better and more cheaply supplied with fish than we are today. Gluts were eaten fresh within reach of the coast. The rest was salted down for storage or transporting .

Throughout the Middle Ages the mode of fishing is described as 'casual' (Hoskins, 1955), if effective, with tidal weirs playing a significant part (Smylie, 2004). The catches from the sea, predominantly from inshore waters, were delivered as far inland as a man could beach a boat. England did not acquire its complement of fishing villages until the age of discovery, when the length of voyages increased, and prospects offshore were realised. Mevagissey and Staithes, spotted as conducive to building programmes, gained breakwaters in the fifteenth century. Newquay, Bude, Polperro and Clovelly, courtesy of the local landowners, the Cory dynasty, followed suit within a hundred years. Investment grew and an industry with it, capitalizing on the cod in the Atlantic, the pilchard off Cornwall and herring migrating down the east coast.

In the 1560s, possibly to encourage boat-building, Wednesdays and Saturdays were added to Fridays and Lent to make a total of 153 days a year in which meat, with arbitrary exceptions,[*] was forbidden. The law, which seems to have been taken seriously, was enforced on at least two occasions. A woman in Dover was pilloried (Pullar, 1977) and a man in London executed for being caught in flagrante with pieces of meat. The remainder, if they could afford it, stationed themselves near supplies of fish when flesh was off the menu.

By the seventeenth century, the navy of England could be 'divided into three sorts, of which one serveth for the wars, another for burden and the third for fishermen' (Markham, 1631–8). Catches were kept alive in watertight barrels and boxes, inshore cages and wet wells in ships at sea. The volume increased with the number of coastal visitors intent on fish, and the accessibility of the markets inland. London was supplied from Kent, Suffolk and Essex by packhorse, cart or boat, and after the 'rippers'' clearance of the woods and Weald, from the Sussex port of Rye.

The invention of steam power during the nineteenth century, and the discovery of the Silver Pit in the Dogger Bank, sixty miles off shore (Ellis, 2001), brought the industry into a new era. Trawling enabled larger catches not only to be taken, but to be stored on board ship in the space

---

* *Puffins, barnacle geese and the extremities of beavers.*

vacated by masts and rigging. From 1861, factories at the dockside provided the ice to keep the fish fresh. Trains stood waiting at newly built railheads to whisk it on its way. The boom, peaking at the end of the Victorian period, accounted for the size of Fleetwood, the wealth of Grimsby, and the fish imprinted on the paving stones in Hull.

With fast days petering out, fish came to be eaten in the same meal as meat. In upper- and middle-class houses, it was cooked in huge copper pans and served on silver salvers, appearing as a course between soup and meat. 'The English are great eaters of fish,' wrote Alexandre Dumas, author of *The Three Musketeers*, in his *Dictionnaire de Cuisine*, with 'sauces prescribed in advance for each species': oyster with cod, egg with haddock or whiting, and butter sauce, confusingly known as 'melted butter' or plain 'butter',* with soles, smelts and so on. It was impossible to entertain in the grand manner without footmen bearing turbot and lobster sauce to which you helped yourself with a fork and trowel (cor!). For country people there were sprats, freshwater fish and eels, and for the London poor cockles, winkles, red herring, and whitebait and shad from the Thames.

The cooking of fish, rising in standard with the quality and quantity available, fell with tinning and the convenience foods that were emerging by the twentieth century. The fishing did not last either. The invention of sonar in the 1960s removed the element of chance. The factory ships, which drew and processed thousands of tons at once, brought the industry to crisis point. The failure to reconcile an infinite demand with a finite supply of fish led to shortages that some had foreseen.

Such was the quantity of cod removed from the sea, wrote an uneasy Mrs Beeton in 1861, she was surprised it had not 'become extinct'. The population appeared to be secure, with nine million eggs born by every female, but not against the world's greatest predator. Less than five hundred years after Cabot had scooped up fish in baskets from North American waters, it was over. The legendary Grand Banks were closed to commercial boats. There were no cod left, wrote Mark Kurlansky. Man had caught them all.

Fish migrate around the coast, following other fish and food, and followed by vessels equipped with every net and device to bring them in. My brother, a pot man for a bit, commuted between Scotland and Cornwall tracking their movements, buying and selling. In the period he noticed that fish were getting small, an indication that there were not enough adults, the UK fleet were still investing.

Of all the fishermen left in Europe, the British feel the most deserted by their government and aggrieved by the lack of consultation. The French and the Dutch appear to be better off,

---

* *A sort of* hollandaise, *but not as good.*

and the Spanish and Russians do as they please – poaching fish, catching it under age and selling it in their markets (video footage is available). For the privilege of joining Europe, the UK's destiny, security, ancestral waters, an equal partnership of the Channel, and a major share of European fish stocks were negotiated away in a weak, cynical and legendary climbdown that continues to hurt. Dead as he is, fishermen will always speak ill of Edward Heath.

The size of the British fleet continues to fall with the total allowable catches (TACs) and closure of grounds. Prices are unstable, and licences expensive. The taxes on diesel and lubricating oil in the UK are the highest in Europe. Plymouth alone has six fisheries officers, working on site. Spain has six in total, based in Madrid, several hundred miles from the sea. The ever-increasing volume of regulations is making it impossible to fish. Some of the decommissioned trawlers, re-registered with foreign owners, are using British quotas. Others have been scrapped, or lie rotting near Fleetwood's ailing market on the banks of the Wyre.

The EU has the impossible task of trying to reconcile the diminishing number of fish with the needs of fishermen and the necessity to have an industry for the future. An attempted balance is struck ever year, but one which seems to offend both the UK's conservationists and its fleet. The Common Fisheries Policy is considered unfair, unevenly administered, and riddled with anomalies which Norway and Iceland – non-European members – do not appear to suffer from. In the time it takes to implement a regulation after a bad season a target species can be kicked while it is down. Industrial fishing is due to be terminated . . . though not yet. There is no end in sight to the waste, the synthetic nets left persistently to fish, and the beam trawlers mangling the underwater meadow that is the ocean floor.*

Where catches were landed in England, particularly on the east coast, they are now overlanded. The trade is global. Fish is caught in the Arctic by a Russian boat, processed in China, and sold with chips in English seaside towns within yards of the quay. It is also sent to Channel Island restaurants in boxes from a depot in landlocked Wiltshire. For how long this can go on is anyone's guess. Fish stocks are difficult to assess and predict, but for more than cod, time seems to be running out. 'Ranching', which effectively means doing to the ocean what enclosure did to farming, has been advanced as a solution.

It was when I saw the tuna caught by the Italians and sold by the hundreds every day in Tokyo's dark and draughty early morning market that the penny dropped with me. The sea, full throughout its history, had more or less been emptied in thirty years. I could either register a personal protest and stop eating fish, or continue to enjoy it, focusing on the species that were not under threat or hoovered up in shoals. The soft option won.

---

* *The trouble with modern nylon nets from the ecological angle is they do not rot when they have broken free from trawlers and lie abandoned at the bottom of the sea. They continue to trap fish for no purpose.*

Six to seven thousand vessels are still UK-registered, employing an estimated fourteen thousand men. For the existing number of 'under tens' (boats of less than ten metres) there appears to be enough fish available. However, they may not be permitted to catch it because of the EU and cannot meet anything like the demand, which currently amounts to three times the supply. The fishing industry, having been shafted politically, is not economically worth defending in its present state. At the same time, the public is encouraged to eat more fish. I do not know where we go from here except into a new phase with close seasons, better international co-operation and the British government minding its own business.

You can tell when there are fish about. On the rising tides at the right time of day and year, bass, mackerel, sprats and whitebait follow each other in to the shore and even up to the sand or shingle. The fish bring the birds and the hopeful beach casters who come at night and remain until morning. Among the pleasure craft and pot men there is the occasional tarred or varnished hull of a coble, lerret, yawl, gaffer, lugger, smack or ketch, reminders of the ochre sails and forests of masts that crammed English harbours, amber-strewn beaches and pebble shores.

The fishing villages and dockside quarters had more in common with each other than with the surrounding countryside or towns. The fishermen spoke different dialects, but understood the same language, faced the same danger and shared the same separation from the worlds of farmers, merchants and labourers. The women wore shawls, barrelled fish, knitted frocks,* and in consumptive cottages lashed by winter gales bore fishing-folk-to-be. The boys embarked for Arctic seascapes and bitter cold, and days of sickness. Some ended it overboard; others returned as frostbitten men who smoked Redbreast Flake, mended nets, sang in pubs and danced jigs on bare wooden floors.

Yet of all the grim faces, photos, and stories of communities where every individual was directly or indirectly involved in fishing, the air reeked of fish, and the cobbles were caked in scales and slime, one impression stuck with me. You could always tell the fishermen from the Hessle Road, Hull, said merchant David Latus, by the smart blue suits with pleated vents they wore into town on Saturday nights.

To be back at sea a day or two later was to be in peril on a heaving deck. Fatalities are higher in fishing than in mining, forestry or construction, the work is tougher, muckier and more

---

The heavy woollen jerseys worn by the fishermen. They were knitted in the round by women and girls, often one-handed, with the aid of a stick tucked into the belt. An experienced knitter achieved 200 stitches a minute. The intricate patterns could differ from one person and place to the next, and helped to identify corpses in the water. The patterns were thought to have been lost, but many have been recorded by Mary Wright in her delightful book Cornish Guernseys and Knit-frocks.

sporadic, and the payment less, in spite of which the instinct to hunt fish remains. Men are born to it, drawn to it, unafraid, tough beyond anything and laws unto themselves. I am not clear whether they are wise or foolish, good guys or bad; only about what they contribute and mean. Nothing is more comforting than the lights on a fishing boat at night, nothing more stirring and defiant than the sight of one by day, flag flying, encircled by gulls and steaming bravely in. That is the moment to drop what you are doing and race to be there waiting on the quay.

Even when the trawlers are berthed side by side, their engines silent and the markets closed until five a.m., it all seems to happen 'down quay'. Everything from slopes to ropes, in a past or present fishing community (Ellis, 2001), leads to the sea. The English are drawn to it, and sit or stand there listening to the waves breaking and the gulls crying, contemplating, or meditating on the swell and the horizon. A crowd collects when the boat comes in, watching as the catch is unloaded. You can do better. Appraise the skipper. Identify the bass or gurnard you might want. Ask the price, have the money ready and don't get in the way. Whilst you may be on holiday, fishermen are at work.

The next best thing to catching fish is buying it from an 'under ten'. I have also struck lucky with beach casters hitting a shoal of mackerel. A man with a dozen fish in his bucket is usually ready to part with one or two.

Otherwise, go to fishmongers while you can. The trade is up against it, increasingly exclusive, and one that England cannot afford to lose. The Guild of Fishmongers and Poulterers is an old and honourable one, which endured for seven centuries until divided and conquered by Environmental Health. Their work requires training, preferably an apprenticeship, and a touch I never tired of showing off to friends in Bob the Fish's shop.

'Go on,' I used to say, pointing to a bream or a dory in his window, 'show us your strokeplay.'

So Bob would take the fish and place it on the slab, saying that the important thing was not to be frightened of it. Seconds later, with a few deft and confident sweeps of an extra-sharp knife, meat and bone were parted and the cleanest of frames remained. A man with one complaint behind him in thirty-eight years. The shop, abandoned by his successor, closed after six decades. We missed it dreadfully in Fordingbridge but another has opened. Hurrah!

For the supermarkets, fish is a loss-leader, often wasted at closing time. Tesco did not compete for service or price with the likes of Bob, but nevertheless handled more fish than all the UK's fishmongers put together by the time he retired. A large amount is farmed because it is easy to get and, having been frozen, to thaw out for presentation (Blythman, 2004). At number two in the industry, Sainsbury claims to employ a 'fishmonger' along with a 'butcher' and a 'baker', but how many have the experience and skills of trained apprentices? Buyer beware.

COOK'S ORACLE

Fish are divided into fin fish and invertebrates. In the white fish, round or flat, which tend to be delicate to eat, most of the oil is contained in the liver. In the oily fish, which are usually cheaper but considered healthier, it is distributed throughout the body. According to scientists, many of the demersal fish, or bottom-feeders, and the long-lived deepwater species are in trouble. However, some of the pelagic or mid-water fish and shellfish are currently sustainable – depending on how and where they are caught. The details, updated every year, are available from the Marine Conservation Society (MCS) at www.fishonline.org.

Fish put on weight in preparing to spawn, which usually takes place in the winter or spring. They remain in peak condition after shooting their roe, but for barely two weeks, losing their strength over the summer until collecting in shoals for the reproductive cycle to begin once again. The game and coarse river fish have seasons. The remainder are caught when available and sold throughout the year regardless of quality, which can vary in the extreme. If chilled immediately, fish keep for longer than people think. The white varieties freeze better than the oily ones. Cod, haddock, dory, gurnard, etc. are prone to an occasional and harmless parasitic worm.

Do not make assumptions about fish, even locally caught at the coast. Appraise their condition. The eyes should be glassy and proud (not sunken), the gills bright red, the smell invigorating but faint, the skin gleaming, and any scales intact. The round fish should be round, the flat ones plump. A certain amount of nonsense is talked about freshness. A white fish just in, betraying stiffness, should be given time for rigor to pass off and the meat to set. Some of the flatties, which can be quite tough, need up to three days. Any curd that emanates from the tissue is a good sign. With oily fish it is better to eat them quickly, or salt them. The fat they shed is promising too. Ironically, the winter is the worst time to be out fishing and the best for the condition of many species caught in and around British waters.

Farmed fish are on the increase, but need to consume three pounds of wild fishmeal to grow a pound of meat: they compare for looks rather than flavour, and raise health and environmental concerns. Salmon and trout are in the dock, oysters, mussels and eels in the clear. The frightening prospect of genetically modified fish and their inevitable escape into the mainstream to breed is looming.

Celebrity fish are those that shoot to stardom and overnight popularity with food writers, having been recommended by a high-profile cook or chef. If the cause is noble, the effect can be a price rise, with restaurants piling in, and potentially increased pressure on stocks. Bass was one of the first celebrity fish. Gurnard was another, though it never got off the ground. My brother will not eat it at all, having used it in the 'rubby-dubby' (bait) at sea.

Billingsgate remains the largest fish market in the world, which is surprising, given England's diminished grasp of its resources. The popularity of fish is dominated by automatic choices, more highly regarded than they deserve. When flat it is still plaice; when round it is still cod. Only market forces will change this. In 2004 my wife and I visited the famous Magpie Café in Whitby, where the obliging Ian Robson and his team do nine hundred covers a day without any apparent loss of composure. We selected the 'fish platter', and the four out of six varieties allowed. Lemon sole came top for flavour. Cod, the nation's favourite, admittedly at its worst time of year, was at the bottom.

All good cooks like to prepare fish. It is the greatest of the culinary arts, but also the most daunting to novices and needs the most carefully laid foundations. Knowing the fish in the fishmonger's window is the first and most important step. I have my favourites. You can find yours, register their texture, and learn to experiment. The dichotomy is that fish is better to eat on the bone, and more manageable off it. If you decide on the easy option – you have chosen a fish and want it scaled, skinned or filleted, but lack the experience – ask an expert to do it. Watch him or her on the job and have a go yourself next time, using a sharp knife and pliers. Open all fish along the back (except Dory) whether they are round or flat and pare the meat from the bones. The alternative is to pass on to feeders work which many of us enjoy. There is an art to eating fish as well as to preparing it.

Here is a selection from English waters that you may run into, mostly with MCS ratings. The species given a rating of 5 are 'vulnerable to overfishing and/or fished using methods which cause damage to the environment or non-target species' (usually trawling). The ones with a rating of 1 or 2 are fished within sustainable limits using methods that do not cause unacceptable damage to the environment or non-target species (usually lines and pots).* The game fish are licensed. The rest, neither rated nor licensed, you need not worry about – yet.

White Fish: Round (cod family)

Cod (5): more familiar than it should be and of variable quality, deteriorating from inshore waters in the summer when it hangs around wrecks and feeds on prawns. I have eaten cod my entire life, like most English people, but only twice in top condition, flaky and emitting the telltale milky white curd. A former favourite for salting (see page 265). The young are codling. Farms are on the way. The head and frame are good for stock. Firm texture at best. Usually comes in cutlets and fillets. Bake, grill or fry.

---

* *The BBC website (I hate this sort of thing) has the rating in the* reverse order.

Haddock (5): allegedly deaf and bearer of the thumbprint, left by St Peter when handling the fish.* A stronger smell than cod, but a superior flavour, the more popular the further north you go. Some stocks are overfished. A favourite for smoking. Firm texture. Usually comes in fillets. Bake, grill or fry.

Hake (5): a voracious fish, you can tell by the mouth, pursued to the edge of extinction by the Spanish, and a former nursery favourite of the English, owing to its absence of bones. The head and frame are good for stock. Pleasant flavour, softish texture. Usually comes in cutlets or fillets. Bake, grill or fry.

Ling (5): a deep-water habitué of rocks known as the 'long cod' or 'long line ling'. A fish with a 'barbe' that reaches great sizes. Still salted occasionally (see page 265) and worth looking out for in shops at the coast. Head, etc. are good for stock. Usually come in fillets. Firm texture. Bake, grill or fry.

Pollack (1–2): an athletic-looking fish, gleaming and gold, but a poor relation of cod, used for fish and chips by at least one chain of restaurants. Dryish meat, but firm, cheaper than cod and a favourite with country people. The skin is tough and easily detachable, the tiny scales can be rubbed off. Usually comes in fillets. Bake, grill or fry.

Saithe or coley (1–2): known as coalfish, owing to its dark skin and grey flesh, which has counted against it until now. Firmish texture. Usually come in fillets. Bake, grill or fry.

Whiting (1–2): former invalids' food, easy to digest, cooked with its tail in its mouth or 'curled'. The texture is firmer than it is given credit for and the taste lovely, but the size can be modest. Comes whole or occasionally in fillets. Bake, grill, fry or soup. Makes some of the best stock.

Whiting, blue (3): an ocean fish occurring more than thirty miles out. It has been taken in unsustainable numbers, but for meal and to fuel power stations. As food and with the right controls, this fish could be the next to partner chips. It eats better than cod, says the MCS and can grow up to two feet long.

Pout whiting (1–2): rarely encountered, not very popular and not much of a size, but a clean flavour and firmish texture. Usually comes whole. Bake, or soup.

---

* *The haddock is supposed to have been one of the fish which Christ foretold would have a coin in its mouth. The Dory is the other.*

White Fish: Round (non-cod family)

Conger (1–2): a sleek and ferocious type of eel, which barks and can be a handful on board boat. The flavour is good and the texture extra firm, popular with the Chinese community. Comes in cutlets. Steam, then remove the skin and bones – a disadvantage of this fish – and commit to a soup or stew.

Garfish (1–2): a queer fellow with the body of an eel, a spike for a nose and luminous green bones, less popular than it used to be. Nice flavour, firmish texture. Comes whole. Bake.

Grey mullet (5): a tame fish, easily caught, good from the sea and poor from an estuary. Needs scaling. Firmish texture. Comes whole and in fillets. Bake, grill or fry.

Gurnard, grey and red (1–2): a bottom-feeder, worth trying. The first time I saw it 'highly recommended' was in Lancaster market in 1986. Good flavour, firm texture. Usually comes in fillets. Bake, grill or fry.

Huss (5): a type of shark, also known as dogfish, rock salmon or plain rock, and an occasional option in chippies. Mild flavour, softish texture. Comes whole and without the skin. Fillet and fry

John Dory (1–2): corruption of *jaune d'orée* – the *saint-pierre* in France – and another bearer of the legendary thumbprint. A singleton of renowned flavour, but a low proportion of meat to bone. Firm texture. Use the small ones, the heads and frames for stock. Comes whole but needs filleting. Bake or grill. Too good to fry.

Monkfish (5): an ugly bugger from the deep that shot to popularity, now endangered as a result. The flavour is fine, the texture very firm. Only the tail is eaten, having been skinned. Comes in a piece. Use for soup or stew.

Ray, skate, thornback (5): a family with over a dozen members which bears young rather than eggs. More people love the flavour than loathe it (like me) so stocks are not looking good. Firm texture. Only the wings are eaten, having been skinned and preferably kept for a few days. Bake or grill.

Red mullet (1–2): no relation of the grey one. Stocks in British waters are better than in the Mediterranean. Another fish that provokes mixed feelings, and needs scaling. The liver and gamey flavour are prized by its admirers. The nickname 'sea woodcock' arises from the custom of baking red mullet whole and with the guts in. I have also eaten it filleted and even pressed, to visual advantage only, in a swanky restaurant. Comes whole. Bake or grill.

Redfish (1–2): not to be confused with the salmon (see page 250); less popular than it was and fairly cheap, possibly owing to colour prejudice. Mild flavour, soft texture. Comes in fillets. Grill or fry.

Sea bass (1–2): another saltwater fish that will ascend an estuary, where I have caught them on a feather. Anglers want bass preserved as a game fish, which is causing tension at the coast. Watch out for the spines (vicious) when handling or scaling. Use the head and frame for stock. To see a Chinese skinning and boning a bass with chopsticks is enthralling. The delicate flavour is much appreciated, but the texture is softer than supposed, even a little overrated. Comes whole or in fillets. Poach a large fish, otherwise bake or grill.

Sea or black bream (1–2): summer visitor increasingly common with climate change. Needs scaling. The flavour is strongish, the texture firm. Usually comes whole, but you can fillet the big 'uns. Bake or grill.

Trigger fish (1–2): another newcomer, appearing in the Solent. The shape and flesh are a little like a dory's, the skin like leather. Comes whole. Bake.

Weaver (1–2): a possible corruption of 'viper'. Its poisonous fin, and habit of burying itself in sand, catches out the occasional bather. It is rarely seen in fishmongers', but not bad: softish in texture. Fillet, avoiding the fin, and fry.

Wrasse (1–2): the male is a gaudy-looking chap, the female more modest. Both are extra bony – stock again.

WHITE FISH: FLAT

Brill (5): one of the best, and consequently one of the quickest to rise in price. Use the heads and frames for stock. The flavour is good, the meat firm, but in short supply on the smaller fish. The larger ones may be poached or baked, whole or filleted, and grilled.

Dabs (1–2): not much on them, but good for stock and soup.

Flounder or flook (1–2): an habitué of estuaries that spawns at sea, on sale in the chippy in Flookborough, Lancashire, where they used to be 'trodden' (i.e. located underfoot in the mud at low water). The quality improves in the winter. The meat is medium to soft – eat very fresh. A fish which is big enough to fillet is best. Grill or fry.

Halibut (5): can reach colossal sizes. The former fishmonger in Falmouth had an eighty-pounder some years ago, and claimed to have seen an eight-hundred-pounder stuck on a lorry. Greenland halibut are with us at present, farmed fish on the way. The best I have eaten came from the van in Wickham Market, Suffolk, about three weeks after Christmas. The flavour is good, the meat firm, the price considerable. Look for steaks containing the bone. Grill.

Plaice (5): one the best-known fish in England, associated with the ports of Scarborough and Bridlington; long-lived but now in shorter supply than it is given credit for. The flavour is good, the flesh soft – eat very fresh. Usually comes in fillets. Fry.

Sole (1–2): linked to Dover, but equally good from other waters, notably Torbay and Lundy. Unlike many others, this is a fish that can be in pretty fine fettle throughout the year – and also too fresh to eat. A sole just caught needs hanging for a couple of days or it will be tough: the engine room was the customary place for fish earmarked for the skipper's table. A restaurant favourite, and expensive, for many years. Remove the head and tail, skin both sides and bake, grill or fry. Makes some of the best stock.

Sole, lemon (1–2): preferred by some to Dovers; the price is rising as a result. Lemons need to be very fresh or else the delicate flavour suffers. The texture is softish. Leave the skin – it is not easy to remove without damaging the fish. Eat fresher than Dovers, comes whole or in fillets. Bake or fry.

Sole, megrim and witch (1–2): poor relations, but abundant and worth trying. Flavour good, meat softish. Look for a fish big enough to fillet. Fry.

Turbot (5): *rhombus* in Latin, after its shape, a mainstay of haute cuisine with a price to match, even higher than brill's. The meat is extra firm with large flakes. An almost festive fish, poached and served whole. Alternatively fillet and bake or grill.

Oily Fish*

Herrings (1–2): the 'silver darling' that spawned a way of life on England's east coast, then

---

* *Herring family come first.*

became eerily absent, but returned in modest quantities and continues to be cured (see page 267). Fresh herrings have a small number of scales, and soft roes in the males that are much appreciated. Bake whole or fry the fillets.

Pilchards (1–2): an adult sardine, still salted (see page 263–4), that was eaten fresh in Cornwall. Good flavour, softish texture. Fry whole, over a coal range if you have one, minding the spits.

Sprats (1–2): occupied the same rank as bacon for generations of country people. Today one of the few surviving examples of the occasional shared catch, given away after the bumper landings on the south coast. For as long as the autumn flush persists, sprats are unlikely to be fashionable. Try them, fry them, eating the whole thing.

Whitebait (1–2): it is no longer permitted to catch herring under 20cm, so all the whitebait are infant sprats. They were a former *pièce de résistance* eaten in Greenwich at an annual supper marking the beginning of term for parliament. There is still a whitebait festival in Southend, Essex. Dust in flour, deep fry until golden brown and squeeze lemon over the top.

Mackerel (1–2): another 'darling', silver and aquamarine, mentioned in connection with a certain type of sky. Charles II permitted this fish to be sold (with milk) on Sundays. So did William III. Gluts were salted (see page 258); smoking has taken over. Mackerel visibly lose freshness. Get them, ideally, straight from the sea and into the pan as autumn beckons, preferably for breakfast, whole or in fillets. Otherwise, bake or grill.

ALSO RAN

Sand eels: an important member of the food chain imperilled by overfishing for meal, which taste of the seabed, but some people cook them.

Scad: sometimes known as horse (possibly 'coarse') mackerel; not as good and no relation to its namesake, but not bad either.

Shad: there are two sorts, both related to herring, which live at sea, spawn in rivers and have a good record as food, in spite of their ridiculous (and obscure) titles. The twaite shad was caught under licence from the seventeenth century in Shad Thames, on a stretch opposite London's Isle of Dogs, which was hit by pollution. The West Country cousin, entitled the allis shad, is bigger and considered better to eat. The Americans are fond of this fish, in particular the roe. I have bought it in Bideford market, but have yet to find a way of cooking it properly or coping with the bones.

QUEER FELLOWS

Cuttlefish (1–2): an oddball with internal shell of great interest to budgies. Sustainable amounts are caught in traps. The body has a gritty skin that should be removed with the guts, gristle, etc., leaving the meat and tentacles. Careful cleaning is essential, though the ink can be kept for adding to the sauce. Cut into pieces and stew. Very tasty.

Squid (5): another oddball, more versatile as a swimmer than it appears, caught with apparatus called 'jigs', but not appreciated as much in England as in the rest of Europe. It is not clear why. The meat does not have to 'eat like rubber' – the usual complaint – provided you stew it for as long as cuttlefish. The young and tender squid are sometimes fried with chilli, garlic, etc.

GAME FISH

Salmon (licensed): a muscular and legendary fish with rank, bravery, strength and glamour equal to any bird or beast. Bob Curtis sold fifty wild salmon a week – a figure that no longer made sense by the 1980s. Numbers were hit by the discovery of their feeding grounds at sea and the effect on their spawning grounds inland of fish-farm and other barriers, pollution and water extraction. In only a few cases have they started to recover. The best salmon I have ever eaten was on British Rail coming back from Scotland. Out of the Tay that morning, the man said. A likely story, I thought, and had to think again. The quality of a salmon is determined by how long it has been fasting and deteriorating in a river after feeding at sea. One school of thought believes that the fish should be eaten extra fresh, another that it should be hung for a few days and became a little whiffy. I can vouch for both. The legal catches are tagged. Salmon is one of those foods that are almost better cold. Bake or poach the whole fish, or a piece like the head and shoulders, and grill the cutlets.

Sea trout (licensed): a brownie that lives and feeds at sea, transforming it into a bigger silver fish that used to be considered a different species. The adults return to fresh water in spring and early summer in order to spawn. Netting takes place by day from the beginning of June till the end of July. The rods cast flies by night over chosen stretches. The legal catches are tagged, the same as salmon. The meat is a little drier, but firm, and has the same pink pigmentation from the intake of crustaceans. Do not hang this one, though. Bake or poach whole fish; grill fillets.

Smelts: a salmon relation, though not a game fish, the size of sprats. They are said to smell of cucumber and taste pleasant. Fry.

I have yet to bone up on shark (5), tusk (5), tope and catfish.

COOK'S ORACLE

Fish and chips are a familiar mismatch. The fish was the bits and pieces from market, fried up, and readily available in Soho by the beginning of Queen Victoria's reign. Chips came in with the peeling of potatoes, it is not certain when or where, but established a heartland in Lancashire. The two remained separate until the 1860s, but by the twentieth century 'had become an established institution over most of Industrial England' (John Walton, 1992). The reaction was mixed, since the shops were seldom in respectable areas, kept late hours and came to be associated with naughty goings-on. The number rose in the glory days to over thirty thousand.

Fish and chips were credited with making life bearable for the working classes, possibly averting revolution, and winning the First World War. They were also considered indigestible, expensive, unwholesome, and a contributor to secondary poverty, culinary ignorance, and the failure to use cheap ingredients to their best advantage.

Sorry, but I am not a fan either. I have never eaten the two together without regretting it – and wondering how the stocks of ever-present cod are doing compared to the other good or better types of fish that are seldom used. As for the chips, they do not provide a balanced combination. The producer-friendly mix in the batter can be one problem, the coupling of two greasy foods is the second. The combination itself is the third. Potatoes do not go half so well with fish as do toast and butter, or even mushy peas. The exceptions are salad potatoes, firm or waxy, late scrapers, boiled or steamed new potatoes and mash – the top storey in fish pie.

Fresh fish is best with vegetables as delicate as itself: beans, peas, chard, spinach, sea kale and green salads. The fashion is currently to put them under the fish, over the fish, anywhere but the obvious place, next to it.

Fennel is the customary herb to pair with fish, having been used by fishermen (see page 413). You may not have to plant it. Look for clumps in the wild, particularly at the seaside, and stuff the fish with a handful.

For dressing, a novice can do no better than a squeeze of lemon or a dash of soy, sea salt on the side, and pepper or sweet paprika on top.

A slightly more sophisticated approach, for fish baked or grilled in butter, is to put the fish on a plate or plates when cooked and keep warm. Then de-glaze the pan with some dry white or even red wine, boiling off the alcohol, and pour it over the fish.

Allow about 6oz (175g) of fish fillet per person, but up to double on the bone.

POACHING

Needs care and the right equipment, but not difficult. Use whole fish, particularly salmon, sea trout and bass, and brill and turbot. They should be cleaned and gutted, but entire, and weigh at least 2lb (900g).

The round fish need an oblong kettle to cook in, furnished with a tray and lid. Mine, a worthwhile investment but modestly priced, measures approximately 24 x 6 inches (60 x 15cm). The flat fish require a wider sort of pan, less common than it was. The Victorian turbot kettles are diamond-shaped.

Poached fish are sometimes referred to as 'boiled', a misnomer which, if taken literally leads to overcooking and disaster. Commit the fish to its pan, barely cover with cold water, and bring up to no more than simmering point.

To eat hot, cook for five minutes and lift out the fish on to a warm dish. Divide by running a knife or trowel along the back from shoulder to tail, peeling off the skin with the help of a fork, and easing the meat from the bone.

To eat cold, cook for two minutes and leave the fish in the pan of water for 6–8 hours. Serve as above.

BAKING

Needs care, particularly with bigger fish. It is customary to use tin foil, but not necessary, and slows the process down. As for timing, it is for most of us a calculated guess. Try taking a consensus to safeguard your position.

Use whole fish, particularly codling, sea bass and bream, Dover sole (skinned), mackerel, salmon or sea trout. Slash the whole fish to the bone twice or three times on either side in order to stop the skin splitting. The heads and tails of white fish may be removed for stock, otherwise leave. Moisten the bottom of the pan with white wine.

Use also cutlets and fillets, skin side up or underneath as required. It helps the texture of softish fillets, like bass, to put the fish back together again with one fillet on top of the other. Melt some butter in a pan and dredge the fish in it.

Commit the fish to a medium to cool preheated oven at 170°C/325°F/gas mark 3 for about 15 minutes per pound, or less as the weight increases. Check on progress a couple of times. When the heat has conducted itself to a skewer, which can be used to probe whole fish, and the meat comes away from the bone, it is cooked. Cutlets and fillets should be firm to the touch. Make haste if they start to leak juice.

GRILLING

Easy. Use cutlets and fillets of any sort. Melt some butter in a pan and dredge the fish in it. Place under the grill and baste at intervals. Remove when firm.

FRYING

Easy. Use: (a) whole fish, particularly herrings, sprats and smelts. Dredge in flour, or fine oatmeal, which is crustier. Soft herring roes, an old favourite, may be done the same way; (b) the softer fillets, bones removed, particularly flounder, plaice, megrim and witch sole. Dredge in flour and fry as above, or wash in beaten egg and coat in fresh white breadcrumbs, then fry.

In each case fry in oil or a mixture of oil and butter, dripping, lard or bacon fat until golden.

N.B. It seems a little mad to deep-fry fish or give instructions for it when many people do not have the necessary equipment, there is often a chippy within reach, and the only reasonably priced edible meal to be had out in many parts of England is deep-fried fish. The result may be better at home, but not much.

STOCK

The quickest and easiest of the stocks to make for soup and stews. Use white fish only, heads as well as frames if you can get them. Some of the flatties make the best stock, particularly whiting, Dover sole and brill. Cover the bones with water, bring up to simmering point and skim until the froth is white. Add a peeled and sliced onion, a bay leaf, salt and peppercorns. Strain through a fine sieve after 15–20 minutes, which is all it takes. Reduce the liquor to make it stronger. You may even cut it with chicken stock, but use only with fish.

FISH SOUP

For 4–6: 3 pints (1.8l) of stock, oil, 1 peeled and chopped onion and 1 clove garlic, 1lb (450g) sliced tomatoes (skins, seeds and all), 1 glass red wine, pepper or chilli (for a kick), 3oz (75g) white rice (unwashed), or 1 ½ oz (40g) couscous or vermicelli, salt and fresh herbs (parsley, chives, etc.) to taste.

Brown the onions and garlic in the oil, add the tomatoes, stock, rice or couscous and wine. Cover and barely simmer for 45 minutes. Press through a sieve, rubbing hard, with the back of a wooden spoon. Discard the solids you are left with, which should amount to no more than 1 dessertspoon. Season to taste. Reheat, giving it a stir. Add the herbs before serving. This soup, kept cool, improves in flavour over two or three days.

FISH STEW

2 pints (1.2l) of soup made as above, a good 1lb (450g) firm white fish fillets, skinned, boned and cut into cubes. Conger (cooked), dory and gurnard are particularly good. Cover with the soup and cook very gently for 5–10 minutes until firm. Do not stir or boil otherwise the fish may break up. Remove the pieces to warm plates and pour the liquor over the top.

From scratch for 4:

1lb (450g) firm white fish fillets, skinned as above, boned and cut into large pieces, some oil, 1 onion and a clove of garlic, peeled and chopped, 4 medium-sized tomatoes (skins and seeds removed), 1 glass of red wine, any leftover gravy, stock or vegetable water, salt, pepper, soy and fresh herbs to taste.

Lightly brown the onion and garlic in the oil until soft. Add the tomatoes and wine. Simmer for 10 minutes until soft. Remove from the heat, and introduce the fish with enough stock, meat gravy, or vegetable or tap water, fortified with soy, barely to cover. Cook very gently for a further 5–10 minutes or until the fish is firm, being careful not to let it break up. Remove to soup plates with a perforated spoon and keep warm. Season the sauce, adjusting the flavour and reducing until thick if necessary. Pour over the fish, and sprinkle some freshly chopped herbs on the top.

Cuttlefish or squid, cleaned and sliced, 1lb (450g). Proceed as above, but cover and commit to a preheated oven for 2–3 hours at 170°C /325°F/gas mark 3. Keep the fish almost covered and moisten with water when necessary. If you have kept the ink, stir it in at the end. I add some chilli sauce or pepper too.

One from Le Promenade des Anglais – *La Bourride*

Imagine a summer evening with Nice lighting up, a warm breeze and a couple of swells out on the town (but only just out of shorts). All we needed was a good feed in agreeable surroundings to fill in time before conquering hearts. Bouillabaisse, which we had heard of, authentic and otherwise, was served almost everywhere. So was *La Bourride* – an unknown quantity. Impressed by the definite article and ready to jump in, we chose a restaurant and ordered wine along with this *Bourride*, then sat back drinking hard and waiting impatiently to find out what it was.

After ten minutes, the maître d' appeared in the customary tail coat and stood behind my confederate. He produced with a flourish a large baby's bib and tied it around his neck. He did the same to me, lifting my hair to do so. A waiter arrived bearing a tray. He put it down on a nearby table, transferring a tureen dish and plates to ours. He raised the lid of the tureen, which erupted with the strong scent of garlic, revealing four pieces of firm white fish basking in a rich cream-coloured sauce. He removed the fish with a slice to the plates, the sauce with a ladle, and potatoes from the dish with a silver spoon and fork. Finally he covered the tureen and with the inevitable 'Bon appétit, messieurs', left me, my mate and *La Bourride* to each other.

The moment had passed when two young lads could wait any longer. We fed and drank without talking until exhausted and darkness enveloped the world outside. We only paused when the waiter returned to empty the tureen. You needed the bib. And the ladies? All over us, naturally. It must have been the garlic.

Bourride lacks the snob appeal of bouillabaisse, an advantage, and seems to travel better, tasting just as good in England as on Le Promenade des Anglais – another *zuppa inglese*.

Proceed in stages. For four people, you need: a few peeled waxy or salad potatoes, 4 fillets of the best firm white fish, say brill, dory or ling; 1 ½ pints (900ml) fish stock; 1oz (25g) *beurre manié*; 5fl oz (150ml) garlic mayonnaise (aïoli), freshly made.

Steam the potatoes and keep them warm. Heat soup plates and a bowl in a cool oven. Put the fish in a pan, with the stock and simmer extra gently until firm. Remove with a slice to the plates and keep warm too. Bring the stock up to boiling point and whisk in the *beurre manié*. Put the mayonnaise in the warm bowl and whisk in the liquor, which will become smooth and thick. Introduce the sauce to the fish. Sup quickly, with the potatoes.

The *beurre manié* is not customary, but helps to stop the sauce curdling. I used to make *La Bourride* adding the local crayfish.

CLASSIC CREAM SAUCE

Of all the ways of cooking fish, this is the most complementary and luscious. Wait to do it until the ingredients are available.

For 4: take fillets of a top-o'-the-range white fish, like Dover sole, bass, dory, hake, brill, turbot, or scallops; dry white wine in the pan or champagne, salt and white pepper to taste, ½ pint (275ml) raw, ripe cream of the best sort – the dread crème fraîche is not up to the job.

Put the fish in a close-fitting pan. Pour the wine over the top, covering the bottom of the vessel. Grill the fish until just firm, basting well. Remove to a hot plate or plates, leaving the liquor behind. Boil up the wine in the pan and reduce until 2–4 tablespoons are left. Remove from the heat and stir in the cream. Continue to reduce until smooth and thick, and the bubbles are getting large, stirring with a wooden spoon and making sure it does not boil over. Season to taste with salt and white pepper. Remove from the heat and check the flavour. If satisfied, incorporate any juices that have leaked from the fish. Whisk a knob of butter into the sauce, then pour it over the fish.

To vary: (a) reduce a cupful of first-quality fish stock with the wine before adding the cream; (b) add finely chopped shallots fried in a little butter, or freshly chopped parsley, chives, chervil or sorrel to the finished sauce.

PLATES

A view from a beauty spot: what it means. The moor is a former royal forest or hunting ground, which provides venison, subsistence grazing for the local breeds of cattle and sheep, whortleberries for pies, and heather for honey bees. Black grouse bred up here within living memory, and bustards before them. A herd of feral goats, originally meat and milk producers, occupies the fringe. Pheasants and rabbits are common wherever there is cover and cultivation; hares are more scarce. The land, which descends to the valley, was modestly enclosed by medieval monks and more comprehensively in the eighteenth and nineteenth centuries in order to rationalise food production. The cereal crops consist of wheat and barley. One of the two mills in the area occupies a site mentioned in the Domesday Book. Cider orchards remain, but the consumption of beer advanced with the opening of a brewery in Victorian times. The hedges, woods and fields contain the usual pickings, including sorrel, garlic, blackberries, sloes, hazelnuts, and fungi.The farms are former self-sufficient units with kitchen gardens, dairies, pig and poultry pens, bread ovens and facilities for curing meat. Until the railways, few of the items on the tables at local inns, came from further away than the eye could see. The coastal towns and villages trapped fowl, dried laver and salted fish, looking to the Severn for its runs of salmon, elvers, eels and lampreys, and large populations of herring, conger and shrimps. The rivers and streams were netted until the 1870s. The main difference in the last 80 years is in the number of working men and horses on the land. Cheddar cheese country begins in the distance.

EXMOOR, AUGUST 2006

The duckling is a genuine Aylesbury, once the commonest of domestic breeds, recorded from the eighteenth century. Its season coincided with new potatoes and peas. There is one producer left. The bird has been sewn up and roasted before a fire in order to conserve the juices. This is an art at which the English excelled before adopting more convenient modes of cookery. The meat hangs in a Victorian 'hastener', a portable device built to stand in front of open coal ranges. A clockwork 'jack' turns the fowl from above. The fat runs clear into a tray below. The fuel is a mixture of dry wood, and green, which burns hotter once a blaze gets going. The door to the bread oven, in use after 150 years, is to the right of the picture.

AT HOME, JUNE 2006

There are not many village bakers left, and even fewer brick or brick housed ovens. They are not listed, however old, and get torn out when businesses close. This double decker was installed when the shop became a bakery in 1841. It is heated with steam tubes that run from front to back, and are visible through the door. The old proving oven is underneath. Colin Honey is holding the peel with which he loads the chamber. He bakes the bread first at around 450°F, followed by cakes and pasties as the temperature declines.

WEST COUNTRY, OCTOBER 2006

Shops make a town or village. This one does everything required of a master butcher. It sells well bred, fed and cut local English meat with all its credentials, grown on chosen farms and hung for as long as it requires. The staff are informed, courteous, and pleased to answer questions, give advice, and conspire with like minds. I bought a piece of beef that cut like butter and would have passed at a Victorian banquet. 'I bet it did not cost you much either,' said the girl in the grocer round the corner.

WELSH MARCHES, JUNE 2006

White Park cattle are the emblem of the Rare Breeds Survival Trust. This Chartley Hall cow, a Staffordshire native, and a member of an exclusive club with a gold star pedigree and royal connections. Her antecedents were stolen goods, possibly of pre-Roman origin, which were driven from the moors above Leek to the slopes below the castle in the middle ages. The cattle moved away with their owner in the twentieth century, but, nearly ninety years later, some returned to their old home. Their meat was exempted from the ban on beef of over thirty months old, which was imposed during the BSE outbreak.

MIDLANDS, SEPTEMBER 2006

Hereford is the most famous name in cattle. A bull prepares to take part in the grand parade. This breed had the world at its feet for a hundred years. Then, in common with other English and British livestock, it floundered in a market dominated by the food giants and lower priced continental meat. Numbers fell from 1960, but by the millennium had started to recover. The beef remains the one which competitors aspire to. It is now poised to make a grand comeback. The owner and his children will make sure.

West Midlands, June 2004

Livestock owner William Dart treads the same farm and even the yard where the ancestors of his North Devon bull rose to eminence in the reign of George III. These cattle, transported by the ship Charity were the first English breed to disembark on American soil in 1623, and the first I noticed 360 years later. Numbers are lower than they were, but stabilising thanks to loyal followers. Look for the sumptuous ruby coat against the grass and amongst the rushes ('daggers'). The beef can equal Hereford.

WEST COUNTRY, SEPTEMBER 2006

Herdwicks at home in Cumbria: at least one of these flocks was driven on foot over the mountains to the show. This is a Trojan of a sheep, capable of surviving any wind, storm or blizzard thrown at it, of eating coarse vegetation, and of supplying some of the toughest wool and tastiest meat around, unofficially called 'royal'. The mutton bacon is called 'macon'. The breed recovered from Foot and Mouth to gain a certified status. After judging, the fell runners climb to the summit behind the pens and race down again.

NORTH OF ENGLAND, OCTOBER 2004

Blue-faced Leicester sheep, seen here at home in the border region, developed from the Border Leicester in the early twentieth century. Their antecedents were promoted by the great Hanoverian farmer Robert Bakewell. In the UK's unique three-tiered system of sheep husbandry, these leggy and Roman nosed ewes are an important link between the different breeds which inhabit high and low altitudes. Their crosses with mountain sheep are called mules. They are strong, fertile and mate with heavier lowland rams to produce most of the lamb for the English table.

NORTH OF ENGLAND, AUGUST 2004

Southdown rams at home on the Southdowns: this quartet belongs to Paul and Stephen Humphreys. They are members of a breed that took on the rest of the world, beat it, and came to represent quality in lamb and mutton throughout the nineteenth century. Their fall from pole position, occasioned by two world wars and super-market forces, was like a deep and prolonged sigh. The turning point in their decline has now been reached. The number of ewes is a fraction of what it was, but on the increase. A resounding comeback is eagerly awaited.

SOUTH OF ENGLAND, OCTOBER 2006

Tamworth sow and young, not far from Tamworth: the pig is the last of the Chinese star signs, but the guardian of the temple, and of great fascination to man for hundreds of years. This one is where she belongs in the woods. She enjoys the shade, roots with her snout, and will dib in uneaten seeds with her feet, helping oak and beech regenerate. Provided they have space, pigs do not feed off bark and saplings. They are far less destructive to trees than sheep or goats, and, by current standards, far better managers than people.

WELSH MARCHES, JULY 2005

York ham curing with Ian Weatherhead. The large white pig, fed to great weights, the long cut and the dry, cold winters of the north of England: these are the things that helped to make the huge celebrated hams that went to master grocers, London, and France for *assiettes anglaises*. This one weighs about 30lb. It lay in salt for about a month, and now waits to mature. Smoking is not part of the process. The sale of two hams covered the cost to the farmer of keeping the pig, providing him with the bacon for nothing. Artisan butchers took up the baton. The bigger and fatter the ham, the more popular it is with travellers and country people, particularly the older generation.

NORTH OF ENGLAND, OCTOBER 2004

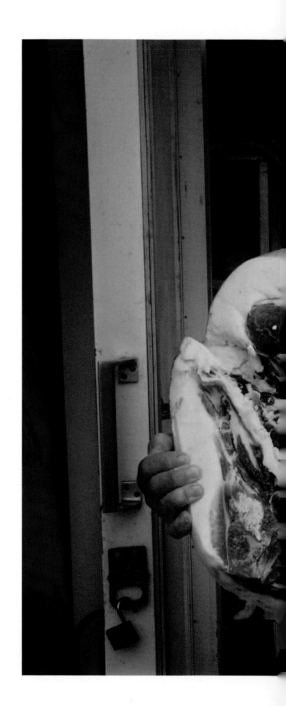

Yorkshire bacon cured by David Brown. Philip, his son, is in the background. The back and belly of pork, boned, salted and rolled, dry more quickly than hams: they are ready to eat at a few weeks old. The shop, located in Otley, sold the full range of items made on the premises by generations of manufacturing butchers. It has now closed. Other businesses may follow taking their specialities with them. Their future depends on whether or not the number of supermarkets in the area, currently standing at over twenty, will be considered enough.

NORTH OF ENGLAND, OCTOBER 2004

Hardy is after teal and wigeon in the Essex marshes. Winnie is a Chesapeake retriever. The birds on the water are decoys. We rowed to an island, before dawn. The light brought every type of duck and wader, from quarry species to whimbrel and avocet. You change from wildfowler to twitcher and back again. You can run over the mud, but not stop, otherwise you sink. You can be in a dinghy, freezing, exhausted, shipping water and rowing into an offshore wind.... A seal joined us, doe-eyed and apparently eager to make friends. It would have drowned Winnie given the chance.

EAST ANGLIA, JANUARY 2005

Home-fed chicken, slaughtered and dry plucked: it is hung for up to two weeks, depending on the weather, then gutted. A supermarket fowl dies, after systematic abuse, at a quarter of the age of a free range bird. It is wet plucked, which encourages bacterial growth, and must be eviscerated and sold before it goes off – and has the chance to develop any flavour. It is also England's favourite food. I pay more for my chicken, but we both benefit.

SOUTH OF ENGLAND, DECEMBER 2005

Harvesting black headed seagulls' eggs. Nothing could be more politically incorrect, more traditional or more sustainable. A marsh dwelling bird's greatest threats are vermin, oil refineries, pollution, and rising sea levels, not a handful of men authorised to take an egg that a black headed gull can lay every day in the spring. Licences are not renewed or passed on. The season is only a few weeks long. Eggs may be tested by putting them in water: fresh ones lie on their sides, addled ones tip up. London takes nearly all.

ENGLAND, APRIL 2006

Seine fishing: another of the world's oldest occupations, which is not unopposed, in spite of surviving so long with the fish it catches and landing so few. The decline in the number of salmon (just netted) has happened in the last 30 years. The discovery of where it feeds at sea, the barriers to its spawning grounds up river, water extraction and pollution are the main causes. By the time the last seining licences are due to run out – they cannot be renewed or transferred at present – there could be no fish left.

SOUTH OF ENGLAND, JULY 2004

Some go to Aldeburgh for the music, some for a swim, some for the fish, some for all three, and to see the marsh harriers further up the coast. It is Sunday morning. The big thing for schoolchildren, real or overgrown, is to meet the boat coming in. This one is an 'under ten' in terms of regulations (i.e. under ten metres in length) and permitted to fish within the twelve-mile limit. The vessel is pulled by cables from the water, rotated on a turntable, and pulled back. The catch is sold from a hut on the beach. A clump of sea peas rambles over the shingle nearby.

East Coast, June 2004

Cockle vendor: Peter Johnson followed his father into the business which started in 1919. Inflation proof prices were painted on the walls of the shop, housed in a blue caravan. When 'weights and measures' called, it was not the sale of cockles in half pints to which they objected, but the word 'pint' – now crossed out. (Beer and milk are O.K.) Passing mothers give cockles to their infants, who keep the taste for life. After the Morecambe Bay disaster, the government banned all collectors in the area, legitimate and otherwise.

SOUTH OF ENGLAND, NOVEMBER 2006

Char fishing: the skiff is designed according to the waves it meets. The rods are sixteen feet in length. Each is equipped with a bell, a line of up to a 100 feet, nine hand made spinners of polished bronze, hooks and a weight. The char is a landlocked salmon with a red stripe, deposited in English lakes in the last glass age. Paul caught half a dozen. He, a caretaker by profession, eats better than an Edwardian parson. He gave us three fish to cook that evening. The meat was firm, delicate, and the colour of peaty water.

NORTH OF ENGLAND, JULY 2005

A St George's flag goes on a prize winner. The Jersey comes at or near the top of a list of unsurpassed dairy cattle, valued more abroad than they are at home. England had the best milk in the world for 200 years, before relegating it to a supporting role, almost non-existent in towns. A perk of being in the countryside is that you can buy quality milk, sweet, fresh, fragrant, untreated, and alive from a small and select number of licensed farms. If such milk is reborn as a health food, via the US, most people will not be able to get it.

WEST MIDLANDS, JUNE 2006

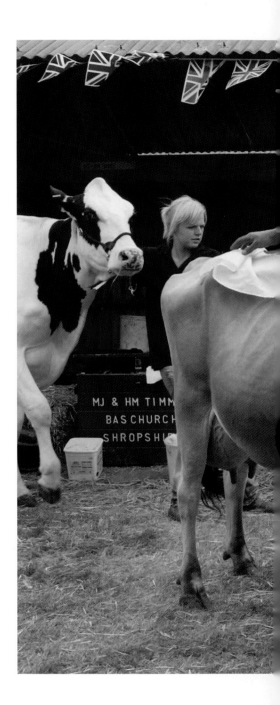

Ayrshire cattle, perfected in Scotland, came south in the nineteenth century. Their milk, almost emulsified, is good for cheese. Jersey, Guernsey and South Devon milk is higher in fat and the best for cream, especially clotted. Shorthorn and Red Poll milk made famous butter. These qualities, along with the climate, vegetation and access to markets, account for the distribution of cattle in England, the foods they produce in the different places, and the standards reached by far-sighted breeders with Nature's permission.

West Midlands, June 2006

Roy holds a plate of 'cut rounds', made with yeast, one of the items necessary for a genuine cream tea. His daughter makes them in the cafe and bakery behind. South Devon tuffs and Cornish splits differ only in shape: they are not cut out but packed together in a close fitting tray and emerge from the oven with a 'kissing' crust rather than a defined rim. The soft crumb and mild flavour are just the thing for clotted cream and strawberry jam or golden syrup. Scones are easier to knock up, and more common, but clumsy by comparison and come from far away.

WEST COUNTRY, JUNE 2006

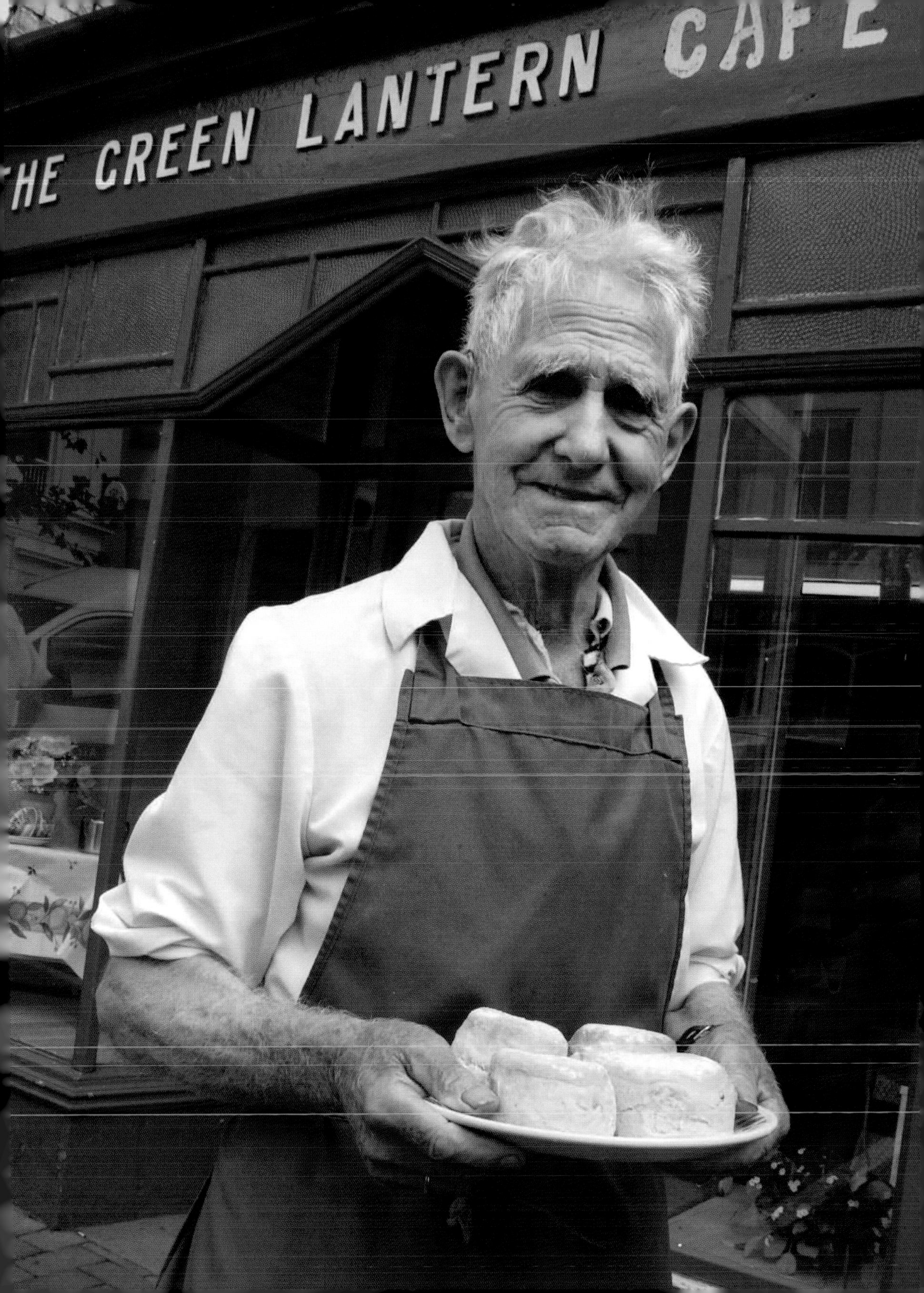
THE GREEN LANTERN CAFE

Laura keeps shop in Butcher's Row, Barnstaple. The cream, incidentally, is one of the first things that visitors expect to see in the west of England – a 400-year-old food-cum-treat lifted off the top of scalded milk, and easily transported to market. The remnants make a distinctly flavoured butter. Clotted cream is widely manufactured, but seldom to this standard. The colour is due to the breed of cow used, their grass, and the season. The crust is thanks to the producer. The vendor, who could sell anything she chooses, chose the best.

WEST COUNTRY, JULY 2006

Kitty Clarke salts the butter in her dairy. The cows are outside. The milk passed through the continuous flow separator behind her, into a barrel churn, and between wooden pats, all by hand. She started making butter twice every day in the Second World War, and finished over 60 years later, a mountain climbed in private and a summit quietly reached. Less than ten other producers are left from tens of thousands. First quality English butter has a scent, not a smell, and almost sheds light. It has two ingredients. A low fat spread can have around twelve.

EAST OF ENGLAND

Joyce Bishop holds a jar of bread and butter pickle, made to go on bread and butter, and a simple, palatable way of storing cucumber. She was introduced to the pickle by her daughter, who encountered it in America, and sells it from a diminutive, curtained theatre of a roadside shed near Thetford Forest. In addition to the apple trees at the front, there is land at the back with a chicken and vegetable plot. Cottage gardens only became a nostalgic design concept in the twentieth century. Their original function was to provide food.

East of England, June 2004

Fen tigress: she obtained these carrots, under cover and fly free, three to six months in advance of the rest of us. Another perk of being in the countryside is buying vegetables, fruit, jam, eggs, and flowers at garden gates. People say they hate shopping, but in what context? A supermarket is a sensory deprivation chamber, where contact is either zero or false. A walk to or stop at the wayside stall is at the other end of the scale. The produce is automatically fresh, local, traceable, and may be measured in food feet and inches.

EAST OF ENGLAND, MARCH 2004

Cobnuts are a cultivated form of hazelnut, introduced to England centuries ago. They grow in plats, or plots, some of which are 200 years old, in Kent. About 10 per cent remains of the acreage covered in 1914. The bushes are coppices, pruned every year. The flowering male is a catkin. The female is a nutkin. They crop in bunches, fresh from St Filbert's day, becoming drier over the next two months. The small and delightful world of nuts is blessed with pretty language, and a stalwart society that fights hard to keep it going.

SOUTH OF ENGLAND, SEPTEMBER 2004

Over 200 different types of blackberries were scattered through the guts of birds, travellers and drovers along the highways and byways of England. They are part of a large repertoire. Country children in Victorian times, charged with doing something useful or wanting a snack, gathered wild fruits, pignut and ramsons like the aboriginals they were. Boys and girls of eight learned from their peers the culinary and medicinal value of plants in and around their village. A modern botanist has a different sort of knowledge.

West Midlands, September 2004

A cider 'cheese' goes up; Joe climbs on to the bed or 'winter' of the press; the beam above is the 'summer'. Martin is at work behind him, Elaine opposite. They pile the apple pulp into the wooden square, put combed wheat straw on top, then raise the square. And so it continues while the mill keeps chugging, the apple keeps coming, and the layers keep mounting till the cheese is done. The wide stripes of fruit and the narrow ones of straw are prevented from toppling by mysterious laws and experienced hands. The juice begins to flow. This is the age-old way of making cider, but not many do it, and not many can. If a food or drink comes with so much meaning, the taste, however good, is next in importance.

<small>West Country, December 2004</small>

John George passes the time with neighbour Norman and his Norfolk terrier. His inverted cider and perry press, ingeniously made from a lorry jack, works against the steel frame above. The bedstone is hewn from the rock which pokes through the topsoil in and around the Forest of Dean. Perry fruit is too hard for eating or even cooking, but makes one of the most delicately scented drinks, now regaining its former status. Single rather then blended varieties tend to be used. The trees are majestic, long lived, and flourish within sight of May Hill. The wood is the colour of yew.

Welsh Marches, November 2003

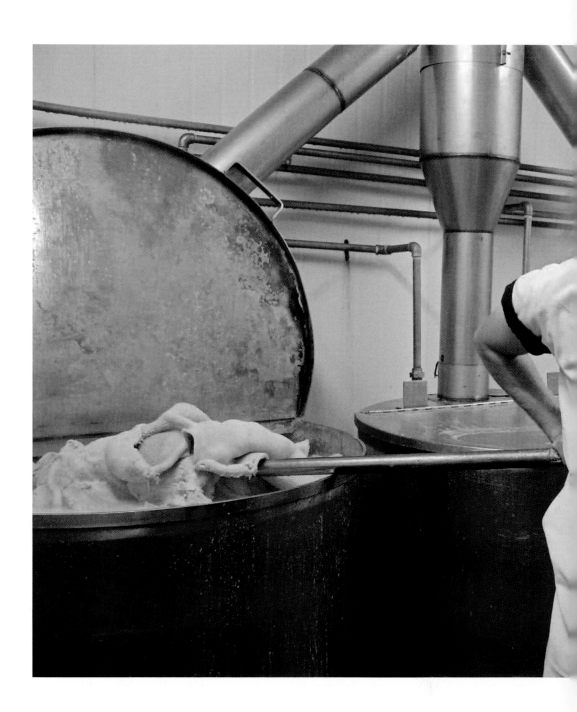

Daniel Heys, son of Chris, works in the family business of dressing tripe. Processing starts with cleaning in a gigantic drum, a job they do for the small number of firms still engaged in the English trade. Boiling (shown here) follows. Tripe was eaten in the swankiest restaurants until the post war period. There are four categories, one for each stomach of an ox. Three are currently prepared. Tripe contains all the goodness of grass fed beef, but takes half the time to digest. Unlike chicken production, it does not involve cruelty to animals. The fat from the factory goes into a pit. From there it goes to make soap, and into the most fragrant of bathrooms.

NORTH OF ENGLAND, JULY 2005

(*Overleaf*) Sold out! England is full of high Victorian market halls, open from two days a week to six, where buyers and sellers of food collect under cover. They are the template for supermarkets, but with the benefit of independent traders, sound values, and goods that matter more than the margin. The meals in the cafes, cooked from ingredients to hand, can be reassuring. Hurrying around a market defeats the object of going. Buying from people like Nancy is one of the simple pleasures, out of all proportion to the cost, which makes a Friday or Saturday morning.

ENGLAND, JULY 2006

C HESIL BEACH, or simply 'Beach' to locals, is made up of millions of tons of elliptical, smooth and desirable stones: a sweeping umbilical cord of a curve and official wonder of the world that parts the waters of the sea and Littlesea. The Portland Race is as infamous a stretch of coast as the Pentland Firth, Morecambe Bay, Goodwin Sands or the Severn Estuary. The waves can break over the Cove House Pub. The local Dorset boat, which takes up to six oarsmen, is called a lerret. The matching bow and stern, which facilitate landing in heavy surf, may be Viking in origin, even classical. The surviving lerrets were clinker-built from the wych elm that used to grow around Eype and Bridport. Gluts of fish are not what they were, but may still be shared out, a nice touch in an age of percentages.

Ash Huddey was the son of a Devon labourer, who walked upcountry during the Depression and found employment in the area. Having turned down an offer to play professional football as a young man, he remained on Beach and fished all his life. His crew, which included one woman, unusual for such communities, worked over the summer months from a hut near the Abbotsbury swannery (a former source of meat) and turned to logging in the winter.

One of the stories I heard about Ash Huddey was that he had seen an Allied bomber come down off Beach during the war, and helped to rescue the men on board. Years later a salvage team turned up intending to find the wreck. After two weeks of trawling back and forth with electronic devices and getting nowhere, Huddey was asked if he knew where it might be. For a small consideration he rowed out, shipped oars and dropped a line on to the plane eight fathoms below.

Ash worked by the tides, beginning as early as 2 a.m. He met the others, drove them to the hut, and, with a single match, lit a tarred rope for the succession of fags he smoked throughout the day. They cooked breakfast, mended nets and played cards. When Ash looked up and saw the imperceptible signs of fish feeding, he would say it was 'time to shoot': to launch the lerret, fling the leads and haul in the shoal hidden at sea. Otherwise, they sat all morning and all afternoon, then went home.

Ash and his crew caught several 'bells' (jellyfish) in the nets over the years, flying fish and the occasional salmon, 'the queer fellows' bound for the Avon or Stour. They landed a shark, which had to be shot, and a turtle, a former delicacy, which went to Weymouth museum. There was a whale in the vicinity whom they christened 'Moby Dick', and a friendly porpoise with a broken fin. The mackerel arrived by day in the spring, the sprats in late summer, and the herring by night on the autumn high tides. Cutty 'Black Hat' Thorner was supposed to buy the catch, but if he could see from the hill above Beach that the lerrets were not out – or happened to be in liquor – he never showed up. The other merchant, appropriately for a man dealing with fish, bore the surname of Laver.

Catches peaked with 1,800 stone of sprats, which took all afternoon to land, then started to tail off and become more irregular. By the time the beach casters arrived, there was not much to cast for. The sea, bereft of terns and gannets diving, the mackerel, the whitebait and the friendly porpoise, looked increasingly quiet from the wooden hut. The end of an era, lasting thousands of years, had come. Ash died after a short illness in June 1973. The others never fished again, and without the fishing – a minor detail of their entire lives – the habit of salting fish for the winter ahead came to an end in the village.

Having caught and eaten mackerel fresh since childhood, I might never have known they packed them in salt in Kilner jars a few miles from me, but for a man whose name kept cropping up and the trail to the cottage where he had lived. Since then, I have seen mackerel salted once to order. They are also mentioned, along with smoked haddock and honey-coloured hams, an English restaurant in nineteenth-century Paris patronised by the Duc des Esseintes in *A Rebours*. I hope Ash Huddey and His Grace will meet. They have something in common.

Curing fish is a process as old as curing meat, a means of storing it, fortifying the texture and making quantities easier to handle. One of the oldest methods is to salt the fish in a barrel, crock or jar, and keep it sealed and submerged in its own brine. The alternative is to salt it on a drainer and hang it up to dry. Smoking is not necessary, but can hasten the necessary loss of moisture and imparts a character to foods – which may or may not be an improvement. A cold smoke enables fish to keep for longer than a hot one, which cooks the meat through. In Japan and Norway, the producer of stock fish (i.e. pole fish, dried aloft), neither salt nor smoke is used in the oldest cures. Wind is the only instrument.

For hundreds of years in England the salting of fish was a common occupation, but a sporadic one dependent on the season, migratory patterns and catches. The number of species and the quantity cured only began to dwindle in the nineteenth century. With improved transport, tinning and refrigeration, dried hake or 'poor john', coley, flounder, gurnard, skate, mackerel and other stand-bys began to disappear from country kitchens. The old, bone-hard cures also gave way to new and industrial ones, and ready-prepared brine baths took over, which provided a simpler and softer option for factories and cooks.

Salt fish might have died out at home, but not for the niche markets abroad. So, some of the oldest and most distinguished cures are simultaneously unused in England and unknown – except as foreign property. If mackerel is reborn, it will probably come as a novelty with an exotic title. Galling as that is, however, it has been good for conservation and for a complement of foods that belong to an historic inner sanctum.

Plain salted herring may still be produced in parts of England and Scotland – they were ten years ago in the Orkneys – but they led the way in smoking. The number of cures is considerable. With each one the 'silver darling' acquires a different character and a change of name. In descending order of antiquity and readiness to keep, it becomes a red or golden herring, a bloater, a buckling, and a kipper.

Red herring: downtown Yarmouth, Yare Mouth, perched on a spit. The sea is on one side, the river on the other – a flood plain clustered with wind pumps, overlooked by a ruined castle. The town has a front, a back and an air. It is also one of the oldest coastal settlements in England, maintaining its place after the earth and waters moved, landlocking the port of Beccles and the village of Herringfleet for the last few hundred years. Imagine carts instead of cars, wagons waiting, ships arriving, the rich and poor, sailmakers, ropemakers, chandlers, curers, coopers, coal miners, all dependent on 'silver darlings'.

A cheerful Karen met us at the door, a short walk from the castle and Time and Tide Museum. No appointment, none necessary, and an unmistakably Cornish voice three hundred miles from home. Mike Kelly, in blue cap, overalls and boots, leading the team of four at H.S. Fish, offered to show us round. The factory, built in the glory days of Yarmouth as a port, is on two storeys. The millions of herrings cured in sunken tanks are down to thousands in barrels, but curing still. There is a passage from front to back and one above it. Each is lined with a row of original doors, painted red, meaning business and reminding me of a school dorm.

The doors opened into a lofty and silent garret, all black: treacle black, pitch black, 'Bible black'. The outer brick walls, running and glossy, were embalmed in a century of tar. The only light came from stark and defined slits for ventilation in the roof. Banks of white wood shavings, crowned with oak sawdust, were piled on the floor. The loft above, divided by metal grilles, allowed for the circulation of the air and smoke.

The fires are lit with a blowtorch. They flare up, especially in an east wind, then subside and smoulder. Jenny and John, she in yellow gloves and apron, he with earring and shades, load the lines of fish from a groaning rack. The 'darlings' go in silver, plump, salted and soft. They come out transformed, after days or even weeks, indifferent to flies, heat and the passage of time, their mouths gaping, skins biscuit-brittle, and complexions ruddy and broken as a 'Glasgow Magistrate's'.* The longer they are in smoke, the harder the cure and redder the herring.

Colin Burgess of J. T. Cole in Lowestoft, a proud man in polished shoes, assisted by his son Paul, produces a golden herring by means of a four-day brine and five-day smoke. They do a

---

* A nickname for red herring alluding to their colour; 'militiamen' was another.

pale herring too, plus other fish for the local buyers who tip up at the works. Colin has been at it since leaving school and the days of using the concrete floor, no longer permitted but the perfect temperature for curing fish. He is a man who will answer any question thrown at him, knowing that it is mostly his experience that converts theory into practice. On herring, he says, holding them up, you could write six volumes.

Silver darlings, when in prime condition, cure as well as pork. Healthy, abundant and reasonably punctual, they moved southward from the Hebrides during the summer, down the coasts of England during the autumn, and round the corner, fetching up off the Kent, Sussex and Devon coasts in the winter, and answering to the various cures on the way. Having provided a staple and an export market in the nineteenth century, catches dwindled to nothing in the twentieth. The North Sea grounds were closed in 1977/8, which helped them to recover, but by the time they reopened, the market had adjusted to Icelandic and Norwegian fish and quotas had come in. Of the healthy and sustainable stocks which now appear to be building up in European waters, 80 per cent is not available to the UK. A further proportion may be landed abroad (Smylie, 2004). And so on. The situation is unlikely to change without positive interference from the UK government. A food shortage will do it.

One of the little touches at H.S. Fish, common to many curers, is that they make and stamp their own wooden boxes. In go the herrings, stacked neatly and closely, shoulder to shoulder. On go the lids and off go the consignments to Egypt, Greece, Italy and the tropics, but rarely to markets at home. Everyone knows what a 'red herring' is as a figure of speech, rather than what it has been: an East Anglian 'ham', 'every man's money' and a universal staple immortalized in song.

'**Fine Yarmouth**' are for diehards who belong to the culinary fringe: an old-fashioned food at its most unforgiving, rarest and best, which satisfied the hungry and in drinkers provoked a thirst. The aroma is more smoky than fishy, the flavour more intense than a salted anchovy's. If you need to disprove any of the familiar charges made against the English kitchen, reach for a red or golden herring, filleted, skinned and cut into slices. Have a bottle ready.

My wife and I never went to the award-winning museum. Nor did any of its thirty thousand visitors go to H.S. Fish. Yet all of us were searching for the same or similar things, an interesting couple of hours, connections to make and a slurp of history. The difference was that we wanted a live and enduring performance without state funding or special effects, which provided a tangible result, and we got one. The pursuit of red herring ended in a catch.

Alan Sampson, a crab pot man in Cromer all his life, told me of a way to cook salt herrings that must have been widespread at one time – and that I later came across in *The Housekeeper's Guide* of 1834 by Esther Copley.* Soak the fish, she wrote, for 'an hour in hot small beer; drain and . . . broil [grill]. Serve with . . . butter . . . and mashed potatoes.'

Another recipe, which appeared in a latter-day version of the anonymous *Everyday Cookery*, indicates that red herrings were holding their own in English kitchens as late as 1963: 'cover the fish with boiled water and after several minutes drain. Soak in milk . . . for one hour. Skin and fillet, then cut into pieces and dress with oil and vinegar. The herrings can be garnished with sieved egg yolk and chopped gherkins. Alternatively mix . . . with diced boiled potatoes.'

A bloated herring, or bloater, is half dried, gutted, brined for an approximate two hours and smoked for a further twelve. The *OED* seems to imply that the word 'bloat' (i.e. soak, 1611) was connected to herring before the word 'bloater' (1832) came into existence. For how long they were eaten before that, and to what extent the cure might have changed, is not known.

Unappealing as they sound, bloaters are highly rated. The annual turnover at Billingsgate in the 1860s was 265,000 baskets, containing 160 fish in each, amounting to a total of nearly 16 million. The French have a word for them, *craquelot*, indicating a knowledge of this particular cure. The *Larousse Gastronomique* says (correctly) that bloaters are eaten for breakfast and high tea in England, but André Simon went one better. A trip to Yarmouth was necessary for 'one in perfection'. It had to be made in October or November and the fish eaten before going to bed. The reasoning was that the herring, plump and ready, arrived off the coast of Suffolk during the autumn. They were caught in drift nets at night, landed by day, and cured over the customary twelve- to fourteen-hour period, ideally for consumption the following evening.

The vernacular way to cook a bloater is to hang it in front of a fire. Put a plate underneath bearing a piece of toast, on to which the fish will start to drip when ready. Otherwise, split and grill with a knob of butter, basting until the bloater is good and hot. The paste or spread, simplicity itself, is well worth making. Mince finely 1lb (450g) of the cooked meat with the roe or milt, but without skin and backbone, and mash it up with up to 4oz (110g) melted butter. No seasoning is necessary. It keeps in a bowl or jar for at least two weeks.

Buckling retain their roe but not their heads, unlike bloaters, and are subjected to a brine of about thirty minutes and a four-hour hot smoke that cooks the meat through. The cure is said to have originated in Germany, but also with a batch of herring committed by mistake to an overheated smoker, from which they emerged with a silver gilt finish and their skin having

---

* *The daughter of a silk merchant from Hackney. She married two parsons, both of whom left her a widow, and published several works on household and other affairs including* The Housekeeper's Guide *(London, 1st edn 1834) and* Complete Cottage Cookery *(1862).*

buckled. Production remained seasonal for longer than it did with other salt fish, and is still local. We used to sell buckling at the Normandy Stores in London, but they tend not to travel, frustrating devotees who do not live in Suffolk: a mail-order service could do well. Buckling have a faithful following. Eat cold with horseradish, tomato or cucumber, and a salad.

Kippers: the London firm of Forman, started by Polish immigrants, believes that it introduced the art of smoking salmon to England in about 1888 – and in commercial terms it may have done. Nearly twenty years prior to that, *The Field* (instructions were credited to the *Rural Almanac*, a journal I have not been able to trace), had published the Northumbrian method of using up 'redfish'. By this they meant a salmon that had entered a river to spawn, hung about without feeding and lost condition. It was identifiable by its pronounced lower jaw and coarse red meat, which is horrid fresh but all right when smoked.

The instructions were to 'gut and wipe a redfish clean; rub it well with equal parts of salt, brown sugar and ground black pepper; and let it lie for two or three days turning occasionally'. The sides were then pressed for another couple of days, 'under stones or weights in the cool, and impaled with wooden skewers to keep them flat – in the sun on a board or against a wall'. The alternative, in bad weather, was to 'dry the fish over oak or seaweed for a final few days, four or five feet up a chimney', taking care it did not get hot. Salmon thus cured were referred to as 'kippered', deriving from the word 'copper', in reference to their colour. 'To cook the fish,' *The Field* concluded unexpectedly, 'cut in slices and . . . fry in buttered writing paper, just sufficient to warm through. By some it is boiled, especially the part nearer the head.'

The story goes that a generation earlier, in the 1840s, a Northumbrian entrepreneur had borrowed the cure used on salmon or kippered herring, and the kipper was born. Brines prevailed over dry salting, smoking became shorter and more concentrated, and the industry expanded, resulting in variations on an original theme, played out in factories both recently built and as old as the cures. The three grey-haired kipper lassies whom I met at Robson's of Craster, established in 1856, were survivors of the annual migration of herring and labour from the north of Scotland to the south of England. They might have moved on with the fish, but happened to stop in a well known magnetic field, with a castle on the horizon and the North Sea breaking a few yards away, to split and gut herrings for a term of sixty years.

The fish are now cleaned mechanically, but fastened to tenterhooks just the same, and hung high in the lums of smokehouses encrusted with the customary slicks of tar. The door closes on herrings for 10–15 hours and opens on kippers, firm to the touch and lacquered by the smoke from below. The fish are slit down the back rather than the belly or filleted, firm to the touch, and vary between factories in both size and colour, from amber to silver. They are usually sold in pairs, and travel and freeze well. A small quantity of kippers used to be exported to

France, 'where they were much appreciated and known colloquially as *jambons de Boulogne* (Hutchins, 1967). Paul Bocuse likes them too. Kippers keep for two or three weeks in the fridge. The impostors, a legacy of the war effort, are imprisoned in plastic with a specious knob of butter, decapitated, dyed and sometimes known as 'Painted Ladies'. Do not look out for them. The kipper sausage is extinct, never to be born again, I hope.

Kippers recovered from the combined efforts of the usual gang (EU, MAFF and Environmental Health) to reduce all manufacturers to the lowest common denominator. They are now exported all over the world not only in the autumn, the former herring season, but throughout the year. Easy to buy and cook as kippers may be, however, their charms do not seem to have registered with English hotels and gastropubs even in their heartlands. Many is the time I have dreamed, and only dreamed, of a grilled kipper served with toast and scrambled egg for breakfast or high tea, and with mashed potato for supper. Whisky is the drink for a kipper, though gin may poured on top: a precaution said in Suffolk to stop the fish 'repeating'.

Pickled herring is another one for the store cupboard: it is useful to have up your sleeve, bone-free, and easy to do at home. When the fish are looking good towards the end of the year, buy a few. Gut and fillet them, or get them filleted, reserving the roe (dust in flour and fry up later).

Commit the herring to a dish or crock. Boil up enough water to drown them, stir in 3oz (75g) salt for every ¾ pint (425ml) and allow to get cold. Pour over the fish and leave for a few hours. Drain and cut the herring into small enough pieces to fit into a jar and cover with white or even red wine vinegar. You may add peeled shallots or sliced onion provided they too are kept submerged. The fish may be eaten after a few days and will keep in the fridge for months. If there are any bones left in the herring, it does not matter. The acid in the vinegar will soften them. So, suck a wedge of lemon if you are choking on a bone.

The pilchard or 'gypsy herring' is a type of sardine, hunted by bass, hake, tunny and shark. It is partly responsible for the harbours, houses, villages and even coastal towns that have drawn the hordes to Cornwall for a hundred and fifty years. Over forty landing stations have been recorded, with lookout or huers' huts in between. By the seventeenth century the Duchy had the largest number of boats in England, apart from Devon, focused on fish in general and pilchards in particular, caught, carted, counted and handled in their millions by fleets of men and armies of women on grey granite quays and stony shores.

In Elizabethan England there was an automatic boat for casting nets, which was propelled out to sea by an offshore breeze and brought back in by a rope. The catches of pilchards were salted down in custom-built cellars and 'fumed', becoming 'fumadoes' or 'fair maids', until the quantities involved made smoking impossible and pressing in hogsheads took over. Once cured, the fish were stacked in a punctured wooden cask and the oil was collected, the two of them providing the invaluable trio of 'meat, heat and light' for fishing communities.

Of all the pilchards salted, only a fraction went by pannier to markets inland or stayed in the villages. The rest were exported to France and Spain, but mostly to southern Europe, which ordered fish from Cornwall for four hundred years. The former factory in Polperro, halfway up the Warren, where the fishermen sat and pondered the harbour and Peak Rock, still bears the name of Teglio. The present and sole surviving one, British Cured Pilchards in Newlyn, a custom-built fishing port and railhead, has dealt with the same Italian family since it opened in 1905.

Nick Howell took over the works in the 1970s. In order to try and stimulate business, he sent some fish to Billingsgate that were rejected on the grounds that they might 'go bad'. For the first time in history some of the pilchards did – thanks to the insistence of Environmental Health that the company change their packaging from natural to approved fibres. With considerable effort Howell changed it back and the quality of his product returned to normal. He also, having been told that his factory was like a museum, turned it into a working one. The presses were new, the boxes made on site, and the pilchards lay together heads out, tails in, brassy and overlapping, waiting to provide the remaining buyers in Piedmont with their age-old annual autumnal treat. Demand failed with eating habits as elsewhere in Europe, and the museum is now closed, but business continues.

There are plenty of pilchards compared with some of the other fish, and boats out of Newlyn and Mevagissey bringing them in. The season begins in the spring and is over by early summer. The English market, which never amounted to much, was hit by tinned South African pilchards. Its recovery is dependent on weaning the beau monde off imported anchovies and a celebrity chef stopping by.

Salted fillets seem more likely to survive than whole fish. The taste is distinct from a red herring's, but equally intense, and provokes the same agreeable thirst. My mother-in-law's family in Polperro used to cook fresh pilchards in front of a coal range, avoiding the spits, peeling away the skin, and stripping the meat from the bones. Howell is married to a Breton, maintaining another connection, but likes cured pilchards Italian-style.

Spaghetti alla puttanesca: this is a recipe from Rome, traditionally made with Cornish sardines. The dish is said to have originated in the Trastavere, one of the oldest districts in the city and a former haunt of prostitutes. *Puttana* in Italian means a whore, 'hence a hot sauce,' says British Cured Pilchards, 'quickly prepared'. It amounts to a basic tomato sauce (see page 58) containing pieces of salt fish. It can be made while the pasta is on the boil.

If starting from scratch, proceed as follows: fry onion, garlic and chilli in a little olive oil and butter, followed by skinned tomatoes. Add slices of pilchard mashed with a fork, some large black olives, stoned and sliced, a few capers, and salt (checking to see if it is needed). Pour over the spaghetti and sprinkle with parsley.

Alternatively, mix slices of pilchard and tomato into cooked polenta with some oil.

Salt cod, Mark Kurlansky's 'fish that changed the world', has been eaten in England since time out of mind. It was dried on shore and on board boat, hung from the rigging as 'yard-arm fish' (Hartley), and imported from Newfoundland from the Tudor period. Another fish-curer, and another unmistakably West Country voice, this one belonging to Richard Turner, London-born and Somerset-bred, explained its position in the modern era. The firm he manages, Cawood of Grimsby, salts thousands of tons of cod a year in its pristine, airy and cavernous factory, stacks them up and dries them on racks. The fish is mainly for export on enduring trade routes to Spain, and also the West Indies, which produce no cod of their own but consider it as much a part of their culture as reggae or cricket. The ling that the factory also cures goes to Italy.

A fishmonger in Dorset salts a little cod for clients, mostly Portuguese. Owing to these and other influences it is re-emerging as *bacalao*. The market in England is small and propped up by minorities, of which country people are one. A few old-timers in the south and west still refer to dried cod as 'tea fish', or even 'toe rag', consigning it to a 'toad in the hole' status, regarded as a treat and customary on Good Friday.

'Wide as a bucket' people used to say of the sides of cod that arrived in the fishmonger's in barrels. The practice in his day was to 'stream' the cod, which needs soaking before use, by tying it down in the nearest river or brook for twenty-four hours. The alternative is to leave a piece in cold water, refreshing it once or twice if thick. Salt fish, thus prepared, cannot quite be cooked like any other – it needs help – but can hardly be overcooked either. The late Queen Mary ate her dried cod with the customary creamed parsnip. Egg sauce is a good companion, spicy tomato sauce (see page 58) a better one.

Smoked haddock is a fish improved by salting and smoking, which gets more popular the further north you go. Finnan is the real thing, a Scottish speciality with a considerable pedigree, which is split down the right and exhibits the backbone on the left. The London haddock, a Victorian copy but a respectable one, very popular in City restaurants, came the other way round – split down the left with the backbone on the right. There is a natural fillet, which is pleasant enough, and a dyed one called the Yellow Peril, a nickname it shares with the worst type of cod. As in the case of Painted Lady, avoid.

CHAPTER
TWENTY-ONE

SHELLFISH

ETER THE DANE RETURNED TO ST MAWES in the late afternoon, gun in pocket, people said, the red flag flying for the trippers on his launch and beard stiff upon his cheeks and chin. The lusty brothers **Vinnicombe**, loaded with salvage from the bay, docked at their yard on the granite quay. A familiar quartet arrived for a game of golf on the links, amongst them the shy and ageing but mighty 'Gar', Cornwall's longest hitter for twenty-five years. A boy cycled home with a ten-pound pollack dangling from the handlebars. The lanes emptied. The evening had come.

By six o'clock the little beach was quiet and the sun sparkling on the river. The tide ebbed and flowed in the silence overnight, resuming its position an hour after dawn. The early mornings were fresh, inviting and often still. The boats lay motionless at anchor, their images reflected in water calm as glass. The squadrons of oystercatchers, piping and crying, made their way to feed in the sheltered reach known as Abraham's Bosom. The wreck rotted near a whitewashed cottage where the Cornish oaks came down to the sea.

My brother and I swam every day. When the tide came up we went in the boat, explored the creeks and spun for mackerel, returning home from a choppy sea with salt on our lips and spray on our faces. At low water we climbed the rocks and combed the foreshore, paddling in the shallows with a bucket and net, catching crabs, or bringing in cockles, mussels, winkles and 'queens'.

Came the 'r' to the month and autumn to Cornwall, always too soon but with compensations, we rowed over to the farm and bought a dozen oysters. We took brown bread and butter, two glasses in a towel, and a bottle of white wine attached to a string and trailing in the water. The picnic that followed was the final and most precocious act of two boys with riches enough, and anxious for more in the dying moments of the holidays. The Hodges family were there then, having laid out, collected and cleansed the oysters for many generations. They also purified the stowaway clams that arrived with the liners and successfully bred in Southampton Water.

The two oyster boats, moored near the farm, had been used for seine fishing off the Lizard. They had square grey cabins, large rudders and sleek, almost classical tarred hulls that went in the ribs after a hundred years. The pair left every now and again on their mysterious trip upriver to the beds past Frenchman's Creek, which lay off Groyne Point. I was tempted to follow in the dinghy but never did. Disturbing the oysters invited a fine of £200 – an outrageous sum in those days – and if you took them from the beach at low water there was hell to pay.

As a boy, I thought the Duchy kept the world in oysters. It came as a surprise to hear that Frank Vinnicombe, and later Marshal, his son, caught them under sail on the Carrick Roads.

The Fal, the Flete, the Dart and other sheltered waters upcountry all had oysters. So did the Greater Thames Estuary, which included the Crouch, the Blackwater, the Stour and the Orwell. The oysters in the city of London, where I worked for a miserable year, went under the names of Whitstable and Colchester. Only Gow's Restaurant stocked Helfords. They always tasted the way the sea smells, whether you were pleasantly near or, as I was, painfully far.

One night in a grimy pub up north, I sat next to an old couple guzzling oysters and drinking stout at a marble-topped table – he in a cloth cap, she in a woollen coat and blue feather hat fastened with a pin. Nothing seemed closer to the world of Dickens or Gaskell, yet oysters by their time were already becoming scarce. The beds that fed the poor were depleted within a century. Near Maldon in Essex they were wiped out by disease and had to be restocked. Pollution and the occasional big freeze are perpetual threats. No one can call himself an oyster farmer who has not lost half a million spat (spawn). The price is consequently high and the mystique about oysters has risen with it.

Native oysters are flat, graded and numbered one to six. 'Rocks', which have started to breed in England owing to climate change, are eaten all year. When laid out in the cool they retain salt water, and should keep for a couple of days. Restaurants use a gadget to open them. The best way to do it at home is with a special knife, an instrument about four inches long that every cook should have, and used to come free with orders from the Duchy. A screwdriver is the alternative. Bind your hand with a cloth for protection, then place the oyster on a table. Press down and insert the knife in the foot and turn the blade. You may have to struggle to prise the shell open. If you apply a squeeze of lemon and the beard shrinks, the oyster was 'tight alive'. Thanks to refrigeration and water quality, instances of poisoning are rare.

Oysters are credited with strange properties, not only aphrodisiac. You can eat any number without gaining weight. Ideally, select a seaside location and order stout or Chablis. Some swallow the meat, others chew it. If you must cook oysters, deep-fry them in batter. For Carpet Bag Steak, see page 117.

Scallops, or pectens, (derived from the Latin for a comb), are relatives of the oyster. They have been used as a motif by such varied people as the ancient Greeks, medieval pilgrims and Shell Transport and Trading. As a Christmas present in 1957, the company gave a book on the scallop and its place in art, the natural world and gastronomy, to each and every one of its shareholders. It must have been the last public relations exercise of the kind.

The scallop lives in colonies and could be gathered in parts of the West Country at very low tide. They are surprisingly nimble and supposed to be sustainable, but are preyed upon by starfish, and are no match for the fearsome dredgers raking up tons from the ocean floor and leaving God knows what devastation behind. Scallops thus taken are water-blown to remove the sand and grit, and shelled so that the cups can be sold on, both of which diminish the flavour.

The best and sweetest scallops are selectively picked by divers in the early summer, and cooked on the flat part of their shells – an unheard-of practice today. This involves steaming them open and removing the cup, the frilly mantle and blue-black trail, leaving the muscle and the orange horn. Brush with butter and bake them for fifteen minutes in a medium to hot oven. Otherwise, detach from the flat as usual, fry gently for a minute or two on either side and serve while still tender to the touch. Deglaze the pan with white wine and cream and you have a sauce.

Crabs: my brother worked on crabbers and drank a barley wine called Crabber's Nip, which came in small bottles with an invisible health warning. I have seen a boat come in with a ton or more of crabs in a net, hoisted high over the side and on to the quay, wriggling and furious, their mouths blowing bubbles and arms and legs flailing through the dripping mesh. The catch went to a local factory, where a gang of women sat round a table in waterproof pinnies cracking the claws and cleaning out the shells at a furious pace. The gossip was incessant.

England favours the 'brown' crab with black pincers. They are taken in baited pots, and may be 'gaffed' at low tide as they lie up in the rocks around the south and west coasts. You advance a hook into a likely crevice; the crab, if at home, will grasp it and not let go. The grip he exerts is slow but fearsome, and amounts to over four tons per square inch. The claws contain the delicate white meat, the shells the stronger dark meat or 'soup'.

The crabs of the east coast come from the shallows, notably off Cromer and its predecessor Shipton, an underwater ruin lost to the North Sea. The area has a higher density of family fishmongers, businesses and pot men, assisted by winches and tractors, than any other part of England. There is plenty to watch and discuss, buy and cook in the area as a result. The beach crab has a greater proportion of white meat than the West Country one, but tends to be smaller. To gastronomes, they are different creatures.

The common spider crab is the largest of the European varieties, and an inhabitant of French and Spanish waters which has pushed north complete with its crusty coat of tubercles and barnacles. It favours the south-west coast of England but has yet to find favour itself: there is no explanation. My mother-in-law never ate brown crabs as a fisherman's daughter in Cornwall, only the inexpensive spiders or 'skerries'. She still describes them as 'picky', though there is plenty of meat in the limbs of the larger specimens and a little 'soup' in the shell. Also the number caught at present appears to be sustainable. Most go for export with velvet crabs, which are made (shell and all) into paste.

Crabs enjoy the occasional glut, which can be difficult to manage and gives a false idea of numbers, which may be precariously balanced. They are better to eat in winter, when a crab feeds up and is easily attracted to the bait in pots, but are wanted in summer at the very time the creature retires to moult. If the tummy of a crab is white, he has only just acquired a new shell and needs time to fill it. A good specimen is rusty underneath and heavy for its size.

A crab will shoot its claws when dropped into boiling water, which causes them to cook inconsistently and is bad for presentation. To prevent this, the creature is either immobilised beforehand or confined to warm water for an hour or two, making it sleepy and indifferent to its fate. The majority of crabs come to the market cooked. The vendor may be prepared to open one for you and check the quality, which, even for an expert, can be difficult to predict. The meat is more abundant in the cock, the 'soup' in a hen; she is distinguished by the large fold in her abdomen or 'purse'. A mixture of male and female provides the perfect balance.

Cooking a crab takes ten minutes: an amateur dressing one will take fifteen. It is time well spent and can be therapeutic provided you have no more than one or two to do. Remove and crack the claws and legs with pliers. Insert a knife in the rear of the crab, where the shell joins the body, and twist, prising the two apart. Remove the feathery grey lungs and discard. Remove the 'soup' from the shell with a knife, and the meat from the body and limbs with your fingers and a skewer. You may keep them separate and repack into the shell, or (as I do) mix them together in a basin. Chill for at least a couple of hours and no more than a day. Decorate, if you wish, with a little paprika or chopped parsley. Serve with a crisp lettuce and brown bread and butter. Mayonnaise is not needed.

A crab is better cold than hot, but can be combined with a white sauce and returned to its shell. Dust with Parmesan and grill until brown. Eat with boiled rice and a salad. Rich.

Lobster: the boat was a sturdy-looking vessel, high in the water, with an upright cabin, a tarred hull and a winch for the pots. I swam out to it in the evenings, climbed up over the gunwale and sat for fifteen minutes in the sun, listening to the drone of the odd 'Seagull' – the outboard of its day – or voices carrying over the water from hundreds of yards away. The lobsters were known as 'blues' by the fishermen, or 'clickers' from their grip, which is quick, noisy and to be avoided, though it lacks the pressure of a crab's. In select and lonely spots on the coast, you could peer down between the rocks and see the ghostly outline of fully grown lobsters foraging for food.

The plenty lasted until the 1970s, then the price began to rise and at twice the rate of inflation. The law states a minimum size of lobster, which does not apply to all European fishermen alike, enabling the French to take smaller specimens than English boats. A close season, starting when the hens are in berry (eggs), has been discussed for over twenty years, but is yet to be translated into law. Farming is not easy either. Lobster are skittish, prone to cannibalism and take seven or eight years to reach a pound in weight. The biggest specimen I have ever seen, and bought from a boat, must have been over fifty years old. It was covered in barnacles and weighed nearly a stone.

Most of the lobster caught in England and Scotland go to Europe. Fishermen usually keep them at sea until they have enough to sell. Robberies are considered below the belt, but are not unknown. The claws of captives are pegged or bound. The lobsters that have lost a limb in battle or from shock, and failed to grow another, may be sold off cheaply. Look out for the spiny lobster (crawfish) too, the French *langouste*, a vegetarian that has no claws in the first place, but has ample meat in the tail and is used for scampi.

Lobsters moult like crabs, improving in the back end of the year, and vary just as much. The best I have ever eaten came from English waters, which are noted for their salinity. It is not in my interest or the lobsters' to disclose where. The cocks, which are right- or left-handed, grow one arm bigger than the other. The hens, though less well equipped, are broader in the beam and considered more tender to eat. Lobster is a treat when fresh, but can be mushy early in the season and when the creature is ailing. Lobsters from Maine, USA, can find their way into supermarkets and restaurants. Eat something else.

It is safer to buy a lobster live because you can control the length of time it is cooked – rather than overcooked, a common fault. Pick a healthy specimen that kicks vigorously, wrap it in wet newspaper, and keep it as cool as possible until you get home. Approach the task positively. Take a large vessel like a Burco, fill it with sea- or salted water. Bring to the boil and immerse the lobster. It will not scream, struggle or shoot its claws like a crab, merely turn from blue to red. Remove a 1–3lb (450g–1.3kg) lobster after only 5–10 minutes. Give a monster a quarter of an hour. Plunge it into cold water to stop it cooking. To clean, lay the creature on its back and insert the point of a large and rigid knife into its middle. Cut in half lengthways through the shell, open and pull out the trail, which is black. Crack the claws. Lobster is almost better cold than hot. Mayonnaise.

To grill lobster, kill the creature by inserting a screwdriver into the front of its head. Cut in half as above and cook over a fire for 5–10 minutes. Boil the claws separately for 5 minutes and serve with melted butter.

Shrimping was for fine days, an occupation shared with people digging for worms, and an absorbing one accomplished at low water. Shrimps move hither and thither with the tide. You need to know where they go. You also need a D-shaped push net, a bucket and a free afternoon in the summer. No bait is required. Remove your shoes, roll up your trousers or skirt, and walk into the shallows. The sun keeps you warm, the wind cools you down, the water laps your legs and swishes to and fro, putting cares aside.

Prawns, a large family, can grow bigger than shrimps. They prefer deeper water and cover, and are taken in pots but also when they come inshore and get marooned in rock pools with shannies and dogfish. Autumn is the time. You dip a net under a clump of weed, scoop it up and turn out the jitterbugging catch into a bucket filled with seawater. Handle with care, preferably not at all. The bigger prawns are armed with claws, the smaller ones with vicious little spears. The tiddlers are sometimes called 'soldiers'.

Shrimps are brown when cooked and sweet in taste. Prawns are pink and salty. There is age-old confusion between the two, in spite of their preferences and colour differences, even in the trade. You could queue for chips at Wells-next-the-Sea, or shrimps cooked in a cauldron on board boat: for me no contest. Large catches have been taken from sandy stretches around the English coast since before they were licensed in the Middle Ages. The Wash, the Dee, and the Duchy of Lancaster's Kent and Leven sands are famous for their shrimps and shrimping. In a flat, quiet crook of the Bristol Channel known for its sleepy water and failing light, the Sellick family race out to the nets and back to dry land on their wooden 'mud horse'.

The shrimp population in Somerset was affected by the Hinkley Point power station, which sucks in water and marine life to cool the reactors and belches it out cooked to perfection. Numbers elsewhere have been hit by the plundering of breeding grounds and young too small for human consumption but suitable as duck feed. The future for shrimps could be secured by confining us all to manual operations (or mud horses). To ply a net is good for the health and for mental health too. Keep an eye on the tide and prepare the catch that evening.

Potted shrimps can be more than a nice little bite. They made the famous teas up north, shared at a table in Betsy Tattersall's with a tame robin (Hartley, 1954), and justified in my case the trip across England. The best potted shrimps I have eaten were caught, picked and buttered with the patience of Job by a fishmonger on the north Norfolk coast. Thanks to EC sensibilities, factories may no longer process their crop in seawater, but you may. The cognoscenti say it is the only way. Bring to the boil, empty in the shrimps, return to the boil and drain. Pull off the head and eat, shell and all.

Cockling was for wet days, the wetter the better somehow. We dressed for it in oilskins, sou'westers, and plimsolls destined for a soaking – not that it mattered: a hot bath afterwards was part of the event. The smaller cockles seemed to live in colonies, the larger ones further apart. Collecting them is solitary too. A group of people out cockling together soon separates, each one seeking his own beds. The lone figure on Sprat Ridge, a bar in the Taw estuary that appears at low water, was Archie Hooper – a former skipper of the Lundy ferry. A boat took him over, cast its nets for salmon and sea trout, and brought him back on the rising tide. 'Enough for a feed,' Archie used to say as he stepped ashore.

The shell of a cockle is plump, frilly and recalls the sand it came from – light in North Uist, dark in Poole Harbour and Southend, blue in Stiffkey ('Stewki') in Norfolk. The inside is smooth and white as porcelain. The occupant, cradled nicely, has an orange horn. There are *palourdes* in selected spots off the south coast, liked by the French. The 'hen' cockle is a type of clam less abundant and oval in shape, which my brother and I (incorrectly) called 'queens'.

Cockle spat are washed here and there by the tide, then settle and grow quickly. The dead leave shells on sandy beaches, indicating beds, the living burrow. Take a kitchen spoon, look for a hole a bit smaller than a peppercorn and excavate the cockle that may be lurking an inch or two underneath. Alternatively, use a garden rake to bring the cockles up. Leave the smaller ones to grown on. Put the larger ones in a bucket. Do not throw them in or the shells might break, mortally wounding the creature within.

Cockling can be a hazardous occupation in thickening mists and rising tides, and was in Morecambe Bay. There can also be clashes between the teams of getters. The commercial beds are protected by quotas and a close season, but respond to working and seem to be sustainable. The Thames estuary, which is closely monitored and cleaner now than it has been for centuries, is one of the happiest hunting grounds. The cockles are hoovered up by boat and landed in the morning. They are processed by roaring state-of-the-art machines in the brilliant green sheds, emitting plumes of steam, that stand next to the flyover at Leigh-on-Sea. Having been dispatched to Holland for processing within hours of capture, the same cockles return to UK supermarkets at inflated prices, deprived of their flavour and packed in jars labelled 'Dutch'. The shells, collected in huge heaps, are sometimes used to fill potholes on unadopted roads and drives.

P. Johnson of Salisbury market, now in his sixties, has been selling cockles all his life. He scoops up the cockles into neat little bags and on to white dishes, intent on each one, as instructed by his father. The exterior of his caravan is blue, the interior pink, and the price of cockles so indifferent to rising, like the former cost of a cinema seat, it is painted in red on one of the walls. Vinegar, pepper and salt are provided. A clock, which goes anticlockwise, registers the time.

Fresh cockles are a delicacy. They can occasionally be obtained in fishmongers'. To prepare and cook them: rinse and drain a couple of times at home, refresh with cold water and throw in a handful of flour or fine oatmeal to scour them out. Leave in the fridge for 24 hours. Rinse again, drain and discard any whose shells remain defiantly open, even after a squeeze. Commit to a saucepan without water and cover. Cook over a highish heat for only 2–3 minutes, or as long as it takes the cockles to open, and remove with a perforated spoon. Do not overcook or the meat shrinks. The finished cockle should be as plump as the shell it arrived in. Eat them when they are cool enough to handle, while still warm.

The liquor is salty and also full of grit, but improves a fish stock, soup or sauce more than cockles themselves. Strain through a cloth before using it.

The Hanoverians incised legs of mutton with cockles, rather than with garlic.

Mussels lie about the beach in blue-black clusters, thicker and stronger in favoured spots than blankets of chain mail, but curiously vulnerable under foot. They grip to ropes, stones and, on exposed parts of the coast, to rocks. The anchors are tiny webs of natural fibre, or 'beards', which, drab as they look, were employed to make a tunic for Henry VIII (now in the Victoria and Albert Museum). There are river mussels too, inedible by modern standards, but able to produce a pearl. I have found them in the Thames. The shells appear after dredging in the mud on the banks of canals.

The mussels exposed to the rough Atlantic seas and storms are small, salty and hardly worth gathering. The ones in the Wash, the biggest I have seen, are taken in large quantities by Eider duck, a cause of friction between the fishermen and the RSPB. The creature does not thrive except in shelter, and likes a trickle of fresh water from a feeder stream. Collect from the point where the low tide turns, or as near to it as possible. Avoid the hottest weather and human habitation (i.e. drains).

The mussel is a 'little pumping station' (Hartley, 1954), able to recycle ten gallons of water a day. It is easily polluted but also easily purified, and attaches itself to ropes or sticks laid out by the farms. Cultivated mussels are sweeter and tastier than the ones in the wild. The crops from the Exe, taken by divers, are worth any premium. A man buys exactly sixteen a week from a van near me.

Mussels will keep in a refrigerated bucket of water, changed occasionally, for several days. Biff any that are open on a hard surface. Reject if they do not close, along with any broken shells. To clean, scrub with a wire brush or scrape with a knife. Either yank out the beard or remove later.

Mussels can be cooked and eaten like cockles, but if they are farmed (and therefore less salty) you can go further. Commit to a dry saucepan and cook over a high-ish heat for 2–3 minutes until open. When done, remove to hot soup plates with a perforated spoon. Strain the stock through a fine sieve or cloth and add chopped onion or shallot softened in butter. Boil up with a glass of white wine and finish with cream. Pour the sauce over the mussels, and dust with chopped fresh parsley or chives. You may use one mussel like a pair of tweezers to eat the next. Sup the liquor with a spoon. The restaurants in Antwerp, the birthplace of *moules marinières*, can do no better than you.

Periwinkles (also a naturalized plant) are a sort of maritime snail with a spiral shell, which may be picked from rocks and stones between high and low water marks.

They were eaten in huge quantities in Victorian England, and brought from as far away as Scotland to London, but considered too impolite for a mention in middle-class cookery books. Winkle eaters have a punctuated outlook on life, says Dorothy Hartley, speaking of a night watchman she knew.

> He used to sit by his big red coke fire-bucket, a bit of folded blanket over his knees, his mug of hot tea, and a little enamel bowl full of winkles: he would turn up the little tab-end at the bottom of his waistcoat, pull out a long pin, and take a winkle . . . then he would chuck the empty shell over his shoulder into the canal . . . He did it quite slowly . . . red in the firelight, head aslant, his huge hand still half open like a hoary brown shell. He . . . paused a second till he heard the tiny plop, before he bent and picked up the next winkle . . . 'They do pass the time very pleasantly,' he said.

Winkles are still measured by the pint in places (I can feel a citizen's arrest coming on) and sold from stalls in seaside towns. Hastings is the home of the Winkle Club – a charitable organisation – and a former Winkle King. The population of this fish is currently sustainable. The meat is black when cooked, fresh-tasting and pleasantly chewy.

Razor shells, empty and plundered by gulls, litter the coast like discarded pencil boxes. The spat, which burrow out to sea, are washed inshore by storms. They leave two small holes in the sand at extra low water, joined by a half-inch thread. I know what to look for, where and when to catch them, and how. So it is only a matter of time. Dust the holes with salt and wait for a spout of water to appear, followed by an armoured column of white flesh. 'Don't snatch,' a fisherman told me, out digging for bait. Many reasons have been advanced as to why the method works (a 'reverse osmosis', apparently), none of them watertight (as it were). Razor shells crop up in fishmongers' occasionally. The meat is firm, sweet and often overlooked, though not by the Chinese. Clean carefully, leaving only the white flesh, and cook as follows:

Fry up some onion and garlic, peeled and chopped, in oil or butter. Add some tomatoes, skinned, minus seeds, and a glass of water or white wine. Cook gently for 5 minutes, then add razors. Heat through for a further 5 minutes until firm, season to taste.

Whelks: and so, by a fifty-year roundabout route to West's Whelks of Whitstable. Graham and son run a quayside business housed in a black wooden shiplap hut. Upstairs, a balcony and rooms overlooking the harbour; two generations in baseball caps, pinnies and jeans, sitting and silently picking whelks by hand. Downstairs is the mighty cauldron in which to cook them, emitting clouds of steam. Outside is the wooden grader, standing on stilts, that separates the big ones for boiling and the small ones for breeding and returning to the sea. There is a boat coming in with fish to gawp at, a market to buy in, and a huge heap of shells for filling wayside holes. Somerset Maugham called it Blackstable. You can swim between the groynes in the middle of town.

Fishing for whelks is hard, messy and persistent work, done in all weathers. The bait smells and has to in order to serve its purpose. The pots are heavy too. Some of the catch, which comes in from Hastings, is redistributed to the north and Midlands. Birmingham takes considerable amounts. The English eat more whelks than anyone else, except the Italians. The Chinese are catching up, but the *beau monde* is unlikely to, even assisted by chilled white wine. Whelks are another food consumed by the ton which is too impolite to mention in print. They may be cooked for market, or be seen oozing and schmoozing in fishmongers' trays. To prepare whelks, soak in salted water for at least two hours and simmer for 15–20 minutes. Hartley dropped them into boiling water, turned off the heat and left them until cold – a method I have yet to try. Remove the protective cap before eating and souse in vinegar – at the last minute – or the meat will be tough.

PS

'Tell me again, Marshy.'

'First thing is,' he said, 'Dad never told a lie in his life.'

I knew that. I had met Frank a couple of times. He was not the type. Now, Martin Vinnicombe, his cousin, was a different matter, he was full of stories. He kept the salvage boat on the quay where my brother and I used to muck about as boys. There was scrap all over the place, unexploded shells full of cordite brought up from the bay – no Health and Safety in those days. Martin said there was a Spanish galleon out there too, implicitly full of treasure. I still believe him.

'Anyway,' said Marshy, 'Dad was on his way out of Newlyn with another bloke. It was a warm, clear day, flat calm. A few hundred yards off, they saw what appeared to be an upturned dinghy in the water and went to investigate. Drawing close, they could see it was not another boat, but a huge grey, green rounded shape, a creature sunning itself which seemed to awake. A head, like a horse's, rose from the water. It was about the size of a horse's too, but small compared to the great long neck and huge body. The eyes were like saucers . . .

'Was he frightened?' I asked.

'Dad's been out in a boat surrounded by whales,' said Marshy by way of explanation. He continued: 'The creature remained head above water for a few seconds, then sank beneath the waves. They saw it on the sonar before it disappeared off the screen. Dad did not tell anyone about it, but he passed a fisherman later in the week who stopped him with the words "So, you seen Old Nick, then.'"

The news got out, Marshy went on. A couple of scientists descended from upcountry armed with diagrams. Frank pointed to the creature he had seen. One of the boffins all but accused him of telling stories – and that was that for their conversation. There was a television film about the sighting, but it was short, unlikely and inaccurate, with a couple of daft actors pretending to be Cornish.

A monster was reported when I was a boy, another by some friends of my mother-in-law's near the King Harry Ferry. Deep water up there, deep enough for tankers. Marshy said he knew about six people who had seen Old Nick. One of them was a roofer working on a house overlooking the sea. There was also a man going home in a boat after a party, who thought for a moment it might have been the drink.

CHAPTER
TWENTY-TWO

FRESHWATER FISH

**T**HE GROUND ROSE TOWARDS PETERBOROUGH in the north. Ramsey, to the south, had a long main street of early houses that passed the ruined abbey and went out into the fen. The leaves of the poplars, glinting in the sun, shimmered in the wind like showers of silver coins. There were regimented crops on either side of an empty road. The fertile basin in which they grew had once been under water and flanked by reeds the height of a hayrick or cottage roof. It was a bright and lonesome summer evening. I was standing on the bed of a former lake, which in its time had been the biggest stretch of water in the English lowlands.

The brooding and ague-ridden Whittlesey Mere,[*] swelling to three miles wide and six long after heavy rain, was fed by the streams of Cambridgeshire and Huntingdonshire. An island stood in the middle where a 'great store' of fish and snakes, geese and duck, bittern, stork, mosquitoes and lacewings bred together. In some places, the lake was clear, in others black and said to be bottomless – 'like some sea' – wet and marshy at the edges but marked with tributaries accessible by boat. The mouth of the 'Mer' was 'formidable', its disposition 'dangerous' and its winds 'sudden', and rising 'like hurricanes' (Fiennes, 1982). The storms were called waterquakes.

The Mere dwellers carried coal on barges, and cut peat and sedge for fuel, exchanging them for pots and pans with local chapmen. The reeds they harvested for thatching houses were said to last a hundred years. The starlings that could descend in murmurations on the stalks, breaking every one, were trapped and eaten in tens of thousands. The fishermen, exercising rights called boatgates, originally held by the Church, made runs through the beds for their traps. Nets were limited. Baited lines were not, and laid out all year round except in Shelerode, a lunar month divided in two by St George's Day. Rents were paid in kind. There were fairs after Christmas with horse-drawn sleighs, and regattas in the summer, with feasts and dancing at Blackhand Point. Landowners, trippers, and Cambridge undergraduates liked to attend.

As the price of wheat rose in the nineteenth century, the squirearchy entered into an agreement to divert the River Nene, run off the water from the Mere, and put down the land to agricultural use. There was no opposition to the scheme from powerful people, so none went down in history. As for the powerless remainder, it is unlikely they believed anything so extreme would be allowed to take place. Promises of a better future were made, no doubt, and the ground work done. Drainage, completed before a crowd one day in late summer, left thousands of fish floundering, panting and finally rotting in mud, soon to dry out and surrender to the plough. Onlookers with boards strapped to their feet to stop them sinking

---

[*] *Information from the* Peterborough Advertiser, *April 1887 and September 1931;* Whittlesey Mere, *a WEA project pamphlet by Paul Middleton.*

collected what they could for food. The night passed and the dawn broke as usual, but not on the waters of Whittlesey Mere.

The last big catch of fish taken from the receding lake amounted to two tons of mainly perch, bream, gudgeon, tench, roach and rudd. The Coles family, assisted by 'Old Piscator' of the *Peterborough Advertiser*, wheeled off the spoils in a couple of wagons. They also received £50 for finding a medieval incense burner on the bed of the Mere, which was claimed by Squire Wells after a tussle with a fellow landowner, and sold on for £5,000. The other discoveries included stones from Ramsey Abbey, the skeletons of wolves and wild boar, and the legendary rogue pike, which weighed three and a half stone and measured four feet seven inches from eye to fork.

Whittlesey Mere rose from the dead and refilled with water in November 1852, when the new river broke its banks. It was drained again. The whole operation, including a pump house and the digging of channels, cost Wells a fortune that he never recovered, the fenmen a way of life, and the wildfowl and fish life itself. 'Oakey' Phillips, the last full-time fisherman, emigrated to America. The reclamation of the land was declared 'progress' at the time and within a few years renamed 'The Great Mistake'. Today, a tattered map printed on silk in 1786 and displayed in a local museum is all that remains of the dark and stormy stretch, where the waves came and went in the quickest of successions and a boat went down in the 'shortest' of seas. The deaths of King Canute's two boys, drowned in a waterquake on the way to their baptism, are commemorated in Peterborough Cathedral.

Malvern and Shaftesbury are the only two English towns of any size that are not built on lakes or rivers. Fresh water is too valuable a resource to be parted from. It is life-sustaining, a means of transport and a supply of food for which people competed. I lived for years near the Hampshire Avon, Queen of Rivers, which had the lot in terms of fish: a good run of salmon and populations of trout, grayling, perch, barbel, carp and the rest. Before the war, the weed was cut by the prisoners from the gaol in Winchester, working in pairs with a giant saw, one man on either bank. A paddle-boat replaced them, then maintenance declined. There was soil erosion from road- and house-building, masking the brilliance of the feeder streams, nitrate-heavy leaching and effluent from the fish farm all washing their way to the sea. Rivers were abused and abandoned all over the country. The next time you are in the industrial heart of Sheffield, look for a road called Salmon Pastures. It may still be there.

Tarka the otter's home stretch of the Torridge in Devon was one of the most polluted. There were conspiracy theories and alleged cover-ups. The former National Rivers Authority, simultaneously poacher and gamekeeper, was at one stage faced with prosecuting itself. The new and privatised water companies, with shareholders to oblige, would never spend money unless they had to. Then it happened. The EU commitment to clean up the environment can take the credit. In the mean time pollution still occurs. There have also been casualties: crayfish (see page 292–3) and a little chap called a burbot, a relation of the cod, which was declared extinct in the 1990s.

Until a couple of hundred years ago, freshwater fish were no less important to the English diet than the fowls of the air and the fruits of the forest. They were acquired with the same ingenuity with which trappers caught fair game, transported in barrels, and held by landowners in 'stews' or 'basins'. The oldest fish keep I have come across, dated about 1200, was at the castle in Dovedale. Breeding programmes were probably advancing under the Church when hit by the dissolution of the monasteries. Meare Pool in Somerset, which was five miles in circumference and overlooked by the warden's 'Fish House', was drained in the sixteenth century. In spite of local opposition, the flood plains and east-of-England 'fishing fields' disappeared in the seventeenth. The Enclosure Acts denied country people access to many of the rivers where they had plied their nets; a prohibition on the nets themselves (except under licence for salmon and sea trout) followed in the 1870s. Meanwhile, trawling, refrigeration and the railways increased the supply of sea fish to even the most landlocked markets.

The ancient practice of angling (from 'angel' – hook) entered a new phase with split cane rods, made from foreign wood, in the nineteenth century. Like hawking and shooting, it evolved into a two-tier occupation. The trout family emerged as a coveted game fish, the piscatorial equivalent of grouse or partridge. To get anywhere near it required money, connections, even the purchase of a house in Hungerford, Berkshire, plus rights to the Kennet. The rest of the fish population was dismissed as 'coarse'. The difference between the two amounted to more than habitat and fin formation. A cachet and mode of capture were involved. It was fly versus worm, art versus craft, and gentlemen versus players, who, in spite of the gulf between them, had one thing in common. As the twentieth century progressed, increasingly fewer people in either camp cast a line with food in mind.

Freshwater fish lost their culinary status to sport, the game ones partially, the coarse ones almost completely. Anglers wrapped in thought (presumably) sit all day catching fish only to weigh them, keep them for a few hours, and put them back at close of play. The prospect of catching an ever bigger trophy and setting a record is behind it all. The notion of eating a coarse fish plays no part in the exercise. To suggest that it could provokes a mixture of reactions from incredulous to hostile. So, it can start with a yarn on the bank and end with a fat lip, river and rivals playing their enduring and habitual parts.

Char: from England's largest lowland lake, extinct, to the largest extant. Windermere runs up the cleavage between slate-grey shaley fells, green and tidy foothills, and the girdle of trees that hangs like a browse line above the dark water. After a night in a Lancashire field, and a gale that threatened to pick me and my wife up with our belongings, tent and all, and pitch us into the next county, the sun rose on a clear, kind and breathless morning. It was warm by nine, hot by ten, and 'right snug', as they say, in the shadow of Crinkle Crag.

Paul, a well-built, quiet man with a firm handshake who had lived by Windermere all his life, seemed to have things all his own way. Fishermen often do. He was out on the lake in the morning, worked in the afternoon and returned home in the evening often to barbecue what he had caught. We met at a busy road junction in the middle of town, and followed him down a twisting lane, around corners and through a farm gate to a shady and secluded beach.

A char boat lay ready at the water's edge, a sleek-looking skiff the colour of honey, lowish in profile and designed according to the wave length on the lake. It was varnished every winter and kitted out with custom-built clasps for rods and rowlocks for the oars. We put in the bung, loaded the gear and moved out into the North Basin. We were making for a spot where the Arctic char collect, having been dumped, frozen alive, in the last 'glass' age.

The char is a landlocked salmon with a skin translucent as a bright night sky. A strawberry mark appears on its belly in whichever of the two seasons – early summer or autumn – the fish prepare to spawn in the feeder streams and becks. For the rest of the year they shy away from the light, confining themselves to the deeper and colder waters of select English and Scottish mountain lakes and tarns, notably Windermere, Buttermere, Thirlmere, Crummock Water, Hawes Water, Wast Water, Coniston Water and Ennerdale Water. The vendace and schelly, relations of the char, enjoy a similar distribution, but are now protected. An American brook char is farmed in England too (one of our local bailiffs has a dog that catches and eats them).

The lakeland char fishery was originally held by the abbey of Furness. It passed into temporal hands after the Reformation, yielding up to four thousand pounds' weight of fish a year. The meat was committed to nineteenth-century Staffordshire pots about the size of wine coasters, painted with an image of the char. Controls were enforced in 1878, along with the prohibition of netting, which brought an effective end to another cottage industry, but induced the current method of catching the char.

Paul was taught to fish by an elder brother. His rods, made of bamboo, are sixteen feet long and mounted either side of the boat. Each is equipped with a bell, a line of up to a hundred feet, nine spinners of polished bronze, hooks and a single weight. We trawled at the slowest pace. You wait, watch and contemplate the farms and fields, the fells beyond, and lakeside houses big and small. The fish strike, the rod bends, and the bell jingles more than usual. Then Paul brings in the line, laying out the spinners side by side on the seat before him in the morning sun, as neatly, unhurriedly and delicately as a duchess drinking tea.

One, two or even three fish may come in together. They have tender mouths and do not fight much for such muscular little chaps. The net is ready, the hook extracted. The char goes into a freshwater safe to keep him cool if he is over ten inches, or back into the lake, gently again and without being handled. The human touch is always a shock to a cold-blooded creature. Paul had said we would not be disappointed. Between nine o'clock and noon he caught eight fish of about a pound or less and returned three. It was an average and sustainable haul on a soft and unspoiled morning, with our skiff bobbing up and down and the water lap-lapping its elegant contours as the pleasure craft moved past.

I dozed off, and learned I was lucky to be able to. After twenty years of mayhem, noise, injuries, and the death of a man garrotted by a water skier's tow rope, a ten-knot speed limit had been introduced to Windermere. The lake was back to its old and pleasant self, and more like it had been when Paul was a boy. Yet, as a breeding and feeding ground for game and coarse fish, water quality continued to cause concern. However tight EC controls are, with people there is pollution. In Elizabethan times it did for the char population in Ullswater. Today, the question is whether the acidity can be kept to a level at which the salmon family can continue to survive. At present, the roach, a newcomer and an invasive one, is putting up the stiffest opposition.

I first acquired char from a fishmonger in Windermere, then from a van, and also from Booths, who may be the least offensive of the supermarkets, but who no longer know the local fish, let alone stock it. The restaurants and hotels I contacted about char, with one exception, did not bother with it either. Meanwhile, Paul feeds like an Edwardian parson. I took three of the fish he caught, gutted them at the lakeside, and put them on ice obtained in an off-licence. After gawping at the topiary in Levens Hall gardens (the finest in existence and worth every minute), my wife and I fried up the char at the campsite that evening. The meat was as good as any salmon, better than any trout, and had an orange blush that can also be pink. It is equally delicious hot or cold.

Potted char: 'Gut and clean [the fish] thoroughly, then rub the insides with a little salt and close up again. Let them stay till the following morning. Pack evenly into a stew dish or casserole with a lid. Cover with butter and char seasoning.* Cook very slowly for 8–10 hours, then let get cold, when the heads and backbones should be carefully removed, so as not to spoil the shape of the fish, and lay the fish straight in the char dish and cover with melted butter' (from Outgate WI, Westmorland, 1962).

---

* *Char seasoning, which probably contained salt, pepper, mace or nutmeg, and cloves, used to be available from the Bowness branch of Boots the chemist.*

Loe trout are another curiosity, whose antecedents spawned in the River Cober and fed in the estuary below that provided Helston with access to the Atlantic. By the Middle Ages, a succession of storms had created a shingle bar that grew into a dam. The water, slowly made fresh by the rain and streams, became Cornwall's biggest lake. It is entitled Loe Pool. The trout that commuted between their feeding grounds at sea and spawning grounds inland were trapped as a result. 'The eye is large, the back a deep purple on which the scales are of a silver hue,' said William Borlase in his *Natural History of Cornwall* (1758). 'The belly, from the straight line which passes from the gills to the middle of the tail, is of a bright pearl colour. The spots are hexagonal annulets . . . scarlet . . . in general . . . the tail remarkably large and very little forked.'

In the nineteenth century, the build-up of water on the River Cober stopped the local flour mills working. On payment of a due to the owners of Penrose, which overlooks Loe Pool, the bar was cut to effect a release. A number of trout were washed out to sea on these occasions, and caught as far away as the Scillies, though not in large numbers. Enough stayed at home breeding amongst themselves and sharing their existence with bathers in the summer, bitterns in the winter and otters throughout the year.

In the twentieth century, Loe Pool registered as the last lake in England to receive untreated sewage. In the long, hot summer of 1976, the algae, feeding on the nutrients and the run-off from the hills, were out of control. The trout lay gasping on the surface of a putrid pond. The former vicar of Constantine, fisherman, fowler and naturalist Canon Mossop, wrote countless letters to the council, Water Board and National Rivers Authority about the problem, and did his utmost to see it addressed.

The situation today is that the pool receives treated waste from Helston and Culdrose Air Station. The lie of the land is not in its favour, but the water quality is better than it was. Licences to fish are administered by the National Trust on behalf of the Penrose estate. Between two and twenty tickets are issued every year. The Loe trout is still with us. 'The flesh is very red in season and much esteemed,' Borlase concluded. I have not had the pleasure.

Grayling are the lady of the stream to the trout's lord, and another surface feeder, shadowy in the water and mercurial on a line, fighting and flashing on an autumn day. 'What a beauty he is when landed,' said *The Field* in 1869, 'with his . . . rainbow-coloured dorsal fin, his lozenge-shaped eyes and small square mouth, a stripe of silver lace running down his sides, the tinge of gold on the belly . . . delicious eating too'. Grayling are indigenous to the upper reaches of English rivers that flow into the North Sea; a popular fish where it belongs, which extends the fishing season, and a favourite with Dorothy Hartley:

I believe the grayling the most beautiful fish in the world. Where Kilsey Crag stands up like a rampart below Hatton Gill there is a stone bridge over clear water, running over pebbles white as mushroom tops, spotted with water snails black as ebony. The fine turf either side of the Wharf is grey green. In the swift place the grayling rests, a fish of silver and pearl fanning the stream gently with graceful fronds of bronze silk. He looks as if he rested still, and let the stream ripple through his soft fins, but he is keeping his place with effortless grace. Sometimes he lets go and drifts downstream, swift as the shadow of a flying bird; and then a flicker of pearl light, and he is back at rest again. At evening time when the stream is dark, he shines like white pewter in the moonlight.

Meanwhile, in the south of England's chalk streams, few creatures are less welcome than a grayling. The Hampshire Avon is electro-fished (the river is cleared by electric charges, which stun the fish causing them temporarily to float to the surface of the water), enabling the bailiffs to remove the species that consume or compete with trout. The grayling are mostly wasted, though some are taken in tanks for distribution to more hospitable rivers. I have been around at the time and been given fish by water bailiffs only too pleased to be rid of them. A one-pound grayling is a delicate and much underrated feed. The meat is white, superior to a trout's. Stuff with the sprigs of wild thyme that he is said to smell of, and bake until firm.

Perch are dandies of the stream, fit for any tank, with green backs, broad bands, orange fins, and spines that keep them safe from attack. They have sticky eggs, which are easily and frequently carried on the legs of birds between gravel pits, ponds and rivers, and move in marauding shoals, around and about landing stages, jetties and bridges. The latest news is that perch are multiplying in Loe Pool and producing whoppers. A fish within a few ounces of the national record was caught – and eaten – in 2005.

As food, perch are next to the salmon family: a former favourite with anglers and country people, which has been farmed, and a lingering one in the restaurants around Lakes Annecy and Neuchâtel in Switzerland. Once caught, they do not deteriorate as quickly as other coarse fish. A two-pound perch is a good one. The skin comes off like paper. The meat, which separates easily from the bones, is usually white but can be tinged with pink from a diet of crustaceans. Again, I have not had the pleasure.

From *A Book of Angling* by Francis Francis (1867):

Now you shall see some real sportsman's cookery. Give me half a dozen of those perch, Patsey, and that copy of the *Times* newspaper . . . take each perch separately, merely wiping him dry without cutting or scraping him in the least, as that would break the skin and let out his juices; then take a piece of paper and wet it in the lake, and roll the perch in it, three or four folds, then screw up the ends and thrust perch, paper, and all into the embers. In . . . five to ten minutes your fish is cooked. Rake him out, take off the charred paper, and carefully remove his scales, which will come off en masse; rub the white succulent side with butter, pepper and salt to taste, make an incision along the backbone and flake off all the beautiful firm white flesh . . . it is a dish fit for a king, or an angler.

Pike: on summer mornings the rods would wait outside the shop for Bob the Fish to open and make an offer for the salmon they had killed below the bridge in town or downriver by the weir. This time there was a boy standing in the doorway with a pike. The tail of the creature was touching the ground, while the head came up to the middle of his chest.

A few minutes later I joined Bob and the boy in the back of the shop. The pike was lying on the concrete floor. It was deep as a salmon and over a yard long. The huge distended mouth was inches wide and open, showing the fearsome teeth.

'Some fish, isn't she?' said Bob. 'Glad I didn't carry her back.'

While paddling in the shallows looking for crayfish, a pike had slipped past me. This one, twice the size, was every bit as sleek and firm. The boy smiled proudly.

'She fight?' I asked.

'She ran.'

The morning sun shone through the window on to the pike, lighting up her eyes and skin. She was silver underneath, streamlined in gold, and a deep, dark green along her back, the colour of the reeds in the river.

'Do you want her?' I asked Bob.

'Don't mind.'

I turned to the boy.

'How much?'

'Fiver.'

I was not going to argue, and paid him. The boy pocketed the money, thanked us both and left by the back door. Bob picked the fish up off the floor by the eyes and, with some effort, hooked it by the mouth on to the scales. We stared at the weight.

'Having a party?' he said.

'No.'

'Cooking for one?'

'Not at the moment.'

He took down the fish and laid it on the counter.

'What are you going to do with eighteen pounds of pike, then?'

I felt the broad shoulders of the fish, and ran the palm of my hand down the cool and gleaming body, over the fin, to the wide sweep of the powerful tail.

'I don't know,' I said. 'I just had to buy it.'

The pike is a luminous shadow amongst other fish till he feels hungry, and they, sensing danger, keep away. Then he moves to the cover of a tributary or reedbed and waits. He is stealthy, uninhibited, swift and savage, striking with a violent flourish and leaving the water ominously still. A pike is more than a river shark; he is certain death. He will attack every fish his own size or bigger except the spiny perch and the anodyne tench, swallowing them in stages if necessary; frogs, birds and next of kin too. It is not unusual to find pike inside pike inside pike, or to see baby wild duck, out for a swim behind their mother, disappear from the surface of a lake with a sinister plop. Nothing can be so destructive in fresh water, reach a larger size, or perform feats more frequently exaggerated by man but never, quite, to be discounted. One look into a dark, forbidding rhine or pool is enough to provoke an image of a monster pike seizing swans, drowning dogs and attacking mules, milkmaids and fully grown men parted from their skis in the water. For most victims, once bitten, to struggle is useless. The only safe place for that terrible mouth encrusted with teeth all pointing inwards is nailed to a keeper's hut. The only safe condition is detached from the body, dried up and grinning.

Pike, which have an emetic roe, were taken 'on the shed' from Whittlesey Mere. Two-minute-milers with names like 'Fish' and 'Turkey' (Nicolson and Sutherland, 1986), flashing down frozen fens on mutton-bone skates, pursued adult pike to the point of exhaustion. Then they broke the ice and hauled out their dinner. This is a fish with plenty on him, highly priced and rated in the past, but worth little or nothing at present. Another one that may be given away by water bailiffs.

Most of the pike I have acquired were obtained by electro-fishing. They can have a broken back from the charge: cut round the bruise and discard. The meat is dry and not particularly pleasant when freshly cooked, but responds well to cold-smoking by a professional. Bob the Fish used to do the honours for me. The alternative is to roll up your sleeves, turn the mobile off, the classic serial on and wind back the kitchen clock to the Victorian era.

Quenelles of pike[*]: First, fillet and skin a pike. Remove the awkward right-angular bones with pliers. Liquidize the meat or put it through a mouli: a process that transforms the texture and turns it into a jelly. For every 1lb (450g), which makes 14–16 quenelles, assemble the following ingredients:

[*] *Adapted from* Memories with Food at Gipsy House *by Felicity and Roald Dahl.*

For the choux paste, which binds the quenelles: 2oz (50g) butter, 10fl oz (275ml) water, 4oz (110g) plain flour, 2 eggs; for the fish, a seasoning: ¼ pint (150ml) cream, ½ level tsp salt, ¼ level tsp white pepper; for the sauce: 1 pint (570ml) of béchamel (made with 1oz (25g) butter, 1oz (25g) flour, 1 pint (570ml) milk), 2 tbsp dry white wine, 4oz (110g) mature Lancashire or white Cheshire cheese, grated or crumbled, ¼ pint (150ml) cream, salt and white pepper to taste.

1. To make the choux paste, put the water in a pan with the butter and boil. When the butter is melted, remove from the heat and add the flour all at once. Stir vigorously to get rid of any lumps. Cook gently, still stirring, until the paste leaves the sides of the pan. Remove from the heat, cover and allow to cool slightly. Beat in the eggs.
2. Mix the fish seasoning and paste with the pike. Push through a sieve with a spoon or plastic scraper and chill (a cold preparation is easier to handle).
3. To cook the quenelles, fill two pans with hot water. Bring one up to simmering point on the stove, but do not boil. Meanwhile, wet your hands in the other to stop the mixture sticking to the skin, take a small quantity, and roll up into bombs about the size and shape of a hen's egg, smoothing over the cracks and washing your hands in warm water between each one (some cooks use dessertspoons, which I find more difficult). Drop into the simmering water. The quenelles will sink at first, then rise to the surface. Poach for 15–20 minutes, prodding them gently. When the texture begins to feel firm, the quenelles are done. Remove with a perforated spoon and drain. Cover with greaseproof paper and set aside.
4. Make the béchamel. Enrich it with the wine and cream. Add the cheese and heat gently until melted. Adjust the seasoning.
5. Commit the quenelles to a buttered baking dish, covered in greaseproof paper, and heat through in the oven for about 1 hour at 150°C/300°F/gas mark 2.
6. Strain the hot sauce over the top.

Why bother?
1. Pike are best when made into quenelles.
2. Quenelles are best when made from pike.
3. They can be prepared in advance, freeze well and cost very little except in labour.
4. They are an excuse to spend an afternoon playing around in the kitchen.
5. A tangible result is achieved.

Nothing is more likely to impress favoured guests, or trump the aces of competitive ones. Restaurants seldom make quenelles today, but when they do, the mixture is usually baked like a terrine in a bain-marie for about 1½ hours at 170°C/325°F/gas mark 3. The preparation is done when it leaves the sides of the vessel. Easier, but less visual.

Zander are spiny and slender pike-perch, natives of Eastern Europe. They were introduced to Woburn on two occasions around the turn of the twentieth century and into the Great Ouse in 1963 by the Rivers Authority, an extraordinary decision given their predatory habits and capacity to breed. The population of other fish has suffered as a result. In their defence, zander are terrific to eat and increasingly popular with restaurants in the fens. Fish of between five and ten pounds are not uncommon. The meat, which a game dealer in Cambridgeshire says he cannot get enough of, is white, flaky and sustainable with demand and supply as they are at present. Watch out for it.

Elvers: from a bridge over the Severn, where the boar can be seen and heard to roll upriver and crash into the nearest weir, a succession of winking lights on either bank marks the way to Tewkesbury, itself lit up and visible in the night. Voices can be heard. The fishermen arrive and stake a claim to indicate a tump is taken, then wait with bags and nets, or slope off and return after a pint. There are rumours every year that unwelcome people, in pursuit of cash, come to spoil a sport and occupation that is centuries old.

The elvers are born in the doldrums, the deepest and darkest of 'shoreless' seas (Fort, 2002) choked with clumps of sargassum weed. Sensitive to light, wispy and transparent, they have a thin red backbone visible through the skin, black spots for eyes, and a mind set on the infiltration of every dark and hospitable home in fresh or brackish water. Struggling, wriggling and borne forward, elvers come up and out of English rivers and make off into the night. They can rise and fall on the current, but not steer. The Severn, with its thirty-foot tides, is the glass eels' favourite conveyor.

The elvers move as the night wears on, but cannot be predicted. A fisherman may dip his great net again and again and get little or nothing for season after season, or bring it up full of stranded orphans out of the river and into the torchlight. His face, meanwhile, remains in darkness. You can chat with a man for hours, get to know him and exchange warm farewells – without even seeing what he looks like unless he lights up. There is competition and secrecy, brought on by the anticipation and gloom. Elvering is not what it was. The visible waves they came in are like the flocks of plover.

Elvers were sold from buckets and baths door to door in Gloucestershire's Severnside villages. They keep and thrive in conditions they like, but throw up a protective and unpleasant slime when distressed, known locally as 'vomp' (Hart-Davis). It is important to eat, smother, or move them on quickly. The beasts drank elvers live from pint pots at contests. The beauties, ever so politely, spat out the eyes. The rest ate elvers hot, fried up in omelettes or cold in sandwiches every spring and early summer. The flavour is faintly fishy, the texture like jelly and the effect romantically stirring, they say. I may never find out. The price, rising fast by 1990, stands today at £400 per kilo, which amounts to some two thousand elvers. The catches go to farms abroad for fattening, a tricky business mastered by the Dutch, then mostly to Japan. The adolescent elvers, which have started to acquire pigmentation, are known as bolts.

Eels, into which little elvers grow, are sleek, slimy, sinuous, secretive and tactile creatures, permanently present in rivers, rhines and lakes. The darker and more gruesome and creepy the habitat, the better. Abundant and well fed on tiddlers, snails and the occasional slug, eels have been a staple for the poor for centuries. No fish, clinging to life and line tenaciously, kept better when caught and transported. The meat was rent for the abbeys, mounted on sticks twenty-five at a time. The skin was used for twine. The body, when parted from the head, twitches for hours.

The life of an eel is destined to come full circle. Up to ten years can pass before, triggered by oncoming sexual maturity, it leaves for its first and final resting place halfway down to the bottom of the world, back in the Sargasso Sea. The return journey is over four thousand miles. The depth at which they couple is five hundred fathoms. The pressure is an estimated one ton per square inch – or thought to be. No one knows exactly where they breed. No one has seen them do it. No one can describe the mass copulation ending in the most secret of deaths. No wonder people are obsessed. No work on the subject, or almost any other, is more thorough and explicit than Tom Fort's elegant *Book of Eels*.

A stormy night in the dark quarter towards the back end of the year, when the rivers are coloured up and filling, is when the eels come slithering out of the pingos and ponds and make for the sea. Up go the sluices, projecting the flow of water on to the risers and the riparian stage. With it goes the weed, the occasional flapping fish, and writhing eels, large and small, coiling and cool, smooth and serpentine, nosing instinctively ahead and lashing with their tails. The man steps forward in oilskins and boots, returning the fish to the river and helping the eels into a tank. He does it again as many times as there are eels, all night long in the driving rain and wildest of winds until after the day dawns. The roaring of water only decreases when he shuts off the flow, though the noise continues to ring in his ears. He leaves the stage delighted or disappointed and barely awake. A living can still be made, but a tough one.

The bag or fyke nets (from the Dutch *fuik*, fish) used for eels come in pairs about ten feet long. They are stretched either across rivers, flowing with the current like an air sock, or in the tidal reaches nearer the coast. The eels get in on their way out to sea and await collection by fishermen in a boat. There have been many nifty ways of catching eels, from lines and gleavers (tridents) to blocked-off pipes, which do not even have to be baited. The victim, seeking a dark place to lie up, invites himself in and stays there until morning.

Eel fishermen are regulated. Even so, they can be cagey, operating as many do near footpaths and busy roads, city centres and supermarkets. Curtain-twitchers are suspicious, habitually reporting licensees for poaching after twenty years of legitimate activity. The 'antis' do not like them either. They would rather cut loose a fyke net, condemning the eels inside to the slowest and nastiest of deaths instead of a short, sharp and terminal electric charge that provides an organic, free-range food.

The worldwide demand for eels increases. The supply falls. The elvers can be farmed, but only from infancy using wild stock. They cannot as yet be hatched and survive. Fishing has been blamed for the downward cycle and may be targeted but is only part of a problem that is yet to be understood, made increasingly worse by the voracious hydroelectric power stations in Scandinavia and Ireland. Another environmental issue with more than one slant.

A 2–3lb eel is a good one. To kill it humanely at home, use the creature's instinct to hibernate – and send it to permanent sleep in a deep freeze. Thaw, then gut and wash like any other fish. To strip, make an incision around the neck, and separate a little of the skin from the meat. Nail the head to a tree or post, or hold it in a cloth. Pull off the skin towards the tail with pliers. There is no quick or easy way of doing it, or sweeter fish to eat.

The muscle-bound migrant eels have blackish backs and silver bellies. They are high in fat and liked for smoking in England, but sought after au naturel by markets abroad. To eat fresh, chop into pieces two or three inches long and dry-fry on either side in a pan until firm. Alternatively, make into a stew like any other fish.

The immature eels are shoelaces by comparison. They have brownish backs and yellow bellies if they come from fresh water, greenish from the saltings, and a lower fat content. This condition is desired by purveyors of jellied eels, a taste that few people are ambivalent about, and that depends for me on the amount of seasoning used. A big splash of vinegar in the jelly does wonders for the flavour. The catch goes to the London and Essex pie shops, of which about eighty remain.

To cook an eel Norfolk style (according to a friend Rodney Portman): 'Chop the fish into pieces two or three inches long, cover in batter, deep fry, and eat 'im like a mouth organ.'

Lampreys have suckers for mouths to attach themselves to stones or other fish, negligible fins, and respiratory holes that appear to have been punched by a nasty child in the side of their heads. They look queer and undistinguished, but kept a place in history for hundreds of years. Having possibly killed off Henry I in Rouen, they went into a festive pie sent annually to his successors from their city in the Gloucester heartland, a custom discontinued in 1836 on economic grounds, but resurrected with knobs on – i.e. gold, crayfish and truffles for decoration – during Queen Victoria's Diamond Jubilee.

Lampreys were eaten by the fancy in Bath, potted like shrimps or char, and made the journey to leading fishmongers from the Severn. They were also bait for cod and turbot. Numbers are down in many rivers owing to pollution and exclusion from their breeding grounds by dams and weirs. A run occurs in the spring and early summer.

There are three types of lamprey, each of which spawns in fresh water and seems to have been cooked. The sea lamprey, the biggest at 2–3lb, was the most highly sought after in Victorian England (Walsh, 1879). The river lamprey, at half the size, was half the price. The brook lamprey was the smallest and cheapest. Their flesh is rich, in need of strong seasoning and said to be like eel, but firmer. The bones and head of the tiddlers are soft enough to eat. I await the pleasure.

Lampreys, Worcestershire style* Clean the lampreys thoroughly by rinsing well in salt and water; then rub a little mixed white spice** over them and leave for twenty-four hours. Quite a lot of fluid will ooze out, but do not throw it away; this will be put in the saucepan with them to stew. If this fluid does not completely cover the lampreys, unseasoned beef gravy may be added when they are nearly done. A glass of port wine . . . is also advocated. Any of the lamprey species may be treated in this way, the larger kinds, of course, will have to be cut up.

Crayfish (from the French *ecrevisse*) are like little lobsters, greenish, brown or pink, and opaque in the moult. They are occupants of alkaline water and chalk streams, and a tragedy waiting to happen. Crays lie up in the sun during the day or hide under stones, scuttling backwards away from danger, and often quitting rivers at night. It is possible to nab them by hand or with a dog. To catch them overnight, leave meat in a river wrapped in a bag net secured with a cord, and pull it out in the morning: the crays will cling to the mesh. I used to pay the mudlarks in Hampshire ten pence each for big ones. A hawker supplied Stow-on-the-Wold only twenty years ago.

It was during the 1980s that MAFF (now DEFRA) stood by whilst a death sentence was passed on the English crayfish. The American 'signals', named after the conspicuous white flashes on their claws, were permitted (as invertebrates rather than fish) to enter the UK.

---

* *From* The Observer's Book of Freshwater Fishes of the British Isles *(1961)*.

** *A variety of the usual spices and herbs went with lamprey, including white and cayenne pepper, ginger, mace or nutmeg, bay leaves, etc.*

As predicted, they escaped from confinement and spread the well-known virus that had already wiped out indigenous crayfish in French and Swedish rivers. The disease, automatically transmitted to natives downstream, created an ecological problem that has yet to hit home. The Republic of Ireland did not make the same mistake.

So, the gluts of the past (described by seventeenth-century diarist John Evelyn) will never happen again. Crayfish may no longer be taken from the wild, but they can be farmed and occasionally appear at market. The natives are not unknown: the signals are more common, sold alive and capable of giving you a nasty nip if you lose concentration. To cook, drop into boiling salted water, leave for a minute and drain.

Sturgeon are a well-armoured fossil of a fish with bucklers for scales, used in the East as ornaments. The mouth is a toothless funnel employed for mud-sifting. The Lord Mayor of London may claim the sturgeon caught in his jurisdiction. The sovereign is or was entitled to the rest. After a rich and respectable woman had run off with her groom, who bore the name of Sturgeon, the fish enjoyed a run of popularity at fashionable dinner parties in Hanoverian London. Two centuries later priorities had changed, and diminutive pond specimens were available in garden centres.

Sturgeon are always making names for themselves. In May 1911, a fish exceeding 200lb lay up in the Frome at Wareham, Dorset, watched for several days by a crowd. A Bulldog Drummond was called for – and arrived in the form of one Captain Radcliffe, a well-known sportsman with the tattooed back of a circus performer and the build of a weightlifter. He landed the beast with a salmon rod, fly and outsized net, offered it to the King and had it stuffed by Rowland Ward (a dealer in game books and former taxidermist, still trading in London). The last time I saw the fish, it was hanging like a prehistoric spaceship, surrounded by dusty furniture and boxes, in a decommissioned church used for storage by Dorchester museum. Sturgeon over three times the size have been recorded in English waters, and appeared as far inland as the Nottingham reach of the Trent. They have been quite common.

In the days of our dining club, my wife and I were asked by a confederate to find and cook 'something unusual' for a party. The lot fell to a sturgeon, probably farmed in France, that appeared in our fishmonger's window the following day. We baked the head and shoulders of the beast and served them up with soy and chilli sauce. The meat, which I have also eaten in Moscow, is firm and pleasant, 'tasting of fish, flesh or fowl according to whether is is nearer the backbone or skin' (Wells, 1982). The Russian sailors who frequented the Normandy Stores used to offer me the caviar, which they smuggled out of the USSR. The tins varied in weight from one to an incredible six pounds. Sadly, I was not able to buy or shift the largest.

Carp are members of a large family indigenous to the Black Sea area and parts of China. They are quick to grow and capable of reproducing three times a year, which led to their early domestication. In due course, the most precocious of the common carp were selected for breeding and collectively entitled 'king'. Mirrors and leathers are variants of the same fish, whose antecedents were introduced to England at some point in the Middle Ages and possibly farmed in ponds with bream, tench and others, establishing a large population in Sussex by the seventeenth century. Escapees were distributed by floods and other means. They blossomed into the stately 'queen of rivers' (a title shared by the Hampshire Avon) and an angler's trophy that fights like hell and lives to a good age, though probably not the great one people say.

We used to sell carp at the Normandy Stores, a box of fish weighing 2–3lb each, flown in fresh every Easter from farms in Holland. The Polish community bought them for Good Friday. The roe is appreciated by the Jews, to whom caviar is forbidden owing to the sturgeon's lack of scales. Escoffier said that English carp tasted muddier than the others, though they do not have to (see page 295), and went down as Queen Anne's favourite fish. I have eaten carp once, in China, when it leapt out of a bucket and under my table in a restaurant – begging to be cooked.

Carp, Somerset style:* '"When the water was a nice height and the sun . . . shining down," said Mabel Stuckey, "you could see the carp all laid out . . . sunning themselves. What a beautiful picture. We used to gut and split them, put them in a pig salter, hang them on the beam, let them dry. When we got short of grub, we'd wash all the salt out . . . stuff them with sage and onion, and cook them in a deep dish with fat in them. You never tasted anything so nice."'

Chubb: 'He [the chubb fuddler] came. He walked along the river bank, and sowed upon its waters some magic seed, which soon bore magic fruit, for up to the surface, flapping, swooning, fainting, choking, thoroughly and undoubtedly fuddled, came hundreds upon hundreds of chubb. The entire population of the village, warned beforehand and armed with rakes and landing nets, fell upon the fish, several wheelbarrows were filled and the contents taken off to be used as manure for cottage gardens or chubb pie according to taste. Henceforward, chubb fuddling became an annual event at Alconleigh, the fuddler appearing regularly with the snow drops . . . to watch him at work was a pleasure which never palled' (from *Love in a Cold Climate* by Nancy Mitford).

Chubb is said to be the worst of the freshwater fish to eat. Barbel is next, but what a fighter!

---

* *From* Wetland *by Patrick Sutherland and Adam Nicolson (1986).*

COOK'S ORACLE

Freshwater fish continue to be eaten in countries and communities that have no choice, or have retained the knowledge of how to treat them. The market in England is dominated by rainbow trout: a farmed fish permitted entry on the grounds of being unable to spawn in the UK (not true). It looks good, tastes dull and suspect, and has provoked concerns about what it eats and discharges. The eel and the zander are the only other species that have a culinary purpose.

It would be stretching Izaak Walton's point to say that all freshwater fish are worth eating, but unwise to reject an entire tribe that might be useful in an emergency and capable of coming up with the odd surprise. It is only necessary to go back a couple of generations to find roach from the River Parrett in Yeovil market, gudgeon praised by André Simon, and dace described as 'dainty', especially when fried up on a river bank or punt. Between a fish cooked within minutes of being caught, and another one killed with a 'priest' and taken home, there is no contest.

Freshwater fish deteriorate quickly. The trout family, grayling, perch and zander may be addressed like any sea fish and with a positive result if cooked the same day. The coarse ones are more of a challenge, regardless of the environment they come from. They need help. Go for a specimen weighing at least 2lb if possible, preferably an eel, pike or carp, and proceed as follows:

To begin with, gut and wash the fish as usual, skinning the eel. Split, fillet and dust with salt and leave for a day. Some people soaked the fish in three successive brines, cutting the last with vinegar. Drain, then commit to a pan and cover most of the fish with a beef or other gravy, a tablespoon or two of soy sauce and plenty of black pepper. Bake or simmer gently until firm. Remove the fish and keep warm. Add a glass of red wine or port to the liquid and reduce by two-thirds, then pour it back over the fish. Dried mushrooms, sweet herbs or chopped chillies may be used in the sauce.

Fish from sluggish or standing waters are off the menu for now, and deserve to be. There is no point in transferring them to a crystal-clear pond and hoping for the best. It does not work. They still taste muddy, everyone knows that. Or do they? Did, perhaps, a family of fishermen and fowlers, born to self-sufficiency before it was thought of and rooted to their spot since Ely was an island, understand a thing or two? Dorothy Hartley, forever curious, found out the following:

> Muddy-bottom fish has to be specially cooked . . . the skill was taught to me by an old fisherman of the Fens, where I first cooked bream: he showed me why all [such] fish have special overlapping and fringe scales – these keep the mud clear from the . . . skin

while the fish is full [alive], and swims against the stream: but once it is limp [dead], and the scales are disturbed, the mud gets under them and touches the absorbent skin of the fish. Therefore pond fish must never be washed, or even moved, more than can be avoided. Take the fish by the head, and smooth it down lightly towards the tail . . . [applying] clay or paste, and bake it quite flat without turning . . . raised on a bed or a handful of twigs, anything that will allow the underside of the fish to cook dryly. When done, this crust can be broken off, skin and all, and the fish will be clean tasting and of very fine quality.

CHAPTER TWENTY-THREE

GREEN TOP

I ROSE AT DAYBREAK EVERY MORNING, crossed the lawn and climbed the railings into the four-acre field, beating the cowman to it. I called to the cattle, just as he did, opened the gate and walked them up the lane. They moved sedately, bags swinging from side to side and hooves flip-flopping on the tarmac under foot. Now and again a cow stopped to drag a clump of weeds from the hedge and needed coaxing on with a gentle pat. Alice, a shorthorn, was queen. Kate, Sunshine and Daisy, all Guernseys, followed her up the drive and round the corner to the places waiting for them in the barn. I doled out their hay by the warm, weak glow of the bare lightbulb hanging down through the cobwebs and rafters from the roof.

Churchill, the cowman, entered wearing gumboots and a rough coat. He took the fag from his mouth, putting it out between finger and thumb, and lodged it behind his ear. He placed a pail underneath Alice and a stool beside her on which he sat down. Then he bent forward and took an udder with each hand, plying them alternately while his head in its cloth cap rested against the flank of the cow.

I preferred to watch, and he to work, than to talk. The jets of milk spurted out between his fingers and into the pail with a low hiss. A white froth, punctured by every jet, rose towards the rim. He filled one pail, and another, and bore them across the yard, his arms rigid, face a weathered red and gumboots scraping on the gravel and grit.

It was getting light now, but still darkish in the dairy. The milk, strained into wide white enamel pans, flowed thick and clean, the bubbles subsided, and the cream was left to rise for clotting. Churchill poured the last few pints into a jug for us and an enamel three-pint can for himself and his family. Then he rinsed out the pails with a clatter. The echoes died and he trudged home for breakfast.

I seldom strayed into the dairy for the rest of the day, yet did not hurry to leave it. There were runnels to finger on the bare slate shelves, and gauze on the windows to look through at the world outside. The stone floor rippled in the sombre light as the water from the hose drained away. The atmosphere was calm and still; the smell, peculiar to dairies, pungent, clean and morning-fresh. They were bound to leave impressions on the senses of a boy.

In Cornwall, in the summer, we had to buy milk. It came to the door in pint and quart bottles capped with green tops, and emblazoned with the name of the dairy. The delivery woman drove a black Morris Traveller filled with crates. My mother, a Scot, used to keep milk back to bake a giant scone, firm on the outside and gooey in the middle. She made it with sour milk. The bottles, with their distinctive green tops, sat in pairs on the windowsill in the kitchen, separating into cream, curds and whey.

* * *

Twenty years passed. I, new to the Forest, was standing chatting with a local when a black Morris Traveller drove up. The back was full of bottles with the same green top, which was rare by this time with so many of the smaller dairies going. The milk, the delivery woman told me, came from a farm up a track beyond the water splash. There would be someone around in the house or yard later on in the afternoon.

The dairy was owned by some people called Sevier, an old name in Hampshire, spelt a variety of ways and pronounced 'Siveer'. The family had lived in the Forest since the seventeenth century, treading bricks, digging peat and keeping livestock. Len bottled the milk and separated the cream. Mabel and Anne, his wife and daughter, made the butter. They had two cows with shorthorn in them, a dozen Guernseys, a Hereford-cross bull, and a few New Forest ponies.

Len was born in a cob cottage adjacent to the farm that had finally crumbled and returned to the earth. He had inherited common rights, and about thirty acres of land drained by his antecedents centuries ago. One crop of hay was taken from two of the meadows.

The Swiss do not consider pasture fit for cattle consumption unless it has twelve types of vegetation in it. The blanket crops of rye grass used in England have one. The poorer of Len's two meadows had eighty herbs and grasses. The richer had over a hundred. In the brook that divided them, the sea trout spawned. Boffins would come, look at it all, and leave nonplussed.

'I don't know what you're doing,' one of them said, 'but for God's sake, keep doing it.'

The milk from the cattle, expressing the meadows it came from, was rich, sweet, fragrant, untreated and alive – an obvious health food. The cream was the colour of butter and the butter the colour of gold. Nothing, with or without a label, could have been more organic, free range or environmentally friendly. The Seviers were born conservationists.

I went to the farm on misty mornings, autumn afternoons and in the drizzle on winter nights. It was hard to keep away from the sound of the cows coming up the lane and the sight of them turning a corner and settling in the warm, weak glow. The cobwebs hung down. The milk filled the pails just the same, and this time, my white enamel three-pint can.

Of all the rural amenities, this little farm, its flagship of a dairy and meadow, seemed the most important. By my patronage I helped to extend their lives. In a dozen ways they enriched mine.

Worth fighting for? When the moment came, there was no question.

Cattle became the main milk producers in England because of their higher yield. Sheep and goats persisted until the seventeenth century. Niche marketeers have included asses and other biddable creatures, including mares, fallow deer and prostitutes (Pullar, 1977). 'Rent breasts' were especially popular in cities owing to the widespread adulteration of milk from other sources. Not that just anybody would do. If taints were to be avoided, a well-fed and even-tempered woman was the one to go for.

Little whole milk was consumed except by invalids and children until the railways and refrigeration opened up the liquid market. Even in my lifetime, country people drank their milk watered down or after processing. It is of great amusement that skim, having been classed as a health food, fetches a premium. The higher price it commands is put down to the cost of removing the cream, which is sold separately. What a racket!

Milk as a natural product, like meat or vegetables, varies. The quality and quantity that a cow gives forth are partly determined by where she lives, when she calved and what she eats. The altitude, climate, herbage, soil, subsoil, minerals and season can all affect the character of milk, and to a fine degree, particularly after processing. The terms 'butter pasture' and 'cheese pasture' have not yet lapsed.

The breed of cow makes another huge difference to the flavour of milk and its properties, helping to decide what it is good for. Some breeds give milk whose cream rises to the surface and separates, making it good for butter. Others yield more of an emulsion, desirable for cheese. When winter feed was scarce, so was winter milk. Cattle calved in the spring with the months of plenty ahead, but must now calve all year for a dairy farmer to remain in profit. However, there are still months in which milk and cream are at their peak and butter and cheese are best produced. No substitute has yet been found for a bite of young grass on an English cow, and no normal cow can meet all our demands.

Raw milk straight from the cow, through a cooler and into a bottle, comes without E numbers, additives or any interference from man. It is as natural and nourishing as mother's milk, live as yoghurt, and went with honey in biblical times. To a 'lactose friendly' pastoral country like England, milk is as important to the kitchen and culture as beer or bread. It is the mother of clotted and separated cream, of butter, cheese, junket, ices, a long list of puddings and white sauce.

To pasteurise milk is to heat it to a minimum temperature for a given period (70–80°C/158–176°F, I think). The result is to eliminate the differences between one batch and the next, and kill off bacteria. The process does not necessarily extend the life of milk, though the claim is frequently made. It enables bulk distributors to handle thousands of gallons a day, mixed together from hundreds of farms.

If, however, a cow is healthy, her dairy undefiled and her milk respectfully handled, pasteurisation is not necessary. 'Under modern standards of hygiene,' said *The Wonder Book of the Farm*, 'it is not often that disease germs are found even in raw milk.' And that was forty years ago. Today there are bacterial tests. A supplier of untreated milk who exceeds the count is fined, and may also lose his licence to produce it. In the mean time, people will continue to be poisoned, but by all sorts of food and drinks, pasteurised and otherwise, including tap water. It is an occupational hazard of being a consumer. The French understand.

As far as the flavour and fragrance of milk are concerned, there is no contest – put your head in a cooler, then remove it to a pasteuriser and compare the two. Raw milk smells fresh and goes sour: it can be used for baking. Treated milk smells cooked and goes bad: it is thrown away. The cream is the same. The riper it is up to five or six days, the better to eat and the better for butter-making too.

On the dreary subject of health, the word is that heat treatment kills good bacteria with the bad, neutralizes the calcium in milk, and causes allergies and heart conditions for which all milk is blamed. The alleged perils of pasteurisation are numerous. Not that consumers of green top are sufficiently obsessed with their organs to heed the latest gossip. I suspect that all foods that taste good and of what they ought, if clean and eaten in moderation, are good for you. To stroll up a lane, chat in a barn and listen to cattle tearing grass is good for you too, but, again, waiting to be ratified by medicine men. They should try a scoop from a churn on a May morning – wine writer Oz Clarke's desert-island beverage. When he said so in a BBC studio full of people, you could hear a pin drop. Evidently, the others had never drunk it.

The farms that sell untreated milk are one of the last obstacles to corporate management of a land still green and pleasant in places. If an owner who has held out against it is forced to pasteurise, he is not only charged with being unable to operate cleanly, he must pay for new equipment and often a new dairy. Though he may not be ruined, he will be stretched. The alternative is to give up selling milk and possibly cream and butter, auction the cattle and let the land to a livery stable. So, the loss of milk means more than the loss of the milk alone.

By the 1970s, the brave green bottle top of unpasteurised milk was of increasing significance. It stood for one of the only foods in the UK that remained unprocessed, unadulterated and traceable to the producer. The skim milk on the shelves of the major distributors failed on all counts. It also filched the characteristic raw milk top and trademark in the drive to appear greener than thou – with conservation-conscious petrol stations and ornithological food giants. The supermarkets love to play the environmentally friendly bunny-, bird- and badger-hugging card. We shall hear lots more of this.

Meanwhile the genuine green top was and remains under persistent threat, and the impostor may ultimately be rewarded. Raw milk is of no economic importance and suspected by scientists. It has also been irksome to administrators and constituted a soft-looking target for bullies in Whitehall and Environmental Health to pick a fight with.

At half past six on a dark February morning in 1989, the BBC announced that the government, its back to the wall over the most recent food scare – involving intensive *chicken* – intended to ban *raw milk* (understand?). Such was the outcry that the first attempt failed, thanks mainly to Sir Julian Rose, an Oxfordshire dairy farmer. On the second occasion, he and I formed the Association of Unpasteurised Milk Producers and Consumers.

A few weeks later, the AUMPC took a stand at the Food and Farming Fair in Hyde Park. Assisted by a group of enthusiasts, we gave away raw milk – as obliged to by law – and sold clotted and separated cream, home-made butters, unpasteurised cheeses and a few provincial dainties to tempt the uninitiated and revive memories. The question was, again and again, what happened to foods and flavours like these? The answer: you chose something else.

Julian gatecrashed an official breakfast waving a bottle of green top and was practically roughed up. The Minister of Agriculture was accosted. A minor celebrity came to the stall, drunk, troubled and seeking attention that had temporarily escaped him. When asked to sign our petition, he replied that he did not like milk ('Well I don't give a pinch of shit for your preferences, pal, and anyway, we are talking about more than milk . . .'). Tempers and temperatures soared. It was the hottest day in May since records began, with pigs, near to death from thirst, refusing to drink the London water.

After the fair, I rang a journalist and asked her to help with our campaign. Not, she said, unless there was a story in it. Obligingly, one broke. The Queen drank unpasteurised milk from the cows in Windsor Park – and appeared to be healthy, fulfilled, and in command of her faculties. Green top was saved from that minute, but remained in the sights of persons official, powerful, and sometimes unknown. It had foes, as well as friends, in high places.

In 1996, five out of eighty thousand cases of food poisoning were traced to unpasteurised milk; six to pasteurised; the remainder mostly to poultry, eggs and processed goods. Yet green top was the only one amongst them to have faced a ban. It was nonconformist, in the way, and loved or loathed on that account, representing farm versus factory and cook versus technologist. Nothing in my experience, apart from foxhunting, so raised the temperature of debate. The two sides were united in being unable to change their opinions, and divided in the matter of thinking for oneself. We knew, but they knew best. Prohibitionists always do. They wanted to control my habits and had the power to do so, even if I had no plans for theirs.

It was only a matter of time before another ban was proposed, and on the advice of scientists, who, in addition to providing information, were initiating government policy. Julian called a meeting at his house, attended by half a dozen tired old lags from the press. Early in the proceedings I ran out of puff. My campaigning days were over. The opposition had been difficult to grapple with, but not half as draining on the emotions and pocket as trying to gun up support from foes mistaken as friends. If lovers of solid milk (i.e. cheese) were not interested in saving the liquid market, and nor were the Guild of Food Writers, the Rare Breeds Survival Trust and the WI, what were the chances of the comatose member for Yawnshire South getting out his ear trumpet, hearing the arguments and attempting to influence the law?

'I can't *think* why anyone wants unpasteurised milk,' said one MP after the campaign. Quite.

The Milk Marketing Board (MMB) was disbanded in 1994, whereupon the food giants took over distribution. Dairy farmers started giving up at the rate of one a day. Julian Rose was amongst them, though he kept on some cattle for the company and milk they provided. From doing doorstep deliveries he recalled the number of customers who did not know what pasteurisation meant but did not like the sound of it either, or milk 'mucked about with'. They helped to save us.

So, contrary to rumours emanating from the corridors of power, green top may be produced under licence in England and Wales. In Devon it is increasingly scarce, thanks to pressure from Environmental Health; in Dorset increasingly common owing to demand. For all the confusion, the law is quite clear. Suppliers must declare a government health warning on containers, which no other product in the UK is obliged to carry – except tobacco. They must pass certain tests and sell direct, or deliver within a certain area. With retailers out of the picture, people have come forward who act as distributors free of charge. They helped to save us too.

Meanwhile, 'the fine, fresh milk of her native Scotland' is sorely missed by an expatriate mentioned in *Laurel's Kitchen Bread Book*. She will be sorry to hear it does not exist any more. North of the border, green top has been banned – except on a single farm – begging several questions. Is it a menace to public health or not? Have the locals developed stronger immune systems? Are they due to the milk? And how many Scotsmen know that a genuine sour-milk scone like my mother's can only be legally made in England?

Dairy shorthorns, like our Alice, are sisters of the beef breed and deserve their own niche. With Southdown sheep and Berkshire pigs, they were the foundation of English farming, summit of rural achievement and more or less the national cow for a hundred years. It used to be said that all the best people kept Shorthorns, which was not true in our case, but many did – a measure of the breed's status, thriftiness, and uncomplaining disposition, which held no terrors for a little boy. No beast on earth continues to generate the same affection. It remains both stirring and comforting to see Shorthorns in a cattle tent, tethered by a roadside, or on a vestigial common. The milk is economically produced and the cream, though white, went into the world-famous English butters and cheeses of the nineteenth century.

Guernseys are a light brown marked with white. They are descended from cattle that became extinct in France, but prospered in the Channel Islands under the name of Alderneys, and made their way to Hanoverian England – an almighty loss to one country and gain to another. A single Guernsey in a commercial herd usually supplies the farmer and his family. The milk is rich and abundant. It does wonders for a beef-cross calf, goes into chocolate, and roundly deserves the brave gold bottle top that is the Channel Islands trademark. The cream, perfect for clotting and butter, is more highly coloured than any of the others, especially in early summer.

Jerseys are smaller than Guernseys, at home in their island confinement smaller still, I gather: the doe-eyed family favourite of Mrs Gaskell and Christopher Robin, with a black nose and tongue and usually a light tan coat. This park, house and 'blighty cow' is still found in Darjeeling. She loves people, to lick your hand and nuzzle up. The bulls are little sods by contrast, testy, vicious, ready and loud-mouthed. They come to shows double-ringed and blinkered. Jerseys used to make beef. Their milk is high in protein, their cream the easiest to lift and, again, perfect for clotting and butter.

South Devons are the South Hams (i.e. 'meadow') cow, and a big one, golden in colour. They come from the temperate country between the North Hams, or Dartmoor, and the cliffside village of Hallsands, washed into the sea. The breed is a mixture of the local Ruby Reds and the first Channel Island cattle brought to England. The occasional black nose reappears. The modern South Devon is closer to the European idea of good conformation than any other native beast, and a beef producer. The loss is to milk so rich it bore the gold top trademark. The cream went into local teas. The butter set a pre-war record that continues to stand (see page 317).

Red Polls, a magnificent plummy red, belong to the neat fields and short horizons of East Anglia. They are claimed with the sheep and horse as part of the Suffolk Trinity, but are strong in Norfolk too, and had antecedents in both counties. From the combination of the local cow and thrifty steers, driven from Scotland to fatten, Red Polls emerged as a dual-purpose beast in an age of specialists. The herd that made the trip to the Food and Farming Fair in London inspired in John Cocksedge, their keeper, a greater love for cattle than anyone I have known. The breed has fluctuated in numbers, but found buyers in America, and seems to be on the increase once more. It provides small beef, sweet milk and excellent butter on little keep.

Gloucesters are black with a white finch back, tummy and tail, a smart beast in a red halter with smashing horns and a fine record. They provided some of the last oxen to be used for draught, the first serum for smallpox, and once covered the Cotswolds, north Wiltshire and parts of Somerset. The population fell before competitors, disease and neglect, for want of benefactors in England's richest county, almost to become extinct. The sole surviving herd of Gloucesters, belonging to the Misses Dowdeswell of Wick, was saved in 1972. Numbers have recovered since then, and spread to Cornwall and Exmoor, but insufficiently. The beef of Gloucesters has the virtue of Welsh blood in it, acquired from the cattle driven through the marches. Their milk goes into the local cheeses.

Ayrshires are a dashing light or dark tan and white, longish in the leg. They were chosen for William Harley's inspirational Glasgow dairy in the 1830s (Trow-Smith), spread over the border into the Morpeth area, and further south with the Scots renting farms during the Depression. The 'vessels' give moderate amounts of milk over many years. The 'producers' give large amounts over a shorter period. Numbers peaked around the Second World War, then subsided, leaving scattered herds in the Derbyshire Peaks, Fylde and the West Country, where they continue to take prizes. My father had Ayrshires for a bit. They were active, independent, of moderate appetite, and produce milk that is good for cheese.

'As for milk,' said Cobbett, ranting away as usual but close to the truth, 'no country yields to England on the face of the earth.' There is a wonderful selection of beasts to provide it, a sympathetic climate, and every opportunity to be self-sufficient in a natural food that contains a long list of vitamins and minerals. So what have we done with it?

After the demise of the Milk Marketing Board the price of the UK's milk fell to the lowest in western Europe and stayed there. In order to increase footfall, the supermarkets sold it at a loss which they made up on other goods. Soon, they were able both to increase the price and negotiate better deals with the wholesalers to whom farmers were contracted. By 2006, consumers were paying almost three times more for their milk than the producer was obtaining. A sworn enemy could not have done the industry more harm. It is still less comforting to know that the supply is capped by EC quotas, which cannot legally be increased even in a shortage. Holsteins and Friesians, top for quantity, bottom for quality, dominate production.

The supermarkets' 'breakfast' and other milk is allegedly 'like it used to be'. This is an admission that the quality of yesteryear is to be desired, and also a damned lie. The milk on their shelves is pasteurised, homogenized, standardized, and equalized – even from a Channel Islands cow – a daft, unnecessary and unbelievable way to treat a resource that no other country in the world has got. Economically, milk performs well as a loss-leader and brings in the hordes at the expense of producers. It comes with every nutritional detail a man could wish for. There have been tastings of milk, all from the biggest retailers. But why?

By comparison, the milk available from a small and select body of producers is what it always was rather than 'like it'. Green top can be obtained direct from the farm gate or the dwindling number of delivery men. If the milk is untreated, from a native breed of cattle, and also organic, in the language of darts it amounts to 'three in a bed'.

Most of the vestigial signs proclaiming 'Milk For Sale' are located in the West Country and the Pennines. As in the case of cider, they are an invitation to stop. Make it the hottest day of the year, and ask for a pint glass. When you have satisfied your thirst, and descended from heaven, check out the cows, the cream, and any possibility of home-made butter. The farmer will be busy pulling in a quarter of the minimum wage, but might make the time for a natter as well.

John Gibson, a dairy farmer in the Peaks with a committed family, a cosy kitchen and a capital view over humps and hillocks called The Nabs, was full of chat and positive ideas. He does not sell raw milk because there is no demand for it in Derbyshire at present, but there could be, forcing existing laws into reverse. Untreated milk has returned to some of its English heartlands, and will return to more if its predicted rebirth as a health food, takes place in New York. As for John's uncle he did not like pasteurisation in the first place.

'These dead bugs it leaves in our milk,' he asked a rep from the brave new world over fifty years ago, 'are we supposed to drink them?'

Milligin: one September evening, my wife and I fetched up at the Red Lion, one of the least artificial of England's remaining pubs, also in the Midlands. There was beer in bottles but not on draught, and a cooler on the bar that had once contained milk from the cows on the farm attached to the pub. The landlady, Barbara Belfield, untroubled by custom from anyone in the village, was only too pleased to serve the two strangers who took to her wooden and leatherette bench, foxhunting scene and electric fire. Time was when we would have drunk her 'milligin' – a one-to-one mixture of milk topped up with Guinness, which she had considered marketing on health grounds, especially good for the hair, skin and pregnant mothers.

Curd tarts: during the Association of Unpasteurised Milk Producers and Consumers campaign, Miss Janet Morris (aged 65) wrote to us from Leeds, pledging her support. She wanted to keep raw milk to make curd tarts with. This is how she did it all her life:

1 pint (570ml) unpasteurised milk, left to go sour, 2oz (50g) butter, 2oz (50g) caster sugar, 1 egg, 2oz (50g) raisins (optional), pinch of mixed spice or grated nutmeg, 6oz (175g) shortcrust pastry (see page 60).

Hang up the milk overnight in muslin (with a bowl underneath) to let the whey drain off. Cream the butter and sugar until soft and light. Stir in the curds, the egg and the raisins if used. Line a greased tart tin or patty pans with the pastry and half fill with the mixture. Dust with spice or nutmeg. Bake for 20 minutes in a preheated oven at 220°C/425°F/gas mark 7. A larger tart needs a little longer. Eat hot or cold.

Beestings, bisnings, firstings, etc. are the new milk a cow produces immediately after giving birth. It is high in colostrum, which is Nature's way of protecting a calf from infection. The milk returns to normal after a few days. During this time farmers do not sell it (and are not allowed to) but often they have more than they need and give the remainder away. The jug that you collected beestings in, you never washed out. It meant an empty cradle.

Beestings is thick, salty, yellow and looks on the point of curdling. The first meal after calving is the strongest, the next less strong and so on. It does not make a pleasant drink, or butter, but will produce a soft cheese and can be used to cook with.

To bake the best custard, fill a dish with beestings, put in a vanilla pod and commit to a medium oven for 30–40 minutes or until firm. Dust with sugar and brown under the grill.

One teacup of beestings equals two eggs in a batter pudding or pancakes. This is another example of proper farmhouse cookery.

CHAPTER
TWENTY-FOUR

CREAM

UNCLE NED LIVED THROUGH three park gates in splendour and seclusion. He had a cold, clear eye and the hair, skin and smell of a baby. He arrived in the back of a black pre-war Rolls, wearing a hat and stiff collar, and carrying a silver and ebony cane. The man at the wheel was Harry Thorne, who liked to tell stories and whistled like a nightingale through his teeth. One week, Uncle Ned came to tea with us. The next we set out for the great, grey, thirty-four-bedroomed house he shared with a drunken butler and a dark-eyed cook who kept a creepy and cavernous kitchen.

My brother held open the three iron gates for the car to pass through, saluting as he did so. The park had cattle at one time, and two shire horses put out to grass. In the dark waters of the kidney-shaped lake, overlooked by trees, someone had drowned. The beeches on the Quantocks above, visible for miles, were called the Seven Sisters. A massive cedar, pinned and propped, reached for the rows of headstones where dogs lay buried in a tangled arboretum. There was a rose garden, an elevated path to a pond with fish, and a spooky back drive that led to the stables, a coachman's former quarters, and a damp and dripping courtyard overgrown with moss.

The teas at Uncle Ned's, held at the dining table, were more elegant and toothsome than any other tea could ever claim to be. There were cakes and splits – never scones – strawberry or whortleberry jam, and two glass dishes of clotted cream, weeping slightly and piled up like the petals of a rose. We drank from ornate Victorian cups coloured blue, white and gold, and ate to the hollow sound of the clock in the hall. A powdery distemper clung to the walls. The chairs and floorboards creaked. The windows thundered on cords when raised and lowered. The glass ran with age, distorting the view of the fields that rose to the woods and wild, unenclosed country beyond. The dust lay thick upon the sills. The musty smell increased as two daring boys crept along the passages, around the corners, and deep into a house that was breathing its last.

Uncle Ned went first, for burial in the family vault. His cook and butler went next, to prison for the lifelong theft of silver, jewellery, ornaments and plate, not to mention claret and port. A sale took place. The building was stripped and left empty. Before demolition, the local hunt chased a fox into the hall, up and down stairs, and past the abandoned room where we had eaten our tea.

The gypsies camped in the summer on the hill, probably taking a few pheasants, but deterring other poachers. The manor had an arch where the rebels were hanged after Sedgemoor, leaving a mark on Somerset never quite erased. The village had a pub with a fives court, and two or three cottages, pink and pebbledashed, serving teas like ours. The post office had a large mixing bowl and a spoon ready for the cream, so thick it came not in a pot, but wrapped in greaseproof paper and a bag. The striking yellow buttercrust was ever present on the counter, at market, or in the mind's eye as the clock approached the hours of one and five. At the family-run hotel where we broke our journey to Cornwall every summer, when you ordered pudding, a rosy-cheeked waitress would lean forward and say, 'And what would you like with it, my love, clotted or separated?'

When milk is left to settle overnight, the cream rises to the surface. It was then, by generations of women, lifted with a spoon or saucer and processed into clotted cream for market or butter for storing. Little was eaten fresh until refrigeration prolonged the shelf life, the railways improved transport and a machine was invented in the 1870s to replace hand-skimming. This saved time and proved more efficient. The 'continuous-flow separator' has a mechanism that is slow to pick up, but generates momentum and, whirring like a spinning top, emits cream from one of its spouts and skim from the other. A few dairies still use one; the rest have gone electric.

With North and South Devon cattle confined to beef, by far the sweetest and most luscious cream on the market comes from the Channel Islanders. Jersey has a little more butterfat, while Guernsey has more colour owing to the cows' retention of vitamin B, especially from new grass. When I worked briefly in Harrods, pint and half-pint bottles of cream arrived on the train from Par every morning. They went to several other shops and most of the hotels. The consistency was thick, the colour bright, the scent sweet and the flavour complex. It was the one thing in London that reminded me of home, and the first thing in the country I looked for, especially when returning from places like France. Supplies faltered in the 1970s, then started to peter out.

The cream in the supermarkets, which took over, is from Friesian or Holstein cattle. The choice of double, single, pouring or whipping cream is a specious and illusory one: it is dull in the first place and automatically pasteurised. The consistency is pasty, the colour white, the scent neutral. Only cream substitutes are worse, and probably worse for you.

Untreated cream may still be supplied under licence and even to retail outlets, in which respect it differs from untreated milk. The remaining suppliers are in good heart and worked off their feet in the soft-fruit season. Nature has arranged for cows to be out in the best of the grass at the same time of year.

Raw cream thickens naturally and should keep for up to ten days, ripening all the time. When sour, it can be used for making butter and for sauces. Cream, said Mrs Miniver, who ordered a pint a day, 'will do for everything'.* In cooking the quality always comes through.

---

* A domestic goddess, brave heart and fictional character, created by Jan Struther and based on her own experiences. Miniver started life in 1937, graduating from a column in The Times into a film with Greer Garson, intended to fortify the English in wartime and bring the Americans on side. A smash hit in both countries.

It is astonishing how many chefs and food writers, with the best in the world available in England, mention cream without reference to the type, use the worst, and descend to *crème fraîche.*

Clotted cream probably arrived with the increasing quantities of cow's milk, which is the most suitable for separating. It is a speciality of Devon and Cornwall that crept into Somerset, then Dorset, Hampshire and Wiltshire, and has also been recorded in Surrey, Suffolk, Yorkshire and Wales, thanks to the traffic in people and customs back and forth across the Bristol Channel. The act of clotting cream does not preserve it for as long as butter or cheese, but enables it to be transported to market – and as far as California by post.

With North and South Devon cattle occupied for beef, Channel Islanders are again the first choice. If the milk of shorthorns or Ayrshires is used for clotted cream, it should be mixed with an equal or greater part from Guernseys or Jerseys in order to obtain cream of the desired flavour, colour and consistency. We did this in Somerset.

The huge, circular, exotic-looking brass creamers, up to nine inches deep and four feet wide, were used by generations of West Country farmers to scald the milk in. The pronounced lip was to carry them by. The creamer was placed over a stick fire for preference. The more intense heat of coal caused the milk to heave and injured the butterfat. It was also a demand on the metal, which had to be thin or else the pan was too heavy to handle, and easily burned through. Most of the vessels that still exist today, including my own, are worn or mended.

The original way of clotting cream is to scald whole milk left overnight.* From the dairy every morning, my mother's cook collected five gallons in a white enamel pan with a blue rim and matching lip. Staggering slightly with the weight, she set it on the lowest flame of a gas stove in the corner of the kitchen. She peeped at the cream in passing over the next couple of hours. When it had developed a brilliant golden delta-like crust with apricot-coloured arteries protected by a membrane, she took the pan from the heat and put it in the larder. The following day she lifted the cream with a perforated spoon and put it in a dish for lunch and tea. It is supposed to make you fat. This is not what happened to me.

The practice of clotting the cream without the milk, common to many farmhouses and most factories, developed with the separator. A pan of cream was heated over embers in one of the purpose-built brick or stone hobs that can still be found in parts of Devon. Then came double boilers. By this method, which is the more convenient of the two, the cream thickens and acquires flavour, but not the same consistency or desired crust.

---

* *Small quantities of clotted cream can be made in a preserving pan over a* bain marie. *This takes a couple of hours. The disadvantage is that the cream is not as crusty as when it lies thickly on five gallons of milk.*

Bideford, a former tobacco port and once the second busiest in England, was one of the towns known for its cream. The Victorian market hall was to sell it. Two world wars and agricultural slumps took their toll, but business was not too bad. In 1964, more than thirty farmers' wives came in on Tuesdays and Saturdays with clotted cream, and also home-made 'cut rounds', yeast cakes, hog's pudding, black pudding, brawn, eggs, veg, etc. The trouble started with a proposed regulation to cover the bowls of cream. A lone councillor objected: it was what the visitors came to see. He did not make any difference. The motion was carried. The number of producers sank to four. The last held out against Environmental Health until about 1998, then turned to an easier life racing ferrets at a local leisure centre.

'Nowadays a considerable amount of cream is made in West Country creameries,' said a former MAFF leaflet, '. . . although some of it may lack the finer points of the best farmhouse product.' The reasons are as follows. The milk is unsuitable. The cream is: (a) separated; (b) pasteurised, which serves no purpose except to prevent an overnight ripening and oblige the regulations (indifferent to the argument that the cream is scalded anyway); (c) baked or run into pots before cooling, rather than lifted. The quality varies from acceptable to a slur on the memory of the cheery, familiar and heroic women who sold their cream from home or brought it to West Country markets by pack saddle, trap, then motor car.

To single out one is unfair and meaningless, as a name without recognition can be, but Mrs Congram deserves a mention. Despite ill health for many years, she kept a house cow and the neatest little dairy. She came to Barnstaple every Friday with a dozen white beakers containing her cream. At the sight of the yellow buttercrust, the sound of Devon voices and the cosy exchanges in the hall, I used to stand before her trestle table lost in thought and in the way. To get at the cream on a busy day, a few carrots or a bunch of beetroot, she would have to come round to the front and, placing her hands lightly on my hips with a reassuring 'There, my love, I must just get past', move me to one side.

First-quality clotted cream, of which only one or two producers are left, should not be put in the fridge or else it goes hard. Try it from a saucer, glass or cup, like an ice, but with a sprinkling of demerara sugar on top. Clotted cream is not a food, but a treat, which deserves a silver spoon. When my wife and I are asked out to dinner, we take our own cream as a precaution. An English pudding or soft fruit served without it is like meat and no veg.

CREAM TEAS

And so to cream teas. The constituents are cream, of course; jam, preferably strawberry, or golden syrup for 'thunder and lightning'; and a plain yeast bun. This important little item of confectionery is known in Cornwall as a split. In Devon it is a 'cut round', a 'tuff', 'three-a-penny' or 'Chudleigh', according to location, and whether it has a defined rim or 'kissing crust'.

The baker's version is different to the home-made split owing to the flour, and more like bread in consistency. Both are acceptable, both rare.

The scone may be in demand and fine with butter or cheese on it, but it is no more appropriate with cream than a croissant or bagel. The flavour is too strong, the texture too stodgy and the double indemnity of sultanas a mixture made in hell. It does not matter whether scones are bought in or 'home-made to a special recipe'. They are not suitable partners for cream and not authentic; nor, therefore, are the vast majority of cream teas billed as 'traditional' (that word again) in West Country resorts. Subscribers to the Radio Cornwall phone-in in 1994 were all agreed: the scone is an impostor.

Meanwhile, splits or 'cut rounds' remain a feature of the teas in the Cornish cricket league, at Carwinion Gardens in Falmouth, and in other bastions of resistance to the scone. The Green Lantern café in Torrington sells thousands a year. I put the cream on first, followed by the jam or syrup*. My mother-in-law, born, bred and a former owner of a tea shop in Polperro, does it the other way round. The difference is a small one, but unlikely to be resolved.

Splits: 1lb (450g) strong plain flour, 10fl oz (300ml) milk, 2oz (50g) butter, 1 tsp salt, ½oz (10g) yeast, ½oz (10g) sugar.

Same method as Francillons's white bread (see page 77). Sift flour and salt together in a bowl and leave in a warm place. Melt the butter in the milk, add half (luke warm) to the creamed yeast and sugar and set the sponge. Make into a dough using the remaining liquid, knead and leave to rise. Knock back and form into twelve balls and prove on a baking sheet quite close together so that they form kissing crusts when risen. Cook in a preheated oven at 230°C/ 450°F/gas mark 8 for 15 minutes.

The huffkin is very similar, but flatter and made in Kent for butter rather than cream.

ICES

Kennack Sands 1959. There should have been a monument. The women in the café remembered me for years. The number of cornets? Ten or twelve, possibly more, I was not counting or even doing it for a bet. It was just that the ices from the Falmouth Dairy were so hard to refuse, especially with chocolate hundreds and thousands on the top. Later the firm was bought out, and that was that. At Bradfield in Berkshire, my place of education, the ices were even better. They were made by 'Chief' and Mrs 'Chief', proprietors of a tuck shop entitled

---

* *Originally molasses.*

Grubs, who were evacuated from wartime London and brought their ices with them. The story was that a huge corporation had offered the couple one thousand whole pounds for the recipe, and they had turned it down. The afternoons spent idling away with a 'double' watching the cricket on Pit, the most attractive cricket ground in England, were worth every penny my family forked out.

There is an underground store for ice at Heveningham Hall in Suffolk and another near Wallingford in Oxfordshire – humps in the ground with brick portals dating from the eighteenth century. Their construction is linked to the first 'ices' eaten in England, the elegant glasses they were eaten from, and the Italian manufacturers who had beaten the rest of Europe in the race to make them. The old London cry of 'Hokey-pokey, penny a lump' is a possible corruption of '*Ecco un poco*' (Hutchins, 1967).

Jane Grigson could understand the quantities of ices eaten in England, but not given the quality. Proprietary brands are divided into two types. 'Dairy' ices must contain a measure of dairy produce, i.e. milk or cream. 'Vanilla' ices are made with a product base and have a longer sell-by date. Variety is the thing, but whatever the disguise, it cannot make a bad mixture taste any better. The underlying false and medicinal flavour and claggy texture always hit hard. The worst seem to taste of their colour, i.e. pink.

Plain vanilla ices are the yardstick to judge the others by. They are easy to make at home and a hundred times better, cleaner and lovelier than anything you can buy. Vanilla, less successful than cinnamon in a warm custard, triumphs in an ice.

Vanilla ice cream: 1 pint (570ml) milk, ¼ pint (150ml) double cream, 2oz (50g) caster sugar, 6 egg yolks, split vanilla pod.

Bring the milk, cream and vanilla pod up to simmering point in a saucepan. Remove from heat and leave the pod to infuse for 30 minutes with the lid on. Meanwhile, beat the egg yolks and sugar together in a bowl. Reheat the milk, and whisk it into them, discarding the vanilla pod. Cook over a double boiler until the mixture has started to thicken, whisking constantly. Do not let it stick to the sides. Cover with a disc of greaseproof paper, in direct contact with the custard, to prevent a skin forming. Leave to go cold. Whisk it up, pour into a plastic container, and freeze. Take out and whisk until smooth every hour for 3 hours, without letting it melt, and return to the freezer. Keeps for up to 2 months. Remove from freezer to temper for half an hour before serving.

Try a cornet with clotted cream on top. There is no name for it, but one or two come to mind.

CHAPTER
TWENTY-FIVE

BUTTER

THERE WAS SOMETHING ABOUT THE MAN, or shaman, as my wife described him, with his woollen cap, ragged clothes and eyes the colour of forest peat. With the same huge hands that cut the turf and kept wicket for Godshill, Len made butter. He began by half filling with raw, ripe cream an end-over-end fifteen-gallon barrel of a churn. To avoid the heat in summer, he started at dawn. To beat the cold in winter, when the cream could be 'sleepy' and the butter take all morning, he added warm water from the kitchen kettle. Come, butter, come, the maids used to say as they worked away, rising and falling with the handle in their grasp.

Every few minutes Len paused to let some air out of the valve on the top of the barrel and have a rest, then started up again. He wound away until the glass peephole was no longer clouded with cream, but clear, and the contents of the vessel had started to feel solid, bumping and sloshing around inside. Then off came the lid and the cream had gone. A lump of golden butter and a moat of blushing buttermilk lay together at the bottom of the churn.

Len drained off the liquid, which he gave to the cats, and refreshed the barrel with water. He rinsed the butter until it was clear, and lifted it out into a large pan that he bore to the kitchen. Mabel and Anne were waiting at a table, sleeves rolled up, pinnies on, scales ready and paper cut. They divided the butter in two, working out the moisture and working in the salt by hand before weighing it up. Then, taking pats, they tossed, patted and biffed the butter into shape, flattening the top and smoothing the sides with humour, flair, and firm no-nonsense smacks.

The wooden pats, or 'hands', scalded and rinsed before use, were not quite a pair. The master was slightly bigger than the mistress. With a final flurry of deft and artistic little dabs, and a telltale criss-cross on their ridges and furrows, the half-pounds of butter were ready for market and me. Often, on coming round the corner and entering the yard, I could hear it being made from the smack of the pats and bump of the butter landing on the table.

The Hampshire meadow, which became of such fascination to botanists, was butter pasture to Len. It peaked in early summer. The butter peaked too, thanks not only to the grass and herbage, Mabel said, but to the bramble tips the cows took in the lane. The scent of the butter was so intense it could fill my kitchen, the colour so brilliant it shed light, the flavour so clean it only needed bread.

First-quality English butter is a luxury, a necessity and a treat. An elegant roll or golden brick on a dish, rich and inviolate, bearing the impression of wooden hands, leaves an impression too. When my wife and I had a dining club, whatever else we gave people to eat – and we went the distance from snipe to the royal mutton – it was the butter they remembered. It seemed to represent the Forest, and took pride of place with a knife of its own above the salt on the table.

* * *

Butter is a means of storing milk discovered thousands of years ago, possibly by accident. It has been of great value to cooks, traders and legatees of English yeomen, who have gone on record as leaving large quantities of butter in their wills. A solid lump is formed by agitating the fat particles in cream at 60–65°F, which can be done with a variety of implements from a rocking churn to a whisk, causing them to break or 'pinhead up' and stick together. The flavour of butter is improved and the condition preserved by adding about ¼oz of salt (and in the past a little saltpetre) to every pound of butter. There is a simple scientific explanation for every part of the process except one: by what alchemical route people rose, women mostly, from being good buttermakers to great ones, local legends and national champions.

Pastoral England is divided into butter- and cheese-producing regions. Where there was an emphasis on one, the other suffered, since they both compete for the cream. The choice of which to make was decided by market forces. It remained fixed for long periods in some areas, but also changed with demand, butter manufacture yielding to cheese and vice versa. The smart money went on suitable cattle. The pigs fed off the waste.

The amount of butter supplied by a given quantity of milk used to be noted in a ratio. Jersey cattle were at the top of the league, but South Devons hold the daily record of 4lbs 10oz, established before the war. Guernseys, with the brightest butter, were close behind. Shorthorns and Red Polls came next, and Friesian cows last. On average one quart of cream makes one pound of butter.

Home-made butter changes with the seasons and the diet of the cattle. In winter it is naturally pale and from part-time sources still in short supply. Spring butter, a better colour from cows out in new grass, is eagerly awaited in our household – as it has been by initiates for centuries. Summer butter, owing to the flower development in old pasture, is the epicure's favourite but does not keep. Autumn butter is the one to stockpile, and always was, in the cellar or on a rack in the cool compartments located in farmyard wells – or butterwells.

Some of the English butter crosses and markets are medieval. However, the golden age for producers was the mid nineteenth century, when steam opened up the cities to manufacturers large and small. Arthur Roland, a commuter and a hobby farmer, took his wife's butter to confederates in the City, and returned to deepest Surrey every evening for more. Supplies were packed in a variety of shapes and containers, sold in a variety of weights and measures, and bore a variety of stamps, giving local food a truly local pedigree.

English butters are divided into four types:

Full-cream butter is the most widespread. The Victorian heartlands were 'High' Suffolk (around Debenham) and Dorset's 'Vale of Little Dairies'. In north Wiltshire, the county council ran a school of buttermaking for the smaller concerns: a brand called Moonraker represented the creameries. Lincolnshire, Yorkshire, Hampshire, the Isle of Wight and Epping Forest played a supporting role. The flavour of these butters was due to the natural ripening of the cream, and the quantity of salt added. They varied from one region to another.

Clotted cream butter comes from Devon and Cornwall. It is a way of using up unsold cream, simplifies operations in the dairy, and squeezes more fat from the milk than a separator. The best way of making this butter is to rinse your fingers in warm water to stop the cream sticking, and beat it by hand in a bowl. The cream should not be left to ripen after scalding, and pinheads up quickly. The flavour of this butter is different to the others.

Wholemilk butter was last heard of in the Midlands, north Wales and Scotland. It was undermined by the separator and disappeared at the turn of the twentieth century, thanks to the (misguided)* prohibition of the dog wheel. Wholemilk butter was made from 'loppered'** milk, which consisted of 4–6 sessions and left to ripen and settle. For the solids to 'come' it is important to keep agitation to a minimum before churning, and start at a slightly higher temperature than if cream alone is used. The clean and tangy tastes of the butter and buttermilk were both highly regarded.

Whey butter or 'after' butter, a by-product of the cheese industry, mostly comes from Somerset and the north-west of England. It was once used to grease Cheshire and Lancashire cheeses prior to clothing, but now constitutes most of the butter considered 'farmhouse'. A hundred gallons of whey contains enough fat to make about four pounds. A very few creameries whose custom it is to dye their cheeses colour their butter too, a regional nicety going back centuries which took me by surprise a long way from home.

At the Devon Show there is still a butter class, much diminished, but a reminder of the craft that runs in the blood. Gone are the horses and carriages, men in frock-coats, and women in bonnets and crinoline stretchers, all sculpted in butter. However, bouquets of flowers remain.

English butter ran into difficulties when foreign imports started arriving in the late nineteenth century, often to be adulterated and repackaged as home produce, knackering its reputation.

---

* *Hartley said the dogs enjoyed the work, and the drink of buttermilk afterwards.*

** *Dr Ron Schmid, author of* Traditional Foods Are Your Best Medicine *(1986) and a fan of unpasteurised milk, speaks of cultured or 'clabbered' milk, which is similar to 'raw home-made yoghurt'. I wonder if there is a connection.*

During the First World War many of the smaller manufacturers gave up; in the Second, butter was rationed. Then the factories swept the board with a blended facsimile made from pasteurised and often imported Friesian cream, mid-range in quality between Len Sevier's butter and a low-fat spread. The taste is consistent whatever the label, the smell recognizable and the length of its life suspect. Continental butters get more credit from the *beau monde* than they deserve. They are produced from treated, cultured and unripened cream, that is unable to compete with the Seviers'. There is a nasty rumour that English buttermakers may take the same route rather than sticking to their guns.

Of all the niche markets left, craft butter occupies the smallest – and that may have saved it. The producers are too few in number to threaten or bother corporate thinkers. The AUMPC was able to scrape up seven farmers' wives from seven counties who made butter, a number that has remained constant in spite of the casualties. To find a new pair of hands, or an old one still at work and attending to her mother in a pure and silent Victorian house, is something that only happens in England every five, ten or even fifteen years. On the next occasion I visited Kitty, her mother had died and she had stopped producing her butter. A loss to us, and a milestone for her, quietly passed after making butter every day, twice a day, since the Second World War.

Mabel died too, and Len did not last much longer than his bull. Anne took over the farm, its meadows and gift of wild flowers, kept on a few cattle and bought an electric churn. Since she cannot afford the equipment prescribed by law, and no one else has asked for the butter, my wife and I are her only customers. We are supplied by an 'arrangement', and an increasingly precious one. To unwrap half a pound of butter, put it on the table and tidily cut the corner reminds me every time.

Natural butter improves with a little age, parts cleanly, smells alive and keeps for about a fortnight in the fridge, a year in the freezer. When rancid, it can be used for cheese straws or choux pastry. Buttermilk is not in much demand any more, but is a refreshing and digestible drink for man and beast, which is said to help alcoholics, and can be used as a marinade for venison, to bake with, to bathe the skin and to limewash dairies. For 'resurrection butter'.

CHAPTER
TWENTY-SIX

CHEESE

'D O I LOOK LIKE A DAIRYMAID?' SAID SHE, ARCHLY.

Pretty enough, I thought.

The woman before me was fetchingly dressed in blue gingham and white gumboots, her dark hair underneath a scarf. The eighteenth-century building behind her, originally three cottages, appeared to be the creamery. A yard, enclosed by former pigsties, stood across the road. It had all been worked out eighty to a hundred years ago. The cycle was continuous, the waste zero. The milk arrived from chosen farms. The whey fed the pork, ultimately made into Melton Mowbray pies, and the cheeses went to local shops, London clubs, country grocers and homesick expatriates. In another incarnation I had found half a pound of Stilton in a Bombay fridge – far beyond my will or inclination to resist after three months in India.

I asked if I could see cheesemaking in progress, a wish denied by other creameries. The 'dairymaid' thought it over. She said it was the end of the month: the accountant was coming, but if my wife and I cared to return the following day, there would be time to show us round. The hour was fixed and she introduced herself as Margaret. I had always liked Margarets and Marys. It is all, so often, in a name.

We returned to the dairy at 10 a.m. and knocked on the cottage door. We were shown into an office still bearing marks of its previous identity: a beam, a cosy brick fireplace and original windows. We put on the necessary white coats and hair nets. My wife removed her jewellery and left it in the bag provided. Then Margaret led us down a passage and into a room as different from the first as it is possible to get, as warm as a greenhouse and steamy as a Turkish bath, equipped with pipes and drums. Talking all the time, she stopped at one of the giant architectural stainless-steel vats and, in the most elegant of positions, bent over and felt the clean, white, almost bouncy contents with the flat of her hand. A moment passed and the verdict was announced: the milk was milk no longer and the curd had come.

A girl entered stage right and after a brief exchange took a cheese cutter with vertical blades. She sank it into the vat, trawling it back and forth, and from side to side, leaving tiny streams in its wake that closed ranks behind her. She took another cutter with horizontal blades and did the same, leaving a morass of floating cubes. She plunged her hands and arms into the separating sea of curds and the warm, wet whey, coaxing them apart, stirring all the time, moving to the far end of the vat, round the corners and back to where we stood. I bet that felt nice. I wanted to get in.

The heat was increased. The temperature rose in the vat, and the acidity with it, to the desired level. There would be draining, milling and salting of the curd, after which it was piled into tall perforated drums, the shape of a large top hat, and left to settle. A Tess, no less, was working on the cheeses, cracked, defenceless and released into the world from their previous confinement. Gently and mother-like, using a knife to smooth their sides, she spruced up her infants for the nursery to come.

The adolescent cheeses upstairs, standing in racks shoulder to shoulder from floor to ceiling, were punctured with spikes to help them go blue. The older ones, veiny within, crusty without and filling the air with their developing scent, were apricot in colour in the morning light. Turned by hand, moving forward and forever watched over by an imperious Margaret, they made their way to the cutting room below for wrapping and boxing. Then it was time for the world outside.

The dairy was not so much a farmhouse producer as a cottage industry. It was located in the country, though Margaret had come from 'hot concrete'. Her father had started a firm of cheese distributors entitled the House of Callow, which she now ran with her sister. They had taken over the creamery some years previously, but kept the name of Webster and remained the smallest manufacturer of Stilton, working throughout the year. They had customers far and wide, but none in the village. They could not have kept me out.

The staff were all women. I raised the point with Margaret. The men did the mucky jobs, she said, or used to. The women made the cheese. 'A lovely place to work,' one of them said.

I tasted four of the oldest cheeses and bought half of the strongest. The rest of the day developed unexpectedly. Twenty years before, I had winkled out George Allen, the baker in Scalford, Leicestershire, who had used an eighteenth-century brick oven (see page 68), and had married into the last family to produce a farmhouse Stilton. I knew that he had gone, the oven and business too. I wondered about his widow. We went to the village and enquired. The vicar had buried her that afternoon.

On the street called the Straight, the one in England not Damascus, I met a mother and daughter who made the village cheese by renneting the pail. The milk, warm from the cow and mixed with the rennet, curdled without any further heating or agitation. The flavour of the cheese was clean and fresh, the chance of contamination minimal, and the manner of its production the oldest and simplest known to man. The cheese also came from Suffolk, a county famous throughout history for butter.

The chances are that cheese was another accidental discovery, made in ancient Persia or Turkey, when the heat of the sun and contact with an animal's gut or a wayside herb separated milk into curds (casein) and whey. Regional cheeses were recorded in England by Roman times (Layton, 1957), monastic cheeses by the Middle Ages, and corporate cheeses by the seventeenth century. The names mostly came later. To the older people in Somerset even today, Cheddar is simply 'cheese' – the one they know. It is the same in Lancashire.

The differences in milk are magnified a thousandfold in cheese, particularly when it has cured. Subterranean limestone and deposits of iron, saltbeds and permanent pasture are amongst the reasons why a cheese may be copied outside its heartland, but not authentically. Beyond the boundaries assembled by Nature and observed for centuries by man, a new and often inferior cheese can emerge. Jenny Harker's mother found this out when she moved from the top of Swaledale down to Reeth fifty years ago, and never got such good results again.

The cattle preferred for cheese are those that supply an emulsified type of milk rather than one that is high in fat and good for cream and butter. Shorthorns and Ayrshires lead the contenders, though Friesians are predominantly used, and a niche market exists for Gloucesters, Dexters and Channel Islanders. Sheep and goats, after flirting with extinction as dairy beasts, are making a comeback too.

With the quality of milk varying 'in the factory of the cow' (Rance, 1982) from one month to the next, so do cheeses. Skilful hands in the dairy, born or bred to adapt, respond to the moment as well as the market. In parts of England it has been customary to produce a succession of cheeses: a soft one to eat immediately in early summer (the hungry gap); then, a lightly pressed one to store a little; and finally a harder-pressed one in the autumn to keep and mature. The season, having begun when livestock went out to grass in May, ended with their return to housing in September. Winter cheeses, now the rule, used to be the exception.

For centuries, the majority of cheeses in England were not made from whole milk, which was expensive and took the cream. They were produced from partly skimmed milk (like Parmesan), radically skimmed milk, and even buttermilk. The finest cheeses, an acknowledged 'drunkard's biscuit', were the perfect match for imported wines – notably claret. The worst, a source of protein for ship and poorhouse, were soaked and pounded before use. Where the Banbury, Suffolk and mighty Essex cheeses lay in all this is not easy to interpret from conflicting reports and the convenient lumping together of entire counties under one banner.

As the eighteenth century drew to a close and the population expanded, so did the demand for food. Factors (dealers) travelled to the farms bearing news and views and bespeaking futures yet to be made. Cheeses travelled by cart, wagon and barge. The season opened in May and closed with the first frosts. Fairs took place every three to four weeks from Leyburn to Lechlade, Weyhill to Whitchurch, and Highbridge in Somerset to Stourbridge in the Fens. Writers praised the cheeses not only of Cheddar and company, but of Buckingham, Bideford, Daventry, Harrogate, Kingston in Nottinghamshire, Loughborough, Willingham and York. At markets there were giant cheeses, medium-sized cheeses and small cheeses; different colours, consistencies and shapes; hard hats, blue millstones and mighty drums; wheatsheaves, dolphins, and rows of curds wrapped in butterburr, reclining on rush mats and waiting for the fancy to take them home. Each one was organic, each one from a farmhouse, and each one represented its vale or dale. You can tell some of the former cheese farms by the clumps of alkanet that are still growing in the vicinity and were used to dye the milk.

The price of cheese was volatile. It rose after a good summer, when the quality was high and supply short, and fell after a bad one and in agricultural slumps. Farmers might drive their cheeses to fairs, return with them unsold and, dispirited, leave home. Some took their skills to North America and New Zealand, and lived to make cheeses that competed with our own. In parts of the south and west, dairies turned to butter, which could be sold immediately, or sent their milk by rail to the towns.

English cheeses have been coming and going with people for centuries, never more so than in the last few generations. Progressive dairyman Joseph Harding is said to have engineered the greatest changes, in his native West Country, then almost worldwide. The first factory opened in the 1870s under his son. It used raw milk, recruited experienced staff, and tried to maintain traditional values. But the thrust was to turn out large quantities of cheese both in and out of season – including a 'Cheddar' miles from its home – and to encourage producers to act as one. Cheesemaking in Derbyshire, where the plant was located, never recovered. As farms were swallowed up and the number of creameries increased, getting their own way, the individuality of cheeses and the secrets of their manufacture came under assault.

My impression of industrialists is that they neither produce nor appreciate the sort of cheese that the average Frenchman would have in the house. They are proud of their achievements all the same. In response to a query on a course about past practices, I was told by an instructor that there was 'no good cheese in the old days'. A gross and inaccurate assumption that has turned the order of merit upside down, infiltrated the Nantwich Show and glorified push-button techniques. The rest of Europe is not impressed. Ask the producers and consumers of Cantal and Parmesan.

The finest cheesemakers are alchemists, not chemists. They have skills inherited, tricks up their sleeves and powers of improvisation gained from mother or mentor that can defy analysis. The acidity tests used today for Cheddar, originally intended to be a guide for students only, were calculated from readings taken when the legendary Mrs Gage (née Cannon of Evercreech, another famous name in West Country cheesemaking) declared the milk ready, the curd come and the time right to proceed at every juncture. To arrive at her conclusions she employed her senses, particularly that of smell.

In the early days of research, experts were recruited from farms and ordered to produce bad cheese in the interests of science, which proved against their nature. If left unsupervised, they could not stop themselves from saving the day and turning out a good one. Tony Rich, who has held demonstrations all over the world and now works in Cheddar, does it all the time.

Yet, he says, 'You do not make cheese, for cheese makes itself. All you can do is try and control the milk.'

'If there is a weak side to . . . progress,' wrote Lord Ernle, 'it lies in the fact that butter- and cheesemaking are becoming too elaborate and scientific for the ordinary run of agriculturalists. There is . . . some risk that this branch of the farming industry may become confined to creameries and associations and that the wholesale dealers may refuse the products which have not come from a factory.' That was in 1912.

A year later the Milk Marketing Board was formed, enabling thousands of farmers to sell their milk in bulk rather than process it. The grading of cheeses, with a utilitarian slant, had already been introduced. During the war the Ministry of Food recognized only four varieties, Cheddar, Cheshire, Leicester and Wensleydale, all of which they classified as 'hard'. This had devastating consequences for dairies that were omitted from the list or failed to conform. As long as rationing continued, cheeses were distributed anonymously. There was no reward for the good ones, no reprimand for the bad and no respect for the differences. Cheeses for keeping went straight into the shops, and cheeses for eating went bad in store. A lot of farms, rather than abide by the rules, gave up. A few expanded into creameries, bought in milk and in so doing accumulated problems. The diehards soldiered on and even reopened for business, anticipating that industrial standards would be relaxed. In the short term, it was not to be.

While the French cheese industry was returning to normal after the war, artisans in England had a continued battle on their hands – with the authorities; with foreign competition; with creameries taking the name and quality of the greatest cheeses in vain; and with the British appetite for the vacuum-packed pasteurised blocks. The worst may now be over, but problems remain. The European-style cheeses that are quick to turn over, easy on the palate and may have only temporary appeal are doing well. Meanwhile, some of the greatest names in cheese, for lack of new producers and free use of the word 'traditional', have become rare breeds.

English cheese is typical of English food, offering the best and worst in the world under the same banner. It is a credit to the purists that they have managed to stay in business with none of the encouragement given to their peers in France and Italy. They deserve to be famous, on both sides of the Atlantic in some cases, and well represented. The Artisan Cheesemakers' Association has proved an effective figurehead for a cottage industry. It has shops to match in London's Neal's Yard and Borough Market, so slick and accomplished they could be in Paris. The cheeses are individually chosen and matured, and constitute the decoration of their premises. The staff know their job; the paper is greaseproof. You feel proud and uplifted when you walk in.

England's Hall of Fame

Cheddar comes from the flat, fascinating patchwork beneath the Mendips where the ground shakes when you jump up and down, the ague was endemic and rabbits climb trees to escape the winter floods. It is quiet, still and brooding countryside under lots of sky and formerly water, where the houses lean, the roads subside and the reeds bend in the evening breeze. The caves in the Cheddar Gorge, a constant temperature throughout the year, are said to have been the original stores for Somerset cheese. There are rumours that the practice may be revived.

DNA tests have located people whose antecedents were in the area thousands of years ago, possibly making cheese. Records date from the twelfth century. The higher ground was common grazing, and the dairies were communal, paying for milk in kind and producing large, even monstrous cheeses from May to October. Cheeses of between 50 and 60 pounds were customary, and 120-pounders made for the East Brent harvest supper. The mould for the 200-pounders, commissioned by Harrods, still survives. Cheeses of over a ton have been recorded.

One of the Cambridge colleges owned a farm in Somerset whose *raison d'être* was to keep them in Cheddar. In 1976, the British government, given the opportunity to protect the name of the cheese, opposed it on the grounds that housewives knew what they were buying. As a result they kept the door open for industrial or foreign copies to corner 60 per cent of the British market, and condemned the genuine article to a niche with sins committed in its name. J. Evan Jones, the American writer and cheese buff, cites the debate in which it happened. He also reckoned that the last pre-Harding type of Cheddar was made by a woman in North Carolina whose mother had emigrated from Somerset in the nineteenth century. It survived until her death, also in the 1970s.

Today, only about a dozen producers in and around Somerset are making a Cheddar that their antecedents might have recognized. Three use raw milk. Two are sold in Neal's Yard. Of all the cheeses produced in England, this is the one that needs the most careful selection and the most time to come round. The age-old formula was three months to set, six to ripen, nine to mellow and two years to cure, an order too tall and costly for most manufacturers.

Cheddar occupies a unique position, holding the offices of both laughing stock and icon, inviting scorn and invoking love. I have tasted good cheeses all my life, and two great ones, each of which was a Cheddar. At its rare and precious best it has a flaky texture and a depth and subtlety of flavour that stay in the memory, surpass competition and unlock doors to the senses that cannot be opened by any other cheese. For devotees of Cheddar, no substitute exists. No pretender is worthy of the throne.

Gloucester cheese is the most illustrious of Cheddar's neighbours, enjoying a long history and rise to eminence, followed by an inexplicable decline. The county took nearly a hundred years to recover from having its dairies vandalized by inverted Luddites paid by the creameries. It is now back to producing its two native cheeses, even from the milk of its native cow, helping to save both from death by indifference.

Double Gloucester is a pleasant whole-milk cheese. It is coloured with annatto, shaped like a millstone and weighs about twenty pounds – elegance itself standing on its rim in a mahogany cheese cradle. The age-old custom of salting the outside accounted for the characteristic waxiness of the texture within. Imagine the boatloads of cheeses painted red or brown and polished for the London market drifting down the Thames on the current from the Lechlade meadows. The rolling ceremonies that marked the start of the dairymaids' year and proved the notorious crust of the cheeses still take place on selected hillsides.

Single Gloucester is made from partly skimmed milk and is distinguished by its smaller size and natural colour. Though half the weight or less of its stablemate, it is not half the cheese, and worthy of mention in a Cruikshank lampoon.* I was given a single Gloucester by the Smart family that they, as one of the best cheesemakers, felt was too old and mitey to offer the public. It was like Parmesan, but harder and more tangy, a cheese from another century with a gripping flavour that offered a glimpse of what people used to look for in food.

Wiltshire: the chalk turned to cheese where Salisbury Plain and its outlying plateaux drop through juniper and bullace to pig and cow country, and milking herds came to the sound of the horn. Two principal types of cheese were made, large and small, which seem to have corresponded with the size of the farms and cottages they came from. The whole-milk Wiltshire cheese, reminiscent of both Gloucestershire and Somerset cheeses, could be natural in colour, annattoed, or tinged with green from bruised sage. The weight varied from about twelve pounds off season to forty. The north and west Wiltshire or Marlborough 'loaf' was a small skimmed-milk cheese of about nine inches in diameter. It had a tendency to blue, many variations, and sometimes contained caraway and cumin in the form of a ready-prepared spice sold by local grocers in the nineteenth century.

Significant though it was, cheese production in Wiltshire fell to butter in the nineteenth century, then fell away. Its recent revival is due to a single producer who found a family recipe tucked into a cottage wall. For her cheese, she uses the milk of sheep as well as goats, and the sweetest little baby's bath of a vat I have ever clapped eyes on.

---

* *Cruikshank alludes to the wedding of Mary, the Regent's sister, to her cousin the Duke of Gloucester in 1816. She is on his knee declaring her preference for a 'bit of single Gloucester' rather than a German suitor or 'sausage'. The cheese, partly eaten, is beside them on a table.*

Red Leicester could not be more different than its famous neighbour, Stilton, but occupied its own class at the pre-war dairy shows in London. The texture is similar to Cheddar. The size is handsome, a forty-pound millstone about six inches high and nearly two foot across. The colour, synonymous with the cheese, is as rich as the pastures of its birthplace and warm as the sandstone cottages in between. Prize-winning Leicesters were bound in a lighter than usual cloth and stripped a few weeks before their release into the world at about nine months. This gave the crusts the mouldy coats that aficionados looked for and indicated ripeness in the cheese.

The 'red' in a Leicester is a misnomer. It is a deep and brilliant orange obtained by using an ounce of annatto for every gallon of milk. The flavour is not affected, but the character is dependent upon it, though the cheese did recover from the wartime prohibition of the dye. The title of red was a later acquisition intended to flag up its regained colour and reclaim popularity. The last of the artisan cheeses was made in Melton Mowbrey, but only when there was milk to spare, and in the proportion of one Leicester to every sixteen Stiltons. After the creamery was taken over, local production ceased and the cheese disappeared from its heartland. When buying cheese in the years that followed and enquiring about its origin I hoped to find Leicester back where it belonged. It happened in 2006. David and Jo Clarke revived production for the first time in two generations and on a farm (mentioned by Bakewell) which had made the cheese from about 1745 – 1874. The milk is unpasteurised and their own, if not from their long horn cattle. The cheese is springy in texture, charming in flavour, and handsome as ever.

'Leicester claims to be the finest of all the mild hard cheeses of England' (Burdett, 1935). It was sometimes cut for distribution into halves and quarters, revealing the dark crust against the orange interior in all its glory. The curd is rarely attacked by mould growth, but can be. On one occasion, a factor appeared at the Normandy Stores with a blue Red Leicester, which neither of us had seen before, and which he had not been able to shift anywhere else in London. We took it instantly! I have a soft spot for this cheese, its companionship with watercress and the cheerful sight of the two on a plate. The 'rarebit' a Leicester makes, used to be handed round out hunting (Hutchins, 1967). Welcome back.

Cheshire bestrides the mighty salt beds of north-west England, which feed the soil, which feeds the grass, which feeds the cattle, which make the difference. There is no milk like it and consequently no cheese either, a fact that registered with the French, a former export market. '*Il [le Chester] doit sa saveur particulière,*' wrote Christian Plume in *Le Livre du Fromage*, '*à la composition saline du lait des vaches qui paissent dans les prés salés.*'

The county of Cheshire and its neighbours claim to have been making cheese by the time of the Roman occupation. It was one of the first regions to abandon milking ewes and goats in favour of cattle, and one of the last to surrender to the plough. The towns ending in 'wich', like Nantwich and Middlewich, produced the salt. Most of them had fairs and their own dairy farmers' association capable of shifting two hundred and fifty tons of cheese in one day. Within living memory Cheshire provided over half the nation's cheese, half its manufacturers, and a greater variety of nuances than any product given a single title.

At Paxton and Whitfield, the London grocers, a request for Cheshire brought forth the response 'Red, white or blue, sir?' This meant a pale orange and faintly dyed cheese, a natural-coloured one, or a specimen with 'green fade', a desirable form of mould growth. Cheshire's quality and identity were compromised when Cheddar became the declared choice of ration books, and hard-pressed cheeses were mandatory. Today there are a handful of craft producers left, though none in Ellesmere, the self-proclaimed 'cheese capital of the world', and only two using unpasteurised milk and cloth bandages. So there is cause for worry – and scope for entrepreneurs.

A classic Cheshire is a tall semi-pressed drum of up to fifty pounds. The current demand is for red Cheshire rather than the white. The fashion chops and changes. The cheeses attacked by mould growth, originally natural, which the Hutchinson Smith family of cheesemakers learned to induce, rose to compete with Stilton and Wensleydale in quality and price. The name of 'Blue Cheshire' was registered and subsequently sold, the enterprise failing when production was moved out of its heartland and into another county. By the 1990s, the supermarkets had long since decided on what given cheeses should be like. This meant mono-coloured in the case of Cheshire. Veining was perceived as a form of damage – and that appeared to be that for an English *pièce de résistance* that the 'cheese-eating surrender monkeys' would never have surrendered. It is wonderful to report that the loss was temporary and that Blue Cheshire is back.

'*Le Chester est probablement le seul fromage Anglais digne d'être employé en grande cuisine,*' Plume continued, though he had not discovered the merits of Lancashire, and had missed an important fact of gastronomic life. The moist, firm texture and salty-cum-fruity taste of a Cheshire is the best of the 'drunkard's biscuits'. No cheese on earth is better with red wine.

Lancashire cheese is a local hero. The farms that make it, and creameries too, are situated in the neat cow country that descends from the mighty Trough of Bowland to the Irish Sea. Beacon, Wolf and Longridge fells stand together. The geology is complex. The landscape is a maze of lanes, hedges, woods and fields that can remain green and lush even in the hottest and driest of summers. The weather side of the Pennines gets more than its fair share of rain.

'Lancashire cheese had become a distinct style by the 18th century,' writes Laura Mason, made in a complex and time-consuming fashion that accounts for the strong and characteristic flavour. Historically, the cheeses north of the Ribble were like those of the Yorkshire Dales in texture, and the cheeses to the south like those of Cheshire, though standards have levelled and none are made today outside the Fylde. They travelled little and not very well, being lightly pressed and fragile, but did survive the journeys by pony and trap into the markets. In Garstang and Preston there was no other cheese.

A classic Lancashire is a tall drum, weighing up to fifty pounds, which has reappeared since the war. There are three craft producers, two of whom use unpasteurised milk. A cloth jacket is customary, a wax one more common, but can get good results. Creamery production dominates, with cheese ranging from extra tasty ('burn yer lips') to mild. The crumbs are also sold. Rather than cutting cheeses, then cutting them up, retailers are in the habit of taking wedges from the entire drum. The single-acid Lancashire, by far the most popular, is regarded by aficionados as bottom of the pile. The Leigh Toaster, allegedly from the village near Manchester, was a brand name thought up by Burdons, the former cheese factor in Macclesfield.

Lancastrians are proud of their cheese and miss it away from home, to the extent of calling for supplies from visiting relations. It is said to link town-dwellers to rural roots, and, as a 'melting' cheese, breaks down to an unrivalled custard-like consistency. John Rodgers, author of *English Rivers*, never got over it. The piece of Lancashire he ate on toast in Rochdale, 'in a filthy temperance hotel . . . was worthy of the Gods'.

Stilton is a cheese of the vale, possibly the most famous in England, where the scattered line of horses and hounds will complete a twenty-mile point over field, hedge and ditch. Given a bright, frosty morning and an elevated position, you can watch them all the way. The land has been more considerately laid out by Nature, elegantly tweaked by man, and sympathetic to livestock than almost any other part of the world. The castle, one of the newest, stands guard. The farms retain the stores outside where cheeses were left to blue in a climate that helped them on the way.

Stilton is the Mouton Rothschild of English cheeses, regarded as a Johnny-come-lately in its time, which rose to *premier cru* and left most of its competitors licking their wounds. So exalted was the reputation of the cheese before the war that master grocers would not cut it except in half: wedges were not considered fitting. Its history is well known, its name protected in the courts, and its limit of production restricted. Attempts have been made to copy Stilton in Holland, but they were not successful and are now forbidden.

Stilton is the one English cheese that the French have heard of and will ask for when in London. In spite of its reputation, popularity and the opposition to change from cheese-lovers, however, Stilton has moved with the times. It has been made in creameries since the nineteenth century. Today it is produced with pasteurised Friesian or Holstein whole milk, and sold at as little as six weeks, all of which are economic decisions. One of the factories used organic shorthorn milk for a bit, which made 'beautiful cheese', but the supplier (a local agricultural college) did not consider production worth continuing.

Craft Stiltons were made with one session of unpasteurised Lincoln Red whole milk *plus* the cream of the next. They were matured for up to *two* years. Production ceased in 1939. Exciting moves are now afoot to produce a Stilton more like the original, starting with untreated milk. Such is the law, it may have to be called something else. The original name of Sticheldon is the most likely choice.

The best Stiltons have been made in dry, hot summers when the milk is high in butterfat. Retailers, running scared of full-flavoured cheeses and imaginary sell-by dates, have been known to sell prime Stiltons at reduced prices in the post-Christmas period. This is a cheese much liked in the cold months. The more concentrated the network of blue veins, the better. To cut a whole or half Stilton, do not use a scoop: pare the cheese in slivers from the top. Eat it with a glass of port, not with a glass of port in it.

From the north

At the end of the nineteenth century, 'most of the . . . dales had their own special cheese and pride in it' (Morton Shand, 1927). The valley of the Ure is one. Cradled in the Yorkshire tundra and cradling Hawes, it sweeps down past Lovely Seat to the Aysgarth Falls. The name of Abbotside recalls the monastic overlords and commissioners of cloth and milk whose lands were broken up into farms making cheese that came to be known as Wensleydale. The presses and conduits, which ran the whey down from dairy to piggery, remain in place.

Wensleydale was the best-known of the Yorkshire cheeses owing to its quality, quantity and availability. The cows moved from the farms up to summer grazing and back when the meadows had been cut. Grass, pasture, aftermath and a few hay cheeses came in succession. The finest gained their reputation from the cattle browsing the alders growing locally, and the crisp vegetation that 'feeds rather than fills' (Rodgers, 1947). The higher up a bite is obtained, the better the cheese.

The Wensleydales that lined the former grocers' shops in Dent and Leyburn were tall semi-pressed whole-milk cheeses of up to about sixteen pounds. Veining was allegedly brought on by the stone in the area. The size and shape of the cheeses were calculated to make them split under their own weight, enabling the desired mould spores to enter through cracks. The story goes that some of the cheeses were dropped on the ground to make sure. White Wensleydale, a newcomer with a closer texture, supplied the cheaper end of the market.

By the turn of the twentieth century, about two hundred farms were producing Wensleydale cheese. The bulk collection of milk did for most of the small-scale manufacturers in the 1930s. The remainder fell to utilitarian grading standards imposed by the Ministry of Food, which had failed to distinguish between hard- and semi-pressed cheeses, and condemned prize-winners to processing. Wensleydale faced extinction after the forced retirement of the last artisan producer, twice a national champion. Photos of the donkey that carried the milk from field to dairy by saddlecan kept the memory going.

The creamery in Hawes underwent a management buy-out in 1992. Blue Wensleydale was born again ten years later, but in pasteurised form. The white is named after one-time boss Kit Calvert. Fruit cake, an age-old companion to cheese in Yorkshire, is produced as well.

Swaledale: with Raven's Seat and Lady Seat looking on, pursued by the promise of a summer snow shower. Beneath a tawny wilderness the fields are laid out like pieces of green cloth cut to fit the valley floor and rise a little up the skirting board. The clutches of stone houses look like models. The cheeses are rare compared to Cheddar and survivors of the war on English dairycraft, thanks to North Country grit, and the occasional excess of milk from suckler cows. They are made by a creamery in Richmond, and by at least one privateer, who came to the door, dog in arms, and swapped a cheese for a pot of jam. Her cousin from over the fell takes the prizes at the show in bejewelled hands. The three-pound, four-week-old brine-washed millstones and drums are clean, delicate and all bespoken, even before judging begins. I barely had the charm, a dirty word in Yorkshire, to obtain one.

Cotherstone cheese comes from a farm at the end of a drive on a windblown precipice. A rushing and gushing River Tees runs through the trees below. I first saw the cheese in a well-stocked grocer's in Barnard Castle, selling quickly and softening slowly – an unexpected treasure for a browser to find in the dark days before the present interest in artisans. The producer was Joan Cross. She was tall, fair, gentle and delighted to meet someone who was interested in her work – who would not be? John, her late husband, referred to some of their fields as cheese pasture. Over tea, she thoughtfully produced a nineteenth-century copy of the local newspaper, which contained an advertisement for Cotherstone cheese.

A collection of Victorian cast-iron presses, bearing the names of local foundries, and looking indestructible, occupied the half-light in the dairy. Some were quite ornate. Joan was a natural, reticent about her skills. She had learned to make cheese from her mother, but always wanted to do a course at agricultural college. Fearing a scientific outcome, I begged her not to. People far and near have shown interest in the cheeses, and the business. It is hoped that Joan's son will take them on. The wheels and drums with smooth golden crusts that she had in the store weighed up to about eight pounds. Their texture varies from soft and cloud-like to firm for longer keeping. The milk is now pasteurised, but the cheese truly local, and the only one in the dales named after a village.

The North York Moors are not known for cheese today, and there is no obvious record of it being made, but made it was until the war, particularly on the farms too far from Pickering and Scarborough to complete the return journey with butter. Flora Dale, who moved to a village near Pickering, had a recipe from her mother's notebook. Four gallons of milk were used to produce a lightly pressed cheese, eaten 'fairly young'.

Two more

Bath cheese was an elegant one prone to changing fancies, an 'erstwhile favourite' in fashion and out with powdered wigs, macaronies and fluttering fans 'from a remote but unrecorded period' (*Encyclopaedia Britannica*). 'Dear Horatio,' wrote Edmund Nelson to his son on 16 July 1801, 'on Tuesday next (God willing) intend to leave Bath . . . recollecting that Sir William and Lady Hamilton seemed to be gratified by the flavour of a cream cheese, I have taken the liberty of sending 2 or 3 cheeses of Bath manufacture . . .' (Naval Record Office)

The old Bath cheese was nine inches square and one inch deep, and a 'cream' cheese inasmuch as it was produced from full-cream milk. It was surface-ripened, soft in consistency, and could also be circular in shape. By 1908 there was one woman left manufacturing the cheese, a Mrs Loxton in the local creamery, 'yielding a comforting profit to the maker and a gratifying food to the consumer'.

Bath cheese must have disappeared around the time of the First World War. Sixty or seventy years later it was reborn on a farm in the hills nearby. The producer, Graham Padfield, a convert from science to art, makes other cheeses too. A pupil of his, very accomplished, comes to Salisbury farmers' market. Until there is a shift in consciousness, Bath Soft will be described as being like a Brie or a Camembert, rather than the other way round.

Blue Vinny: the Blackmore Vale is a rolling and pastoral basin, seen to its greatest advantage from Shaftesbury's Abbey Walk or one of the steep surrounding hills. The land is embroidered with hedges and ageing oaks, and has mostly been enclosed in the last 150 years. The odd common remains. My father took me there for the first time since baptism, aged about ten, to see where the family had come from. In the early days of the local hunt, founded in January 1826, a Henry Serrell led some hounds to the Rev. Jack Russell (the terrier breeder) on behalf of an antecedent of mine. I wonder if the cheese with which he coaxed them across Dorset and into Devonshire, a distance of seventy miles, was Blue Vinny?

The Blackmore Vale was pork- and butter-producing country, connected to the London market by the Southern Railway. Its cheeses were randomly and thriftily made from hand-skimmed milk, often left naturally to sour, bagged up and punctured to promote mould growth, and help soften the occasionally notorious texture. The quality fluctuated. It plunged with the invention of the continuous-flow separator, which removed all the cream, but improved with the use of rennet and the simple determination to get better results. By the twentieth century, a more successful Vinny was produced with semi-skimmed milk, weighing from seven pounds and worthy of a mention with England's leading cheeses in the *Encyclopaedia Britannica*. A firm in Blandford made the presses.

Dorset, in contrast to its 'timeless' image, was on the move from the Second World War. By the time I first saw Hardy's 'vale of little dairies' there were hardly any left. The milk was contracted, the cream and butter unavailable, and the blue-veined cheese, owing to the failure of visitors to get it, growing more mysterious every minute. An enterprising Londoner and Cheddar producer took up Vinny in the 1970s, but failed to make it pay. I bought a piece in Weymouth, cut from a millstone of about twelve pounds, and kept it as a curiosity for several years.

The present Blue Vinny is more like a Stilton in size and shape, but a different proposition as a cheese, and enjoys a longer period in storage before leaving the producer. It is connected to the Blackmore Vale by AC status and made by a farm on the Stock Gaylard estate, from which Jack Russell acquired his hounds.

Anyone interested in making cheese, particularly those relating to where they live, can obtain recipes from agricultural colleges. The books listed below, which may be ordered from dealers or libraries, contain instructions for the following past or present cheeses:

Eliza Smith, *The Complete Housewife* (1729, republished): Newmarket and the Queen's cheeses
Hannah Glasse, *The Art of Cookery Made Plain and Easy* (1747): brickbat cheeses.
Mary Jewry, *Warne's Model Cookery* (1900): Cheshire (imitation), new milk, cream, and egg or 'artificial' cheeses.
Encyclopaedia Britannica (11th edn, 1910): Rutland slip coat cheeses.
Farmhouse Fare (1935–73): cottage, Cornish, Cumberland, Devon smallholder, Lincoln, Nottinghamshire, Colwick, Old English herb, Shropshire sage, and Suffolk (soft) cheeses.

OUT OF THE WOODWORK
'Huntingdonshire . . . its chief commodities are corn, malt, and cheese; and they fatten an abundance of cattle' (Moule, 1830).

Butter or cheese?[*]

Question: Can any of your readers tell me the exact method of making what is called resurrection butter – that is, cream tied in a napkin and afterwards buried? We tried it and failed; but we are ignorant of the principle which converts the cream into butter. M.F., October.

Answer 1: If M.F. can find a book called *The Ladies of Beever Hollow*, he will also find the full instructions for making resurrection butter.' Foxley, November.

Answer 2: Resurrection butter or Harrington[**] cream cheese is made as follows. Tie a quart of thick cream in a close thick cloth and tie another cloth over that. Dig a hole in the garden nearly two foot deep, put in the cream and throw the soil over it until the hole is filled, but do not press it. In twenty-four hours take up the cream, remove carefully the outer . . . cloth, then untie the other and put the cream into a wooden bowl; beat it for a short time until the whey is separated from it. Line a small cream cheese vat with a piece of wet muslin and put in the cream. The lid should be made to fit into the vat. Place a weight on it, and in a few days, if the weather be warm, the cheese will be ripe. These cheeses are very rich and good. Fanny, November.

Cottenham cheese: 'at Cambridge I went into an inn . . . for lunch and had such a good cut of cheese that I asked the waiter what it was. He didn't know, but sought out the manager, who, in a voice made thick by drinking tawny port, told me . . . it came from a neighbouring village called Cottenham' (Layton, 1957).

SHEEP'S CHEESES

The milking of ewes, from being one of the most common sights in the medieval period, was relegated to pockets in the north of England and Wales by Hanoverian times, and was rare by the twentieth century. Trow-Smith's photograph of a flock in Radnorshire awaiting the pail, their heads secured in a horizontal ladder and peeping through the rungs, is the only evidence I have seen that the practice continued after the Second World War. The cheese, which may have died out for a few years, re-emerged with the introduction of quotas affecting cattle in 1982. Since then, sheep have had a modest revival as dairy beasts, assisted by the fashion for Mediterranean foods. Ewes' milk can be mixed with cows' milk in order to make cheese, and was used thus for centuries, as well as on its own. It lacks colour, but has plenty of bite.

---

[*] *From correspondence in* The Field, *1869.*

[**] *No explanation given – the correspondent's family, perhaps? And use unpasteurised cream.*

Goats' cheeses

Goats have as long a history as any domesticated animal, if a less distinguished one. It is not clear whether they were so seldom mentioned in early records because there were too many or too few. There are four feral herds in England, a couple in Wales and a couple north of the border. Legend has it that the one in the Cheviots left Lindisfarne with the monks bearing St Cuthbert's body (en route to Durham) and strayed from the party. They may also have arrived with migrants seeking summer pastures (Werner)*, or as escapees from the herds employed to keep Wooler in milk and whey during its term as a health resort in the nineteenth century. Whatever their origin, these goats are of the rough, tough old English rather than the Swiss commercial type.

The Valley of Rocks in Devon has a herd, also feral, which was reinforced by Cheviot goats in 1976. Some of Lynton's newer residents tried to get their descendants run out of town, but without success. The goat survived: it usually does, roaming, browsing and climbing, the billies looking hellish but smelling to high heaven, and the nannies falling in behind. The Bagot goats, one of England's rarest breeds of livestock, were emparked at Blithfield in Staffordshire around 1380. They used to be hunted after a fashion, like deer, and survived a wartime extermination order. The legend is that the survival of this goat and that of the Bagot family are linked.

Goats are consummate heath croppers, which eliminate young vegetation. They fell from popularity with enclosure, but continued to be credited with all sorts of powers from trampling on adders to preventing abortion in cattle. So, the goat in England never quite died out, I have cooked kids a couple of times. Their meat should be stewed or curried like mutton or venison. Mabel Sevier's family kept goats for milking on a common near the Forest, and sold the cheeses locally before the war. The softer quick maturing French types have increased in popularity since milk quotas came in. Pleasant as they may be, you cannot seem to get away from them, grilled and served up with a multi-coloured salad, in certain pubs and restaurants.

A few points about cheese

England's strongest suit in terms of cheese is in its heritage of hard- and semi-pressed millstones and drums. Of these, only a handful are manufactured as custom dictates in or near their county of origin, bound in cloth and left to breathe – enabling them to lose weight – an important part of the ageing process. With the passing of grocers' shops, a still smaller number is selected and stored until it reaches the condition that the rest of Europe regards as prime.

---

* Ray Werner, an authority on the history of livestock.

Too many excellent cheeses are not allowed to mature for long enough and, as a result, are half the quality they could be.

The word 'farmhouse' used to mean what it said: that a cheese was made on a farm, implying by hand, from the raw milk of one herd of cows (except in the case of communal dairies). No longer: anyone can use the word and for any purpose. Do not be deceived. If you are interested in cheese, wise up about the makers.

Awards and credits are suspect. The star performers do not win prizes every year. Others must be allowed to. An eminent cheesemaker told me that she produced her best cheeses as a novice. Her current efforts were not so good – she did not know why – but won lots of prizes owing to her higher profile.

No cheese has ever been improved in flavour by pasteurisation. The hard ones do not suffer from its effects as much as the rest, though they take longer to come round and seem to lack complexity. Semi-pressed cheeses tend to taste uniform after heat treatment. Soft cheeses are ruined. Farmhouse producers and sophisticated palates, notably in London, are against pasteurisation. Environmental Health and the National Dairy Council are still mostly in favour, though they are not so zealous as they were, and acknowledge that the older the cheese, the less likely it is to have a problem with bacteria. Most of the factories pasteurise their milk automatically, maintaining it does not affect the quality. Art versus science again.

With 'thermised' cheese, the milk is brought up to temperature and immediately cooled. It is obviously a gentler process, but why, apart from obliging regulations, does it take place if milk can be tested for harmful bacteria?

Within weeks of manufacture, cheeses are tried by tasters who can tell how they will develop. This is done with an iron, an implement for removing a plug from a cheese, sampling a little and putting the rest back. The cheeses that pass inspection are released on to the market bearing the retailer's label or none. The failures go for processing.

At the shows, out of a maximum of 100 points, 40 are awarded for taste and aroma, 40 for texture, 10 for body and potential keeping quality, and 10 for looks.

A good cheese cannot be improved, and a bad or immature one cannot be disguised by smoking it, marinating it, mixing it with fruit or nuts, wine or herbs, or anything else. Annatto, a harmless West Indian dye used in England since the eighteenth century on account of its neutral smell and flavour, is the only cosmetic to have stood the test of time.

All traditional English cheeses are made with animal rather than vegetable rennet. They are said to taste better for it.

In the shop, make sure your piece of cheese is neatly and cleanly cut: an ugly piece is an ugly experience. Also, if you find an exceptional cheese, do not chance it. Leave with as much as your pocket can stand. You may not get anything as good for some time.

Try eating cheese with a drink before dinner, an American habit and a good one, as well as afterwards. With bread it is a snack, said broadcaster John Arlott, but with bread and a glass of wine it is a meal. As for cheese and biscuits, a fairly recent invention, be careful of the biscuits. Most of the brands on the market are too big, sweet and clumsy for cheese. Plain water biscuits are best. The late John Fothergill, innkeeper, made his own.

COOK'S ORACLE

The stronger and better the flavour of a cheese, the less is needed in cookery and the more the quality comes through. It is a mistake and also a false economy to use a cheap or mild cheese.

Cheese for toast (Welsh rarebit)* or to spread on pork chops
Lancashire is best, Cheshire comes next, Cheddar and Leicester are also good:

2–4oz (50–110g) grated cheese, 2–4oz (50–110g) cream, 1 egg yolk and a little white pepper or made mustard.

Mix well and spread. It browns quickly. Be careful not to burn.

Cheese pudding
More substantial than a soufflé. A strong cheese like Cheshire or Lancashire is best, Cheddar and Leicester are also good. Feeds at least 2:

8oz (225g) grated cheese, 1 pint (570ml) of milk, 4oz (110g) fresh white breadcrumbs, 2 beaten eggs, salt and white pepper to taste.

Heat the breadcrumbs in the milk and leave for at least an hour. Reheat gently when ready to use, stir in the cheese and allow it to melt. Remove from the heat, add the egg and the seasoning and put in a close-fitting buttered ovenproof dish. Bake in a preheated medium oven at 170°C/325°F/gas mark 3 for 30–40 minutes or until firmish. Eat with mustard. If you have any left over, cut in slices and fry until brown on the outside.

---

* *Rarebit: is a possible corruption of 'rear bit', meaning a savoury that came at the end of dinner, as opposed to the 'fore bit' at the beginning of the meal (Evan Jones).*

CHAPTER TWENTY-SEVEN

Vegetables

M Y MOTHER'S KITCHEN GARDEN was enclosed by walls ten feet high, square in shape, solid without and safe within, a sanctuary overlooked by the sky and bushy or skeletal tops of trees. You entered through one of the glossy green doors and left through another, reassured by the quiet, the stillness, the privacy and plenty, the growth, dormancy or growth to come. A grid system of paths, edged with box, divided the beds. Plums and pears, their trunks erect and arms outstretched, clung to the weathered and mottled brick. A gnarled and bushy vine, tethered to the roof of a hothouse in one corner, hung with tapered and tempting bunches of purple grapes.

William John Churchill planted, weeded and cropped the garden for over fifty years, and still found time to milk the cows, feed the pigs, mow the lawns and rake the leaves before they gathered in dark sodden drifts on virgin grass and around the cedar. The red, blue and yellow rosettes with frilly halos and forked tails that he had won at shows for fruit and veg were mounted on a board in the stables. I was given my own patch in the corner of 'his' garden, but never used it. I, a youngster on whom youth was wasted, took for granted the dew-fresh lettuce, the earthy carrots, the frosty cabbage and the squeaky greens that came in a trug to the kitchen door.

The disdain for vegetables with which the English are credited is hard to reconcile with the number of walled and market gardens, the allotments and the greatness of names like Scarlet Emperor, Kelvedon Wonder and Jersey Royal. There are a few natives (notably glasswort, sea kale, and watercress), a few that may be (fat hen, purslane, sorrel and rock samphire), some casualties (brooklime and wild celery) and a long list of old favourites and new faces. The number of vegetables in cultivation is thought to have peaked at 120 varieties around 1500, slumped at the Reformation and fluctuated according to fashion after that. Having fallen to less than 50 in the 1970s, it is now rising again.

All the vegetables in cultivation today are descended from palatable selections of wild plants that may no longer exist. Many of the Roman introductions reappeared in the sixteenth and seventeenth centuries – we do not know which ones, nor can we trust received information. I have a copy of Gerard's *Herball*, and was preparing to quote it along with everyone else, when I read that it was 'laced with myth', a source of error and a mere translation of a work in Dutch written by a bloke whose day job was as a barber (Roberts, 2001).

Over the centuries, however, rustic landowners, well-to-do yeomen and cottagers on the bread line toiled away to fill the hungry gap and pinch days before the harvest home. They were all self-sufficient and had to be, or perished. Immigrants added to the fund of knowledge.

Travellers brought and distributed seeds, which gardeners kept going as a matter of course. By the time La Rochefoucauld arrived in Suffolk in 1784 there was drilling, crop rotation and fertilisation going on. He found beans grown commercially, vegetables going to London, and the squire of Mistley planting four acres of carrots for his own consumption, to say nothing of what he sold, and pineapples and peaches ripening in his hothouse.

As for cookery, advice was at hand. 'All kinds of vegetables should have a little crispness,' wrote John Farley of the famous London Tavern, 'for if you boil them too much you will deprive them of their sweetness and beauty.' Salads were appreciated too. Mrs Beeton feared they were 'apt to ferment in the stomach', but she was out of date, as well as out of touch. By the late Victorian period, watercress was in commercial production. Lettuces, tomatoes and celery were booming.

My mother's walled garden must have been built around 1850, retaining heat, concentrating crops and protecting them from wind, rabbits, deer and pilferers. It covered one acre. The one at Helmsdale in Yorkshire, laid out between the castle and park, covered five acres, and kept twenty men and boys busy in its heyday. Then, during the First World War, people left the land, never to return, and a long list of gardens with brick, cob and even serpentine walls became too big to manage and fell into disuse.

The Victorian cottage garden, which is now visualised as a dreamy and glorified herbaceous border with a Gertrude Jekyll twist, was not devoted to pleasing flowers and shrubs. It contained green vegetables, currant bushes, and a few herbs. Potatoes were grown on allotments, or in fields with cereals and certain types of beans. In some parts of the country, particularly in Northamptonshire and the Midlands, there are traces of the arable strips where generations of labourers sowed their crops until enclosure. Look for the evenly spaced ridges ten to twelve feet wide, with furrows either side, reclining under grass in the much-loved patchwork, designed by civil servants and funded by developers, which spelt the end of the working village.

I might never have plunged a spade into the earth but for getting married, and acquiring an abandoned garden of almost two acres and an opportunity. A timely encounter with 'permaculture' drawings, manorial in conception, made it all seem possible – and I was off.* There would be a formal area, and a diminutive park, with woods and wilds, leading to an old

---

* *Permaculture: a word coined by Australian Bill Mollison to describe the permanent or sustainable form of agriculture which he practises and preaches. It is based on sound principles old and new, no-dig and irrigation.*

coach road and a common beyond. Fallen trees provided for the fire, hazel coppice made the bean poles and pea sticks. Bracken grew for mulch, and a rich topsoil, moved and mucked for generations, capped a moisture-retaining seam of light brown clay.

I knew what vegetables should taste like, that was all, and that was enough to start with. There proved to be no greater advantage than to begin at the beginning, free from prejudices and assumptions, eager to learn and anxious to succeed, however many questions there were to ask and leads to follow up. Books helped, but not as much as personal contacts, racial memories and getting to know the land under foot.

The plan for the kitchen garden was:

1. To grow a succession of crops that could be eaten fresh throughout the year, to dry, pickle or bottle the excess, and to freeze nothing.
2. To entertain any idea until it failed, whether it was based on 'permaculture' methods, Old Moore, common sense or local gossip.
3. To be chemical-free.
4. To single out the star performers in terms of flavour, paying special attention topersonal and proprietary recommendations, the Heritage Seed Library*, local and organic selections, and Awards of Garden Merit from the Royal Horticultural Society, Wisley.

The project consisted of:
1. Marking out the plot.
2. Covering it with black plastic for twelve months.
3. Repeating the whole thing five years later (having started in the wrong place).
4. Raising beds (to minimise weeding and beat the wet).

Further considerations were:
1. Feeding the soil – mucking, liming and applying green manures.
2. Feeding the plants.
3. Composting.
4. Seed-saving.
5. Irrigation (have not got round to it yet).
6. Protection, speaking of which . . .

---

* *Maintained by the Henry Doubleday Research Association (HDRA).*

The realities are:

1. Beginner's luck applies to unbroken land in particular. It will probably draw you in, cocooning you warm and safe in the foetal position, and also in denial, untilplague and pest descend for good. Face the music in advance.

2. The sentimental thought of all God's creatures living together in symbiosis, eating each other in preference to your plants, and performing to your advantage, is an emotional crutch and pipe dream, no better than hope itself. Again, meet it head on.

3. Few people like their soil; it is always too wet/dry, acid/alkaline, etc. And it may be.

4. There is usually something you cannot grow to your satisfaction – if at all.

I was told by a man in the Gammon (my favourite drinkers' pub) that the success of veg gardening is directly related to the hours put in. It takes time and trouble to prepare the soil, erect the poles, plant the seed, kill the slugs, shoot the deer and pick the crop. The work is hard, constantly thwarted, unremitting, and unnecessary in modern England, but rewarding too. It may save money, win prizes at the show or realise a need to connect with the earth even if you only have a window box or tub. There are the drastic effects of intensive farming on the soil, subsoil and wildlife to consider, the elements of control over chemical input, the food miles, and the quality of crops to a fine degree. The first peas and broad beans, picked and cooked within a few minutes, and consciously tasted, are worth a wagonload of recipes.

After seven years of thrills and disappointments in the kitchen garden, my wife and I felt we had completed our apprenticeship. A plate of vegetables is no substitute for meat, fowl or fish, but a necessary companion, and the satisfaction of growing one proved equal to the pleasure of eating the other. The health benefits are obvious and the emotional ones too, hence the feeling of calm and contemplation to add to the continuity and endeavour that characterise allotments. You get fat from potato crisps and exhausted from strenuous exercise, not from lifting a few spuds. And if you have the luxury of doing it for fun, after a tough or pointless day on the road or meeting deadlines, it quietens the mind.

Here is a list of the veg we grow, or intend to:

ALLIUMS

Leeks: A lily and member of the large and widely distributed allium family, cultivated for thousands of years in the Near East, but equal to colder climates. The present garden leek, which is probably of Mediterranean descent and another Roman introduction, is biennial. There is also a 'sand leek' or rocambole, a form of garlic, found in the wild in Cheshire and the north, which I have yet to clap eyes on. The Babbington leek is a perennial with a round purple head, handsome in a border, which can reach six feet tall.

Leeks are obliging to grow once planted, provide winter interest, and help to break up heavy ground. They do not mind the wet in Wales, the cold in Scotland, or the wind in the Fens. Rust is occasional. The different varieties are distinguished by their height, thickness of stem and to a small extent by colour, with flags varying from green to bluish. The choice of seeds, particularly in the north-east of England, has been influenced by exhibitors, who raise early-maturing giant leeks for show. The smaller types are sweeter, the immature ones sweetest.

Leeks are winter vegetables in season from about November to April (just the wrong time for a cooling Vichyssoise). The flags should be firm and fresh. Remove the tops and outer leaves, reserving them for stock, discard the tails, and stand upside down all day in a jug of cold water to remove the grit. Slice, fry quickly in butter and season well.

Older, larger leeks can be slimy. Barely cover with stock, gravy, or water, soy and pepper, with butter on top. Simmer gently for about half an hour or until soft. Reduce the liquid to a few tablespoons before serving. Alternatively, use in soup as a substitute for onions or garlic.

Onions: Another allium and biennial, spread by the Romans, hardened off by the Dutch in the eighteenth century, and long since adapted to English climes. Sizes vary from petite in spring and pickling onions to the mammoth entrants in country shows. The colour can be white, pink or red, as well as the usual brown; the body round, squat or spindle-shaped. The easy way to grow onions is from sets, which are treated to retard their growth and perform when planted out. The serious way is from seed. The all-important onion bed, raked, weeded and preened by an exhibitor, has the air of a final resting place.

We have in Hampshire a textbook 'Onion Johnny' from near Roscoff, who shrugs his shoulders, wears a beret, smokes Gauloises, and has been coming to England for nearly fifty years. He has a cottage and warehouse nearby. He visits towns in the south- and mid-west with his van and bike, selling strings of pink Breton onions and shallots. To the question '*Combien, m'sieu?*' (the limit of my French), he replies, 'Ze same price as las' time, m'sieu.' Nobody is counting, nobody is fooled; perhaps he is not fooling: you pay up regardless.

Another Breton came to the Normandy Stores: red face, blue eyes, and a threadbare grey suit over a spare frame and a warm heart. He was always pleased to see you, to shake hands, and eager to talk in a mixture of languages about *Cornouaille*. The last of the Onion Johnnies, Frenchman all through, but a part of English life since our two nations last met in battle at Waterloo and peace descended after hundreds of years.

Look out for two heritage varieties of onion: the eponymous James Longkeeping, raised by a market gardener in Lambeth Marsh, and mentioned by the RHS in 1819; and Rousham Park Hero, introduced in 1887 by Deverill's Nursery, Banbury, Oxfordshire.

Onions are intended to keep, making them available from summer and overwintered crops almost throughout the year. Imported onions from hotter climates tend to be milder. Their seminal importance is undiminished, though baked onions, which sometimes had a lamb's kidney inside, have more or less dropped off the provincial repertoire. The skins of the brown varieties improve the colour of dark soups and sauces. Remove before serving.

SHALLOTS

A miniature onion in all but the detail. The optional name, scallion, is connected with Ascalon, a ruined city on the Palestinian coast occupied by Crusaders. If you are thinking of growing veg but doubt your ability, start with shallots. Plant a handful a foot apart in a sunny weed-free bed between the shortest day and the end of March, and each obliging bulb should open into seven or eight more, in the course of the summer. Some people plant shallots in rows and eat while young and green, like spring onions; they are less vulnerable than seeds, and hotter too. Otherwise, pickle. The less trouble you take, the better. Peel off the skins and fill a jar, adding a couple of chillies if you want a kick. Cover with malt vinegar. Put on the lid and leave for three months. Do not add salt or sugar; shallots are sweet enough. You can bottle them with cooked beetroot as well (see page 351).

GARLIC

The strongest flavour of the alliums, introduced to England from the Mediterranean in 1548 (says Mrs Beeton in one of her footnotes). Garlic, which was less favourably regarded by the Victorians than by their antecedents, has now swung back into fashion. It likes dry locations and is doing well on the Isle of Wight. Some gardeners overwinter garlic, others plant from the shortest day until mid-March. Take a bulb, divide it up and poke a few cloves into the ground a foot or so apart. Lift on a dry day at the end of the summer. After taking and using seed for four years, you have your own subspecies. A chef told me that it is the green or dormant shoot in a clove that lingers on the breath. Pickled garlic is increasingly popular. And smoked? Surely it does not need any more flavour.

ARTICHOKE

The globe is a daisy and perennial, originating in the Mediterranean area, known to the Romans and recorded in England in the sixteenth century. It is a tall, dramatic and amusing plant with silvery foliage and green or purple edible heads. The cardoon is a cousin with edible ribs, even more statuesque, though it is now regarded as ornamental. The word is that the artichoke family does not thrive on clay – nonsense! I have never seen a stronger vegetable, more inclined to look after itself. Purple or purplish heads are tastier than green ones, but seldom appear on the market. We grow half a dozen plants in both the kitchen garden and herbaceous borders.

English artichokes crop in July and August. The youngest are cooked whole Italian-style, the older ones before they flower. Some say that, unlike most other vegetables, artichokes should be cut and left to go a little stale for two or three days before preparation. Then boil upside down in plenty of salted water for 10–15 minutes or until you can pull out a leaf, and serve with a pot of melted butter per person. If you have an embarrassment of riches, dispatch the foliage and the fluff, and bake the hearts in tomato sauce (see page 58).

'Jerusalem' artichoke is more likely to derive its name from the coastal village of Tersensen in Holland, its first port of call in Europe (Roberts, 2001), than from the Italian *girasole*, meaning sunflower. The heads range from small and yellow in culinary plants to a deep and beguiling red in 'Velvet Queen', an ornamental one. The stems can grow to seven or eight feet tall. The root, which is the edible part and looks like a knobbly or elongated potato, is thought to have arrived in England in the early seventeenth century. Chickens love the seeds. The main disadvantage of Jerusalem artichokes is that they multiply like mad. Either dig up every last one as required, saving a few to replant for the next crop, or confine in a bed. The smoothest variety is 'Fuseau'.

Jerusalem artichokes are in season over the winter, from about December until March. They are compared to potatoes marinated in Dettol when boiled (quite apart from causing wind). Yet a single artichoke peeled and grated into a beef or mutton stew, without making its presence felt, improves the gravy out of all recognition. Chips, thinly sliced and deep-fried, are not bad either.

To make a soup, take 1lb (450g) peeled artichokes and a medium onion, peeled and sliced, add 3 pints (1.8l) of game stock and season to taste with salt and white pepper. Cook for half an hour until the veg is soft, liquidize and finish with cream.

Asparagus

A lily and a perennial. The native form is a wind-cheater designed by Nature to lie prostrate in order to survive the westerly gales. It is linked to Asparagus Island in Cornwall (though not around in 2005 – we checked it out). The erect form is originally from the environs of Turkey and a possible Roman introduction, cultivated with enthusiasm by Huguenot immigrants in the seventeenth century, particularly around Ipswich and Colchester. The berries have been carried hither and thither by birds – making feral asparagus too. The domestic plant underwent improvement under the Hanoverians, reaching a wider audience, particularly in London, and was grown in large quantities near the Raven pub in Battersea, where market gardeners of the day drank. Bath asparagus is a shade-tolerant member of the same family (see page 411).

For couch potatoes, especially those on a diminishing income who enjoy luxuries, asparagus is ideal. It is also vigorous, sending out a root system like a huge man o' war, long-lived, prolific and fills the hungry gap. The plant is associated with light soils, but can thrive on clay provided it is not waterlogged in winter and choked by perennial weeds in summer. It benefits in old age from a dressing of salt. Pests are few, but include a beetle, slugs and ants, which tunnel up the stems. Cut with an asparagus knife, allowing up to twenty crowns per person for a feed almost every day in season.

The age-old English way of growing asparagus is over a corpse,* provided for country people by a much-loved hunter, or a road kill. Two deer, struck by cars in successive seasons outside our house, supplied my wife and me with the necessary footings. After preliminary work and a slow start which takes two or three years, the plant can grow for a further fifteen with little attention, and at no cost after the initial outlay.

Evesham asparagus, flushed with purple and originating in Worcestershire, is pick of the bunch. It is raised by men like Gary Andrews, a third-generation grower and nurseryman, but is absent from the usual catalogues. The only other heritage variety is Connover's Colossal, which now has an RHA Award of Garden Merit. The all-male hybrids are thicker than the female sprue grass or simply 'grass'.

The English asparagus season opens when the first shoots appear in April and closes on the longest day, 21 June. It is extended by commercial growers of hybrids. The heads should be tightly knitted, and the spears eaten within hours or even minutes of cutting, or else they become stale and tasteless or sour. If a bundle must wait, wrap the top in a plastic bag and immerse the tail in a bowl of ice. Steam in a vertical or horizontal position (don't bake). Eat hot with home-made butter and Maldon salt, or cold with mayonnaise, either on its own, or with other seasonal dainties – sea trout, sweetbreads and new potatoes.

To make soup, put the heads aside and cook up the stalks with a chopped onion and a few fresh peas in a chicken or duck stock. When soft, rub through a sieve. Add the heads and simmer gently for five minutes. Season to taste, and finish with cream.

AUBERGINE

A perennial grown as an annual, related to the spud, which underwent early domestication in its native India. The aubergine was introduced to Europe from the East by the Moors (along

---

* *The experts may not agree unless the carcass is well rotted.*

with citrus fruits and cultivated carrots). It was known in England possibly by the end of the sixteenth century, but was initially regarded with suspicion and offers little in the way of food value. A deep purple colour is the most common. The white variety accounts for the name 'egg plant'. There are long aubergines, round ones and babies, all requiring sun and light. Plants do better in a greenhouse, but may be raised outside in a good summer. Try pots against a wall.

Home-grown aubergines are in season in August and September. Their condition should be firm, the seeds unformed. Chop into large dice, dust with salt and leave to sweat for a couple of hours (some people do not bother). Cook like marrow. Alternatively, slice, brush with oil and grill.

Beans, broad

A legume, and another Mediterranean plant, eaten as a staple in England by man and beast, possibly since the Bronze Age. To feel 'full of beans', to eat baked beans (see page 57) and to proceed to the village of Barton in the Beans would not have been possible without broad beans. There are three types. The longpods are field beans or close relations. The Windsors are for garden use. There are dwarves too.

Broad beans like a heavy soil and space, but they are easy to grow and beat the slugs in the race to get going. The two main pests, blackfly and chocolate spot, need not be crippling. The seed, left to dry on the vine, is easy to save for the next generation. All beans leave nitrogen behind through their roots.

Heritage varieties include Martock, a close relation or actual descendant of the bean mentioned in the manorial rolls of 1293: 'If you shake a Martock man he rattles,' the saying goes (HDRA) in Somerset. In the 1970s, conservator Steve Oxbrow acquired seed from the Bishop of Bath and Wells' kitchen garden in exchange for a donation to the cathedral roof. The taste, welcome on former fast days, is described as 'meaty'. Bunyard's Exhibition (1884) is what it says (popular with exhibitors). The Windsors Green (1809) and White (1895) are rated for flavour on both sides of the Channel. The Crimson Flowered bean is an eyecatcher in the garden. Lovers of broads plant a succession, starting with Aquadulce, which is able to overwinter.

Broad beans are amongst the first of the summer veg, in season from May until July. It is possible to eat the whole pod when young, along with the tops of mature plants, but customary to wait until the seed is just firm and tender to the touch. If the pods are going brown and swollen, and the beans within showing a black 'eye', they will be starchy. The youngest broads can be eaten raw with an oil and vinegar dressing. To cook, pick and boil within twenty-four hours in fresh water; salt makes them tough. Season after draining (reserving the water if you are making gravy) and eat a surplus cold. Remove the skins of the older beans if you can be bothered, boil up, drain and mash with butter.

Beans, French

A perennial in its wild state in Central and South America, cultivated for millennia and grown as an annual. It was introduced to England via Europe in the sixteenth century, acquiring the title 'French'. The originals were green climbers, tweaked by generations of breeding programmes to produce many different guises and sizes including dwarves, all with abundant foliage and cheerful flowers. The fleshier types of bean are grown for their edible pods, which can be oval, round or flat in shape, and purple, yellow or striped in colour: these are usually eaten fresh. The thinner-skinned varieties are sown for their edible seeds. These can be black, brown, pied or mottled, and either eaten fresh as 'flageolets' or dried as 'haricots'.

Beans are not fussy, but respond to being well treated. The climbers deliver more than the dwarves and over longer periods, but offer less choice and need a structure. Slugs attack the infant plants and deer eat the shoots and flowers; otherwise pests are few. Some gardeners do no more than stick them in the ground. The haricots, as well as being eaten, can be saved for seed.

Many types of bean are no longer commercially grown, but the choice of seeds remains good. The heritage climbers include Kew Blue (pre-1950), Mr Fearn's Purple Flowered (c.1900), Jack Edwards, Ryder's Top o' the Pole (pre-1970) and Veitch's Climbing. Mrs Fortune's, a well-connected bean, was named after an enthusiast in Bristol who acquired the seed in the 1960s from a retired head gardener at Windsor.

The dwarves include Black Valentine (1897), Early Warwick (1890), Magpie (1913), May Bean (pre-1800), and Scott's Bean (pre-1946). Brighstone (no 't') is named after the village in West Wight, notorious for shipwrecks, where seed is thought to have been landed or washed ashore, and used on allotments since the turn of the twentieth century.

In terms of flavour, a bean seems to be a bean, so go for the texture, size and appearance you like, remembering that the coloured pods (unless yellow) revert to green when cooked. I grow one climbing green bean to follow broads and peas; one dwarf usually of the refined 'Kenya' type; and one haricot for drying, which is left on the vine until the end of October, then shelled and stored in a jar.

Fresh beans are in season from July until the first frosts. If the whole bean is to be eaten, pick or buy before the seed swells and the jacket becomes loose. Boil hard in salted water for five minutes, no more (reserving the water), and serve hot with butter and crushed garlic (see page 348). Eat cold with a dressing or in salad too. Cook flageolets in unsalted water or they become tough.

Newly dried crops need only soaking for two hours and cooking for a further two, no more or they can start to ferment. The older the beans the longer they take. Haricots which have been stored for months require soaking overnight and cooking for up to a day (see page 57). After a year, they are too hard to cook at all.

Beans, runner

A perennial in its wild state in central America, grown as an annual and appreciated on three counts: for its habit, flowers, and flavour. This bean was introduced to London as an ornament in about 1600, taking over a century to make its way into the kitchen. The Victorians knew the plant as a scarlet runner, or kidney bean, owing to the shape of the seed (along with the rest of the tribe), and promoted it to a national favourite that gardeners grow in astonishing quantities. Nothing can be more English, and look it on an allotment, than a row of transatlantic runner beans. Plant-breeders have concentrated on length of pod, their tendency to curl, and fibrosity, eliminating the 'string', but have not made sweeping changes to the composition of runner beans. There remains one principal type – a green climber – to which a couple of dwarves have been added.

Runners are like French beans, responsive rather than fussy. The climbers require support, or work, but you can put up a wigwam in a confined space a few feet square. I have erected a three-dimensional arch for beans to run up, which, in late summer, becomes a leafy alleyway splashed with colour from the flowers and hung with pods. The soil in the trench is replaced every year. Runners, like French beans, are prey as infants to slugs and as adults to deer; otherwise they are reasonably pest-free. Once away, if you keep picking, they keep cropping. Seeds are saved like haricots or broads.

Heritage varieties include: Ivanhoe (pink seeds), Painted Lady (1855, red and white flowers) and Churchfield Black (grown for generations in the Black Country). There was a nasty rumour in 2001 that Scarlet Emperor (1906) was to be deleted from the national list. Again, be vigilant.

The flavour does not seem to vary much, but the exhibitors' uniform choice and stringless varieties may be suspect: watch out for them in the seed catalogues. I plant one variety, obtained from a neighbour who inherited seed from his father, also a lifelong gardener, over fifty years ago.

Runners are in season from July until September, following broad beans and peas into the spotlight. If large and swollen they are past their best. String if necessary, slice diagonally and boil hard in salted water for five minutes, no more (reserving the water). The leftovers heated in melted butter always taste better to me.

The customary English way of storing runners was to pack them in layers of salt. From the previous owner of our house, my wife and I inherited a jar, dated 1986. It is treated as an antique.

Beet, leaf

A biennial, and a maritime one, from the Mediterranean and beyond, which crops for about a year. Leaf beet is a member of the goosefoot family and has been popular for centuries. It was first cultivated by the Persians or Greeks, and spread with the Romans, establishing itself in England as an escapee (see page 416). Few edible plants are so little trouble. You can grow it in a confined space or herbaceous border. Cut and it will come again until flowering, if covered in cold weather. Pests are rarely tempted, except deer and rabbits. Use a net or join a gun club.

The seeds are little cluster bombs. The choice is adequate. Leaf beet is closest to its wild cousin, tough and useful. The plant is sometimes referred to as 'perpetual spinach' or 'sea kale' beet, both misnomers, since it is not perpetual nor an actual spinach, and no relation of sea kale – muddling indeed. Chard has fleshier leaves and whiter ribs and lacks the constitution of leaf beet. Ruby and rainbow chards are less hardy still, but their colourful stems are lots of fun.

The leaf beets are in season from July until winter in their first year and from spring until bolting in their second. They differ less in flavour than in appearance, squeaking when fresh and limp when stale. Wash well to get out any grit. The young leaves can be eaten raw. Wilt mature leaves in a steamer, and stir-fry in a little bacon, chicken or duck fat, or sprinkle with soy sauce. Alternatively, blanch, drain and stew in cream or butter, reducing any excess moisture to zero, making sure it does not burn. Season well.

BEET, ROOT

The Romans developed the swelling on leaf beet from which root beet and ultimately sugar beet and mangolds emerged. A humble trio compared to chards, but more valuable, useful and persistent, cropping up on land today where they ran to seed in the Second World War. Beetroot has never been as popular in England as in Europe, with exceptions – it is part of a genuine York ham tea. A neighbour of mine in Hampshire, who looks perfectly normal, grows enough beetroot to eat every day. Globes are customary, elongated forms for exhibition and amusement. The flesh, apart from red, can be white, golden or striped. 'A fantastic change,' says Geoffrey Grigson, 'from the wild species in the sand to the scarlet slices in vinegar.'

The seeds are again cluster bombs. The choice is not bad. Heritage varieties include Bull's Blood, Cheltenham Green Top (1905) and Dobies' Purple (c.1900). I do not aim for a crop in the summer, when there is plenty of other stuff about, but in the autumn, lifting roots of cricket-ball size for pickling.

Fresh beetroot is in season from July through November, and stores well in the cold. Remove only the top before cooking. Do not cut the tail or any other part unless you want the vegetable to bleed (i.e. for some recipes). Bake the larger beetroot: this concentrates their flavour. Commit to a slow oven for several hours, cool and peel. Boil the smaller ones, or else the volume shrinks to nothing. To pickle, put in a jar cooked and cold, and add a few peeled shallots or cloves of garlic. Cover with white wine vinegar and seal. Wait for 2–3 months before using. Beetroot leaves may be eaten like chard or spinach.

Brassicas in order of their development, leaf first

Kale: a large family of wild, domesticated and feral plants, annual or biennial, cultivated for thousands of years. Kale (i.e. colewort, the stem plant), a headless form, introduced to the British Isles by the Romans or Saxons (Rix and Phillips, 1993), is thought to be the common ancestor. It is the least fussy and troublesome of the brassicas, an early starter and late finisher, indifferent to many of the pests that do for the others. Kale may be sown direct into ground vacated by early crops. A secret weapon, albeit a humble one.

The coarser kales are fodder, the finer ones food, but not always easy to obtain. Nero de Toscana, an Italian variety, and Red Russian are increasingly popular in England. Asparagus kale and Pentland Brig, known as the 'Green Doctor' in Scotland, are not popular enough. Hungry Gap is a variety of kale nicknamed after the season in spring and early summer, which it is supposed to fill when food is short (it actually crops earlier). It is rather drab in colour when cooked, but a lot less bitter than alleged, and was in the shops until fifteen years ago. I grow two varieties.

Kale is a cut-and-come-again crop that produces leaves in summer, offers little over the winter and ends in a flourish with spears, coming into its own during February or March until May. Stir-fry the younger leaves, boil the older ones and shoots, and discard the oldest.

Cabbage: an improved form of kale, grown for its edible or ornamental head and even to make walking sticks. The stalky ones on the cliffs of the south and north-east coasts are considered escapees, from which I have taken seed. In countries like Germany and Poland the cabbage is of national importance; in England it is of mixed reputation, mostly evil. Beau Brummell claimed to have ended an engagement to a woman because 'she actually ate cabbage'. Yet he could have done worse and so could she.

Cabbages like a sunny spot and free-draining, firm, even stony alkaline soil. Think twice before trying to grow them, and be content with one good specimen in your lifetime. With breeding, the cabbage tribe has become weaker and moodier. Pests are legion, there is no getting away from it: flies, caterpillars, pigeons and worse. The dread club root, which stays in the ground for at least seven years, at most indefinitely, and has no known cure, is my reward for relocating the entire veg garden, building twenty raised beds and shifting over fifty barrowloads of soil and muck. To cap it all, there's that girl in Salisbury market flaunting organic January Kings, each of which costs less than half a pint and feeds four people. I can't stand it.

Summer cabbages are ball-headed, red or green. The winter ones are ball-headed, white or green, with crinkly foliage in the Savoys. Spring cabbages have immature leaves, entitled collards ('colewort') or greens, from which pointed hearts usually develop. Heritage varieties include Flower of Spring (1905), Jersey Wakefield (1860, summer crop), Christmas Drumhead (1903) and January King (1867). Summer cabbages are for addicts, and a failsafe in the event of other crops doing badly. I plant a winter cabbage (hoping pointlessly for the best), and one to overwinter, delivering in the spring. Durham Elf (RHS Award of Garden Merit) did not do badly.

Cabbages are available throughout most of the year, the new season's crop starting on or around Derby Day. The Savoys have the best flavour. A fresh cabbage squeaks and has a clean and moist cut stalk. Boil in a little salted water with the pan uncovered for about five minutes: boil too long and the house will smell. Drain the leaves well, pressing out as much moisture as possible and reserving the water for gravy. Young cabbage can be sliced and stir-fried. Dust with black pepper, paprika or soy sauce.

Cauliflower: a glorified cabbage, probably from Greece, imported into England via Italy in the sixteenth century, and thought by Kings Seeds of Essex to be 'the test of a real gardener'. The disadvantage of collies is that they need space and tend to come at once. The curds range from the usual white or cream in the hardy winter–spring cauliflowers to purple and lime green in some of the precocious summer–autumn varieties. The choice of seeds is good. I have planted two old favourites, Maystar and St George, and got better results than with other brassicas.

Cauliflower are in season from about March until November and store pretty well. The best collies I have eaten were cream-coloured, visually past their best and stacking up in my garden, the curds having sprung apart and acquired stalks prior to flowering – a condition that would make them a market reject. I divided the florets and cooked them like carrots 'Vichy', i.e. in barely enough water to cover, boiled away with a good lump of butter and a pinch of salt. The conventional route is to trim the head, leaving some of the foliage, steam it for about fifteen minutes and serve it whole to be cut like a cake. To make a real fuss of a colly, pour a *sauce hollandaise* over the top.

Broccoli: a broken-headed sprouting cabbage, developed in seventeenth-century Italy, which crossed the Channel in the eighteenth and is now considered well and truly English. The summer varieties are a quick-to-mature stocking-filler. The hardier ones can be picked and picked again over a longer period. They are distinguished by colour. The choice of seeds is adequate and includes a perennial entitled Nine Star with which I have not had much luck. I plant a purple-sprouting winter broccoli, which is tough and fairly resistant to pests like club root, to come in after carrots and cabbage. I have also tried white-sprouting, which seldom appears in the shops, and is of less interest to pigeons, but lacks the constitution.

Broccoli can be available for most of the year, the winter varieties from as early as Christmas almost until May, cropping at least twice. The first cuts from a plant are the meatiest. Summer broccoli is a favourite in the dread 'selections of vegetables' found in pubs. Purple-sprouting is better. White-sprouting is the best: boil in salted water for five minutes or so and eat on its own with melted butter.

I hear tell that some gardeners peel the stalks of the plants they pull up, and cook those too.

Brussels sprouts: first recorded in eighteenth-century Belgium and eaten in England within fifty years. With game and the Christmas turkey, sprouts are 'traditional': They are currently out of favour with the *beau monde,* and accused of being bitter. They are not half as bitter as some of the fashionable salad crops, and twice as welcome in cold weather. The pity is that the choicest varieties do not appear in retailers, large or small. If, therefore, you want to eat the best sprouts, you must grow them yourself. Do not worry about caterpillars – plants recover – and pick from the bottom of the stalk. There are two 'gourmet' varieties available in the UK, which stand well over long periods and which I have tried. One is green, entitled Beurre Noisette, the other red.

Sprouts are in season from September to March. The smallest, firmest buttons have the sweetest flavour, especially after a frost, and keep best on the stalk. Peel away discoloured and outer leaves, cut crosses in the bottom and boil in salted water in the usual way for 5–10 minutes or until they start to give. Save the water for gravy. Eat the tops in the autumn and spears in the spring.

Radishes: known to the ancient Egyptians but first mentioned in England in 1548. The original radish was black: the winter varieties still are, and of considerable size. Whites appeared in the late sixteenth century, followed by reds in the eighteenth, and ultimately other colours. The tendency in Europe (the very opposite to Asia) is generally to grow small, round or longish radishes and pick them young. Heritage varieties include French Breakfast (1885) and Icicle (1896). Many gardeners start right here – with a strip of soil, a packet of seeds and, a few weeks later, a miraculous home-grown crop of blushing, healthy and crunchy bite-sized radishes.

'The tender leaves are used as a salad in early spring,' said *Blackie's Modern Encyclopaedia* in 1896, 'the green pods are used as a pickle, and the succulent roots are much esteemed.'

Turnip and swede: a brassica with a swollen stem, related to oilseed rape. White-fleshed turnips (entitled 'white turnips' in Cornwall), which provide a summer crop, are for addicts. Swedish turnips, or swede (entitled 'turnips' in Cornwall, see page 62), are the product of an accidental cross with cabbage that arrived in England during the eighteenth century. They are purple without, yellow within, hardy and 'like a field', as the saying goes, meaning an open site, company and perhaps a bit of wind, as opposed to a garden. Swedes can thrive on red West Country soil, but do not grow well elsewhere, even in the Fens, which grow everything else. I buy them in.

Swedes are in season from November to February. They are treated with scant respect, but store well, improve stocks and, if you take trouble, come into their own with every sort of game. To do justice to a swede, peel, cut into four and slice thinly with half an onion and a clove of garlic. Barely cover in cold water, adding a large lump of butter, dripping or fat, a pinch of sugar, and salt and pepper to taste. Boil vigorously as you would for carrots, adding more water if necessary until the swede is soft and the water is sizzling and has all but disappeared. This can take between 15 minutes and an hour, depending on the age of the swede, which does not matter. Then turn down the heat to low and let the bottom of the pan caramelise. Mash, stir well with a wooden spoon and keep warm until needed, or gently reheat. If the flavour is lacklustre, add a bit of soy or vinegar.

CARROTS

A biennial which grows a root in its first year and an arresting flower, blushing at first and blossoming white, in its second. The carrot's relations includes the edible or medicinal angelica, fennel, glasswort, lovage, pignut and sweet cicely, the neutral hogweed, and poisonous hemlock. The chances are that the English wild carrot is a native, and the cultured plant arrived via Europe from the East. Yellow and purple varieties were eaten in the Middle Ages, but were more or less eclipsed by the orange ones imported from Holland (where else?) in the sixteenth or seventeenth century. They are now staging a comeback.

The carrots in Bahrain are grown in the desert, and irrigated by saline water piped up from underground through bore holes. They like the sand and salt, but struggle on heavy ground in England. There is also the notorious carrot fly. Unless you erect a two-foot barrier or hit the chemicals, this pathetic little nuisance – which cannot even do what it was built for, i.e. flying – will reduce every last root to a network of ugly black tunnels.

There are short, round and precocious varieties of carrot, intermediates ones, and long, tapering roots grown in bins of sterile compost by exhibitors. The choice of seed is average. Heritage varieties include James Scarlet (1870), Oxheart (1884) for the intermediates, and Red Surrey (1834). John's Purple, yellow under the skin, was named after John Purves of Oxford, who lost his allotment to developers but saved the seed. I plant main-crop carrots to follow summer veg. They keep in the ground until it freezes, and in the cold for a couple of weeks. I have not had much luck storing them in clamps, sawdust, wood ash or any other time-honoured way.

Freshly pulled carrots are in season from July until the winter. The rounder or stumpier the shape, the sweeter the flavour seems to be. Use before they go soft, which happens quickly when they have been washed and bagged in plastic. The best way to serve carrots is in a beef or mutton stew, where they exchange flavours with the gravy.

To cook carrots 'Vichy' style: top, tail, peel and slice. Barely cover with cold water and boil it away with a pinch of sugar, a little salt and a knob of butter. When the carrots are sizzling, they are ready to eat: be careful not to burn them. To vary, you may use stock instead of water, and give the carrots a final dressing of black pepper, chopped parsley, or a squeeze of lemon juice. You may also, instead of butter, cook the carrots and add cream, reducing it a little before serving.

Celery

A biennial, an umbellifer and English native, growing freely in maritime ditches and marshes, also known as 'water parsnip' or 'smallage', whose broadish leaf and strong taste I have yet to register. Alexanders, a relation that likes drier soils, introduced by the Romans and considered an improvement, is now itself relegated to the wild. Cultivated celery arrived from Italy via France in the seventeenth century, persisted in the eighteenth, and emerged in the nineteenth as one of the most important crops for the urban market, grown on the fertile plains near Manchester, Deeside and the Fens. I have a handsome pint-sized glass to present the stems in, shaped like a rummer, which had made its way to a sale at Monticello, Thomas Jefferson's former house in Virginia, USA, from Victorian England. A ten-dollar bid and it was mine to bring home.

Celery is not only green or yellow. The 'Solid Pink' variety dates back to 1894. There is also a red one, grown specially for soup. The strings and residual bitterness are diminished by 'blanching', which involves trenching and earthing up the crowns, as well as tying them in collars for exhibition: all hard work. 'Self-blanching' varieties have inevitably emerged, but lack winter hardiness and flavour.

Stem celery is in season from September to February, a long and useful stretch. It goes very well with English hard cheese, 'yellow farm butter . . . and water biscuits', says Sheila Hutchins, and until the 1960s it often did. Was it Betjeman who paused on a Sunday afternoon and heard the sound of the nation 'munching celery'?

To cook celery, braise until tender, not al dente – it does not work. Remove the top and feathers, reserving them for stock or soup. Trim any root (an advantage of lifting your own plants) leaving a cone. Put in a baking dish with a quarter-pint of stock, or water and some soy, and season to taste. Cover and commit to a medium oven for an hour. Reduce the liquor to 3 or 4 tbsp; either add cream, or crown the veg with butter. The heart of celery is the 'best bit'. Pheasant is the usual companion. The leaves and trimmings are good in a stew or soup. Pound surplus seeds and mix with fine salt for seasoning.

CELERIAC

A basal development of stem celery, inaccurately called the root. It reached England in the early eighteenth century, but never became as popular as it did in Europe. The larger modern varieties are an improvement on the older ones, and easier to grow than celery, but difficult for the amateur gardener to perfect.

Celeriac is in season from September to February. It should be crisp and solid. The best way of cooking this vegetable is in a winter salad, French style – *à la remoulade*. Peel, cut into chunks and process in a mandoline. Blanch for two minutes in boiling salted water and drain. Add fresh mayonnaise while the celeriac is still warm and eat cold.

CUCUMBERS AND COMPANY

A big family of annuals and perennials, edible and inedible, sprawling and gripping, distributed naturally and artificially throughout the world. It includes melons, gourds, and loofahs for back-scratching. A great-aunt of mine, a dead ringer for a twisted and malevolent Bette Davis in *Whatever Happened to Baby Jane?*, kept a huge wooden bowl of stripy, shiny, warty and exotic Turks' Turbans and other specimens in her gruesome and Gothic horror of a house. Some species, leafless and strung out, grow in impossible conditions on impacted sand in the Sahara Desert. The larger ones are used as pots, which women, with the strength of an athlete and poise of a model, pick up without thinking and carry on their heads.

Lilly, a Chinese girl married to an Englishman near us, gave me some seeds. I planted several by a structure intended for beans. They grew and I tied them up. They grew more and I tied them up again. They grew to the top of the structure, along to the end, down and out from the sides, growing so hard and fast I was hacking them back like Captain Blood. By the end of the summer, a couple of dozen fruits or vegetables, I do not know which, ovoid in shape, weighing several pounds and protected from falling by my wife's tights, hung through the leaves from the bars of the structure. They did not taste of much, but went to our pigs rather than to waste – and what energy in a single seed.

Cucumbers: Originated in India, spreading westwards to the Mediterranean, and probably northwards through Europe with the Romans. After disappearing at least once, the chances seem to be that cucumbers reappeared for good in fifteenth-century England. A bloke in Somerset claimed to have produced 2,000 lb of fruit from a single seed a couple of years ago. I believe him. Crops may be grown outdoors and left to sprawl, or indoors, which needs more attention, but extends the season from June through September. Cucumbers can be bitter near the stalk. They are considered 'cold' to eat, meaning hard to digest, but the skins are thought to make them easier – unlikely as it seems. Perhaps we have forgotten something else. Sheila Hutchins knew an old Thames waterman who complained that his wife ate cucumbers like a beast, not fried in bacon fat 'like everyone else'.

Gherkins: A coarse variety of cucumber grown for preserving, which is almost a staple in Eastern Europe, a *cornichon* in France, and a 'wally' in fish and chip shops in England. So thick and fast do gherkins come, I wilted under the strain of trying to keep up with them. Great to have in the larder, though, and popular with chickens. Our neighbour Walter Lavis told me how to pickle gherkins Polish-style in jars,* with dill and by steam-sealing:

4½ lb (2kg) cucumbers, no more than 4 inches long; 1 clove garlic, 1 tsp black peppercorns, 2 bay leaves, 1 heaped tsp dill seeds, 1 tbsp salt, 2 tbsp sugar and 10fl oz (275ml) white wine vinegar per jar; 2½ pints (1.5l) water.

Wash, dry and pack the cucumbers into clean sterilized jars with the garlic, peppercorns, bay leaves and dill. Heat the vinegar and water, add the sugar and salt and boil until dissolved. Leave to cool. Pour over the cucumbers, making sure they are covered, and seal. Put the jars in a large pan with enough water to come up to the shoulders of each one. Bring the water up to the boil and simmer the jars for 45 minutes. Check that the tops are tight. If not, continue cooking until they are. If so, buckle down and store.

If you have difficulty opening the jar, heat it in water. Allow the cucumbers to cool before serving, keep in the fridge and eat within a few days.

Vegetable marrow: An American native that, having registered in England at least 150 years later than the squash (1651) and pumpkin (1685), left them standing in terms of popularity. This is surprising. The marrow does not taste any better, keep as well as some of the squashes or reach the size of the pumpkins. You can buy plants at sales and garden centres in the early summer. They need a yard in every direction, but not the customary dung heap, cause little trouble, and lurk naughtily under cover of the darkness created by the leaves. I would not bother eating the flowers: wait for the fruits. The flavour does not seem to vary much between varieties.

The season for marrow is from July until the first frosts. The flavour needs help. Top, tail, peel, pip, quarter and cut into slices half an inch thick. Dust with salt and leave to drain for an

---

* *Kilner has gone, a sign o' the times. You will have to use 'Le Parfait' from France.*

hour. Rinse and drain. Put some oil in a pan (a wok is best), add the marrow and fry on all sides, stirring well. Add a sliced onion, a clove of crushed garlic, and a couple of large tomatoes, flesh and juice only, a dash of vinegar and soy. Season to taste with black pepper; no more salt. Cook uncovered gently for an hour or until the marrow is tender. To vary, fry a little freshly chopped or powdered chilli with the marrow. The onion, garlic and even tomato can be omitted and a decent result still obtained.

Baby marrows: Known as courgettes. They are selected to give more fruits, and have more uses and flavour. There are some yellow ones. Pick or buy whilst firm to the touch, when the seeds are still small enough to eat. Salting is not essential. Top and tail but do not peel and pip. Cook like a marrow or cut into chunks and bake in a medium oven for 45 minutes.

Herbs aromatic

How they dart about! Dill, so popular in Sweden, is a native of southern Europe. Basil, an Italian standby, originates in India. The English used to grow many herbs like lovage and borage, an umbellifer and constituent of Pimms, which have fallen from fashion. Thyme grows wild on the downs in the south, sweet cicely in the north, and mint on the riverbanks with brooklime and cress. Tansy is one of the strongest plants in our garden, throwing up 'bachelor's buttons' in summer, and leaving stalks for kindling when winter comes along. Rosemary is said to like willful women, sage billows purple or green, marjoram sprawls, and chamomile makes a labour-intensive lawn: they are all perennials that can look after themselves in warm, well-drained conditions. There is also the artemesia family: tarragon; wormwood, a component of absinthe; and wispy, scented southernwood or 'lad's love', my favourite alive, but a sorry sight at the end of the year.

English gardeners and cooks favour parsley, a long-term resident, but one which needs propagation every year. One variety has a curled leaf, another has a flat one, a third has a root entitled Hamburgh parsley, which performs like a carrot out of doors and a herb in the kitchen. Spare a thought for chervil, and also chives, a spikey native, escapee and member of the onion family, which has a lilac flower and tolerates acid soils.

Horseradish

A brassica and possible Roman introduction, originating in eastern Europe but not recorded in England until the sixteenth century. The 'horse' implies coarse. The leaf is like a dock and can be an unwelcome sight, barging in on other vegetables. The root is difficult to get rid of, but constitutes the edible part of the plant and is a cash crop in Germany grown as an annual. Horseradish used to provide the edge in wholegrain mustards. It can be eye-wateringly hot when young, losing its punch when stale, and does not come good from any manky old plant in your garden. The sauce has accompanied beef since the 1840s, and goes with smoked fish. It is seldom freshly made, but is simply done and delicious with it. Top, tail, peel and finely grate a stick, then mix with a similar amount of cream. Simpson's in Cornhill in London did without the cream: good, plain cookery.

MUSTARD

A member of a worldwide family grown for its leaves, shoots, roots and seeds that includes cabbage, radishes and many of the oriental vegetables. It is possible that charlock or 'wild mustard', a Roman introduction turned invasive weed and 'vegetable rat', was the big player in England hundreds of years ago. The European white and black mustard plants (*Sinapis alba* and *nigra*), also introductions, emerged triumphant at some point between the sixteenth and nineteenth centuries. The white variety remains a constituent of the teatime favourite mustard and cress, or 'hot and cold', which is sold in punnets. 'Even flat-dwellers may grow this,' says E.R. Janes. All you need to do is line a tray with old sacking, felt or blotch, moisten and cover it with soil or compost, then sprinkle seed thickly on the top. You will get mustard in a week, and cress three days later (see page 376). So if you want the two together, stagger sowings. Common rape will do as well.

Is mustard and cress less common than it was, even becoming a little hard to get, or is it my imagination? Watch out. The French, who cannot get it at all, take home supplies from our local hardware shop when they come to Fordingbridge on twinning excursions.

The mustard eaten for centuries with meat, and mentioned by Shakespeare, was coarse in texture, dried with horseradish, and sold or stored in balls for reconstitution as a paste. A woman in eighteenth-century Durham, by grinding and sifting the seeds, goes down as the first person to arrive at the hot taste and smooth texture now regarded as characteristic. A London firm entitled Keen, as in 'keen as mustard' (Mason, 1999) took up the baton. Colman's of Norfolk came along in 1814 and bought them out, establishing a powder of world renown and opening a shop in the Royal Arcade, Norwich. Taylor's, founded by a Cornishman who came to rest in Newport Pagnell, Buckinghamshire, developed an extra-strong ready-made paste in amber stoneware jars, presented to 'Sailor Billy' in the 1830s, which kept as well on ship as it did on shore. Two in the eye for those who think that English food and light industrial standards mean tasteless.

Eliza Acton's *Modern Cookery*, published in 1855, continued to mention mustard in connection with Durham. So did Mrs Beeton, copying her almost word for word, though there seem to have been several producers, and a number of cooks making their own. Walsh reports a leading manufacturer in Newcastle on Tyne, in common with others, using tiny amounts of turmeric to heighten the colour by the 1870s. Then as now, the mixtures used were trade secrets. A combination of white mustard seeds and an Asian variety (*Brassica juncea*), brought to Europe in the 1950s (Vaughan and Geissler, 1997), provides the legendary flavour.

To make mustard from a powder, and avoid lumps, use a fork or whisk. To prolong its life, try mixing it with gin. To reconstitute mustard that has gone hard, cover with water for a few hours, drain and remix.

Parsnips

A biennial and umbellifer with an uncertain history, owing to its early confusion with carrots. The wild parsnip, an occupant of hedgerows with a broken yellow head and one of the last to flower, is probably native. The cultivated form with the swollen root, imported into England, was common by the sixteenth century – and eaten with sugar – rising to a position it lost in Europe.

Far be it from me to disagree with Dr Hessayon, but I do not find parsnips easy to grow, let alone well. The seeds take ages to germinate, often fail, and do not reproduce if more than a year old. The roots fork in all directions, sprout whiskers and get canker. Yet East Anglian farmers bung in the same seed as me, and lift perfect parsnips six to eight months later. Infuriating. Heritage varieties include Tender and True (1897) and the Student (1865). Dig as required over the winter, weather permitting.

Parsnips are in season from the end of October until March. Three or four long frosts concentrate their flavour. Take trouble with this French reject and humble vegetable, and it will rise to the occasion. Peel, and commit to cold water acidulated with vinegar or lemon juice to stop the flesh going brown. Cut in half lengthways and half again, removing the core of the older and larger roots. Reduce to chunks of more or less the same size. The secret is then to *steam* the parsnips for five to ten minutes. Remove when they are soft enough to pierce with a fork. Commit to a pie dish with plenty of cream, or gravy and butter, season and bake in a moderate oven for a couple of hours until brown on top. Alternatively, mash. Oven-roast parsnips, usually hard or burnt, are overrated.

Parsnips are legendary with salt cod (see page 265), and better with game than potatoes.

Peas

Another legume, originally Mediterranean, from a large and complex tribe that includes groundnuts, lentils and vetches. It is thought that wild peas came to England in the Bronze Age, field peas with the Romans and garden peas from France under the Tudors. Dried peas made coarse bread, a soup, and a pudding that combines with ham and a 'stotty' (see page 78) to make a popular Northumbrian sandwich. Fresh peas do not seem to have been eaten until the seventeenth or eighteenth century, and only then as a snack, before rising in popularity to occupy more space than any other vegetable in the UK. I have a photo of women hoeing peas in fields as far as the eye can see, dressed in long skirts, aprons and white headdresses, dated . . . 1950.

Sweet peas, in spite of being ornamental, take their place in kitchen gardens. The variety Matucana is attributed to a very Sicilian monk who introduced them to England at the end of the seventeenth century. Wiltshire Ripple is another favourite of ours. Dave Manston, a champion grower of sweet peas and everything else – a man to whom crop failure is unknown – lives only a few hundred yards from me. Sea peas are a bushy little creeper, found in the shingle on the East Anglian coast.

Culinary peas are divided into three groups. Common or garden peas are grown for their edible seed, round or wrinkled; mangetout for their edible pod; and sugar snap for both. However, mangetouts are emerging that go on to produce a seed big enough to eat, like a sugar snap, and may be referred to as 'sugar pods'. Muddling again. Read catalogues carefully.

Peas are less fussy and fragile than they look, but need a well-structured soil, space and support. Pests include a moth. Seed can dry on the vine. The plant leaves nitrogen behind. The number available has been diminished by the needs of mechanical harvesting and the patenting of seed, but the choice is still outstanding. Heritage varieties include Alderman (1891), Champion of England (Cambridge, 1843), Duke of Albany (Lancashire, pre-1885), Eat All (Suffolk, pre-1900, 'mangetout'), Early Onward (1908), Forty-First (Gloucestershire and Devonshire, pre-1900), Gradus (1890), Kent Blue (pre-1940s, 'mangetout'), Lancashire Lad (pre-1911), Little Marvel (1900), Pilot (1904), Purple Podded (pre-1911, edible pods and seeds), Time Out of Mind (Cambridgeshire, pre-1900), Veitch's Western Express (Devonshire, pre-1975, overwinters).

Prew's Special peas were allegedly collected from the tomb of King Tut. They came to the Heritage Seed Library via Lord Carnarvon and Lord Portman, whose gardener in the twenties, and the seeds' conservator, was a Mr Prew. The quality of his peas is described as 'reasonable'. Curse-free, one hopes.

Carlin(g)s are a light brown dried or 'parched' pea, known in the border counties of England since the sixteenth century. Both Geordie and Cumbrian folklore credit a shipload with relieving famines. 'Tid, mid, misery – carling, palm and pace* egg day' goes a commemorative rhyme, referring to the Sundays leading up to Easter – though Carling and Palm Sunday are one and the same and the fifth in Lent, not the fourth as suggested. On this

* 'Pace' from 'Pasch', meaning 'Easter' (OED).

and other occasions, bowls of the peas were eaten at home and in pubs. Carlins began to disappear with family grocers in the 1960s, but are still found in parts of the north, fortified with salt, vinegar or rum. They are served at the Aspatria rugby club dinner, and fed to pigeons.

There are purple-podded peas to catch the eye. Salmon-flowered peas grow in clusters at the top of the plant, making them easy to pick. Pea 'beans' climb a pole. The taller varieties crop for longer and you do not have to stoop to them, but require netting or hazel fans. The pretty asparagus pea does not need support. Farmers choose self-clingers. I plant the three main types in succession, ringing the changes between them.

The season begins with first earlies during May and ends with maincrop in the autumn. The wrinklies are preferred for flavour, but all peas must be cooked within an hour or even minutes of picking, or else their sugar turns to starch – a disadvantage of obtaining them fresh from any other source except the garden. Do not wash young peas (say Sutton and Sons in *The Art of Preparing Vegetables for the Table*) or disguise their taste with mint. Boil for a couple of minutes in water with a little salt and sugar, which is said to prevent the juices escaping (reserving the water for gravy). Peas have a special or seasonal relationship with spring lamb, sweetbreads, duckling, pigeon (see page 208) and farm butter. They may also be stewed in a little well-seasoned stock with a whole crisphead lettuce or two if you have a surplus.

PEPPERS

An annual or biennial related to the potato, which came from Central America – Bolivia, Brazil and Peru. The plant was distributed around the world by the Spanish and Portuguese, spreading in all directions, and changing the food cultures of the countries where it came to rest. The colour is usually red, or green, but can also be purple, orange or yellow. In culinary terms, there are two very different sorts.

Hot or chilli peppers, recorded in England in 1662 (*OED*), vary from mildly hot with a background sweetness to the scalding *habaneros*. The strength is measured in units called scovilles, ranging from zero to several hundred thousand. It will no doubt break the million barrier. Chillies are used as a spice. The shoulder of the pod is hotter than the tip, the seeds are hotter still, a test of manhood and a turn-on for some, though most of us look for the break even point where heat encounters sweetness and flavour. For me this means the *jalapeños*. Initiates look for a blemish or corking on the skin, which is regarded as a sign of quality and the very thing which has made this particular chilli a supermarket reject (Matt Simpson, *Chilli, Chili, Chile*).

There are at least two chilli festivals in the autumn, and over sixty varieties available from five categories. In a temperate climate, plants must be started early: they prefer a greenhouse, and crop from July or August through October. Do not handle a hot variety and blow your nose, wipe your eyes or do anything of an intimate nature with either yourself or anyone else without washing first – unless you want to inflict punishment.

Chillies are dried for processing, either in the sun or hydrators. I am obliged to have a go now that the best of the sauces on the market in England, an Egyptian harissa, is no longer available. The secret of its success lay in its confinement to the only three ingredients a good sauce needs: chillies complete with seeds, a neutral oil and salt.

Chilli powder, imprisoned in tins in England, appears in fiery red piles next to the yellow turmeric, the wads of *pan*, the shifting silks and rustling satins in brassy and technicoloured candlelit bazaars the far side of the world. I have been told by Asians to grind my own powder from dried chillies; alternatively to buy it from East Africa, the least capable of producers – and therefore the least likely to cut the product with industrial waste.

Sweet peppers, originally 'pimento'* (1697), are derived from the same species as chillies (capsicum, 1725). They come in a variety of shapes, from bells to bananas, to be cooked fresh as a vegetable and dried as a spice. I have grown a few, and eat them raw or in a stew with aubergine and tomato.

The spice, entitled paprika, was introduced to Hungary by the Turks around 1820, filtered upwards from peasant kitchens and registered in England in 1898 (*OED*). The best-known type is *edulsuss*, meaning 'noble sweet', an ingredient in goulash (see page 120–1). It is marketed under the name Kotanyi – the final two letters implying nobility – and has a flavour as sweet as it claims. Buyer beware, there is a *scharf* (sharp) paprika too.

POTATOES

A perennial in the wild, found in North and South American mountain ranges, but 'small, watery and tasteless' (*Blackie's Modern Encyclopaedia*) without cultivation. The potato comes from a family of mixed benefit to mankind that includes tomatoes, tobacco, henbane and deadly nightshade. It was considered a narcotic and a source of disease, before becoming as an ornament, fit for royal consumption, a staple, a hand-warmer and a packed lunch, which also made a rotgut called 'British Brandy'. The prior appearance of the sweet potato, no relation, added to the mixed messages delivered by history. These included a monument in Baden, Germany, crediting Sir Francis Drake with being the 'Introducer of Potato to Europe in the Year of Our Lord 1580', demolished by the Nazis in the Second World War.

---

* *A change of definition here. 'Pimento' now means allspice.*

A rising industrial population, and its proximity to Ireland, where the potato had done well in the seventeenth century, made the flat and fertile Ormskirk district of Lancashire the first part of England to grow the crop in large quantities. Development was slow elsewhere, but quicker than in France and ultimately sweeping. The temperate regions of Jersey, Pembrokeshire, Kent and Cornwall's Golden Mile worked on a 'new' potato, which could be shifted by rail and dug in places like Polperro on Good Friday – the first free day of the year in the rural calendar and the customary date for planting with parsley upcountry. The blight of the 1840s and 1870s, the boom years of 1903, 1904 and 1905, and the potato shortage of 1917, whatever their social and economic consequences, all had a favourable effect on the development of this cherished, respected and necessary vegetable.

Potatoes are a culture within agriculture, horticulture and gastronomy into which you may dip a toe, immerse your whole self or stop at any level en route. I am in it up to the neck, sinking fast, and as the end of January approaches can hardly contain my excitement at the prospect of our local potato day – which offers over four hundred varieties of seed. The event is attended by experts and enthusiasts from all over, including a King and Queen of Spuds and Taffy the Tatty up from Monmouthshire, who buys for the whole allotment and unwisely gave me the chance to invade his space (he never recovered either).

There is more than one reason to grow your own potatoes. The crops that are available in supermarkets receive a greater quantity of biocides than any other vegetable. They are often described as 'reds' or 'whites' and confined to no more than half a dozen types better known for bulking up than anything else. Maris Peer, an English variety, if you regard the label closely, is grown abroad. M. Bard is imported as well. Ready-cooked potatoes come in the form of rösti, mash and so on. These are sold at a price for two portions that would buy enough seed to produce a sack, and keep a house going for several months.

According to Robert Hart, no slouch himself, a gardener in Sussex raised potato mountains several feet high from a mixture of seaweed, straw, compost and soil, accommodated in a pit one foot deep and sixteen feet square, which he dug every year. From these he claimed to produce half a ton of tubers from a single seed. His name was Tom Cooke, his nickname 'The Ace of Spuds'.

'Potato-growing reflects life. It is the product of a number of compromises,' says another buff, the enlightened Alan Romans (all you need to know, really). 'Purchasing reasonably high-grade seed, tools and fertiliser, organising a three- or four-year garden rotation, and making some physical effort will result in a worthwhile crop.' Selecting the different varieties is addictive, and planting child's play. Then there is the pleasure of plunging a fork into the soil on a summer evening (usually through the middle of your champion tuber), holding the tops, and unearthing the potatoes from their nest underground. It's like collecting eggs; it never seems to pall.

There are potatoes to suit every taste and most conditions in England, waiting to be slotted into place. Trial and error is the best way. Potatoes like a light loam, plenty of sun, and muck or compost. Pests are many, but so is the number of varieties with increased resistance. Cover with fleece to beat the late frosts. For an extra-early crop, bury a potato in a black plastic bucket of soil and leave it in the greenhouse. And it's true, slugs will take one potato and leave another.

Potatoes are round, oval, kidney-shaped, irregular or knobbly and vary considerably in size. The skins and flesh can be white, cream or coloured, including blue, purple and red. Over the years there have been losses to commercial requirements and disease, with strains growing weaker. The UK has come out of the twentieth century with fewer varieties of potato than some countries and more than others, thanks to new names appearing every season and old ones born again. Conservators and enthusiasts are doing a fine job, with Scotland in the forefront of breeding programmes and provision of seed, and England bringing forth two of the most loved and respected varieties. The International Kidney (bred in Berkshire in 1879) became the Jersey Royal. The enduring King Ted was renamed after the coronation of Edward VII, having begun life in Northumberland as Fellside Hero in 1902. We may also have saved the Pink Fir Apple (1850) from extinction, crossing it with Désirée to beget Anya (the name of my wife). Golden Wonder made the crisp, Ireland favours British Queen . . . and so on. I go to the beach, to bed and the bog, plus several other places, armed with potato catalogues and beguiling photos of the Ladies Christl and Felicia, Mimi and Belle de Fontenay. For the fair sex, there is Duke of York, Ulster Prince and Winston.

The age-old basket for carrying potatoes, made of ash by hand in Devon until about 1990, is called a maund. The man's measure takes 56lb, the woman's 48. I have acquired a pair, without the strange and wondrous powers of a potato wizard, but grow almost enough to last for most of the year (and haricot beans to fill the hungry gap). I plant an extra-first early, first early, second early, a maincrop and a latish salad potato, some of which are tried and tested and some experimental. For those with limited space, a new potato is the popular choice.

Potatoes are available throughout the year. They are stored when dry in the dark, which stops them going green and poisonous. The potatoes in supermarkets, like the carrots, if washed and imprisoned in plastic, do not keep. A lowish temperature helps to delay the late winter sprouting, which coincides with the end of their dormancy and loss of eating quality. The spring is a thin time for home growers and aficionados, when the old potatoes are finishing and new ones are imported or very expensive. Jersey Royals come into my local greengrocer during April. The crops from the mainland appear in May and June, followed by the second earlies in July. The rest are lifted in August and September.

COOK'S ORACLE

The character of a potato is not determined solely by variety. It can be affected by soil conditions, and the length of time it spends in and out of the ground. For most people, and the dishes they like, the consistency is the most important characteristic. Elizabeth David said that English potatoes were no good, and indeed they were not – for what she wanted. Waxy potatoes, yellow of flesh, were more to her taste, holding their shape when boiled, but gaining in texture what many think they lose in flavour compared to dry, mealy white potatoes, or 'melters'.

New potatoes are often allowed to 'set' for a day before use. The skin may be rubbed off with your finger when they are in good condition, and removed from freshly dug late scrapers and salad varieties with a blunt knife. On old potatoes, the skin constitutes a wrapper, tasting of the earth, that can have a considerable effect on the flavour. Waxy potatoes take longer to cook than mealy ones. It is essential to have a steamer.

Several million people have turned to Dr Hessayon for gardening tips: he is not bad 'in the kitchen' either. He singles out with his usual clarity half a dozen excellent ways of addressing the potato, which 'can all be found in a good cookery book'. Here is my choice:

Pan haggerty: adapted from *English Recipes and Others* by Sheila Hutchins).
For 4: peel and finely slice 1lb (450g) potatoes, using a grater or Magimix, patting them dry with a cloth, and half the quantity of onions. Heat 1oz (25g) butter in a frying pan and put in a layer of potatoes, then a layer of onions, then about 4oz (110g) grated cheese. Add salt and pepper and cover with a lid. Let the contents fry very gently for about 40 minutes, until the onions and potato are nearly cooked, then brown the top under the grill. Serve straight from the pan. This was a Northumberland recipe but needs a melting cheese. Use Lancashire or white Cheshire.

Potato cake: serves 6. Any old potato will do. Take 3lb (1.3kg), peeled and finely sliced, using a grater or Magimix, and some rendered goose, duck or chicken fat. Place an 8-inch cast-iron frying pan on a moderate heat. Cover the bottom with fat and distribute a little around the sides. Starting in the middle, arrange the slices of potato neatly in circles on the surface of the pan so they overlap. Do not leave any spaces. Build up the layers, frying the potatoes gently, meanwhile. Finish off with two tablespoons of fat, cover with greaseproof paper and bake in a preheated oven for one to one and a half hours at 180°C/350°F/gas mark 4. Cut round the edges of the potato, shake it loose and drain off excess fat. Turn out carefully on to a large heated plate, dust with salt and keep warm until required. Slice like a cake. *Pommes Anna*, the French equivalent, contains clarified butter rather than fat.

Gratin: a dish that can sit around when cooked, keeping warm until needed, which improves with age and never fails to please. Butter a fireproof dish and rub with garlic. Peel and finely slice enough old potatoes, using a grater or Magimix, to fill up to three-quarters of the vessel. Distribute the slices neatly in layers. Season each one with salt and white pepper and cover with milk. When finished, dot with butter, put greaseproof paper on top and bake in a preheated oven for two hours at 170°C/325°F/gas mark 3, uncovering the dish for the last 40 minutes. Sliced onion may be put between the layers of potato.

Another quicker and easier gratin, using waxy potatoes: peel and slice, but not so thinly. Put into a pan and cover with a mixture of milk and cream. Season with salt and white pepper. Heat for 5 minutes, stirring gently so that the potatoes do not stick. Transfer to a buttered dish, rubbed with garlic, and cook as above – uncovered but not for more than an hour.

Rösti: *'Mit bratwurst mit ei!'* – battle cry of skiers and a favourite in the German-speaking region of Switzerland, where it is sometimes confined in rings. I have seen a similar dish in markets in Tsingdao, a former colonial town on the east coast of China with a schloss and brewery, where potatoes remain a staple food.

Use waxy potatoes. Parboil in the morning, draining while still firm, and leave in the cool until the evening. Put some oil or fat in a pan, and add the potato coarsely grated. Cook gently, browning the bottom, and turn over. Dust with salt before serving.

To vary: pieces of cooked bacon, onion or leek may be added to the potato before it is fried.

Game chips: peel a medium-size potato and shred in a mandoline. Wash and dry in a salad spinner. Deep fry until just golden, shaking the basket to stop them sticking together. Drain, then fry again until golden brown.

Mashed potato: one of the things that epitomizes English cookery – heaven done well, otherwise hell. In spite of all the culinary gossip, the message does not seem to have got through that mash must be free from lumps at any price, smooth and rich, and that takes effort. Floury old potatoes are essential. Peel and cut into chunks of more or less the same size. Steaming is better than boiling the potatoes, particularly if they are extra floury (like Sharpes Express or Catriona). When tender enough to pierce with a knife, drain. Return to the saucepan and mash as if your life depended on it. Gather the potato to the side of the pan and cover the bottom with milk. Season to taste with salt and white pepper. Heat the milk until it froths and stir into the potato with a wooden spoon. Beat the mixture – again, for your life. Pause for a breather, add twice as much butter as you planned, and resume operations. The chances are, unless you are exhausted, you will end up with the charmless and utilitarian sort of mash you find in pie shops or at school. To serve, make a well in the centre of the potato – or even each helping – and put a knob of butter in it. A couple of spring onions may be boiled up in the milk and incorporated into the potato.

Potato pancakes: makes 4–6. If you have a small quantity of mash left over, proceed as follows: for every 6oz (175g) of potato, add 2oz (50g) flour, 1 egg and 5 tbsp milk. Mix well and season to taste. Heat some oil or lard in a frying pan until smoking, turn down the heat and add a coffee cup of the mixture. Give the pancake a minute or two to brown. When it starts looking solid, flip over and do the other side. Flip back if necessary, remove to a plate, fold in half and keep warm while engaged with the others.

Steamed or boiled: to keep them warm when cooked, cover with a cloth or newspaper, as in Ireland. A lid makes them soggy.

Saffron

Imagine the fields of two or three acres enclosed by dead hedges cut from hazel coppice; the gentle contours of well tended land; the orderly strips of pale purple flowers inches apart in beds up to ten feet wide; the women, in headdresses perhaps, stooping to lift the crop on damp and dewy September mornings; the ladies, no less, and wives of the 'crokers', carried to church in the finest of silks; the busy autumnal markets, and the prosperous half-timbered Essex wool town of Chipping renamed Saffron Walden, whose arms, tithes and gifts to the monarch were calculated in a rarefied spice (Hirsch and Evans). It was in such a spot that the Lord High Chancellor of England chose to build a house great enough for himself, but as James I remarked, rather grand for a king.

Saffron comes from the *crocus sativus*, not *colchicum autumnale* or 'naked lady', the semi leafless type. The three or four tiny, thread-like stems in the lilac flower are grown for their yellow dye, pungent flavour, and the elusive scent which reminds my wife of summer holidays, saffron buns and the former bakery in Polperro. Tens of thousands of these stigmas are needed to make one pound of dried filaments – 'hay' – or powder. The plant, indigenous to the Near East, has been cultivated since the dawn of civilization. It spread to India with the Persians and to Europe with the ancients, the Moors, Crusaders and itinerants, waxing in East Anglia from the reign of Edward III (1327–77) and waning with competition from other spices and commercial dyes in the eighteenth century. By André Simon's day, saffron was well and truly a 'fallen monarch of the English kitchen'.

Saffron is propagated through its bulbs or corms, which are dug up every year and resown. It likes a gentle south-facing slope and the sort of light, fertile soils, which are found between

Walden and Cambridge. Crops were grown in the villages of Littlebury, Duxford, Whittlesford, Ickleton, Hinxton, Cherry Hinton, and Fulbourn, and in college and monastic gardens, but modestly elsewhere. Given the prosperity that saffron brought to his locality, William Harrison could not understand why other parts of England were not inclined to grow it. The Vale of the White Horse was amongst the areas which he considered suitable.

Another conundrum is how one of the poorest and remotest regions in the country became the largest and most persistent consumer of the dearest spice: perhaps the dealers sold it on. Legend has it that saffron came earlier to Cornwall, where it was exchanged for tin by maritime traders, possibly Phoenician, and stayed later than in other parts of England. Production was sparse, but may have continued on a small scale in Penryn and Launcells, near Bude, until the turn of the twentieth century. A charming feature of Cornish life today is the sale of saffron in chemists, a custom established by apothecaries hundreds of years ago, who kept it as a cure for respiratory diseases (herbalist Nicholas Culpeper).

An Irish boy at my prep-school wore a saffron-coloured kilt. The Biharis use turmeric, a root present in meat and other curries, on their dhotis. The two shades of yellow are easily, frequently and deliberately confused by food producers. Several other dyes are employed to mimic saffron, and always have been, with heavier penalties the further back in history you go. The best way of telling whether or not you are being offered real saffron in a market is the price. If it ain't expensive, then it is cut with something else.

The biggest current producer of the *crocus sativus* is Spain, followed by Iran and Kashmir, with France, Italy, Greece and Morocco supplying small amounts. 'The saffron cultivated in Essex . . . was considered . . . the best in the world, albeit by Englishmen', says John Humphreys. 'I wonder if the industry will ever be re-established and . . . England could again become an exporter of the most highly esteemed spice in the world.' Some people are having a go at growing it. Corms are available from the museum in Saffron Walden.

In order to release its colour, flavour and scent, hay saffron must be infused in hot water or alcohol. Try a modest pinch at a time; bottle, cork and leave for a week.* Powder is over twice as strong. It does not need infusing, but is easier to adulterate and a less reliable purchase. I put saffron in cream sauces with top o' the range white fish and chicken.

SALAD, SUMMER

Lettuce: 'sal' in 'salad' refers to the salt, an age-old ingredient in dressings. Lettuce are a form of daisy, annual or biennial, widely distributed in Europe and the Mediterranean area and cultivated for thousands of years. They were spread by the Romans and reappeared in England

---

* *Says Colin Honey, baker of South Devon.*

in the sixteenth century. The Latin name for lettuce, *lactuca*, comes from the bitter and narcotic milk which is contained in the stalk, and did for Peter Rabbit.

We take lettuce for granted. They will tolerate some shade and can be fitted in around other crops, but are demanding in terms of labour, attract slugs and tend to mature all at once unless you stagger them or plant a cut-and-come-again. The tribe may be divided into two main groups. Cos lettuce are tall, upright and crisp. 'Cabbage' types are round or flattish, with various types of leaf – firm, soft (or butterhead), fussy and loose. The choice of seed is good and improving. Heritage varieties include All the Year Round (1831), and Bath cos. Little Gem is just that. The curiosities are Chinese stem lettuce and the red brigade – Little Leprechaun, Marvel of Four Seasons, Mikola, etc.

Outdoor lettuce are in season from about May until October, indoor ones for a month or two longer. Texture and looks are all-important, so it's cos type for me every time. The flavour ranges from zero in hydroponically grown lettuces to bitter. The Edwardians believed that washing impaired the subtlety – you are on your own here – making 'hotel and restaurant lettuces unfit to eat' (Sutton & Sons, 1888). If you have a surplus, try heating through the hearts in a little stock or gravy with a few freshly picked peas.

To beef up salads, look around the garden for bittercress, chickweed, hedge garlic, wild sorrel, etc. Opinions are divided as to whether an oil and vinegar dressing should contain sugar as well as salt and pepper.

Rocket is an annual and a native of southern Europe, which still manages to seem 'Italian' or even faintly exotic, yet appeared in England in the 1530s – several hundred years before marrow and Brussels sprouts. And rocket it does too. You sow the seed, watch it crop within about a month and see it bolt, all in a matter of weeks, having got flea beetle on the way. The taste is nutty, distinct and increasingly familiar in restaurants. Wild rocket, also available in seed form, has smaller, darker leaves and a flavour even more intense.

SALAD, WINTER

Not many English varieties take mild degrees of frost, but there is one that has been around for nearly two hundred years. Winter Density, a semi-cos, is a smasher that we have planted outside in the autumn and forgotten about until the spring. It is uncomplaining, strong, crisp, tasty, and up and away before the slugs get going. It helped to fill the hungry gap since 1800.

Lamb's lettuce is a native of northern Europe related to valerian, known as corn salad in America and *mâche* in France. The leaves are like those of forget-me-nots. The plant is naturalised in England, if not indigenous, crops up in the wild and may have been more popular in the past than it is today. Lamb's lettuce is slowish to grow, but excessively hardy for such a delicate-looking flower. A candidate for the window box too, says E. R. Janes. The mild flavour of lamb's lettuce and the stronger one of watercress are a well-established and pleasant combination.

Miner's lettuce or winter purslane is a native of the Californian coast. It acquired its title during the Gold Rush, keeping prospectors in reasonable health, and carries loads of vitamin C. The European species, spread by the Romans, is a maritime summer plant that grows wild in salt marshes near me. You find it bedded down in the occasional wreck. Purslane, a corruption of 'porcelain', has saucer-shaped shiny leaves to match. No trouble at all and quite nice to eat.

Chicory and endive are first cousins, related to the daisy, one a perennial that appears in the wild, the other an annual. They were known to the ancients, and in England in the sixteenth century, but never rose to the position they acquired in Europe. The confusion between the two may have something to do with it. The Italian *radicchio*, meaning chicory, is what it says. The Belgian *witloof*, i.e. 'white leaf', obtained by bleaching plants – which is not a difficult task but needs an outdoor shed or cellar – is chicory too. The flat, densely curled and lettuce-like varieties are endives. In England, that is. In France, the opposite applies. A problem for bureaucrats to solve.

Chicory has a strongish taste, even a slightly bitter one, reminiscent of dandelion, which appeals to lovers of Campari. The root has been dried and used to adulterate coffee, and suffered adulteration itself (Rix and Phillips, 1993). Endive is milder, and another useful winter crop, at home in a polytunnel and OK outside. Those who like the piquant flavour, says E.R. Janes, rarely eat lettuce if endive is available.

Oriental veg could have come in with azaleas and rhodies, but failed to tempt the English plant-collectors, gardeners and cooks of the nineteenth century. A hundred years later the mood had changed, owing to fashion, travel and people like Joy Larkcom, whose *Salad Garden* was published in 1984. The seed companies now have a respectable list of oriental vegetables for autumn planting, which are quick to grow, frost-hardy and a useful addition to the winter repertoire. Their disadvantage is that many are brassicas, and susceptible to club root, and must fit in with your rotation. You can have too much of certain flavours as well. I have grown Green in Snow, mibuna and mitsuna.

SALSIFY
A perennial related to the daisy, and a native of the Mediterranean, cultivated since the sixteenth century and mentioned in England in the seventeenth (Rix and Phillips, 1993). The wayside

flower 'goat's beard' is similar. The leaves are edible and grassy. The long, thin roots, off-white on the outside, offer more. The nickname 'vegetable oyster' is likelier to come from the colour within than the flavour, pleasant as it is. Salsify requires a deep, rich soil, and is slow to mature but reasonably pest-free. Heritage varieties include Mammoth (1899).

Salsify is one of those plants you come across in catalogues rather than in people's gardens (Hessayon, 1991) or on the plate. I remember it appearing on hotel menus in Cornwall in the 1960s, but time was running out. The dwindling popularity of this vegetable is probably due to its low productivity compared to other crops, and the small amount of trouble needed to cook it properly. Makes a change, though.

Salsify is in season over the winter from about October. Wash, top, tail and cut into three- or four-inch pieces. The flavour and whiteness of the flesh is preserved by boiling roots for 10–15 minutes until tender, then peeling off the skin. Drain as usual. Then season to taste and serve with melted butter, a dressing of soy, freshly chopped parsley or chives.

Scorzonera, or black salsify, a native of southern Europe, is lumped together with the above, but is broader of leaf, darker of skin, and was sooner to arrive in England by about a hundred years. It is credited with beating many afflictions, including snake bites – hence the nickname 'viper's grass' – and deterring carrot fly. Scorzonera was widely grown and appreciated in Victorian kitchen gardens, then almost disappeared, clinging on as seed but seldom appearing in the flesh. I have bought it once, from a woman in north Devon. Constance Spry, a champion, liked it more than salsify. Cook the same way.

SPINACH

An annual from Asia, said to have been domesticated by the Persians. It spread eastwards to Japan, westwards to Europe, and to England in the sixteenth century, possibly via the Dutch (Simon, 1939–46). New Zealand spinach, a sprawling plant that returned with Captain Cook, never became so popular. There are two main types of this vegetable. The summer crop is a makeweight. The winter one has a superior flavour and a fleshier texture. Modern breeding programmes have reduced the bitterness.

Spinach of one sort or another can be eaten almost throughout the year, a penance to some, reassuring to others. Wash well. Young summer crops can be eaten raw in salads. Otherwise, cook like chard, remembering that the legendary iron content dissolves in water (Rix and Phillips, 1993). So in health terms, stewing is better than wilting.

TOMATOES

A half-hardy annual or short-lived perennial originating in southern and central America, brought to Europe by the Spanish in the sixteenth century. The tomato acquired the name of *pomme d'amour* in France and a reputation for being an aphrodisiac or worse. It was slow to start in Europe, but gathered an incredible momentum from about 1800. Once established, it became a favourite in Victorian England – grown in London's peripheral market gardens – a mainstay of Italian cookery and a performer worldwide. The largest quantity of tomatoes I have ever seen under cultivation was on floating turfs (negotiated by boatmen who 'punted' with one leg) on Burma's Lake Inle.

Tomatoes can be striped, yellow, pink, or blackish as well as red. The skins are usually transparent, revealing the flesh within. The body can be heart-, pear-, plum- or gourd-shaped, or squat, as well as round. Plants are usually 'indeterminate' or cordon and grow vertically up a stake, or 'determinate' bushes and sprawl. The size of tomatoes ranges from that of a cherry to that of a cricket ball. It is related to flavour and the capacity to ripen in the English climate. The smaller the tomatoes, the more intense they taste and more likely they are to thrive out of doors, particularly against a wall, but do not plant near potatoes or the two crops will exchange blight. Plum tomatoes, which are low in water and used to make paste, can have good flavours too. In common with other medium-weight fruits, some varieties are happy out of doors, while others are not. Check up when buying seeds or plants. The larger, milder types of tomatoes need a hothouse.

It is hard to understand why people, even those addicted to indifferent flavours, put up with the tomatoes in the supermarkets. The choice is feeble and the condition is unripe. The quality is outstandingly low compared to the fifty to eighty heritage and other varieties available from specialist suppliers, and the heady scents and flavours they can deliver. Old favourites include Brandywine from the nineteenth century, Essex Wonder and Harbinger (1910). Tomato days are taking off. I grow up to six types both to eat and cook, trying at least two new ones every year.

English hothouse tomatoes can appear as early as March and last until November. Outdoor ones are in season from July. The riper the condition, but still firm, the better. The aroma tells all. I suspect, though it could be fancy, that the tomatoes with green-girdled pips have that 'old-fashioned flavour' people recall (or imagine) that intensifies to an exquisite sweet-sour degree.

Baked tomatoes are heaven: cut fruits in half and give them 40 minutes in a greased pan in a preheated oven at 180°C/350°F/gas mark 4. You may put fresh white breadcrumbs on the top, mixed with melted butter, freshly chopped parsley and shallots, or crushed garlic. Season well.

Dried tomatoes are the rage. They can be done in the slowest of cool ovens, cut in half, but take up to a day. Hydrators claim to get better results.

WATERCRESS

The Hichens clan left north for south Wiltshire the century before last. Five generations later they are still in business growing watercress, laid out in the beds in front of their houses like carpets on show. Keith is in charge. Two men were cutting; Jeff was one, clad in gumboots and black and blue checked top. He was bending over and moving forward with quick, even and economic strokes of a Sheffield steel knife: the latest in use after forty-six years in hot sun, gentle breezes and bitter winds. Billions of bunches, crisp as wafers and taken by hand at less than knee height. Millions of boxes filled by packers in the company shed. Thousands of journeys to local kitchens and markets upcountry.

In April the cress begins to flower and the concrete beds are cleared. Seed is taken for propagation. The infants, bursting forth and soaking up the clean spring water, go out in orderly rectangular clumps. They look lonely as stepping stones at first, then colonize the space around them, join forces and, spreading thickly, revert to the lush green carpet that covers the valley as before. The new season's crop is what the supermarkets want for summer salads. The rest of us wait for the months to pass, the colder weather to kick in and the cress to thicken and leaf up. You look forward to the growth, maintained over the winter by the constant temperature of the feeder streams, and leave it behind with the snowdrops in the spring.

Watercress is an annual and a native from the same huge family as cabbage that grows in Geoffrey Grigson's 'viridian tufts and pillows' in southern England. It has been eaten for hundreds of years, possibly millennia, and farmed for the urban poor since the early nineteenth century. The estimated three thousand acres once under cultivation, local and communal, and connected by Hampshire's watercress line to London, is down to about 5 per cent of what it was. The odd concrete bed remains, which is no longer used.

There are several types of watercress, green all over or brown at the edges. Most if not all of the cash crop in England and France today is of American origin, but descended from plants taken by the British to the far side of the world, New Zealand included. The commercial beds, being spring-fed, do not get liver fluke from sheep upstream. They are tested for pollution, and invariably pass, and are covered or rested in long frosts and snow.

Watercress is blessed with a crunchy texture, and a fresh peppery taste that feels as if it is doing you good. It is a mainstay of many English kitchens, but underrated by the *beau monde* owing to a working-class cachet, its ticket as a garnish, and more fashionable salad crops. Aficionados say that, of all the cheeses, Red Leicester is the one to accompany watercress: and a handsome couple they make too, contrasting in colour and from different parts of the country.

Dorothy Hartley kept her watercress in a vase in the larder, like a bunch of flowers, not in the refrigerator. She maintained that the flavour only came through when the leaves had turned yellow a day or two after cutting. Opinions vary. The word in Wiltshire is that a bunch picked in the morning will do for lunch, and another picked in the afternoon for tea or supper. The wise guys, having dropped their money down a drainpipe and into the Hichens' honesty box, pop round the corner to Robert Fry and pick up a steak. A journey worth making.

THE EXTENDED FAMILY OF CRESSES

Common or garden cress (*Lepidium sativum*), a native of the Mediterranean cultivated for centuries (Larkcom), and known to the Italians as 'English', is the one used with mustard (see page 360) to fill punnets and make egg sandwiches.

Winter cress (*Barbarea vulgaris*), very tough, was cultivated in England until the end of the eighteenth century (Rix and Phillips, 1993), and grows in the wild. Land cress, the North American species, appears in seed catalogues.

Fool's watercress (*Apium nudiflorum*) grows in the wild. It is 'brooklime' to some people, but so is one of the speedwells (*Veronica beccabunga*). Confusing.

Indian cress arrived from Peru in the seventeenth century. There are two types, referred to as 'nasturtiums' (*Tropaeolum majus* and *minus*), the botanic title of watercress, owing perhaps to the hotness of their leaves. This plant can draw blackfly from broad beans. The seeds have been used as a substitute for capers. The flowers are eaten in salads (see page 415). Colours vary. 'Black Velvet' is a smasher.

PS AKRAM AND BARRY

Akram was tall, and studious. Barry, his cousin, was more secular and talkative. They were two East African Asians who knew more about English vegetables, and grew them more abundantly, than any other people I have met. The walled garden, which they rented, was tucked away behind a nursing home near me. Akram and Barry saved their own seeds. They raised plants on moist and elevated trays of gravel. They heated the greenhouse with a cast iron boiler fed with the wood which lay round about. Their chickens ate grain and the waste from the garden, and drank the rain water collected from the roof.

Akram and Barry had pace as well as knowledge and application. I never saw them working at breakneck speed, but always found another crop in, or another batch of compost from their custom-made steamer ready for spreading on the stony soil. From every visit, I came away with plants, vegetables, eggs or a surplus cockerel to put in the pot at home. At length, they had to leave their secret garden. Thank heavens they never came to mine.

CHAPTER
TWENTY-EIGHT

Fruit and Nuts

THE LAND WAS THROWN IN with the house. Nearly two acres of tangled grass, impenetrable scrub, and reaching brambles, forty feet long and thick as a man's wrist, with a choked understorey and towering standards looming in the background. There were sixteen oaks, three or four beech, numerous ash, dying elms, infant yews, wild cherry, birch, hawthorn, hazel, holly and 'sally' (sallow) as they say in these parts, with a couple of top fruits hidden in the bush. Such was the emphasis on the house or 'property', however, and so remote the chance of planning permission, that the abandoned garden was not part of the calculations. 'The land is the land,' people used to say, clutching deeds, a masonic handshake of a remark hinting at sanctity, power and meaning, almost as weighty as C. S. Lewis's 'God is God'. You bought the land first and, if you did one thing, you sold it last or not at all. You clung to every inch, infirm as you might be, and useless as it might be to you. The previous owner, born in the house and carried out, had done just that. And now the land was worthless, barely measured let alone maintained or fenced: thrown in.

The house was a glorified cottage. The land, fantastic though it was, needed clearing to deliver food and fuel and reveal the succession of wild flowers fighting to break through. The fruit trees amounted to a parent plum and several seedlings, one standing greengage and one stricken, which I came upon by accident while selectively slashing, digging, pulling and burning to get it all into working shape. I was not in a hurry to expose them. I liked plums and gages, though not nearly as much as an English mulberry or cherry, an orange in Morocco or an Alphonso mango.

Came the second year. The plum, having been shy in the first, delivered. The fruit was medium-sized and longish, even pointed, with a smooth cleft and a taut, shiny purple or powdery light blue skin. I bit into it with neutral expectations, releasing the juice from pearly green flesh, and awoke. The flavour was like an alarm call, jarring, provoking, revealing, exciting, sweet and subacid, almost too intense to bear. My first, brief encounter with a two-year-old York ham, a flaky Cheddar, and Maris Otter malting barley had brought forth similar feelings. So that was how a plum should taste, and I had never known.

To rank highly in some countries, trees must be double- or triple-purpose. In England, the opposite applies. With very few exceptions, dessert fruit tends to occupy one compartment and culinary fruit another. I had known this since a boy, mistaking a quince for an apple. There did not appear to be any way that a plum so stirring to eat fresh would perform when cooked – but it did. Stewed or bottled in a blood-coloured bittersweet syrup, or made into a treacly damson-like jam, the result was the same. It was sad for the greengage, an ace in its own right, to be trumped by a glorious plum.

The trees were in a mess, or so it seemed. The temptation was to prune them. I asked neighbouring gardeners how to do it. No one seemed to know, so I went ahead, thinning branches here and there, but taking no more than a third of the wood. It was when the job was complete that I was told I should not have done it like that, or even done it at all. So, the course to take with trees is to leave them alone until the mist clears.

The next move was to get the fruits identified. I chose an institution run by worthy people and, as instructed, sent three unripe samples of the plum and another three of the greengage for committal to cold storage and examination at their leisure. A few weeks later I received a letter saying that my fruit had been too rotten to serve their purpose. I waited till the following year for the tree to crop again, picked three more samples – hard as bullets – and sent them off in bubble-wrap by Special Delivery. The same thing happened. I felt angry at first, then increasingly uneasy about the trees and their future.

A girl turned up at the door one day, having disturbed the peace overhead, selling aerial photographs of people's 'properties'. Mine was amongst them, including a snap of the house and its environs taken in about 1960. Since then, the vegetation had changed more than anything else, with parts that were covered now bare, and vice versa. It looked as if the plum and greengage had already been planted and got well away. That made them forty to fifty years old and coming to the end of their lives. I had been right to feel uneasy. There was no time to lose.

Opinions vary as to whether stone fruits breed true from seed. Unwilling to take the chance, I needed to get them grafted or budded privately and quickly. After two false starts, I found a man for the job up in Essex – Will Sibley. His authority was obvious, his tone reassuring, the procedure clear. I would look for fresh growth about one foot long, take some cuttings, and he would do the rest.

It was not a bountiful year: that can be the way, thanks to Nature, frosts in May and bullfinches after the buds. I set aside a weekend to pick and bottle the fruit and stood by for the anticipated gales. After two days of storms, the wind dropped to a breeze and calm descended overnight. From the bedroom window in the morning, it seemed that the woods had been spared. Then, going downstairs and walking out, I saw the plum, partly naked and sustaining a huge gash where the biggest of its limbs had been ripped from the trunk. Not far away, the greengage lay in a tangle of broken branches, splinters and twigs on a wet battlefield of autumn grass.

The plum will go too, before long. He is tall, too tall and top-heavy, all wood and leaf, bearing little and reaching for the sky in a final fight to live. I am on the case, but with no trees like him in the vicinity and books unable to help, I still do not know the name. I came to the 'property' looking for a bacon loft, a bread oven and original lime plaster, and got them – with the plum, a greengage and the rest thrown in. The fruit may be found elsewhere in England, rare or even unique, a casualty and cultivar that came within a whisker of extinction.

The trees were symbolic, one standing but mortally wounded, the other uprooted – like so many living and life-giving orchards torn from the earth by the hand of man in the last fifty years. To people like my late father-in-law, whose mother had been in service in London, Kent meant the summer, the boxes, the fruit and the nuts called by the cockney shouters. Somerset and Devon meant the rash of blossom from the Cornish Riviera. Pershore meant the smell of plums cooking in the factories. Southwell meant an apple, along with a cathedral. Barnack meant an 'orange', Wye meant a cherry and Taynton meant a pear. Many thousands of places in England bear the names of cultivars born, raised and cared for in some cases since women made lace and men carried swords.

Most people in England only ate wild fruit until two or three hundred years ago. Cultivation was slow to start or possibly restart after the monasteries went. John Tradescant, father (1570–1638) and son (1608–62), serial plantsmen, travellers and importers originally of Suffolk stock, who laid out the grounds at Hatfield and other noted houses, are held responsible for getting English gardening going. They made shiploads of introductions, kept a nursery in Lambeth (later developed) and left an incomplete catalogue, dated 1634. But for a confidence trick, the Ashmolean Museum in Oxford, where the document is housed, might be called the Tradescantean.

Fruit cultivation took off in the nineteenth century, thanks to go-ahead breeding programs, the demand for food, and purchase of trees for country estates, cottage gardens and suburban plots. The number of cultivars rose from tens to almost ten thousand. Nurseries remain, with up-to-date selections and out-of-date courtesy and charm. There are some unusual orchards too. After-hours on a summer evening I happened on one in Norfolk with over thirty varieties of early, mid and late September plums. Orchard owner Garry Maufe planted the trees on the clay they like in the 1970s. His daughter, Nina, who now runs the business as a 'pick your own', was destined to become a Mrs Plum (OK, Plumbe). She enjoys her title, but only modest profits from the historic fruit on offer.

Fruit-growing has not been part of the EC's plans for the UK. A lot of crops need hand-harvesting. Foreign competition is strong in terms of price. The supermarkets buy as cheaply as they can. England's conservation programme, which does not apply to food in general, applies to fruit least of all. A sycamore with 'amenity value' may have a tree preservation order slapped upon it – albeit one overcome by Tesco (as in Shaftesbury). An orchard grazed by pedigree cattle, regardless of its age and contents, may not. There should be no fruit industry by rights, but there is one, bravely hanging on.

I have twenty-four cuttings, new growth, new life, taken just in time. If I look after them, they will prosper. Twenty million viewers watched *The Darling Buds of May*, H. E. Bates' nostalgic fantasy set in post-war Kent. They only have to buy the fruit and nuts to secure the real thing.

STONE AND OTHER FRUITS

Sloe: a large and complex tribe. Sloes are wild plums, indigenous to England and domesticated in Asia, producing a succession of cultivars that infiltrated Europe thousands of years ago. The blackthorn, which bears the sloes, is a mixture of good and evil with a poisonous spike: hedge-layers beware. The flower is the whitest and earliest of the lot, appearing before the leaf, but bad luck in the house and frequently coincides with a late cold spell that is known as the blackthorn winter. The fruits are small, round, blue-black, tart, and will make a jelly with crab apples if you are pressed, and a superior gin. Pick the sloes after a frost when their skins are shrivelled or broken. Then cover with Plymouth, Beefeater or any gin at least 40 per cent proof and leave for three months. The Victorians did not add any other ingredients. Contemporary recipes mix equal measures of sloes, ground almonds and sugar, then add the gin. Winemakers use the lees.

Bullace: are an early form of plum, domesticated in Asia, whose stones have been found on prehistoric sites in England. The trees, which are gangly, tough, and have been used as root stocks, persist as seedlings in the wild. The fruits are bigger than a sloe, round, black or green. I used to pick them on an old road near Salisbury Plain. So did the locals, whom I never saw or met, leaving me with nothing on two or three occasions. So, if you find a supply of bullace, mark it and keep mum. They are sour to eat and fiddly to cook, but can make one hell of a jam (see page 397).

Cultivated plums, European or Euroasiatic, came with the Romans or possibly before. They are larger than bullace, with the exception of the cherry plum or myrobalan, and more versatile. Tradescant noted forty varieties. How astonished he would be to find the twenty-first century market dominated by a gross and artificial American plum, and a single English one, which belong at the bottom of the range. From the dull and overrated Victoria, with only popularity on its side, there is usually no escape. The name is synonymous with plum.

Time was when you walked into Evesham and smelled the plums cooking on the breeze. The factories used the Purple Pershore, the gardeners grew it, and the stalls sold it along the road to Broadway with up to half a dozen other sorts. The Worcestershire climate is good for plums, Bedfordshire is better, and Hertfordshire better still in terms of the varieties they can offer. The West Country is disappointing, but has a couple of surprises. The Kea plum is one, a dark little chap for making jam, which I have in my larder. You can find him near Truro – if you are quick enough. The supply is finite and locals do not wait.

Greengages: a variety of plum that arrived in England via France in 1490 (Brogdale*), lost its label, and acquired its present title in the eighteenth century. Both skin and flesh are green with perhaps a delicate bloom, or yellowish. Half a dozen cultivars are available, a modest but sufficient number considering the 'exquisite' quality of the fruit (*Blackie's Modern Encyclopaedia*). Cambridgeshire is thought of as the 'home of English greengages' (Marshalls**). I am acquainted with the trees on Ray and Marion Mannings' farm, but not yet this variety of the fruit. The word is that it would be well worth the journey from Hampshire.

Damsons, or Damascene plums, arrived in England from Syria at more or less the same time as greengages. Their lineage and oval shape differ from the bullace, though the blue-black colour can be the same, and the two are often confused. Damsons are associated with the Lythe Valley in the foothills of the Lake District, which has a growers' association and a continuing tradition of sales at farm gates and markets. There is also an excellent damson gin I cannot stop drinking, made in a house I cannot take my eyes off (Cowmire Hall), and a beer on sale in local pubs that the Belgians would recognise. I flirted with a Godshill damson, a seedling from the Isle of Wight, then planted a Shropshire Prune – without the need to. The number of trees wasting their crop year after year is a crying shame. It says a lot for the intensity of the damson's flavour that it has survived when there are so many cooking plums to choose from. Make the jam and you may forget the others.

One of the more curious aspects of the English countryside is the use of plums as windbreaks and field margins, up to a quarter of a mile long: hundreds of trees that could provide tons of food, planted so as to economise on land that could be used for other crops. I have seen Warwickshire Droopers in Kent, greengages in Cambridgeshire and damsons in Wiltshire all serving as edible hedges. My father, at the other end of the scale, had a single plum that delivered more than three hundred pounds of golden fruit one year. Many people know they have a local apple even if they do not know what it is: they also have local plums. There are hundreds of heritage, self-fertile and other varieties, which need little looking after unless fan-trained. A healthy proportion appear in nursery lists and may be sampled at tastings. Good for the gout, they say, too.

There is at least one plum day. The season can start in July. The later varieties hang on until October. When processing fruit, you must act quickly – and beat the wasps to it. The French

---

* *Houses the national fruit collection, near Faversham, Kent.*

** *Seedsmen.*

have their *mirabelles* and *prunes d'Agen*. So, what have the English to compare? My plum, of course, whatever it is, and a *pièce de résistance* of our own . . . Derek Wadsworth, a horticultural heavyweight and former head gardener at Longford Castle, told me his late employer liked to eat plums. The fruit, picked before it ripened, was attached by its stalk to a cotton thread and hung in the cellar to dry. The plum was ready when shrivelled to the stone, and kept until the following season, improving all the time. More than one daily, after lunch, was too much of a good thing.

Cherries: *Prunus avium* is another English native found growing in the wild. The tree is too large to net, the fruit too small for modern tastes to eat, and hardly worth guarding – but that may be the point. Mine is probably a diversion or 'trap', planted by a wise old codger, and intended to distract predators from the crops of fruit and vegetables in the adjacent garden. The blossom will pollinate other cherries, and the wood is much liked by cabinet-makers and turners. A tree with more to it than it seems.

The cultivated form of the wild cherry is one of the few selections in England or Europe not of Asian origin. The fruit has been eaten since prehistoric times. It is known in the West Country as a mazzard, after an Anglo-Saxon bowl or maser, rather than its other Frenchified title, gean (*guigne*). The trees, pyramidal in shape, can reach sixty feet and thrive in damper conditions than most. They are more or less confined to north Devon and the Tamar Valley, which received in the glory days two waves of water-borne trippers, one to see the blossom and the other to buy the fruit.

The parish of Landkey in north Devon, which drew people from Barnstaple, and to a lesser extent Swimbridge and Goodleigh, was famous for its mazzards. The trees occupied hedges, closes, garden and greens, rather than orchards, though they could partner apples and cover up to four acres of ground. Bird scarers of various sorts were employed, from men with pop-guns to cats borne aloft in cages. By the nineteenth century an estimated 300 tons of fruit was obtained in a good year from a total of 100 acres in the area, bought as a 'future' and auctioned off, sold in the local pannier markets, and taken to Chulmleigh Fair, Ilfracombe, Crediton and the London train. One of the local vicars noted that during hymn singing in the mazzard season all his congregation had scarlet mouths.

The decline of the mazzard industry is attributed to predation by bullfinches, thrushes, blackbirds and squirrels; lack of skilled pickers and distributors; poor weather; and the demand for milk, causing farmers to grub up trees and turn the land over to cow pasture. By the end of the twentieth century there were more people in north Devon who had not eaten mazzards than those who remembered the taste, the juice, the pies and cream, and the colour of the dye made from surplus cherries.

Dick Joy, born in the parish of Landkey and a councillor for years, was determined not to let mazzards go. He got a local nurseryman to graft a few trees, which are now sold by Thornhayes of Cullompton. Thanks to private and public funding, donations of land, and the involvement of organisations like Common Ground, sixty-five mazzards were planted on an open south-facing slope in the village that opened in July 2000 as the Millennium Green. All are doing well and should be fully grown in twenty years. Meanwhile, Michael Gee's charming little booklet on mazzards and their history has sold out. The conundrum is how the fruit can be obtained now that wildlife or predators, is so 'cherished'.

There are five known varieties of mazzards: Bottlers, Duns, Hannafords and Large and Small Blacks, plus a few synonyms. Perhaps we shall see them back in the markets. There is or was an eighteenth-century press in Newport, near Barnstaple, for wine or liquor. Imagine the colour alone.

Cherries are said to come from the name Ceresus, a port in Italy where fruit was unloaded and spread throughout the Roman Empire in the first century BC. It seems that these were sour cherries, and progenitors of the Morello (as in morel, implying Moorish or blackish, 1678), but the name attached to all such fruit and was recorded for hundreds of years. The chances are that it was the improved sweet cherry, which arrived in England with hops from Flanders in Tudor times and became the focus of gradual improvement. In the nineteenth century new stock arrived from France and produced a family of sour-sweet intermediates entitled Dukes or Royals, and *Anglais* over the Channel.

It was not in Devon, but upcountry in Oxfordshire, that I ate my first cherries – and never recovered from the thrill of it: the taut skin ready to burst, blushing on one side, creamy on the other. Then there were the gangs of gypsy pickers in their bow tops, the men wearing belchers and the women in multicoloured clothes, ready then as now to predict your fate. The Harwell area, clinging to tradition, still has many cherry orchards. If you are in the vicinity in summer, do not miss the fruit.

To leave home at dawn, reach Kent in time for a brew-up, and find the cherries selling on market stalls and people queuing to buy them is 'leisure' and pleasure in one. My wife and I went to a tasting too. Of the three hundred varieties we might have had, twenty was sufficient to undermine my power to separate them. I started with pencil poised, but ended up with little on paper apart from the Merton tribe and the firm Kent Nap, and Napoleon Bigarreau, a name I knew already. Time for one church, one garden, a swim on an empty beach, and a walk in those bird-infested Dickensian marshes. They are trying to ruin Kent, grub up its remaining orchards and eliminate links to Tudor England. Enjoy them while you can.

The good news is that cherries are coming through on smaller root stocks, making them possible in modest-sized gardens for the first time. The Morellos and perhaps the Dukes will take a north wall. There are self-fertile varieties too. I admit never to having eaten cooked cherries, except in the form of jam, but look forward to being converted. The season for sweet cherries runs from June to July. Cookers are slightly later.

The pub in Sarre, in Kent, where you can buy flour from the windmill, has made its own cherry brandy for a hundred years – a nice nip with a cheerful colour. According to her notes, my grandmother did it by filling a jar with ripe Morellos, then the brandy or whisky, and letting it all lie for at least three months. She finished the drink by dissolving 1lb sugar to every gallon of liquor.

Mulberry, black *Morus nigra*, are a native of the Middle East, known to the ancients, and probably introduced by the Romans, which is happy in England and loved in return. The tree is of medium size and spread, requiring the open or central position it usually gets. James I, keen on the production of silk, encouraged the planting of mulberries, but not of the type (*M. alba*) that feeds the appropriate moth. And so he commissioned trees by mistake, specifically the one in the Chelsea Physic garden that stood for over three hundred years. Come the war and the need for a bomb shelter, his mulberry made way, but not before it had served a final and well-considered purpose. From the cuttings that were taken, I have been able to plant a Jacobean tree and for a fraction of the price it would take to buy a contemporary painting or chest of drawers. You can too.

My tree grows less slowly than anticipated and bore within a few years. It is late into leaf and hardly the 'bush' of the nursery rhyme, but delivers every day in late summer, provoking you to 'go round' it. Mulberries are for those who complain about 'bland food'. I am surprised that people do not waste them less, gather them more, and fuss over a fruit as shocking in flavour and intense as the purple stain it likes to leave behind.

'The juice of the fruit mixed with apples,' says *Blackie's Modern Encyclopaedia*, 'makes a beverage of a deep port wine colour called mulberry cider.' Now there's a thought.

Medlar, *Mespilus germanica*, known to the Romans, is now largely ornamental and more popular in England than in the rest of Europe. The wild tree, which I cannot recall seeing, has thorns. The cultivars have none. They are medium to small, with gnarled and brittle branches that make them top-heavy and catch the autumn gales, but leaf up early and grow a canopy you may enter like a tent. The white flower is one of the prettiest, the fruit one of the most peculiar: a bit like a large dull yellow rosehip with a tail-end sunburst, known as 'open-arse' since the Middle Ages. There are five pips to each medlar. I have planted a variety called

Nottingham, possibly a corruption of 'Neapolitan' (Mason, 1999), and pilfered the fruit from unlikely places. Ringwood town centre (see page 41), Salisbury Cathedral Close, and St James's Park in London, a stone's throw from Downing Street, are amongst them. A ripe medlar is an acquired taste, slightly grainy in texture.

Medlars are in season at the onset of winter. The ritual in England was to wait for them to soften and turn brown or 'blet', and eat them raw with a piece of cheese and a glass of port. To make the jelly, watch the tree from the middle of November, and select a mixture of the harder clingers for their pectin and fallers for their 'bletted' flavour. Add the juice of one strained lemon along with the customary pound of sugar for every pint of medlar juice (see page 399).

Worth considering

Apricots are a native of Armenia, cultivated in England for over four hundred years. The tree or bush is small, and is likely to do best in a hothouse or fan-trained. Buckinghamshire, Oxfordshire and Gloucestershire are associated with apricots. Hartley mentions the thinnings (the sacrificial fruits taken from the tree, enabling the rest to prosper), 'which hang so golden against the Cotswold stone walls' and were used for stuffing the local hams, boned and baked in brick ovens (see page 176) for special occasions like Wool Fair. How surprised she would have been to hear apricots referred to as the latest 'thing' in English gardens in 2006. Moor Park is the usual variety, now two centuries old, but there are others. 'A fresh-picked English apricot has to be tasted to be believed,' say Chris Bowers and Sons of Norfolk in their specialist fruit plant catalogue. And I have come nearly sixty years without the experience. Shameful.

Fig: a relation of the mulberry, and a native of the Near to Far East, which came to England in the sixteenth century. The tree or bush is spreading, and the leaves can be prickly – not the obvious choice for Adam and Eve to cover their modesty with. The Victorians knew a thing or two about the fig that we seem to have forgotten. If you cannot hang a leg of mutton or rib of beef for the time it requires (Beaty-Pownall), leave it overnight in the branches of a fig tree and the result will be the same. That may be why so many trees are planted close to kitchens, and the fruit goes into a product known as 'meat tenderiser'. Crops can be taken more than once a year in congenial surroundings. Figs are dried abroad, and have been used to 'cut' coffee since the Turks invaded Hungary. I would not plant one before an apple or plum, but would not waste it either.

Grapevine: an Asian shrub, cultivated since time immemorial, probably introduced to Europe by the Phoenicians. The Romans did the rest. Several vineyards were mentioned in England in the Domesday Book, but they fell into an early decline with rural depopulation from the Black Death, competition from France, and climate change. The production of table grapes began to pick up in the eighteenth century and flourished in the hothouses built by the Victorians. My mother and stepfather, who were well supplied in Somerset, did not make a big enough fuss of them. My wife and I have planted Black Hamburgh, which is pruned every year and trained up a wall, and a sprawler called Brant on a chestnut structure. We have not been troubled by the vine weevil. Growth is vigorous. The plants' ornamental value is almost enough. The leaves begin to turn in September, then curl and catch fire, shot with yellow and burnt sienna. The grapes are small, but ripen out of doors and should be protected from the birds. The trick is to break the skin with your teeth, releasing the flavour, and leave your digestion to deal with the pips.

Peach: a native of China, which reached Europe via Persia, and England along with apricots and figs in the sixteenth century. Peaches 'are amongst the most delicious of *our* fruits,' said Mrs Beeton, if expensive. Nectarines are a smooth-skinned variety, or sport, originally occurring by chance. They get leaf curl and blossom early, which can affect crops, but do not mind the cold and can thrive in sheltered positions. There used to be a tree behind the High Street in Fordingbridge much appreciated by Bob the Fish and Kevin the Chip. 'Big as that,' they'd tell you, indicating a three-inch girth, 'juicy and yellow inside – better than the Italian ones.' They reckoned that the tree sprouted from a stone someone threw away. After it died, probably from root poisoning, Bob planted another at home which delivers up to a hundred peaches each August, quite delicious, with white, almost greenish flesh.

Quince: are a native of western Asia, related to the medlar, known to the ancients, and a contender for Adam's apple – golden, fragrant and most of the things the Bible said it was, above all present in the Holy Land when the eating apple was still in China. The positive twist to the tale is that the quince is much more palatable and tempting in its chosen habitat (according to reports) than in locations man has chosen for it. This fruit is taken less seriously in England than in Europe, but continues to be admired. I prefer the Japanese form, japonica, a different genus, usually regarded as ornamental. The flower is early. The fruit is late, characteristically hard and yellow or greenish and lies on the cold, wet ground in people's gardens without going rotten until Christmas. Another pleasant jelly, equal to redcurrant or medlar.

For apples, see Chapter 32.

SOFT FRUIT

Wilkin and Sons, 'Wilkinsons' to everyone, the jam wallahs of Tiptree, are still going strong. I cold-called, expressing an interest in seeing around their factory, to be told that Health and Safety, and the dread insurance sector – a powerful combo – had other ideas. I asked whether I could I sign a disclaimer to say that if I tripped over a carpet, stubbed my toe or fell into a pot of Little Scarlet I would hold myself responsible. No. They were sorry. If, however, I cared to write and make an appointment, they would see . . . Never mind. I would retain my unrequited love for the company, its big green lorries, and unchanging labels. The product is too hard-set for me, but remains true to itself. It has also, with Elsenham down the road, helped to save a few fruit-growers from at least one of the twentieth century's agricultural depressions.

A year later an Essex girl came to live near us in Hampshire. Her first instinct in her new garden was 'to get the soft fruit in'. I was so impressed with the connection she had made, simple as it appeared. The next best things are to buy English produce or 'pick your own', a pleasant occupation that saves the land from set-aside and equestrianism, and provides work and food in good condition. Growing your own gives you control over the varieties.

Here are most of the soft fruits available in England, and their implications. They need different degrees of maintenance and protection from vermin, but mostly can find a place in small gardens.

Blackcurrants are a native, found in the wild near me and cultivated – as much for its medicinal as culinary value – for up to five hundred years. They shoot from a basal stem, and need good soil and pruning to crop well. The fruit makes Ribena in England and *cassis* in France, but is almost unknown in parts of Italy. The Scots are in the forefront of breeding programmes with the up-to-date 'Ben' varieties, which may be the wise choice, though not so tempting as the comforting number from the archives. We have planted Baldwin, Goliath (pre-1847), Seabrook's Black (1913) and Wellington XXX (1927), hoping to obtain up to eight pounds of fruit from mature bushes.

Blackcurrants are in season in July and August. The leaves can make a tea, or be used to cut it. The fruit, which contains in a handful your daily requirement of vitamin C, is ready to eat when it has turned black. It should dominate in summer pudding (see page 431), makes an excellent tart, and is the jam you should begin with.

Redcurrants: Geoffrey Grigson was not sure whether they are native or naturalised, but often saw them in the wild. I have too, for the first time, in Dovedale. Bushes are notoriously long-lived (Roberts, 2001), but new varieties are coming through all the time. We have gone for Roxby Red, which cropped up at the top of the North York Moors and should find it easy going in the south. The fruit is pippy and seems to have a shorter season than blackcurrants, but if you are planting one you may as well plant the other. If also you want fruit for jelly and your garden is too small for a tree, the obvious solution is to choose a redcurrant. Some people like them raw, dipped in sugar. Use in summer pudding (see page 431), and strawberry jam too (see page 393) as well as jelly. Whitecurrants are a sport without the pigmentation of blacks or reds, more fragile and high in pectin. They make a pinkish jelly.

A way with currants: a neat bit of food writing from gardener Tom Petherick (*Daily Telegraph*, 15 July 2006): 'Sprinkle the fruit with sugar, leave for a couple of hours until the sugar has drawn out the juice and eat with whichever type of cream you favour.'

Gooseberries are a native, christened in 1532, when a cultivated form is thought to have arrived in England from France, and slang for a chaperon since 1837. They are related to red- and whitecurrants, not black. In the course of losing popularity elsewhere, the gooseberry or 'feaberry' became something of a national obsession. A total of a hundred and fifty clubs were formed (Mason, 1999) with size as their objective, obtained by selective pruning and stripping of the fruit, which is weighed in competitions on apothecaries' scales. I shall proceed to the heights of Yorkshire and the depths of Cheshire to find out what mental process lies behind it all, and 'monitor' (sneak on) anyone failing to use *metric measurements*.

An allotment and cottage garden favourite is the goosegog, which can also be found in commercial orchards. Standards of three or four feet high are available, as well as bushes. Colours vary from green, which tend to be cookers and the most popular, to yellowish or red. Some of the names are terrific – Crown Bob, Dan's Mistake, Heart of Oak, Hero of the Nile, Howard's Lancer, King of Trumps, the Queen of Trumps too, Lancashire Lad, Sultan Juror . . .

The gooseberry season begins with the culinary varieties in May. It ends with the dessert ones in June, which are a lot less popular but can amount to fruit from one and the same bush, left to grow bigger and riper. The berry for the goose, it is claimed, but only for a green goose eaten in the summer and the other from Michaelmas on. And mackerel? A disaster for both parties. Cobbett opted for a gooseberry batter pudding – a sponge is delightful (see page 431). Look out for Oldbury tarts, baked in a hot-water pastry, last heard of in Gloucestershire.

Gooseberry ices, *très recherché* for a hundred and fifty years, can still be found in rural Lancashire. To do them yourself, make a fool and freeze it.

Raspberries are a native, originally hindberries; one of the hart and hind's favourite bites, renamed obscurely by 1620s and an affront to decency since 1915. Wild and wayside plants, in common with gooseberries and strawberries, were selected over the centuries for cultivation in gardens.* They occur from the south of England up to Scotland, which has long been in the forefront of production, supplying dye as well as food for the rest of the UK. Recent breeding programmes have delivered in terms of quantity, virus resistance, and shelf life, but at a cost to the flavour in many varieties. It is a treat to buy home-grown raspberries in a shop or market, provided they are simultaneously sweet, tart and remarkable enough for Jersey or Guernsey cream. We are flirting with Glen Moy, which has an Award of Garden Merit and Lloyd George amongst its antecedents, the connoisseur's choice in the past; and a couple from the Mallings stable. For those who like a firmer texture and bigger hit, higher in acidity, there is J. H. Logan's loganberry, a vigorous and bountiful American hybrid (I think) that crossed the Atlantic in 1891.

Summer raspberries are in season in and around July for about six weeks. Autumn varieties crop from mid-September until the first frosts, and do not seem to attract birds. They have an excellent flavour. Examine for wounds when buying. Use quickly and do not wash. Another jam to make (see page 393).

Strawberries are a native and a shade-tolerant one, widely distributed in the wild and grown in people's gardens for hundreds of years: mine is no exception. Europe has an Alpine variety, modestly improved, which enjoys a small commercial market. The larger cultivated strawberry resulted from a chance cross between plants originating in Chile and Virginia that occurred in eighteenth-century France. A controlled experiment, conducted by amateur John Knight in about 1820, followed in England (Vaughan and Geissler, 1997). Nurseryman Thomas Keen entered the arena with his sensational seedling (Mason, 1999), the Laxton brothers bred Royal Sovereign in 1892, and the industry was away.

Strawberries and cream! How English! How exquisite! Provided they are both top of the range, otherwise disappointing: a big, watery mouthful of Elsanta, the supermarkets' choice, bred in Holland, accompanied by dead white cream, 'fragrance-free' and pasteurised to within an inch of its life. A national dish diminished to the point where an Edwardian would hardly recognize it. You've been had. You might just as well put balsamic vinegar on your Royal Sovereign – people do.

Strawberries are moody. They run out of puff as cultivars, attract pests and dislike land vacated by potatoes. There is also their condition. A Belgian girl told me that her father grew the best ever strawberries for jam – provided they were picked and used the same day. The fruit not only damages easily, but leaches goodness in doing so. Then you find a strawberry that

---

* *From the text of Thomas Tusser's poem recording the country year,* A Hundreth Good Pointes of Husbandrie *(1557).*

'tastes like it used to', the cream to go with it, and all is forgiven. Dream England is back on the rails.

To put the rural idyll in perspective, having planted strawberries in mother earth and paid for the privilege in slug damage, we are committing them to white and 'visually challenging' custom-made plastic containers – and a corner of the garden known henceforth as 'Industrial Unit One'. However, I am anticipating results. With regard to variety, breeders are at it all the time. One makeweight and one shy but star performer on the flavour front would be a good balance. Cambridge Late Pine, a pineapple shape, not Alpine, is in the spotlight.

English strawberries are available increasingly earlier and later. An original six-week season has been extended by polyculture and 'ever-bearers' to more like six months. That, perhaps – the effect of artificial heat on a temperate plant – is where the flavour goes. Mrs Beeton thought so. The jam is unusually made (see page 393).

RHUBARB

A perennial vegetable from the colder parts of Asia, related to the common dock, and the buckwheat used for flour, *kasha* and horticultural green manure. The plant, used as a laxative since early times in China, was known to the Romans in powdered form. It was grown in England from at least 1500, partly in the belief that it cured VD (Rix and Phillips, 1993), increasing in popularity as sugar came through under the Hanoverians and it could be eaten as a fruit. Forced rhubarb, accidentally discovered in the same way as chicory (see page 374), emerged in about 1817. The result was the same as with sea kale: a more tender and palatable crop than the ordinary, obtained early in the season, and of particular interest to people lacking teeth. By the reign of Queen Victoria, the name of a well-known cultivar, rhubarb and sea kale appeared at market together.

The forcing sheds in the triangle created by Wakefield, Rothwell and Morley outside Leeds went up in 1877. The crop, known to some as 'tusky', lit by candles, heated by coal and fertilised by refuse from the woollen mills, or 'shoddy', thrived in conditions it seemed to find familiar. The railway station was conveniently close, as the motorways are now. The number of producers is down from about two hundred to ten. There is competition from Holland, fruit coming in and easier work to do, but the industry persists. A festival takes place every February, which I cannot go on missing. They say you can hear the rhubarb splutter and pop as it struggles to grow, jostling for position in its beds in the dark.

Rhubarb is strong, even strong enough to grow through a hard tennis court. The stems are the edible part of the English plant, and the only edible part: the leaves are poisonous and will kill chickens. The status of rhubarb, which was available during the war and momentarily unfashionable in peacetime as a result, is now back to normal. There are over a hundred and twenty cultivars, bred over the years in such diverse locations as Yorkshire, Norfolk, Deptford and Lewisham. I have planted an early variety called Stockbridge, a couple of rarefied Champagnes, and Strawberry Surprise for flavour.

The season for forced rhubarb begins in January and ends at Easter. The garden plant follows on until July. Pull the stalks, do not cut them, and remove the string when they are getting coarse. This fruit makes another excellent sponge (see page 431). The best way to stew rhubarb is to concentrate the flavour: commit to a pan over a low heat with about 1 tbsp of sugar per pound. Cover and cook gently for a few minutes until the juice runs and the fruit is soft. Strain through a sieve, return the juice to the pan and reduce until it is almost a syrup, being careful not to burn it. Reintroduce the rhubarb and check for sweetness.

Cook's Oracle

Fruit is about variety, condition and, when preserving is involved, using each fruit to its best advantage. Home-made jams, bottled fruits and drinks are useful and comforting to have in reserve, pleasant to look at (and show off) in the larder, avoid waste and make good presents.

Jams

Our policy is to 'cherry-pick' – to make quite a lot from a few chosen types rather than to try and cover the full range, which is hard work and leads to disappointments. You will need: (a) a pan at least twice the volume of the fruit you pick; (b) a kitchen thermometer – jam sets at around 104°C/220°F; (c) muslin for strawberry jam, and jelly, which must be scalded before use and washed out afterwards in hot water, not detergent; (d) jars, which must be washed and committed to the oven on a tray to sterilise when it comes to filling them; (e) covers for the jars, preferably their lids, washed as well, though papers will do; (f) sugar, pure cane or preserving sugar, not demerara, dark brown, etc.

Choose a dry day, or else you and the jam will suffer. Pick ripe fruit. Unripe, it sets well but lacks flavour. Over-ripe or blemished, it can ferment. If you are a beginner, start with a small quantity, up to 4lb. Allow a whole afternoon to make a mess and complete operations, probably to your dissatisfaction. Don't worry, and don't overcook the jam: if it is too soft for your liking, you can boil it up again. If caramelized, it is beyond hope. Put on the lids when hot, or cold the following day, not warm or else the jam will go off. After three or four attempts you should be motoring.

The following quantities can be scaled up or down.

Blackcurrant jam is the easiest to make because it is high in pectin and sets easily. Take 4lb (1.8kg) fruit, 4lb (1.8kg) sugar, 2 pints (1.2l) water. Wash and pick over the fruit. Mix in water, bring up to simmering point and cook gently for about 20 minutes or until soft. Mix in the sugar all at once. Boil for a further 10 minutes, stirring well and testing the temperature. Best to pour into a jug, then pot and cover immediately.

Damson jam has the best flavour, bullace comes close. It is a little more trouble than blackcurrant and takes longer to set. Proceed as above, but using slightly less water, say 1½pints (900ml). As you boil the fruit and sugar, the stones will keep coming to the surface. You should be able to remove the majority with a spoon before 104°C/220°F is reached. I boil up the stones in water for a couple of hours, extracting the almond flavour, then add the liquid as syrup to the jam. To make damson cheese, press the fruit through a sieve with a wooden spoon rather than picking out the stones.

Strawberry jam is the one for splits and cream, but a palaver, even a little eccentric, so start with a small quantity. The redcurrants provide the pectin that enables it to set. Take 2lb (900g) strawberries, 2lb (900g) sugar, 3lb (1.3kg) redcurrants (makes 2 pints (1.2l) of juice).

Take a clean bit of muslin or cheesecloth, scald it in boiling water and wring out when cold. Lay it out, put the raw redcurrants in the middle, wrap them in the cloth and squeeze out every last drop of juice. Discard the currants, and bring the juice up to simmering point. Add the strawberries and the sugar. The jam should reach setting point in about twenty minutes. Pot, and ideally leave for a few months before eating. Try this method with loganberries or mulberries.

Raspberry jam is the one with a culinary rather than teatime value, used in Bakewell and Queen of Puddings (see page 430) and eaten with milk puddings too. Do not overcook. Bake 2lb (900g) fresh raspberries for 1 hour in a cool oven at 150°C /30°F/ gas mark 2 until the juice runs. Heat 2lb (900g) of sugar in another vessel for the last 15–20 minutes. Rub a wok with butter and put in the raspberries, sugar and strained juice of a lemon. Cook gently, beating with a whisk all the time for 15 minutes. Finally bring up to boiling point, and pot.

JELLY

The candidates are crab apple (with or without rowan), gooseberry, medlar, quince or japonica, and red- or whitecurrant.

Up-end a chair and put it on the kitchen table. Take a piece of muslin big enough to tie by each corner to a chair leg with string, making a hammock. Press down with your hand to make sure it is secure and will bear a certain amount of weight. Place a bowl underneath. Wash the fruit and cut it up into chunks if large, commit to a pan and barely cover with water. Bring up to simmering point and cook for 20 minutes or until soft. Pour the lot into the hammock and leave undisturbed overnight. Compost or feed the fruit to livestock and test the liquid in the bowl. If it feels slimy, it contains enough pectin to set. If not, add the juice of one strained lemon for every pint. Weigh out 1lb (450g) of sugar, again per pint (600ml). Put the liquid in a pan. Bring up to simmering point and add the sugar, stirring well, until it has dissolved, then boil hard, removing the scum as it rises. Crab apple, gooseberry and the currant jellies will set within 10 minutes; the rest may take longer. A molten jelly sets at a higher temperature than jam when it falls from a wooden spoon in lazy drips, rather than a stream. The conventional test is to put a blob on a plate, leave it to set and poke it, looking for wrinkles. Remove the pan from the heat while you do this.

BOTTLING

The candidates are plums, particularly cookers, and greengages. Cherries I have yet to try, but they must be in the same league: the Dukes and Morellos would be the ones to go for. With Kilner jars having gone there is no alternative except to use the French equivalent. The rubber seals should ideally be replaced every year, but can be used again if they still feel soft.

There is a good deal less to bottling fruit than people imagine – in fact, nothing. You need, apart from the fruit and sugar, serviceable preserving jars and a pan big enough to put in at least two at a time.

Pick a quantity of firm, even unripe plums, gages or cherries. Wash them and cram them into the jars. Cover with water, then empty it out, measure and heat it, adding and dissolving 6oz (175g) sugar for every pint (600ml) of liquid. Refill the jars to the brim, closing the lids, and put them in the pan, submerged up to their shoulders in water. Bring up to the boil and simmer for about 10 minutes or until the lids are stuck fast. Remove the jars and wipe with a cloth in case they are sticky. The fruit will have risen from the bottom of the jar, which I redress by turning the vessels upside down for a month. As long as the preserving process has worked and the tops are secure, they will not leak. If they do, you must eat the fruit before it ferments. Plums and gages get an almond flavour from the stones within a few months, and lose it after a year. To open the jars, rather than wrestling with a knife and stabbing yourself, reheat in water. This one is worth home-made custard.

NUTS

Cobnuts: Kent again. The north and south are as different as north and south Devon. The Isle of Thanet, Romney Marsh and the Weald are different again. In a quiet corner described as 'out of the way', but surprisingly close to the M25, between hung-tile houses, neat fields and short horizons, the cobnuts cluster on wonderfully crooked, gnarled and spreading trees not a bit like mine at home, on account of being two centuries older. The acreage they covered has fallen from seven thousand throughout England in 1913 to a few hundred. The coppices grow not in an orchard, a thicket or even a wood, but in a platt, a term attached to the village down the hill, St Mary's Platt (sometimes spelt with one 't' – a possible corruption of plot).

The hazel, along with birch and juniper, was one of the first trees or bushes to recolonise the British Isles after the last Ice Age (Rackham, 1986). The wood has been used since wolves inhabited the 'wild' of Kent. If cut every eight or twelve years (and there are prohibitionists), the life of a hazel is prolonged almost indefinitely. The coppice, protected in enclosures during the Middle Ages, was more valuable than standing timber. The stakes are used for hedging and charcoal, the poles for thatching spars, hurdles, and thumbsticks: my one-legged stepfather was never without one. The fans are for peas and the brash for kindling. The fruit came to be known as cobnuts, a cob being a shape, but also a children's game played with nuts that pre-dated conkers. The hazel is a useful and a magical tree, associated with knowledge, fertility and divining buried treasure as well as water.

The filbert may be named after the saint's day on which it more or less ripens, but also after its 'full beard' or husk. It is bigger, longer and more pointed than the ordinary hazel nut, and a native of south-eastern Europe known to the ancients and possibly grown in England since the Middle Ages. Cultivation increased during the seventeenth century, establishing Kent as the chief supplier and source of improved nuts within a hundred and fifty years. Lambert's Filbert, named after the breeder in Goudhurst, emerged around 1830. By the end of the Victorian period, there were more than seventy varieties with up to forty synonyms each. To make matters worse, they took the title of cobnuts from the wild hazel and the two different families appeared together at markets under the same name.

The 'untaught, unlettered Kentish peasant' (Game, 1999) perfected the art of winter pruning, passing it from father to son. The spread of branches into a goblet shape provided easy access to the bowl of a fully mature tree. The restricted height caused it to bear fewer nuts, but larger. A round of summer pruning, or 'brutting', removed unwanted shoots and spawn or suckers. Fertiliser included turkey feathers, a dead ringer for a late snowfall, though it is now more likely to come from animals grazing in the platts. The wild-flower count is through the roof.

The harvest in Kent was a busman's holiday for Londoners until the Second World War, but employed more local people than hop or fruit farms. Pickers either stood in the bowls of trees or in couples on the ground opposite each other, moving in a clockwise direction around the outside (there must have been a dance). The baskets were called 'kipsies'; aprons were used too. The nuts went on to the evening train in osier sieves holding twenty pounds of green cobs and forty of ripe ones, covered in blue paper and bracken, and secured with hazel wands.

The flowering male is a catkin or blowing: he arrives with the snowdrops. The female is a nutkin. The fruit come in singletons or rough little clusters of two to five. Siamese twins are lucky. All sorts of different nuts may grow together, whose flavour and performance vary. The offspring do not breed true. Propagation is effected by selecting a wand from a coppice, bending it over and pegging the upper middle part into the earth, leaving two or three feet to the tip above ground. It is left to strike, then dug up and severed from the parent, and grown on for two years before planting out.

Nut nuts? Of course. Richard Webb was one, a man who did not believe in pruning. His twelve-acre garden near Reading, enclosed by a six-foot wall and described as an exuberant thicket, was protected from intruders and vermin by six mastiffs and sixty cats, and from anything else that slipped through the net by a brawny forewoman dressed in the black habit of a Quaker. Most of the land was occupied by nut trees, the largest of which yielded 110lb a year. Webb introduced several cultivars, which he exhibited and named after the celebrities of his day. His Prize Cob is still available. He died in 1877. Meg Game, author of *In a Nutshell* and the lifelong owner of a platt, went looking for his house – and found it – but the estate was carved up and most of the trees cleared for 'exclusive homes'.

The Kentish cob faces opposition, not only from developers, infillers and equestrianism. The supermarkets, apart from buying meanly, insist on a standard approximating to imports, which many self-respecting growers do not care to meet. Then there are squirrels, dormice, deer, nuthatches and, of course, the layers of bureaucracy. Having been informed by DEFRA's predecessor, MAFF, that the UK did not produce any nuts, never mind fresh ones, the EC addressed the dried market only. The growers in England, omitted from talks, marginalised by the rules and forced to register their existence, responded by founding the Kent Cobnuts Association – a small but proud and united body of people – intent on a result. They sought a derogation, got one, and now have twenty-two members, including a total of four in Herefordshire, Essex, Pembrokeshire and Cornwall, and ten nurseries supplying them.

Cobs can be purchased from quality greengrocers, directly from producers and from the Association at the Kent County Show. St Filbert's Day falls on 22 August. Firstings are light in colour, soft, moist and milky: some eat them with salt. Secondings are riper, firmer, browner and better keepers in the fridge, ironically reaching perfection as prices tail off. Thirdings, the fallers, come last. Cobnuts share the same season as game, light lambs, fungi, apples, blackberries and pears. I have an implement for cracking them after dinner, which is shaped like the legs of a principal boy.

To roast cobnuts, shell and bake in a cool oven, 150°C/300°F/gas mark 2, for 1 hour.

Sweet chestnut: the Royal Horticultural Society kicked off with a disagreement as to whether *castanea sativa* was native or naturalized. The contention that it comes from Asia Minor, and spread throughout Europe with the Romans, won the day. The sweet or Spanish chestnut can grow to a handsome size in conditions it likes, and provides the optimum material for coppicing, splitting, quartering, fencing and poles. The wood hardens off, lasts for years and is sometimes bought as it stands and cleared by contractors. It is not to be confused with the horse chestnut which arrived in the sixteenth century, complete with 'conkers'.

The French use all the sweet chestnut they can get. The English have not used enough since the National Health Service stopped buying it to make walking sticks for the blind. The husks, too prickly to handle, drop to the ground in October. They lie amongst the serrated leaves, then burst open to reveal the starchy and edible seed within, cushioned in velvet and wrapped in imitation leather. Home-grown chestnuts are smaller than the European ones, but my wife eats them, a habit she acquired during childhood in the Forest. For her, the sound of the fallow deer rutting and the sight of fallen chestnuts go together. The vendors in London buy supplies in from abroad.

Walnuts: a native of many locations from the Balkans to China, spread by the Romans again, and treated with a mixture of reverence and contempt. 'A woman, a dog and a walnut tree, the more you beat them the better they be' is an English saying that has spread as far as Italy (Bianchini and Corbetta, 1976). As far as the walnut goes this is nonsense, for if you draw blood or sap it is certain to result in the death of the walnut. Like thousands of others, I have planted a specimen that is too big for the land around it and will have to come down. In the mean time, it is growing a honey-coloured, ripple-rich wood, for which makers of furniture, treen[*] and stocks for shotguns will in theory be offering me a fortune. The green, soft-shelled nuts appear in early summer, and could be the nuts gathered on 'cold and frosty' May mornings. They are used for pickling. The hard ones, which have none of the bitterness of dried imports, fall in the autumn.

---

* *Wooden vessels/ornaments.*

CHAPTER
TWENTY-NINE

FIELD, FOREST AND
FORESHORE – FAVOURITES
TO FAMINE RATIONS

 EN SEVIER WAS BORN AT A TIME, said his daughter Ann to the congregation, when nobody walked in the Forest except for a reason. He went to dig turfs or pick fruit. In his grandfathers' day it was the children who gathered wild food the adults were too busy. Culpeper is full of plants that every child knew, and unlike a modern botanist many times his or her age, also appreciated for their food value.

With the change of pace and people in the English countryside, a huge amount of local knowledge was pushed aside and lost. It started to return with acupuncture, herbal remedies and the interest in medicinal and edible plants growing in the wild, but had also held its own in scattered locations since the first hunter-gatherers exercised their skills, and man rubbed a leaf on a nettle sting.

As a reborn country-dweller with the time to walk and the inclination to learn, the obvious course for me was to combine the two. A veil parted and an increasingly fascinating world opened up that could only be seen at walking pace, and that brought a seasonal succession of gifts from the high-water mark to the depths of the Forest. I was accused of robbing the 'environment' only twice in twenty years, and had no competition. Bikers, riders, runners, ramblers and twitchers continued on their way, heads down or in the clouds, with nary a thought for the harvest right and left a Frenchman would die for.

Having started out with a pocket guide, I began to make sense of edible fungi within two years. I found most of the favourites within two more, decided on the best, and returned to their haunts every season. I sold mushrooms to a local restaurant and shared them with friends, but rarely divulged my happy hunting grounds. I had more than mixed feelings, even strong reservations, about giving such valuable secrets away.

The paper said one year that the south of England had been 'picked out', thanks to the mushroom wallahs on TV. It was not true. The fungi repeated for ten to twelve seasons, providing me with enough to dry until the next time round. Then the weather turned against them, I drew a blank for weeks, and December arrived. I would give my circuit the final once-over and call it a day. I did not expect to find any mushrooms so late in the year, let alone a quantity so large and in such perfect condition. Bugger! For the first time ever, I had come unprepared and without a knife and basket. It was also getting late. So I resolved to leave my discovery overnight, return, and pick them in the morning.

My wife and I set out at 8 a.m. In order to increase our chances of finding more fungi, we separated. She, by a shorter route, reached our destination within fifteen minutes. I heard her shouting, then saw her, white and breathless, running towards me. What on earth was the matter? Had she found a body, hurt herself or been attacked? No, it was worse than that. Our mushrooms had gone. They had all been picked.

We rushed through the trees and bracken to the spot, and stared at the forest floor. Someone, out even later than us at night or earlier in the morning, had scooped the pool. The person who had done it was not a novice either. The fungi had been lifted with care and obvious satisfaction down to the last one. I was gripped, and by a cold and clammy hand. My thoughts returned to a girl I had seen exercising hard on a treadmill in a gym that summer, rather than in the lush woods and rolling hills outside. Best place for her, I now realised. I had wanted to see people connected to their surroundings. I had been granted my wish. I had reaped the reward. From then on, nothing was more agitating than the sight of a person out walking with a basket, and nothing more reassuring than one white-knuckled in a car, on a bike or a treadmill in a health club, going nowhere and seeing nothing except their pulse rate on a screen.

Mushroom-hunting has a varied history, suffused with prejudice, superstition and myth, especially in England. Records of it are scarce, and for the same reason as fowling: the people involved were not in the habit of writing diaries and were of no interest to those who did. There are woodmen alive today who were brought up on fungi gathered in the course of a working day. The knowledge of crops and where they grew was handed down, but went no further when people changed jobs, moved house and bought cultivated mushrooms instead. It decreased, leaving botanists and chefs to take up the baton.

The one thing about fungi, universally understood, is that they can be poisonous. The sickness and suffering caused by a wrong 'un are just the job for a Gothic novel. They are also documentary evidence, taken from hundreds of actual cases (a disquieting thought), and not to be regarded lightly. The majority of accidents occurred during crop failure and famine in nineteenth-century Europe. Today, Italy sustains the greatest number of deaths from mushroom poisoning – up to twenty every season.

The English, by comparison, who have registered four deaths in the last seventy years, not only fear wild mushrooms more than any other nation, we fear them more than processed foods, crossing the road, and all the other risks of greater magnitude we face every day. People can accept that you know about anything from Staffordshire pottery to sandpipers and sedum, but not that you can tell the considerable difference between a panther cap and a penny bun. There is no changing their mind either. A tasteless mushroom from a packet will forever be more popular than a fungus twice as palatable and freely available, whose identity is 100 per cent certain. The mother-in-law will not eat a horn of plenty even after watching me and checking for any symptoms (actually, she has). And yet, with caution, no one need be poisoned by a mushroom, or even exposed to the chance.

Mycology is a daunting subject, but not for a cook, who can afford to be minimal. Of the estimated five thousand fungi that grow in England, about five hundred are officially edible, and only a fraction of those are either worth pursuing or poisonous. Once found, by attention to detail and a process of elimination, it is not difficult to establish what they are. From then on, mushrooms hitherto invisible, situated next to the kitchen, by the roadside or in a park, start springing into view. The autumn, rather than being the death of summer and melancholic prelude to winter, comes as a bonus at the end of the year. A word of warning, though. Do not eat too many fungi either at once or for days on end. You can get sick of them – I nearly did – and ruin your enjoyment for ever.

COOK'S ORACLE AND GAME PLAN

1. Organized mushroom hunts are not a bad idea. You can feed off your discoveries, and the confidence of an expert, and learn a lot in a few hours.

2. Buy a pocket book for the field and a comprehensive guide, preferably with photos, for home.

3. Examine the differences in colour, texture, size and distribution of fungi. Note the formation they grow in, if any, and the habitat. A field mushroom likes open spaces, as does a peregrine falcon and a sun-loving plant. If you see something similar in a belt of trees, it is something else.

4. To register the smell of a fungus, cup it in your hands.

5. Do not eat fungi you cannot identify, mix varieties (until you are confident about what they are) or listen to old wives' tales or rules of thumb. A slug can eat a death cap without ill effects. A fairy cake is not as charming as it sounds.

6. Do acquaint yourself with the poisonous fungi, particularly the *Amanitae*, *Inocybes* and yellow stainer, which resembles a field mushroom.

7. There is now a limit to the weight you may pick, but an ineffective one. Do not be greedy: leave plenty for the field or forest.

8. Fungi respond positively to moisture at the right time, and negatively to frost. They enjoy both good and bad years, which can surprise you either way.

9. Fungi will repeat in an area, but seldom in exactly the same spot.

10. Fungi can absorb a lot of water. Pick only good specimens, using a penknife, if possible in dry weather, and collect in a basket. They sweat in plastic bags. Wipe clean rather than wash.

11. Fungi, with exceptions, deteriorate quickly. The majority go soft within twenty-four hours of hatching and lose their colour.

12. If committing fungi to cream, soups and stews, use the lighter ones (i.e. chanterelles) and the darkers ones where appropriate (e.g. horns of plenty).

The old favourites are as follows. There are few surprises, but you may learn something from my encounters and order of merit. All but the St George's mushroom and the morel are found mainly in the summer and autumn.

THE A TEAM

The boletus family is known by its pores rather than gills.

Boletus edulis, the cep or penny bun, is easyish to identify: it is the roundest, plumpest, naughtiest, most magnetic and outrageous fungus of the lot. To find him awaiting you in his elf-like hat and fit your hand around his firm little stalk is the greatest thrill in mushroom-hunting; to feel him softening and past his best, the most painful disappointment. The biggest can weigh several ounces. Look for singletons or groups under oak, holly, etc. and Scots pine. Ceps seem to prefer clearings, heather and moss to leaf litter. Check for worm infestation. A year's supply, dried and awaiting use in the larder, is an important part of a cook's repertoire, and a comfort, which can make any good soup or sauce into a great one. Fry, stew, soup and dry: the best will freeze – 3 star.

Boletus aereus, the summer cep, is a variation which comes and goes earlier in the season. The cap is suede-like, the stalk is darker and the flavour equal to *Boletus edulis* – 3 star.

B. badius, the bay boletus, which bruises blue, is eaten as well as the cep – but is hardly worth it when both are available.
    N.B. *AVOID* any members of the family that are born coloured blue or red.

Agaricus campestris, the field mushroom, is easyish to identify. The cap is white and the gills are pink or chocolate, with a veil or the remains of one on the stem. Look for rashes in fields. Crops are said to be carried by stallions, but are less common than they were owing to the corn subsidy. The old-fashioned field mushroom beats most of the rest for flavour, provided it is in peak condition. Check for worm infestation and peel the old ones. Fry, soup, stew the buttons, ketchup – 3 star.
    Look out for the following members of the agaricus family:

A. augustus (the prince).
A. arvensis (horse mushroom), smells of aniseed, can get very big.
A. silvicola (wood mushroom), smells of aniseed again.
A. bisporus, the progenitor of the cultivated mushroom.

A. bitorquis, one of the few mushrooms that can grow under yew.

A. macrosporus, an habitué of road and motorway verges, larger than most.

N.B. *AVOID A. xanthodermus* (yellow stainer), an habitué of field margins, which visibly turns yellow when cut with a penknife and smells faintly of ink.

Morchella esculenta, **the morel,** is easyish to identify. The cap is brown and crinkly, the stalk white, the effect rude, and the season early summer. Look in wood edges on the chalk. I have eaten morels, in France, but have yet to capitalize on information gained about where they grow in England, or find lookalikes *M. elata* and *vulgaris*. Clean well. Fry, stew, dry – 3 star.

N.B. *AVOID Gyromitra esculenta*, the false morel.

Pleurotus ostreatus, **the oyster mushroom,** is easy to identify. The cap is grey and the gills are white. Look for brackets on dead, dying or fallen beech. I once found a clump on a Portakabin on an eel farm outside Nottingham. Oysters are often missed when growing above head height, but are not uncommon and are able to crop throughout the year. I have impregnated oak logs with the spores, which are available from seed companies, and await results. Fry, stew – 2 star.

Craterellus cornucopiodes, **the horn of plenty,** is unmistakable, but can be missed. You may be standing in a wood and suddenly see one dark and mysterious *trompette de mort* then find yourself surrounded. Look for rashes under beech. I go to a grove that delivers almost every year at the end of October and beginning of November. The colour of the fungus is transformed by cooking into a glossy and funereal black, made for a white plate and a cushion of scrambled eggs. Fry, stew – 2 star.

Sparassis crispa, **the cauliflower mushroom,** is unmistakable too. The fruit body looks like an old-fashioned Mediterranean sponge. The biggest can weigh several pounds. The 'colly' is a greater pleasure to find than almost any other fungi. Look at the base of pines and on stumps. It has a choice flavour, but needs careful cropping and cleaning. Cut neatly from the forest floor. Pull out unwanted bits of heather, grass and bracken, and scrape off any remaining soil with the point of a knife. Serve whole or in slices. Keeps well. Braise whole, fry, stew – 2 star.

Cantharellus cibarius, **the chanterelle,** is easy to identify. The fruit body is Dorothy Hartley's 'torn golden shawl' of the autumn woods, a flower amongst fungi, 'egg yolk yellow, the stem coming up straight . . . springing and spreading, stiff as a tiny fountain'. Look for clusters, particularly on banks under beech. They can be abundant but have never performed that well for me. The scent is mild, of apricots, and the flavour subtle. Keeps well for a mushroom. Fry or stew – 2 star.

N.B. The false chanterelle is closer to orange in colour, more pliable, less crinkly and grows individually among pines. The edge is rounded rather than blunt. It is falsely accused of being hallucinogenic, but is harmless, tasteless and not easily confused with the real thing when the two are seen together.

Tricholoma gambosum, **the St George's mushroom,** is easy to identify because of its season. It occurs on or around St George's Day on 23 April, which singles it out from other fungi. The cap and gills are white. Look for arcs and groups under lime, hazel, etc. The smell is floury and the flavour mild, but crops are a welcome sight after a long winter. Fry, stew – 1–2 star.

The B team (all 1 star)

Lepiota procera, **the parasol,** is easy to identify. The scaly light and dark brown global caps open out into umbrella shapes with white gills underneath. They can grow within yards of each other, hundreds at a time, marching into the distance like extraterrestrial props in *The War of the Worlds*. Look in open pasture and on rides. The flesh is better and less bulky when the cap is closed, the flavour pleasant. Fry or stew.

N.B *Lepiota cristata*, the shaggy parasol, which has a slightly rougher edge to its cap, grows in wood edges. It is said to cause tummy upsets in some people (not me).

Hydnum repandum, **the wood hedgehog,** is unmistakable. The cap is cream, its underside distinguished by spines rather than gills. Look under beech and hazel. The flesh is meaty, but can be bitter. Blanch and drain before cooking. Fry, stew, dry.

Lepista nuda, **the wood blewit,** is pretty unmistakable. The fruit body is blue all over, making it one of the prettiest fungi of all when collected in a basket and turned out on to the kitchen table. Look for disparate groups under oak, beech, hazel, etc. It was the first wild mushroom I found and cooked apart from *A. campestris*, and is the only one I have never found again, though it is supposed to be reasonably common. Fry, stew, dry.

Lepista saeva, **the field blewit,** is also pretty unmistakable. The cap is grey, the gills white, the stalk blue, hence the nickname 'blue leg'. Look for clusters. The 'field' prefix is a bit of a misnomer: field edges and hedgerows would be more accurate. Fry, dry.

Lycoperdon giganta, **the giant puffball,** is unmistakable. It is a brilliant white and can repeat in large quantities and grow to the size of a football or more. Horses, normally the most sure-footed of beasts, will inexplicably stumble into puffballs if they get the chance. Fifty or sixty in a field adjacent to a radar station, a mushroom in itself, is the oddest sight I have encountered on a 'fungus foray'. The fruit body, after being such an unearthly presence in the grass, when lifted and naked, its private parts revealed, looks almost pornographic. It also leaves a cute little nest behind. Puffballs are said to have been eaten at the Lord Mayor's former banquets in the City of London. A firm, fresh specimen sounds hollow when you tap it. The flesh is bulky. Fry.

Sarcoscypha coccinea, **the scarlet elf cup,** which fills with dew for the elves to drink, is unmistakable. Look for singletons or small groups on dead wood, usually fallen elm. They occur in my garden. Hallucinogenic? I do not think so. The flavour is mild but the colour cheers up egg dishes and salads. Fry or stew.

Coprinus comatus, **the shaggy ink cap,** is pretty unmistakable and compared to a lawyer's wig; it is white in infancy but soon degenerates into an inky, runny mass. Look for groups at road edges. Use extra-fresh.

    N.B. *AVOID C. atramentarius,* the common ink cap, if you like a drink. It may be edible but reacts with alcohol within a couple of hours, necessitating a couple more on the khazi. Take it from me.

I have also tried, but not returned to: the beefsteak fungus, chicken of the woods, common yellow *Russula,* fairy ring, Jew's ear, saffron milk cap, tawny grisette and yellow legs, amongst others.

FRYING

Every sort of edible mushroom can be used. Slice the large ones, and the largest into strips. Make sure you have a pan big enough to take them, preferably a wok. Put in a knob of butter or bacon fat, melt over a high heat and add the fungi before it burns. Cook quickly; if they shed water, until it evaporates. Otherwise turn down and cook through, stirring gently. When the mushrooms are tender, and have absorbed their own juice, season to taste. Serve on toast or with grilled meat, bacon, scrambled eggs or in omelettes.

To vary: put a chopped onion or shallot or crushed garlic in with the mushrooms, or finish them off with fresh parsley or chives or sweet paprika.

BRAISING

Use large fungi – particularly horse mushrooms, 'cauliflowers' or parasols – and a wok. Fry whole, as directed, but over a lowish heat and in a covered pan to cook the mushrooms through. When they are tender, uncover and reduce any cooking juices to a minimum. Season to taste, present whole, and carve in slices.

STEWING, IN CREAM

Use fungi of a light colour – ceps, morels, oysters, 'cauliflowers', chanterelles, St George's mushrooms, 'hedgehogs' or field blewits. Fry or braise as directed in butter, add ¼ pint of cream (150ml) for 2 people and stir it in. Stew gently until heated through, smooth and thick. Season as usual, using white pepper. Serve with sippets or as a sauce with pasta or roast chicken, pheasant or partridge.

DRYING

Use ceps thinly sliced, or whole morels and horns of plenty. A Rayburn or solid-fuel cooker gets the best results. Commit the fungi to a basket and suspend over the stove for six to eight hours; separate and repeat the process two or three times until they are dry. If you only have gas or electricity, lay the fungi out on a rack. Put it in the oven, set at the lowest possible temperature and leave for an hour. Do not let them turn black. Then put in a basket and leave over the radiator for a couple of days or as long as it takes the fungi to get thoroughly dry. Store in a jar. Use in soup (see below), stews and potato gratin.

KETCHUP

Use field mushrooms and family, or 'lawyers' wigs', gathered in dry weather, or else the ketchup will go musty. Put in a bowl and dust with fine sea salt. The fungi will shed their ink. Leave for three days, stirring occasionally, and strain. Add to the liquid obtained an equal quantity of port, and for every pint a blade of mace, a dozen black peppercorns, and a clove or two of crushed garlic. Reduce by half. Strain again, bottle and keep in the fridge. Use like soy sauce in soups, stews, dark sauces and gravies that need a kick upstairs.

SOUP

Special (for 4): use dried ceps. Sweat a chopped onion in 1oz (25g) of butter until soft; do not brown. Add ½oz (10g) flour to absorb the butter and cook over a gentle heat for a few minutes, stirring well. Heat 2 pints (1.2l) of game, chicken or duck stock and whisk it in a little at a time, increasing the heat. Add 1oz (25g) ceps, season to taste with salt and white pepper, cover and simmer for 30 minutes. Liquidize, but not until smooth. Finish with cream.

Everyday (for 4, adapted from Elizabeth David): use fresh field mushrooms and family, horns of plenty or parasols. Sweat a clove of crushed garlic in 1oz (25g) butter until soft. Add 1lb (450g) sliced fungi, 2 pints (1.2l) of stock, a thick piece of crustless white bread, a tablespoon of fresh parsley, a little grated nutmeg or mace and season to taste. Bring up to the boil, simmer for 20 minutes and liquidize. Finish with cream and more fresh parsley if you like.

TREES

Crab apples: are indigenous to England and Europe, occurring as far east as the Balkans. They are a remnant of ancient woodland, rare and often confused with the seedlings of cultivars. Any tree with indifferent fruit found growing outside a garden tends to be called a crab apple. The trouble is that there are ornamental varieties too, very statuesque and good pollinators.

One or two trees growing in the Forest may be the true crab apple. They are of medium height, tough, thorny and densely packed with branches. Both trees and fruit, which is small, yellow and falls in November, conform to the description 'crab' or 'crabbed', meaning gnarled or sour. The fallers do not go far, but may have provided the first cider. They can also be used to fortify perry. I made my first jelly with crab apples after the blistering summer of 1983, but have never got close to anything approaching the toffee-like richness from any other fruit.

Elder: 'So, what's all this about?' said the Asian girl working in our chemist.

'Cordial,' says I, paying for the tenth packet of citric acid she had sold that morning.

The month was June, and the lanes were overflowing with dreamy, heavily scented blossom. Elder surprises you. It is more evil than good, a tree that requires an explanation before felling, and provided Judas with a gibbet. There are several varieties including ornamental ones with 'black' or purple leaves. The wood is a brute, tough and non-combustible, but thought to have been used for sackbuts and grows a brown and flabby fungus known as Jew's ear, which some like to eat (though not me). The stems, which are hollow, made peashooters for children and plover calls for fowlers. An elder smells unpleasant, then throws up the most delicate white or pink flowers, fragrant as vanilla, that make the well-known cordial.

Take 20 heads of elderflower, fully opened, minus stalks, 2lb (900g) caster sugar, 2 lemons, cut up, 2oz (50g) citric acid and 2 pints (1.2l) boiled water left to cool.

Mix all well together in a large bowl and leave for five days, stirring a couple of times. Strain through muslin, commit to screw-top bottles, and keep in the fridge over the summer in order to stop the drink fermenting.

The commercial cordial, from coppiced elder groves, is pasteurised. There is a 'champagne', fizzy, which must be quickly drunk.

'Try elderflower pancakes,' says Geoffrey Grigson in *The Englishman's Flora* (a desert island book), 'circlets of the blossom held by the stem, dipped into batter, fried, and eaten with sugar.'

Wine-makers use the blue-black clusters of fruit.

Juniper is an evergreen English native and cypress, mistaken in the distance for yew, and one of the first to appear after the last Ice Age. 'The other trees spring up protected by the . . . prickles and eventually a wood is formed' (Rackham, 1986). Juniper's ability to colonize the chalk or limestone can be seen on the steep slopes of the cut through Twyford Down. I have also seen it growing near Roundway in Wiltshire, a Civil War battle site, and in the Derbyshire Peaks, the Yorkshire Dales and the Lake District.

Juniper starts as a compact bush and spreads into a gangly tree. Without competition and in full sun it can live to a great age, and takes years to rot down. A bough, placed over the lintel of a cottage door, is thought by the Scots to repel troublesome fairies. The wood is not highly valued except on the fire, giving out little smoke but filling the room with its beguiling scent. In some houses a juniper log was bound in a red ribbon to distinguish it from the others, put on to smoulder after dinner, and removed at bedtime.

The seeds are little green cones in their first year, and mature in their second, blue-black and high in oil. The English word 'gin' is a corruption of 'genever', from the Latin *juniperus* with which the drink is made. The seeds were used in excessive doses to end unwanted pregnancies in women, as was gin, linking ancient and modern, to kitchen-sink to folk lore. From a long and diverse history, Plymouth has emerged as one of the purest and least toxic of alcoholic drinks and Juniper as one of the most charming English surnames.

Juniper berries are strong, pungent, and inevitably used with venison in England, but popular abroad with a wider range of game, pork dishes and in sauerkraut. Use sparingly and pound in a mortar beforehand. For every 2 measures of pepper, use 1 of juniper. Gin, says Elizabeth David, is underemployed in cookery.

Rowan, the mountain ash, is another magical tree, and also a municipal one, with the combined powers of being able to ward off evil spirits, grow at high altitudes and adorn public parks and motorways. It lacks the stature, long life and burning qualities of the ash, but is used to make tools, and throws up plenty of fruit. The berries vary from orange to red. They are high in vitamin C, low in pectin, and should be combined with an equal quantity of crab apples in order to set. The different-coloured jellies that can be made from rowan look very becoming on a larder shelf. The bittersweet taste, not unlike marmalade, goes with venison and duck.

Wild service, *Sorbus torminalis*, a native of ancient woodland, is one of the most overlooked of English trees. Its title is more likely to be derived from the old English word *cyfre* than from the Latin *sorbus,* or *cervisia* meaning beer, though the fruit is known to have made and fortified alcoholic drinks as well as provided food from neolithic times. The seeds, which were mottled or chequered and called chequer berries, appeared before Christmas in Victorian markets (G. Grigson). Their name is shared by the PM's residence and other farms and houses located mostly in the Weald, where service trees grew in abundance, a connection muddled by pub signs bearing draughts or 'chequer' boards. There is also a *Sorbus domestica*, and a *S. devoniensis* available from specialist nurseries.

The service is having a toughish time. It is one of the species that may be hit by climate change. It grows slowly, coppices poorly and displeases foresters, but has a pretty maple-like leaf and white flower with a strange and elusive scent. There is no explanation why the tree has failed to register with garden designers and conservationists. I have planted three of four specimens to give them a leg up. The fruits should be picked in the autumn and left outside in bunches to 'blet' like medlars (see page 389), and sweeten during the first frosts. They are said to improve stomach disorders. The taste is almost exotic, the texture gritty. Service berries may be steeped in gin or vodka, the same as sloes (see page 381), or used to make a wine. The following house recipe (adapted) comes from the Chequers Inn, Smarden, Kent, via Richard Mabey in *Flora Britannica*.

Hang fruit on strings like onions until ripe. Cut off with scissors – do not pull out stalks. Put in a stone or glass jar with 1lb (450g) sugar scattered on the top of every 5lb (3kg) berries. Keep airtight until juice comes to the top, giving the occasional shake. Add brandy if you wish. The longer the liquor is kept, the better. Strain before drinking.

Bushes

Blackberries, brambles in Scotland, are a rose with the vigour of Rambling Rector and a blushing white flower. They stride across the ground and through the woods, the tip rooting and a new shoot walking on the following year. The only check to their progress comes from grazers and diggers like deer and pigs, a garden spade and seasoned hedge-layers – who will use the stems for binding hurdles. The seeds of the plant were carried in the guts of man and beast from one place to the next. There are thought to be over two hundred subspecies. The dewberry, Geoffrey Grigson's 'token blackberry', is smaller and comes earlier.

Blackberries are the last remaining link to the countryside that many people have, and the most familiar of hedgerow plants, but are not utilised as much as they were. The crowns of thorns, lined with cloth or leather, made rustic hats. The leaves went into stuffings. The fruit, which dyes the mouth, can also be used on cloth. It is very high in vitamin C. The large single berry on the end of a cluster, the first to ripen, is best eaten raw. The smaller ones last until Michaelmas. Use in a pie with apple (see page 428) or in blackberry junket:

> 'This is a very old recipe,' [says Hartley], good for people who cannot eat the seeds. Take a square of coarse strong cheesecloth and pile it full of the ripest blackberries . . . knot the four corners, slip a stick under them and twist, over a china bowl, pressing the bag with a wooden spoon, till it is full with rich, thick blackberry juice. Don't add anything . . . it should set solid in about two hours if left undisturbed in a warm room. It will be the consistency of junket, and is delicious served from the bowl with thin rolled brown bread and butter or sponge fingers [and of course Devonshire cream].

Dust with caster sugar. The taste is mild, the process intriguing.

Whortleberries: come from a low-growing shrub that likes acid soils, cropping up on moors, heaths and verges under dry-stone walls. They are known by several names, including bilberries and wimberries, a corruption of 'wine-berries' used in the north-west. Whorts are taken by deer, sheep and grouse but also human hands, patiently and sometimes armed with combs to tease the fruit from its bush. Some families claim exclusive rights of usage to land over which they have bent double to pick the whorts since their grandparents did the same.

'You recognize the same bottoms every year,' says Tessa Reitman, a Somerset girl born and bred. Also the telltale purple stains on hands and mouths.

Whorts are less than half the size of the American blueberry imported into England, of a deeper colour and an explosive flavour that goes a mighty long way and whisks me back to boyhood quicker than a plume of steam from the Taunton branch line steam train of my youth. They share the same flowering and fruiting season as most of the blackcurrants, finishing by the end of August, and should be eaten as soon after being picked as possible or lose their scent. I have never seen whortleberries in any form in a pub or restaurant, but did once buy a plastic cupful at a church fête on Dartmoor, and the tastiest ever pie at a market in Lytham St Anne's. Put with apple in a pie (see page 428). A tablespoon goes a long way.

The hedge lanterns: I have yet to make use of haws, gelder rose, and dog rose, another fruit high in vitamin C. The best home-made wine I have ever drunk, which looked and tasted like a medium dry sherry, was made from rose hips.

VEGETATION

Bath 'asparagus' is a curiosity: the spiked star of Bethlehem, *Ornithogalum pyrenaicum*, a former source of birdlime from the Pyrenees, highly regarded as a food. It was introduced by the Romans to the vicinity of Aquae Sulis, and appeared at markets in bundles within living memory. The plant is found elsewhere in the region, and on roadside verges closer to London, mostly in Wiltshire. The stem is slender, up to three feet tall, and bears a yellow flower. It has been happy in unimproved locations and ancient woodland, but cannot compete with the stronger vegetation let in with the light by the loss of elms to disease, and with man's passage through its ancestral sites.

One of the families in Bath used to go on expeditions to pick 'Sally in the Woods'. On moving to south Wiltshire after the war, they took a few plants to a farm near Teffont.* A colony was established, which is probably still there, but is of no interest to the present generation. Having been treated with contempt by a large majority, the usual thing has happened: a tiny minority is prohibited from picking the plant in the wild. I was able to obtain seeds from a specialist supplier that failed to germinate, and shall send for more. The bulbs take three years to develop and need to be protected from badgers. The crop, a former 'dainty of spring' that tempted Fortnum's (Geoffrey Grigson, 1958), should be treated like asparagus.

Bistort: *Persicaria* is a large perennial family with broad and pointed leaves, a dot in the middle and a light purple bottlebrush of a flower, which is related to the dock. The species plant occurs uninvited in many gardens. It is called by a variety of names, some of them obscure: Easter may- or man-giant is probably from *manger*, and ledge or ledger (I submit) a corruption of hedge. It is also known as adderwort or snake weed, after the twisted root. Bistort is eaten in the spring in parts of the north of England, notably Cumberland, Westmorland and the Pennines. It is considered to be medicinal and popular with deer and chickens.

I was not on location at the right time of year, but contacted Dorothy Rawson of the WI in Kendal who sent out an SOS requesting information. Over the next couple of weeks, a flood of heavenly handwritten and carefully typed recipes ebbed in my direction for Easter ledge, herb, herby, yarby or dock pudding, plus a coloured photograph of the genuine article from Jan Sargeant, nestling beside a pile of carrots and a splendid lamb chop on a green and white plate. The other correspondents included Jean Denney, Mrs Brearley, Mrs C. Nicholson, Mrs Powley, Mrs Stoker, Mrs Tetlow and Mrs Wadsworth. My telephone conversation with Laura Brough of Dalston lasted half an hour. Mrs R. Bowes of Shap, Mrs Nelson of Old Hutton, and Miss Garston of Burnside should not be forgotten, nor an anonymous contributor from

---

* *From botanist Barbara Last's article on Bath asparagus in* Wiltshire Life.

Witherslack. I emerged from the experience having found out what I wanted (to present *Housewives' Choice*).

Easter ledge pudding is cooked with meat in the north-west of England, fulfilling the same function as a batter pudding in Yorkshire, a suet pudding in Devon, and a vegetable pudding in the Newcastle area. It was sometimes eaten instead of meat on Good Friday. A variety of ingredients was used, of which Easter man-giant was one. The others were nettles, dandelion, lady's mantle, parsley, mint, gooseberry, raspberry and blackcurrant leaves, watercress, onions and all manner of vegetables and greenery (including the odd rhubarb top, which I have always understood to be poisonous, but in small quantities may have some homeopathic value). Local legend has it there was once an old lady in Staveley who put a hundred herbs into her pudding.

The recipes I was sent varied considerably. Some used a lot of Easter ledges, others more vegetables. The quantities were often unspecified, an increasingly rare indication of how cooking evolved from the food available (I love this sort of thing). Pearl barley was used by most contributors to bind the mixture, but so was oatmeal. Pinhead, perhaps? Again, there were considerable differences between the amounts in relation to the bistort and other ingredients.

Pearl barley takes a couple of hours to cook, less if soaked overnight. It is boiled in salted water in a muslin bag, or loose (watch the levels), then drained. The Easter ledges, etc. may be washed and cooked with the barley, stalks removed and chopped up – or cooked separately, drained and mixed in. To finish the pudding, season it, add butter, dripping or beaten egg and stir well. Commit to a dish and heat through for a few minutes.

Oatmeal does not take as long to cook as pearl barley. It is mixed with Easter ledges, etc., prepared as above, and cooked in water to the consistency of a porridge. Alternatively, bind the ingredients with beaten egg and steam for a couple of hours. In both cases, allow to cool, then slice or fry spoonfuls in bacon fat.

Chickweed is a low-growing bushy plant popular as chick feed, which resembles the scarlet pimpernel but has a star-shaped white flower – hence *Stellaria media*. It grows in gardens past and present near human habitation, gatecrashing the sites used for other vegetables and making useful ground cover. The texture of chickweed is dense and the flavour rather nutty – a pleasant addition to a salad.

Fat hen is an annual goosefoot, and member of a family including Good King Henry (see page 413) and orache, all of which are edible. It appears in fields, gardens and borders, in muck, unsterilised compost, and imported topsoil, and could be Europe's oldest vegetable. The plant was known in England as *melde* by the Anglo-Saxons, underwent cultivation, and was remembered in villages like Melbourn in Cambridgeshire, Melbourne in Derbyshire (Grayson, 1976) and Milden in Suffolk. When the door opened for spinach, it closed on fat hen, which is quicker to wilt, though the taste of the two after seasoning and their benefits to health are similar. Stir fry.

Fennel, a Roman introduction and escapee, is tall and feathery, soft but tough, and green or bronze in colour; a relation of the cultivated bulb. It will colonise both waste and prepared ground and likes maritime locations. Fennel is a handy fly repellent, accomplished cook Betty Butt told me, in which the fish on her native Dorset coast were packed.* The two entered kitchens in the same box, they were cooked together and a long association began. The smell of the plant, which is said to inhibit other vegetables as well as insects, is one of aniseed.

Garlic, hedge is an upright biennial, which tolerates the shade and populates the margins of field, road and track. The soft heart-shaped leaves appear in late winter, and release the smell of garlic when rubbed; the delicate white flower breaks open by May. The taste is a little bitter, but lovers of Campari and endive will take to it in salads.

Garlic, wild is a native of dark, damp places, with leaves like lily-of-the-valley and a fragmented white flower. It grows in clumps on banks and in all-consuming carpets in a favourable wood, excluding any other understorey. The old English name of 'ramsons' lives on in Ramsbottom (Lancashire) and Ramsey (Cambridgeshire), though the plant is more abundant in the West Country today. The smell of wild garlic is pungent, the taste strong when raw, mild when fried or in a soup.

Good King Henry is a perennial goosefoot from southern Europe, known to the Greeks, spread by the Romans, 'Mercury' to classicists and 'Henry' to the Germans. The 'King' is an English twist (Geoffrey Grigson, 1958). As a crop, GKH seems to have been of some importance in Tudor gardens. It endured in certain areas, then fell into neglect with competition from spinach and ultimately joined the ranks of escapees. Or so the story goes. Having failed to find any plants in the wild over the course of several years, I was obliged to send for seeds. In its second year, Good King Henry is strong, to say the least, indifferent to being moved and looking forward to being split. The leaves and flowers, which are said to be edible, taste bitter. To obtain

---

* *Betty Butt: dairywoman of the old school, born and bred on the Isle of Purbeck. Her parents rented a farm from a landowning Roman Catholic family, whose every last tenant, labourer, gardener and servant were also Catholics.*

'poor man's asparagus', you force the stalks, pick them before they go hollow, and steam or boil them in a bundle. They do it to a nicety in Lincolnshire. What is the secret? I wonder.

Hairy bittercress is a frilly little annual with a white flower, early to appear. It likes bare and rocky places, appearing between the bricks on my terrace, but also deep soils, popping up when there is little else about except snowdrops and hellibores. The plant needs careful washing but, with lamb's lettuce and watercress, makes a nice winter bite. The taste is like mustard.

Hops are natives as well as escapees of plants in cultivation; a perennial with a soft little fir cone of a flower that climbs like runner beans, but to twice the height and in the opposite direction around a pole. They are or were intensively grown in Kent, Herefordshire and Worcestershire, and were more widely distributed elsewhere than imagined. There is a field in a neighbouring village registered on old maps as Hop Garden. The shoots appear uninvited in the semi-shade in May in my Hampshire garden and next to the local allotment. The younger the plant, the more like asparagus it looks. The taste, characteristically, has a little of the agreeable bitterness it gives to beer. Cut a small bunch of hop shoots when three or four inches long, steam and eat with butter, or commit to an omelette.

Pignut is an umbellifer, coming from the same family as carrots, parsnips, cow parsley, sweet cicely, etc. It is short, slender and delicate, with a toothy leaf, and likes a variety of soils both acid and alkaline. I have found plants within sight of the last eagle's nest in England, within sound of the Cornish sea, and within yards of my door on the edge of the New Forest. Pignuts, a children's favourite, could be the 'nuts in May' gathered in the nursery rhyme (but so could green walnuts). The root or tuber is the edible part. It is not easy to locate even with a penknife, and still less easy when the stalk breaks off, as it habitually does. The skin is like a hazelnut's and the flesh white and crunchy: another test for a Clever Dick. Eat raw or cook.

Sorrel is a ground-hugging perennial that competes with grass and looks like a small dock, but has an inverted, arrow-headed leaf. The plant, cultivated in France, is the texture of spinach and tastes of lemon. A lot of sorrel goes a little way, but impresses itself on lacklustre dishes. Put it raw in salads and soups, and softened in butter in a cream sauce for chicken or fish .

Stinging nettles have more saving graces concealed behind a vicious and indomitable front than almost any other species. Standing nettles break hard ground, condition the soil and, in full sun, feed the larvae of the peacock butterfly. Stricken nettles help along the compost heap and, after soaking in water, make an excellent fertilizer for the vegetable garden. Young nettles are high in protein; old ones are poisonous but can make a form of cloth. The sting, the Romans discovered, makes you tingle and keeps you warm. It is also good for arthritis, and neutralized when plants are cooked. 'Granny's nettle drink' was a country favourite associated with Lancashire, sold at the cottage door to cyclists, walkers and passers-by, which seems to be coming back. It is made like tea, with dried nettles or fresh. A soup was popular during the war. Use the tops before they flower. Cut in March and April wearing gloves.

I have tried but not returned to alexanders, cow parsley, ground elder, hogweed, etc.

Flowers

Alkanet, evening primrose, violas, and nasturtiums 'in' one moment and 'out' the next, are the commonest in salads. Rose petals may also be used.

Snails

My father took me out from prep school one Sunday in the 1950s. We spent the whole afternoon on the chalk belt of the Surrey downs collecting snails that he claimed were edible and a Roman introduction. We took over a hundred home, let them loose in the garden and moved house, never getting to eat any. I subsequently heard that labourers on the Mendips used to grill snails, or 'wallfish', on ranges in some of the local pubs. Snails have also been Lenten fare in England and gathered by country children for pigs.

When Roald Dahl's wife, Liccy, was fifty, I cooked for them. He was terrific to work for and a great host. She, also kind, lent me a book of recipes going back several hundred years. It belonged to the Throckmortons, her mother's family, confederates of Guy Fawkes, and came from Coughton Court in Warwickshire. There were standard entries and references to things like truffles, morels and coxcombs, also instructions for potting an otter, and for viper soup, which was said to deter leprosy. Snail broth was made as follows:

> First gather 40 or 50 snails in a garden, slit them and take out all the green but more of the fat, then wash them in water with a little salt and wipe them with a cloth till all the slime is off them; have ready a chicken cut in pieces with a little bugloss, agrimony, and the leaves of endives, and so boil them in the broth. When the chicken is half boyld, put in the snails being clean wiped, so let them boil till all the strength is boiled out. When the broth is ready to take off, put in eaither a little mace . . . or Rosemary, which herb pleaseth the taste. Drink this a fortnight.

FROM THE SEASIDE

Beachcombing is in the blood. The bigger the wreck, the bigger the crowd of people that can materialise on a cliff, the greater the swarm down below absorbed with ropes and baskets, the louder the cries and more frantic the signals to haul up the timber, crates and cargo washed ashore. Even an empty cove will bring the odd prospector, out for more than a stroll or swim. Diggers for bait may be encountered, or collectors of driftwood, but not so often a smart 'bag lady' busily engaged above the high-water mark on the Cornish Riviera. I, trying to keep three OAPs in order with cream teas, stole a minute to ask what she was doing. The woman said she was picking wild 'spinach'. Her grandfather, a mounted customs and excise officer in Cornwall, removed to the Isle of Wight, had introduced her to it over fifty years before.

Sea beet is a version of leaf beet, a possible Roman introduction, biennial and an escapee with a taste for maritime locations. It is found overlooking beaches, poking through the grass, earth, rocks or stones. The larger clumps throw up hundreds of firm, fleshy, shiny bottle-green leaves, the size and shape of a blunt spearhead. Sea beet can be eaten all year round, even in spring and early summer if denied the light to flower, but tends to attract dogs near footpaths and civilisation. It is now illegal to pick this plant – the most pathetic of bureaucratic decisions, seeing as how only new-age cooks and seasoned country people ever bother, and it is not endangered anyway. Forever on the lookout for such developments, I gathered seeds on the Essex coast that have prospered in the garden and taste better than spinach. A good one for the hungry gap.

Sea cabbage is another possible Roman introduction, biennial and escapee. It grows along the cliffs of the Channel coast, notably in Kent and Dorset, and up north as well. There may be a problem with cross-fertilisation with the neighbouring brassicas grown on farms – rape in particular. Country people have gone on record as selling wild cabbage in various markets until the twentieth century. I gathered seeds on the Yorkshire coast and sowed them with sea beet in the garden. The plants proved as strong and resistant to pests as I had hoped, each one branching out from the main stalk rather than throwing up a single head, like a January King. They need a good boiling – the flavour is strong – but you may cut and come again over the winter until flowering takes place in May.

Sea kale is a perennial famously advertised as one of the few native vegetables. It belongs to pebble banks. The colonies on the south coast look from a distance like a rash of fungi creeping slyly towards the shore. They root very deeply in the shingle, dying back to straw in the winter and bursting through in the spring. The leaves are a powdery blue-green, the stalks purple, the flowers yellow and the seeds imprisoned in little brown balls. Wild sea kale goes on record as having been sold in Kent, Sussex and Dorset. You are not permitted to dig it up – or anything else: I am not sure of the position with seeds. Garden plants are either propagated annually, earthed up and fitted into the rotation, or blanched under cloches on a permanent site – processes that are not understood by the seed companies. Cut sea kale as low as possible, once only, allowing it to regrow. Only the stalks are worth eating. Top, tail, steam and serve with melted butter or *sauce hollandaise.*

Marsh samphire or glasswort is a hardy and invasive annual, and former component of glass. It begins as pink or green stubble and rises in spiky, bushy beds from mudflats and banks covered by the tide. The plant is associated with Norfolk, but is picked throughout East Anglia, in Lincolnshire and along suitable parts of the coast from Kent to Cornwall. It is delightful to find bunches, in a country greengrocer's and fishmonger's. Samphire, a feature both at royal banquets and on pub menus, is the best known of the wild vegetables sold in England – though the earliest crops on sale are from Brittany. Pickers were endangered by EU bureaucracy and hardline conservationists, which provoked a flood of correspondence in the newspapers and enabled them to survive. My wife and I have struck out over many a mudflat and returned with samphire. The plant reaches perfection with asparagus on the longest day, 23 June, and becomes woody by August. Pull, wash and eat raw, or blanch in boiling water, stripping the flesh from any stalks with your teeth.

Rock samphire, the true samphire as opposed to glasswort, is a small spare bush. It pokes out from cliffs and stony ledges overlooking the sea. Shakespeare's reference to the harvesting of samphire as a 'dreadful calling' is due to the number of people who allegedly fell to their deaths while trying to get that elusive bunch. The trade, once considerable, seems to have been ruined by the attempt to pass off weeds as the real thing and the improvement in garden vegetables since the eighteenth century. The plant crops in the spring and used to be pickled in salt and vinegar. It is probably health-giving, but tastes strongly of iodine and, to my knowledge, has not been eaten within living memory except as an experiment.

Seaweed

Rises with the tide and falls too, lying draped over the rocks, lank and limp as the hair on a wet poodle, or spluttering and gurgling to itself on the foreshore. It is something to pop in your fingers and treacherous to walk upon, often taken for granted, but of great practical use. The amounts collected by farmers are recorded in William Borlase's eighteenth-century *Natural History of Cornwall.* A woodcut of a characteristic horse and cartload on a Devon beach, with Lundy in the background, appears in Mrs Webb's twentieth-century *Farmhouse Cookery.* For some, seaweed is still an important crop. There is a man known as 'the Greyhound' in his locality after the quick and sure-footed way he scrambles over the rocks collecting a particular type of seaweed. His itinerary is secret.

Livestock, if permitted and fodder is short, will go to the foreshore in winter. The sheep on the island of North Ronaldsay are famous for doing so. The seaweed is said to give their meat more flavour, a pig more weight, a cow more milk, and a hen more eggs with yolks of a deeper colour. When gathered, seaweed breaks down into an excellent fertiliser, repels cats, and makes gelatine. Kelp provided a mainstay of the Hebrides. It was used in the production of iodine, soap, glass and bleach for linen, and to cure a long list of ailments by family doctors. Seaweed is healthy, sustainable, natural and magical stuff.

The seaweeds are green from the chlorophyll they contain or coloured by a pigment. The greenest occur at the high-water mark, the brown ones (the largest and longest) at half-tide, and the red ones further out. Four native species are considered good to eat, of which three are marketed in the west of England, Wales and Northern Ireland, and one for the table. Their flavours vary. They are strange to the uninitiated, but 100 per cent natural and, for me, worth getting used to.

Laver: mentioned by Pliny, laver is the 'black butter' of north Devon and Somerset, really dark green, which clings to the rocks in satin-like ribbons from Watchet to Hartland Point and beyond. It is laverbread in Wales and *algue celtique* to the French. A cool summer and a calm sea produce a good harvest; a week of storms tears it from the beds. Crops are cut with scissors when there is an 'r' in the month, and improved by the first frosts.

The age-old way of washing laver was to stream it in a brook, allowing the current to do the work. On the coast of north Devon and Somerset it was then dried in one of the huts overlooking the Bristol Channel. Today it is washed and left overnight for the creepy-crawlies to make an escape. Next morning it is boiled to a pulp for several hours in water, acidulated with vinegar and refrigerated or frozen. Laver is not difficult to gather, clean and cook, but seems to taste better when the experts do it.

In the established victuallers and market stalls of north Devon and south Wales, the laver or laverbread comes loose. Steve the Fish in Barnstaple, formerly of Taylors in Butcher Row, used to sell a quarter of a ton a week in season. Upcountry, laver is occasional. In supermarkets it is unknown. The seaweed in London is more likely to be imported from Japan.

Country people swear by the iron content of laver, and its ability to purify the blood. It is welcome as a vegetable, especially when cabbage and greens are short, looks like spinach and tastes all the more delightful for a squeeze of orange juice, sweet or Seville. Salt and pepper are not required. The pungent flavour seems to signal it is doing you good. Laver is too much for fish, moderate with beef, good with fowls, lamb and pork, excellent with bacon, and better with a hot ham than anything else on earth. A couple of spoonfuls will also improve a lacklustre soup. In Northern Ireland, laver is known as sloke and sometimes goes to the table in a special pot.

Carragheen: *Chondrus crispus*, 'though now thought of as an Irish speciality,' said Dorothy Hartley in 1954, 'was called Dorset Moss. Near Cerne Abbas I found it hung up in cottages, where they used it medicinally. In Yorkshire it is made into blancmanges.' The appearance is like lichen and the colour almost purple, but blanched by the sun and wind after being washed up by the tide. Crops can be gathered from beaches in the summer already 'processed' by Nature, or picked from rock pools earlier in the season and left to dry, either protected from the wind or under a net. Plain 'moss', as it is known to brewers like myself, is used to clarify beer. To cook, cover with milk and sweeten to taste with sugar. Heat gently for about fifteen minutes or until the mixture thickens and begins to resemble a white sauce, and strain. Serve hot as a custard, or cold as blancmange, having been poured into a shallow jelly mould and turned out when set. The flavour is a curious one, faintly of iodine, but not disagreeable.

Dulse, or *Palmaria palmata,* consists of paper-thin red straps. It is found swishing around the sea at low water, often clinging to the holdfasts of kelp. Crops can be gathered and dried like 'Dorset moss'. It is ignored in England at present, but treated as an edible chewing gum in Northern and Southern Ireland, sold in packets, and said to make a cracking hard liquor. Dulce, which looks as fragile as laver, is cooked for just as long. Cover with water and leave in a cool oven for the afternoon, then reduce the consistency to a porridge.

Pepper dulse: *Laurencia pinnatifida*, is a wild card and misnomer, neither peppery nor dulse. It clings to the rocks at half-tide, peaking nicely in time for the summer holidays. The tips are a brilliant yellow, bright as gorse in flower. The texture is crunchy. The flavour, rather than being of iodine, is hard to believe – a mixture of oil and garlic. No vegetable is more unexpected: another one for a Clever Dick. Wash and eat raw as a snack, or chop and sprinkle over salads.

I cannot recommend picking the following for food:

Sea holly (an eryngium), a relation of the ornamental favourites Blue Star and Miss Wilmott's Ghost, used to provide roots for candy but is now protected.

Sea purslane has a garden equivalent, entitled 'miners lettuce', which is overwintered, easy to grow and better to eat.

Sea pea is pleasant to look at, no more.

CHAPTER THIRTY

TRUFFLES

RANK WOULD ARRIVE IN THE NORMANDY STORES, where I worked as a grocer, on Fridays and Saturdays. He wore a tweed coat and boots, a high chef's hat for the occasion, and stood in the corner by the counter with an air of great importance, chatting to customers. To people he favoured he said boldly, 'Come,' in a Germanic accent. 'I show you de vay to de Connaught.' To the rest he did not speak. To those of us who served, he barked the occasional order. Frank never did much, but was fun to have around and swept the floor at the end of the day. We used to give him a couple of quid to take home.

Frank was born around 1900, near Pilsen, formerly part of the Austrian Empire and known for truffles and *foie gras*. He fought in both wars, survived a firing squad, cooked throughout Europe and worked as a valet for Gregory Peck. He came to England in 1942, made for London, and found employment with a butcher in Ladbroke Grove who traded horse meat and included Winston Churchill among his customers.

After the war, Frank took a day trip to the south coast. On the return journey, the coach stopped for a breather. Frank disembarked with the other passengers and found himself sniffing the air. The scent that hung in the autumn woods took him back to childhood and the countryside around Pilsen.

'*Les truffes!*' Frank said, waving his hand. 'Everyvair.'

In those days, I never even knew they grew in England.

In *The Domestic Dog*, Brian Vesey Fitzgerald revealed the following. He had lived for forty years in what he called 'truffle country', meaning south Wiltshire. The number of dogs he had seen used as finders was 'a good many'. By 1957 half a dozen remained, implying a trade that may have been going, but had not gone. In the same era, Sheila Hutchins used to buy English truffles from a cooked-meat shop in the King's Road, Chelsea. An old man brought them up from the country every season, then failed to reappear, and the line went dead.

The truffle is a subterranean fungus and parasite that favours mainly beech, oak, lime, cedar and hazel, cropping well from adolescence onwards with the nuts and mast. It thrives on a substratum of chalk, moisture and a warm back end (autumn), suffering in droughts and from predation by vermin. The first English truffles were recorded in Northamptonshire over three centuries ago. Since then they have been found all over the South Downs, in private gardens, and in locations as diverse as Durham and Dorset, Bristol University and Wormwood Scrubs. The truffles dug up in Scotland were probably carried north on the roots of trees transplanted earlier this century.

Truffles, 'trooffles' (patrician), 'trubs' (Wiltshire) or 'fossils' (Sussex) come from the genus *Tuber*. There are about twelve natives. The summer or garlic truffle, *Tuber aestivum*, sold in Victorian markets as 'green' (i.e. fresh), is the most precious. The winter truffle of Périgord, *T. melanosporum*, which looks very similar, is not supposed to grow in England. The white truffle, *T. magnatum*, has yet to be recorded outside Italy: it has nothing in common with pignut except colour, though the two have been confused. The Burgundy truffle, *T. unicatum*, is one of the varieties that is spreading with cultivation.

The type of truffle mentioned in literature has not always been clear, and the use of the name, innocent or otherwise, is freer than it deserves to be. The 'red truffle' was not a tuber but an earthball, *Melanogaster broomeianus*, which came to be associated with Bath. The 'false truffle' was a title given to some of the poorer, mostly harmless and indifferent relations of the real thing that were passed off as worth eating in Victorian England. Crops were 'gathered by Italians and Frenchmen', said a challenging *Encyclopaedia Britannica* in 1910, 'for the inferior dining-rooms of London where continental dishes are served'.

Dogs were used to locate most of the truffles found in England. A poodle–terrier cross with scent over sight, indifferent to game, was the popular choice. The most acute were credited with powers of detection that could be exercised downwind from twenty yards or more. Pups with truffle-hunting in their ancestry, naturally attracted to the scent, fetched a premium. A novice, coupled to an adult, could begin work at three months old.

Sows,* which are attracted to the scent of truffles and rooters by nature, do not require training. They are less easy to transport and control than dogs, but are used in France and were in England by the Kinnairds and other families who lived and worked on the great estates. Most truffle-hunters were part-timers, keepers and woodmen in the winter, labourers and hurdle-makers in the spring and summer, who did other jobs to make ends meet. A William Leach walked up country from Cornwall looking for truffles in the nineteenth century. He stopped and settled in Patching in Sussex. The Olivers of Goodwood and the Jepsons or Gepsons of Northington are mentioned by various sources. The Hatchetts, Annetts and Leroys of Hampshire were said to be of French stock, imported by English grandees in the nineteenth century. Jesse Wells, a Romany, who gathered crops near Southampton, took them by pram around the hotels. The Yeatses of south Wiltshire produced many truffle-hunters. The Brays and Harraways were similarly engaged. It is not difficult to find the names and families in whom the occupation ran.

In 1860, twelve men from Winterslow, near Salisbury, replied with a petition to a proposed tax on dogs. A correspondent from *Longman's Magazine*, speaking highly of the village, its frank

---

* ''ogs and dogs', as the saying went, were used in Sussex though sows seem to have been more effective.*

and independent population, and 'cosy white-walled cottages', declared a visit necessary in order to understand the truffling trade. Eli Collins, a resident, and the best-known of the hunters enjoyed a seventy year career in which he found the biggest ever recorded tuber and in the right company. Edward VII accepted this truffle on behalf of his mother, exchanging it for her 'photograph' on a sovereign (as requested by Collins) which was less than half the market price and shrank in folk lore to a farthing. Queen Victoria is said to have had two truffle hounds herself, a present from Albert she never used.

Collins had access to more than a dozen estates in Wiltshire and one in Berkshire owned by a fellow Moonraker[*]. He was a handsome man from his photos. He worked in a collar, tie and green velvet coat with voluminous pockets given him by a local grandee, in which he was able to carry truffles, food and his dogs when they tired. He also received a certificate that gave him the run of the Longford estate. In common with other hunters, he had a stout wooden staff with a fork at one end for digging, a point at the other for poking, and a hook for brambles. His figure in the woods was locally familiar, but his reputation spread, with correspondence reaching him addressed to only 'Collins, Trufflehunter, Salisbury Plain' (according to local historian Norman Thorne). Trade peaked at the end of the nineteenth century and declined from 1914.

Alfred, Eli's elder boy, hunted on his own from about sixteen. On Monday mornings in season, he set out from home wearing an apron and pushing a bike with his baskets fore and aft. The work paid for the occasional drink in the Pheasant, and a bed or train ticket when it took him further afield. People either went to Alfie's cottage to buy their truffles or received them in shoeboxes through the mail. The post office in Winterslow was known for the scent it bore. The village hall had a picture of local hunters, copied from photographs, which is now in Roche Court.

Alfie was the sixth and last generation of his family to dig truffles. He did not go out much after the Second World War; nor did anyone else. He died aged eighty in 1953, a man much mourned, with an ancillary line in morels and friends in high places, though poor himself. His daughter, Lily, whom I looked up before she died, lived with a companion in Whiteparish. Collins still has descendents in the area, but none to whom he passed on his itinerary and the knowledge of the treasure buried in the soil.

The future of the occupation rests with men like Robbie Williams, plumber, who is admitted to estates in the area. He is well qualified. His antecedents arrived in Winterslow

---

[*] *Occupant of Wiltshire, where consignments of illegal brandy were hidden in ponds from customs officers. Men caught at night in the water with barrels, pretending to be simple, are supposed to have said they were looking for moonbeams.*

during the eighteenth century. At almost the same moment in history, the first truffle-hunting Collins acquired two dogs that had been left by an itinerant Spaniard in a cottage on Salisbury Plain. Robbie has already copied the stout yew truffling iron that Lily inherited from her father and gave to Salisbury Museum. The velvet coat, once famous, is there for the copying too.

Edwin Tucker and Company, seedsmen of south Devon, was amongst the first people to import trees into England inoculated with the spores of truffles. Downy oak and hazel were favoured as hosts, and sold at eighteen months with planting instructions, having been inspected and certified. Crops were expected in 5–8 years. A lime-rich soil no more than 65 per cent clay, and a PH around 7.2 was recommended by the vendors. Truffle UK, based in Dorset, has taken up the baton.

I was prevented from buying a tree by my garden, which failed on all counts to provide the right conditions for truffles. The alternative was to find them. People do in England, often at first by chance, having stumbled on infested woods. They have also kept it quiet, laid false trails and added to the fund of tall and other stories. Diviners with rods, and swarms of yellow flies consorting with truffles, increase the mystique. In the absence of hard facts to go on, my wife and I considered getting a likely-looking mongrel, and training him up on a find-and-reward basis, only to delay every year. It did not make sense to spend the autumn looking for objects unlikely to be there in the first place.

One thing does not lead to another in my experience, but it can. On a brighter November morning than usual, having left my name with a contact the previous day and written it off, the telephone rang. The call was from a woman who had discovered some truffles with her husband. She would not at first tell me who she was or where they lived, but changed her mind during our conversation. There was no need to fear I would broadcast her secrets, I explained. It would not be fair, let alone wise, with so many of my own.

My wife and I went to their farm, highly excited, and exchanged firm handshakes. We were led straight to an outhouse full of things that I hardly noticed owing to the one in mind. A generation had passed since I had met Frank, then Lily Collins, and first harboured an unfulfilled ambition to find a truffle. It was a failure I had learned to live and possibly die with, a familiar and comfortable one that, at the prospect of it ending, brought forth irrational fears. The reasons why a couple would want to share their secret, and with two strangers, at that moment and in this place, were not clear. The simplicity of the situation provoked a flood of complex thoughts. Surely there would be some disaster lurking that would get in the way of events unfolding as intended. None materialized. There, on a shelf, in a fridge, and in my hand, was an English truffle.

It was harder, heavier, lumpier, wartier and crustier than I had anticipated, more durable, dense and resilient. The skin was a bit like a lychee's, but black as soot, and scrubbed up well under the tap. It cut and revealed an interior the colour and consistency of milk chocolate, marbled with diminutive white flecks, fronds and veins. The scent was clean and fresh, hinting at the strength to come. A mushroom is defenceless and fragile, but a truffle is a tough little chap. It has attitude.

The wood in which the truffles had been found did not bear any sign of its enchantment. We followed a path to a spot where the first of many tubers, displaced perhaps by a badger, had fetched up in the open under a tree. We felt on the ground with the soles of our feet for telltale bumps, drawing a blank or falling for onion couch, then moved on and on again, sinking to our knees in the autumn sun. I was not willing to entertain the thought that the season might be over. I was going to find a truffle. My mood had changed; my mind was clear. My heart worked away with my hands as they pulled back the moss and parted the leaves, then almost stopped. A growth, a shape, an orb, firmly embedded and promising more under ground than above, was poking up through the soil. I exposed the topknot, followed by the side, and rocked it to and fro, prising the bottom out of the ground and leaving a cosy-looking hollow. I stood and weighed up the truffle. It was almost the size of a cricket ball, but heavier.

My wife joined in, busily feeling the floor of the wood for any truffles. She found one too, then another and another, growing in the characteristic ring they make around a tree about six feet from the trunk. With the help of our host and hostess, and her little wooden rake, we collected several pounds in a basket. We could have taken more but left them for the earth. At length we noticed the decline of the sun. It was late afternoon, getting cold and time for tea.

The scent of truffles met us in the kitchen and wafted through the door into the hall. We ate them thinly sliced and raw on white bread and toasted muffins, with butter I had brought from my private supply. The day closed on the same open, generous and spontaneously intimate footing that had marked it throughout. We parted with a present I had done my best to make into a purchase. My search for an English truffle had ended; my kitchen would bear the scent as well, my larder would bear the trophy. I had even survived the excitement.

In the light of recent discoveries, and the season observed by deceased collectors, scientific opinion may have to change. Either the summer truffle endures throughout the year, or the winter one occurs in England too. The time may come when they are continually uncovered, cultivated in gardens and sold in shops. It will be a joy to have them, but not the pleasure of waiting for twenty-five years.

Cook's Oracle

The crowning glory of a truffle is its smell – uniquely and deeply fruity, pungent, penetrating and powerful. It ripens and increases over the period of a week or two, and should infuse whatever you are cooking with it. The flavour is subtle, suggestive, elusive, lingering and, as *Tuber aestivum*'s nickname suggests, not unlike garlic. The improvement that a truffle bestows on the flavour of other foods, and a longer life than other fungi, are its main assets.

Truffles will keep in a cold, airy place or refrigerator for up to two weeks. Immersed in olive oil, they store for two months: use a mild variety of oil (the Italians use grapeseed oil) and seal the jar. If a tuber starts to go soft, eat it quickly. Some people remove the skin from the larger specimens.

Truffled eggs: take a dozen eggs, preferably from under the hen, and a truffle the size of a walnut, washed and dried. Put them together in an airtight container and seal the lid. Leave for two or three days to allow the scent of the fungus to permeate the shells. Break the eggs into a bowl and beat with a fork in the usual way. Peel and thinly slice the truffle, adding it to the bowl, and season to taste. Then scramble the eggs, or make an omelette, not too firm.

Dressing for salad: use truffle oil with a good-quality vinegar, go easy on the salt and do not add pepper; grate some truffle over the top.

Unlikely as it sounds, truffles have been cooked as a vegetable in England during gluts. My father claimed to have eaten them steamed for a couple of minutes and brought to the table wrapped in a napkin.

CHAPTER
THIRTY-ONE

PUDDINGS

F THERE IS A GAP in the repertoire of Haute Cuisine,' wrote Delia Smith, 'it is . . . in the area of . . . "proper puddings". You'd have thought it would have taken a really exotic dish to get a Frenchman beside himself with admiration for the cookery of any other country', but that is what happened in seventeenth-century England. And if our visitor had lived 150 years later, he would have been even more impressed. 'Nowadays, of course, he would have been hard pushed to find a traditional pudding on a restaurant menu.' Fortunately, there are exceptions. A pub near me had a customer who used to come for lunch, omit the main course and order two puddings. Most places and all seasons had their own. Here is a small selection.

APPLE PIE

This is a pudding for the autumn and winter made with dessert fruit, which keeps its texture. Blackberries, whortleberries and mulberries add colour, flavour and importance.

For 6, you will need a 8 x 1½ inch (20 x 4cm) pie plate. Sweet pastry (see page 60) using 6oz (175g) plain flour, 1 dessertspoon icing sugar, 3oz (75g) frozen butter, large pinch of salt, 2½ tbsp of ice-cold water, 1½ lb (700g) dessert apples, with core and peel (5 medium sized), 2oz (50g) white or light brown sugar.

Make the pastry and rest in larder. Wash, dry, peel and core the apples. Wrap the flesh in a plastic bag. Put the cores and peel in a pan with a pint (600ml) of water. Bring up to the boil, loosely cover and simmer gently for 30 minutes. Roll out the pastry, cut a strip from the edge and stick it to the rim of the pie plate, brushed with water. Strain the liquid and return to the pan (discarding the cores and peel). Add the sugar and boil hard for about 15 minutes, reducing the liquid to a syrup. Do not let it burn. Slice the apples and arrange in the dish. Pour over the syrup. Brush the prepared rim of the dish with water and cover with the pastry. Press down the edges to seal, and trim. Make a tiny hole in the top to allow steam to escape and glaze with milk. Place on a baking tray and cook in a preheated oven 230°C/450°F/gas mark 8 for 25 minutes. You want the pastry to cook but do not want the pie to lose juice. Let it cool a bit before serving with cream or custard.

CHRISTCHURCH COLLEGE PUDDING

A lemon tart.

For 6, you will need an 8 x 1½ inch (20 x 4cm) fluted tart tin with a removable bottom and a wire rack. Sweet pastry (see page 60) using 6oz (175g) plain flour, 3oz (75g) frozen butter, large pinch of salt, 2½ tbsp of ice cold water. For the filling, 4oz (110g) sugar cubes, 2 lemons, 3 egg yolks, 2 egg whites, 4 tbsp cream, 1oz (25g) melted butter, 2 tbsp brandy. Duck eggs are usually a better colour than hens'. Goose eggs are best – use 1 and subtract some of the white.

Make and cook a sweet pastry case (see pages 60). Rasp the rinds of the two lemons on the sugar cubes. Crush the sugar in a bowl. Mix in the egg yolks. Whisk the whites and fold them in. Stir in the cream and melted butter, the juice of one of the lemons and the brandy. Pour into the pastry case and cook in a preheated oven at 180°C/350°F/gas mark 4 for 30 minutes.

Bachelor's pudding

An autumn or winter steamed bread pudding even bachelors can make. This produces a large pudding which is good cold, or heated up, fried in unsalted butter and dusted with caster sugar.

For 6–8, you will need a large, size 24 (63fl oz) china pudding basin (or a plastic one with a fitting lid), a saucer or ring to put it on, and a pan deep enough to put them in, 8oz (220g) chopped cooking apples (after peeling), 8oz (220g) breadcrumbs, 6oz (175g) currants, 6oz (175g) castor sugar, ½ tsp nutmeg, pinch of salt, 1 lemon, 4 eggs, 2 tsp baking powder and milk to mix.

Peel, core and coarsely chop the apples into a bowl. Mix with the breadcrumbs, currants, sugar, nutmeg, salt and grated rind of the lemon. Stir in the well beaten eggs. Leave to stand for 30 minutes. Stir in baking powder and add milk if the mixture is a little stiff, aiming for the consistency of a thick porridge. Butter the basin, fill it with the mixture. Cover it with tin foil and bind it with string (or fix the lid). Put the saucer or ring at the bottom of the saucepan, then put in the basin. Add enough boiling water from the kettle to come a third of the way up. Bring it up to simmering point, cover and cook gently for at least 2 hours, adding more water if necessary. Use a palette knife to turn it out on to a plate and serve hot with custard.

Chocolate pudding

Moist, crunchy, and super-rich, flat on top and keeps well. For 8, you will need an 8 x 2 inch (20 x 5cm) spring-form cake tin, 6oz (175g) plain chocolate (70% cocoa content), 6oz (175g) unsalted butter, 4oz (110g) white sugar, 2 eggs, 3oz (75g) plain flour, 3oz (75g) crushed ratafias, 2 tbsps of cool espresso coffee, 2 tbsp brandy, icing sugar to decorate.

Melt the chocolate and 2oz (50g) of the butter slowly in a basin over a pan of scalding water, and leave to cool. Cream the sugar in a bowl with the remaining 4oz (100g) butter. Add the whole eggs one at a time, and beat well with 1 tbsp of the flour. Crush the ratafias to crumbs and fold in with the remaining flour, melted chocolate, coffee and the brandy. Butter the tin. Pour in the mixture and cook in a preheated oven at 180°C/350°F/gas mark 4 for 40 minutes. The pudding should be slightly underdone in the middle. Dust with icing sugar. Cream essential.

Exeter pudding

One of the best suet puddings for winter, baked in the oven and very rich. It is difficult to believe that the cathedral city let this one go.

For 8, you will need a large, size 24 (63fl oz) pudding basin, 10oz (275g) ratafias, 10oz (275g) breadcrumbs, 6oz (175g) white sugar, 7oz (200g) suet, rind of 1 lemon, 7 eggs, 4oz (110g) soft butter, 6oz (175g) stoneless damson or raspberry jam, 4 tbsp rum.

Butter a small circle of greaseproof paper and stick to the bottom of the basin (which will help the pudding turn out). Butter thickly the flat side of the ratafias and line the bowl. Mix the eggs, breadcrumbs, sugar, suet, lemon rind, and rum together. Add a layer of the mixture to the basin then a layer of jam, another of mixture, another of jam and finish with the mixture. Bake in a preheated oven at 180°C/350°F/gas mark 4 for 1½ hours or until firm to the touch. Using a palette knife to free the pudding, turn it out on to a plate. Carefully remove the greaseproof paper.

Queen of puddings

Rich and sophisticated. Eat warm, or preferably cold the next day.

For 8, you will need a 10 inch (25cm) (60 fl oz (1.8l) capacity) oval pie dish, 1½ pints (875ml) milk, 2oz (50g) butter, 2 lemons, 8oz (220g) caster sugar, 6oz (175g) fresh white breadcrumbs, 4 eggs, separated, 6oz (175g) damson or raspberry jam.*

Heat the milk to scalding point, stir in the butter, the grated rind of 2 lemons and 2oz (50g) of the caster sugar. Pour over the breadcrumbs in a bowl and add beaten egg yolks. Leave for 15 minutes. Pour into the buttered pie dish and bake in a preheated oven at 180°C/350°F/gas mark 4 for about 40 minutes until just set. Turn the oven down to 150°C/300°F/gas mark 2. Spread

---

* The Ascot range suffices for all pie dishes and pudding basins. It has been made in Swadlincote near Burton on Trent, Nottinghamshire, for 23 years. The original manufacturer was T G Green, who occupied the same premises from 1790 until 2001, before moving next door and becoming a part of Mason Cash.

the jam on the surface of the pudding. Whisk the egg whites and fold in the remaining 6oz (175g) of sugar. Cover the jam with the mixture and cook for about 40 minutes or until the meringue is a light brown.

Sponge pudding

Easy to make. This one is best with rhubarb or gooseberries, bottled plums or greengages (with some juice but without stones). Use margarine for the sponge. Butter (oddly enough) is not so good.

For 6, you will need a 7 x 4 inch (18 x 10cm) round dish, 1½lb (700g) fruit, 2 eggs (or 1 goose egg), 4oz (110g) Stork margarine, 4oz (110g) caster sugar, 3oz (75g) demerara sugar (white will do), 4oz (110g) self-raising flour, milk to mix.

Cream the caster sugar and margarine. Beat the eggs and add to the mixture together with 1 tbsp of the sifted flour. Fold in the remaining flour. Add a slurp of milk if it is a bit stiff. Wash fruit and chop if necessary and cram it into the dish. Mix in the demerara sugar and cover with the sponge, sealing around the edges. Bake in a preheated oven at 200°C/400°F/gas mark 6 for 35 minutes.

Summer pudding

Take a pudding basin out into the garden, fill half with blackcurrants and the rest with a mixture of redcurrants, whitecurrants, raspberries or mulberries until heaped and proud. Wash the currants, then put them in a pan with the other fruit and a tablespoon or more of sugar, heating them gently until the juice runs. Check for sweetness, adding more sugar if necessary. Line the basin with slices of crustless white bread about half an inch thick, sides first, then the bottom. Fill to the rim with fruit, using a perforated spoon. Finish with about half the juice from the pan, or less. Make a lid with more slices of bread. Put a small plate or a saucer on top, then a weight, and leave in a cool place for at least four hours. Turn out on to a dish with a spatula and spoon over the rest of the juice, moistening the pudding and colouring in any patches. Add cream.

This pudding, a favourite in pre-war nursing homes, was sometimes called 'Hydropathic' – not very appealing. My late grandmother referred to it in her notes as Umberslade pudding, no reason given, after a place I have yet to locate. She put the *raw* fruit and sugar in the basin with the bread, *then baked it* and let it go cold.

CHAPTER THIRTY-TWO

APPLES AND CIDER

S O T H E R E W A S I, a guest at the Royal Geographical Society, the lecture finished. People were milling about in the hall chatting to each other and buttonholing the experts. And there *it* was, all by itself, attracting no attention and sitting on a white paper plate: large, conical in shape, ribs north to south, and a few becoming specks on a smooth yellow skin. The story was that the lecturer's daughter had gone out for a walk one afternoon in the environs of Oxford and found a fruit thought to have been extinct for years, and sold in England by medieval costermongers: the grey costard. It was not to be, I later learned, but could have been, such is the wonderful, incomparable and historic reserve of English apples!

The native European apple, which occurs from the UK to the Balkans, is a remnant of ancient woodland and now quite rare. The naturalised domestic apple, we were told at the lecture, was descended from random selections in central and eastern Asia. It was spread by man and beast along what came to be called the Silk Road and still appears in the military zone on the former Sino–Soviet border. The Persians are thought to have discovered the art of grafting trees, which the Romans spread throughout their empire. The cultivated apple, thriving in the English climate, rose to perfection at the limit of its range.

The number of apple varieties in England runs to many thousands, classified, controlled and otherwise, since an apple does not breed true from a pip, but throws up a new seedling, some of which, like the Bramley, have become world-famous. The rest are left to do their best in the wild, all lumped together as crab apples (see page 407).

The apple variety Decio, which is still grown in England, and has an identical twin in Italy, was said to have arrived with a Roman general. A harder fact to emerge is that only one orchard in England was recorded in Domesday Book. Slowly and surely, cultivation increased with the production of apples for cider and cooking, gnawing away at the prejudice against raw fruit (upheld by choosing the wrong sorts to eat and in the wrong condition).

One Richard Harris was dispatched by Henry VIII to France, returning with trees for an orchard near Brogdale, and stimulating interest in England. Within a hundred years, sixty varieties of apples were listed. Leathercoats were mentioned by Shakespeare – they are still in existence – and 'Hot codlins, hot!' cried in London. The distribution of fruit grew under the Hanoverians, encouraging more business, thanks to the improvement in roads and the construction of canals. Thomas Knight and daughter, landowners in the Midlands, are credited with starting the first apple-breeding programme, in the 1790s. The interest taken by powerful patrons was of crucial importance to home-grown varieties and their spread throughout England, the Empire and places far afield, including Mount Vernon.

The English passion for horticulture may be an attempt – not always subconscious – to recreate the Garden of Eden (Morgan, Richards). It was also a form of expression, a way of providing food, and a means of advancement. The appearance of prime, exotic or rarefied home-grown fruit for dessert, bringing dinner to a wonderful close for two dozen grand, competitive and like-minded people, signalled a large hothouse and labour force, and the wherewithal to pay for them. An estate, coupled with a fully operational garden and the observation of certain rituals, gained an auspicious marriage for your son or daughter, and admission to circles and events kept in existence by people who were eager to belong, and run the country too.

In order to maintain their position, and avert any threat, landowners had only to make sure that every aspect of their lives was the finest possible, from the horses in the stables to the dining arrangements. All were noted. Could an *apple* really matter? Of course it could – if a single wrong word was enough to raise an eyebrow or condemn the user as bogus. Men of refinement and discernment had no option but to grow the best of everything and, in the case of apples, to defend their choice of one variety over another as they did the chateaux of Bordeaux.

The Pomological Society, founded in 1854, had big names on board. It was initiated by Thomas Rivers, nurseryman from Hertfordshire, and John Spencer, head gardener of Bowood. The president was Joseph Paxton of Chatsworth, designer of the Crystal Palace. The secretary was Dr Robert Hogg, a respected and erudite Scotsman who recorded the different varieties he found growing throughout the country over an approximate forty-year period. His *Fruit Manual* (3rd edition) was and remains a standard reference work. A medal is given in his name.

The committee members of the Royal Horticultural Society, cast in the same mould in 1861, continued to shape the destiny of the English apple. Their priorities were subtlety and complexity of flavour, delicacy of colour, and as long a season as possible. The distinctions became clearer between cider, culinary, and dessert fruit – a supplement to dinner – and apples were subdivided into early-, mid-, and late-ripening varieties capable of storage. First Class Certificates and Awards of Merit were granted to star performers.

For country people, apples lasted for up to nine months. The trees could be long-lived, intercropped with gooseberries, currants and cobnuts, and planted in hedges to mark a boundary, shelter livestock, save space in fields and gardens, and enter the lottery of pip regeneration. The annual prunings provided kindling. The dying and overgrown limbs supplied a pleasant wood for turning, and an aromatic one for burning after dinner. The bigger the tree, the more fun it was for a family to pick, what with all the ropes, ladders, baskets and carry-on.

Commercial production increased towards the end of the eighteenth century. It was aided by improvements in communications and by sugar coming in from the Caribbean, but hampered by better prices obtained for livestock and other crops, particularly hops, hitting the orchards in Kent and the West Midlands. English growers of any size, in contrast to what was happening in country house and cottage gardens, concentrated on no more than six types. They were undermined by free trade and the increasingly large quantities imported from America, Europe and the Empire. The great apple exhibitions of 1883, 1890 and 1895, with fifteen hundred varieties on show and thousands of people attending, were held in an atmosphere of 'peculiar intensity that arises from a sense of imminent loss' (Morgan). Significantly, many of the agricultural shows and breed societies were founded in this period.

By the 1920s, home-grown fruit was up against it with livestock, cheeses and the rest. Even so, there were acres of orchards throughout the Thames Valley, great swathes of blossom teeming with beetles, butterflies, frogs, newts, deer, badgers and foxes, captivating birds and pollinating bees. They lived with ancient churches, farms, cottages and meadows off hedge-lined lanes on a patch of land now known as Heathrow. Every apple-producing county, even a wee one like Huntingdonshire, has a similar tale to tell.

The Ministry of Agriculture started to take an interest after the war. In 1964, controls were set up to raise the standard of English fruit to those of its European competitors. The grading system, which still operates, established the importance of size, uniformity and appearance over flavour, scent or any other quality. The French, under pressure to invest in fruit, and in an area populated by Algerian colonials (the Loire and Rhône valleys), launched a campaign to promote the standardized American 'Golden Delicious' in the 1970s. British supermarkets, salivating over the profits to come, made sure it took off.

The campaign to promote the Cox in response seemed a good idea, but of the clones available to big retailers, the most regular and cosmetic were chosen. About six other English varieties are on offer in supermarkets, which is no improvement on a hundred and fifty years ago, and an approximate 0.2 per cent of the number in existence. There is also the ultra-dubious matter of how home-grown fruit is treated before it sells, and where it goes for treatment, i.e. waxing. The current destination is South Africa, a round trip of 24,000 food miles after months of refrigeration for that 'fresh local produce'.

If the big retailers had their way, there would be no English apples left. Their persistence is due to default, or being left behind, and a roll-call of champions two hundred years old. The names of Laxton, and Rivers, whose nursery closed in 1990 after 265 years of trading, live on in fruit varieties. Hundreds more names are coupled to apples or plums that mean nothing now, but that helped to create a greater range, depth and diversity in one committed country than in most of the other countries put together.

Apple orchards last for about a hundred years. The loss of trees need not be too drastic provided they are replanted and people keep track of the fruit. Our village in Hampshire, in common with many others, used to have a Sunday School. Before the war, every child grew a tree and sold the crop to raise money for children overseas. There is no written record of where the apples are and what they were called, or how many thousand local varieties have passed into history throughout the country. It will never be known who deserved recognition and never got it for finding, keeping and building the symbolic store of apples that is England's birthright.

To George Bunyard of Maidstone, Kent, a dinner 'ordered with intelligence, prepared with art and served with discretion' required a dessert worthy of its setting; to Edward, his son, it was grounds for a book. In it he mentioned 'An Epicure's Dozen' of apples; I decided to plant one of my own. I would take a few days to choose which varieties, a period that increased to several months. Then I got sucked in. Apples and potatoes have much in common. They both produce nuts. It is the endless names, the people, shapes and colours they are connected to, or the places you might have seen on the map or passed in the car, where a parson or backwoods peer had lived, a friend had rented a haunted house or your maiden aunt had acquired a puppy. You could buy the Leathercoat mentioned by Shakespeare, and Dickens' Biffins. There was Catshead, Chorister Boy, Hoary Morning, Polly Whitehair and Sops in Wine. Fancy 'Gert Bed'yn' having its own apple. I could not stop reading the lists, never mind plant a tree.

Then comes the difficult bit. You have to choose, face perspiring, hands shaking, and no going back. I, obsessed by now, took about eighteen months to complete the order. Not, as it turned out, that completion was effected. I made every mistake in the book. Ten years later it was back to the beginning. To avoid the same course, proceed as follows.

First look at the land. If there are not many trees in the immediate vicinity or revealed in orchards on old maps, they may not like it. Apples will grow in a variety of conditions, but have their preferences and perform accordingly. My garden is damp, which means canker. It is also fertile, claggy and surrounded by cover, causing whips to race away and towards the light. An open spot for each tree would have been better, located on firm and dryish ground that will support the root system. Two happy and contented trees are better than twelve that do not like their position.

Root stocks, along with soil fertility and the genetic make-up of trees, determine size. They vary from standards, which are vigorous, down to pot size. Be warned, the classification is muddling. Big trees require space, but they are longer-lived, and deliver more fruit. They can also work wonders in a smallish garden, and provide shade in the summer or a place to loll about. However, a greater number of small trees will fit into the same area.

In addition to trees of conventional shape, there are stepovers, fans, and espaliers, trained horizontally into shape for beauty or convenience and to encourage flowering. Cordons are amongst the 'performers', but grown on a single stem, sometimes vertically for effect. Do not miss the imposing sky rockets at Powys Castle (home of the artemisia) if you are in the area during May.

The current attitude to planting has recently changed. You do not excavate a crater, fill it with compost and baby trees along. You dig an 'ole, scatter some bone meal in the bottom, cover it with soil and put in the whip, not too deep, supported by a stake. Watch the levels, spread out the roots and fill the hole with soil. Without denying it water, encourage the tree to fight for its life. Do this before Christmas, not after, giving it time to get established. Mulch the surrounding area before it weeds up.

Apples need a certain amount of maintenance if they are to bear well, though it can be good exercise and enjoyable provided you do not have too many trees to prune. Get someone to show you how, and do not plant more than you can manage or you will waste half the crop.

When it comes to choosing varieties, it may help to bear the following considerations in mind:

Apple varieties

History: if the continuity is not enough, think 'value for money'. An eighteenth-century piece of furniture can fetch hundreds of thousands of pounds. An apple tree of equal provenance is yours to plant for less than twenty quid.

Locality: every county, almost every district that people may be proud of belonging to, with well-supported cricket, football and rugby teams, has its own apples.

Rare breeds: they need a leg up. A new tree planted can keep an old variety going. And how clever of you to find it!

Star performers of the past: they may not crop so well, but deserve their status and reputation for flavour. Plant for people who do not believe there was a Golden Age.

England has an estimated one-third of the listed apple cultivars in existence. Some nurseries grow hundreds of varieties, combining up-to-date lists with an out-of-date courtesy and charm. There are several apple days and festivals held throughout the country, very well attended with boffins who can identify fruit. Bear in mind when tasting apples that they can look good too. If the shape, the skin, the blush, the shade of green, the russeting or any other feature instinctively appeals, the fruit is rarely disappointing.

From a modest quantity of land, you can have apples to come in after plums and autumn raspberries and go out before rhubarb (OK – a veg) and the succession of soft and stone fruits get under way. If you have too many to eat or keep, leave the rest in a box at the gate, names attached for people who care, and join the niche market. For specialist growers who sell their own produce and keep overheads low, there is an opportunity.

My Own Epicure's Dozen were a mixture of dessert and culinary fruit, intended to crop or store for most of the year. They were either flagged up by the big names (the Bunyards, Joan Morgan, Everard O'Donnell) or tasted by me.

The top three positions went to the great triumvirate from the Victorian era: Ashmead's Kernel (Gloucester, 1700), Beauty of Hampshire (the local version of the Blenheim, 1850), and Ribston Pippin (Yorkshire, 1707). The other seven eaters were: Claygate Pearmain (Surrey, 1821), Court of Wick (Somerset, 1790), Gascoyne's Scarlet (Kent, 1871), Peasgood's Nonsuch (Lincs., 1853), Rosemary Russett (Middlesex, 1831), St Edmund's Pippin (Suffolk, 1875), and Yellow Ingestrie (Shropshire, 1800). The cookers were: Broad Eyed Pippin (England, 1600) and Golden Noble (Norfolk, 1820).

The shortlist included: Adam's Pearmain (Norfolk, 1826), Allington Pippin (Lincs., 1884), Barnack Orange (Leics., 1904), Cornish Gillyflower (Kernow, 1800), and Lord Hindlip (Worcs., 1896). These are all eaters.

On the 'looks' principle I would buy: Colonel Vaughan (Kent, 1600), Pitmaston Pineapple (Herefordshire, 1785), Suntan (Kent, 1956), and Tydeman's Late Orange (Kent, 1930). These are all eaters.

On their reputation I would particularly like to try: Cheddar Cross (Bristol, 1916), D'Arcy Spice (Essex, 1785), Duke of Devonshire (Lancs., 1835), Ellison's Orange (Lincs., 1904), King's Acre Pippin (Herefordshire, 1899), Sturmer Pippin (Suffolk, 1800). These are all eaters; Annie Elizabeth (Leics., 1857), Cottenham Seedling (Cambs., 1924), Grenadier (England, 1862), Lane's Prince Albert (Herts., 1841), and Thomas Rivers (Herts., 1892). These are all cookers.

European stars: Court Pendu Plat (1613), Gravenstein (1600), Margil (1750), Orleans Reinette (1776).

COOK'S ORACLE

Dessert apples have more sweetness than acidity. Culinary ones are the reverse. Cider fruit is high in tannin. To this classification there are exceptions. Triple-purpose or 'cottage' apples include the Tom Putt (Somerset, 1700) and Forge (Sussex, 1851). Dual-purpose apples, generally subacid, are those that may be cooked when fresh and eaten after storage. These include Charles Ross (Berks., 1890) and James Grieve (Scotland, 1890).

Eating apples, sweet as they are, need a balance of acidity to deliver the legendary impact they can have. The better the summer and late autumn, the more concentrated the flavour and aroma, bringing forth comparisons to aniseed, coffee, nuts, pear drops, spices and various fruits from pineapples and bananas to raspberries and strawberries. The condition and ripeness are crucial. Every eater worth its salt tastes good when freshly picked. The earlies are the charmers, eagerly awaited, though they tend to go soft within a few days. The mid-season apples have more of a bite and can keep for several weeks. The late ones are too intense for some people straight from the tree, but can keep for months.

Some fruits remain on the tree until after Christmas, or even Easter. Others should be picked before they fall and tested for storage. To do this, take a specimen, cut in half and paint the exposed surface with iodine. If it remains all black, the fruit on the tree will never ripen. If mostly white, eat up. A keeper with the right amount of starch having turned to sugar will be about 75 per cent black and 25 per cent white. Pick the rest and commit to a shelf in a dark, dry, cool, frost-proof and ventilated room. Give them a little space and protect from rats and mice. Inspect frequently and remove any rotting fruit. I have an apple store like a tall chest of drawers.

Any apple can be cooked, but only the ones designated 'cookers' have the acidity that causes them to break down into a froth or purée. To country people all cookers tend to be known as 'Bramleys' (Notts., 1809), but that is only one of over sixty varieties, from the lesser-known Edward VII (Worcs., 1902) and the reasonably well-known Lord Derby (Cheshire, 1862), to the Eynsham Dumpling (Oxon., 1960), and Hambledon Deux Ans (Hants., 1750), which keeps for two years.

The English taste for an acid cooking apple provided the different types with specific uses: Dumelow's Seedling was the one for mincemeat. The Norfolk (1698) and Herefordshire Beefing (1700), noted for thick skins, were baked in the declining heat of wood-fired ovens. If a dessert apple is specified for a pudding, then fruit is needed which will maintain its shape. So, do not use a Howgate Wonder (Isle of Wight, 1915) or Lord Derby (Cheshire, 1862) for a *tarte Tatin* and expect the result that is achieved in France.

If I had to choose one sauce and a partner it would be apple for pork. With such a balanced foil for so rich a meat, it is not surprising that the two enjoy the same season. Nor that, by the time the flavour of the apple begins to fade in storage, for aficionados pork is coming to an end (see page 153).

The way to get the most from a cooking apple is as follows: peel and core as usual. Slice into a pan, add a tiny bit of water and cook to a froth over a low heat. Meanwhile, barely cover the peel and core with water and cook that up gently too, for about half an hour. Strain off the liquor (discard the rest), reduce until thick and mix with the apple. Sweeten with the minimum of light soft brown sugar. Do not add anything else. As well as a sauce, you have a purée for cream and a filling for a Charlotte.

To dry apples:

The fruit 'should be ripe but not overripe. Using a silver or stainless steel knife, peel and core the apples and cut into rings about a quarter of an inch thick. Put into a basin of salt water immediately (half an ounce (10g) of salt to 2 pints (1.2l of water) and leave for 10 minutes. The rings should be threaded on a stick which can rest on the runners of an oven, and the rings should not touch each other. Dry at 150 °F (65°C) for some hours. Apples should be like dry chamois leather, moist and pliable. Cool in the air before packing tightly in paper bags, or dry jars or tins. Store in a dry dark place . . . it is best to soak dried fruit for 24 hours before cooking and to use the water used to soak them for cooking too; flavour it with a little lemon or vanilla, a clove or a piece of ginger' (Norwak, 1979).

Cider

'Don't know,' said Rita in her lovely shrill Somerset voice.

'Where does he come from, then?'

'Don't know that either. He rings up once a year, comes over for the straw, and off he goes again.'

'And he collected it yesterday?' I said.

'Yes – sorry – if you'd rung earlier in the week . . .'

'Never mind, Rita. You weren't to know. I'll wait til next year.'

So, one cider 'cheese' was to be built this season, possibly one or two more. It was a warm afternoon in late September, about five o'clock, time for a cup of tea and a bit of sponge cake in a suitable spot. The lanes were quiet and lined with willow pollards, the fields divided up by ditches called rhines. The hills were former cliffs, the humps were islands, and for two hundred years, across the moors, some folks of mine had lain entombed in the bottomless, black and peaty soil. My stepfather used to shoot snipe down here. Once, I saw a swan electrocuted on take-off by cables overhead. There was a crack, a flash and it fell quivering to earth with two red gashes in its long, lifeless neck.

People emit signals: the car, bike or trap they drive, the horse they ride, the job they are doing, the clothes they are wearing. Down the lane, two men were talking, both, on account of their boots and trousers, worth talking to. I approached, we engaged and found common ground. A few minutes later I had the name of a farm to go to.

There was no one about in the drive, no one at home in the house, no vicious dogs barking in the yard, no sign of life, nothing happening. The wife and I separated. I was poking around the outbuildings when she caught the smell of fruit hanging in the air. Leaning against a barn, there were ten to twenty potato sacks filled to the brim with apples. The door was open and the building silent, but for a telltale 'drip, drip, drip'. An ancestral 'cheese' stood proudly on the bed of a press, packed with fruit and held together with straw, leaking juice into an open trough.

A week later, the yard was full of cars. Men, women and children came and went with a cheerful 'hello', all taking part in the English *vendange*. Mary, with whom I was now acquainted, appeared in a smart overcoat. Pete, her husband, followed – a white-haired man diminished by bad health, but strong of heart, with a firm eye and steady grip. David, their elder son, came over and we shook hands too, laughing about the dirt on his transmitted to mine.

The barn, large and open, doubled up as a service bay for the tractors old and new, lorries and other motor vehicles littering the yard. It had a ramp, tools, torches and other equipment for spraying, welding, chopping logs and making cider: a bale of straw, a large wooden shovel and a frame about four foot square and six inches deep. A twin-screw press and bed, silent and inactive for most of the year, was now the centrepiece. The great oak beam, 'vollyer' or 'sow' was poised to descend. The bed was ready for the cheese. A disused headboard hung on the wall. The fruit mill bore the familiar name of its increasingly grand founder – A. Day, then Albert Day, then Albert Day & Sons of Mark. The empty barrels were clean, the apples waiting.

The mill spluttered into life, overcoming the banter. A big fellow tipped the fruit from its sacks into the open top. The apples, ground between the wheels, passed into the trough underneath. Pete took the frame and placed it on the bed of the press, scattering it with straw teased out from one of the bales. David, in waterproof trousers, shovelled the pulp or 'pummy' (pommace) out of the mill, over to the press, and on to the straw.

Pete, leaning forward and working with both hands, packed the fruit into the centre, corners and sides of the frame, levelling it off with more of the straw. This completed the first and bottom storey of the cheese. Then up went the frame and on went the 'pummy', and so it continued as the apples kept coming and the mill chugged on.

The children were getting their hands in the fruit now, sleeves rolled up and pressing it down tight. Up went the square to the next level, and up after that like a castle keep or the cob on its way to making a wall. The thin layers of straw were hardly visible. The thick layers of pummy, massed together and sandwiched in between, showed red, green and white, or brown with exposure to the air. The seventh storey was completed and still the cheese rose – to the eighth, ninth and tenth storeys – as men and girls climbed on to the press, reaching into the square, and the vollyer waited above them.

A cheese is finished when the man says so, regardless of how high. Off goes the square and the motor of the mill. On goes the final layer of straw and the wooden headboard. The garage had fallen quiet again but for the trickle of 'boy's cider', the unfermented juice, already leaking from the press and into the vat, and the murmurs of approval that it was a fine cheese. You found yourself repeating how fine it was as your eyes rested on the wide stripes of apple and the narrow ones of straw, prevented from toppling by mysterious laws. It is no mean feat to build a cheese neither leaning nor collapsing, over one yard high, even for people who have done it all their lives.

Taking a crowbar to the screws, David wound down the vollyer until it met the headboard resting on the cheese. With a little pressure – not too much – the trickle of 'boy's cider' increased to a modest flood. Bubbles, oozing from the pummy, cascaded down the sides and mingled with the treacle-coloured liquid flowing into the vat. I dipped a glass. Got a blockage, the big fellow said, you won't have one tomorrow, and the two of us laughed. I stood back and took a reflective draught. A fine cheese, I muttered again to Pete and he to me. You would not think that a ton and a half of apples and a bale of straw would stand up on their own. It was time to sweep up.

'Bacon sandwiches, anyone?' David's wife called from the door of the garage. We washed them down with glasses of cider made the year before, then followed Pete into the kitchen. His grandson, sitting on Mary's lap, would be putting up a cheese of his own one day. And the new people round about? Were they making cider? Not even drinking it? Well, perhaps they will. It was very cosy. There was family china on a dresser and next to it a photograph of the local Badger Pie Supper taken in 1947. To the backdrop of the Mendips, a heron landed on the roof of the garden shed and the hunt went past flushing out roe deer. The girls had been going to the meet, but got involved with the cider instead.

The slower the process of cider-making, the better for the vintage and the longer the equipment lasts. David pressed the cheese over the next three days until it was a flat fraction of its original size. Then he whetted a hay knife and sheared the sides of the pummy, laying the dismembered bits back on top to make an extra gallon. The cider, piped into barrels, was left for the yeasts to get going. Fermentation would start in about a week and finish in a month. A bung sealed the top of the vat. The remains of the cheese went to the farm supplying the straw that had helped to make the cider in the first place.

Before we left, David opened a bottle of cider wine, which he made every year. He said I looked like a man who appreciated wine, which is true, but in some ways not so much as cider. There are the cheeses to wonder at and the barns to wander into, with taut cobwebs, dim light, dark corners, and perhaps a peat spade or seed fiddle tucked away behind the press. The rows of bloated barrels, the wooden pails, and the sound of the yeasts frothing, fretting and soothing add to the spell.

A year passed. Through Rita, I caught up with a man called Martin. He had been over to her place as usual, collected the straw and was due to make cider the following week. We arranged to meet at the farm. There were four at the press this time, two helping, the usual next of kin, women and children, who would remember the occasion for the rest of their lives. Just as I have. The girls were almost dancing to the rhythm of the mill. Joe Tucker grasped the sheaves of combed wheat straw, shuffling them neatly, tapping them firmly and placing them orderly as a mat between the layers of cheese. It is the purest, oldest way of pressing cider, practised in museums no doubt, but that does not count. People must want or need to do such things if they are to reap the benefit, and we, the rest of us, are to feel reassured that such things are being done.

Christmas – carol; spring – leaf; summer – swimming, sea and river; autumn – apples. The connections will always be there. One year it was Jim astride his cheese with his hay knife, another Mary his wife loading the fruit, and Cath her mother helping in pink rubber gloves, aged nearly eighty, thanks to a pint of cider every night. Could we join them? Of course. We were welcome.

It started for me trailing down a lane to the great, gruff yeoman in a winceyette shirt, breeches, boots and gaiters, who drove a Field Marshal tractor and helped with the hay. My brother, lapsing cheekily but convincingly into broadest Somerset, would bring an empty bottle for him to fill. The cider was dry and strong, too much for me aged ten or twelve, but, blinking hard, I got it down. Sometimes the liquor dropped bright and clear, and sometimes with the 'snarleygoggs in 'er', rough, ropy, and sharp enough to make you cough and a piglet squeal. We drank up, even so. The ciders, though they varied from one farm to another, all shared that familiar and evocative scent. If a drink or food comes with so much meaning, it does not even matter what it tastes like.

Cider comes from the west of England, West Midlands and the Welsh Marches, and to a lesser extent from the southern counties and East Anglia. The Celts are thought to have discovered that the native crab apple was better for juice than food. The fruit they pounded in hollow tree trunks, and pressed by means of a beam fixed at one end and weighted at the other – a practice that lasted for hundreds of years. Single, twin-screw and travelling presses emerged in the eighteenth century, the cast-iron roller mills and scratters in the nineteenth. Some of the orchards are still cropping after sixty or seventy years. The cider they yield has but one ingredient. It is amongst the most natural and unspoiled drinks made by man since giants trod the earth and storks built nests on the Somerset moors.

Cider trees may be encouraged to fruit with wassailing and other japes of pagan or sacramental origin, conducted on old Twelfth Night, but tend to be biennial bearers. Crops are threatened by bullfinches, which used to be vermin, spring gales, and cold weather closing the blossom to pollinators. The word is that a West Country brewer (of beer) sold his soul to the devil for the three late frosts that strike, suspiciously often, from 19 to 21 May. This, not April, is Devon's 'blackthorn winter'.

England's present varieties of cider apples are thought to be descendants of the native crab and Asiatic apples, cross-fertilised in Europe and introduced by the Normans. They are juicy, tannic, unsuitable for cooking, unpalatable to eat and need not be presentable to look at. The bittersharps are regarded as the age-old essence of cider. The bittersweets are more appealing to modern tastes, though still astringent. The rollicking names they share – Fillbarrel, Foxwhelp, Brown Snout and Slap-me-girl – can differ from one county to the next. Blending the apples and knowing how they perform are the key to the drink they make. The Kingston Black, named after the darkness of its juice, is one of the few varieties used for single cider.

Cooking and eating apples will make cider, but a thinner and weaker one, less inclined to keep. Triple-purpose varieties are useful, but need help. If a farm does not have apples suitable for cider, or can get better ones, there is no shame attached to buying them in. After a wet summer, the fruit will be large and productive. After a dry one, it will be smaller and make less cider but of superior strength and flavour; the pummy is firmer too. Two thousand and three was an excellent year.

Cider apples, unlike eaters and cookers, are shaken from the trees and collected underneath. They are then left, preferably under cover in a barn or pound house, until the fruit will yield to the pressure of your thumb, indicating that it is ripe. Brown apples are tolerated, black ones discarded. By the time the wasps are asleep and the corn harvest is in, the crop should be ready for pressing. November is the right month for cider.

The stone and granite horse-drawn wheels that break the apple pips can produce an almond-scented cider. Some like to mill and leave the fruit for a day to macerate, believing that it produces a more mellow drink. As far as I know, only West Country cidermakers build a cheese with straw. Bales are easy to come by. The taller varieties of wheat like the Maris duo Huntsman and Widgeon, used for thatching, and infrequently for bread (see page 73), are grown by a small number of farmers and harvested with binders. In Herefordshire and elsewhere, cloth or nylon sacks are filled with pummy, and stacked up on the press. They are easier to use, but must be cleaned before they are used again.

However sour the fruit, the juice is sweet as it flows – but loses sweetness. A natural cider that has fully fermented out is dry. It is ready to drink within a few months of being made, but can also keep for years. A clearer and swankier cider is obtained by keeving or syphoning it off from the lees into bottles. Vintage quality comes from a second fermentation and racking. Commitment to a rum or whisky barrel has a controversial effect. To some the flavour is improved, to others impaired.

There used to be a song entitled 'The Apple Trees', 'sung in every west of England farmhouse . . . a sort of Georgic', consisting of six verses and a refrain, and giving complete instructions as to how the fruit was grown and the cider made. It was rare by 1900, but recorded in Baring Gould's *Book of Devon*, published in 1899, from notes taken by an ancient sexton.

Cider went with farming until the war. It was payment in kind, safer than pond water and, requiring no fuel, cheaper to brew and buy than beer. The quantities consumed per person were extraordinary by modern standards. A surplus, the original 'tanglefoot', goes to the legs before the head. West Country publicans, wary of selling too much cider to strangers, were happy to let regulars look after themselves. A man near us had twelve pints every night. He was never quite sober, but only drunk once in his life, when he miscounted and had thirteen. My father helped him out of a ditch, fully recovered, the following morning.

Farm ciders have a slight viscosity to go with their fragrance, and a higher alcohol content than the majority of beers, beefed up in the past by adding animal or vegetable protein (parsnips, mangolds, wheat, etc.) to barrels. There is apple brandy or 'whisky' too, legitimised and otherwise. Distilling, I was told as a younger man, was so simple 'a babby' could do it, and either 'everyone did' or, more guardedly, 'it went on'.

Apple brandy is naturally as clear as gin and registers more than 100 degrees of proof. You can dip your finger into a glass and light it. To make strong liquor without a licence has been illegal since the Excise Act of 1763. To sell it is to court a stretch. To drink it with 'thee' and 'thou' ringing in your ears is worth a life sentence without parole.

English cider took awards in France in the nineteenth century, but had none of the controls. It was watered down by unscrupulous wholesalers, then hit by chapel. There were fewer to drink the cider as labour left the land, and fewer to make it as the fruit became a cash crop and people could sell it without going to the press. A proposal to tax cider was made by the Thatcher government for the first time since the eighteenth century. Fifteen hundred gallons is now the limit before duty.

Cider almost died out on farms, thanks to mass production, which now accounts for most of the market. A fault unavoidable in factories is that milling begins when the company rather than the fruit is ready. The cider is pressed quickly and hydraulically, which does not get the best out of the apples, and nearly always pasteurised, bubbly and sweetened. It may contain imported apple juice as well. No image or variety of presentations can improve the quality.

When the UK joined the EC, producers received a grant to grub up trees. Of the twenty-five thousand acres of cider orchards that Somerset had, an estimated 10 per cent remains and much of it is wasted. In Devon, Gloucestershire and Herefordshire, the situation is similar: in Worcestershire and Dorset, not so good. To my knowledge, there are three cidermakers working in Hampshire – including a man who uses a scratter and spin-drier – one in Wiltshire and a travelling press (no longer mobile) in Shropshire. The application for a grant to restore the last pound house in north Cornwall was turned down by the district council.

The positive news is that the worst may be over. Some of the new landowners are planting trees and patiently waiting for them to fruit. A sign at a farm gate proclaiming 'Cider' should be a temptation to call, the news of a man privately selling a drop an invitation. As a rule, the more modest-looking the premises, older the barrels and dustier the floor, the more authentic the drink and the less it has been interfered with. Pay in real money and take a container. Expect to be offered the customary glass and to have a natter.

When a press comes up for sale, grab it; enthusiasts can make their own. The next step is to enquire about any cider apples growing locally, particularly in the western counties, or to plant trees as you would for eaters and cookers. Some varieties need a leg-up – the Black Dabinett has got one; for others it is too late. If you go into production, remember that barrels are agreeable to look at but must be cleaned thoroughly after use. Keep the wooden ones full and 'plimmed up' in hot weather, otherwise the timbers will leak.

Here are some ideas for consumption:

Cider royal: an eighteenth-century recipe. Take two full hogsheads, distil one and a little from the other, then mix the lot in a single barrel. Let it lie for at least three months.

Cider wine: frequently made with cider. To one gallon (3.75l) of apple juice add 1lb (450g) sugar, 1lb (450g) raisins, some fresh ginger, and a couple of oranges, cut up. Leave in a container with an air lock for at least six months.

Cider and black: i.e. a shot of blackcurrant cordial. Drink immediately. Used to be popular in urban pubs as well.

Winchester shandy: the agricultural version of cider royal, also known as a 'snakebite' or 'pig's arse'. Put a large measure of gin at the bottom of a pint pot and top up with cider. Two is the limit (remember the legs).

COOK'S ORACLE

In stews, cider can be a substitute for stock but leaves a sharp edge, so balance with a little sugar and allow the flavour to settle down for a day or two. Add soy and a tea bag (briefly) to make a dark sauce for beef, oxtail, mutton and hare. Add cream to make a light sauce for lambs' sweetbreads, rabbit and pheasant.

Cider turns to vinegar when exposed to air. It can also be made by taking cider and whisking in a small quantity of vinegar. It is between malt and wine vinegar in quality, a useful addition to the store cupboard and an efficient air freshener. Try it hot with honey for arthritis. My mother-in-law used to put it in the bath to condition the skin and hair.

CHAPTER
THIRTY-THREE

Pears and Perry

**T**HERE IS A TREE IN A HAMPSHIRE cottage garden, tall, stately and shapely, with a thick forked trunk and drooping arms. The bark is broken and scaly. The leaves are close, crowded and curled at the edges, shiny on one side, soft on the other. The tree can be shy for years, then, pleasing itself, throw up immense clusters of fruit so thick they compete with the foliage, so high you cannot reach them and so hard they can bruise your head. The pears are a pale green with russet in places, and delicate stripes. They swell in summer, hang through the autumn and remain until the winter, even Christmas, abandoned by the leaves, indifferent to the wind and equal to the cold. The tree and the cottage of mellow brick, timber and thatch have stood together for two hundred years.

'Pears for heirs' the saying went, and this one, along with the village, belonged to an estate. The local grandee still claims the fruit, but does not collect it. Nor does anyone else. The golf balls fly by as the pears fall to earth, land with a bump, accumulate and rot. Half a ton is wasted in a favourable year.

The local pear, known as a 'Barny', may or may not be confined to the area and called by other names. A family of Plymouth Brethren (no bad language, intoxicating drink, or tea on Sundays), who lived in a mobile home about half an hour from me, had the remnants of an orchard. Back along, they took the fruit to Bournemouth and sold it door to door, a round trip of fifty miles undertaken on a pushbike. I used to go over in the autumn and pick up fallers, and often had things to do in the area. There was a nursery nearby, the choicest of pubs, a man selling charcoal and another with a chestnut coppice. I knew the road well.

I was on the way home one afternoon when confronted by some veg and an honesty box at a cottage gate. It was only when I stopped, helped myself and left some money that I took in the surroundings. Then I saw the tree in the garden beyond, the huge silhouette towering above the cottage, the loaded branches and the clusters of pears hanging like glass from a Georgian chandelier. I had not only driven by for ten years without seeing it, but further in order to collect the same fruit. It happens all the time when you go too fast and forget to look. You never know how often.

The history and development of the pear are very similar to those of the apple, a close relative. The domesticated varieties spread from Asia and through Europe, arousing increased interest from the sixteenth century (Vaughan and Geissler, 1997). England has a wild pear of no use to the table, but over four hundred cultivars. The largest, imposing themselves on the landscape, have an ornamental value that has not been made full use of in parkland settings or formal planting. The seedlings can crop up in strange places, often beside a road. There is one on the open Forest, another beside the A338, and a third in the central reservation of the Great North Road (now I am looking out for them).

Pears can be fussy even on their own vigorous root stocks, but are infrequently diseased. They are noticeably absent from some areas and thriving in others, a possible indication of whether or not you should plant. Quince root stocks are often used to control growth in small gardens, which is fine as long as they like your land (and they did not like mine). Trees can be standards, weepers or trained. The shape of the fruit varies from long to round. Such are the differences in taste and texture, dual-purpose pears are uncommon, triple-purpose ones unknown.

Dessert fruit is bred to eliminate the 'sand' or grit in the flesh. The English varieties may not match the apples for choice (in France it is the other way round), but they have been underrated. The well-known Conference pear, named after the International Fruit Conference of 1888, of which the breeder Thomas Rivers was chairman, can be delicious. My wife and I have planted a Hessle (Yorkshire, 1827), a seedling from near Hull, on the grounds of its being hardy, easy, a native, and reputed to bear large crops of small, sweet fruit. Early, mid and late varieties are available, stringing out the season from August until December, but they do not keep as well as apples, and rot from the inside. A pear is ripe when the flesh next to the stalk is beginning to feel tender. Eat soon, or else it will go soft and 'sleepy'.

Cooking pears, languishing in thousands of gardens and on the way to 'nonexistent' status, are high on the list of England's neglected resources. The Barny is already 'inedible' to the uninitiated, rather than equivalent to a Bramley apple and feted. The Warden pear, another cooker, named after its abbey home in Bedfordshire, pre-dates the Reformation. It is also known as the Black Worcester, having brought great prosperity to the city in the sixteenth century and, by royal licence, featured on its coat of arms since 1575. Incredibly, without filling in any forms, imperilling your liberty, health and safety or breaking a regulation, for the cost of a quarter of a tank of petrol, you can buy this pear. I did. The tree took years to bear and the fruit could be larger. So what?

Cook's Oracle

To bake pears, peel the skin off as many cookers as you can fit in a dish, leaving the stalk, and sit them upright. Half submerge in a mixture of red wine or vinegar and water, sweetened to taste and improved with a stick of cinnamon and a strip of lemon peel. Cover and bake for 2–3 hours in a preheated oven at 150°C/300°F/gas mark 2. The pears are done when they are soft enough to penetrate with a fork. Pour off the liquid, reduce by half, and pour back over the pears. Eat cold with cream or a proper custard.

PERRY

The largest pear tree in existence stood beside the deconsecrated church at Holme Lacey in Herefordshire. The trunk is gone, but the rooted branches remain, scattered in a field on a tributary of the Wye. It grew from an unidentified sapling, planted in 1790, to cover three-quarters of an acre and give up to seven tons of pears a year. The fruit went for perry, an alcoholic drink similar to cider, which is mostly confined to Gloucestershire, Herefordshire and Worcestershire. The finest vintages are said to come from within sight of May Hill. The monumental wheels, circular stone troughs and chiselled beds with gaping mouths and blunt corners that populate farms around the Severn valley are hewn from rock in the Forest of Dean. The cost of the wheel, which I have helped to push at Helen's, the big house in Much Marcle, was greater than that of the barn it is housed in. It takes three men to do the work of one horse.

Perry pear trees do not crop as early as apples or bear as regularly, but live for longer and can thrive on soil unable to bring forth cider. They are often grafted above the browse line, leaving a ring on the bark, so that cattle might graze underneath. The blossom from each tree, visible for miles, falls like a white wig from a forty-foot stand. The wood is tough, close-grained, of a rich honey colour, and planes well. It is valued for furniture and treen, and was used for ploughs, passing through the Severnside clay with ease.

Perry pears are harder and usually smaller than cookers. They like late summer sun. The more unpalatable, tannic and astringent the fruit when raw, the better the drink it makes when fermented. There are more than one hundred bittersharps, bearing two hundred names, but few bittersweets, if any. The Taynton Squash produced a result compared to champagne in colour and briskness. The Barland was said to be medicinal. The Blakeney Red made the dye for khaki drill. Other pears to capture the imagination are Bloody Bastard, Dead Boy, Green Horse, Golden Balls, Lumberskull, Madcap, Merrylegs, Painted Lady, Squirt, Startlecock and Stinking Bishop. Their performance can change from one parish to the next. Some of the pears used for cooking, which have been overtaken by bigger and less grainy fruit, might now be classed as better for perry. Dessert pears are not considered good enough to press.

Unlike cider, perry is not usually blended. The tendency is to use the different types of pears as each one ripens over a six-to-eight-week period, starting in the autumn. Fallers from the tree, particularly the early ones, which soon become sleepy, cannot wait. The word is, and is contested, that a bag of fruit that wets the shoulder is ready for perry. A few crab apples do not go amiss. The fruit is milled in the same way as cider. The pears are left to macerate or ripen for a day, shovelled into hessian or nylon sacks and piled up on their great stone bed. The juice begins to flow even before the beam comes down, and increases with pressure.

Pears make a sloppier 'cheese' than apples and more tannic juice, but of a restful grey colour like ginger beer, with a promising scent of the drink to come. The barrels are clean and ready, and sealed after fermentation. First-quality perry, a little sweeter than cider from the unfermented sugar it contains, is loved or missed, and a great surprise to anyone trying it for the first time. I was no exception.

The range of single perries maintained a healthy rivalry and competitive spirit amongst producers. Barrels were drunk or dispatched early or late in the new year and, in a good vintage, guaranteed to satisfy most tastes between them. People spoke of Huffcap perry from this parish, or Moorcroft perry – the Stinking Bishop – from that one. And it's true. Perry is weaker on paper than cider, but goes the same distance. Two pints is enough for most drinkers.

Perry was a democratic drink, popular with landowners and miners alike, with markets in Bristol, Birmingham and London throughout much of the Hanoverian period. Two appraisals of cider and perry fruit or Pomonas, were written in the nineteenth century (Knight's, 1811 and Herefordshire, 1876–85). At the same time perry was being used by merchants to cut imported wines and was failing to compete with mass-produced beer. Farmers turned to cattle and corn, and the drink went into a long decline. Then Babycham appeared, doing for perry's reputation what custard powder did for *crème anglaise*. Between 1955 and 1963, the estimated 115,000 perry pear trees left in the West Midlands had sunk to 75,000. By the time I visited the region fifteen years later, there were fewer still and much of the crop was wasted.

What did I know of perry? Not even that it had a reputation to ruin. Jim Franklin's former sign advertising 'Perry For Sale', located near Little Hereford, where the Stinking Bishops spent the night between dioceses, implied there might be more to the story. Of course there was: a cottage industry retained partly by default. Hundreds of orchards had been grubbed up, but hundreds lived on, their trees too large, inconvenient and expensive to remove from the landscape.

Perry gets little of the attention given to other drinks, microbreweries, vineyards and cheeses, let alone gastro-pubs and restaurants. The Three Counties Cider and Perry Association is due to raise the profile of an occupation that looked like dying out but never did, thanks to a number of enthusiasts that is now increasing. One of them, a lifelong perry- and cidermaker, I was told, took snuff and drove a Morris Traveller. He did not do either, as it happened.

I have two surnames. John George had two Christian names. I watched him, never stirring from his chair, watching me through his front window as I approached. His wife answered the door and let me in. They lived in a modern house flanked by two older farms, perched on a ridge between ranges of hills that caught the wind from all directions. The ponds, front and back, were dug for the only water before the mains arrived. The yard, workshops and Victorian outbuildings were full. There were heaps of coke washed up in bunkers, piles of machinery, and shelves crammed with every device for taking apart the ten to twenty cars, lorries and forklifts and putting them together again.

John was a mechanic, wildfowler, coal-heaver and parish councillor, who fired a musket and a cannon, and helped to save the village pub. He kept chickens for meat, ducks for eggs, and geese in an old caravan. He housed the native pigs in red-brick sties, feeding them on whey and a little cider or perry. The pork he had cooked underground, or 'under the hill' as people used to say.

John was an intent listener and economical speaker with inner resources he acted upon. The fruit press, a mixture of ancient, modern and recycled materials, consisted of a steel frame braced by two lorry jacks and governed by a spirit level. The last of the juice was on its way from the layers of cloth and the pears within. John, saddened by the loss of his drinking partner, did not make much perry now, but liked to keep it going. My wife and I spent a charmed and misty afternoon pottering around his yard and orchard. We were joined by a neighbour called Norman, smartly dressed in jacket, tie, and gumboots, and three high-born Norfolk terriers who liked a drop too.

As the day drew in, John fetched glasses. We tasted a dry and a sweeter perry, dark but clear, and fortified by its twelve-month occupation of an old rum barrel. We had arrived unannounced after lunch, and left after tea and cake in the kitchen. There was much to ponder: the large amount John did, the small amount he said, our feet under his family's table, the perry in our bottles, the colour of the earth and the haunted wood we had left behind as the lights went on in the valley below.

CHAPTER
THIRTY-FOUR

ROUNDING UP

RAINY, MISTY, WINTRY MORNING, the sky pressing down on the rooftops of the houses and spirits far and wide. The dark had lifted on a steep and unforgiving wilderness, partitioned by black-stone walls and empty except for sheep. The road, picking up signs of life, led into an unfamiliar town. I passed a board on a wet and grimy pavement saying 'Duck and Muffin', slowed down and stopped. A light shone through a window advertising Gold Flake and Capstan cigarettes. The shop inside, a faded green and brown, had a lino floor, a counter and shelves of tins mostly containing peas. There were two women waiting in coats and scarves, two being served and two serving, evidently mother and daughter, all chatting together. A steaming pot stood between them belching to itself. I entered, waited, and when my turn came, asked what it contained.

'Duck, luv, savoury duck,' the mother said. 'You 'ave it on a buttered muffin.'

I glanced at the trays in the window, their contents and the signs.

'What's rag meat?'

'Steak pudding,' the mother continued. 'They're steamed in greaseproof paper now. We used to wrap them in rags, an old bit of sheet or a shirt tail, and boil them in a pan.'

The shop had fallen quiet, except for my drawl. I felt a little self-conscious, but spared by the interest we all took in each other and the smiling faces intent on mine.

'And beef?' I could not see any beef.

'There, luv, between the elder and bag. A beast's gullet. Some people call it wessin.'

There was tripe and cowheel also in the window, sitting in their trays. The mother was poised to serve me. I was holding people up and had to choose.

'Duck and muffin it is, then.'

'You won't regret it,' the daughter said.

The mother set to in a no-nonsense way, treating me as one who needed feeding up. She took a home-baked muffin in one hand, open and buttered, and wrapped in a paper napkin. She took a spoon in the other and, stretching forward, plunged it into the pot and removed it brimful. The 'duck', transported to the muffin, settled obediently on the surface, lapping the edges as the top closed and oozing down the sides on to the paper napkin. It was slightly runny in consistency, deeply coloured and richly flavoured, the smell tempting as a siren song. The helping was mountainous, the cost minuscule, the bundle warm. I strung it out, took my time and relished every moment in the mist outside, as the chatting resumed in the shop within.

'Enjoy that?' the mother shouted through the door when I had finished.

I nodded.

'We only serve the best here,' the daughter said.

I had not eaten since dinner the previous evening, the morning was half advanced and the weather custom-made for the food on tap. Could a takeaway be any better? Not in such conditions. I returned to the shop, watched like a member of another tribe, wiping my chops with a silk hanky. I bought twenty Capstan for old times' sake, a box of strikes and a few bits and bobs out of good will. The daughter and I exchanged a few words. Her family had been in business for six generations. You could tell. I, provoked by the shop, the commitment and the 'duck and muffin', started to express the feelings they brought forth. I got stuck a couple of times, but managed to dredge up a new and ever more purple supply of words, cast inhibition aside and finished on a high and grandiloquent note. A silence fell. Then a woman in a headscarf and woollen coat, face upturned and staring at me, spoke.

' 'E don't talk like uz.'

I searched for the shop fifteen years later, but without success, and assume it must have gone. Was it on the Oldham road out of Rochdale, or vice versa? It is no good looking for a place in the north of England if a family called Clough and a terrace of houses is all you have to go on. In a way, I am pleased I never found them. Memories, made of this, should be left to lie.

A 'savoury duck' is a synonym for a faggot, made after pig-killing and by country butchers (see page 161). In towns, it was produced from the ends of cooked meat and bacon, and the bits and pieces that collect on a slicer in the course of its operation (Robin Mitchell, Derby*). The demand led to a 'duck' containing minced and seasoned pork, bound with egg and breadcrumbs, then baked in a tray and served in squares. The quality, like a sausage, is dependent on the proportion of meat to starch: i.e. the more of one and less of the other, the better the result. The 'duck' served by the Cloughs, effectively a sauce and probably a little different each time it was made, must have contained stock and flour.

Muffins: comes from a long list of tea breads, cakes and variations on a theme that were cooked on hearthstones in the north of England, then on iron griddles, and in ovens too. They entered the language in 1706 (*OED*) and may also have been used to describe a bit of 'nookie' before 'crumpet' took over (David). Within living memory, muffins had a wide distribution and fashionable status, particularly during the cold months. History and folklore are full of undergraduates toasting muffins by the fire, and vendors carrying trays on their heads, in spring and summer driving open-topped buses in seaside towns. The only pedlar I can vouch for walked from Theale in Berkshire to Bradfield College, where I became a pupil, on Saturday afternoons until the war.

---

* *Proprietor of the Soul Deli in Derby market.*

Muffins have suffered more than the usual bastardization, which helps to account for their loss of popularity and retreat to a heartland in south Lancashire. The Americans hijacked the name and attached it to a nasty-looking bun containing fruit or chocolate, but have the decency to call the genuine article 'English'. Mass-produced UK muffins, which have none of the desired taste or texture, are just as bad. In Fleetwood they are known as barms, as in yeast, an ingredient that was not always present in other griddle cakes.

Ordinary muffins can be made from a white bread dough mixed to a softer consistency than usual with milk and water. Richer ones, sometimes called 'French', implying sophistication, contain eggs. They were mentioned by Florence White in connection with Scarborough, and sold by the Cloughs almost a hundred years later.

Some recollections from Constance Spry (1956):

> Many years ago, there used to be . . . in Derby a little house with a front door rather high up in the wall . . . approached by a flight of stone steps. On the platform (outside) stood a large table covered in a snowy sheet on which were arranged high piles of muffins, crumpets and pikelets . . . presided over by a wrinkled old woman enveloped in an . . . apron and wearing a white bonnet.
>
> I (pushed there in a mailcart) still remember the smell of baking . . . the sense of snowy whiteness, and my excitement in carrying the purchases home . . . ever since I have wanted to achieve such beautifully made muffins, but . . . never have.
>
> The pikelets were . . . about as thick as pancakes . . . bigger than muffins or crumpets . . . (and) traditionally buttered on both sides . . . The memory of them in some remote way makes me think of Mr. Chadband, whose unctuous speeches we used to . . . learn by heart for schoolroom mimicry and entertainment.

To make muffins (using white bread recipe, see page 77), you will need:

1lb (450g) strong plain flour, 12 fl oz (360ml) lukewarm milk and water, 1 dessertspoon salt, 1 tsp sugar, ½oz (10g) fresh yeast, 1oz (25g) butter, rice flour for baking sheets.

Sift flour and salt together in a bowl and leave in a warm place. Melt the butter in the milk and water, add half (lukewarm) to the creamed yeast and sugar and set the sponge. Make into a sticky dough using the remaining liquid. Cover and leave to rise for about an hour. Knead the dough and divide into nine pieces, form into balls and place on a baking sheet dusted with rice flour. Flatten out a bit and cover, leave for 40 minutes until they have started to rise. To cook, heat a frying pan with a little oil, invert the muffins and press down gently with a fish slice to help the shape. Cook very gently for 15 minutes on each side.

Custom dictates that muffins should be pulled apart with the fingers, then reconstituted with the butter inside. They are best eaten the same day but make a smashing pudding, which appears in Hartley's *Food in England*.

Crumpets: a glamour puss in Betty's Tea Rooms, Harrogate, Yorkshire (my wife's favourite place), told me that the rings crumpets are cooked in expose them as industrial and Lancastrian. The mixture is the same as the one used for a muffin, but with added milk and water, making it a batter rather than a dough.

You will need: at least 2 crumpet rings, 1lb (450g) strong plain flour, 26 fl oz (760ml) milk and water, 1 dessertspoon salt, 1 tsp sugar, ½oz (10g) fresh yeast, 1oz (25g) butter, 2 pinches of bicarbonate of soda.

Use the same method as for muffins adding only 6 fl oz (180ml) of the liquid to set the sponge. Gradually add the remaining liquid until you have a smooth, thick batter. Leave this for 30 minutes, add the bicarbonate of soda dissolved in a little water, and leave another 30 minutes. To cook, heat a frying pan with a little oil, place the rings on the pan and pour in the batter to half way up. In 5 minutes when the bubbles have burst, the crumpet is cooked. Remove rings, cool on a rack and eat toasted.

Pikelets are the same as crumpets but unconfined in rings and easier to make. To cook, pour the batter quickly onto a hot greased pan about 7 inches (18cm) across. Wait for the bubbles to burst after about 3 – 5 minutes, and cool on a rack. To eat, spread with butter, traditionally on both sides and heat through gently in the oven or grill.

TRIPE

There were few if any smoking chimneys left, but there was one steaming in an empty quarter of Dewsbury. You park in a side street and pass out of the sun and daylight into the factory below, entering the humid confines of men in white coats, hats and boots engaged in the process of dressing tripe. Chris Heys, the boss of the firm started in 1953, was on holiday in Spain. Daniel, his son, would show us round. I made a mental note to stop introducing my wife to men of half my age and twice my capability with the looks of screen idols. He led, confident, cool, and wielding a crowbar like an officer's baton. We followed. On the right were two colossal tumblers, the last in England, to clean the carpet-sized pieces of brackish tripe. On the left, two giant stainless-steel cauldrons, bubbling away, to boil them in. Through plastic flaps, an inner sanctum with baths to blanch, soak and turn the tripe out the desired off-white. Another lad, attentive and built for the ring, with the sloping shoulders of a champion boxer, was scrubbing a pig's gut with a coarse brush. The fat he detached ended up in a pit outside. From there, transformed into soap, it would make the journey to the sterile and luxurious death-denying bathrooms of the twenty-first century.

Tripe is mentioned throughout English and other histories in connection with people grand and humble, before establishing a heartland in the industrial north-west. By the end of the nineteenth century, it was not unusual for a town to have over fifty dealers in tripe, plus vendors selling bits on wooden skewers outside the pubs at closing time. In 1876, an Inspector of Public Nuisance brought an action against the Great and Little Bolton Co-operative Society for adding to their number without a licence.

Fifty years later, inspired by a firm in Manchester, the trade received a 'makeover'. So swish was Vose's Tripe de Luxe Restaurant and Tea Room in Wigan, the public were invited to inspect the premises before they even opened. There were seats for three hundred people, white tablecloths, marble counters, and panelled walls with oak divisions. The furniture was in the 'Early English' style, the staircase modelled on the eighteenth century. A ladies' orchestra played amongst palms and plants on a first floor coloured pink and ivory, and exhibiting every aspect of harmony, charm, delicacy and refinement (Houlihan). The Japanese would have saved it.

Lancashire had an estimated one thousand tripe-dressers and dealers between the wars. There were several more in Yorkshire, Cheshire, Nottinghamshire and elsewhere. I can remember two in London with smashing shop fronts, one gone, the other poised to go. The trade was and remains distinct from that of a butcher, requiring totally different skills. A craftsman's or even an artist's approach is needed to display and cut tripe to the nearest ounce for people who watch their pennies. Demand can fluctuate according to the season and habits of localities, with some preferring their tripe hot as a winter dish, and others cold.

James and Henry Gosling, father and son, of Worsborough Common, Wombwell, near Barnsley, were the first tripe-dressers I went to. Their works, powered by coal until the pit strike, was pleasantly positioned on top of a hill. The firm was in business for over a century, closing a few years ago. All but about six others have gone too. Tripe-lovers blame imported meat, changing eating habits and images, and the supermarkets.

The ox, as every schoolboy knows, has a stomach with four compartments. The rumen or cud bag, divided into face piece and thick seam, provides 'jelly' tripe. The reticulum is the honeycomb, the most expensive cut, which catches the vinegar or sauce. The omasum supplies the Bible ('bibble') tripe, which is named after its bookish appearance, awkward to clean, and goes to hunt kennels. The abomasum, manifold or rennet pouch is the ladies' or corduroy tripe, 'slutch', 'shag', 'scragg', 'reed' or 'rag', which is usually unblanched and referred to as 'black'.

The tripe-dealers' repertoire includes the oesophagus or windpipe, the wessin, weasand or 'wazzle', known to the Cloughs as 'beef'. A pig's gut is 'bag' (see page 160). Cowheel (see pages 121–2) is prepared like honeycomb tripe, but imported from Ireland since BSE. Elder, a corruption of udder, another victim of regulation, seems to have disappeared for now with sheep's feet (see page 51). Donkey* 'stones', and 'bree', a broth and by-product from the sale of hot tripe, were before my time.

I was in a market up north when a TV company had just been in, making fun of tripe. This they pulled off by getting a group of adolescents to try it – none did – and pull faces. I can remember how they felt. I, in my teens and growing more clever every second, told my father I did not like tripe. Perhaps not, he said, but you did as an unconditioned and hungry child – a fact I had chosen to forget. The kids in the market would never know, and left, prejudice intact for ever. I wondered what they ate, and whether it contained the goodness of grass-fed beef but took a third of the time to digest. Tripe does.

United Cattle Products' pre-war book on tripe sold over 250,000 copies: no matter. The only way to make a case for such a food in England today is through its status in France and Spain, where it is usually eaten hot, as it is or was in Yorkshire. Tripe *à la mode de Caen* is an old and persistent gourmand's favourite. *Callos*, a form of baked beans that I have eaten in Avila and Ronda, is mine (see page 57). The blanched varieties of tripe are more popular, but the 'black' one, lacking the prolonged soaking, is meatier and tastier.

FRUMENTY

The moorland road plunged to an almost cliffside village. It is odd where a national dish can end up, in one or two houses in one corner of one county. The dark and striking Ella Simpson, a Yorkshire farmer's girl and English graduate, who knew most things, did not know the reason why. What she had, though, was a relic of her childhood – an earthenware jug belonging to a neighbour in which he collected frumenty on Christmas Eve. They ate it round about with the usual apple pies, meats, cheese and Yuletide cakes.

Frumenty, a corruption of 'froment' ('wheat' in French), is a porridge made from polished corn, probably for thousands of years. It was served with meat in medieval England, and mentioned by Kilvert and Hardy. Bowls of 'fermitty' were sold in pubs, at fairs and in the streets of market towns throughout the country where wheat was grown in the Victorian period, and survived at meets in the Midlands until the 1930s. Like porridge, it seems to taste better from a horn or wooden spoon.

---

* *Still eaten in Spain and China.*

The fresh wheat for frumenty was taken to the miller's for husking. It was then covered in water and left in his cooling brick oven to swell and burst, ending up the texture of jelly. Bakers took in dishes of grain to put in their still-hot ovens when they had finished for the day and also sold them in shops as 'cree'd' wheat. When Burgess the miller of Thornton-le-Dale in Yorkshire stopped selling corn suitably polished and prepared, the lingering consumers of frumenty turned to pearl barley: a dish sometimes known as 'fluffin' (*Farmhouse Fare*).

Frumenty was associated with Lent, but also with the autumn and gleaning, the moment when wheat was at its freshest and most suitable for boiling. From there it made the jump to a festive dish, which was made from storable ingredients and kept for a few days when cooked. Ella had not made frumenty for years, but knew someone in the village who did. Half an hour later, the three of us sat with frumenty from the deep freeze heated through in a microwave. It was like a milk pudding, made as follows by Flora Dale: 'Boil 1lb pearl wheat or barley for hours until tender in a quantity of water, adding more if necessary. To half a basin of plain flour mix in enough milk to make a smooth cream with half a nutmeg and half a pound of sugar. Add to the frumenty and boil gently stirring all the time; alternatively, heat it in the oven. Eat with milk and sugar.'

Oatcakes

The pool was still there, not surprisingly. Trees and houses are often gone, but ponds and lakes, provided they have not dried up or been drained, usually remain. I had stopped to admire the view in the Staffordshire Peaks, the black and distant crags torn by a giant from a seam of stone. The pool was about a hundred yards below. How still, dark and mysterious it looked halfway down a mountainside, neither natural nor artificial, in its elevated setting. I was not surprised to hear from a man and wife, who had also stopped, that the pool was a queer one. Livestock would not drink from it, birds would not fly over it, and man had failed to plumb the depths.

Would the shop in Leek be there too? It was – on the corner, large windows, and people queuing out of the door. Last time there had been two busty women in white making oatcakes inside; now, two men. One dips a ladle into a bucket of batter and empties it on to a hotplate, where it spreads out, blowing bubbles and sizzling. He does this ten to twelve times in quick succession. By the time the final oatcake is in position, it is ready for the other man to flip it over, revealing the brown and smoother underside. He then puts the fillings on top, leaves them to heat through, and rolls up the oatcakes. You grab a hot little bundle and down it goes. Was the shop ever called Peggy's, or was it my imagination? Anyway, now it is Asplin's. The boss wears a smart red hat.

In common with other parts of the UK, the English uplands do not favour wheat. They have relied on barley and particularly oats since they were first cultivated thousands of years ago. The bread took the form of innumerable cakes mixed from medium or fine meal, salt and water, milk, buttermilk or cheese whey. North Staffordshire and the Derbyshire Peaks yielded the best-known examples. Some of the surviving equipment used to make them dates from the fifteenth century. The first bakestones, heated over a wood or heather fire, were hewn from local rock. Iron griddles emerged with the Industrial Revolution. A whole range of implements bearing colloquial names went with them, now either lost to kitchen modernisation or collector's pieces. A piece of bacon, buried in the meal, kept in a wooden ark for months. The two were mentioned along with cheese in inventories.

The oatcake did not register with writers and enter history books until the eighteenth century. It is also one of the items in the English kitchen to have successfully made the journey from country to town, arriving on coal- or gas-fired hotplates and in the kilns of Staffordshire potters. This has accounted for its survival, but also a change of identity. The original sourdough oatcake was about eighteen inches across and mixed in a wooden tub called a doshen in Derbyshire (Pamela Murray, 1974). The vessel was impregnated with years of barm and allowed to retain a little batter, especially in winter, which started the next fermentation. The modern oatcake, probably universal by 1914, is less than half the width, thinner, softer, regular and raised with compressed yeast. The babies are called 'little dippers'.

The farm and cottage industry approach to oatcakes continues in a small way. Of the 'front room' vendors operating in terraces throughout the Five Towns, one similar to Asplin's is left. The rest have 'consolidated', i.e. got bigger. The first oatcakes I ever saw were home-produced. They sat by themselves on a table in a pile in Hanley market hall, before an old woman in a hat, coat and mittens, out to make a few bob. A pub round the corner, staffed by Liverpudlians perhaps, had a board outside saying 'Lobby'.

As well as in north Staffordshire and Derbyshire, oatcakes are found in Cheshire and traditionally in Blackpool, where people from the potteries went on holiday in Wakes Week at the end of June. They are a rare thing in modern England: a food with many levels of expertise, which inspires loyalty and devotion. Oatcakes mean a lot to local culture, and because of their resemblance to chapattis have also been discovered by the Indian community. With ingredients varying from one area to another, so does the oatcake. Recipes are closely guarded. The larger firms have abandoned ladles or jugs for hoppers, and use preservatives, but the overall standard is high for a light industrial food. It is a relief to enter the environs of Stoke and know there is something you can eat. Converted on sight, I used to get oatcakes sent down from the potteries to Hampshire.

North Staffordshire oatcakes

Take ½lb (225g) fine oatmeal, 4oz (110g) wholemeal flour, 4oz (110g) strong white flour, 1 tsp salt, ½ oz (10g) fresh yeast, 1½ pints (900ml) warm milk and water mixed.

Sieve the oatmeal and flour into a bowl and make a well in the centre. Dissolve the yeast in a little of the liquid, pour into the well and stir in a little more liquid making a pool in the middle. Sprinkle some flour over the top and leave it in a warm place for half an hour to get going, froth a little and bubble up. Then work in the rest of the liquid and the salt, making a batter. Cover and leave to stand in a warm place for about an hour. To cook, proceed like pancakes: wipe the bottom of a pan with lard or oil, heat until smoking, and cover with the mixture. Turn when solid enough to do so and cook the other side until firm.

Cooked, oatcakes should be eaten fresh, ideally on the day of manufacture, or else they tend to go dry at the edges. Otherwise, freeze or keep in a plastic bag. To serve, heat gently in a greased pan. The filling is up to you. North Stafford Hotel uses a mixture of smoked haddock, cream, etc. A hard or semi-hard cheese melts nicely with onion or tomato. The better the cheese, the better the result, but sadly, the smaller the margin for takeaways.

The North Country oatcake, of which there were innumerable sorts, is a descendant of 'clap'* and 'haver'** bread. It is thin, elongated and probably has more in common with the original north Staffordshire and Derbyshire oatcake than the round and pliable one that is made today. The North Country cousin started as a sourdough mixed to a dough or paste (Poulson). It was distributed onto a bakestone by a cloth or board of the sort that hangs in museums and the occasional pub. A mechanical belt was invented by the Victorians. The practice of drying oatcakes on a kitchen rack or clothes horse, or in a cool oven, enabled them to keep. This form of oatcake is known as 'hard'. When eaten with a beef and cowheel stew, made by butchers, the combination is known as stew and hard.

Of the six hotplate bakers making oatcakes that used to operate in the average-sized industrial town, four or five remained by the 1990s. All were in Lancashire and all retired, including Betty

---

* i.e. clapped into shape.

** As in haversack: Norse for 'oats'.

Wordsworth* of Barnoldswick, whom I met in 1992. Some of the pubs were still doing 'stew and hard' or so it was said, but none did. The scent was getting fainter all the time, the trail growing ever more cold.

In such situations, you can either give up or entertain the thought that there is one person left and waiting to be found. First there was a town, then a market much like any other, a counter manned by two Lancashire lasses, and finally a bowl of 'stew' and the longed-for stack of 'hard'. The boss was not present, but brought in a bowl of 'stew' every week, which was made by her father. The 'hard' she collected from a secret source. Wendy, the woman's name, which I never put a face to, was the person to contact. I was confident she would tell me who her supplier was, then hopeful, then left rocking an empty cradle, a rejection (and a challenge) I did not take personally.

Wendy, thinking of her business, had not even confided in her brother – a butcher nearby, to whom she delivered the same oatcakes. The supply is so limited as to be worth guarding, the demand is not being satisfied. Perhaps some bright spark, who would rather not do a desk job, will take advantage of the situation.

Buckwheat in cakes seems to have gone missing for now. It is a relation of rhubarb which originated in Asia, spread with the Crusaders and came to be known in France as 'saracen' corn. The English name, first recorded in 1548 (*OED*), is derived from the German *buche weizen* or 'beech wheat' and its tiny triangular beech-like seeds. It is grown as a subsistence crop for man and, in common with other cereals, animal consumption. Poultry and pheasants like it. As a garden plant, buckwheat makes a deep-rooting, weed-uppressing green manure which can tolerate and improve poor soils, and in theory (I never benefit from this sort of thing) attracts hoverflies to prey upon aphids.

The buckwheat in Poland, entitled *kasza*, consists of the wholegrain boiled and served like rice. It was grown and milled in the north-east of England, possibly until the twentieth century, and could resurface with real or supposed wheat allergies. The flour is dark, especially when mixed and cooked, and has a distinct lingering flavour which may appeal to those who like rye bread. Mrs Rundell referred to yeast-leavened buckwheat cakes as 'bockings' in 1861, but made them with eggs, an unlikely ingredient for such humble fare. Joan Poulson, looking back in 1975, used only the bare necessities. Make the same way as crumpets but use buckwheat flour. Omit the bicarbonate of soda and the rings.

---

* Betty's husband was born in the poet Wordsworth's house in Whitehaven, coincidentally as it happened – he claimed to be no relation . . .

SHIPS BISCUITS

It is the little things that matter, like the blue and white paper wrapper and on it a picture of a cottage with a crescent moon above. In the same bag there are eight to ten white and biscuit-brown bodies, the shape of half-moons, which is also their name. Bowdens of Barnstaple produced them in thousands for Bristol and the troops. Bulleds of North Molton made them too. Neil Chanter, the baker in South Molton, came by the recipe about twenty years ago.

Half-moons are like latter-day ships' biscuits made from white flour, surviving in a maritime county. They go in after the bread, setting and spreading in the declining heat of a brick oven built in 1928. They are then turned and left overnight in the prover underneath, emerging an inch or two high with a crisp constitution, excellent keeping qualities, and a taste on the cusp of sweet and savoury that is heaven-sent for home-produced butter. Open like an oyster – in the middle with the point of a knife.

The future of half-moons is more or less decided. Neil makes about fifteen pounds a week, or thirty bags, for the older generation. Bulleds has gone, so he is the last producer. His sons will not be following him into the business. I call every time I pass. South Molton has a grand pannier market, fine houses and many shops to recommend it, and a nicety waiting at the end of the high street that is peculiar to North Devon.

Suffolk has rusks. Marshall's bakery in Southwold was the place to get them, now converted to a restaurant, its two-hundred-year-old faggot oven probably demolished. However, Palmers of Haughley – and their rusks – are still going. On the domestic front, interest is not quite dead either. The communications fairy led me into enchanted territory in Sue, a Baker by name and persuasion, who remembered her grandmother making rusks and likes to continue the tradition herself:

8oz (225g) self-raising flour (or plain with 2 tsp baking powder), pinch of salt, 1½ oz (40g) butter, 5 fl oz (150ml) milk.

Sift flour and salt into a bowl and rub in the butter. Mix with enough milk to make a soft dough. Roll out to ¾ inch thick and divide into about twelve with a medium-size pastry cutter. Bake on a tray in a preheated oven for 15 minutes at 220°C/425°F/gas mark 7 and remove. Lower the temperature to 180°C/350°F/gas mark 4. Cut the rusks horizontally in half and return to the oven inside up for a further 15 minutes until crisp.

Norfolk rusks are made with an egg and less milk. Dorset knobs, produced for generations in Morecombelake, and in excellent health, play a similar role.

EPILOGUE

HISTORY AND PROGRESS

**T**HE HISTORY OF ENGLAND is emphatically the history of progress!' says my dictionary of quotations. It is the conflict that troubles me. History is loved conditionally, for as long as it does not get in the way. But progress has the power to stupefy people and ratify corporate decisions. Its dark side eliminates history altogether.

Conservation-wise, England is mid-range – less indifferent to its inheritance than China, less proud than Japan – a Jekyll and Hyde of a society that neither wants to keep history nor let it go. I live in a country that had a Paradise Square and an old George Inn where Pepys, and Buddy Holly, his image of England fulfilled, sat drinking chocolate by the fire. I also live in one that knocked these places down, and put up tokens of remembrance. But why? If the civic authorities in Oxford and Salisbury were prepared to demolish buildings hundreds of years old, I would rather not be reminded, or find that 'Dairy Meadow Lane' leads to Tesco.

A trade association pamphlet was floating about, which I picked up and read. It transported me to chalk downs, sheep and almost shepherds, streams, lakes and trout, thriving beef cattle, cheesemakers, fungi, and herds of wild pigs – all in one county. It was enough to please Cobbett. The landscape was so idyllic, well endowed and carefully maintained, I wanted to live there. I do.

Rural England never used to be heritage-mad, but it is now. It has also changed more than London since I lived there. The more markets, pubs and other living organisms that are cleaned up and dumped as uncommercial or in museums, the more frequently we are invited to 'step back in time', and the more longing are the retrospective looks.

I am with Frank Zappa. Nostalgia – and bureaucracy – will finish us off.

People come to ride and walk dogs on Martin Down, a conservation area near me, and to see any wildlife that can survive the disturbance. Wardens from English Nature are on call 'twenty-four seven'. The land supports hundred-year-old anthills, wild marjoram and thyme, orchids, toadflax, and every other sort of wild flower. Flocks of sheep with Cinderella status are employed to mow the grass. There is a slaughterhouse operating a few miles away, but no demand for the free-ranging rare-breed meat on offer, and therefore no supply. The food required comes from environments like the sprayed, silent and brutally neat chemically infested desert over the hedge. No juxtaposition of values could be more ironic, no contrast more startling and extreme.

The village of Martin is an English mixture of ancient and modern, with a church, manor, cottages and council estate; a village where a famous book was written,* where there is no shop or pub, and where equestrianism dominates. After centuries of self-sufficiency, the community

---

* *A Shepherd's Life by N.H. Hudson.*

progressed to the point of eating almost nothing of its own at all. In 2004, Nick Snelgar, a local visionary, started a project entitled Future Farms, whose aim is to feed the parish from within its own boundaries. Behind the historic front, a new population grapples with the newest of visions and the oldest of ideas. Nick's wonderfully simple plans, cautiously received, have got off to a good start.

When I arrived near Martin, a local blacksmith and descendant of a medieval bishop, made the cider. Come the soft fruit, you went up to Mrs P's cottage, opened the back door and took a pot of cream from the fridge, leaving the money. I loved her and everything about her, though she was never in and we did not meet. Now that the last pail of milk has been drawn in the area, for the first time in its recorded history, it is a round trip of over a hundred miles to obtain the cream I want. May Nick step into the breach. England needs him! He is one bloke who does not consider dairy bygones a fair swap for the real thing. He has his eye on Red Poll cows.

My wife and I had a dining club at the Ship. She did the puddings and waited at table. I, kept a safe distance from the guests, manned the kitchen The house was made for it, as old inside as out, repaired not restored, and retaining the flesh of original plaster on its weathered bones. The menus chose themselves. The beef was hung until black, the mutton and game until dubious, the bacon till dry and the hams for a year or two. The Forest yielded venison and, in those days, cream and butter. Gunners provided hares, rabbits, and every fowl from pigeon to wigeon, pintail and tufted duck. The seasons obliged with the usual fish, veg and bottled fruit, fungi in the autumn, laver in the winter, sea beet in the spring, and bicoloured tufts of 'Dorset moss'.

During BSE, a spirit of rebellion pervaded the English countryside. Having cooked for a small party, I offered anyone who could solve a riddle a free dinner. What united the items on the table? All guessed, none correctly, so I explained. Everything was unlicensed or illegal. The oxtail, included in the ban of beef on the bone, provoking rural outrage, was the *pièce de résistance* in more ways than one.*

Once, a side of Longhorn meat, taken to the limit on grass, and covered with a creamy fat, turned up in the local butcher. I grabbed two ribs, baked them off and dished them up with salad potatoes, beans and a thin complementary gravy. Stuart Wood, who married two excellent cooks, came to dinner.

'Horseradish?' I called from the kitchen as he tucked in.

'No thanks.'

---

* *My solicitor says that this offence, as far as prosecution goes, would not now be past its sell-by date.*

'Salt?'

'Doesn't need it.'

That's how to eat.

Laurie Lee, walking out on a midsummer morning and down a valley towards Salisbury, noted the change in dialect on the way. If you travel around England today, one of my favourite countries to travel in, regardless of corporate influence, the differences still seem so very great and wonderful to me: the changes in language, building materials, altitude, vegetation, birds, cattle, sheep and the meat on sale in a butcher's window.

Everyone eats. Food is a common bond, and when it is specially grown, given or cooked, a communion wafer. Everyone drinks. The more unspoiled the pub they drink in, the more likely you are to hear the truth spoken. The words may not be what you want to hear, or the language what you quite understand, but that can be meat and drink in itself. If you are sitting in silence between two old boys over pint pots and one turns to the other and says, 'You killed that pig yet?' you can take offence or listen hard. It is the history of England speaking.

The people 'fifty years behind' have more than caught up. They are fifty years in front – the template for organic farming, wildlife, conservation, animal welfare and the slow food movement. They taught me everything. I learned about milk from Leonard Sevier, and how he trod bricks. I learned about cream from Mabel and butter from Anne, learning too where they used to cut peat and where the ragged robin grows. I learned about cheese from Betty Butt, of the soft Dorset voice and quiet grey eyes, who started life as a farmer's girl walking with honey to Wareham market. I learned about hares and the course they ran from Bert Lawes, father of David, born on the purlieu and ninety years a commoner. I learned more with Bob the Fish than from an expensive education. I learned from people not with facts in their heads but with feelings in their hearts, who knew where they belonged, what it represented and, deeper still, who they were.

I met a man who said that 'Time Immemorial' dated from the year 1159. I camped on a site with a Catholic priest seeking refuge from a cruel front line, who smoked, drank and looked at the fell, saying nothing at all. I went through a gate and into a marsh an hour from London, so oil-slick black, lonesome and quiet the city was not there. I stood in a shed hearing 'thee' and 'thou' spoken and holding a drink that was clearer than water, stronger than fire and burned like a candle on my naked finger.

I knew Mr Noakes, who was born in the Forest, lived in the woods and served with the Hampshires. He said we were 'spoiled'. I found a deer, hit by a car, and asked him to come. We went to the spot as a winter sun set, the puddles froze, and found her done for, struggling on the ground. He took out his gun from the back of the van with a tin bath for her body. He loaded a bullet into the breech and, standing beside her, broke the silence with a clattering shot. He put down the gun, knelt on the ground and opened a knife. Lifting her foreleg, he ran the blade up to the hilt and into her heart. The fear left her eyes: she was on her way. The blood, let, flowed in the last of a raw red light. It ran down her pelt and on to the heather, and fell to earth in crimson drops.

I can say how a stream flows too, the milk from a pail and a torrent of cider from a huge oak press. I can say what it means to Martin and Joe to build a 'cheese' on a farm above the moors, but not in words. Nor how it felt to shake a hand that was cold from the 'pummy' and warm from the heart. Yann Martel was right, language indeed flounders in such seas.

ENGLAND

A Postscript

THE SPECTATOR WAS FIRST PUBLISHED in 1828. On 27 October 2001, the following appeared:

There can be little doubt, of course, that the transformation of Britain into a cosmopolis has improved the quality of its food out of all recognition. Anyone who remembers the dire nature of British cuisine in its virtually unchallenged heyday could not possibly wish to return to the days of culinary innocence. But, it required no official policy, bureaucracies or governmental guidance for foreign food to conquer: it did so because it was, almost without exception, better than the native variety.

I have tried to deal with most of these points: the overall lack of improvement in raw materials; the need for innocence – or simplicity – in the kitchen; and the policies of cheap food and rationalization. The question of 'British cuisine' remains an idea that Sheila Hutchins 'found almost as unpleasant as . . . British poetry'. The term 'Great British', goes one worse.

'British' is an economical term used by the media, commonly substituted for English, Scottish and Welsh. Each nation must feel it has come off worst. England's position is that, after grabbing the lion's share of power and glory, it stands accused of having a 'battered' image (BBC), and so on. It is obvious why, in a post-imperial, polyglot and politically correct society with competitive neighbours, such precautionary views are taken.

In English circles themselves, I have not found any of the confusion that is thrust upon us by people on the outside. An Englishman who cannot explain what it is to be one, is more likely to be modest or inarticulate than facing a crisis of identity. If, also, England cannot be mentioned without causing offence or inviting slander, it is harbouring a complaint that no other country has got.

A bishop in the Church of England who has carefully declared himself 'British' seems suspect to me. A rabbi who sees himself as an 'English Jew' does not. According to Defoe, he is 'true born English' and belongs in England for as long as he wants to. If the Scots came from Ireland, extinguishing the Picts, and the Welsh and Cornish are more Iberian than Celt, it does not matter where the rabbi's antecedents originated.

A. J. P. Taylor, in his *English History 1914–45*, explains the differences between England, Britain, Great Britain, and the United Kingdom of Great Britain and Northern Ireland. I shall always speak of England too, partly from conditioning and partly because it is what I mean. 'Made in England' carries a message, and a pictorial one; 'Made in Britain', with its official, unromantic and apologetic odour, none at all. A government servant, diplomat, soldier, athlete or business executive can represent four peoples convened in their interests as one. He cannot represent four cultures. Anyone who sees the Mendip Hills, Fish House at Meare and surrounding cider orchards as British is liable to give them blanket surveillance rather than looking for the fine and beautiful distinctions that divided Somerset into marsh and hill folk, Devon into three counties, and made the chalk and sheepwalk of Wiltshire so different from the clay, cow pasture and cheese.

Bibliography

Acton, Eliza, *Modern Cookery* (Longman, 1855; facsimile Elek, 1966)

Allen, Mark, *Falconry in Arabia* (Orbis, 1980)

Ambrose, Alison, *The Aylesbury Duck* (sponsored by Ron Miller, *Dairyman*, 1991)

Ambrose, Ernest (1878–1972), *Melford Memories* (Long Melford Historical and Archaelogical Society)

Anonymous, *Everyday Cookery* (Ward Locke, 1963; Book Club Associates, 1972)

The Ark, quarterly journal of the Rare Breeds Survival Trust (RBST)

Arlott, John, *English Cheeses of the South and West* (Harrap)

Ashton, Chris, *Domestic Geese* (Crowood Press, 1999)

Ashton, Chris and Mike, *Domestic Duck* (Crowood Press, 2001)

Austen, Jane (1775–1817), *Pride and Prejudice*, 1813

Ayrton, Elizabeth, *English Provincial Cooking* (Mitchell Beazley, 1980)

BBC Home Service (*Farming Today*), *Cattle at the Crossroads* (Littlebury, 1944)

Baring Gould, S., *Book of Devon* (Methuen, 1899)

Becket, Arthur, *Spirit of the Downs* (Methuen, 1909)

Beaty-Pownall, S., '*Queen' Cookery Books*, 1902–8

Beef Shorthorn and Galloway Cattle Society leaflet (2005)

Beeton, Isabella, *Book of Household Management* (S.O. Beeton, 1859–61; Cape, 1968)

Bianchini, F., and Corbetta, F., *Complete Book of Fruit and Vegetables* (N.Y. Crown, 1976)

Billings, Warwick, 'Trubs and Truffles' (*Wiltshire Life*, 1988)

Blackie's Modern Encyclopaedia (1896)

Blackmore, R.D., *Lorna Doone* (1869; Pan, 1967)

Blythman, Joanna, *Shopped – The Shocking Power of British Supermarkets* (Fourth Estate, 2004)

Bolland, Maureen and Bridget, *Old Wives Lore for Gardeners* (Bodley Head, 1976)

Borlase, William, *Natural History of Cornwall* (Truro Museum, 1758)

Borrow, George, *Lavengro* (1850)

Bovill, E.W., *English Country Life 1780–1830* (Oxford University Press, 1962)

Brillat-Savarin, Jean-Anselme, *Philosopher in the Kitchen* (1825; rept. Penguin (trans.), 1973)

Bunyard, George, *The Anatomy of Dessert* (Dulau, 1929)

Burdett, Osbert, *A Little Book of Cheese* (Howe, 1935)

Burke, Thomas, *The English Inn* (Herbert Jenkins, 1930)

Calvert, *Kit of Wensleydale: An Autobiography* (Dalesman, 1981)

Carson, Rachel, *Silent Spring* (Penguin, 1965)

Carter, D., *The Strange Story of the Dunmow Flitch* (Dunmow Flitch Bacon Co., *c*.1950)

Cassell's *Bible Dictionary* (late 19th century)

'Cecil', *Records of the Chase* (Longmans, 1854)

Cheke, V., and Sheppard, A., *Butter- and Cheesemaking* (Granada, 1956)

Cheke, V., *The Story of Cheesemaking in Britain* (Routledge, 1959)

Cobbett, William, *Cottage Economy* (Griffin and Co., 1821)

——, *Rural Rides* (1830)

Collins, Wilkie, *The Two Destinies* (London, 1876)

Connolly, Cyril, *Enemies of Promise* (1938; Persea, 1983)

Courtine, Robert, *Feasts of a Militant Gastronome* (Morrow (trans.), NYC, 1974)

Coward, T.A, *Birds of the British Isles*, 3 vols (Warne, 1920)

Cox, Harding, and Lascelles, Hon. Gerald, *Coursing and Falconry* (Badminton Library, Longmans Green, 1889)

Cox, Ian (ed.), *The Scallop* (Shell Transport and Trading, 1957)

Cox, J. Charles, *Royal Forests of England* (1905)

Creasey and Ward, *The Countryside between the Wars* (Batsford, 1953)

Culpeper, Nicholas, *Complete Herbal* (1653; Wordsworth Editions, 1995)

Cumming, E., *British Sport Past and Present* (Hodder & Stoughton, 1989)

Cummins, John, *The Hound and Hawk – The Art of Medieval Hunting* (Weidenfeld & Nicolson, 1988)

Dahl, Felicity and Roald, *Memories of Food at Gipsy House* (Penguin, 1991)

David, Elizabeth, *English Bread and Yeast Cookery* (Lane, 1977)

——, *Salt, Spices and Aromatics in the English Kitchen* (Penguin, 1970)

Davies, Jean, *Straw Plait* (Shire, 1981)

Davies, Maynard, *Adventures of a Bacon Curer* (Merlin Unwin, 2003)

Davis, J.G., *Cheese*, vol.1 (Churchill, 1965)

Defoe, Daniel, *Tour through the Whole Island of Great Britain 1724–6* (Webb & Bower, 1989)

Devon W.I., *The Cookery Book* (Devon Books, 1987)

Drummond, J., and Wilbraham, A., *The Englishman's Food* (Cape, 1939)

Dumas, Alexandre, Snr (1802–70), *Grand Dictionnaire de Cuisine* (1873)

Dunning, James, *Britain's Butchers* (Thomson, 1985)

Edlin, Abraham, *Treatise on the Art of Breadmaking* (British Museum, 1805)

Ellis, Hattie, *Eating England* (Mitchell Beazley, 2001)

Encyclopaedia Britannica, 11th edn, 1910–11

Ernle, Lord, *English Farming Past and Present* (Longmans, 1912, several edns)

Escoffier, Auguste, *A Guide to Modern Cookery* (Heinemann, 1907, several edns)

Evelyn, John (1620–1706), *Diaries*

Ewart Evans, George, *Farm and Village* (Faber, 1969)

Farmhouse Fare (recipes from *Farmer's Weekly*, Agricultural Press, 1935; Countrywise, 1973)

The Field (country journal), quoting *A Rural Almanac*, 1 May 1859

Fiennes, Celia (1685–1712), *Illustrated Journeys* (Macdonald, 1982)

Fishman, Eleanor, *Staffordshire Oatcake Recipe Book* (New Victoria Theatre Appeal, *c*.1990)

Fletcher, Nicola, *Game for All Seasons* (Gollancz, 1987)

Fort, Tom, *Book of Eels* (HarperCollins, 2002)

Fothergill, John (1876–1957), *An Innkeeper's Diary* (Right Book Club, 1931)

——, *My Three Inns* (Chatto & Windus, 1951)

Foulkes, F.W., *Hooked on Cheese* (Shropshire and Cheshire Libraries, 1985)

Francillon, W., and Dent, G.S., *Good Cookery* (Dent, 1920)

Francis, Francis, *A Book of Angling* (Longmans, 1867)

Frohawk, F., *British Birds* (Ward Lock, 1958)

Fuller, Thomas (1608–61), *The Worthies of England* (1662; Ams.Pr.Inc, 1940)

Fussell, G. and K., *The English Countrywoman* (Melrose, 1953)

Game, Meg, *In a Nutshell – The Story of Kentish Cobnuts* (Howkins, 1999)

Gaskell, Elizabeth, *Cranford* (1851–3)

Gee, Michael, *Mazzards: The Revival of the Curious North Devon Cherry* (Mint Press, 2004)

Gerard, John, *Herball* (1597; Bracken Books, 1985)

Gibbons, Stella, *Cold Comfort Farm* (Longmans, 1932)

Gilpin, Rev. William, *Remarks on Forest Scenery* (1794)

——, *Observations on the Western Parts of England* (1798)

Glasier, Philip, *Falconry and Hawking* (Batsford, 1978)

Glasse, Hannah, *The Art of Cookery Made Plain and Easy* (1747)

Goffe, F.H., *Poultry* (c.1950)

Grant, Doris, *Recipe for Survival – Your Daily Bread* (Faber, 1974)

Grayson, Peter, *Recipes From The Peak District* (Grayson Publications, 1976)

Grigson, Geoffrey, *The Englishman's Flora* (1958)

Guinness Book of Records

Haggard, H. Rider, *Rural England* (Longman, 1902)

Hakluyt, Richard, *Journals 1589–1600*

Hall, S., and Clutton Brock, J., *Two Hundred Years of British Farm Livestock* (British Museum, Natural History, 1989)

Hardy, Thomas, novels 1867–95

Harrison, Rev. William, *A Description of England* (1577; Cornell University Press, 1968)

Hart, Robert, *Forest Gardening* (Green Books, 1991)

Hartley, Dorothy, *The or A: add Hart –Davis Countryman's England* (Batsford, 1935)

——, *Made in England* (Eyre Methuen, 1939)

——, *Food in England* (Macdonald, 1954)

——, *The Land in England* (Macdonald General Books, BCA, 1979)

Harvey, G., *The Killing of the Countryside* (Cape, 1997)

Hastings, MacDonald, *The Shotgun* (David & Charles, 1981)

Hawksworth, D., *British Poultry Standards* (revised) (Blackwell Science, 1994)

Hazlitt, William (1778–1830), *Winterslow*

Heath, Ambrose, *Pig Curing and Cooking* (Faber, 1952)

Henry Doubleday Research Association (HDRA), seed catalogues

The Herdwick Flock Book, 1928/9

Hessayon, D.G., *The Vegetable Expert* (1991)

Hillier, Walton and Wells, (eds), *Calcareous Grassland Ecology and Management* (Bluntisham Books, 1990)

Hills, Barclay, *Shepherds of Sussex* (Skeffington & Son, 1921)

Hippisley Cox, A. and A., *Book of Sausages* (Gollancz, 1987)

Hirsch, J. and M. Evans, *Saffron Crocus – History and Cookery* (S. Walden Museum, 1998)

Hope, J., *A History of Hunting in Hampshire* (Warren & Sons, 1950)

Horne, Pamela, *Labouring Life in the Victorian Countryside* (Gill & MacMillan, 1981)

Hoskins, W.G., *The Making of the English Landscape* (Hodder & Stoughton, BCA, 1955)

Houlihan, Marjory, *Tales of the Lancashire Tripe Trade* (Richardson, 1988)

Howey, Peggy, *A Geordie Cookery Book – Recipes from Northumberland and Durham* (Frank Graham, 1971)

Hudson, W.H., *Hampshire Days* (Longman, 1903)

——, *A Shepherd's Life* (Methuen, 1910)

Hume, Susan, *The Book of the Pig* (Spur, 1979)

Humphreys, John, *Essential Saffron Companion* (Grub Street, 1996)

Hutchins, Sheila, *English Recipes and Others* (Methuen, 1967)

Huysmans, J.K., *A Rebours* (Penguin, 1959)

New Forest, Illustrated Guide Book (Warde Locke, 1936)

James, Walene, 'The Perils of Pasteurised Milk', an extract from *Immunization: The Reality behind the Myth* (Bergin & Garvey, 1988)

Janes, E.R., *The Vegetable Garden* (Penguin, 1954)

Jesse, Captain, *Life of George Brummell* (Swan, 1893)

Jewry, Mary, *Warne's Every-Day Cookery Book* (London, 1880)

Johns, Rev. C.A., *British Birds in Their Haunts* (Routledge, 1909)

Jones, J. Evan, *A Book of Cheese* (Macmillan, 1980)

Jusserand, J., *English Wayfaring Life in the Fourteenth Century* (Ernest Benn, 1889)

Kenchington, F., *The Commoners' New Forest* (Hutchinson, 1944)

Kent, N., *The Technology of Cereals* (Pergamon, 1993)

Kilvert, Rev. Francis (1840–79), *Diaries* (O'Donoghue Books, 2006)

Kitchener, Dr William, *The Cook's Oracle* (1817)

Kurlansky, Mark, *Cod – A Biography of the Fish That Changed the World* (Cape, 1998)

La Rochefoucauld, François de, *A Frenchman's Year in Suffolk, 1784* (Norman Scarfe, 1988)

Lander, Hugh, *English Cottage Interiors* (Weidenfeld & Nicolson, 1989)

Landsborough Thomson, A. (text), and Rankin, Ian (illustrations) *Britain's Birds and Their Nests* (Chambers, 1910)

Lane, Margaret, *Tale of Beatrix Potter* (Warne, 1946)

Larousse Gastronomique, ed. Montagne, Prosper (Hamlyn, 1961)

Last, Barbara (contributor to *Wiltshire Life*), article on Bath asparagus

Laurence Wells, A., *The Observer's Book of Freshwater Fishes* (Warne, 1941)

Lawrence, Felicity, *Not on the Label – What Really Goes into the Food on Your Plate* (Penguin, 2004)

Layton, T.A., *Cheese and Cheese Cookery* (Wine and Food Society, 1957)

Lee, Laurie, *As I Walked Out One Midsummer Morning* (Deutsch, 1969)

Luckwill and Pollard (eds), *Perry Pears* (University of Bristol, 1963)

Mabey, Richard, *Food for Free* (Collins, 1972)

——, *Flora Britannica* (Sinclair-Stevenson, 1996)

MacPherson, Rev. H.A., *A History of Fowling* (David Douglas, 1898)

Manwood, John, *Treatise and Discourse of the Lawes of the Forest* (Lymington Library, 1592)

Markham, Gervase, *English Hus-wife* (1615; McGill Queen's University Press, 1986)

——, *A Way to Get Wealth* (1631–8)

Martel, Yann, *Life of Pi* (Canongate, 2003)

Martin, Brian, *Tales of Time and Tide* (Isis, 1994)

Mason, Laura, with Brown, Catherine, *Traditional Foods of Britain* (Prospect, 1999)

Mayhew, Henry, *London Labour* and *London Poor*, 1851 and 1861, reprinted as *London Underworld* (David & Charles, 1987)

McCann, John (Inspector of Historic Buildings for Essex County Council, and lecturer on vernacular architecture), article on bread ovens from *Period Home*, vol. 6, no. 3

Meat and Livestock Commission, *Chief's Guides*, Eblex (English Beef and Lamb Executive) 2006, and BPEX (British Pork Executive) 2006

Middleton, Paul, *Whittlesey Mere*, WEA project (Peterborough Museum)

Ministry of Agriculture, Fisheries and Food with Small Pig Keepers' Council, *Home Curing of Bacon and Hams*, Bulletin 127 (HMSO, 1949)

Mitford, Nancy, *Love in a Cold Climate* (Penguin, 1985)

Mollison, Bill, *Permaculture – A Practical Guide for a Sustainable Future* (Island, 1990)

Morgan, Joan, *A Book of Apples* (Ebury, 1993)

Morphy, Countess, *Recipes of All Nations* (Herbert Joseph, c.1950)

Morsley, Clifford (ed.), *News from the English Countryside 1750–1850* (Harrap, 1979)

Morton Shand, P., *A Book of Food* (Cape, 1927)

Moule, Thomas, *County Maps of Old England* (1830; Studio Editions, 1990)

Murray, A., *The World's Handbook of Dairying* (Clare's Wells, 1935)

Murray, Pamela, *Oatcakes in Staffordshire*, 1974 (County Museum)

Naish, G. (ed.), *Nelson's Letters To His Wife and other documents 1785–1831* (Naval Records Office/Nelson Society)

Newby, Howard, *Country Life – A Social History of Rural England* (Weidenfeld & Nicolson, 1987)

Nicolson, Adam (text) and Sutherland, Patrick (photographs), *Wetland – Life in the Somerset Levels*, (Michael Joseph, 1986)

North, R., *Death by Regulation – The Butchery of the British Meat Trade* (IEA, 1994)

Norwak, Mary, *The Farmhouse Kitchen* (Ward Lock, 1979)

OED (*Shorter Oxford English Dictionary*), 1983

Old Moore's Almanac (published annually)

Ort, George, *The Modern Manna* (self-published, 1984)

Pasmore, Anthony, *The New Forest Commoners* (1969)

Payne-Gallwey, Sir Ralph, *Shooting Moor and Marsh* (Badminton Library, Longmans Green, 1989)

Phillips, Roger, *Mushrooms and Other Fungi of Great Britain and Europe* (Pan, 1981)

Pellowe, Susan, *Saffron and Currants – A Cornish Heritage Cookbook* (Renard Productions Aurora, USA, 1989)

Plat, Sir Hugh, *Delights for Ladies* (1602; Crosby Lockwood, 1948)

Plume, Christian, *Le Livre du Fromage* (Flammarion, 1968)

Pollard, Major Hugh, *The Sportsman's Cookery Book* (Country Life, 1926)

Poulson, Joan, *Old Lancashire Recipes* (Hendon, 1974)

——, *North Country Recipes* (1975)

Poulter, George, *A History of Camberley* (1937; Frimley and Camberley UDC, 1969)

Priestley, J.B., *English Journey* (Gollancz, 1934)

——, *A Prince of Pleasure and His Regency* (Heinemann, 1969)

Pullar, Philippa, *Consuming Passions* (Hamish Hamilton, BCA, 1977)

Rackham, Oliver, *A History of the Countryside* (Dent, 1986)

Ramsbottom, J., *Edible Fungi* (King Penguin, 1943)

——, *Poisonous Fungi* (1945)

Rance, Major Patrick, *The Great British Cheese Book* (Macmillan, 1982)

Richardson, Paul, *Cornucopia* (Abacus, 2001)

Rix, Martin, and Phillips, Roger, *Vegetables* (Pan, 1993)

Roberts, Jonathan, *Cabbages and Kings* (HarperCollins, 2001)

Robertson, Laurel (with Flinders and Godfrey), *The Kitchen Bread Book* (Random House, NYC, 1984)

Rodgers, John, *English Rivers* (Batsford, 1947)

Roland, Arthur, *Farming for Pleasure and Profit* (Chapman & Hall, 1879)

Romans, Alan, *The Potato Book* (Frances Lincoln, 2005)

Rosenthal, Michael, *British Landscape Painting* (Phaidon, 1982)

Ross Williamson, Hugh, *The Sword and the Arrow* (Faber, 1974)

Rouse, John E., *Cattle of the World* (Oklahoma University Press, 1970)

Rundell, Mrs Thomas, *Domestic Cookery for the Use of Private Families* (Murray, 1806)

Schmid, Ron, *Traditional Foods Are Your Best Medicine* (1986)

Serrell, Alys, *With Hound and Terrier in the Field* (Blackwood, 1904)

Simon, André, *Concise Encyclopaedia of Gastronomy* (9 vols, Wine and Food Society, or *Hounds and Terriers*,' Curwen Press, 1939–46)

——, *Birds and Their Eggs* (1944)

——, *Basic English Fare* (Gramol Publications, c.1945–50)

Simpson, Matt, *The Tomato Book* (Simpson's Seeds, 1999, 2004)

——, *Chilli, Chili, Chile* (2005)

Smith, Delia, *The Complete Cookery Course* (BBC, 1978)

Smith, Eliza, *The Compleat Housewife and Accomplish'd Gentlewoman's Companion* (1727; facsimile, Literary Services and Production, 1968)

Smith, Henry, *The Master Book of Poultry and Game* (Spring Books, c.1950)

Smylie, Mike, *A History of the Silver Darlings* (Tempus, 2004)

Soyer, Alexis, *Shilling Cookery for the People* (Routledge, 1860; facsimile, Pryor, 2002)

Spry, Constance, with Hume, Rosemary, *The Constance Spry Cookery Book* (Dent, 1956)

Staniforth, Arthur, *Straw and Straw Craftsmen* (Shire, 1981)

Stevens Cox, J. (ed.), *Dorset Dishes of the Eighteenth Century* (Dorset Natural History and Archaeological Society, 1961)

Sumner, Heywood, *Cuckoo Hill – The Book of Gorley* (Dent, 1987)

Surey-Gent, S., and Morris, *Seaweed – A User's Guide* (Whittet, 1987)

Sutton & Sons, *The Art of Preparing Vegetables for the Table* (1888)

Taplin, W.A., *A Sportsman's Cabinet* (c.1803)

Thirsk, Joan, *English Peasant Farming* (Routledge, 1957)

Landsborough, Thompson, A., *Britain's Birds and Their Nests* (Chambers, 1909)

Thompson, Flora, *Lark Rise to Candleford* (Oxford University Press, 1939)

Thomson, Andy, *Native British Trees* (Wooden Books, 1998)

Thomson, Una, *At Home in the Hills – Fell Sheep Farming in Cumbria* (c.1985)

Toulson, Shirley, *The Drovers* (Shire, 1980)

Toy, Spencer, *A History of Helston* (1936)

Trevelyan, G.M., *English Social History* (Longman, 1944)

Trow-Smith, Robert, *English Husbandry from the Earliest Times to the Present Day* (Routledge, 1959)

——, *A History of British Livestock until 1700*

——, *A History of British Livestock 1700–1900*

Tubbs, Colin, *The New Forest* (Collins, 1986)

Turner, Michael, *English Parliamentary Enclosure 1750–1830* (Dawson, 1980)

Vaughan, J.G., and Geissler, C.A., *The New Oxford Book of Food Plants* (Oxford University Press, 1997)

Vesey Fitzgerald, Brian, *The Domestic Dog* (Routledge, 1957)

Walford, E. (ed.), *County Families of the United Kingdom* (Chatto & Windus, 1902)

Walsh, E., *Lurchers and Longdogs* (Boydell Press, 1977)

Walsh, J.H., *A Manual of Domestic Economy* (Routledge, 1879)

Walsingham, Lord, and Payne-Gallwey, Sir Ralph, *Shooting Moor and Marsh* (Badminton Library, 1889)

Walton, Izaak, and Cotton, Charles, *The Compleat Angler* (1653; Oxford University Press, 1982)

Walton, John, *Fish and Chips and the British Working Class 1870–1940* (Leicester University Press, 1992)

Watts, Mary (ed.), *The Complete Farmhouse Kitchen Cook Book* (HarperCollins, 1984)

Webb, Mrs Arthur, *Farmhouse Cookery* (George Newnes, c.1947)

Wells, John, *A History of the Farmstead* (Faber, 1982)

White, Florence (ed., and founder of English Folk Cookery Association), *Good Things in England 1399–1932* (Cape, 1932)

Whitehead, Kenneth, *Deer of Great Britain and Ireland* (Routledge, 1964)

Whitman, Walt, 'The Ox Tamer' from *Leaves of Grass* (1855)

Willughby, Francis, *Ornithology – with Discourses on Fowling, Singing Birds and Falconry* (London Library, 1678)

Wilson, C. Anne, *Food and Drink in Britain* (Constable, 1973)

Wing, Daniel, and Scott, Alan, *The Bread Builder* (Chelsea Green, 1999)

Wiseman, Julian, *A History of the British Pig* (Duckworth, 1986)

Wodehouse, P.G., Blandings series (1935–77)

The Wonder Book of the Farm (c.1957)

Woodforde, Rev. James (1758–1802), *Diary of a Country Parson* (Oxford University Press, 1935)

Wookey, Barry, *Rushall – The Story of an Organic Farm* (Basil Blackwell, 1987)

Wright, Mary, *Cornish Guernseys and Knit-frocks* (Ethnographica, 1979)

INDEX

Author's Acknowledgements

Apart from those mentioned in the text, I would like to thank the following for information and help received:

Robin Appel (grain merchant); John Leigh-Pemberton (Sussex cattle breeder); Pat Mitcalfe (Shorthorn breeder); Lorna Newboult (Lincoln Red breed society); George Birkett, Ian Fairhurst, Robert Hullah and Tom Lowther (sheep farmers); Kay Harrison, Roly Besant, and Patricia Mabbutt (commoners); Ray Werner (livestock historian); Roger Bell, Roger Castle, Ken Libby, and Alan Sampson (fishermen); Jan Wallace (Turkey Club); Dr. Lynn Browne (Marine Laboratory, Queen's University, Portaferry, N. Ireland); Pippa Colchester (Heritage and Conservation, Essex C.C.); Cathy Braddock (Leek Library); Angela Broome (Courtney Library, Royal Institution of Cornwall, Truro); Sue Andrews (Made In Cumbria); Elizabeth Sheinkman (literary agent); Fiona MacIntyre and Carey Smith (Ebury Press); and countless other contributors including Brian Adlem, Maria Bremridge, Douglas Carr, Peter Convery, Jane Duveen, Judy Fergusson, Sylvia Forde, Roger and Trudie Forster, Clive Gimson, Les and Shirley Goodyear, Jim and Pauline Greenwood, Merrily Harpur, George Hines, Jane Hurst, Nick Ings, Patrick Kinmonth, Pauline Lyle, Brian Martin, 'Dusty' Miller, Brenda Mills, David Norwood, Alison Parks, Chris Pouncey, Sherwood Robinson, 'Smokey' Jim Sadleir, Doris Sambidge, Julia Skinner, Tessa Traeger, William and Jehanne Wake, Liz Wallace, Paula Walton, Martin Weaver, Ellen Whaites and Nicky Wood. Happily, there are too many farmers to mention more than a few, and too many small shopkeepers to mention at all. Anyway, there is nothing like finding them for yourself.